inside
new york
1999

Publisher	Matthew Matlack
Editor-in-Chief	Amy Du Bois Barnett
Managing Editor	Arlaina Tibensky
Art Director	Jessica Sbarsky

EDITORIAL

Editorial Assistant	Genevieve DeGuzman
Copy Editor	Stacie Joy
Photographers:	Laura Kearney
	Tali Gai
	Connie Hwong
Section Editors:	Dana Burnell
	Fran Eipper
	Sarah Fabbricatore
	Gabe Fried
	Hannah McCouch
	Alicia Rabins
	Corey Thrasher
Writers:	Esther Chak
	April Di Como
	Clarence Haynes
	Connie Hwong
	Naomi Imatome
	Maureen Johnson
	Siobhan O'Leary
	Nan Ramnath
	Jenny Shalant

SALES

Vice President of Sales	Daniel J. Greenstein
Account Representatives:	Dina Cheney
	Lani Droz
	Vernon Gibbs II
	James Kane
	Cliff Kuang
	Joe Pine
	Indira Rocha

Printed by: RR Donnelley & Sons Company

Special thanks to:
Patt Mapp, Paul Goldberger, Malik Yoba, Raliegh Neal, Michael Musto, Roshumba Williams, Bill Sweeney, Sharon Brumbaugh, Sam Rivera, James Mbote, Center for Career Services, ACIS, James Billings, Tucker Graphics, Rachel Simmons, Lisa Lugo, Lisa Brettell, The Historical Society, Barry Matlack, Nate Grant, Matt Hong, Joe Possidento, Mark Edgar, Emily and Al Sbarsky, Rick and Carol Brettell, Crazy Art, Janel Joaquim, Gail Parenteau of Parenteau Guidance, Rachel Noerdlinger at the Terrie Williams Agency, Alissa Neil at the Village Voice, and Ana Lombardo at FPG International.

©1998 Inside New York, 2960 Broadway MC 5417, New York, NY 10027.
No part of this book may be used or reproduced in any manner without the written permission of the Publisher, except in the case of short quotations embodied in critical articles or reviews. The opinions expressed herein are those of the authors exclusively, and are not necessarily endorsed by the publication staff, its advertisers, or any university.
For sales or advertising information, call 212-854-2804, email sales@insideny.com, or visit http://www.insideny.com.

Please contact BookWorld Companies at 1-800-444-2524, or Ingram Book Company, if your bookstore would like to carry *Inside New York*.

TOC | table of contents

city living
page 7

- getting around.9
- financial service.13
- NYC media.16
- finding a job.18
- finding an apartment.21
- NYC politics.24
- dating.28
- gay and lesbian life.30
- weekend itineraries.34
- new york by season.36

neighborhoods
page 41

- financial district.42
- tribeca.48
- chinatown.52
- little italy.56
- lower east side.60
- soho.64
- east village.68
- greenwich village.72
- gramercy.78
- chelsea.82
- midtown.86
- upper east side.94
- central park.98
- upper west side.102
- morningside heights.108
- harlem.112
- washingon heights.118
- bronx.122
- queens.126
- brooklyn.132
- staten island.138

shopping
page 141

- NYC Shopping.142
- Store Listings.147

table of contents | TOC

arts
page 169
- Visual Arts.170
- Performing Arts.189
- Literature.205
- Film and Television.221

restaurants and cafes
page 231
- NYC Restaurant Scene.232
- Restaurant Listings.235
- Cafe Scene.267
- Cafe Listings.268

nightlife
page 281
- NYC Nightlife.282
- Bars.284
- Dance Clubs.314
- Music Venues.321

leisure
page 329
- Escaping from NYC.330
- Relaxing in NYC.334
- Sports and Recreation.338

resources
page 345
- Moving and Storage.346
- Getting To and From NYC.348
- Budget Travel.349
- Hotel Listings.351
- Resources.353
- Services.358

introduction

New York is impossible. New York is wonderful. New York is hell on earth. New York is the promised land. New York is the hardest place to live in the United States. I wouldn't want to be anyplace else. Welcome to the city of contradictions, where difficulties are the norm, and those seeking calm and placid lives are urged to apply elsewhere. Why do we put up with it? No, New Yorkers are not masochists, and you are not one for deciding to visit or live here. You have not come here to punish yourself. You have come here to realize what most New Yorkers already know, that there is a tremendous reward for putting up with New York's frustrations. This is the place where the stakes are highest, and that means it is the place where the rewards are highest too. The ratio of daily life stresses to life pleasures isn't much different here from elsewhere--it's just that the numbers are bigger. Bigger stresses, bigger pleasures.

You never get to the bottom of New York. I have spent my life wallowing in the depths of this city (or, if you prefer, studying and writing about it) and I am not so arrogant as to say I understand it completely. If you value a place that continues to surprise you, that you will not understand in the first week you spend in it, then you have to be in New York.

You will be continually surprised by the extent to which normal lives go on in this city--people get up, they have breakfast, they go to work, they go to the movies, they shop, they fall in love, they go home, and start all over again. In an odd way, New York is even more like other places than it once was, since the influx of nationally franchised chain stores and mall-style shopping has edged out lots of unique New York institutions and replaced them with the same kind of places you find in Omaha. Skyscrapers are everywhere now, too; once the whole idea of a skyline was something that belonged only to New York. And finally, because the complex ethnic tapestry that has always characterized New York is also more and more the rule of the day everywhere, New York is now less unusual in the makeup of its populace.

And yet, this is not two Chicagos, or six Omahas, or ten Bostons, and it never will be. Somehow all of these people and things massed together makes for some extraordinary chemistry that exists nowhere else. It is exhilarating, and it is beautiful. Learn to take its frustrations in stride, and celebrate the idea of discovery, and the idea of choice. In the end, vast choice is the city's greatest gift, and this book will help you navigate your way through the worlds that are available to you here, and to make the logistics less painful so that the rewards can shine through all the faster.

Paul Goldberger
Staff writer at *The New Yorker* and Pulitzer Prize-winning architecture critic.

Get an earful of New York!

*At last someone's taken steps
to introduce the ultimate New York guide:
the CityQuest™ series of audio tours.
Each hour-long CD takes you step by step through the history,
culture and myths of a famous neighborhood
in the company of James Earl Jones and special surprise guests
while a mix of sound effects, music and commentary
brings the whole experience alive.*

CityQuest™
Listen...Walk...Discover

Greenwich Village · Wall Street · Fifth Avenue · Central Park
CD and player for rent. Deposit required.

For information call 1.888.HEAR.NYC.

city living

getting around	9
financial services	13
NYC media	16
finding a job	18
finding an apartment	21
NY politics	24
dating	28
gay and lesbian life	30
weekend itineraries	34
new york by season	36

welcome

Welcome to the greatest city in the world. New York is utterly unique. The smells, the sights, the sounds—there's nothing like it in the world. More importantly, there's nothing that even compares. New York has grown from a small port town into a glorious and thriving city. But everyone knows that. The real juicy stuff (like how to get a job, how to pay the rent, how to get around) is what people who actually want to live here need to know. How do eight million lawyers, students, doctors, actors, etc., go to work each day and share the sidewalks without creating utter and complete chaos? Life in the big city is fast, harrowing, frenetic, and confusing, but there is a way to make it all work. The secret is to find the New York way of doing things. Get the insider's scoop, beat the system; don't just survive, thrive!

Eventually, all the frustration directed towards the idiosyncrasies of the Big Apple will turn into love. After all, what other town has a subway system that compares, and a plethora of yellow cabs to chauffeur you around when the subway breaks down? Where else are there so many wonderful ways to rack up a huge credit card bill—restaurants, stores, theater, oh my! Leaving the city limits will soon produce a rather unexpected feeling—longing.

In New York it's important to hit the ground running. Don't hesitate; jump in the city and get established. Find a crash pad, get a steady income, make a date for Saturday. Peruse the next few pages for tips on job hunting, transportation, dating, and other important aspects of New York life.

transportation

For newcomers, possibly the most harrowing aspect of New York is the transportation system. The city's subways are an unfamiliar form of travel, and the thought of descending into certain grimy tunnels after dark strikes fear into the hearts of inexperienced travelers. The yellow cab, a New York icon, seems much less threatening on postcards; the high speeds and the erratic driving style of most cabbies are sure to make newcomers pause before hailing. City buses are pleasant, but who can read the map? New arrivals in New York may opt to walk. What a shame, because the benefits of the city's transportation system outweigh the problems, and with a little practice, all the maps will come into focus, the subway lines will unscramble, and the cabs will stop on a dime.

The subway has an undeserved bad reputation with those unfamiliar with the city. True, stations and tunnels were once much-maligned, but the graffiti has since been cleaned up and the crime rates have dropped. The subway is the quickest and most efficient way to cross the city, which becomes especially apparent at rush hour; when traffic is stopped dead aboveground, things are usually still smoothly moving below. The subway does have a few bad points: trains and stations get unbearably hot in the summer, and overcrowding can make a crosstown trip unpleasant. Keep in mind, though, that for $1.50, Coney Island, Yankee Stadium, and Kennedy Airport are all within reach.

Each subway line is assigned a color and a number or letter for identification purposes. These numbers or letters appear on station signs, subway platforms, and the train itself; pay attention and there shouldn't be a mishap. The conductor usually announces the direction of the train: "Bronx-bound" means it's going uptown, and "Brooklyn-bound" means it's heading down. Of course, everyone's bound to get lost once or twice, and if this happens, don't panic. Ask someone on the train how to get back on course; New Yorkers are nice enough— really! If you're headed downtown instead of up, or vice versa, then get off at a station where you can transfer

city living 9

Address Locator

In order to find the cross street of an address, follow these simple steps:

NORTH-SOUTH AVENUES

1. Cancel the last digit of the house number
2. Divide the remaining number by two
3. Add or deduct the key number (list follows)

*On street or address numbers preceded by an asterisk, omit step 2.

For example, take 1100 Broadway:
1. Cancel the last digit so you are left with 110
2. Divide 110 by two, leaving you with 55
3. Subtract 31, the key number for Broadway addresses over 1000. Thus, 1100 Broadway is at 24th Street.

Avenues A, B, C, D	Add 3
First Avenue	Add 3
Second Avenue	Add 3
Third Avenue	Add 10
Fourth Avenue	Add 8
Fifth Avenue	
1-200	Add 13
201-400	Add 16
401-600	Add 18
601-775	Add 20
*776-1286	Subtract 18
Sixth Avenue	Subtract 12
Seventh Avenue	
1-1800	Add 12
1800 + above	Add 20
Eighth Avenue	Add 9
Ninth Avenue	Add 13
Tenth Avenue	Add 13
Eleventh Avenue	Add 15
Amsterdam Avenue	Add 59
Broadway	
1-754	= All below 8th Street
754-858	Subtract 29
859-958	Subtract 25
1000 + above	Subtract 31
*Central Park West	Add 60
Columbus Avenue	Add 59
Lexington Avenue	Add 22
Madison Avenue	Add 27
Park Avenue	Add 34
Riverside Drive	
*1-567	Add 73
*567 + above	Add 78
West End Avenue	Add 59

EAST-WEST

Addresses for any east-west street begin at the avenue listed below

East Side:
1	Fifth Avenue
101	Park Avenue
201	Third Avenue
301	Second Avenue
401	First Avenue
501	York or Avenue A
601	Avenue B

West Side:
1	Fifth Avenue
101	Sixth Avenue
201	Seventh Avenue
301	Eighth Avenue
401	Ninth Avenue
501	Tenth Avenue
601	Eleventh Avenue

---

colored lines on the map correspond to the paths of the trains, and under each station name are the numbers or letters of the trains that stop there. Note the important distinction between local and express trains; the latter does not stop at all the stations on the line. Listen carefully to the conductor, because sometimes a local train switches tracks and becomes an express, or vice versa, due to construction. For more information on train routes, call the New York Transit Authority (718) 330-1234, or visit one of their booths in Penn or Grand Central Station (see *Resources*).

Though subway crime has dramatically decreased, it's still not advisable to ride the train alone after 11pm; splurge and take a cab instead. For those who must take the subway at night, wait in the designated after-hours areas, and stay in view of the token booth. Avoid taking the long underground tunnels to transfer between trains, as underground (it will save a token). Don't be afraid to yell over the turnstile to the token-booth clerk; they've seen it all, so it won't bother them, and you can get back on the same train if need be. There are maps posted in the interior of the trains, so consult them; remember, the

10 city living

they can be deserted and rather dangerous late at night. Stay away from the subway entrances with no token booths; they're marked by a red light aboveground. A general note on subway safety: keep all valuables hidden, and make sure wallets and money are buried away in a deep pocket.

Buses are slower than the subway, but they certainly offer a more scenic trip. The bus stops every three or four blocks along most avenues. Stops are marked by either a glass shelter or a street sign which lists the lines servicing them; posted schedules at the stops are useful when traveling in the evening or at night, when buses run less frequently. All buses are identified by numbers, which are preceded by a letter that denotes the major route: M for Manhattan, Q for Queens, B for Brooklyn, and Bx for the Bronx. Most buses run continuously from 7am to 10pm, but after that service slows; after midnight on weeknights many lines run as infrequently as once an hour. Most lines run uptown and down, though there are some buses which provide crosstown service. To switch bus lines, ask the driver for a transfer, then present it to the driver of the next bus.

The front of the bus is the designated area for disabled and elderly passengers. It's okay to sit here if the bus is relatively empty, but move to the back during rush hour. It's protocol to give up a seat for someone more deserving; it's a matter of opinion, but usually those with children or heavy packages qualify. Try to use the door in the back of the bus when exiting.

Most important of all, let all the passengers off before boarding the bus; this prevents a traffic jam.

Buses take tokens, Metro-Cards, or exact change ($1.50). Purchase tokens and MetroCards at token booths in subway stations. They can also be found at various stores and kiosks around the city, as can bus and subway maps.

MetroCard Gold is the most fabulous thing to happen to mass transit since... well, you figure it out. Slide this floppy little card through the sensors on turnstiles and bus-fare boxes; do it again in two hours or less, and go for the "money shot," as New Yorkers fondly call it. That's right, transfer with a MetroCard Gold from a bus to subway, or vice versa, and get a free ride. Here's how to get the maximum benefits: plan an errand, take the subway down, come back in two hours or less on the bus, and only pay for one way. The thrill that comes from this process has nothing to do with cheapness; it feels like beating system. Buy a $15 card and get an extra fare;

	Jan	Feb	Mar	Apr	May	June
High	37.6	40.3	50.0	61.2	71.7	80.1
Low	25.3	26.9	34.8	43.8	53.7	63.0
Precip. (inches)	3.42	3.27	4.08	4.20	4.42	3.67

	July	Aug	Sep	Oct	Nov	Dec
High	85.2	83.7	76.2	65.3	54.0	42.5
Low	68.4	67.3	60.1	49.7	41.1	30.7
Precip. (inches)	4.35	4.01	3.89	3.56	4.47	3.91

city living 11

buy a $30 card and get two, etc. When all the fares are used up, take the card back to the token booth with cash and have more added on. It's like an MTA credit card.

Taxicabs and Gypsy Cabs are a pricey way to go, but there's certainly less hassle involved. Head out into the street and wave an arm, and a yellow cab will come to a screeching halt. If one drives on by, don't be insulted; it was probably off duty or already taken. Determine this by looking at the lights on the top of the cab: if it has passengers, the lights will be off; if it's empty, the middle lights (the numbers) will be on; if the driver is off duty, the "off duty" lights will be on as well. Rates for yellow cabs have been steadily climbing over the years and are currently at $2 for the first fifth-mile, then 30¢ for each additional fifth-mile or seventy seconds stopped in traffic. There is an additional 50¢ charge after 8pm. These rates cover all passengers; legally, the driver can carry up to four passengers at a time (though ask nicely for a fifth person and it's usually fine.) Drivers can't refuse service to anyone, even if they're only going a few blocks or, conversely, to an outer borough. Expect to pay significantly more for destinations outside the Metropolitan area. Fares to JFK and Newark Airports from Manhattan are fixed at $30, with a $5 recommended tip.

Car services and gypsy cabs also provide private service; although theoretically restricted to telephone orders, they often cruise for fares and are cheaper than the yellow cabs. Gypsy cabs dominate upper Manhattan and the outer boroughs; they're mainly Lincolns or some other type of large passenger car. Always agree on a price before entering the car.

The Staten Island Ferry is a real thrill. It connects Manhattan to the only borough not accessible by subway. It's free and offers some spectacular views of Manhattan, Ellis Island, and the Statue of Liberty, so even if Staten Island is not on the itinerary, the round trip is worth it. Call 806-6940 for more information. Catch the ferry at the foot of Whitehall Street.

12 city living

financial services

At the bank, different types of accounts allow account holders to write and deposit checks, call for financial advice, obtain travelers' and certified checks, rent a safe-deposit box, and secure a loan. When choosing a bank, select one that is conveniently located near your campus, home or work, and has a 24-hour automated transaction machine, ATM. Most banks issue ATM cards which can be used to obtain cash or balance information from machines owned by other banks, though a fee may be imposed. Fees, loan rates, and interest rates vary, so check around; smaller banks tend to pay higher rates and charge lower fees. Those who attempt to do their banking by phone will most likely find themselves chatting with an apathetic machine.

Checking Accounts

There are two types of checking accounts: "Regular" accounts, which have no fees and accumulate absolutely no interest, and NOW accounts, which do. Generally, there is no limit to the number of checks written, but many institutions charge one or several fees: monthly maintenance regardless of the balance, a penalty fee if the balance falls below a minimum, and a fee for every transaction. However, a certificate of deposit, money market, or savings account linked to a "regular" account gets customers free checking. Two signed pieces of ID (a driver's license, a student ID with photo, etc.), two references, and the names of a customer's employer and current bank are needed to open a checking account. Many banks offer some type of student checking account that requires a lower minimum balance, but there are usually a great deal of restrictions (only ten transactions a month, for instance).

Savings Accounts

In a savings account, capital will earn about five percent interest, although rates vary among institutions. It's common to have both a savings and checking account. Checking is separate; funds can be deposited into savings and transferred to checking as necessary. Most banks will regularly mail an itemized statement of all transactions made. There is usually an average minimum balance of $1,500 to avoid maintenance charges.

Money Market Deposit Accounts (MMDA's)

MMDA's combine the aspects of both checking and savings accounts: they often require a higher minimum balance, and allow fewer transactions, but interest rates are typically higher than with NOW or savings accounts.

city living 13

Certificates of Deposit

CD's are the most restrictive type of account. A sum of money is deposited under the provision that the account holder will not touch it for increments of six months, but the interest rates are higher than with MMDA's. Some institutions allow customers to withdraw the interest accrued on the initial deposit, but any withdrawal of the principal before the agreed upon date, or before the account reaches maturity, may result in penalties.

Debit Cards

Banks usually issue these cards automatically to new customers. The cards are used to make ATM transactions; the money is drawn straight from the customer's checking accounts. Lately, more and more stores and services are accepting debit cards for payment, which has its benefits and drawbacks: unlike credit cards, there's no monthly bill, so lax account holders may overdraw their accounts if they don't keep track of their transactions. Chase Manhattan is currently offering a debit card that is similar to a VISA; it's accepted wherever there's a VISA sign, and customers must be credit-approved.

Banking Online

Most banking can be done right from home with a PC, modem, and an account in any major bank. Use the software provided by the bank, or purchase Intuit or Microsoft programs designed for this purpose. Customers can review accounts, transfer funds, check the latest stock figures, assess their current worth, buy and sell stock, and pay bills all while sitting in the Lay-Z-Boy. There are monthly service charges, and some worry about the safety of online transactions. But all and all, it's a great service for the computer literate.

Banking by Phone

All the transactions performed by an ATM can be accomplished via touch-tone telephone, except deposits and withdrawals. Schedule bill payments (like rent, mortgage, or car) or set up payments by request to designated payees (like stores or credit card companies). A small monthly fee or a minimum account balance is usually all that's required. Call the bank's customer service line for specifics.

Credit Unions

Credit unions are member-run, nonprofit organizations which offer accounts similar to those at banks: in the credit union world, a share draft is a checking account, a share account is a savings account, and a share certificate is like a CD. Because they're member-run, credit unions tend to be friendlier and more sympathetic than regular banks. They offer higher interest rates but unfortunately have fewer services, and the hours of operation are usually limited. Before joining, make sure that the credit union is insured by the National Credit Union Share Insurance Fund.

Credit Cards

Aside from being a shopping convenience, a wisely used credit card can help build a good credit history, which is essential for taking out loans and mortgages. Some also provide frequent flyer miles, which is an excellent advantage for hard-core travelers.

American Express
All cards have a minimum income requirement. The Optima True Grace Card costs $25 per year and gives users 25 interest-free days for all purchases. The regular Green Card is $55; forget about the Platinum.
(800) 528-4800

Diner's Club
$80 a year with a minimum income of $25,000 annually.
(800) 234-6377

Discover Card
Issued by Dean Witter, there is no annual fee for the card, and the minimum income is judged on a case-by-case basis. There may be cash back at the end of the year.
(800) 347-2683

VISA and MasterCard
These cards can be obtained just about anywhere; walk out of the dorm and there's probably an information table set up right on the sidewalk. Interest rates may vary, and some cards offer frequent flyer miles, so shop around.
Call banks for specific rates.

Income Taxes

April 15th is the deadline for filing taxes; don't forget, it happens every 365 days. New York State taxable income is arrived at by adding and subtracting various state "modifications" from the Federal Adjusted Gross Income. New York City Income Tax is based on state guidelines. If all this is just meaningless drivel, call (800) CALL-TAX or 732-0100 (for residents of Manhattan). New York City and New York State use a combined income tax form; call (800) 462-8100 to receive one. Computer-friendly people can file online; the IRS office in Manhattan (800) 829-1040, provides information on this process. There is also an IRS Tele-Tax hotline (800) 829-4477, which gives recorded tax advice 24 hours per day.

city living 15

Newspapers

Daily News
New York Post
New York's tabloids that brashly headline everything lurid. These rags provide a certain hometown pride you can't find anywhere else.
(800) 692-6397 or 932-8000

El Diario
New York's award-winning Spanish-language daily dishes out the same coverage as its corresponding English local dailies, but with an eye to Hispanic issues.
807-4600

Amsterdam News
A historic black-owned newspaper, providing an insightful perspective on New York's African-American community.
932-7400

New York Times
Excellent coverage of metropolitan and international issues, as well as the goings-on in the Arts. Friday's Weekend and the Sunday Times are most popular.
556-1234

The Wall Street Journal
A conservative paper geared to the business world, with extensive coverage of economic and corporate news, and no pictures, only drawn portraits of people in the news.
(800) 568-7625

Free Papers

Manhattan Spirit
What the city would rely on were it stranded about 200 miles to the north. Still, a useful read amidst the hubbub and the hype.
268-8600

New York Press
This weekly contains columns that read like journal entries, and the writing is among the city's best; the Mail never fails to amuse.
941-1130

Resident
Several *Resident*s are published throughout Manhattan, each covering a different neighborhood.
679-1850

Village Voice
The bastion of liberal politics, this free weekly keeps its readers abreast of the machinations of city politicians and provides good coverage of gay and lesbian concerns. Snap up a copy on street corners Tuesday nights.
475-3300

Magazines

Black Book
Provocative and offbeat, with much attention to the hipper-than-thou downtown subculture. Articles are arranged as if in an address book.
334-1800

Free Time
This monthly gives comprehensive listings for every event in New York that's either free or under $5. It's available at some newsstands throughout the city or by subscription for $1.25 each.
545-8900

New York Magazine
Check out this glossy for breezy interviews with or articles about New York celebs. Comes out Mondays for $2.95.
447-4749

The New Yorker
A literary staple sometimes featuring fiction and poetry by heavyweights like Munro and Brodsky. Film reviews tend to read more like dissertations on cinema than strings of soundbites. Available everywhere every Monday for $2.50.
1-800-825-2510

Paper
The shiny bible of the downtown scene, dishing out weekly pronouncements on the latest in fashion, entertainment, and lifestyle. The perfect accessory for every hipster's coffeetable.
226-4405

Time Out
The most comprehensive listings for entertainment in the city, as well as short articles on different aspects of all things social and cultural in New York.
539-4444

Radio
More interesting and less predictable than commercial radio, the city supports a number of college and public radio stations.

WNYU, 89.1, New York University radio, shares its frequency with WFDU, Fairleigh Dickinson University. NYU's format varies from hard rock to jazz, and their new music show is every weekday afternoon. WFDU leans towards alternative programming.

WSOU, 89.5, Seton Hall University, plays metal, hard core, and punk throughout the day, more than any commercial station.

WKCR, 89.9, Columbia University, is the WNYC of college radio, programming jazz, classical, world music, country, bluegrass, opera, and an evening news broadcast.

WFUV, 90.7, is public radio from Fordham University. Programming covers various genre, but leans toward college rock.

WFMU, 91.1, Upsala College, programs everything from the latest in underground and indie rock to specialty shows like the Hebrew music show.

WNYE, 91.5, programs for New York public schools and also broadcasts Radio France International late at night and early each weekday morning. On weekends, the station programs a Hellenic broadcast and various talk shows.

WNYC, 93.9, New York's National Public Radio Station, programs mostly classical, but runs a number of weekly programs of world music, new age, and other modern instrumental genre. Besides NPR, WNYC also broadcasts "A Prairie Home Companion" and works in conjunction with Symphony Space (see *Arts*).

16 city living

Television Networks

ABC	Channel 7
CBS	Channel 2
FOX	Channel 5
NBC	Channel 4
PBS	Channels 13, 21
UPN	Channel 9
WB	Channel 11

Public Access

New York 1 is the city's all-news station featuring only local news and community issues; NYC's own version of a community bulletin board.

Channels 41 and 47 are the two major Spanish-language stations.

Cable

Cable in Manhattan is provided by Paragon Cable above 59th Street and by its parent company, Time Warner, below. Channel correspondence differs slightly between the two, so check your carrier for detailed information.

Several public access channels are legendary in New York City for testing the limits of the first amendment: Channels 16, 34, 35, 56, and 57 are all public access channels, which means pretty much anything goes, and that means anything.

radio station guide

AM

Format	Station	Frequency
Adult Contemporary	WALK	1370
Adult Contemporary	WICC	600
Adult Contemporary/Talk	WPAT	930
Big Bands/Talk	WLIM	1580
Christian Music	WWDJ	970
Ethnic	WWRV	1330
Gospel/Talk	WWRL	1600
Korean Language	WZRC	1480
Music	WNYG	1440
New/Talk	WGBB	1240
News	WBBR	1130
News	WCBS	880
News	WINS	1010
News/Sports/Talk	WEVD	1050
News/Talk	WNYC	820
News/Talk/Nostalgia	WGSM	740
Nostalgia	WRHD	1570
Oldies	WHLI	1100
Pop Standards	WMTR	1250
Pop Standards	WQEW	1560
Religion	WMCA	570
Rhythm and Blues	WNJR	1430
Spanish Language	WADO	1280
Spanish Language	WKDM	1380
Sports/Talk/Mets	WFAN	660
Talk/Caribbean/Black	WLIB	1190
Talk/News	WABC	770
Talk/News	WOR	710
Talk/Nostalgia	WVOX	1160
Westchester News	WFAS	1230

FM

Format	Station	Frequency
Adelphi University	WBAU	90.3
Adult Contemporary	WALK	97.5
Adult Contemporary	WBLI	106.1
Adult Contemporary	WEBE	107.9
Adult Contemporary	WFAS	103.9
Adult Contemporary	WHFM	95.3
Adult Contemporary	WKJY	98.3
Adult Contemporary	WMXV	105.1
Adult Contemporary	WPAT	93.1
Adult Contemporary	WWHB	107.1
Adult Rock	WEHM	96.7
Barnard College	WBAR	87.9
Big Band/Nostalgia	WRTN	93.5
C.C.N.Y.	WHCR	90.3
C.W. Post Campus	WCWP	88.1
Classic Rock	WXRK	92.3
Classical	WNYC	93.9
Classical	WQXR	96.3
Columbia University	WKCR	89.9
Comedy/Rock	WPLR	99.1
Community Services	WNYE	91.5
Contemporary Jazz	WQCD	101.9
Country	WYNY	103.5
Easy Listening	WEZN	99.9
Fordham University	WFUV	90.7
Hofstra University	WRHU	88.7
Jazz	WBGO	88.3
Light Contemporary	WBAZ	101.7
Light Contemporary	WHUD	106.7
Light Contemporary	WMJC	94.3
Multi-ethnic	WNWK	105.9
Music/Public	WFDU	89.1
Nassau Comm. College	WHPC	90.3
Oldies	WCBS	101.1
Oldies	WKHL	96.7
Oldies/Adult Contemporary	WLNG	92.1
Progressive Rock	WDRE	92.7
Rock	WAXQ	104.3
Rock	WBAB	102.3
Rock	WDHA	105.5
Rock	WNEW	102.7
Rock	WRCN	103.9
Rock	WRGX	107.1
Seton Hall University	WSOU	89.5
Stony Brook University	WUSB	90.1
Top 40	WHTZ	100.3
Top 40	WPLJ	95.5
Top 40	WPSC	88.7
Top 40/Urban	WQHT	97.1
Urban Contemporary	WBLS	107.5
Urban Contemporary	WRKS	98.7
Varied	WBAI	99.5
Varied	WFMU	91.1

17 city living

finding a job

searching
Searching

for work in New York City can be overwhelming, because there's simply so much to choose from. The oddest of the odd jobs can be found here; for proof, just peruse the *Village Voice* classifieds. Those with a particular dream job in mind will surely find it offered somewhere in the city; surviving the competition, however, is another story. Remember, work is always available to the innovative, creative, and persistent; by marshaling all possible resources and using lesser positions as stepping stones, most will succeed in finding satisfying, well-paying jobs in New York.

New York is the headquarters for many big-name companies, and tons of postcollegiate professionals flock to the city for a chance at corporate stardom. The market is incredibly competitive for all those who dream of working at Miramax or Morgan Stanley, simply because there are so many qualified candidates. The best way to land a juicy position, of course, is to contact someone directly within the company or organization; unsolicited résumés usually don't generate much response. For those who are new to New York or who find themselves staring at an empty rolodex, there are sneakier methods. Call a potential employer and ask to speak to someone in Human Resources; if this works, ask about position openings and offer to send a résumé. Remember to always send a cover letter, and call information for company numbers, if need be. Persistence and confidence pay off in New York, so save the number and keep calling. If information won't give out the number, or if Human Resources can't be reached, search for contact names on the Internet; enter the company name in Yahoo or some other search engine and browse through the home pages. As a last resort (really last resort), hang around the lobby in the company's building, and listen in. You never know.

For those who don't have a specific workplace in mind,

18 city living

there are several resources available to help narrow the search. For a casual first glance, turn to that old standby, the classifieds. The *Village Voice* and the Sunday edition of the *New York Times* boast pages and pages of full- and part-time jobs, as well as listing of employment and temp agencies. Classifieds are particularly good for finding work in the restaurant, bar, and club industries.

Most universities in the New York area have a career counseling center which is open to both matriculating students and alumni, and ideally offer accessible, regularly updated listings of jobs and internships, information on file about alumni in specific fields and geographic locations, trade publications from various industries, mock interviews, and other services which help prepare for the application and interview process. Some schools also maintain online databases of job openings, which are often accessible via the school's website on the Internet. Contact numbers are not available to nonstudents, however. Those out of school can make a friend on one of the New York City campuses in order to reap the benefits of these career centers.

There are many websites which provide service to everyone and contain job listings sorted by field, duration, and geographic location. However, postings are often outdated and somewhat slim; while searching online may not yield a job, employer profiles and other associated resources are nonetheless very helpful. Some popular sites: www.monster.com includes employer profiles and takes applications online; www.job-hunt.com has profiles and useful resources such as university career service sites; www.jobweb.org can search for jobs using keywords; www.jobtrack.com gives an excellent field breakdown and helpful tips for searching online; www.careerpath.com includes classifieds from the *New York Times* and five other papers.

Internships are often the best way to get a foot in the door. Companies in almost every field need eager beavers who are willing to slave away for peanuts, so internships are fairly easy to get, but their quality varies greatly. Large businesses are notorious for employing interns as glorified errand-runners, and those lucky enough to get a stipend will surely be working long, exhausting hours. Those determined enough to hang on and tough it out will be

city living 19

rewarded with networking opportunities (and a ton of free promotional merchandise). The easiest way to find out about internships is from a college career center, but calling a targeted business and inquiring directly can also be fruitful.

Part-time jobs are a good way to fill the time between college graduation and the first day of a dream job. Temping is a lucrative livelihood for the few who can stomach living on the edge. Start by asking friends or a counselor at a college career center before signing up with an unfamiliar agency, since some are better than others; in addition, some agencies cater to special-interest groups like Rainbow Temps, which serves a gay clientele. Sign up with three or four agencies to ensure continuous employment, and make sure to become friendly with an employment officer at each. Those who don't can spend the next few weeks waking up at 8am every morning to call into the agency, rather than receiving a call offering employment a day in advance. Most jobs fall somewhere between babysitting the phone for $7 per hour to raking in $17 per hour as an executive assistant. Unfortunately, there's no way to pick and choose.

There are other part-time jobs around the city which provide some extra cash for little stress. Look in the windows of stores and restaurants around your neighborhood; the close proximity will allow you to work longer hours. Unfortunately, most New York restaurants won't give out the better positions unless the applicant has some hard-core city experience. Try bussing or hostessing before waiting tables.

Bust out the designer labels for interviews; good looks greatly improve the chance of getting hired, especially at trendy places (sad but true). Large department stores like Macy's are always hiring—spend the weekends selling perfume and get a great discount on your next Macy's purchase. Anyone with a bike can get some exercise and a little extra money by making deliveries. Stay outdoors and hand out flyers; look for help wanted ads in the back of magazines and other New York publications (see *City Living* section). Bilingual folks can make tons of dough working as part-time translators, tutors, or tour guides. For those students who don't want to stray far from campus, the library calls (but doesn't pay much). A little creativity is all it takes to find a part-time employment opportunity.

20 city living

finding an apartment

While New Yorkers often dispute the merits of Mayor Giuliani's hard-core master plan to whip (literally) the city into shape, most agree that Manhattan is better than it has been in years—lower crime rates, cleaner streets, and some sense of civic duty prevails. The city's soaring reputation, however, has unfortunately brought soaring rents. Everybody and his brother wants a piece of the Manhattan real estate pie, and most are willing to pay dearly for it. Labor under no illusions: the perfect apartment is not out there. There are, however, plenty of places that will suffice, and the real estate market will seem more manageable if approached with an open mind. Here are a few guidelines to assist with the search:

Find a rent bracket. Rents vary in Manhattan according to neighborhood; the more desirable the location, the higher the rent. Decide what's affordable, then concentrate on neighborhoods that have rents in this range. Newspaper ads are arranged by location, so this method will save time. Expect studio and one-bedroom apartments in Chelsea, Nolita (the north end of Little Italy and east of SoHo), the West Village and SoHo to go well over $1500. The same apartments in Hell's Kitchen, the Flatiron District, and the Lower East Side are slightly less; a one-bedroom can be found for $1400. The East Side, Upper West Side, and Gramercy Park area are extremely desirable neighborhoods, and the rents reflect that. Surprisingly great deals can be found on the Upper East Side; one-bedrooms are available for just over $1000. Get a fabulous sublet for the summer (or maybe the whole year) by cruising college neighborhoods around graduation time. Professors and students post listings on walls, street signs, and store fronts in the Village and Morningside Heights. For a real deal, though, look outside of Manhattan. Brooklyn, for instance, has spacious apartments at much lower rents.

Search through available resources. The *Village Voice* and *The New York Times* are excellent sources for real estate listings. *The Wall Street Journal* and *The New York Post* list rentals as well. The *Brooklyn Heights Press*

21 city living

and *The Phoenix* are both great sources for rentals in Brooklyn; pick them up at newsstands in the neighborhood. The *Times* real estate section officially comes out Sunday, but pick up a copy at a local kiosk late Saturday night to get a head start. Get the *Voice* Tuesday night, or go online. Listings are available even earlier on the Internet. The *Voice*: (www.villagevoice.com), updates their file at 1pm on Tuesday, and the *Times* (www.nytimes. com) updates theirs at midnight on Friday. Real Estate Online's Metro New York Real Estate Guide (http://www.ny realty.com) is another fine online source.

Of course, real estate brokers are another way to go, albeit not a very pleasant one. They can be pushy but they'll find you an apartment fast—for a fee. Many brokers charge between 10 and 15 percent of the first year's rent for their services. Smaller firms may only charge one month's rent. Find a broker by perusing the classifieds. Call the agencies that list appealing apartments and make an appointment to see their other, "exclusive" listings (rentals not listed in the paper). Avoid agencies that ask for an application fee; it's just a waste of money.

Never make an appointment to see a place without enough money in the bank to cover the first month's rent and a security deposit. A security deposit is another term for damage insurance. It's usually about one month's rent, and if all goes well (and nothing in the apartment is destroyed), it will be returned when the lease is up. If an open house is advertised, arrive fifteen minutes before the starting time with a check in hand, just in case. Apartments go very quickly, and it pays to be prepared. Be sure to read the lease in its entirety before signing. Be wary of any deviations from the standard (a standard lease can be obtained from any office supply store).

When in doubt, share. Sharing an apartment with a roommate or two significantly cuts costs. Be

real estate Lingo

Decode the codes. Real estate has a lingo all its own. Ads are filled with abbreviations, and brokers drop phrases like, "one-month's security," and "fourth-floor walk-up." Most of the ambiguous terms apply to the condition of the apartment. "Flrthru," means that the apartment is a duplex, or a two-level living space. A "walk-up" refers to an apartment in a building without an elevator; an "eleventh flr walk-up" should generally be avoided. "Stu" is the abbreviation for a studio, or a one-room apartment. A two-room place, generally known as a one-bedroom, is abbreviated as "1BR." "Wbfp" and "EIK" are particularly ambiguous; they simply indicate, however, the presence of a wood-burning fireplace and an eat-in kitchen. An apartment described as "cozy" is undoubtedly small, and anything labeled "small" outright is probably closet-like. "No Fee" means no broker's fee will be charged.

careful, though; some landlords are picky about the number of people sharing their apartment, and subletting without his or her permission can result in an eviction notice. For those who want to forge ahead, it might be wise to try a roommate-finding service. Roommate Finders (250 West 57th Street, Suite 1629, NYC 10019, 489-6862) and The Roommate Solution, Inc. (488 Madison Avenue, Suite 1700, NYC 10022, 717-0144) are two good agencies. Both have about a $200 up-front processing fee.

Try a housing alternative. If all else fails, snag a room at a YMCA. There are three locations in Manhattan: McBurney YMCA (206 West 24th Street, NYC 10011, 741-9226), Vanderbilt YMCA (224 East 47th Street, NYC 10017, 756-9600), and Westside YMCA (5 West 63rd Street, NYC 10023, 787-4400). All three rent rooms on a daily basis. Rates vary with location, but a single can generally be had for about $40 to $50 per day.

For something a little more permanent (but less permanent than, say, a year lease), try the 92nd Street Y (1395 Lexington Avenue, NYC 10128, 427-6000). Rooms go for about $525 to $650 a month, and there is a two-month minimum stay. The Markle Residence (123 West 13th Street, NYC 10021, 249-6850) offers rooms with private baths for about $400 a week, which includes two meals a day.

Roaches.

They are unpleasant reminders of the filth and violence that city-dwellers have grown used to. Finding a flurry of the crawly things in your kitchen, bathroom, closet, or bed can break your heart and invite nightmares of alien abduction. You can be the cleanest homemaker in Gotham but this doesn't guarantee a roach-free environment. Taking a few precautions may not eradicate the antennaed menace but it may give you peace of mind:

1. Keep food out of sight and covered.
2. Roaches like water. Keep kitchens and bathrooms as dry as possible. Make sure faucets don't drip.
3. Place baited roach traps beneath refrigerators, ovens, and other electrical appliances that make heat. These innocuous little discs are worth their weight in gold.
4. Roaches like to nibble on the glue that keeps paper bags together. Don't save them.
5. Throw garbage out at least once a day.
6. Use an insecticide in cracks and around baseboards.

If all else fails, stomp on them with a heavy-soled shoe and rest easy knowing that you, with the rest of New York, are fighting the good fight.

politics

"Don't you see, the rest of the country looks upon New York like we're left-wing Jewish homosexual pornographers? I think of us that way sometimes, and I live here." Although Woody Allen's words in *Annie Hall* may have rung truer in the late '70s, the city's relatively large percentage of open-minded, ultra-liberal residents means that registered Democrats outnumber registered Republicans here by two to one. Manhattan is the most heavily Democratic of the five boroughs, and together with the Bronx, Brooklyn, and Queens, it has supported Democrats for President by significant margins in every election since World War II. As the most conservative of the boroughs, Staten Island votes Republican with the same consistency that the other boroughs vote Democrat.

New York is unique in that as a city, it contains five counties; nearly everywhere else in the United States cities are within counties and not vice versa. Each borough is its own county: Manhattan is New York County, Brooklyn is King's County; Staten Island is Richmond County; the Bronx is Bronx County; and Queens is Queens County. An 1898 charter established the office of borough president in hopes of preserving borough pride despite consolidation into one city. Each borough president ("beep" for short) serves as a cheerleader, spokesperson, and advocate for his or her own borough. Large, well-funded offices allow borough presidents to hold investigations and commissions, and issue reports and recommendations, but nothing is binding and they possess little real power aside from the fact that the press will quote them regularly. The borough presidents also appoint members of local community boards, neighborhood citizen bodies which deal with zoning issues. Community boards can raise objections to building projects, thereby stopping them permanently or just temporarily. (Call 788-7453 to find the contact information for the nearest community board.) Meetings can range from a real snooze to a royal battle: one meeting in the East Village had squatters hurling cat feces at board members unsympathetic to their plight.

As mayor, Rudolph Giuliani is the city's chief elected official. He is responsible for collective bargaining with the city's unionized workers, overseeing the city's budget, and making political appointments that run the city's bureaucratic machinery. By appealing to white, ethnic voters living in the outer boroughs, exploiting David Dinkins' supposed mishandling of racial tensions in Crown Heights, and taking advantage of the paranoia over the city's rising crime rates, Giuliani became the city's first Republican mayor in twenty-eight years, currently in his second term. Next in command is the public advocate, currently Mark Green. Elected by popular vote, the public advocate serves as an

city living 24

ombudsperson dealing with complaints regarding municipal government. Since the mayor and public advocate do not necessarily have to come from the same political party, they may have dissenting opinions; this relationship serves as checks-and-balance, resulting in healthy but sometimes gridlocked politicking. When Mark Green dislikes a particular Giuliani administration policy, his staff can investigate and issue a scathing report about the inadequacies of city services.

The city's legislative branch, City Council (and its 51 members), share power with the mayor. The Council votes on everything regulated by city government, including zoning, sanitation, quality-of-life issues, recycling, and setting city-wage taxes. Also, the Council investigates the actions of the executive branch. Traditionally, the Council has been monopolized by Democrats. Representation in the Council is roughly proportional to a district or borough's population. In 1990, Brooklyn had the largest population at roughly 2.3 million, followed by Queens at 2 million, Manhattan at 1.5 million, the Bronx at 1.2 million, and Staten Island at 379,000.

Political involvement in New York City can start with a political club. New York City Democratic political clubs are a holdover from Tammany Hall, New York's legendary Democratic political machine, which controlled city government from the late 19th century through the early 20th. Initially organized by local district leaders who were part of Tammany, the clubs gave the machine its strength by providing constituent services and favors, particularly to immigrant populations. In 1933, mayor Fiorello La Guardia won a three-way race as a fusion candidate who opposed Tammany, and after his three terms the institution was powerless. Despite its early demise, the clubs still exist today. Each club covers sets of election districts based on groupings of several city blocks. Particularly thriving are the five clubs on the Upper West Side, a traditionally intellectual, liberal neighborhood. The four Democratic and one Republican club keep West Siders the "most politically active in the city." To find the name and number of a club near you, call Manhattan's Democratic County Committee (687-6540) or the Republican County Committee (599-1200).

Perhaps the best way to entrench yourself in politics is to vote. Students may register to vote in New York after they have been in the city for 30 days. After you register here, don't be surprised when you're called for jury duty, since the many federal, state, and civil court cases in the city necessitate lots of jurors. While school is in session, you can postpone jury duty by responding to summonses with a letter explaining your status.

25 city living

Students who move to new housing each year need to update their address in order to vote. If you are attending school here and prefer to continue voting at your permanent address, contact your home state Board of Elections and request an absentee ballot in advance of the election. For more information about voting in New York City, or to request a registration form, call (800) 367-8683.

Surviving the rigors of the city involves a little resilience, a little savvy, and the most important weapon of all—information. Armed with phone numbers and an indomitable sense of justice, triumph over municipal bureaucracy is guaranteed. Hard to believe, but there are people out there who can help ease many urban dilemmas. Now crack your knuckles...let's get ready to rumble:

How to dodge jury duty:

To be or not to be (in court)—that is the question. Serving on a jury is a civic duty, and over the years the process is becoming more and more stringent; it's harder now to slip through the cracks and escape. While anyone can come up with a reason to be rejected from a selection panel ("I have a bias against civil suit lawsuits," "I'm writing a piece about how to dodge the jury draft," etc.); the most effective way is to get personally banned by a judge. If a person is a defendant with a case pending, he or she will be difficult to place, and therefore gain immunity from the jury-selection process. Usually, jurors are allowed just one deferral any date up to six months after the summons. Try shirking the responsibility around the summer months when supply and demand of the juror commodity is in the draft dodger's favor. Summer sessions slow down the courts because of judicial seminars and judges' vacations. Civil and Criminal Court Division of Jurors: 374-0614.

How to beat the housing market:

If an apartment is rent stabilized, these conditions are met: the rent must be lower than $2000, and it must be in a building that was built before 1974, contains six or more units, and is not owned by a hospital, university, or other institution. To research an apartment's rent regulation status, call the DHCR's information line (718) 739-6400. Make sure to find out if a landlord is raising the rent above the legal limit, though DHCR won't reveal an apartment's rent history unless you're the tenant in that apartment. To bypass this, perform a minor act of civil disobedience: Take a blank lease form, fill out your name and the landlord's name and address. Make it look authentic and bring it to DHCR with an ID. When former landlords won't return security deposits, try the small claims courts. Metropolitan Council on Housing Tenant Line: 693-0550, Mondays, Wednesdays, and Fridays 1:30-5pm.

city living 26

*How to get the most
out of your MetroCard:*
The Straphangers Campaign, a watchdog group for mass transit, suggests taking advantage of the Block Ticket. Though usually distributed to subway riders after breakdowns and disasters, this pass entitles the bearer to use the transit system free for seventy-two hours after issuance. A delay of more than twenty minutes or if a delay is announced, obligates customer service to hand out passes. However, it is a bargain that comes at a price. In order to pull it off, some haggling and clenched fists may be needed. Ask to see a supervisor and request an official delay. MetroCard Customer Service: 638-7622, Transit Authority Inspector General: (800) MTA-IG4U.

*How to stop
a noisy neighbor:*
For irritating neighborly noise pollution, the City Council's decision to raise the penalty from $175 to $525 will not do the trick. These laws usually don't get enforced strictly enough to get adequate revenge. According to Ray Alvin (author of the Get-a-Grip New York series of reference books), the best way to do battle is to try this lawyer-free strategy: First let your neighbor know that you mean business by taking out a harassment subpoena at the police department as a scare tactic. Local precincts can assist with the forms so ask for the community-affairs officer. Second, get the landlord to open a second front of pressure by compelling him or her to back-up the claim. If the landlord doesn't want to be involved, boycott the rent. Thirdly, get your noisy neighbor to agree to an impartial mediation with the Community Disputes Resolution Program office. Police will then serve the offending neighbor with a summons. Once resolutions are signed by both parties, peace and quiet can be had by all. New York Police Department: 374-5000, Institute for Mediation and Conflict Resolution, Manhattan: 233-2405.

*How to nail
the phone company:*
Out of the 30 thousand pay phones in the city, 10 thousand are run by Bell Atlantic, and the rest are run by third-party companies that are basically unregulated. Call the complaint line if problems arise, especially with the unregulated companies. These companies come and go quickly, changing their services without notice. Policing these upstarts remains extremely difficult, and the only way of fighting back is to call and complain. By blowing the whistle, people help the city keep tabs on the pay phones that steal coins or don't work at all. United we pay what we want, get what we want, but divided we end up missing the bargains and losing our quarters. ITT Street pay-phone complaint line: (718) 403-8216, State Public Service Commission comment line: (800) 335-2120.

Converting an out-of-state driver's license to a New York license:
As long as the license has been expired for less than a year and was active for more than six months, the defunct piece of plastic can be the ticket to get a New York license. Avoid the crowds and go to the License X-press Office, which handles any DMV matter that doesn't involve written tests. For top-speed service, check out the X-press around holidays when the last thing on people's minds are licenses. Since the DMV uses a scoring system (six points=new license) make sure to bring lots of identification in order to score high: An out-of-state license=three points. A credit card=two points. Bank statements=two points. For the desperate: Parole papers=one point. Divorce records=2 points. Department of Motor Vehicles License X-press Office, 300 West 34th Street at Eighth Avenue 645-5550, Mondays, Tuesdays, and Wednesdays, 8am-7pm.

27 city living

dating

It's Saturday night, there's a new pair of shoes in the closet, every hair's in place—now, who to call? New York has an inexhaustible supply of nighttime glitz and glamour; the trick is finding someone to share it with. Contrary to popular belief, New Yorkers are not cynical about love; they just don't know where to find it. Though New York City probably offers the country's largest and most diverse dating pool, most natives find it difficult to keep their heads above water. Many claim that New York, despite the overcrowding and the constant noise, is the loneliest place on earth. Most eager daters find that it's all too easy to mix, mingle, and socially mangle a perfectly good evening. Never fear; dating in the city may be tough but plenty of New Yorkers are optimistic about dating and love. Glitz and glamour aside, most are just looking for "someone nice" to spend time with.

Meeting the right people is what New York City is all about. Business contacts are one thing but getting that coveted number takes a different kind of finesse. Most New Yorkers are skeptical about meeting their mate in a club or bar, but that doesn't stop them from trying. Love, in Manhattan, is dictated by zip codes. The location and type of bar or club is a strong determinate of the sort of people found within. Upscale trendies mix with their kind in SoHo and the Upper East Side, and downtown bohemians find love, of course, downtown. Lounges are generally populated by models and are better suited for people-watching than cruising. Clubs bring all kinds of folks together—the good, the bad, and the ugly. The most important thing to remember is that aesthetic codes at all bars and clubs are not the same; what's attractive in one nighttime dive can be horribly disfiguring in another. For a successful pick-up, do the research, know the bar and its clientele, and dress appropriately.

There are a few important pointers for those venturing into the nighttime singles scene. First, try not to give out a number; always get the other person's instead. This will save a lot of space on the answering machine, and maybe preclude a few calls to the police. Also, to avoid the glares of fellow dating peers, look around the bar and see what everyone is drinking, then order one, too. That said, here are a few bars and clubs that are particularly profitable for nighttime (and

28 city living

daytime, of course) company: NV, Life, and Nell's are clubs with an upscale, fashiony crowd; there's a refreshing variety at Mother, Tunnel, and Twilo; Spy, Bowery, and Chaos Bars cater to a snooty but fun group; the patrons of McSorley's Old Ale House, Belmont Lounge, and Ludlow Bar exude East Village chic; and Hell, appropriately buried deep within the meat-packing district, has an incredibly hip and trendy clientele (see Bars and Clubs for locations and reviews). Any crowded bar on the weekend is sure to generate at least one interesting conversation, and maybe a bull's-eye.

There are other ways of meeting people besides trolling through bars. New Yorkers generally make connections through friends. Take the blind date the next time its offered, and just go somewhere nice for drinks—see, not so hard, is it? For those who want to try something different, there are some interesting dating services available in the city. Many combine food with an introduction: Brunch Buddies, It's Just Lunch, and Single Gourmet all arrange meetings around meals. Of course, the notorious *Village Voice* personals are entertainment in themselves, but they could be profitable. *The New York Press* and *New York* also offer an extensive personals section. The important thing is to be creative and open-minded; with eight million people walking around, there are opportunities everywhere to make some kind of connection.

The date's for real, now what to do? After snagging that precious first date, plan something that will really impress. Don't go drop a lot of money, though. There are plenty of romantic spots in New York City that inspire love without depleting the wallet. A favorite spot of New Yorkers is Central Park (see *Neighborhoods*). Rent a boat and drift out on the lake. The Promenade in Brooklyn Heights and the Brooklyn Bridge (see *Neighborhoods*) are beautiful spots for romantic interludes. The Cloisters (see *Neighborhoods*) offer many secluded areas for a private picnic. Or make a weekend of it (see *Romantic Weekend*). However, if money really does buy love, then go for broke and dine at Windows On The World (see *Restaurant section*) and enjoy the breathtaking views.

city living 29

gay + lesbian

The bronze plaque outside 53 Christopher Street commemorates the climactic event that launched the gay rights movement in the United States almost three decades ago. On the night of June 27, 1969, more than 100 men, patrons of a gay bar called the Stonewall Inn, stood their ground in defiance of policemen who raided the establishment as part of an ongoing bullying tactic to subjugate homosexuals. The confrontation was violent and lasted several nights as word and outrage spread through the community, but it was a defining moment for gay men and women, one that resonates to this day.

Gays have always been part of New York City's colorful and eventful history. Though it is easy and understandable from our current perspective to look back at a singular event like the Stonewall uprising and call it the turning point in American gay history, the truth remains that the so-called turning point is part of a much longer curve, veering toward the mainstream and extending back through many generations.

In the early days of the 20th century, a burgeoning community was establishing itself in the West Village. Stewart's and Life Cafeterias, now defunct but formerly situated on Sheridan Square, were well-known gay hangouts, serving essentially as halfway houses where young gays could "come out" and gather with others.

The East Village, and the well-known Greenwich Village, became magnets for artists eager to make their mark. The numerous gay playwrights, actors, painters, sculptors, novelists, poets, photographers, and musicians who flooded into the Village contributed to the area's bohemian flair and intellectual prowess, and made them the city's most famous gay enclaves.

Before emigrating to Paris, a young James Baldwin penned *Giovanni's Room* while living in a $100 per month apartment on Horatio Street. Playwright Edward Albee, very much a part of the Village gay scene in the late 1950s, walked into the restroom at The Ninth Circle, a no-longer extant bar he frequented, and found "Who's Afraid of Virginia Woolf?" scrawled across the mirror; he later used the question as the title for his most famous play. Djuna Barnes, best remembered for her novel *Nightwood*, lived the last reclusive years of her life in a small apartment at Patchin Place, and some of the century's most accomplished poets, Allen Ginsburg, Frank O'Hara, and W.H. Auden, lived in the perennial

30 city living

nonconformist East Village.

In recent years, the West Village has remained as much the core of the gay community as it was almost one hundred years ago. Many political organizations have offices in the area, and help organize and publicize local goings-on. Chelsea has also become a predominately gay area, with many young gay professionals calling it home. Every June is Gay History Month, and fun, informative events and celebrations abound. In addition to two popular film festivals, the most anticipated event is, of course, the pride march.

Every year, on the last weekend in June, the march begins with "Dykes on Bikes." The motorcycles are lined up in alternate rows of three and four: the perfect spacing reflects the militaristic discipline of the black-clad women. Only a few smile to acknowledge the explosive adoration of the crowds lining Fifth Avenue. Most of the women are stone-faced, however, aware that their purpose is to intimidate as much as to exhilarate. The march culminates in a huge street fair around the Stonewall Inn, and at night, the top of the Empire State building is illuminated in lavender and white.

Gay New York, however encompasses much more than its notorious downtown enclaves. Many Village thirty-somethings have migrated to the Upper West Side, where Lincoln Center's great performances reinforce the city's commitment to the arts and friendly night spots line Broadway and Amsterdam Avenues. Their corporate counterparts have, for the most part, resigned themselves to the Upper East Side, renowned for its high-end art and comfy living. Harlem has supported a vibrant African-American community, and many who were instrumental

RESOURCES

Plug yourself into the most diverse gay and lesbian community in America. The following publications will keep you abreast of local and city-wide gay events, usually in enough time for you to plan the perfect date:

The New York Blade, 223-1181
A relatively new addition to the growing number of gay and lesbian New York publications, this free weekly can be found throughout the city.

MetroSource, 691-5127.
A comprehensive listing of community businesses, this quarterly also features articles on various gay-related topics.

Time Out: New York, 539-4444.
An essential guide to everything that's happening in the city, it's a must for everyone and includes a special gay and lesbian section in every issue.

Homophobia is a reality that all gay men and women take seriously. The following organizations can provide help when needed:

The Gay + Lesbian Switchboard, 777-1800.
If you have a question about almost anything gay-related, or don't know where to turn for help, the Switchboard can provide answers.

Lesbian + Gay Community Services Center, 208 West 13th St., www.gaycenter.org, 620-7310.
Founded in 1984, the center sponsors many gay events, including lectures and dances. It also houses an extensive gay historical archive.

Gay + Lesbian Alliance Against Defamation, 150 West 26th St., Suite 505, www.glaad.org, 807-1700.
GLAAD is a media advocacy organization established to ensure fair and accurate reportage of issues and events concerning homosexuals.

in the Harlem Renaissance struggled to eradicate both racism and homophobia.

Although Manhattan is the gayest of New York City's boroughs, and is home to most of the city's exciting clubs, quaint coffee houses, and entertaining cabarets, Brooklyn and Queens both have substantial numbers of ethnically diverse individuals, who have created their own gay focal points in Park Slope and Jackson Heights.

Though New York is ultimately one of the greatest cities in the world for fine dining, shopping, museum-and-movie-going, bar-hopping, dancing, sight-seeing, outdoor R + R, and other activities enjoyed by gays and lesbians, the city is no

clubs, cabarets, coffeehouses, etc.

The New York City club scene is simultaneously fun and exhausting. Check out the following hot spots for the time of your life:

Mostly Male:
Stonewall, 53 Christopher St., 463-0950.
This isn't the original, which was next door, but its proximity reminds patrons of that night many years ago when a spontaneous act of solidarity galvanized the gay rights movement. Patrons are diverse in age, with some neighborhood folk mixing with out-of-towners.
The Bar, 68 Second Ave., 674-9714.
Black-clad guys who probably grew facial hair in anticipation of coming here rock to a jukebox of wildly divergent musical styles.
The Works, 428 Columbus Ave., 799-7365.
The drinks are cheap at this popular Upper West Side haunt where the majority of young men hanging out seem to be rehearsing for a GQ photo shoot.

Mostly Female:
Crazy Nannies, 21 Seventh Ave. South, 366-6312.
Can you say Lesbian Central? Go on the weekends for a fun, racially-mixed crowd of trucker-types and femmes.
Julie's, 204 East 58th St., 688-1294.
Yes, you read the address correctly. This classy nightspot is no downtown bar, and the women are well-heeled, with an air of consummate professionalism.
Meow Mix, 269 East Houston St., 254-1434.
Fast becoming the né plus ultra-hip scene thanks to Ellen Degeneres' and Anne Heche's pop-ins. This club is best known for its pulsing jukebox and frequent literary events.

Manhattan cabarets feature some world-class talent in an intimate, subdued environment. Say you want to spend an evening at the theater and can't quite afford Broadway or opera tickets. Voila:
Eighty-Eights, 228 West 10th St., 924-0088.
Quite simply, one of the most charming piano bars in the city, featuring name talent in the upstairs lounge, and laid-back jamborees downstairs.
Don't Tell Mama, 343 West 46th St., 757-0788.
Class acts, usually big names from the '50s and '60s, abound in this small Midtown gem.

Ah, the ubiquitous coffeehouse! How do you choose which one to go to when there are so many? Relax, and sample the following standbys:
Tea and Sympathy, 108 Greenwich Ave., 807-8329.
A little bit of old England in the Village, this sophisticated haunt is a favorite of gay men who take their tea seriously.
Drip, 489 Amsterdam Ave., 875-1032. Scrubbed and spiffy uptowners frequent this popular spot with its colorful decor and collection of pop culture tchotchkies.

Hey, you've arrived in the most exciting city in the world! There's more to life than bar-hopping, lounge singing, and sharing a room with coffee-crazed hipsters:
Columbia University Dance, Earl Hall, Broadway and 116th St., 854-1488.
For a nominal fee you can dance till you drop at these mixers sponsored by the University's gay students alliance.
Lesbian + Gay Community Center Dance.
The kind, activist folks at this organization sponsor a dance on the second and fourth Saturdays of every month. (see Resources)

gay religious groups

Whatever religious fundamentalists and the conservative press choose to think, gays and lesbians, and organized religion are far from mutually exclusive. The many gay and gay-friendly congregations that march every year in the Gay Pride Parade signal not only their existence, but the need that many gays and lesbians have for a spiritual community. The following is a modest sampling of these organizations. Contact the Lesbian and Gay Community Center (see Resources) for additional information and a comprehensive list.

Metropolitan Community Church, 629-7440.
Founded in the early 1970s by Troy Perry, the MCC welcomes all individuals and is an amalgam of the Catholic, Anglican, and Lutheran Churches.

Congregation Beth Simchat Torah, 929-9498.
This lesbian and gay synagogue lies in the heart of the West Village where New York City's gay community began.

Dignity, New York, 627-6488.
The largest Catholic gay organization is unrepentantly vocal in its opposition to the faith's traditional position on gays and lesbians.

It's Episcopalian counterpart is called Integrity, 691-7181.

West Park Presbyterian Church, 362-4890.
The day after the official Presbyterian Council struck down amendments that would have sanctified same-sex relationships, this progressive church defiantly flew the rainbow flag.

Saint Paul's, 265-3495.
This Roman Catholic Parish is always in hot water with the Archdiocese for sponsoring a very active gay and lesbian congregation.

utopia. "The biggest myth," says 26-year-old gay-rights activist Keith, "is that New York City is a giant gay playground and no one ever gets hurt. Homophobia does exist here, and every new gay resident should be aware of that, if only to spare themselves the shock if they find themselves in a harmless but uncomfortable situation. But in comparison to other American cities, New York seems to have realized that diversity is a tremendous strength and is, in many ways, light-years beyond them in terms of gay-friendliness."

{real} New Yorkers' Weekend

It's Friday evening, you're exhausted from your grueling work-week. You'd love to quit your job, but rent is due on the first. The last two weekends you wasted under the covers with the phone off the hook. Make this weekend different. Head home and call a friend who knows how to give a really mean massage. Afterward, grab some grapes out of the fridge and the hand of your new best friend and head out to the Roosevelt Island Tram (see *Cheap Thrills in Upper East Side Neighborhood section*.) Watch how the sun sinks behind the towering buildings of your favorite city.

Head out Saturday morning as early as you can. First hit the Farmers Market in Union Square (see *Sites + Parks in Gramercy Neighborhood section*), pick up some fresh basil, some strawberries and oranges, a few postcards, and some apple cider, then head over to Little Italy and buy some mozzarella, marinated mushrooms, and fresh bread. Call some friends and pick a picnic spot in Central Park (see *Central Park Neighborhood section*) Avoid Sheep Meadow, which is teeming on the weekends. Choose a sunny patch of grass, make a few sandwiches, then write a few postcards to far-away friends. Once the sun sets, hop from bar to bar in the West Village and catch a show of your favorite local band who's drummer's brother you used to date.

For real New Yorkers, Sunday doesn't start until noon. The Screening Room (see *Restaurant section*) offers a great brunch and screening of Breakfast at Tiffany's at 1:30pm. Afterwards you might want to head to Orchard Street in the Lower East Side to do a little vintage shopping at great spots like Cherry, Shine, and Rose is Vintage (see *Shopping section*). Finally, check out The Strand's, "eight miles of books" (see *Literature section*). Head back to your tiny-over-priced-but-charming apartment. Try on all your new clothes again, then curl up under the covers with your new used book and put off Monday for as long as possible.

{fun-filled} Sporty Weekend

New York is an urban arena for the modern gladiator. On Saturday, fuel up on complex carbs at the Empire Diner, before jogging over to the world famous Sports Center at Chelsea Piers (see *Leisure section*). Day passes are available for $25; get two and take a friend. Throw a few punches in their boxing ring, spike to your heart's content playing volleyball in their sand volleyball courts, and play Spider Man on vertical climbing walls, all under one roof! Wind down after your workout with a massage at the Origins Feel-Good Spa.

Still haven't had enough? Take an evening trip to BowlMor Lanes (see *Sports + Recreation section*) and learn to bowl with the lights out. There's a full bar for those who want to improve their game and a DJ to keep you out of the gutter. Afterwards, have a light dinner at Clementine (see *Restaurant section*).

On Sunday, get up early the next day and enjoy the sun in Central Park (see *Central Park Neighborhood section*), New York's favorite place to push their limits. Rent a pair of rollerblades then skate into the park at 81st Street. The road west of Sheep Meadow around 69th Street was designed specifically for skating, but any scenic trail will do; just watch out for other skaters. Bring a picnic basket and have a healthy lunch. Rent a rowboat from the Loeb Boathouse (see *Central Park Neighborhood section*) and drift the afternoon away on the Central Park Lake. Cross the Park to Lexington Avenue and take the 6 train to the Brooklyn Bridge (see *Brooklyn Neighborhood section*). Time it right and arrive at dusk; cross the bridge on foot and enjoy the spectacular sunset. Have a well-deserved dinner at Brooklyn's River Cafe (see *Restaurant section*).

{cool} Sightseeing Weekend

Visiting New York without seeing a Broadway show (see *Performing Arts*) would be like visiting the Riviera and not going to the beach. Currently, hot shows include *Rent* and *Cabaret*. Choosing a pretheater restaurant is made easy by Restaurant Row on West 46th Street, a street that lives up to its name with hundreds of eateries.

Tavern on the Green (see *Restaurant section*) for brunch or lunch the next day should fuel you for the day, on both food and opulence. If the weather's nice, take a ride through Central Park (see *Central Park Neighborhood section*) in one of the horse-drawn gigs lining Central Park South.

Make your way over to the east side of the Park, where Museum Mile (see *Sites + Parks in Upper East Side Neighborhood section*), features some of the city's finest exhibitions. Or, if you're up for a long walk, promenade down Fifth Avenue where you'll pass grand hotels, the Humanities Library (see *Sites + Parks in Midtown Neighborhood section*), the Empire State Building (see *Sites+Parks in Midtown Neighborhood section*), the Flatiron Building (see *Sites +Parks in Gramercy Neighborhood section*) and—whew! Haven't you stopped for a drink yet? Head to Greenwich Village, where the Avenue ends at Washington Square Park (see *Sites + Parks in Greenwich Village Neighborhood section*), stomping grounds for the students of New York University. There is a wonderful diversity of restaurants in this area, everything from Ethiopian to French.

Sunday is another day to explore. Of course, there is much left in Manhattan to see. However, if you want to get a sense of "real" New York, head out of Manhattan. After all, New York does consist of five boroughs. Take the subway out to Coney Island (see *Brooklyn Neighborhood section*) for the good 'n' greasy life of the boardwalk. Clearly, you'll want to grab hot dogs at Nathan's (see *Cheap Thrills in Brooklyn Neighborhood section*), but after spending the day by the surf, come back for dinner at Windows on the World in the World Trade Center (see *Sites + Parks in Financial District neighborhoods section*) and a panorama of the Big Apple's celebrated skyline.

{sweet} Romantic Weekend

So, you're in the mood for love and have a whole weekend to nurture Cupid's wound? It's Friday Night: Go on a traditional date. Start out at the Metropolitan Museum of Art's Cantor Roof Garden (see Cheap Thrill ih upper East Side neighborhood section) for some white wine and a spectacular view of the city. Stroll arm in arm over to Erminia (see Restaurant section) for a quiet dinner. Then it's off to the Hotel Carlyle (35 E.76th St., 744-1600) for one of their featured cabaret performances.

On Saturday head dowtown for brunch at the Pink Tea Cup (see Restaurant section). After a relaxing meal, go to the 10th St. Baths (268 East 10th Street, 473-8806). Their "Platza" rub, Turkish Baths, and saunas will awaken your senses to all possibilities of touch and make you both feel like you are on cloud nine.

"Recover" for the rest of the day and then head to Jean Claude (137 Sullivan St. between Houston and Prince.) for dinner. Always mobbed with the art-house crowd, this SoHo fave serves imaginative French cuisine at Bistro prix. Curl up afterwards on one of the cushy couches at Scharmann's (see Restaurant section) for drinks or one of their fabulous desserts.

Although you may still be reeling from the night before. Force yourself to wake at noon on Sunday. Buy the New York Times and go to Sarabeth's (see Restaurant section) for a lazy brunch and order the house favorite--Goldilocks Eggs with smoked salmon & Cream Cheese and play footsie under the lace table cloths. Work those calories off by renting a boat at the Boathouse in Central Park (East Park Dr. on 73rd St., open 9am-5:30pm on the Weekends. $7/an hour + $20 Deposit); this is the most undeniably the most romantic way to enjoy Central Park. Read poetry to each other as you canoe gently downstream.

Finish up at the Boathouse Cafe (Central Park near East 72d Street, 517-2333), where the lake view and smooth jazz quartet combine to provide wonderful ambience. Make sure to share the luxurious warm chocolate cake for dessert. Afterward step into a gondola and let someone else do the work, while you navigate the sea of love.

35 city living

JANUARY/FEBRUARY

Chinese New Year
Celebrate Chinese New Year in Chinatown during the first full moon on January 19th. Parades, fireworks, and food make it worth the crowds.
❻❼❻❼ *to Canal St.*

New York Coliseum Antique Show
Yearly January antique-a-thon with vendors from all over the world.
Coliseum at Columbus Circle, 384-0010, 19 to 59th St.

Dick Clark's Rockin' New Year's Eve
While the rest of the country watches it on TV, see the ball drop in person along with thousands of delirious New Yorkers. Other highlights of the evening include fireworks and a midnight run through Central Park
Times Square, midnight, **❶❷❸ ❹❺❻❾❼** *to Times Square*

New Year's Day Beach Walk
On Rockaway Beach, Jones Beach, and Sandy Hook; Champagne and cookies provided.
(718) 634-6467

Empire State Building Run Up
22nd annual mad dash to the 86th floor, for those who have something to prove.
Every February. Contact New York Roadrunners Club for more information.
(see Sports + Leisure section)

Black History Month
Black History Month is Celebrated throughout the city throughout the month of January, with readings, concerts, theater events etc.
Consult the New York Times and call museums of interest for more specific information.

FOCUS!
Free Festival of Contemporary Music, in its 13th Year, 3rd and 4th weeks of January.
Alice Tully Hall, 65th St. (at Broadway), 768-7406

New York International Motorcycle Show
Dream machines from around the world sparkle under the florescent lights of the Javits center every year in February.
Call Jacob Javits Center for details, 216-2000

Tisch School of the Arts
Free theater in February from this talented student theater group.
Call for reservations, 988-1921

MARCH/APRIL

St. Patrick's Day Parade
An annual political event featuring the wearin' o' the green', baby-kissing and gay and lesbian protesters.
From 10:30am to 4pm at Fifth Ave. at 44th St., March 17th.

"Wall to Wall" Marathon Concert
The 24-hour music marathon features a multitude of performers and a different theme each year; it's always fun.
Second or third Saturday in March, 11am-11pm. Symphony Space, 2537 Broadway (at 95th St.), 580-0210, **❶❷❸** *to 96th St.*

Annual English Handbell Festival
Features 100 ringers from New York plus guest choirs.
March 29th, 3pm. Riverside Church, 490 Riverside Dr. (at 122nd St.), 870-6722, **❶❾** *to 125th St.*

NY Flower Show
The Garden of Eden comes to New York City.
Piers 90 and 93. 51st St. (at 12th Ave) Tickets: $10. First week in March.

Art Expo New York
The world's Largest Show of Pop Art comes to the Javits Convention Center featuring landscapes, posters, sculptures, decorative arts and more.
Call Javits Center for more information, 216-2000

Easter Parade
"On the Avenue, 5th Avenue" the annual exhibit of the good life has become more interesting since it has become a drag-rehearsal for Wigstock.
Fifth Ave. (at 44th St., heading up to 59th St.) Easter Sunday.

Opening Day at Yankee Stadium
A few baseball legends always show up.
Call Ticketmaster or Yankee Stadium (718) 293-4300, for details

Whitney Biennial
Whitney Museum's display of "the most important " American Art. Controversy, every time.
945 Madison Ave. at 75th St., 570-3600.

Cherry Blossom Festival
A great reason to see what's in bloom at the Brooklyn Botanical Gardens.
1000 Washington Ave., **❷❹** *to Eastern Parkway.*

MAY/JUNE

New York Philharmonic
The Philharmonic performs at the Cathedral of St. John The Divine on Memorial day at 8pm. The line starts forming at 3pm.
Amsterdam Ave (at 112th St.) **❶❾** *to 110th St.*

Ukrainian Festival
Sample some of the city's best festival fare on Seventh Ave.

Fleet Week
On Memorial Day weekend, the city's harbors fill up with naval vessels while the streets and bars fill up with sailors. Land ho!

Bike NY: The Great Five Borough Bike Tour
All the boroughs on one bike! 932-0778, Early May.

Martin Luther King Jr. Parade
Celebrate Dr. King the 3rd Sunday in May.
Fifth Ave; 44th St. to 86th St.

Ninth Avenue International Food Festival
Food galore from around the world, pick what you eat carefully because there is a

36 city living

staggering amount to choose from! Also jewelry, music, and vendors too.
Between 37th and 57th St., Mid-May.

Met in the Parks
The Metropolitan Opera gives performances in the city parks; call for a schedule.
Begins in June, 362-6000

JVC Jazz Festival
Well-known performers give free outdoor concerts in Byrant Park and at venues all over the city.
Begins in June, 787-2020

Bryant Park Free Festival
Dance, food, comedy, music, films!
Sixth Ave. (at 42nd St.) call 983-4142 for information

Puerto Rican Day Parade
Salsa music, dancers, food, and pride in Puerto Rican culture.
Fifth Ave to Central Park South, early June

Mermaid Parade
Celebrate Coney Island boardwalk's season opening. Last year's parade king was David Byrne. Enjoy the freaks in all their glory and marvel at the innovative ways women dress up as mermaids, waddling down the boardwalk.
❸❹❻ to Coney Island; late June

Celebrate Brooklyn
Music and fun in Prospect Park.
Weekends in June and July

AIDS Walk New York
Late June annual walk to raise money to fight AIDS, 6.21 miles. Call Gay Men's Health Crisis for information, 807-6655

Belmont Stakes
Longest, and last Triple Crown stakes.
Belmont Long Island, Mid-June, (718) 641-4700

Gay Pride March
The annual Gay Pride Parade gets bigger and better each year.
Late June, Columbus Circle to Greenwich Village

Midsummer Night's Swing
Dance the night away under the stars and tango around the Lincoln Center fountain; also jazz, zydeco, swing—all for $8
Free dance lessons from 6:30 Lincoln Center, ❶❾ to 66th St. (at Broadway), begins in June-August

JULY/AUGUST

Philharmonic in the Parks
The New York Philharmonic gives concerts in city parks; call for a schedule.
875-5709

July 4th, Macy's Fireworks on the Hudson
Oooh and Aaah at the gala fireworks on display over New York Harbor. Find a spot in Battery Park or call a friend with a 20th floor penthouse with a downtown view.
July 4th, check media for specifics

Concerts in the MOMA Sculpture Garden
Concerts of classical music among world-renown sculpture; free, on Friday/Sat. nights in July and August.

Lincoln Center Out of Doors Festival
Free Music and dances performed, held outdoors.
Call for information, 875-5400

US Open
The drama of championship tennis makes its way to Queens every year.
Flushing, Queens, (718)760-6200

Harlem Week
A slew of cultural activities, including concerts, outdoor fairs and educational workshops.
August 15-17th

India Day Parade
Celbrate Indian Independence, August 21st.
Madison Ave (bet. 24th and 31st Sts.)

Dominican Day Parade
The DR celebrates its culture on August 10th at 1pm.
Sixth Ave. (bet. 39th and 56th)

Pakistan Independence Day Festival and Parade
Turn out to support South Asian freedom on August 24th.
Parade at 10am, Madison Ave. (bet. 41st and 26th Sts.); Festival 2-9pm, Madison Ave. (bet. 23rd and 26th Sts.)

SEPTEMBER /OCTOBER

Broadway on Broadway
See the stars of the hottest shows on the Great White Way belt out their signature tunes.
Noon-2pm, September 7. Broadway and Seventh Ave., (bet. 43rd and 48th Sts.), ❶❷❸ ❼❾ⒶⒸⒺⓇⓃⓈ to 42nd St.

The Cloister's Medieval Festival
The Cloisters transforms into a New York that never was with falconers, jesters, knights, fair maidens and medieval food and music.
Each September, call the Parks Department/Special Events, 360-2777, for information

West Indian Day Carnival and Parade
Eastern Parkway from Utica Ave. to the Brooklyn Museum is lined with food, floats, and shopping; the parade begins at 8am on September 1st.
❹❺ to Eastern Parkway, ❷❸ to Grand Army Plaza

Washington Square Outdoor Art Exhibit
Great Art outdoors and all for free! September 6-7 noon-7pm.
ⒶⒷⒸⒹⒻⓆ to West 4th St.

Brooklyn Promenade Show
Good art and a beautiful view of New York Harbor and the Manhattan skyline from a historic neighborhood.
Last weekend in September. Brooklyn Heights Promenade (bet. Ramsen and Clark), (718)625-0080, ❷❸ to Clark

SoHo Arts Festival

Readings, performances and talks at SoHo galleries. September 11-21.
524 Broadway (at Spring St.), Suite 203 (headquarters), 925-4200, ❶❽ to Prince St.

San Gennaro Feast
Little Italy's yearly bash, with or without Vinnie the Chin.
September 11-21.
Fifth Avenue (bet. 48th and 57th Sts.) and 52nd and 53rd Sts. (bet. Madison and Sixth Ave.)

WIGSTOCK
Come see RuPaul, Lady Chablis, Sherry Vine et al., dressed up and showing how to work it on Labor Day.
Pier at 11th St. on the Hudson. Info: 620-7310

Atlantic Avenue Street Festival
Vast, Multicultural Street fair in Brooklyn in September.
(718) 875-8993.

Halloween Parade
What used to be a carnival of subversion has become a parade of drunken innocents but it is Halloween after all and the goblin turn out in all their fabulous glory.
Greenwich Village, on Broadway from Spring St. to Union Sq. ❶❾ to 14th St., ❶❻❹❺❻ to Union Sq.

Hispanic Columbus Day Parade
An alternative rendering of popular history.
11am, October 12th. Fifth Ave.

Columbus Day Parade
Cheer on Christopher's "discovery" on October 13th.
Fifth Ave.

NOVEMBER/ DECEMBER

NYC Marathon
20,000 runners take over the city. It's fun to watch them don silver, insulated shawls so they don't die from exhaustion after their trek.
Tavern on the Green.

Holiday Windows Along Fifth Avenue
New York outdoes itself with whimsy and holiday cheer especially Saks Fifth Ave + Lord and Taylor.
Fifth Ave.

Nutcracker Suite
New York City Ballet and Student of the School of American Ballet unite to perform this beloved Christmas classic.
New York State Theater, 870-5570 NYC

Macy's Thanksgiving Parade
Beware of a giant Bullwinkle loosing his tether. Wear your mittens and be on guard for pick-pockets. Seeing it once is enough.
Fifth Ave. on Thanksgiving Day

Palm Tree Lighting at the World Financial Center
Over 100 thousand holiday lights lit right after Thanksgiving.
545-0505

Rockefeller Center Tree-Lighting
Gather 'round the city's favorite tree for the ceremonial lighting and celebrity ice-skaters at the ice rink.
Rockefeller Center ❽❶❻❻ to 47th/50th St./Rockefeller Cntr.

Park Avenue Tree-Lighting
Over 45 blocks of trees light up at the flip of a switch at the Brick Presbyterian Church on the first Sunday of December at 6:60pm
Park Ave (at 91st St.), 289-4400, ❹❺❻ to 86th St.

The Chorus Tree
Famous tree sings at the South Street Seaport.
Call SEA-PORT

Marathon Reading of a Literary Classic
The reading begins on December 31st and ends in the wee hours of January 1st when the book is finished. Celebrity writers show up. Last year it was Nabokov's Lolita.
Paula Cooper Gallery, 155 Wooster St., 255-1105

Times Square New Year's Eve Countdown
Dick Clark is ageless, New Yorkers become warm and fuzzy, and the City counts down in delirious unison waiting for that ball to drop.
Times Square, ❶❷❸❹❺❻❼ to Times Sq.

YEAR 'ROUND FUN

Films at MoMA
See avant-garde and classic films during MoMA's pay-what-you-wish Friday, 6-8pm.
53rd St. (bet. Fifth and Sixth Aves.), 708-9480, ❽❶❻ to Seventh Ave.

Barnes and Noble
Talks and readings by famous, unfamous and infamous authors at locations across the city. Pick up a schedule at every store.

Tour Grand Central
Learn about the design and features of one of the nations' most important urban landmarks, Grand Central Station. Wednesdays at 12:30pm.
Meet at information kiosk, Main Concourse of Grand Central Sta. (42nd St. at Park Ave.), 935-3960, ❺❹❺❻❼ to Grand Central

Moon Bike Ride
Join other bikers for a safe ride through Central Park in the peace and quiet of night. Last Friday of each month, 10pm.
Meet at Columbus Circle entrance to Central Park, 802-8222, ❶❽❶❶ to 59th St.

Urban Park Rangers
Walk with the Urban Park Rangers in New York City Parks for entomology, ecology, ornithology, and plain old fun.
Saturdays/Sundays 11am + 2pm. 1-800-201-PARK

Orchard Street Bargain Tour
Over 400 stores and boutiques offer merchandise at up to 70 percent off in this historic district. The tour includes a visit to sites like the Tenement Museum and the Eldridge Street synagogue.
Sundays at 11am. Katz's Deli, 205 East Houston St. (at Ludlow St.), 226-8742, ❻ to Second Ave.

38 city living

new york city's neighborhoods

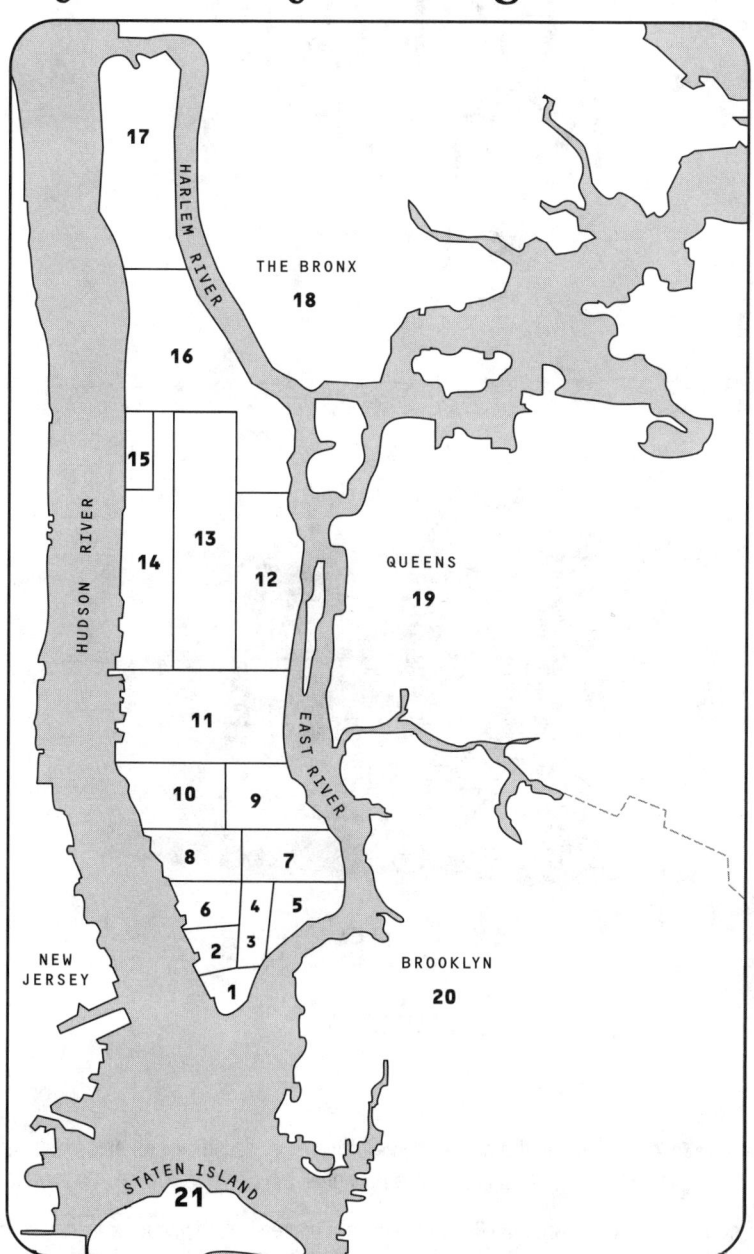

1. Financial District
2. TriBeCa
3. Chinatown
4. Little Italy
5. Lower East Side
6. SoHo
7. East Village
8. Greenwich Village
9. Gramercy
10. Chelsea
11. Midtown
12. Upper East Side
13. Central Park
14. Upper West Side
15. Morningside Heights
16. Harlem
17. Washington Heights
18. Bronx
19. Queens
20. Brooklyn
21. Staten Island

College is a great start.

Here's another.

The New York Times starts the day for some of the most accomplished and ambitious people in all fields. It provides a big-picture view of all the news transforming our world.

Discover new worlds. Learn more about the ones you already care about. Order now and benefit from our special education rates. Call 1-800-631-1222 for information and mention the name of your school.

The New York Times

Newspaper in Education | **Expect the World**™ | www.nytimes.com

neighborhoods

financial district.42
tribeca.48
chinatown.52
little italy.56
lower east side.60
soho.64
east village.68
greenwich village.72
gramercy.78
chelsea.82
midtown.86

upper east side.94
central park.98
upper west side.102
morningside heights.108
harlem.112
washington heights.118
bronx.122
queens.128
brooklyn.132
staten island.138

financial DISTRICT

The Financial District is still the center of the world's big money transactions, but you don't need a suit and an agenda to appreciate its finer nuances. The district sits below Chambers Street, and is covered by a motley assortment of architectural styles: 18th-century Georgian-Federal, 19th-century neoclassical, and modern skyscrapers.

Anyone interested in hurling themselves into murky waters over a deal gone bad will be faced with a plethora of options: the Hudson River? The East River? Or maybe consider pulling a Darryl Hannah and *Splash* into the Upper Bay of New York Harbor. If you want to go out with a bang, the Brooklyn Bridge is close by. However, by the time you've walked halfway to Brooklyn Heights, you may find yourself in a more reverential state of mind. The awesome view and the splendor of the bridge's architecture will probably be enough to make you feel as though life in the Financial District is, indeed, worth living.

Despite the neighborhood's moniker, activity in the Financial District is not limited to financial concerns. At the district's eastern edge, trucks from New England make daily 5am deliveries to the Fulton fish market, while lawyers and politicians make their daily journeys to the municipal buildings and City Hall, where Rudy Giuliani holds court. Ironically, Century 21 and a smattering of dicount designer stores make the Financial District their home as well.

Tourists, numbering a billion per year, flood the narrow alleyways and take refuge at the South Street Seaport, whose mixture of quaint cobblestone streets, sidewalk cafes, cozy bars, all right on the water, is oddly reminiscent of San Francisco.

By twilight, stockbrokers wallow in pints of Guinness in nearby TriBeCa while other professionals head home to the suburbs and tourists trudge back to their hotels. But even as Lady Liberty lights up the harbor and silence spreads over the deserted streets, the view from atop the Twin Towers reveals that the rest of the city is still on the move; taxis honk their way up Broadway, as, further south, party boats laden with tourists circle the island's southern tip, admiring the panorama of towering buildings. Meanwhile, each round trip of the Staten Island Ferry pulls the city closer to the next dawn.

local color

Name: Ellen Fabbricatore
Age: 23
Occupation: Actress / Waitress

Q: How long have you lived in the neighborhood?
A: Since I was 2.

Q: What do you like about the neighborhood?
A: The fact that we were pioneers. No one used to live here, but it's slowly transforming into a more residential neighborhood.

Q: Where do you like to hang out?
A: Battery Park City.

Q: Where do you buy groceries around here?
A: Associated Supermarket on Gold Street.

Q: Are there any good places to buy shoes in the neighborhood?
A: Yeah, I'm ashamed to admit this, but I have a pair of those $19.99 boots they sell on Nassau Street. The shoes they sell there are great -- they're cheap but they look expensive.

Q: Do you ever go out in this neighborhood?
A: To be honest? Not really. I usually hang out in the Village.

Ellen Fabbricatore: Financial District Pioneer

history

One of the most famous real estate transactions in history occurred in the Financial District in 1626. For the equivalent of $24, Peter Minuit, the Director General of New Netherland, bought the island of *Manahatta*, now known as Manhattan, for the Dutch East India Company from the Manates tribe. He encountered little trouble, since the Native Americans could not conceive of private property, much less transferring that property to someone else.

But the Dutch had already claimed the island long before Minuit's purchase. In 1609, the Dutch East India Company hired Henry Hudson to find a passage to India and China. Instead, what he found was a harbor and the river that now bears his name.

After news of the harbor's high-quality spread, the Netherlands claimed the island called Manahatta, which was populated by several tribes. Because of its access to the Hudson River, the Atlantic Ocean, and points east, the island quickly developed into the biggest center of commerce in America. This wealth of opportunity attracted many immigrants long before the Statue of Liberty was presented by France.

Shipping gave way to finance as the neighborhood's predominant industry, just as marinas and Victorians ceded ground to progressively larger buildings, culminating in skyscrapers. These cathedrals of commerce, which became less and less ornate over the years, form New York's trademark skyline.

Andrew J. Tobin Plaza
Dominated by a Twin Tower on either side, this five-acre square with a mammoth fountain at its center hosts free concerts and temporary art projects during the summer as well as the permanent work of modern artists.
Between One and Two World Trade Center, 1 9 to Cortlandt St., C E to the World Trade Center.

Battery Park
A gun battery in Colonial times, later an entrance point for millions of immigrants, the park's beautiful river view calms tourists waiting in line for a ferry to Lady Liberty.
South of State St., 1 9 to South Ferry

Battery Park City
Palm trees and remarkable cleanliness seem transplanted from a kinder, gentler city, though the skyscrapers looming in the distance bring back the familiar vertigo; meander alongside the Hudson on this commercial and residential complex's well-maintained esplanade and pretend that the "City Beautiful" movement really did find its way into municipal government.
Bounded by Chambers St., West St., Pier A, and the Hudson River, 1 9 to Rector St.

Bowling Green
The oldest extant public park in the city, this spot where Peter Minuit supposedly purchased Manhattan once boasted the famous statue of George III which irate Revolutionary patriots toppled and used for bullets.
Broadway and Battery Place, 4 5 to Bowling Green

National Museum of the American Indian
The Old Custom House contains this extensive, well-curated museum, one of the few Smithsonian institutions outside of Washington. The exhibits are fascinating, though the federal architecture and the beautiful rotunda alone merit the trip.
One Bowling Green (foot of Broadway), 668-6624, Admission Free, 4 5 to Bowling Green, 1 9 to South Ferry

City Hall Park, City Hall
This grassy triangle marks the northern boundary of the district. Washington's army gathered here for a reading of the Declaration of Independence.
Broadway and Chambers St., 6 to City Hall

North Park
This small waterfront park provides good views of the harbor and the sailboats at the picturesque Battery Park City marina.
Chambers St. and River Terrace, 1 2 3 9 to Chambers St.

Ellis Island/Statue of Liberty
The city's first immigration center, in use from 1892-1932. A single fee covers the ferry ride and admission to both the Statue of Liberty and Ellis Island; visitors can trace an immigrant's path from baggage room to registry room and view the American Immigrant Wall of Honor. "Your tired, your poor, your huddled masses, yearning to breathe free," also applies to the bedraggled tourists laboring up her spiraling steps; the crown offers a spectacular view of the Harbor. Ferries depart from Castle Clinton in Battery Park every 30 minutes during the summer.
Ellis Island, 883-1986, Admission $7, 1 9 to South Ferry, &

Schermerhorn Restored Buildings
The buildings now house the Seaport Museum's Visitors' Center and a standard array of upscale, franchised shops like J. Crew, Banana Republic, and The Gap. Beware of street performers who gather here and prey on tourists.
Fulton St. (bet. Front and South Sts.), 2 3 to Fulton St., &

St. Paul's Chapel
After George Washington was elected president, a magnificent service was held here in his honor. Completed in 1766, this Georgian building is the oldest in continuous use in Manhattan, sponsoring services, lectures, social programs, and free noon-time music concerts.
Broadway and Fulton St., 602-0874, J M 2 3 4 5 to Fulton St., &

44 financial district

South Street Seaport
Within the complex are the Fulton Fish Market, the Fulton Market, harbor cities, Pier 17 shopping, the South St. Seaport Museum, and a life-size ship collection at Pier 16. Gaze at the Brooklyn Bridge from the benches along the water.
Bounded by Pearl, Water, John, and Beekman Sts., and the East River, 732-7678 or 962-4729, harbor cruises (two-hour tours around New York Harbor in the museum's 1885 schooner) $16 adults, $12 students, $4 seniors; ❷❸ *to Fulton St.*

New York Stock Exchange
The world's largest security exchange and the site of some of the greatest disasters in city history. Watch the frenzied activity from a safe distance at the viewing gallery, but please, don't feed the traders.
20 Broad St. (bet. Exchange and Wall Sts.), 656-5168, Admission Free, ❷❸ *to Wall St.,* ♿

Trinity Church
This 1697 Anglican parish has been primped and polished in time for its 300th birthday. Check out the tombstones of Alexander Hamilton and other New York notables resting peacefully in the graveyard. Call for more information about free lunch-time concerts.
Broadway and Wall St., 602-0872, Admission Free, ❷❸ *to Wall St.,* ♿

Federal Reserve Bank of New York
Occupying an entire city block, this edifice holds one-third of the world's gold. Don't get any funny ideas: security cameras watch from every possible angle. Free tours of the vaults are available; make reservations one week in advance.
Liberty St. (bet. William and Nassau Sts.), 760-6130, Admission Free, ❷❸ *to Wall Street,* ♿

World Financial Center
The centerpiece of Battery Park City houses American Express, Merrill Lynch, and Dow Jones, among other financial institutions, in its four postmodern towers. The Winter Garden is the focus of the center, with palm trees, sweeping views, and upscale shops and restaurants.
West St. (bet. Liberty and Vesey Sts.), 945-0505, ❶❾❸❺ *to World Trade Center,* ❶❶ *to Cortlandt St.*

World Trade Center
The 110 stories of aluminum and steel make the Twin Towers the tallest buildings in New York and the second tallest buildings in the country, after Chicago's Sears Tower. A car bomb exploded in a parking garage underneath the towers in 1993, closing them for several weeks. Check out the mall in the lower level, filled with upscale shops.
Church St. (bet. Liberty and Vesey Sts.), 435-4170, Admission Free, $4 to observation deck ❶❾❸❺ *to World Trade Center,* ♿

---

cheap *thrills*

Money Makes the World Go 'Round
The visitor's gallery at the World Trade Center gives a bird's eye view of the beehive of activity of the Commodities Exchange.
Four World Trade Center, 938-2018, ❶❾ *to Cortlandt St.*

Clocktower Gallery
The 13th floor houses an avant-garde sculpture gallery. Continue up the winding stairs for views of Manhattan, and an up-close look at the giant clock's inner workings.
346 Broadway (at Leonard St.), 233-1096, Suggested Donation: $2, ❹❸ *to Chambers St.*

Ride the Bull
Try to climb atop this most emblematic of Financial District Statues before the cops pry you off.
❷❸ *to Wall St.*

financial district 45

A Saturday in the Financial District

1 Fraunces Tavern Restaurant
Start your morning with some old-world history in this tavern where George Washington is reported to have said farewell to his officers at a reception in 1783. With a healthy assortment of fruit, omelets, and muffins, the breakfast here is considered one of the best buys in New York.
(see Restaurant section)

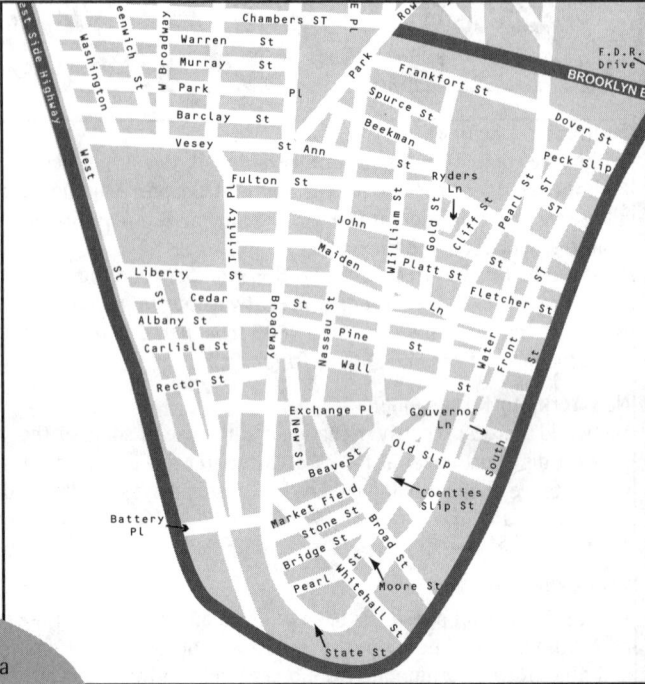

2 Statue of Liberty, Ellis Island
Hop a ferry at Castle Clinton for a large dose of New York history. You'll get to see how beautiful Manhattan looks from the water.
(see Sites + Parks)

3 McDonald's
You will be able to tell disbelieving family and friends that you ate in the fanciest McDonald's in the world. A Big Mac will always be a Big Mac, but when do you get to eat one in a Micky D's that has a doorman, pianist, and table service?
(see Restaurant section)

Most Lepidopterists Under One Roof
Mariposa
That means "butterfly specialist." Check out the carefully mounted specimens in their infinite variety behind clear Plexiglas frames as New Age music wafts past your ears.
South Street Seaport Pier 17, 233-3221, MC, V, AmEx,
 Ⓙ Ⓜ ② ② ③ ④ ⑤ *to Fulton St.*

46 financial district

4 Century 21
This discount department store is well-known to native New Yorkers for offering some of the best clothing, housewares, appliance, toys, and electronics deals in the city. It's a good place to start before heading over to the more expensive and touristy shopping destinations in this neighborhood.
(see Shopping section)

5 South Street Seaport
Over 100 years ago all goods that were shipped in and out of the city passed through this port. Now you'll find upscale shops, food, and history at this "mall" which begins at Water and Fulton Streets. There's the Fulton Fish Market which sells seafood to most of New York's restaurants, Pier 17 shopping, the South Street Seaport Museum, Pier 16's life-sized ship collection and 19th-century buildings line Schermerhorn Row.
(see Sites + Parks)

6 Bridge Cafe
An unpretentious place to eat some of the seafood this neighborhood is famous for and wind down your day. The intimate waterfront setting makes the experience even more of a treat.
(see Restaurant section)

Festivities at South Street Seaport

Most Inexpensive and Classic Way to View Manhattan
Staten Island Ferry
Grab a camera and some friends and be dazzled by NY's skyline along with the gaggle of tourists that will accompany you aboard.
Staten Island Ferry Terminal, South Ferry,
❶❾ to South Ferry

financial district 47

TriBeCa

After angry editorials, near brawls, community board meetings, and plenty of pouting, the artists who pioneered TriBeCa's minimalist, neo-industrial aesthetic have been forced to accept this neighborhood's latest stage of transition. Having preserved their galleries and performance spaces, the artists have yielded their living spaces to the financiers and other yuppies who can afford the skyrocketing rent.

Just twenty years ago, the Triangle Below Canal slumbered as an industrial wasteland of warehouses, loading docks, and back alleys. The area was ripe for refugees from SoHo who filtered down and converted the cast-iron buildings into art-friendly living spaces. Slowly, new tenants have inherited the extensive renovations done by these artists who were forced from the neighborhood by the steep rents and the onslaught of expensive shops and high-priced restaurants.

By day, Donna Karan-clad moms push strollers and shop for gardening tools or baby clothes that would swallow most people's daily salary. Washington Market spills over with school kids around 2pm, and CUNY coeds mill around West Broadway and Church Street between classes. At night, Wall Street sends its suits and gold cards up a few blocks to descend upon the clutch of restaurants along Hudson and Franklin. Robert DeNiro, the neighborhood's most famous resident and restaurateur, finances upscale eateries like Tribeca Grill, Bouley Bakery, and Nobu, where prospective patrons must reserve a month in advance.

TriBeCa is far from an insular overpriced play space like SoHo, however. The side streets can be foreboding and dimly lit after dark, the swanky restaurants and bistros tucked away into converted storage spaces surrounded by unconverted storage spaces and loading docks. However, it is indisputable that TriBeCa is going the way of SoHo and will soon have its very own branches of J. Crew, agnès b, and Marc Jacobs.

Despite TriBeCa's increasing ostentation, the Knitting Factory, a longtime presence on the TriBeCa scene, hosts everyone from Naked City to folk and roots rock to marginalized drama. Franklin Furnace still utilizes its space to give public exposure to experimental productions; CityKids, a grassroots organization that promotes youth-to-youth communication, still flourishes; and Biblio's keeps the area's artistic and spoken word tradition alive.

48 tribeca

sites + parks

White Street
Typical of TriBeCa's architecture melange: juxtaposed alongside Federal-style buildings are 19th-century cast-iron warehouses. Number Ten is notable for its creative stonework. Numbers Eight and Ten feature shorter stories on the upper levels, a design intended to make the building look taller.
White Street (bet. Church St. and West Broadway), **❶ ❾** *to Franklin St.*

New York Mercantile Exchange
Built in 1884, this former poultry and dairy product exchange offers visitors a glimpse of TriBeCa's commercial character, new and old. Note the Victorian architecture and stunning rose window.
6 Harrison St. (bet. Hudson and Staple Sts.), 334-2160, **❶ ❷ ❸ ❾** *to Chambers St.*

AT&T Long Lines Building
With its windowless pink granite exterior, the Long Lines Building stands in stark contrast to the nearby loading docks and cast-iron column. The interior contains little except switching systems which route long-distance calls.
Church St. (bet. Thomas and Worth Sts.), **❶ ❾** *to Franklin St.*

TriBeCa Film Center
Established by TriBeCa's most famous resident and restauranteur, Robert DeNiro, this space contains screening rooms, production offices, and the New York offices of Miramax Films, TriBeCa Films, and other filmmakers. Downstairs is DeNiro's famous TriBeCa Grill and across the street his TriBeCa Deli, with less expensive but equally exquisites sandwiches.
325 Greenwich St. (bet. Franklin and North Moore Sts.), 941-4000, **❶ ❾** *to Franklin St.*

Harrison Street Row
Recalling Federal-Era New York, these restored houses complement the cobbled walkways of TriBeCa's warehouse district.
Harrison Street (at Greenwich), **❶ ❾** *to Franklin St.*

history

Derived from the misnomer "Triangle below Canal Street," TriBeCa was so named by real estate developers in the mid-'70s. Beginning modestly in 1813 with Bear Market, which dealt in fruit and produce, by the mid-19th century TriBeCa was a major point of transfer for the increased shipping and commerce moving through lower Manhattan. Its cast-iron facades and spacious five-and-six story buildings housed stores, factories, and storage facilities, as TriBeCa became a thriving light manufacturing zone.

By 1939, Bear Market and the surrounding area were renamed Washington Market; the market itself did more business than all others combined. It remained a vital part of the city's produce market until most companies made an exodus from the city in the early '60s and were quickly replaced by the real estate developers. The Washington Market Urban Renewal Project was launched almost immediately and office buildings, institutions such as the Borough of Manhattan Community College, and public parks sprang up in the neighborhood. In the '70s alone, the area's population jumped from 243 to more than 5,000 people taking advantage of TriBeCa's new ammenities.

Development continued into the '90s, although at a slower pace. Construction of Stuyvesant High School, the city's most competitive public high school, was completed in 1993. Lofts were quickly converted to residences as they had been a decade or two earlier in SoHo, with the important distinction that these lofts were open to both nonartists and artists. As a result, TriBeCa has become a one of the most desireable neighborhoods in New York, with many shops, cafes, and a rich population.

tribeca 49

A Saturday in TriBeCa

Bubby's
1 There's often a wait at this trendy neighborhood brunch standby but since it's Saturday, hang out and do some people-watching. The cheese grits, omelets, and gourmet sandwiches are worth the wait.
(see Restaurant section)

Seeing the Sites
2 Stroll off your meal by checking out some of the neighborhood's historic sights. White and Harrison Streets have an array of federal-style buildings. The firehouse at 114 Moore Street is where Bill Murray and Dan Ackroyd fought against some of Manhattan's deadliest paranormal activity in the film, *Ghostbusters*. Pick up a copy of the *TriBeCa Trib* and chill out on the grass at Washington Market Park.
❶❾ to Franklin St.

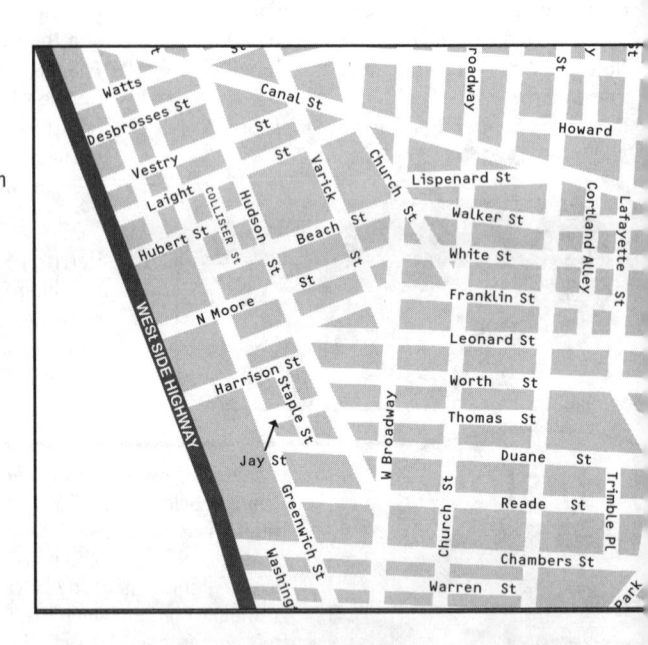

Biblio's
3 Browse through the unique book selection and have a light bite to eat. Don't overdo it on the snacks, you'll want to save room for dinner.
(see Literature section)

TriBeCa Potters
Watch the artists at work at TriBeCa Potters and browse among the items for sale between 9am and 5:30pm.
443 Greenwich St., 2nd Floor (bet. Vestry and Desbrosses Sts.), 431-7631, ❶❾ to Canal St.

Hanging Out
Take a seat on one of the many loading docks to relax and people-watch.
❶❾ to Franklin St., ❶❷❸❾ to Chambers St.

Celebrity-Spotting
Camp out on Greenwich Street, and look for interesting, famous, and just plain odd people. Robert DeNiro, Kurt Loder, and Christopher Walken are all known to make appearances.
1 Greenwich St. (bet. Duane and Moore Sts.), ❶❾ to Franklin St.

{cheap thrills}

50 tribeca

4 Rosemarie's

Settle down to an intimate dinner in this elegant yet relaxed Northern Italian restaurant. It will make you understand why TriBeCa is known for the quality of its restaurants.
(see Restaurant section)

5 The Knitting Factory

No matter what your mood at the end of this day (and we hope it will be good), you'll find an assortment of comedy, theater, and music at this neighborhood hot spot. Kick back with a drink and enjoy.
(see Music Venues section)

Well-known TriBeCa restaurant

Most Retro-Opulent Movie Theater
The Screening Room
Dinner and a movie is a classic; finding them under the same roof is not. Divine food and a comfy little theater. The $30 prix fixe includes a three-course meal and movie admission.
54 Varick St. (at Canal St.), 334-2100, MC, V, AmEx, Diners, D, Entrées: $16-$23, ❶❾ to Canal St.

Most Affordable Breakfast
Kitchenette
Low prices and the cute setting keep this place hopping with everyone from neighborhood artists to refugees from the nearby World Trade Center. For lunch, try the Soup Pot across the street, which is owned and operated by the same people.
80 West Broadway (at Warren St.), 267-6740, AmEx, Breakfast: $3.50, ❶❾ to Chambers St.

chinatown

Rusty red pagoda-topped phone booths, slick fish eyes on blue plastic, Chinese soft-rock drifting down between the laundry lines, the scent of rotten fruit and deep fry are just some of the sensations that characterize Chinatown. Crooked alleyways, ancient tea parlors and barber shops still exist in this neighborhood below Canal Street and east of Broadway. On Sundays, vendors hawking Chinese-style crullers with hot soy milk, fresh tofu, and bean sprouts congregate under the Manhattan Bridge. The drugstore on Grand Street still weighs out deer antlers and "dragon's eyes" with brass hand scales the way they did in China at the turn of the century, while, on Canal Street, dozens of merchants each promise a better deal on imitation wristwatches and designer handbags.

Chinatown is far from the typical residential community. With over one-third of New York's Chinese population of 300,000 (and counting) residing there, the community is growing larger by the day. Once confined to the vicinity of Mott Street, the neighborhood's burgeoning population has pushed its boundaries past the edges of SoHo and the Financial District. With new arrivals and refugees from Southeast Asia, including Vietnam, Cambodia, Thailand, and Malaysia, the community is in the midst of radical change in both its geographic size as well as its racial composition. Strips of Vietnamese, Thai, and Indonesian restaurants have joined the rows of Cantonese noodle and tea shops. The oldest part of Chinatown is centered around Mott and Pell Streets, the area's main tourist drag. But this part of the neighborhood is also slowly changing with shop owners moving to the suburbs and the disappearance of mom and pop stores. In addition, since Hong Kong's repatriation, businessmen are transferring funds from abroad, turning Chinatown into what one woman described as "a little Hong Kong." It will be interesting to watch the developments in this neighborhood over the next few years.

sites + parks

Chatham Square Library
Four stories of books, including an impressive Chinese Heritage Collection featuring classics, keep Chinatown's avid readers busy. Available resources include free computer workshops, art, poetry, pre-college information sessions, live performances, magazines, popular fiction, videos, and Friday-night Internet training classes.
33 East Broadway (near Catherine St.), 964-6598, **F** *to East Broadway*

The Chinatown Manpower Project
A nationally funded intensive bilingual vocational class aimed at teaching recent immigrants English and cooking skills before placing them in jobs in the tristate area.
70 Mulberry St. (at Bayard St.), 571-1690, **NR** *to Canal St.,* **BDFQ** *to Grand St.*

Columbus Park
There's more asphalt than grass at this bustling niche: pick-up basketball games and bladers share the space with Chinatown's elderly, who gather to play cards, gossip, and sun themselves.
Between Bayard and Worth Sts. (north and south borders), and Mulberry and Baxter Sts. (east and west), **NR** *to Canal St.*

Eastern States Buddhist Temple
The devout flock here daily to kneel and burn incense before the imposing porcelain Buddha. Pick up trinkets at the gift shop.
64 Mott St. (at Mulberry St.), 966-6229, **ACE** *to Canal St.*

H.T. Dance Company
"Dance is not only doing your own good work," says company director H.T. Chen, "it should have a social value as well." Since 1978, the company's small black-box theater has hosted the Arts Gate Center, which offers dance classes to children and adults, and commissioned other programs from contemporary choreographers.
60 Mulberry St. (at Bayard St.), 732-3751, **NR** *to Canal St.,* **BDFQ** *to Grand St.*

The Museum of the Chinese in the Americas
No Chinatown experience is complete without a visit to this community-oriented museum, the first ever dedicated to the history of Chinese in the Americas. The award-winning permanent exhibition, entitled, "Where Is Home?" features a moving collection of memorabilia, photographs, and commentary exploring the diverse identities and experiences of Chinese Americans.
70 Mulberry St. (at Bayard St.), 619-4785, Admission $1, **NR** *to Canal St.*

history

In 1858, a merchant from Kwantung moved to 8 Mott Street and became the area's first Chinese resident. By the 1870s, there were almost 2000 Chinese within the boundaries of Canal, Worth, Mulberry, and the Bowery—the area which became Chinatown proper.

Migration was not easy for the Chinese. Isolationist leaders forbade them to leave China until the early 18th century, and immigrants were greeted with fear and even hatred when they arrived in the United States. Most settled in California, working in mining and railroad construction, and were dubbed the "Yellow Menace." After the Chinese Exclusion Act of 1882, many Chinese moved to larger cities and urban Chinatowns began to grow across the country.

Immigrants were restricted to a few types of businesses, but soon, there were restaurants and shops to attract visitors. The population grew as restrictions and prejudice began to wane in the late '60s, Chinatown expanded into parts of the Lower East Side and Little Italy, becoming the largest Chinese community in the West.

Recent immigrants continue to arrive in Chinatown, and the neighborhood's borders are stretching as the population grows and becomes more ethnically diverse. The boundaries between Chinatown and Little Italy are blurring and eastern SoHo and the Lower East Side now have a significant number of Chinese residents. Despite a population of around 100,000, and it's contribution to New York culture, Chinatown has little representation in city government and its residents remain wary of city politics.

chinatown 53

A Saturday in Chinatown

1 Bird Warming at Sara Delano Roosevelt Park
Get up early and head to the corner of Chrystie and Delancey Streets between 7am and 9am. From spring to fall, you can join in while men do their exercises and wait for the sun to warm up enough for them to unveil their cages filled with songbirds which welcome the morning.
NR to Canal St.,
BDFQ to Grand St.

2 Dim Sum
After all of that warming and stretching, head over to The Golden Unicorn for some of the best dim sum in Chinatown. Be adventurous and try one of everything. Just be careful not to get run over by any of the food carts.
(see Restaurant section)

3 Shop on Mott and Pell Streets
Head over to the commercial center of Chinatown and either shop 'til you drop, or just look at the wild assortment of merchandise. You'll find everything here from Walkmans to dragon-shaped clogs. But be careful, just because that walkman says Sony, doesn't mean it's made in Japan.
NR to Canal St.

Most "Authentic" Trinkets
The Eastern States Buddhist Temple Gift Shop
Want a Buddha, complete with red Christmas lights from head to toe? Whatever you want, it's here.
64 Mott St. (at Mulberry St.),
966-6229, **ACE** to Canal St.

Most Informative Wall
Wall of Democracy
A mind-boggling collage of posters, news articles, and hand-lettered statements on current events in China are pasted to this giant wall. Bayard St. (bet. Mulberry and Mott Sts.), **NR456** to Canal St.

Most Adrenaline for a Quarter
Chinatown Fair
If you have forgotten how exciting old-school arcade games like *Ms. Pac Man* and *Centipede* can be, spend a quarter and remind yourself.
8 Mott St., **JMNRZ** to Canal St.

54 chinatown

4 Chinatown Ice Cream Factory
Walk over to 65 Bayard Street between Mott and Elizabeth and treat yourself to an ice cream taste sensation with flavors like lychee, ginger, papaya, and almond cookie.
(see Restaurant section)

Chinatown Fair 5
Even if you're not a video game fanatic, you'll find something to interest you at this arcade at 8 Mott Street. You can play tic-tac-toe with a chicken or get your picture taken in a photo booth with a friend.
8 Mott St., J Z M to Canal St.

Bo Ky 6
Settle into a light end to an active day at this excellent Vietnamese restaurant which specializes in noodle soups. Like most things in Chinatown, you'll find it's a bargain.
(see Restaurant section)

You can buy anything in Chinatown

Noodle Stands
For less than it costs to do your laundry, you can enjoy a big container of lo mein or a handful of egg rolls bought at one of the food carts lining Canal Street.
Canal St. (bet. Lafayette and Mulberry Sts.), Cash Only, N R to Canal St.

{cheap *thrills*}

The Museum of the Chinese in the Americas
Learn all about the heritage of one of the city's largest ethnic populations for only $1.
70 Mulberry St. (at Bayard St.), 619-4785, N R to Canal St.

chinatown 55

Little Italy

Once home to Italian and Irish newcomers whose transatlantic journey at the turn of the century landed them in tenements lining the narrow streets, Little Italy is getting littler and littler. Mulberry Street and the Italian flags that wave above it, scores of restaurants with a choice of white or red sauce, and the few remaining specialty food shops that still carry stuffed peppers, black olives, and cannoli dripping with ricotta, are the only vestiges of the neighborhood's prior incarnation as an actual ethnic enclave that once stretched as far east as Orchard and Ludlow Streets, and as far west as Broadway. Chinatown is crowding in from the South and East and you might be hard pressed to find any Italians still living here.

If it's Mama Leone you're looking for, you might do better to visit Bensonhurst, Brooklyn or Belmont in the Bronx, where Italian communities flourish. In order to get the gist of what the neighborhood used to be like, you can watch Martin Scorceses' *Mean Streets* and Francis Ford Coppola's *The Godfather Part II*.

The neighborhood rallies during the 10-day festival of San Gennaro, the patron saint of Naples. Mulberry Street shimmers under twinkling lights and you might find yourself humming "That's Amore." Enjoy the festival by having some Italian "specialties" at stands selling sausage, zeppoles, Italian ice, and fried calamari.

Of course, this street carnival only contributes to an atmosphere that more resembles the Italian section in Epcot Center than the Little Italy of yesteryear. But, after you feel as if you've eaten your way through Sicily and won a bear for your girlfriend, consider the advice of every fledgling mobster who's ever said, "If you can't beat 'em, join 'em." Don't offend anyone while having a good time though, or you might end up like Joey Gallo, who was gunned down at Umberto's Clam House on his birthday after he allegedly bad-mouthed a rival family.

56 little italy

sites + parks

Elizabeth Street Company Garden Sculpture
Most Manhattanites couldn't even fit these sculptures in their living rooms, let alone any "garden" to which they may have access. However, this patch of green off of Elizabeth Street is the perfect place to escape the bustle of Houston and to dream of the English countryside.
Elizabeth St. (at Spring St.), ❻ *to Spring St.*

Old St. Patrick's Cathedral
Though it's difficult to tell now, the church was New York's first Gothic Revival structure, built in 1815 by Joseph Mangin. A fire in 1866 destroyed the historic façade, necessitating Henry Englebert's 1868 renovation. It served a predominantly Irish immigrant population after the consecration of the new St. Patrick's Church at Fifth Avenue and 50th Street in 1879.
264 Mott St. (bet. Prince and Houston Sts.), 226-8075, ❶❿ *to Prince St.,* ❷❹❻❽ *to Broadway/Lafayette St.*

St. Michael's Russian Catholic Church
With its rosy-pink façade and onion domes, this Orthodox church adds a distinctively Eastern flavor to the area, complementing its better-known Catholic neighbor.
266 Mulberry St. (bet. Prince and Houston Sts.) ❶❿ *to Prince St.*

The Police Building
The domed edifice built in 1909 by Hoppin and Koen served as the city's main police headquarters for nearly 65 years. Its new copper dome was crafted by the same French artisans who restored the Statue of Liberty's flame and now shelters 55 co-op apartments.
240 Centre St. (bet. Grand and Broome Sts.), ❶❿ *to Prince St.*

history

Beginning with the explorer Giovanni da Verrazzano's 1524 arrival in Manhattan's bay, Italians have been an important part of New York City's history. Immigrants from Northern Italy arrived in the early 17th century, but their numbers were dwarfed by larger waves of Southern Italians, who came in the late 19th century. From 1880 to 1900, the number of Italians in New York rose from 12,000 to almost 220,000 and doubled to 545,000 by 1910. Most of the Italian immigrants settled in lower Manhattan, an area packed with poor immigrant families living in crowded, unsanitary tenements in neighborhoods dotted with religious institutions. Immigrants tended to cluster according their relations in the Old World, with Genoans, Calabrians, and Sicilians living on the east side, and Piedmontese, Tuscans, and Neopolitans living on the west side. This was the era chronicled by Francis Ford Coppola in *The Godfather II* when Sicilian Vito Corleone established himself as the benefactor of his small community.

However, by the mid-20th century, like the fictional Corleone, most Italians had moved out of the old neighborhood to greener places such as Staten Island, Brooklyn, Long Island, and New Jersey and throughout the United States. Despite Little Italy's romance, most Italians now consider the Italian section of the Bronx to be the real "Little Italy."

little italy 57

A Saturday in Little Italy

1 **Di Palo's / Piemonte Ravioli Company / The D+G Bakery**

You will swear you're shopping in Italy when you enter this little market run by gourmet Italians. Di Palo's is the perfect place to find fresh mozzarella, mascarpone, ricotta, and homemade sausages. Just down the street you will find Piemonte Ravioli Company where they sell homemade pasta of every description. Don't forget to pick up some freshly baked, crusty Italian bread at the D+G Bakery, in business since 1963.
(see Shopping section)

{cheap *thrills*}

The San Gennaro Festival
Get yourself a humungous Italian ice and ogle at the macho men trying to win oversized stuffed animals for their girlfriends. Mingle with tourists, natives, and dancers along Mulberry Street. Food is overpriced, but delicious so make sure you eat something beforehand, or you won't be able to resist the aromas from the stands.
Second week in September, Mulberry St. (bet. Canal and Grand Sts.), Cash Only, N R to Prince St.

58 little italy

2 La Mela

Before heading home to prepare your dinner feast, fortify yourself with lunch at this Mulberry Street standby. The food is nothing to write home about, but you won't leave hungry, and you might even be a bit tipsy after a 1/2 carafe or two of the house wine. You will leave inspired to put your recently purchased fresh ingredients to good use.

(see Restaurant section)

3 Ferrara

Relax with an espresso and Italian pastry at this neighborhood institution after a day at the markets.

(see Cafe section)

Most "French" Joint in Little Italy
Cafe Gitane
French through and through, from the menu offerings to the aloof waitstaff. This place offers the perfect ambiance for flipping through fashion rags, drinking coffee, and the standard downtown sports of posing and people-watching.
242 Mott St. (bet. Houston and Prince Sts.), 334-9552, Cash Only, Entrées: $7-$10, ⓝⓡ to Prince St., ♿

Most Dangerous Place for a Glutton
Italian Food Center
Stock up on hard-to-find gourmet goodies.
(see Shopping section)

little italy 59

Lower East Side

It's 10am and the sun is already beating down, serving up the first presummer scorcher. Cunning Lower East Side locals adapt; they set up folding tables and chairs and resume their Saturday morning activities. The residents compete for sidewalk space on the cluttered side streets of Essex and Norfolk, gathering in front of beaten-down chop shops and yellow-and-red-bannered bodegas. Some nibble at early lunches and mingle, and others play cards or dominoes, as salsa music pours out of windows and passing cars.

Up and down the main streets of the Lower East Side you'll find a string of shabby boutiques brimming with leather jackets and fabrics, frilly dresses and kids' clothing. Stepping onto Delancey Street is like stepping back in time; there are dime stores and lingerie stores still run by families who arrived in the U.S. fifty years ago.

The Williamsburg Bridge bestows on the area a transient feel, presenting the perfect metaphor; as it shuttles passengers onto Delancey, it is reminiscent of the first major wave of immigrants who passed through Ellis Island and landed in the towering tenement landscape of the Lower East Side. The Lower East Side was once the most overpopulated, integrated neighborhood in world. One of the largest ethnic pockets was the Jewish one that, in 1920, was home to 400,000. Nowadays the Puerto Rican and Dominican presence dominates, but the Jewish culture lingers on in Yiddish theaters, kosher delicatessens, and popular food shops like Katz's Delicatessen and Kossars Bakery.

The Lower East Side was hit hard by drugs and other criminal activity in the '70s, and locals had to pool their strength and resources in order to reclaim "Loisaida." The Centro Cultural Clemente Soto Velez champions local Hispanic culture, housing theaters, art galleries, and studios for local artists, and is a stabilizing presence in the area, devoting much energy to improving the quality of life and instilling a sense of local pride. Thanks to their efforts, combined with those of local block associations, the crime rate and drug traffic have plummeted, making it a safer neighborhood. Evidence of this is the influx of trendy shops and nightspots, mostly along Ludlow Street. East of Essex Street, when the trendy bars and boutiques all but peter out, and the salsa music and smell of salt fish permeate the senses, you are reminded that the Lower East Side is not simply the latest area for the hipper-than-thou crowd to invade, but a diverse and evolving neighborhood with a long and interesting history.

sites + parks

East River Park
Every Saturday and Sunday in the warmer months, the park fills up with families from the nearby projects who come here to barbecue, fish, play ball, bike, or just hang out in the shadow of the Williamsburg Bridge. A walk through this riverside park reveals romantically derelict urban landscapes of industrial Brooklyn. Don't venture here after dusk or on rainy days, when it can get a little sinister.
Jackson to 15th Sts. (east of the East River Drive), **F J M Z** *to Delancey St.*

Eldridge Street Synagogue
Eastern European Jews erected the Lower East Side's first large-scale building in 1887. With its multihued stained glass windows, brilliant frescoes, and intricate woodwork, the synagogue stood out for many years amidst the notorious Lower East Side tenements. It fell into disrepair during hard times, but in recent years, the Eldridge Street Project has made significant renovations.
12 Eldridge Street (bet. Canal and Division Streets), 219-0888, Admission: $2.50, students; tours on Sun., Tues., Wed., and Thurs., **B** *to Second Ave.*

Hamilton Fish Pool and Recreation Center
Just $25 per year buys membership to this and many other municipally run pools and fitness centers around the city. The pools are generally clean, the gyms basic but friendly. Don't expect state-of-the-art equipment or classes; just a workout without an attitude.
127 Pitt St. (off Houston St.), 387-7687, **F** *to Second Ave.*

Lower East Side Tenement Museum
These are permanent, interactive exhibits dubbed the "Confino Apartment" and the "Gumpertz & Baldizzi Apartments." The Confino is the exhibition of a Sephardic-Jewish immigrant family in 1916 and the others were restored to look like they did in 1870 and 1935.
90 Orchard St. (at Broome St.), 431-0233, **J M Z** *to Essex St.*

play ball!

history

For immigrants traveling from the provincial areas of Europe, the tenements which dominated the landscape of the Lower East Side must have been a chilling sight. Infamous for providing the worst housing conditions in the city, these five-story firetraps absorbed most of the first major wave of immigrants who passed through Ellis Island and could not afford anything better. During the last two decades of the 19th century, the largely Irish population was joined by Italians and Eastern European Jews who crowded in by the thousands.

New laws and housing plans failed to alleviate the situation. The first city housing project, built in 1936 as a last-ditch effort portended the limited success of projects in general. But great spirit arose out of poverty and the neighborhood soon became as well known for its wealth of intellectual and artistic life as for its overcrowding. During the early part of this century, Yiddish theater flourished along Second Avenue, area newspapers grew into forums for intellectual debate, and many famous performers like George Gershwin, Irving Berlin, and the Marx Brothers cut their teeth here. The '50s and '60s saw revolutionaries, writers, and musicians populating the northern boundaries, an area that later expanded and became known as the East Village.

The Lower East Side fell into decline as rents once again decreased and crime, drugs, and dilapidated housing became prominent neighborhood features. In the '80s, the area stabilized somewhat after an influx of Latinos who dubbed the area "Loisaida."

lower east side 61

A Saturday in the Lower East Side

1 Tonic

Stroll over to Tonic for an early brunch of waffles and fresh berries. This cavernous spot is equal parts hair salon, cafe, and performance space, so after you've eaten, head down to the basement where they'll wash your hair for you and give you a new 'do.
(see Restaurant section)

2 The Lower East Side Tenement Museum

Don't miss the free video "South of Delancey" featured in the gallery which tells all about Lower East Side living. For a more personal look there is a guided tour for $8 ($6 for students) of several apartments in the building that look as they originally did from 1864 through 1935.
(see Sites + Parks)

3 Vintage Shopping

There are some great Vintage clothing shops, especially on Orchard Street (visit Cherry) and on Ludlow Street (visit Shine), where you can find good deals on button-down shirts, slips, and dresses.
(see Shopping section)

Most Retro Deli
Katz's
Pastrami and corned beef sandwiches and more await at this somewhat dingy, but superior delicatessen, where little has changed since 1888.
205 East Houston St. (at Ludlow St.), 254-2246, MC, V, AmEx, Average Entrée: $7, ❻ to Second Ave.

Most Hip Kosher Lounge
Lansky Lounge
Named after Jewish Mafia kingpin Meyer Lansky, this hot nightspot (located in Ratner's Delicatessan), channels the spirit of the celebrated speakeasy whose site the club now occupies.
102-106 Norfolk St.; follow the lights up the iron staircase to the unmarked door, MC, V, AmEx, Average Entrée: $9, ❻ to Delancey St.,

Babylon

4

Stop in to Babylon for a leisurely lunch and another time-warp experience; you'll actually feel encouraged to sit for hours and enjoy the '70s vibe in this clean, olive-hued cafe. The organic vegetarian food is delicious, especially the quiche.
(see Restaurant section)

5 Walk off Your Lunch in the East River Park
Hang out with the local families from nearby projects who'll be fishing, barbecueing, and playing ball in the popular park.
(see Sites + Parks)

6 Torch
Slip into one of the half-moon booths at this sexy '40s-style French supper club, sip on a Martini, have a fabulous meal, and enjoy a live blues performance right in front of your table.
(see Restaurant section)

7 Dharma
Mellow out in this upscale bar where candles scale the walls. The design is enough to draw a healthy crowd, and there are seven single-barrel bourbons to choose from—ooh la la!
(see Bars section)

Baby Jupiter

Dance some of that poison out of your system at this hot new club. DJ's rock the house till 4am, **8** when everyone starts to crash out on the couches around the dance floor. When they finally get you out the door, take a cab home and keep your eyes opened until you get there.
(see Clubs section)

Hanging out at the Pink Pony Cafe

Luna Lounge
Pay no cover to see some of New York's most eclectic performers and grab a shot at open mike success.
171 Ludlow St. (bet. Houston and Stanton), 260-2323, **F** to Second Ave.

Liz Christy Garden
Take a midday stroll with your paramour in this most intimate and beautiful of Manhattan's private flower gardens.
F to Second Ave., **6** to Bleecker St.

Delancey Street
Stores offering cheap but cheerful shoes and hip-hop gear crowd along this vibrant if somewhat derelict commercial stretch.
F to Delancey St.,
J M Z to Essex St.

{cheap *thrills*}

lower east side 63

SoHo

Climbing the precipice of a sooty five-story warehouse toward the vast blue sky is an intricate maze of wrought-iron fire escapes, landings, and steps. A pigeon perched in the shaded iron frame swoops out into the light and feathers down to the sun-drenched cobblestones on Crosby Street. A woman in strappy platform sandals and black pantsuit strolls onto the deserted street, leafing through stacks of gallery postcards. She navigates the uneven pavement with the confidence of a SoHo veteran who intuitively knows her streets, their slopes and widening cracks. She turns west onto Prince Street, through the lively lunch crowd, jaywalking to one of many booming art galleries lining the block. Before disappearing into the immense pillared entrance, she waves to a friend who is smoking on the loading dock a few doors down, promising to stop by later.

At night, dark buildings caked with paint seem to encroach upon the already cramped cobblestone streets, and the intricate grillwork casts twisted shadows upon the unevenly paved sidewalks below. A Checker, one of the last of the city's luxury cabs, pulls up and deposits three black-clad and reed-thin women who silently disappear into what seems to be an innocuous storefront. Instead of an abandoned warehouse, it's a cavernous art gallery, where sculpture reaches for the ceiling as white-wine-sipping guests mix and mingle below.

Yes, those cast-iron buildings still exist, as do the many galleries that cropped up as a result of the early influx of artists. However, alongside the galleries, many of those old buildings now house a veritable mecca of stylish stores ranging from J. Crew to Marc Jacobs to Portico.

The neighborhood now attracts a mass of shoppers with platinum cards and tourists eager to soak up New York City bohemia and get some shopping done, all in one day. This has meant that the cost of living in this once dirt-cheap neighborhood has skyrocketed, forcing many of the artists who originally gave it character, out into surrounding areas. While SoHo is still arsty and funky, expect more stores than galleries, and more trust-fund-kids than up-and-coming artists.

sites + parks

New York Open Center
A holistic learning center which offers lectures, workshops, and weekend retreats on topics ranging from screenwriting to flamenco dancing; call for a catalogue. The meditation room is open to the public free of charge, pillows provided, if you forgot to bring your own.
83 Spring St. (between Crosby and Lafayette Sts.), 219-2527, MC, V, Amex, NR to Prince St., 6 to Spring St.

The Puck Building
Erected in 1886, this building was originally a printing plant for Puck, America's first humor magazine. Today, the first floor hosts galas and the upper floors have been converted into apartments and offices, including those of the *NY Press*. Puck still grins from the northeast corner of the building.
295 Lafayette St. (at Houston St.), 274-8900, BDFQ to Broadway/Lafayette St.

Poet's House
This free reading room and resource center houses the largest collection of poetry books in the country. Current poetry and literary periodicals are available for browsing, and Walkmen are provided for listening. Call for information about live readings.
72 Spring St. (bet. Broadway and Lafayette St.), 431-7920, BDFQ to Broadway/Lafayette St.

SoHo's most famous resident stands guard over agnés b.

history

In the early '60s before SoHo had its name (**S**outh of **Ho**uston), it was an abandoned commercial slum known as "hell's hundred acres." By the late '60s and early '70s, artists with little money and a greater vision for both themselves and these desolate streets, took a risk, and on the sly packed up their drawing tables, canvasses, and paint brushes to invade these vacant and decrepit, but large and light-filled commercial warehouses, converting them into combined studios, galleries, and living spaces.

This powerful colony of artists fought to make their presence legal in the neighborhood and began attending community board meetings to convince the New York City Landmarks Commission to designate an area of 26 blocks in SoHo as a Historic District by 1973. Their passionate dedication led to the preservation of the elaborately ornamented, wonderfully spacious cast-iron buildings, which define SoHo's unique architectural style.

SoHo is going the way of Greenwich Village in transforming from a hotbed of cultural revolution to a more staid standard-bearer of respectability. As rents climb into the stratosphere, expensive boutiques and galleries populate the creaky warehouses; designers and the models who don their wares hold court at the bars and restaurants which line Mercer, Prince, Lafayette, and Spring Streets. While visitors may never achieve a real intimacy with SoHo, they can at least enter the orbit of SoHoites by poking into one of the galleries lining Greene and Wooster Streets.

There used to be more galleries than stores in SoHo

soho 65

A Saturday in SoHo

1 **Jerry's**

Get your butt out of bed, pick up the *Times*, and get on line for brunch at Jerry's as early as possible because every else in SoHo is doing it. Once you've settled into your comfy booth, spread out and stay awhile.

(see Cafe section)

Shopping

2 SoHo is one big shopping mecca, with stores filled with everything from designer clothes to expensive housewares to upscale cosmetics. The whole of SoHo is worth exploring, but Prince and Spring Streets are lined with shops. One special recommendation: check out Ina. This fantastic designer consignment store has the best selection of hip Prada, agnés b, and Helmut Lang designs at almost half the price.

(see Shopping section)

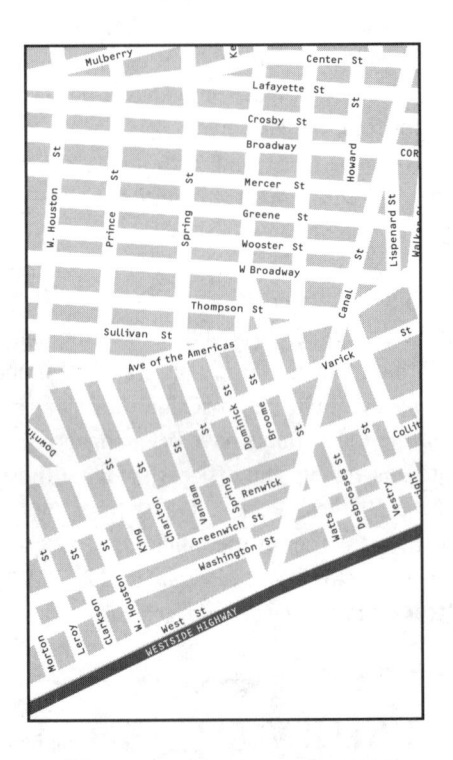

3 **Fanelli's**

Tired and hungry after a hard day of shopping? This dark and smoky bar has opened its arms to SoHo survivors for over 100 years. Crawl in and order a well-deserved beer and burger with the rest of the hipsters who pack this longtime neighborhood hangout.

(see Restaurant section)

Most Passionate Flamenco Night
ñ
Flamenco dancers perform every Wednesday night and make it easy to order one more pitcher of *sangria*.
33 Crosby St. (bet. Broome and Grand Sts.), 219-8856, Cash Only,
N R 6 to Canal St.

Most Models Per Square Inch
Spy
If you can't get in, just remember, money and beauty aren't everything.
101 Greene St.
(bet. Prince and Spring Sts.),
343-9000, MC, V, Amex, Diners,
C E to Spring St.

Most Thrilling Bathrooms
Bar 89
It's glass doors must be latched precisely so they become opaque when occupied.
89 Mercer St. (bet. Spring and Broome Sts.), 274-0989,
MC, V, Amex, **C E** to Spring St.

66 soho

4 The SoHo Grand Bar

Show off your hot new outfit in this new hotel lounge for the hipper-than-thou crowd. Partake in a fancy predinner cocktail and watch as the fashionistas come and go.
(see Bars section)

5 Rialto

Join the beautiful crowd for dinner, but don't expect food for waifs: Rialto's wild mushroom sausage with roasted shallot vinaigrette, and creamy risotto with peas and mozzarella will help you fill out your already hip-hugging pants. The romantic ambiance makes this the perfect place for a date.
(see Restaurant section)

6 M+R Bar

You don't have to go far for a great place to drink in this neighborhood; after dinner, stroll across the street to M+R Bar. It's always packed with a fun crowd and the drinks aren't that expensive.
(see Restaurant section)

A drag king performs at Club Casanova

7 Don Hill's

Top off your night by dancing until dawn. No one at Don Hill's is shy. Shove up to the front of the stage with the rest of the downtown kids, and cop their moves.
(see Clubs section)

{cheap *thrills*}

Gallery Hop
You're in SoHo after all, so pick up a free copy of the *Gallery Guide* at any major gallery and spend the afternoon checking out the interesting shows.

Cheapest Tailor
Go to José Tailor for a $5 hem and other good deals, it's quick and easy on your wallet.
30 Spring St. (bet. Mott and Mulberry Sts.), ⑥ to Spring St.

east village

Two women in saggy corduroys round the corner of East 11th Street and wheel a heaping pile of vintage coats in a plastic dumpster. Having shimmied it to the curb, they heave the bin onto the street where it steers itself into an oncoming car and chucks loose a leopard-print blazer. The driver manages to swerve around it, and the women, giggling, chase the dumpster down the street. Further down the block, a couple sits on their stoop with bowls of Raisin Bran cupped in their hands. He slurps milk off his spoon, his girlfriend raises her sleepy eyes, and says, "Hey, are you selling that stuff?" One of the girls slings the loose jacket back onto the heap, and says, "No... sorry, man. They're going to the homeless."

The East Village simmers with a unique sense of community pride. It can be seen in the efforts of its residents toward rebuilding the neighborhood's parks and community centers and in the way neighbors actually talk to each other here. The area has absorbed artists, anarchists, Puerto Ricans, Ukrainians, blacks, whites, gays, lesbians, Asians, and Indians who contribute their rich culture to the neighborhood. One resident said, "One of the great beauties of the East Village is that if you are smart enough and want to seek out something you can tap into pretty much anything around here from people to experiences."

Walk down Second Avenue and see what they mean. Stroll past security gates which roll up to reveal vintage clothing shops and take-out pierogi vendors, past young locals who emerge from crumbling tenements with cigarettes dangling from their lips. Walk further east on 6th Street, where Indian restaurants creatively compete for business, towards Tompkins Square Park where a row of old-timers lean back on benches and hock used books for 50¢ a pop. Watch tattoo-covered dads push strollers. Find a place on the grass and stay until the orange sun sinks into the west and Latino men break out congas and timbales for an evening drum circle.

After the area went through rough times in the '70s, the East Village is popular again. More and more residents are willing to scale the alphabet toward Avenue D, pushing further out toward the East River, where they wouldn't have before. The East Village seems to represent young ambition. A resident asserts, "The kinetic power of the East Village is still pretty amazing."

sites + parks

Community Gardens
Explore the nooks and crannies of Alphabet City, and you'll be sure to come upon at least one of a number of community-owned-and-operated gardens, such as the lovely retreat on 6th Street and Avenue B, where poetry readings, performances, and festivals are frequently held. When it's open during the day, take advantage of the shade.
Throughout Alphabet City, ❻ to Second Ave., ❶ to First Ave.

Tompkins Square Park
Major renovations in 1992 improved the park's facilities and safety, and the recreational courts, working bathrooms, and open green space attract families, tourists, and local oddballs alike, enlivening the park year-round. On any given weekend, you may stumble across a free concert or arts-and-crafts festival in the park, but the best events are spontaneous, like the drum circles, impromptu chess marathons, and the endless parade of East Villagers walking their dogs.
7th to 10th Sts. (bet. Aves. A and B), ❻ to Second Ave., ❶ to First Ave.

Ukrainian Museum
A small museum that highlights contemporary Ukrainian culture and history. Exhibits on the two floors rotate, so call ahead to find out what's on. Recent exhibitions have included student art, folk art, and Easter eggs from the Ukraine.
203 Second Ave. (bet. 12th and 13th Sts.), 228-0110, Admission: $1.50, students, ❶ to First Ave.

Bullet Space
This "Urban Artist Collaborative" in a deteriorating building showcases city artists known for political and challenging works. The stark gallery also as a musical space, community center, and residence for artists.
292 East 3rd St. (bet. Avenues C and D), 982-3580, ❻ to Second Ave.

Cooper Union
A "free" college (tuition is paid by alumnus) specializing in art, architecture, and engineering education, Cooper Union's standards are some of the highest in the country. The school houses the Houghton Art Gallery and the Great Hall, the site of an 1860 speech by Abraham Lincoln.
51 Astor Pl., 353-4120, ❻ to Astor Pl.

history

Long a haven for social dissidents, the East Village supports a cult of permissiveness. Much of the popular mythology of the East Village centers around its beatnik past and its cast of characters, including LeRoi Jones (now Amiri Baraka) and Charles Bukowski. The recreational drug use of literary luminaries like William S. Burroughs also set the stage for the East Village's darker side.

Drug traffic exploded during the economic plunge of the '70s, and led landlords to torch and abandon buildings, leaving the area depressed and undesirable. Drawn by the same low rents which attracted artists, anarchists, and squatters to Alphabet City, immigrants settled in the area. Puerto Ricans founded the community of Loisaida, which blurs the boundary between the East Village and the Lower East Side; Indians crowd around the mecca of 6th Street, and an enclave of Ukrainians claims lower Second Avenue.

The sense of community which these disparate groups have achieved is largely due to their joint efforts toward rebuilding their neighborhood. Villagers reclaimed their neighborhood from drug dealers and prostitutes by planting gardens and founding community arts centers on the rubble of abandoned lots.

In the early '90s, the East Village was "discovered." Since then, its popularity has grown exponentially, and pricey restaurants and cyber cafes have followed the crowds. Now that the area has become economically viable, the city wants its property back to accommodate the upwardly mobile college kids and trendies who want to live in this bastion of "authenticity." Only time will bear out the results of this struggle, but the indomitable spirit which pervades the East Village will not submit quietly.

A New York Legend

east village 69

A Saturday in the East Village

The First Street Cafe 1
Breakfast at this authentically grungy East Village joint will be a memorable experience. All around people are playing chess, reading magazines, and smoking excessively. It's a laid-back, one-man operation; the guy behind the counter fixes your eggs, steams your milk, flips the tape when the mood strikes him, and occasionally steps into the center of the tiny cafe to tell a story and entertain. If you just ask, he will send you home with a list of his favorite obscure jazz riffs he always has playing.
(see Cafe section)

2 **Community Gardens**
Explore the nooks and crannies of Alphabet city's community owned-and-operated gardens. The one on 6th Street and Avenue B has a famous sculpture standing four-stories high and lots of live performances. On Houston Street a lazy dog peeps you as you enter his paradise.
(see Sites + Parks)

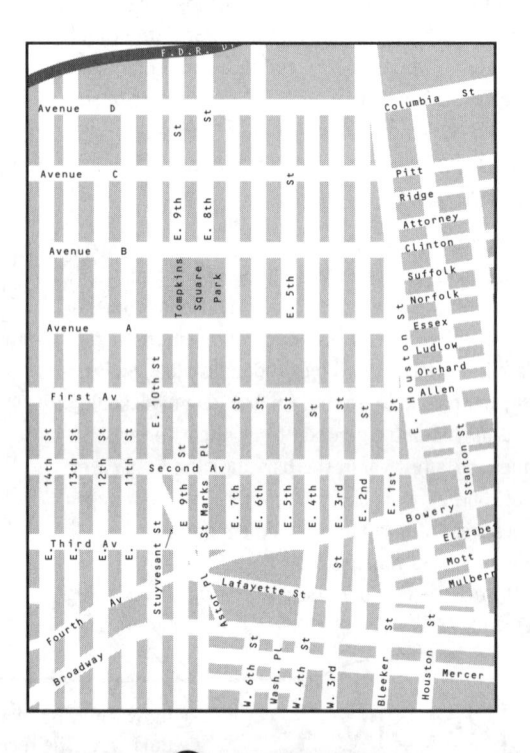

3 **Mama's**
Belly up to the counter and order the "best Mac and Cheese you'll ever have," and a side of beets and carrots, or perhaps the lemon asparagus. Awesome food at very reasonable prices. Tons of regulars crowd in for lunch; you're bound to launch a conversation or two with an artist neighbor in the close but cozy quarters.
(see Cafe section)

Most Board Games
Limbo
The hottest nonbar in the East Village. There's a decent selection board games, if enough space becomes available to play.
47 Ave. A (at 3rd St..), 477-5271, Cash Only, ❻ to Second Avenue

Most European Fries
Pommes Frites
Pretend you are in Amsterdam for dinner and have French Fries slathered in vinegar with a side of garlic mayo. A lucky few can fit inside, the rest get theirs to go.
123 Second Ave., 674-1234,
❻ to Second Avenue

Most Likely Place to Inhabit Your Nightmares
Korova Milk Bar
This is the milk bar from *A Clockwork Orange*, in every detail.
200 Ave. A (bet. 11th +12th Sts.), 254-8838, cash only,
❶ to First Avenue

70 east village

4 The Russian Bathhouse

The East Village is teeming with historic spots like this one. The Russian bathhouse was founded by Russian immigrants when they got off the boat one hundred years ago. Hop in for five minutes or three hours, either way it's $20 for a steam in any of the four authentic rooms, and an hour massage is just $45.
(see Shopping section)

Prowling the East Village

5 Mesopotamia

What this restaurant lacks in style it makes up for in service and great Belgian entrées. It is new and discovered by few, but as Avenue B gentrifies at the speed of light, more and more people are flocking here, so hurry up and carve your name under a table.
(see Restaurant section)

Members of the Groove Collective, grooving in the East Village

6 Opaline

Relax with a cocktail or a cup of tea at this dark and intimate lounge. With jazz acts on the weekends and a crowd that acts its age, Opaline is a laid-back foray into mellow East Village culture.
85 Avenue A (bet. 5th and 6th Streets), 475-5050, AmEx, MC, V, D
F to Second Ave.

Free TV
See Stomp, without buying a ticket, by watching the TV monitors outside of the Orpheum Theater. 126 Second Ave. (bet. 7th and 8th Sts.) **N R** to 8th St., **6** to Astor Pl.

Lakeside Lounge
Come every night with no cover and no minimum for good music. 162 Ave. B (bet. 10th and 11th Sts.), **L N R 4 5 6** to 14th St.

Bags O' Bags
Only $5 for bags at this store, the "Five Dollar Handbag Shop." Get pocketbooks, shoulderbags, big bags, and stuff your still-thick wallet into it. 147 Ave. A, 677-5001, **L** to First Ave.

{cheap *thrills*}

Greenwich VILLAGE

In most of downtown Manhattan changing trends dictate the attitudes and appetites of residents, redefining hip on a daily basis, forcing those in search of the harbingers of all things cool to look in increasingly obscure areas. Greenwich Village, however, has earned its reputation as the elder statesman of hip, having sheltered generations of artists, revolutionaries, and writers like Dylan Thomas and Edna St. Vincent Millay. It hosts a cluster of coffee houses, jazz and cabaret clubs, taverns, and New York University.

The Village's predictability supplies a large part of its tourist-friendly charm: Washington Square Park is an open playground for residential and visiting masses alike, and the shops which crowd the NYU area foist their schlocky wares upon the newcomers 365 days per year, be they tourists or the fresh crop of gawking freshman who arrive each fall. After dark, most nightcrawlers emerge from the subway station at Sheridan Square, thrust into the big city atmosphere of the Village's busiest and most confusing intersection, before dispersing into the various cafes, clubs, and theaters which fan out along the nearby streets.

The Village is not simply a commercial center and tourist destination. It's also one of the city's few neighborhoods which has artfully blended its past and present, supporting an ever more radical and diversified gay and artistic community while still accommodating the many families who quietly thread through the sea of tourists on their way to Balducci's to pick up dinner.

Just when nostalgic critics begin to arm themselves with accusations of the neighborhood having sold out, the Village reveals its ability to surprise. The area west of Seventh Avenue South, known as the West Village, is one of the most quiet and beautiful neighborhoods in the city. This cloistered area shelters a grid of tangled, tranquil streets, where it's very easy to lose yourself, literally. Each street is lined with slender trees, fussy federal style doorways with fluted columns on either side, flanked by ornamental windows webbed with ivy. This area has held true to its roots as a genteel enclave, remaining remarkably settled and serene, despite being nestled at the center of a wildly fluctuating downtown area. So when the city has gotten to you and your only desire is to take a drive through a country village, windows down, taking in the smells of bark moistened by dew, buck up! This quaint section of Greenwich Village will restore your faith in New York City life.

As long as Greenwich Village maintains its historic dignity, its tolerance and radical politics, its art and intellect, there will always be a spirit which will continue to attract and surprise even the most jaded New Yorker.

Name: Gina Tarigo
Age: 27
Occupation: Store Manager/Banana Republic

Q: How long have you lived in the neighborhood?
A: All my life. I'm an official native, born in St. Vincent's Hospital. I've lived in the same building on the same block all my life. My parents grew up on the same block, four doors down, fresh off the boat from Italy. When they were courting or whatever in those days, my dad wasn't allowed to take my mom past Sixth Avenue.
Q: Do you have a crazy New York story you always like to tell?
A: Well yeah, we got smart one night and decided go down to the piers at the Hudson River around 12th St. where no one was around, and one of my friends fell backwards into the water with her pants around her ankles while taking a pee over the edge. A drag queen in a cape and sequined mini skirt threw her whip down to my friend and rescued her.
Q: Tetanus shots?
A: Yes, at St. Vincent's, 3am.
Q: Give me one word which describes Greenwich Village.
A: One word... home.

local color

You haven't seen it all until you've spent an afternoon in Washington Square Park.

history

In the mid-19th century, as New York University was built around Washington Square and beautiful churches sprang up, the neighborhood became host to art clubs, private galleries, literary salons, and hotels, shops, and theatres clogged lower Broadway.

As the art scene increased in importance, the Village's removal from the financial constraints of Midtown's Broadway theatres and publishing powerhouses resulted in the development of a phenomenon for which the neighborhood would become world-famous: the Bohemian lifestyle. Experimental theatre, galleries specializing in avant-garde art, and irreverent "little magazines," the forerunners of today's "zines," exploded onto the scene. Wild parties, candle-lit tearooms, novelty nightclubs, and bizarre boutiques soon followed.

Just prior to the Depression, "artistic flats" became the era's local euphemism for luxury apartments that displaced the longtime residents that had spawned the artistic revolution that first put the neighborhood on the map.

Following the Depression's end, the Beat Generation arrived and the Village saw the first stirrings of gay culture. Again, writers and artists of all kinds congregated here, fueling the genesis of the hippie movement and the gay revolution. Novelist Norman Mailer started the *Village Voice* in 1955; the paper remains a leading organ of the left wing throughout the city and beyond.

Near the Village's still bustling Sheridan Square, a 1969 police raid on a local gay bar resulted in the Stonewall Rebellion, a seminal moment in the developing movement for gay and lesbian rights. With the '80's came the AIDS epidemic, which hit the community hard and sparked increased activism that continues today.

greenwich village 73

movies + books

Washington Square, 1881
Henry James' novel about the upper classes of the 1830s and 1840s was based on experience: as a child he lived in his grandmother's house, at 18 Washington Square North.

The Age of Innocence, 1920
One of several Edith Wharton novels set in New York. This look at lower Fifth Avenue society of the 1870s was turned into a film by Martin Scorcese in 1993.

Kids, 1994
This controvsersial chronicle of youths coming of age in New York was filmed in and around Washington Square Park.

Searching for Bobby Fisher, 1994
The story of a chess prodigy and his father, played by Joe Mantegna, with scenes filmed on location in the southeast corner of Washington Square Park.

Grace Church
Designed in 1846 by James Renwich, Jr. In a Gothic Revival style, Grace is the city's greatest Episcopal church. NYU students in the residence hall across the street whose windows face Broadway can wake up in the morning to the sight of the church's climbing white marble spiral.
802 Broadway (at 10th St.), 254-2000, **NR** to 8th St., **6** to Astor Pl.

The Jefferson Market Library
High Victorian Gothic pinnacles, gables, and a patterned slate roof crown this former courthouse, erected near the site of the former produce market for which it is named. Voted as one of the country's most beautiful buildings in 1885, it served as a Women's Detention Center, Police Academy annex, and temporary housing for the Census bureau until the city decided to landmark it and convert it into a much-needed branch of the New York Public Library in the '60s.
425 Sixth Ave. (at 10th St.), 243-4334, **FL123 9** to 14th St..

Washington Square Park
The park is now almost unrecognizable as the public gallows and potters' field of its 1780 origins. Most of the surrounding 19th-century Federal-style brownstones have been taken over by NYU; the elegant houses known as "the Row" on Washington Square North, which now accommodate university bureaucrats, once housed such talents as Henry James.
ACEBDFQ to West 4th St.

Judson Memorial Church
King Juan Carlos II of Spain provided funds for the renovation of this Romanesque church, whose modern minimalist interior clashes with its elaborately etched exterior designed by McKim, Mead, and White in 1892. Originally constructed to bring together the poor populace living on the south side of the square and their upscale northern counterparts, the building now houses seven floors of NYU administrative and academic departments, including the new King Juan Carlos II of Spain Center.
55 Washington Square South (bet. Thompson and Sullivan Sts.), 477-0351, **NR** to 8th St.

74 greenwich village

Parsons School of Design
Get a sneak peek at this crucible of young talent at one of the two exhibitions open to the public or by attending one of the ever-intriguing openings.
2 West 13th St. and 66 Fifth Ave., Ⓐ Ⓑ Ⓒ Ⓓ Ⓔ Ⓕ Ⓠ *to West 4th St.*

Sheridan Square
A major hub of the West Village, the square gets noisy and raucous on the weekends when its subway stop starts hatching nightcrawlers.
Between Seventh Ave., Christopher St., West 4th St., and Grove St., ① ⑨ *to Sheridan Square*

Stonewall Memorial Statues
General Sheridan calmly gazes down upon a standing gay male couple and a sitting lesbian couple which commemorate the 1969 gay rights riots at the Stonewall Inn.
At Sheridan Square, ① ⑨ *to Christopher St.*

St. Luke's in the Fields
A church that remembers a time when there were fields. The grass has given way to The Gap, but you can still get a taste of old-time Village life within the church when the adjacent elementary school is not in session.
487 Hudson St. (bet. Grove and Christopher Sts.), 924-0562, ① ⑨ *to Christopher St.*

cheap *thrills*

Washington Square Park
Watch the antics of street performers around the park's fountain or kick back with one of the neo-Dylan guitarists. Watch the hustlers playing speed chess on the outdoor tables and Rasta men hawking low-quality weed to tourists and prep-schoolers.
Ⓐ Ⓑ Ⓒ Ⓓ Ⓔ Ⓕ Ⓠ
to West 4th St.

West Side Highway Park Development
One of the best rollerblading, jogging, and biking stretches in Manhattan.
① ⑨ *to Christopher St.*

Gorilla Repertory Shakespeare Performances
Check out the free interactive performances scheduled in Washington Square Park at 8pm, from late summer through early September.
Ⓐ Ⓑ Ⓒ Ⓓ Ⓔ Ⓕ
to West 4th St.

greenwich village 75

A Saturday in Greenwich Village

The Grey Dog's Coffee

1 Once you've eaten in this friendly, rustic cafe you'll be back every week (every day if you have time). Its picket fence and dried flowers make you feel like you're in a country kitchen. Order a big piece of fresh-baked olive or basil bread and some eggs, and bring a pad and paper because this place inspires poetry. By the time you look up it'll be lunch time so order up a chicken caesar salad.
(see Cafe section)

2 **Our Name's Mud**
Drift uptown a ways to Our Name's Mud, and engage in the perfect Saturday afternoon activity: pottery painting. You choose an unpainted mug, pitcher, vase, etc... and all your favorite colors and then create your own design; they make great personal gifts.
(see Shopping section)

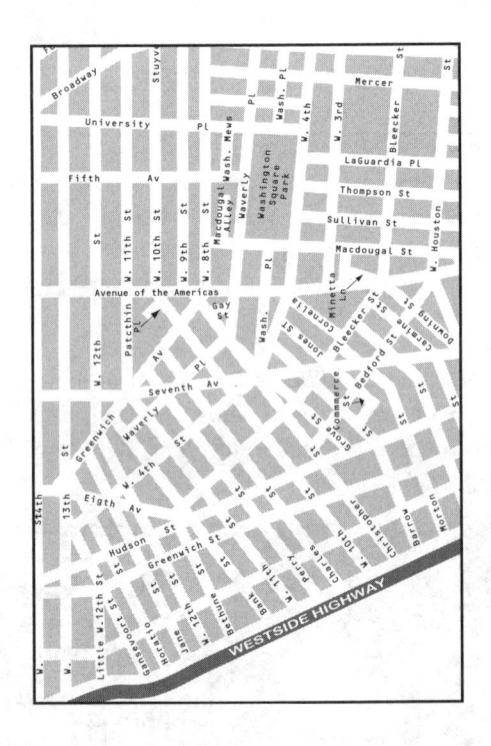

3 **Washington Square Park**
You can't go to the Village on a Saturday without taking a walk through Washington Square Park. Stop and watch the grumbling chess players, and preschoolers climb the slide, then wander over and listen to guitar players strum, or just lie down under the shade of a tree and close your eyes for awhile.
(see Sites + Parks)

Most Gourmet Food served at 4am
Café Milou
"Warm red cabbage salad with goat cheese" before sunrise; perfect for gourmet vampires.
(see Restaurant section)

Most Interactive Antiques Restaurant
Il Buco
This Italian-Spanish gem is an experience not to be missed. Come for a beautiful antique setting, a fabulous wine bar, and tantalizing tapas.
47 Bond Street (bet. Bowery and Lafayette Sts.), 533-1932, **6** to Bleecker St.

Pão! 4
Have a relaxing feast of wine and Portuguese seafood with a friend.
(see Restaurant section)

5 UDO
Sit at the upstairs bar for a bit, listening to your favorite songs on the juke box, or chatting with their charming bartenders, then climb down the stairs after 10pm to see a gritty blues band. You'll walk out sweating and re-energized for the rest of the night.
(see Bars section)

6
Hogs and Heifers
Hogs and Heifers is a unique New York experience. When you walk through the door the cowgirl bartenders in bras and short-shorts start yelling obscenities and threatening that if you don't get up on the bar and dance and then throw your bra into the crowd, "you're gonna get kicked outta here!" You must believe her and accept the challenge. The crowd will roar and the bartender will lighten up and pass you a shot of whiskey on the house.
(see Bars section)

Most Hard-to-Find Bathrooms
Jekyll and Hyde
In the haunted house decor it's easy to miss the bathroom door, cleverly hidden behind a bookshelf a lá the Addams family.
(see Nightlife section)

greenwich village 77

gramercy

When Sinatra belted out "I wanna be a part of it, New York, New York" he wasn't talking about Gramercy Park. But even 'Ole Blue Eyes would have been pressed up against the bars of this private oasis unless he had a pad in one of New York's most elite areas of real estate. Only those living along the park itself receive a key to the serenity resting snugly behind its gates.

Of course, there's more to the area than just the park. The region between Union and Madison Squares-known now as the Flatiron District after the triangular building at the intersection of Broadway and Fifth Avenue-sits between Gramercy and Chelsea, and is full of bars and shops, some with a slightly more laid-back atmosphere than in Gramercy proper. What's more, this formerly commercial zone has a surplus of converted warehouses, now used for expansive (i.e., expensive) residences. According to disgruntled Flatironer Evan Halper, a journalist, the neighborhood has assumed a "see-and-be-seen" air, similar to that of its neighbors to the west and east, filled with "rich kids with as much space between their ears as between the first and last digits of the their trust funds."

Gramercy has become a hub for fashion models and photographers, as well as for an eyeful of young celebs; at the right moment, you might catch an informally dressed Winona Ryder on her way to one of the spacious, pricey restaurants that fill up for brunch on Sundays.

With a literary history of Melville and Edith Wharton dating back to the 1920s, Gramercy has maintained its patronage for the arts. Though the area may seem indifferent to the world outside, it makes a point of taking care of its creative institutions; the National Arts Club and the Poetry Society of America are both housed in the stately building at 15 Gramercy Park South.

Though perhaps an ideal urban landscape; clean, residential, with elegantly commercial avenues, Gramercy may feel to some more like a fantasy land. Still, it's impossible not to admire its beauty, best taken in on a walk up from the bottom of Irving Place at 14th Street, where charming houses (alas, no key included) sit alongside prim restaurants and markets. Unfortunately, once you reach the top of the street, blooming out into the square around the Park itself, you may feel as though you've walked the yellow-brick road, only to find the doors of Oz closed to the public.

sites + parks

Flatiron Building
While 20 stories barely constitutes a skyscraper in modern parlance, this triangular office building at the intersection of Fifth Avenue and Broadway, erected in 1902 by Daniel H. Burnham, certainly impressed turn-of-the-century tourists; the men were especially eager to see if the unusual flow of air created by the building's angle really did lift ladies' skirts above their ankles. For many, its rusticated limestone facade and steel frame symbolized the dawn of the skyscraper era.
23rd St. and Broadway, ❻❼❽ to 23rd St.

Theodore Roosevelt's Birthplace
Saturday afternoons are the best time to visit the birthplace of our 26th President for a spin around his childhood home, a couple of museum galleries, and admission to a chamber music concert. Ask about Roosevelt's playboy uncle Robert, who lived in the brownstone next door.
20th St. (bet. Park Ave. and Broadway), 260-1616, Admission $2, ❻ to 23rd St.

Madison Square Park
Dog walkers and baby-sitters bask in the serenity, just as Edith Wharton and Theodore Roosevelt once did, on the site of the original Madison Square Garden.
23rd to 26th Sts. (bet. Fifth and Madison Avenues), ❼❽ to 23rd St.

Gramercy Park
Only the créme de la créme of Gramercy possess a rusty key to the gate of this manicured private park, where time seems to stand still. The park is opened once a year to the general public, but for the other 364 days, membership is a privilege.
20th Street and Irving Pl., ❻ to 23rd St.

Union Square Park
On Mondays, Wednesdays, Fridays, and Saturdays, one of the city's largest-though not cheapest-greenmarkets, chock-full of farm-fresh produce and nongreen goods like used books and fat pretzels made from scratch, commands the park's western edge.
14th to 17th Sts. (bet. Broadway and Union Square West), ❶❼❽❹❺❻ to Union Square

Union Sq. Greenmarket

history

Although originally a swamp, the area surrounding Gramercy Park has long been one of the most fashionable addresses in New York. Thanks to its intellectual residents at the turn of the century, the historical Gramercy has been called "an American Bloomsbury." Past residents include James Harper, founder of the Harper Collins publishing house, Theodore Roosevelt, Edith Wharton, Eugene O'Neill, and O. Henry, who wrote *The Gift of the Magi* in a local restaurant, Pete's Tavern, also called Gramercy home.

In 1831, Samuel Ruggles, longtime trustee of Columbia College, drained the swamp and laid out 66 English-style lots around a private park, still standing as the neighborhood's famed Gramercy Park. In the 1920s, the development of high-rise apartment buildings, the extension of the Third Avenue El, and the onset of the Depression meant that an address around Gramercy Park was no longer as desirable as it once was. The neighborhood's majestic mansions crumbled a bit, and the turn-of-the-century elite shopping mecca dubbed "Ladies' Mile" became the "temple of love" after an influx of brothels. On the heels of capital flight came a vibrant population of leftists and artists, including Andy Warhol, who instituted his legendary Factory. Gramercy became an enclave for groups of rebels, ranging in identity from communists to junkie divas, and heavy drug traffic and drifters plagued the area.

Today, the revitalization which has spurred development in most of the downtown area has returned some of the old panache to Gramercy, and a Union Square address is desirable once more.

gramercy 79

A Saturday in Gramercy

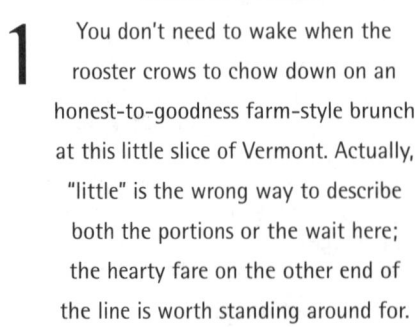

1 **Friend of a Farmer**
You don't need to wake when the rooster crows to chow down on an honest-to-goodness farm-style brunch at this little slice of Vermont. Actually, "little" is the wrong way to describe both the portions or the wait here; the hearty fare on the other end of the line is worth standing around for.
(see Restaurant section)

2 **Gramercy Park**
Walk off your Farmer's feast with a stroll up Irving Place to Gramercy Park. Walk around it heading east—you can't walk through it, after all—and take in the beautiful architecture and beautiful people, the old hotels and the old money.
(see Sites + Parks)

3 **National Arts Club**
Having completed the tour of the park and its surroundings, duck into the National Arts Club and see what's on display (or for sale!) in this beautiful architectural specimen. Upstairs is the Poetry Society of America, solidifying Gramercy's role as patron of the arts.
(see Sites + Parks)

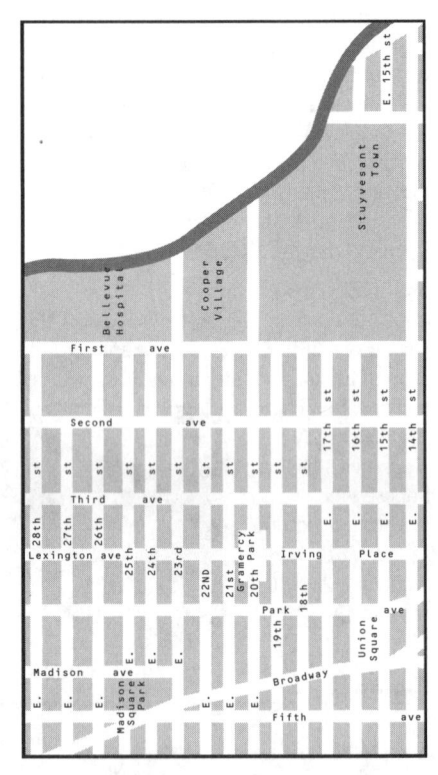

4 **Union Square Greenmarket**
Walk west to Park Avenue South and down to Union Square, where the busy park will be filled with, among other things, a thriving market of produce and baked goods (though you can't possibly be hungry yet, after the brunch at Farmer's!). There's also a superlative Barnes & Noble on Union Square North.

{ cheap *thrills* }

Model-Spotting
Beautiful women over six-feet tall and impossibly fit men seem to congregate in large groups in this fashion-industry-heavy neighborhood. Stroll down Park Avenue South from 23rd Street to Union Square and count all the faces you recognize from magazine covers.
6 to 23rd St.

Oldest Beer in New York
If you want to check out a historical New York site, but have had it with museums and churches for the day, then go to Pete's Tavern and have a beer at the oldest bar in the city.
129 East 18th St. (at Irving Place), 473-7676, **4 5 6 N R** *to Union Sq.*

Movie Filming at the National Arts Club
During the Summer months, movies seem to be shot on a near weekly basis in or around the National Arts Club on Gramercy Park. Hang nearby with a pen and wait for autographs.
15 Gramercy Park South, 475-3424, **4 5 6 N R** *to Union Sq.*

80 gramercy

5 Theodore Roosevelt's Birthplace

Strange that a Rough Rider like Teddy was born in genteel Gramercy, but it's true. The locale is marked by a five-room display and guided tour for $2, just up Broadway from Union Square. *(see Sites + Parks)*

Flatiron Building 6

Continue up Broadway to New York's best-known architectural anomaly, induced by the intersection of Broadway and Fifth Avenue. While you're there, head up a half-block to Madison Square Park, for a relaxed eye in an otherwise commercial storm. *(see Sites + Parks)*

Lady Mendl's Tea Salon

7
For that missing refinement in your day, complete the walk back to the park with some fine sippin'. Wouldn't life be grander if everyone made time for tea? 56 Irving Place, 533-4600, **456NR** to 14th St.

Union Square Cafe 8

Doesn't life sometimes seem like it's all about biding time until the next meal? A wonderful way to close out your day, New York dining doesn't get better, or more popular.

(see Restaurant section)

The Flatiron is one of the most unique buildings in the city

Most Scenic Park Not Requiring a Key
Madison Square Park
While it's not as quaint as its elite cousin to the southeast, this beautifully landscaped oasis offers a serene alternative for those of us not lucky enough to own a key to Gramercy's exclusive little sanctuary.
23rd St. (bet. Fifth and Madison Aves.),
6NR *to 23rd St.*

Most "In" Restaurant
Union Square Cafe
Past the point of trendy, this hotspot has graduated into one of New York's culinary benchmarks, the perfect blend of old and new styles.
21 East 16th St. (bet. Fifth Ave. and Broadway), 243-4020,
V, MC, AmEx, D; Entrées: $16-26,
456LNR *to Union Sq.*

Most Celebrity Sightings
Lexington Avenue
Winona Ryder is just one of a handful of celebs reported to be living in this oh-so-expensive residence on Gramercy Park. There's probably a better chance of sneaking a peek at some pretty face here than there is in the park itself.
Lexington Ave. (at Gramercy Park),
6NR *to 23rd St.*

gramercy 81

chelsea

Of all of the neighborhoods in New York which have made the climb from rags to riches, Chelsea's has been perhaps the least meteoric and, therefore, the most profound. While it has become known as a residential center for gay men, it has a huge variety of inhabitants and seems to be shaping up as a stylish, diverse district. Grittier than Greenwich Village to the south, Chelsea has nonetheless developed a remarkable restaurant scene.

Uprooted by high rent and close quarters, a number of art galleries have quietly resettled not just north of Houston but also. The social scene on Eighth Avenue (Mom, why are there no women in that bar?) contrasts nicely with the shopping on Sixth Avenue and regal townhouses between Ninth and Tenth Avenues, making Chelsea as varied and interesting a neighborhood as you'll find.

Plus, it's one of the friendliest places in Manhattan, with its eateries spilling out into the streets, creating a sense of common space and community.

Spending time in Chelsea will force you to watch your waistline. The gym scene is huge here and you can watch (from the street) the pecs of the men pumping iron as they sweat during window-front workouts. Chelsea afterdark possesses many night life activities for folks of all persuasions. It seems appropriate that Chelsea was home of the old meat-packing district. Get past all this and you can enjoy a cool night out. Finally, Chelsea is a neighborhood of varied and interesting buildings, including the London Terrace, a glorious block-long expanse on 23rd Street between Ninth and Tenth Avenues, and the Chelsea Hotel, site of myth and mischief, scene of the death of Sid and Nancy, and New York address for Leonard Cohen and Dylan Thomas, among others.

Parts of Chelsea may be too "exuberant" for some, but by and large this section of town has found its niche. Between an ethnic pocket right out of old Spain, the flower district on 28th Street, an enormous movie multiplex, and enough restaurants to challenge the effect of those plentiful gyms, Chelsea has muscled its way into being an integral part of New York City life. Taking the weight off of the Village as another gay-friendly section of town, it would be a shame to look at Chelsea as one-dimensional. Although the Chelsea Boys do thrive, God bless 'em, bringing the average body-fat percentage down a point or three, they make up just one aspect of neighborhood which is bursting at the seems like Arnold Schwarzenegger's shirt.

sites + parks

The Chelsea Hotel
From its opening, the residential hotel has lured literati and pop-culture icons to its fabled halls: Mark Twain, Dylan Thomas, William S. Burroughs, Vladimir Nabokov, and Arthur Miller all crashed here at some point. Even sometime girlfriend of Sex Pistols front man Sid Vicious, Nancy Spungen, met her untimely end here, allegedly at the hands of hunting-knife-wielding Sid himself. Rooms aren't readily available, but swing by and survey the plaques commemorating the most venerated guests and gaze at the residents' artwork, which crowds the walls.
222 West 23rd St. (bet. Seventh and Eighth Aves.), 243-3700, ❶❾ to 23rd St.

Little Spain
Though the population of Spanish sailors that burgeoned after the Civil War has since waned, snatches of Spanish still drift by on the streets, salsa music pours from the windows, and a few bookstores and restaurants persist as remnants of the past.
14th St., west of Sixth Ave.
❶❶❶❷❸❾ to 14th St.

Chelsea Piers
Restless New Yorkers recreate at this insular arena of sports and recreation facilities: indoor soccer, the sky rink, and an open-air roller rink help city-dwellers relive starry-eyed junior-high romance. Boutiques galore, too.
Piers 59-60, near 23rd St., ❸❸ to 23rd St.

General Post Office
A beautiful example of McKim, Mead, and White architecture, circa 1913, this imposing, columned structure on the cusp of Chelsea and Clinton bears the famous postal slogan.
Eighth Ave. at 30th St., ❶❸❸ to Penn Station

General Theological Seminary Gardens
An enclave of serenity hides behind the wall of this Episcopalian seminary. Afternoons, the garden is open to backyard-deprived urbanites.
20th St. and Ninth Ave., ❸❸ to 23rd St.

Chelsea Flower District
Sunrise heralds the aroma of roses and snapdragons wafting along this stretch of Sixth Ave., where vendors meet the horticultural needs of every urban green thumb.
Around Sixth Ave. and 27th St., ❶❾ to 28th St.

history

The core of the area known today as Chelsea was originally Thomas Clarke's family estate, and subsequently divided into homogenous blocks of one-family residences. Warehouses, factories, and piers later shot up along the Hudson as the economy shifted from agriculture to industry in the 19th century. At the end of the Civil War, the area between 14th and 23rd Streets on Sixth Avenue constituted the city's shopping nexus, but construction of major department stores nearby lured consumers away. The creation of the fur trading market has remained a vital segment of the economy through the '40s.

Shortly before completion of Pennsylvania Station, the firm of McKim, Mead, and White was asked to design a post office to complement the beautiful new railroad station whose grandeur rivaled that of Grand Central. Their answer was the white-columned structure that still stands opposite the site of the original Penn Station, marking the height of New York City's architectural Golden Age.

Today, the historical flourishes still contrast with the modern accents. The '80s ushered in a renaissance of commercial prosperity with the arrival of superstores; in the last decade, entrepreneurs capitalized on Chelsea's bevy of vacated warehouses to create monster dance emporiums, attracting the sex-and-drug trades to the area. Depreciated land values by the Hudson River led to low rents, attracting galleries as SoHo prices began to soar. Residential development promises to intrude next, as brokers seek out the few remaining inexpensive areas in Manhattan.

Extreme blading at Chelsea Piers

chelsea 83

A Saturday in Chelsea

1 **Paradise Muffin Co.**
In Chelsea, where brunch reigns supreme, this casual counter cafe is often the quickest and/or most relaxed fix. Get your lattés to go, or hang around reading provided newspapers and magazines in the open-air seating area. A super-friendly spot to start your day.
(see Restaurant section)

2 **The Cooler**
Only in New York (and perhaps only in Chelsea) would a former meat-room convert so seamlessly into a nightclub. A variety of musical genres perform at this A-1 venue, which opens at 8pm and usually has a cover.
(see Bars section)

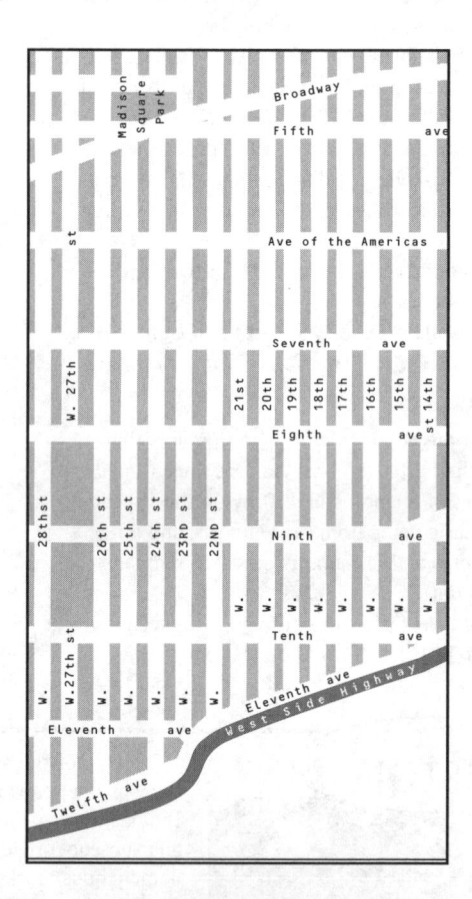

3 **Sixth Avenue**
Borderline-Chelsea, the Avenue of the Americas has become an avenue for shopping in a serious way, with fine clothing stores and boutiques, book and music stores, and some quick-bite pit stops.

People-watching at Big Cup
Nurse a cup of joe from behind one of the gigantic windows of the ever-hip coffee shop and see more butt-cheek exposure in an hour than in all of your embarrassing baby photos. *228 Eighth Ave. (bet. 21st and 22nd Sts.), 206-0059, Cash Only,* C E *to 23rd St.*

Enjoying Some Silence
Read amidst General Theological Seminary's greenery. *Ninth Ave. at 20th St. Admission: free,* C E *to 23rd St.*

Blading by the Hudson
The outer rink on the water is fun, but avoid crowded time when the slow-moving, flat-footed folk turn into so many bowling pins. *23rd St. at the Hudson River,* C E *to 23rd St.*

{cheap *thrills*}

84 chelsea

Teeing off at Chelsea Piers

4 Alley's End

This wonderful hideaway is a less hectic way to approach the frenetic Chelsea meal scene. Cute, contemporary, and relatively cheap, it's getting more and more popular, to the point where there's actually a wait on weekends.
(see Restaurant section)

5 Chelsea Architectural Tour

Heading west on 20th Street affords views of some of the city's most striking 19th-century buildings. Between Eighth and Ninth Avenues, the gothic St. Peter's soaks up most of the attention, while a block west, gorgeous Greek-style town houses line the north side of the street. Swing up Tenth Avenue and back east on 23rd Street, where the London Terrace Apartments regally occupy the entire block. Also on 23rd Street, between Seventh and Eighth Avenues, is the Chelsea Hotel, of Sid Vicious and Leonard Cohen fame, more impressive for its lore than its design.

Flower District 6

A sweet-smelling addition to your day, don't wait too long after rosy-fingered dawn to get the full effect. For obvious reasons, spring is the best time of year to visit here.
(see Sites + Parks)

Most Brownie for Your Buck
Taylor's Prepared Food and Bakeshop
Brownies the size of Buicks. For $3, it's the cheapest "meal" around.
228 West 18th St. (bet. Seventh and Eighth Aves.), 378-2895, Cash Only, ❶❾ to 18th St.

Most Beef
Chelsea Gym or the Meat-Packing District
Take your pick, Chelsea Gym, for fab abs, or the less appetizing meat-packing district..
267 West 17th St. (bet. Seventh and Eighth Aves.) or 14th St., ❹❻❸ to 14th St.

Most Sublime Meal in the Flatiron District
Bolo
Gastronomic ringmaster, Bobby Flay offers a colorful circus of his "Fantasy Spanish" cuisine, one beautiful plate at a time.
(see Restaurant section)

midtown

From grandiose to gaudy, Midtown is the New York which many New Yorkers know least about. The 30 or so blocks below Central Park include the city's famous theater district, Restaurant Row on 46th Street, and a gussied-up Time Square sits between the country's most famous meat market and the seedy Port Authority Bus Terminal. The no-nonsense corporate world to the east sidles up to the United Nations' often chaotic world of diplomacy and diplomatic immunity.

While these are the most famous aspects of Midtown, pockets of residential areas have become popular as people scramble from the high costs of living both up and downtown. The area between 34th and 59th Streets, Hell's Kitchen, has gone from a disjointed refuge to a bustling neighborhood. Tenth Avenue in the 50s is buzzing with television studios while glam hipsters pour in and out of loud, dark, lounges and a variety of Indian restaurants on Ninth Avenue dubbed Little Calcutta.

Directly across town is the Murray Hill. Centered around Third Avenue in the 30s, some of the city's most well-preserved brownstones are there for the gawking. The neighborhood, though, isn't exactly a social mecca. Its primarily Yuppie denizens tend to keep to themselves. "There are these beautiful brownstones, which I never see anyone coming in or out of," regrets resident Mika Dashman.

Stroll down Madison and Fifth Avenues to window-shop at some of the city's most luxurious stores. To the west, by the Hudson, sits the Javitz Exhibition Center, with trade shows of everything from Studebakers to greeting cards. For sports fans, there's the "world's most famous arena," Madison Square Garden, home of the Knicks and Rangers. For the a more cultural outing, look for the row of standout art galleries west of Fifth Avenue on 57th Street.

With no shortage of distractions, Midtown is virtually inexhaustible, if you don't mind thick crowds and the frenzied pace of Midtown city life. One way or another, mind your wallet. If the pickpockets in Times Square don't get it, the cashiers at Saks will.

movies + books

King Kong
Staked his claim at the top of the Empire State Building.
The Manchurian Candidate
This 1962 thriller, starring Frank Sinatra, culminates with a Presidential convention in the old Madison Square Garden, at Eighth Ave. and 50th St.
Breakfast at Tiffany's, 1961
Audrey Hepburn, dressed to the nines, wistfully looks into the Tiffany's window on Fifth Ave. and 57th, over coffee and a danish.
Welcome to the Dollhouse, 1995
Dawn looks for her kidnapped sister in Times Sq.
Night on Earth, 1991
Armand Mueller-Stahl, the Russian clown-turned-taxi driver, picks up his first passenger, Giancarlo Esposito, in Times Square.
The Cricket in Times Square,
George Selden's classic 1962 children's story. A mouse and cat, live in a drain pipe in Times Square station, and befriend a cricket with talent.

history

Formerly known as Long Acre Square, the several blocks which comprise Times Square have long been held in the American imagination as a hotbed of vice. Turn-of-the-century "silk hat" brothels first brought carriages and cabs into the area for quite a different reason than to visit the Astors, who maintained the neighborhood's exclusivity until the 1890s. A few years later, the *New York Times* erected a new building on 43rd Street, and the square was renamed. In commemoration of the Times new home, publisher Adolph Ochs hosted a New Year's Eve gala, complete with the famous ball drop, paving the way for Dick Clark.

By WWI, Times Square had attracted theaters from their former areas of concentration along the Bowery to East 14th Street and the stretch of Broadway from 42nd Street to Union Square. Visits to Times Square increased during this decade, silencing the voices challenging the amusements for which the area was steadily gaining a bad reputation.

WWI disrupted theater production and further developed the area's more sordid entertainment as servicemen on leave made Times Square a mecca for prostitutes and live nude revues. Zoning laws in the '50s attempted to control the growth of such businesses but met with little success. Recent laws have resulted in redevelopment by Disney, who celebrated their takeover of the area with a parade in honor of Mickey Mouse's anniversary. This government-sanctioned sin-cleansing led columnist and city resident Fran Liebowitz to quip: "I didn't move to New York at the age of seventeen because it was clean. I moved here because it was interesting. Now, it's less interesting."

Columbus Circle

Reminiscent of Parisian traffic circles, complete with antipedestrian sentiment, endless honking, and maniacal motorists; Christopher Columbus is the American touch, presiding over the madness which grew out of his expedition. Donald Trump's gaudy tower of overpriced condos, completed in 1996, and identified by the burnished replica of the Unisphere out front, dwarfs everything in the vicinity.
Intersection of 59th St., Central Park South, Broadway, and Eighth Ave., ABCD1 9 to 59th St.

Intrepid Sea-Air-Space Museum

Marvel at the ingenuity of the Masters of War and the military-industrial complex at this World War II aircraft carrier, now parked permanently on the Hudson and open to the public. A Stealth bomber, a guided missile submarine, and an Iraqi tank are among the goodies on display.
Pier 86, 46th St. and Twelfth Ave., 245-0072

Madison Square Garden

As "The World's Most Famous Arena," the Garden is home to the Knicks, Rangers, college basketball, and the Paramount Theatre. The complex underwent massive renovations in 1992, including the addition of 98 box suites renting for $20,000 each. The original arena was on 26th Street and Madison Ave., where turn-of-the-century New Yorkers packed themselves in like sardines to watch boxing, horse racing, and live cabaret.
31st to 33rd Sts. (bet. Seventh and Eighth Aves.), 465-6751, 1 2 3 9 to Penn Station

Theater District

Home to bloated musicals like *Cats* as well as the more innovative productions that keep it respectable; the heart of it all is Times Square. Eschew McDonald's and check out Restaurant Row on 46th St. between Eighth and Ninth Avenues for great deals on pre- and post theater prix fixe dinner menus.
Around 42nd St. (bet. Broadway and Eighth Ave.), NRS 1 2 3 7 9 to Times Square

The fountain at Rockefeller Center

Pennsylvania Station

McKim, Mead, and White modeled the original station (commissioned by the Pennsylvania Railroad), on the Baths of Caracalla in Rome, intending to upstage Grand Central and put another feather in the City Beautiful movement's cap. Completed in 1911, its subsequent demolition in 1965 prompted the formation of the Landmarks Preservation Council to ensure that buildings would no longer be sacrificed to the postmodern aesthetic. Today's Penn Station recently got a facelift and is as busy as ever, serving up to one thousand passengers every 90 seconds.
Between 30th and 34th Sts. (bet. Seventh and Eighth Aves.), 1 2 3 9 to Penn Station

National Debt Clock

A running tab on what Uncle Sam owes, including the average family's share. Clinton's campaign manager will be happy to point out that the speed of increase has been favorably adjusted twice since Bill took office.
Sixth Avenue (at 43rd Street), NRS 1 2 3 9 to Times Sq.

Times Square
Huge efforts to transform this notoriously sleazy strip of 42nd Street into a family-oriented funland have resulted in such ham-fisted ironies as moving a former burlesque theater down the block to serve as the entrance of a new multiplex. A seedy aura still clings to the area, especially at night, despite the throngs of tourists dazzled by Broadway's lights and the towering underwear ads. Grittier outposts of hustling and dealing remain, though they're much subtler.
42nd St. (at Broadway), **NRS123079** *to Times Sq.*

Bryant Park
Strangely enough, in a city where everything not bolted down disappears, the elegant movable chairs never stray far from their designated spots. Walk around and note the funky statues; Gertrude Stein's is one of the city's few statues of historical females. Summers, classic movies projected onto a large screen draw after-work crowds toting cheap wine and blankets.
40th to 42nd Sts. (bet. Fifth and Sixth Aves.), behind the New York Public Library, **BDFQ** *to 42nd St.,* **7** *to Fifth Ave.*

Rockefeller Center
The 19 commercial buildings and a subterranean network of shops and tunnels are dwarfed by attractions immortalized in the popular lore of New York: seasonal highlights include the ice rink and the tree lighting, at which thousands fenced in by the NYPD stand around with their kids, muttering "when are they gonna light the goddamn tree..." Also, in the winter slip and slide among twirling would-be Ice Capades at the skating rink or just park yourself on the sidelines and take in the scene while sipping a cup of hot cocoa.
49th to 52nd Streets (between Fifth and Seventh Aves.), **BDFQ** *to Rockefeller Center*

Radio City Music Hall
The Rockettes kicking grounds were opened in 1932 with a gala performance by the decidedly classier trio of Martha Graham, Ray Bolger, and Gertrude Niesen. The brainchild of Samuel Rothafel, the hall was designed by Donald Deskey, whose flair for art deco opulence continues to astound tourists much as it did Depression-era theatergoers. These days, everyone from the Moscow Circus to Michael Jackson has graced its stage; the annual Christmas show is a New York tradition. "The Grand Tour" costs $13.75 and leaves from 1260 Sixth Avenue every half hour, 10am-5pm, Monday through Saturday; 11am-5pm, Sundays.
50th St. (at Sixth Ave.), 247-4777, **BDFQ** *to Rockefeller Center*

---

cheap *thrills*

Bryant Park
In the summer, free classic movies on Mondays at dusk, and afternoon and evening concerts entertain in this charming and tranquil oasis.
(see Sites + Parks)

Marriot Marquis Hotel
Check out the vertigo-inducing glass elevators, which shoot up to the 49th floor.
NRS123079
to Times Square

New York Public Library
The main branch of the NYPL offers free exhibits, lectures, and programs year-round. Pick up a calendar of events in the entrance hall.
(see Sites + Parks)

Roosevelt Island Aerial Tramway
Pay just a token to dangle precipitously from the exoskeleton of the Queensboro Bridge for spectacular views of Midtown. 6am-2am weekdays, until 3:30am Fridays and Saturdays.
NR *to Lexington Avenue,* **456** *to 59th Street*

midtown 89

The most famous library in New York

Center for the Humanities, New York Public Library
Housed in a monumental Beaux-Arts building, books don't circulate at the NYPL's flagship branch, though they may be perused by anyone in one of the enormous oak-paneled reading rooms. The retrieval system is refreshingly efficient and the comprehensive reserve collection holds almost a million rare books, holographs, and manuscripts. In warm weather, brown-baggers and tourists cool off in the shadow of the two limestone lions guarding the main entrance, which provided the exterior shot for the opening scene of Ghostbusters.
Fifth Ave. at 42nd St., 340-0849, ❻❼❽❾ *to 42nd St.*

Grand Central Terminal
With its soaring ceilings, leaded lunette windows, and stolid, ornamented façade, this cathedral to industrialization is also one of the world's busiest and most spectacularly efficient train stations. Designed in 1889 by Reed and Stem, Grand Central Terminal has thus far eluded the sinister machinations of real estate speculators. A recent facelift restored some of the twinkle to the constellations painted on the vaulted blue ceiling. Seafood enthusiasts should be sure to check out the elegant old-fashioned Oyster Bar on the lower concourse.
42nd St. (bet. Park and Lexington Aves.), ❺❹❺❻❼

The Chrysler Building
This building is 1,045 feet of art deco madness. Completed in 1930, its glory days as the world's tallest building (at 71 stories), have gone the way of the milkman and Mayor LaGuardia, yet the African marble lobby and the silvery tip immortalized by Carol Burnett's Miss Hannigan in Annie, among others, are as impressive as ever.
42nd St. (at Lexington Ave.), ❺❹❺❻❼ *to Grand Central*

United Nations
Built atop ground once occupied by slaughterhouses, the United Nations Plaza is international territory, so if you've never left the country, here's your chance. Though San Francisco, Boston, and Philadelphia were all contenders when the site was planned back in 1944, its first Secretary General, Trygve Lie, preferred New York. The U.N. has its own fire department, police force, and postal service; the city provides protection for diplomats. When the roses are in bloom, they make even the East River seem appealing. Students can tour the building for $4.50; tours leave every half hour, 9:15am to 4:45pm.
First Ave. at 46th St., 963-7713, ❺❹❺❻❼ *to Grand Central*

Fifth Avenue
Trump built his tower here, hundreds of couples a year are married here, and both ACT-UP and the Irish parade down this legendary thoroughfare. The most famous stretch bisects Midtown, beginning with Bergdorf's and FAO Schwartz, and getting progressively less glittery as it approaches Gramercy to the south. Follow in the fashionable footsteps of Holly Golightly by window-shopping at Tiffany's.
❶❷❸❹ *to Fifth Ave. will stop at the top of the stretch*

90 midtown

Empire State Building

Snow falls up at this archetypal symbol of progress, which rose during the Depression and still sways in high winds. King Kong climbed it, a B-52 bomber crashed into it, a sniper randomly shot at people from its top, and the first person jumped a year-and-a-half after it was completed. On the observation deck, a high fence effectively discourages potential suicides but doesn't obstruct panoramic views of the city. Go at night for the best view and the fewest tourists. Striking the balance between exhilaration and terror, the view from here provides an accurate metaphor for why native New Yorkers feel a little bit bored anywhere else in the world.
350 Fifth Ave (bet. 33rd and 34th Sts.), 736-3100, Admission to observation tower $4.50 adults, $2.50 seniors and children under 12; **B D F N**

St. Patrick's Cathedral

The Roman Catholic behemoth looks a little out of place amidst all the glass and concrete; a $200,000 rose window, bronze doors for its Fifth Avenue entrance, and neo-Gothic spires built in 1885 all lend a European air to the church's design.
Fifth Ave. (at 51st St.), 753-2261, **E F** *to Fifth Ave.*

midtown 91

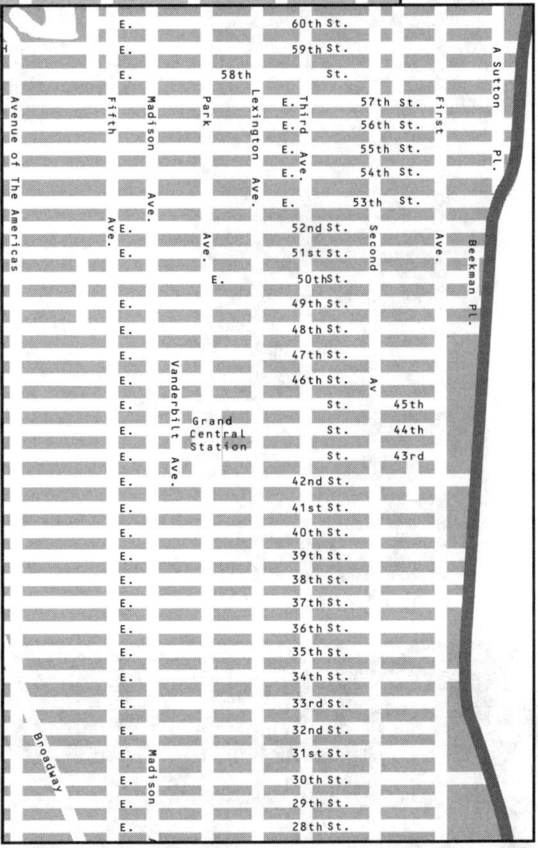

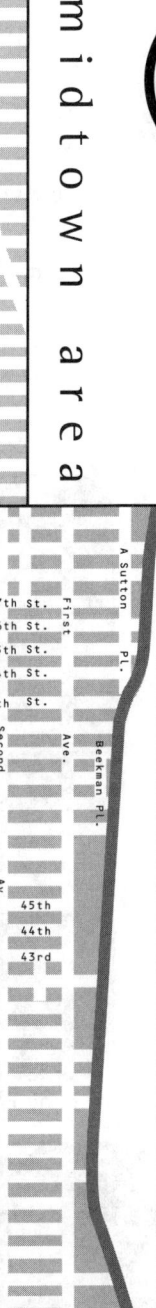

A Saturday in Midtown

1 Cafe Europa

Start with a light meal at Cafe Europa, one of the slickest cafes in Midtown and some of the best coffee in the city.

(see Cafe section)

2 Window-shopping

Stroll east on 57th Street to Park Avenue and check out some of the most expensive stores in Manhattan. Unless you've got a gold card with lots of room, don't even think of going inside Prada or Burberry or Hermés...

3 FAO Schwartz

Stop at this classic toy store and pretend you're shopping for a young niece or nephew. This most exclusive shop will make you forget you're not a kid anymore.

(see Shopping section)

The huge FAO Schwartz clock

Most Irish Pub
DJ Reynold's
This area has pubs a-plenty, but not only is the staff here Irish, nearly all the clientele is as well.
West 57th St (bet. Eighth and Ninth Aves.), 245-2912,
①❾ⒶⒷⒸⒹ to Columbus Circle,
ⓃⓇ to 57th St

Most Generation X-driven Musical
Rent
All the hype is earned. This poignant play is what *Hair* must have been to hippies...
208 West 41st St (bet. Seventh and Eighth Aves.),
Nederlander Theater, 307-4100,
①②③❾ to 42nd St

4 Empire State Building

Head down Fifth Avenue to the Empire State Building. At the top, snap pictures of Manahttan's spectacular cityscape. Back in the lobby, grab a snack at one of the myriad eateries.

(see Sites + Parks)

5 Bryant Park

Relax on a bench in Bryant Park and people-watch while you rest up for the rest of the day.

(see Sites + Parks)

6 Sight-Seeing

Spend the rest of the afternoon visitng more of midtown's famous sites. Stop in to look at Grand Central Terminal's recently redone ceiling. Check out the art deco design in the Chrysler Building. Walk around Rockefeller Center; in the winter and watch the ice-skaters twirl around the rink.

(see Sites + Parks)

7 Torre di Pisa

For dinner, make reservations at Torre di Pisa. Excellent Italian cuisine and disctinctive decor make up the slightly pricey menu.

(see Restaurant section)

Relaxing in Bryant Park

Most Beautiful Reception Space
Celeste Bartos Forum at the Humanities Library
Used for a variety of lectures and events at the New York Public Library, this remarkable space can also be rented out for wedding receptions and the like. Exquisitely elegant and expensive, it's out of most budgets, but is nonetheless worth a visit.
455 Fifth Ave. (entrance on 42nd St.), ❽ ❹ ❼ ❻ ❼ to 42nd St.

upper east side

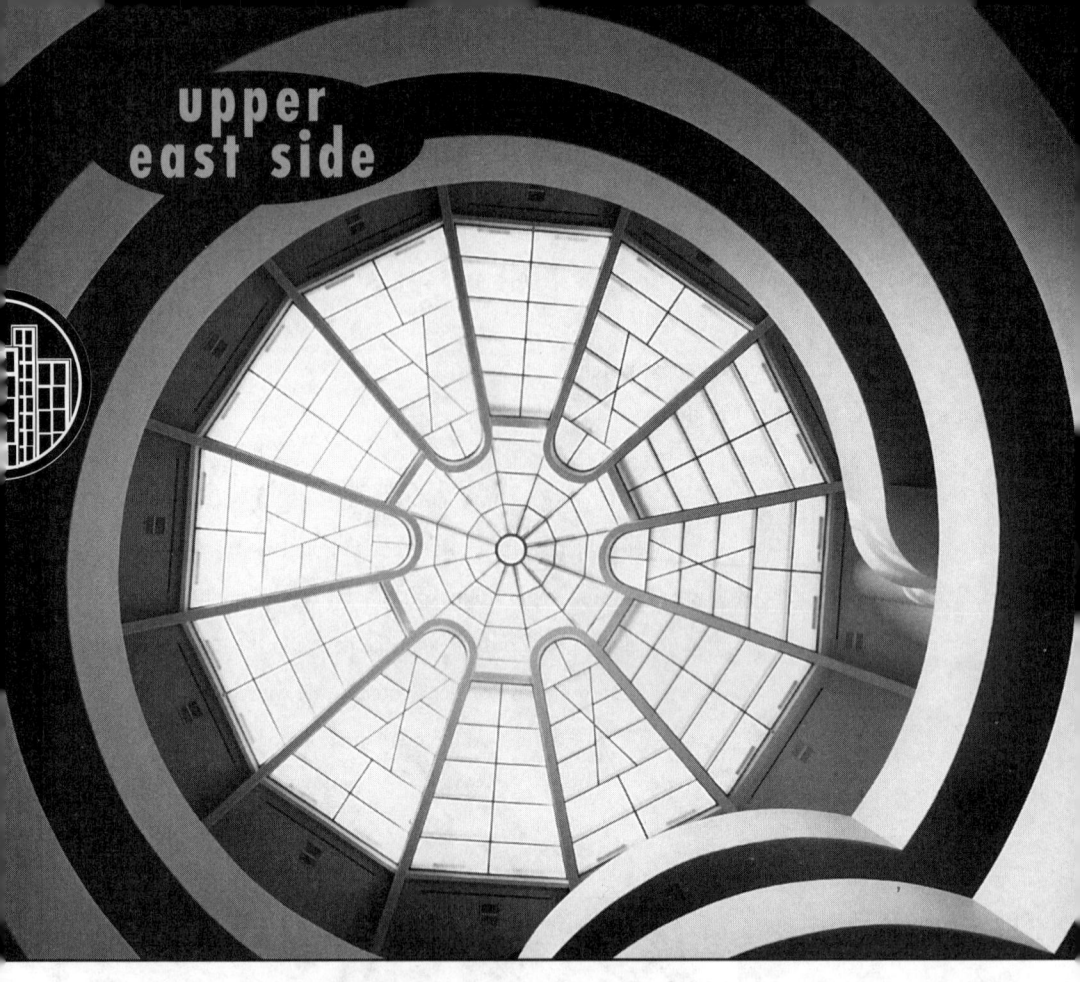

Fifth Avenue, Madison Avenue, Park Avenue: How often do streets become household names, synonymous with wealth, corporate power, and exclusivity? In the late 19th and early 20th centuries, the Upper East Side was home to the Astors, Carnegies, and Fricks, among many other wealthy families. Their palatial residences have, in some cases, been converted into foundations, galleries, and museums. Manhattan's Gold Coast, above 60th Street and west of Lexington Avenue, is home to luxurious apartments with price tags that would make even Donald Trump hesitate, luxurious restaurants that don't bother to list something so crass as prices on their menus, and exclusive clubs like the Knickerbocker, the Metropolitan, and the Union.

Exploring the Upper East Side can be an intimidating experience for the uninitiated. Gloved doormen still hail cabs, caterers still have their own entrances, nannies still take the kids out for a stroll, and navy-suited adolescents still get shuttled to exclusive private schools where they are groomed for inheritance. Gradually, however, the luxury of Fifth, Madison, and Park Avenues begins to vanish after crossing Lexington.

Despite all its associations with old money and power, the Upper East Side is ultimately a neighborhood of many minds. The area beyond Third Avenue has a decidedly middle-class charm, which becomes increasingly blue collar near the East River. Many Eastern European and German immigrants reside in this modest area called Yorkville. This neighborhood within a neighborhood still boasts an active Hungarian patronage, old-world delis, and moderately priced ethnic restaurants. Long-time Yorkville resident Bridget promises, "It's easy to feel comfortable on the Upper East Side. All my neighbors are warm and friendly, and I've never felt excluded because I earn a modest income." Indeed, an area as large as the Upper East Side has, as Bridget says, "a lot to offer, and room for everyone. You be sure to print that!"

sites + parks

Carl Schurz Park
Picturesque views of the East River, Queens, and the Triboro Bridge are the draw of this green locale, not to mention Gracie Mansion. Get a feel for the east side amidst the rollerbladers, joggers, and well-groomed dogs that frequent this site.
East End Ave. (bet. 84th and 90th Sts.), ❹❺❻ to 86th St.

Gracie Mansion
Constructed in 1799 by merchant Archibald Gracie, this retreat from the urban gridlock of the city continues to stand as an elegant reminder of a bygone New York elite. Bought by the city in 1887, it became part of Carl Schurz Park and housed the Museum of the City of New York from 1924-30. Since the 1940s it has been the official residence of New York mayors. Tours are conducted Wednesdays; call in advance for times and reservations.
East 88th Street (at East End Ave.), 570-4751, suggested admission $4, ❹❺❻ to 86th St.

Henderson Place
Rumor has it that the 24 Queen Anne-style townhouses built in 1882 by fur importer John Henderson are haunted, either by ex-residents or by vengeful beavers.
86th St. (bet. East End and York Aves.), ❹❺❻ to 86th St.

Museum Mile
Fifth Avenue along the length of the park, houses a great many of the city's best and most famous museums. Here are just a few:

- **The Metropolitan Museum of Art** contains an impressive collection of Western and non-Western art; it is the most comprehensive art museum in the western hemisphere.
- **The Solomon R. Guggenheim Museum**, designed by Frank Lloyd Wright, is an architectural wonder that exhibits works of modern art along its curved central ramp and galleries.
- **The Museum of the City of New York**, which inhabits a Georgian East Side mansion, holds artifacts from old New York.
- **El Museo del Barrio**, located in a former public school building, displays art exhibits dedicated to preserving and documenting the heritage of Puerto Rico and Latin America.
- **The Whitney Museum of American Art** exhibits a premier collection of modern works by American artists.
- **The Frick Collection**, mansion, displays great European works from the Renaissance to the end of the 19th century.
- **The Cooper-Hewitt Museum**, located in the former Carnegie Mansion, exhibits decorative arts, including prints, drawings, and patterns.

history

Until Central Park opened in the 1860s, much of Manhattan's uptown landscape resembled an affluent countryside. However, as the city expanded northward it was soon dotted with masses of attractions and buildings.

The eastern section of the region developed rapidly as the Second and Third Avenue elevated lines, completed in 1879, facilitated transportation between the urban center and outlying regions, attracting Irish and German immigrants who settled in the brownstones and tenements lining the area that would become Yorkville.

The development that earned the area its elite reputation, however, was construction astride the park along what would become the luxurious Fifth, Madison, and Park Avenues. From Astor to Tiffany, New York's wealthiest barons erected park-side mansions. Although most were later demolished, the Carnegie and Frick survive as the Cooper-Hewitt Museum and the Frick Collection, respectively.

Park Avenue's glamorous reputation developed after the New York Central Railway buried its above-ground tracks. Elegant apartment buildings lined the newly cleared blocks while Madison Avenue's wealthy inhabitants attracted opulent boutiques to the ground floors of the street's row houses. The Upper East Side cemented its reputation for both ethnic diversity and upscale living with the construction of high-rises as even the former working-class, immigrant-packed Yorkville area became desirable in the 1950s. Upper-class immigrants from Europe and Asia arrived in the '80s, making the area have one of the most exclusive and expensive zip codes in the continental United States.

upper east side 95

A Saturday in the Upper East Side

1 **The Regency**
If you have never seen a big business deal conducted before regular business hours, rest assured, you will here; where corporate Manhattan brass butter their muffins and sip champagne at 8am. City regulars can feel more than at home here if they dress smartly.
(see Restaurant section)

2 **Carl Schurz Park**
Small but picturesque, this is a nice place to relax after your ritzy meal at Regency. The Park also affords probably the best sweeping views of the East River.
(see Sites + Parks)

Mayor Rudy Giuliani and friend

3 **Gracie Mansion**
The New York mayor's private residence since 1942 is in Carl Schurz Park. There are tours only on Wednesdays, but you can photograph the building anytime.
(see Sites + Parks)

Most Marvelous Marzipan
Elk Candy Company
More than 60 years have gone by since this Yorkville landmark opened its doors.
240 East 86th St.,
❹❺❻ to 86th St.

Most Overpriced Clothing
57th Street bet. Sixth and Park Aves.
Unless you belong to the Knickerbocker Club, you probably can't afford anything on this street of fantasy.
❸❼ to 57th St.

Most Exclusive Club
Knickerbocker Club is inclusive only to those whose ancestors were present in America during colonial times.
2 East 62nd St.,
❹❺❻ to 59th St.

96 upper east side

4 Burritoville

The best burrito deal in town can be found here. They cater to carnivores as well as strict vegetarians, who can request soy cheese and tofu sour cream instead of the real thing. The Route 66 burrito is outta sight!
(see Restaurant section)

5 Fifth Avenue and Museum Mile

Some of the best addresses in the city are along this stretch of Fifth Avenue, and many of the museums, including the Cooper-Hewitt and the Frick Collection were the former private residences of the richest men in America. You could either walk the mile or spend the whole day in any one of these world-class museums; they will not disappoint.
(see Sites + Parks)

6 Match Uptown

Lively and candlelit, this uptown twin of the popular SoHo restaurant serves excellent, eclectic New American cuisine and is a place to see and be seen. Dress up and walk in with attitude.
(see Nightlife section)

7 Manny's Car Wash

Reserve your table early for the nightly blues fests at this hot nightspot.
(see Nightlife section)

{cheap thrills}

Roof Garden
Summers, the Met's Roof Garden caters to a white-wine-sipping, after-work crowd and others just admiring the gorgeous view.
1000 Fifth Ave. (bet. 79th and 84th Sts.), 535-7710, ❹❺❻ to 86th St.

Pay-What-You-Wish Days
The museums along Museum Mile, as well as the MoMA and the Whitney, host "free" nights approx. once a week with hours into the evening.
(see Arts section)

Window Shopping
Just admiring the view is half the fun of shopping at posh boutiques and designer showcase stores along Madison and Fifth Avenues. from the 60s through the 90s.

upper east side 97

central park

Central Park is the place where bronze, scantily clad sunbathers attempt deeper shades. It is where every kind of in-line skater, from the seamlessly gliding expert to the tentative novice, enjoys a long afternoon. Tieless businessmen chat with dredlocked Rastas. Musicians open their guitar cases and serenade a crowd reclining on a gently sloping hill. Lovers curl together in its few intimate enclaves. Statues of *Alice in Wonderland* characters hold court, and a poignant memorial called Strawberry Fields reminds us of John Lennon's legacy. Central Park is everything that is magical about New York, condensed into ten million cart loads of rock and soil, 843 acres carefully landscaped over twenty years.

It is difficult to fathom any visit to New York City without a trip to Central Park. An estimated 15 million people come here every year. "It's such a beautiful place," smiles 17-year-old Ashley. "My family and I try to come here every weekend during the spring and summer for a picnic, and we walk around for hours." Miles of paved and unpaved paths allow hiking, biking, skating, or jogging enthusiasts to get their share of exercise. "There's something for everyone here, not only for the athletically inclined," says John, a park ranger for the past eight years, "but for the aesthetically inclined as well. Some of our city's most striking apartment houses have been built along the park's perimeter, so the skyline is really spectacular, especially when the sun begins to set behind the buildings."

In a city that's notorious for draining cash flow, Central Park is welcome relief. Although the antique carousel costs 90¢ per ride, almost all of the park's attractions and events are free, including Belvedere Castle, the Swedish Cottage, the Conservatory Garden, Shakespeare in the Park, and the dog run.

The park is also a popular place for bird watchers. Ostentatiously plumed, the Scarlet Tanager spends the early summer here and the stark winter brings bright yellow Cape May warblers. Even swarms of Monarch butterflies spend a few months in autumn before embarking on their long journey to Mexico. The contrast between Manhattan's overwhelming concrete-and-steel, and Central Park's earthly communion of soil and water is a reminder that although city business and commerce are crucial to New York's survival, humans cannot survive without having places to retreat, reflect, and relax.

Name: Tyrone Bastien
Age: 21
Occupation: Waiter

Q: How long have you been visiting Central Park?
A: 21 years
Q: What do you like best about the park?
A: I just started going to Shakespeare in the Park a few years ago, and I love it. It is rare to find free things to do in the city, but in Central Park you can.
Q: What attracts so many people to Central Park?
A: The park is a happening place! It seems like, throughout my life, there has always been a reason to come here. When I was a kid I used to watch the ducks nibble at bread thrown into the water. When I was a little older I was playing Frisbee or baseball with my father. Now I go to the performances. Who knows, maybe much later in my life sitting on this bench will be my favorite thing. Central Park is a playground for everyone no matter how young or old.
Q: There has been so much talk over the years about muggings in Central Park. Do you feel safe when you visit the park?
A: Yeah, I do. I mean, I use common sense. I come here during the day, leave some of the wilder, secluded areas before dusk if I happen to be alone. Honestly, though, the police patrol the park all the time. There's even a special "precinct" near the reservoir.

local color

Tyrone Bastien
Central Park devotée

history

In the 1800s the beautiful sanctuary that we know today as "The Park" was predominantly undeveloped camp territory known as "Squatters' Sovereignty". Primarily composed of poor immigrants, blacks, and American Indians who dwelt in shacks, huts, and caves alongside livestock, this social and geographical wasteland, as it was seen by wealthy citizens and government, could be put to better use in terms of social reform as a center for leisure and recreation. The conception of the park was inspired by the public grounds in London and Paris and in 1857 a contest was held to choose a design. The winning entry, submitted by Frederick Law Olmsted called the "Greensward Plan," consisted of a pastoral, romantic, English landscape which combined picturesque and formal elements. In the building of the park, over four million trees, shrubs, and vines were planted while 1600 shantytown residents were displaced, including Irish pig farmers, German gardeners, and the black Seneca Village population. It took sixteen years and today's equivalent of $20 million to realize this plan.

Although the designers opposed the idea, ball fields were introduced in the 1860s and public sculptures installed, though only Bethesda Fountain was included in the original design. Grazing in Sheep Meadow was discontinued in 1934 and the sheepfold became Tavern on the Green. In 1965, the park was declared a national historic landmark, and as a part of urban renewal and countercultural movements during the '60s, the park hosted rock concerts and "be-in's." Deterioration during the 1970s led to a revival of the Greensward Plan by the Central Park Conservancy in the 1980s, reinstating the park as the public respite it was constructed to be.

The Park is composed of many different neighborhoods, each with its own character and attractions:

Belvedere Castle

One of the main attractions at the Castle, apart from the view, is the Henry Luce Nature Observatory, which identifies local bird and plant life. Also located here is the Weather Center, the source for New York local weather forecasters.
Mid-park near 79th Street

The Conservatory Garden

This garden is one of New York's best examples of formal landscaping in the European tradition, with fountains, flowers, and shaded pathways.
East Side, near 105th Street

The Harlem Meer

The Meer is a haven for locals, many of whom have fished there for as long as they can remember. The Charles A. Dana Discovery Center is situated on its northern bank and to the south and west lies the pool, with its lush greenery, a running stream, and even a small waterfall.
Northeast corner of the park

The Jacqueline Onassis Reservoir

The Reservoir lies directly to the north of the Great Lawn, recently refurbished by the Parks Department. It is still used occasionally to distribute water to Harlem and the Upper East Side and is circled by the park's main running track, which is about a mile-and-a-half around.

The Mall

A stately avenue lined with trees and statues of great literary figures leads up to the bandshell and fountain at Bethesda Terrace.
East Side of the park, 65th-72nd Sts.

The Ramble

This 37-acre natural woodland has winding paths and open lawns; the perfect place to bring a book and read in the shade.
Northeast side of the lake

The Shakespeare Garden

Leading upwards to Belvedere Castle, is reminiscent of the villa gardens of Northern Italy. In this formal garden grows every species of flower or plant mentioned in Shakespeare's plays.
West side of the park, at 80th Street

Sheep Meadow

The hot spot for sun-worshippers, Frisbee-players, and kite-flyers of all ages, sizes, and shapes. On sunny afternoons in summer, the grass cannot be seen for all the bodies, hence the nickname, "Gettysburg."
West side of the park, mid-60s

Strawberry Fields

The heart-shaped grove, a memorial to John Lennon, is right across from the Dakota Building where Lennon was shot and where Yoko Ono still lives. The name references a famous Beatles song.
West side at 72nd St.

Sports/Recreation

For the urban athlete, activities abound in the park. From softball to "stroller-cise," don't be afraid to go up and ask the participants about joining the group.
(see Leisure section)

Bike Rentals

Contact the Loeb Boathouse, East Drive at 74th Street (517-2233). The cost is between $8 and $14 per hour, depending on the bike; ID required.
(Rental info: 861-4137)

Bird-Watching

Over 270 different species of birds populate the park. The Central Park Conservancy and New York City's Audubon Society (691-7483) organize bird-watching expeditions which begin and end at the Charles A. Dana Discovery Center.

Board Games

Chess players are welcome at the Chess and Checkers House at 64th Street, west of the Dairy.

Boating

The Boathouse rents boats at $10 per hour plus a $30 deposit; model boat regattas and races are held on weekends on Conservatory Water.
(Fifth Avenue at 72nd Street)

Dog Walking

Expect to see dogs, cats, or ferrets out for a stroll with their owners. Dogs must be kept on a leash at all times but unofficial dog runs exist in a couple of like the Great Hill near 107th Street and Central Park West.

Fishing

The Harlem Meer stocks widemouthed bass for fishing on a strictly catch-and-return basis. Bamboo rods and other equipment are available free of charge at the Charles A. Dana Discovery Center.

100 central park

Horses
Contact the Claremont Stables, 175 West 89th Street (724-5100). The cost is $38 per half hour for experienced riders only. For the more sedentary, horse-drawn carriages leave from 59th Street on the east side *(246-0520)*

Ice-Skating
The park has two rinks: Wollman, located mid-park at 62nd Street (396-1010 for skate rentals and fees), and the Lasker Pool (534-7639) and Rink (396-0388). During the summer, Wollman Rink is used for rollerblading, the Lasker for swimming.

Organized Tours
The Central Park Conservancy (315-0385), Columbia University's Big Onion Walking Tours (439-1090), and The New York Historical Society (873-3400) all give historical tours of the park. The Urban Park Rangers (427-4040) lead nature walks each week. Steve Brill, famous for converting the park's plant life into dinner, gives environmental tours of the park. *Call (718) 291-6825 for information*

Rides/Amusement
The Carousel (mid-park at 64th Street) and the Zoo (east side, low 60s) are open year-round. The Dana Discovery Center runs a series of after-school and weekend educational programs, including art and natural history classes. *Call 280-6525 for information*

Performance

Dana Discovery Center
A performance space for multicultural dance and music where the Harlem Meer Performance Festival is held. *110th St. and Fifth Ave., 860-1370,* ❷❸❻ *to 110th St.*

Delacorte Theater
Shakespeare in the Park lures stars like Patrick Stewart and Andre Braugher to its leading roles. Tickets are free at the box office at 1pm on the day of the show. Be prepared to arrive as early as 4am on weekends for the most popular shows, though you can sleep later on weekdays. *West side of the park near 81st St., 861-7277,* ❻❸ *to 72nd St.*

Metropolitan Opera
Bring wine and a picnic basket and listen to arias as the stars come out and the skyline lights up; arrive early for a good seat. People seated farther from the stage treat the opera as background music for their conversations so be prepared to shush. *North Meadow, West 64th St. where Broadway and Columbus intersect, 362-6000, Free,* ❶❾❸❸ *to 96th St.*

SummerStage
A summer-long program of concerts, poetry readings, modern dance shows, and other events; last year, among the festival's highlights was a poetry reading by Patti Smith. *Rumsey Playfield, mid-park at 72nd St. near Fifth Ave., Free, 360-2777, East Side:* ❻ *to 68th St., West Side:* ❸❸ *to 72nd St.*

Swedish Cottage Marionette Theater
For information about shows, call the numbers given above or keep an eye on the *Times*, the *Voice*, or *Free Time* for full programs of events around Memorial Day. Performances take place on Saturday afternoons; call for reservations. *Mid-park at 81st St., 988-9093, Cash Only, Admission $5, $4 children,* ❸❸ *to 81st St.*

central park 101

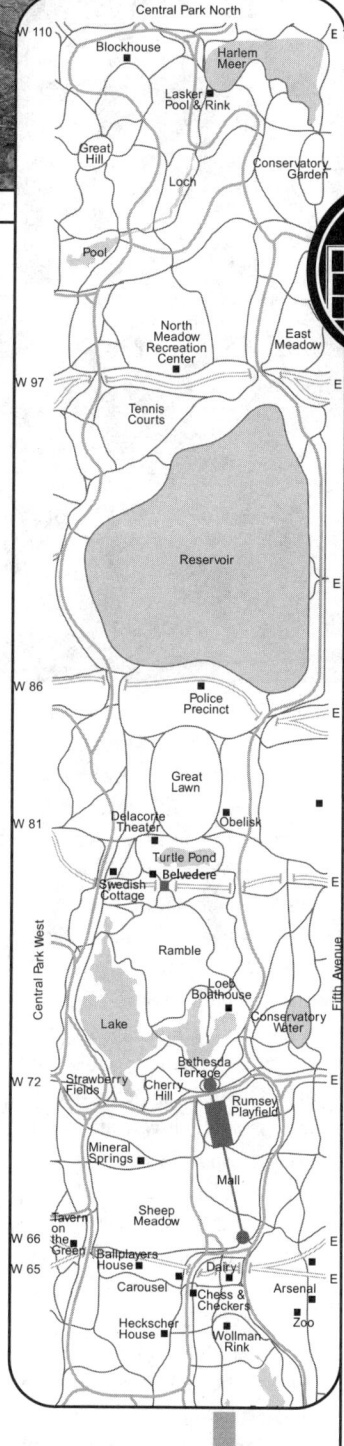

upper west side

"We're a kind of grown-up Greenwich Village," says 32-year-old Peter Nelson about the neighborhood where he has lived for the past three years. "Life up here seems more leisurely and mature than in the Village. It's also domestic, so much so that I'm always side-stepping baby carriages!" At night, the Upper West Side's stretch of Broadway pulses with activity, but its shine is friendly. Taxis make their way along the avenues, shuttling uptowners between historic and lively restaurants like Café Des Artistes, and one of the neighborhood's most esteemed venues for the Arts, Lincoln Center. The Center's enormous illuminated fountain reflects the glow of surrounding theaters, as well as the beckoning neon of bars and restaurants clustered across its expansive plaza. Collegiate types from nearby Fordham Law School and academic outposts further north barhop along Amsterdam Avenue, while those with a more refined palate sample tortes and ladyfingers at the superb dessert cafes tucked away in sidestreet brownstones.

During the day, young professionals grab a cup of coffee at Zabar's and a bagel at H & H before catching the subway to work, while parents drop off their kids at one of the "progressive" private schools on West End Avenue. Lucky stiffs who have the day off can spend the afternoon in either Riverside or Central Park, enjoy a margarita at one of Columbus Avenue's sidewalk cafes, or browse through one of the area's many boutiques. Ballerinas and opera hopefuls stream out of the Julliard School at dusk, eyeing the arriving performers at Lincoln Center with wistful determination.

Though the Upper West Side has traditionally been associated with moderate-to-liberal academics with a soft-spot for politically correct products, investment bankers and account executives climbing the rungs of the corporate ladder have moved into the area. Urbane and ambitious singles have also come to inhabit the enormous apartment complexes of Broadway and the classier apartments and brownstones of Amsterdam and Columbus Avenues; their presence supports an active singles scene in Amsterdam Avenue's bars. With its strong community spirit, the Upper West Side strives for a balance between being a tight-knit neighborhood and a sophisticated part of a massive metropolis.

local color

Name: Anne Sullivan
Age: 27
Occupation: Columnist/Animal Rights Activist

Q: How long have you lived in the neighborhood?
A: 15 years

Q: What do you find most attrative about the Upper West Side?
A: I think the Upper West Side has a really relaxed feel. There's lots of stuff to do. West Siders have the adantage of living near two amazing parks: Central and Riverside.

Q: How has the neighborhood changed since moved there?
A: Noisy construction on Columbus Avenue was very irritating. There were a lot traffic back-ups, particularly during rush hour. After that, everything was fine. Several businesses have come and gone, many have hung on. But the people in my neighborhood have pretty much remained the same: progressive and friendly. Every year my neighbors and I get together to plant flowers, which is nice; it makes the neighborhood feel like a real community.

Q: As an ethical vegetarian, do you think the neighborhood has a lot to offer you?
A: Absolutely. There are some wonderful restaurants in this area that offer delicious vegetarian dishes. As far as food stores are concerned, the Whole Foods Market has a big selection of veggie foods. There's even a place called Cafe Lalo where I can get amazing nondairy chocolate mud cake.

history

Though difficult to envision now, the Upper West Side was once a distant suburb of New York. Before the completion of the Ninth Avenue elevated train line in 1879, the area known as Bloomingdale was a popular refuge from the crowded city. The Dakota, a famous west side apartment building, received its name in the late 19th century because residents felt it was so far from downtown that it might as well have been in the Dakotas.

The area did not truly become the Upper West Side until the development of Central Park, from 1856 to 1873. Its completion spurred a wave of construction, and by the turn of the century, cultural institutions such as the American Museum of Natural History moved into the neighborhood.

In the 1960s, a successful attempt at urban renewal transformed the area with the construction of Lincoln Center on the site where West Side Story had been filmed just a few years earlier. A number of multipurpose skyscrapers were erected in the early 1990s. Today, the Upper West Side currently grapples with Donald Trump's proposed development project at the West Side Rail Yards. Running from 59th to 72nd Streets along the river, it is the last undeveloped plot of land in this former country retreat.

upper west side 103

movies + books

Rosemary's Baby, 1969
Director Roman Polanski's breakthrough, starring Mia Farrow as a housewife who makes a creepy Faustian bargain, filmed in The Dakota, at 72nd Street and Central Park West.

West Side Story, 1957
Filmed in the tenements in the lower 60s, just before they were torn down to build Lincoln Center. Leonard Bernstein wrote it while living in The Osborne, on West 57th Street.

Single White Female, 1992
Bridget Fonda discovers that Jennifer Jason Leigh is the roommate from hell as they share an apartment in the Ansonia Hotel, at Broadway and 72nd Street.

Marathon Man, 1976
Shot on location, including the final confrontation between Dustin Hoffman and Laurence Olivier, filmed in the 86th Street pumphouse, at one end of the Central Park Reservoir.

Pomander Walk
This private fairy-tale street of quaint Tudor houses, complete with flower-lined walks, old-fashioned lampposts, and colorful trim, was built to resemble the set of an eponymous play by the same name; tough-guy Humphrey Bogart was a former resident.
94th St. (bet. Broadway and West End Ave.), ❶❷❸❾ to 96th St.

Soldiers' and Sailors' Monument
This 100-ft. tall memorial was erected in 1893 in memory of fallen military heroes. Declared a municipal landmark in 1976, the monument stands in the center of a cannon-lined, leafy esplanade in Riverside Park.
Riverside Drive at 89th Street, ❶❾ to 86th St.

The Ansonia
Completed in 1904 with the intention of bringing Parisian architecture to the Upper West Side, the building's interior has since been drastically altered. Most of the grand, irregularly shaped rooms have been subdivided. The ornate exterior is still intact and a landmark.
Broadway (bet. 73rd and 74th Sts.), ❶❷❸❾ to 72nd St.

The Apthorp
Commissioned by William Waldorf Astor, who dreamed of a new, monumental style of building in New York, this enormous limestone structure was built around an elegant courtyard which is only open to tenants. Rumor has it Rosie O'Donnell lives here.
Broadway (bet. 78th and 79th Sts.), ❶❾ to 79th St.

Dakota Apartments
The turrets and shutters were more imposing when the whole building was black with over a hundred years of soot. After its recent bath, it is harder to picture it as the haunting backdrop for the film *Rosemary's Baby*. As one of four famous twin towered buildings so distinctive on Central Park West—the others being the Majestic, the San Remo, and the Eldorado—this exclusive apartment building attracts celebrity residents. Since 1980, the doorman has spent most of his time answering questions about the spot where John Lennon was assassinated.
72nd St. and Central Park West, ❶❷❸❾ to 72nd Street

Riverside Park
Frederick Law Olmsted, co-creator of Central Park, also designed this less crowded three-tiered neighborhood retreat. Courts, playing fields, and a half-pipe are available for public use.
Riverside Drive (bet. 72nd and 103rd Sts.),
(see Sports + Recreation section)

104 upper west side

New York Historical Society
Established in 1804 in an effort to preserve and document the history of New York and the United States, a vast collection of art, Americana, crafts, printed material, and artifacts are available on display here at the oldest continually operating museum in the country.
77th St. and Central Park West, 873-3400, ❶❾ to 79th St.

Public Plaza at Fordham
Built by Robert Moses, the Upper West Side branch of the Bronx university was established in the early '60s in an effort to revitalize the area. Located above street level, this quiet sunny plaza has a marble wall and a sculpture of St. Peter casting his net.
60th to 62nd Sts. (bet. Columbus and Amsterdam Aves.), ❶❾ to 59th St.

New York Society for Ethical Culture
This secular humanist association began in 1876 on the philosophical basis of ethical idealism. The group is dedicated to bettering human relations in the city. Active social and political reformers, the society has advocated rights for workers, women, and the poor and is right at home in the traditionally liberal Upper West Side.
2 West 64th St. (off Central Park West), ❶❾ to Lincoln Center

Lincoln Center
San Juan Hill, the setting for *West Side Story*, was leveled in the '60s to make way for the city's cultural heart, which now draws over five million people a year. The New York State Theater, Avery Fisher Hall, the Metropolitan Opera House, the Juilliard School, the Performing Arts branch of the New York Public Library, and the Walter Reade Theater are all housed within the complex, designed by Robert Moses and funded largely by the Rockefellers. To the left of the Met, Damrosch Park hosts free summer performances on the outdoor stage.
62nd to 66th Streets (between Columbus and Amsterdam Avenues), ❶❾ to 66th Street

West Side Community Garden
Paths lined with benches and all kinds of flora surround this old-fashioned patch of greenery. The park extended over the entire block until eight years ago, when developers moved in with high-rise apartment buildings. There is a waiting list for free plots in the vegetable and flower garden. Call for information about community group activities.
90th Street (between Amsterdam and Columbus Avenues), 580-1399, ❶❾ to 86th St.

---

cheap *thrills*

Student Discount Tickets
Check the box office at the City Opera and Alice Tully Hall a few hours before evening performances for dirt-cheap student rush tickets. You may get to sit in the front row for your favorite opera, content with the knowledge that you paid $50 less than the person sitting a few seats down.
❶❾ to 66th St., Lincoln Center

Symphony under the Stars
Lincoln Center and the New York Philharmonic offer free summer concerts in Damrosch Park, complete with fireworks displays.
875-5709, ❶❾ to 66th St., to the left of the Met

Three Dollar Movies
The Cineplex Odeon Worldwide Cinema offers first-run films at discounted prices. Call for listings.
340 West 50th St.
(bet. Eighth and Ninth Aves.),
246-1560, ❶❾ to 50th St.

upper west side 105

A Saturday in the Upper West Side

1 **The Royal Canadian Pancake House**
"Pancakes make people happy," is their slogan, and do they ever! A single order from their selection of over 60 varieties will get you nine, thick, CD-sized pancakes. Be prepared to wait on the weekends and literally rub elbows with the couple next to you, but it's worth it.
(see Restaurant section)

2 **American Museum of Natural History**
Feel like a kid on a field trip as you circumnavigate dinosaur bones and then continue your tour of historic apartment houses.
(see Sites + Parks)

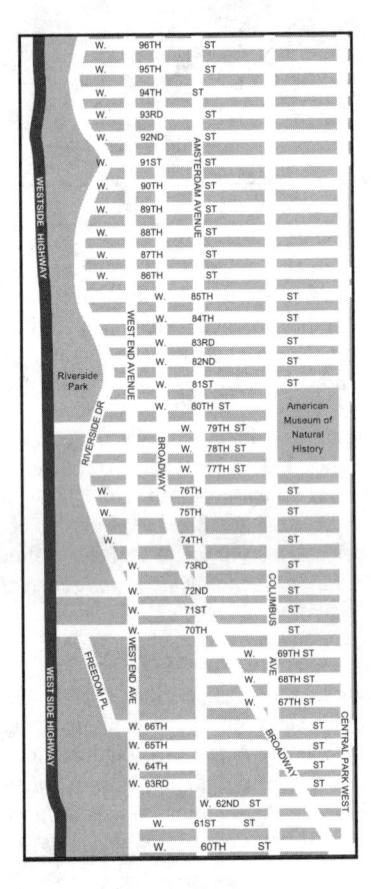

3 **Lincoln Center**
Take a right on 62nd Street at Century Apartments and walk to Broadway. Home of Avery Fisher Hall, the New York State Theater, Damrosch Park, the Vivian Beaumont Theater, and the Metropolitan Opera, this world-renowned center for the arts is a must-see attraction even if you're not seeing a show.
(see Sites + Parks)

Most Fishy Window Display
Citarella
The windows of this fresh seafood gourmet grocer are most definitely fishy, swarming with both the exotic and the everyday fruits of the sea. Public art at its best.
2135 Broadway (at 75th St.) 874-0383, MC, V, AmEx,
❶❷❸ to 72nd St.

106 upper west side

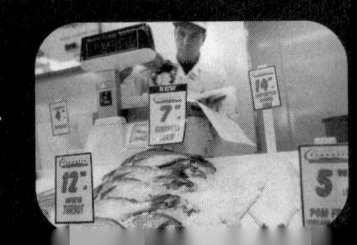

4
Café Des Artistes

Five blocks to the north of Lincoln Center, plus a few blocks east on Central Park West is this newly renovated Manhattan icon that some consider the ultimate romantic restaurant. For anyone looking to have the quintessential New York experience, having a meal here is a must.

(see Restaurant section)

5
Beacon Theater

This eclectic concert hall featuring name acts used to be a movie theater. In fact, it was one of the great New York movie palaces, and one of the few that escaped demolition.

(see Nightlife section)

6
The Shark Bar

This rowdy and culturally flavorful haunt

is an excellent place to scope for celebrities

and end your day on a glamourous note.

They also serve food, so if you skip

Café Des Artistes and have a taste for

soul food, this may be your best bet.

(see Nightlife section)

Scary stuff at the Museum of Natural History

Most Mouthwatering Samples
Zabar's
Delectable foodstuffs such as olives, pastries, nuts, and cheeses. Walk in, have a look around, and take a taste, or two, or three...
Zabar's at 2245 Broadway (at 80th St.), 787-2000, ①⑨ to 79th St.

upper west side 107

morningside HEIGHTS

Morningside Heights is a small town in the big city. As removed from Manhattan's exceedingly developed urban core today as it was at the turn of the century, the neighborhood lies outside the perimeter of most sightseers travels and affords a welcome reprieve from expected city noise and congestion.

Here, the business of education harmonizes with the restful quietude of a largely residential area. Many small communities exist within the larger academic communities of Columbia University, Barnard and Bank Street Colleges, and the Jewish and Union Theological Seminaries. A congenial air pervades the neighborhood. Even the many panhandlers become familiar faces though sobering reminders of the urban blight that creeps around Morningside's edges.

Sandwiched between two parks, Morningside and Riverside, Columbia University is the neighborhood's largest landholder. The University has been instrumental in influencing the character of Morningside Heights, not only because of its presence, but also its sweeping control over residential property.

During the week, bookbag-toting students with busy schedules rush into Columbia Bagel, Tamarind Seed, or other popular eateries for a meal-on-the-run between classes. Area businesses range from bars that draw both working-class crowds and local bookworms, to street vendors peddling plastic sunglasses and inexpensive dog-eared books.

Columbia University's pedestrian-only Campus Walk interrupts 116th Street between Broadway and Amsterdam and is a great place to people-watch. The steps outside Low Memorial Library provide lounge space for students on a break from classes. Riverside Park, the neighborhood's largest, is often packed with sun-worshippers during the spring and summer, and remains a perennial favorite place to walk the dog or go running.

Morningside Heights also supports a thriving and highly visible Hispanic community, whose restaurants, barber shops, botanicas, and other businesses flourish several blocks south of 110th Street on Amsterdam Avenue.

In the summer, when most students are on vacation, the area often seems deserted. Locals who normally avoid student hangouts reclaim their turf, giving the neighborhood an equally pleasant, but refreshingly different atmosphere until classes resume in September.

Cathedral of St. John the Divine
The largest Gothic cathedral in the world and principal church of the Episcopal Diocese of New York, it is both a place of worship and the host to a multitude of community events, including a 4am Winter Solstice celebration, an all-night recitation of Dante's Inferno, a Halloween showing of Nosferatu, as well as the more traditional chamber music and candlelight Vespers.
1040 Amsterdam Ave. (at 112th St.), 316-7540, ❶❾ to 110th St.

Columbia University Campus
Architecturally and financially the centerpiece of the neighborhood, this heavily symmetrical creation of McKim, Mead, and White appears uncannily like a walled city from the outside; recent construction and renovation projects solidify this Ivy's presence just under Harlem. Low Library was once voted one of the most beautiful buildings in North America. The 'Steps,' recognized as one of the best hangouts in NY, is a great spot for people-watching and lazing in the sun. The plaza below is a grassy playground for co-eds and families alike.
From 114th to 120th Sts. (bet. Broadway and Amsterdam Aves.), 854-1754, ❶❾ to 116th St.

Grant's Tomb/Sakura Park
Pay your last respects to the General and his wife at America's second-largest mausoleum. The tomb, once plagued by spray-paint-wielding youths, is now in prime condition to celebrate its legacy as one of America's most highly acclaimed buildings. Recently, the neighborhood has put up a fight to preserve the mosaic benches that skirt the imposing structure. Sakura Park, located across the street, is a favorite family retreat.
Riverside Drive (at 122nd St.), 666-1640, Admission Free, ❶❾ to 116th St.

New York Buddhist Temple
This branch of the Japanese Buddhist sect Jodo Shinshu welcomes all visitors to the Sunday services, which are conducted in Japanese and English, and to meditation workshops.
331-332 Riverside Drive (bet. 105th and 106th Sts.), 678-0305, ❶❾ to 110th St.

Riverside Church
Based on the Cathedral at Chartres, this interdenominational church boasts spectacular stained-glass windows, the world's largest carillon (a set of bells), and an impressive view of the city from its tower; take a free ride to the top on Saturdays. Lectures and concerts held regularly.
120th St. (bet. Riverside and Clairmont), 222-5900, ❶❾ to 116th St.

Riverside Park
Walk along this two-mile stretch for pleasant views of the river and the European-style apartment buildings along Riverside. Playgrounds, tennis courts, and a half-pipe exist alongside landmarks such as the Soldiers' and Sailors' monument, Grant's Tomb, and the Firemen's Memorial.
Riverside Drive (bet. 72nd and 125th Sts.)

history

A 17th-century stretch of farmland known as "Vandewater's Heights," would become the site of the Battle of Harlem during the Revolutionary War, and the location of present-day Barnard College in Morningside Heights. Just before the turn of the century the area was still backwater, though development was encouraged by the paving of area roads, the construction of Riverside Drive, and the promise of subway accessibility. The Anglican Church began construction on the world's largest cathedral, St. John the Divine, which remains unfinished to this day; its bizarre hybrid of architectural styles reflects the varied visions of its several collaborators over a century. Grant and his wife were reburied in Grant's Tomb, constructed in 1897, by which time Columbia University was busily moving into its present location, soon to be joined by Barnard College, and the Jewish and Union Theological Seminaries. Today it is an intellectual bastion and a neighborhood on the rise.

Stonecutter at work

movies+books
Hannah and Her Sisters, dir. by Woody Allen, 1986
Barbara Hershey takes an adult education class and hangs out with her new friend on Low library steps.

morningside heights 109

A Saturday in Morningside Heights

1 **Tom's Restaurant**
Start the morning off with breakfast at this popular Columbia haunt, its exterior made famous by TV's "Seinfeld." The standard diner fare is tasty and inexpensive.
(see Restaurant section)

2 **Cathedral of St. John the Divine**
A mere two blocks from Tom's. When completed it will be the largest Gothic cathedral in the world, with an interior composed of 14 bays depicting mankind's vocations, and 7 chapels, each paying tribute to a different ethnic group. The Cathedral is very much under construction, with stone cutters and other artists working daily on various projects.
(see Sites + Parks)

3 **Columbia University's Low Library Steps**
Walk over to Columbia and hang out on the steps. A great place to relax and people-watch, these steps provide an almost bird's-eye view of the University's Campus Walk, which used to be 116th Street before the area between Amsterdam and Broadway was closed to auto traffic.
(see Sites + Parks)

Most Delicious Veggie Burger
Metro Diner
What appears to be your standard diner proves to be a veggie-friendly haven of salads and vegetable platters.
2641 Broadway (at 100th St.), 866-0800, MC, V, AmEx, ❶❾ to 103rd St.

Most Overwhelming Slice
Koronet
Possibly more than two people could handle, the 'jumbo slice' is the Godzilla of the pizza world.
(see Restaurant section)

Most Striking Contrast
The Mosaics at Grant's Tomb
Winding around the base of this neoclassical mausoleum is a chaotic tile mosaic structure composed of interconnected benches, arches, and tabletops.
Riverside Drive (at 122nd St.)
Admission Free, ❶❾ to 116th St., ♿

110 morningside heights

4 Barnard College

Cross Broadway at 116th Street and walk north. Barnard was established as a women's college at a time when Columbia was exclusively male. It was named after Frederick Barnard, a pioneer in the fight for women's rights in higher education.

(see Sites + Parks)

5 Riverside Park

Walk south along the bike path for excellent views of the Hudson. The impressive architecture of many of the residences along Riverside Drive, which abuts the park along its entire length, is also worth a look. Leave the park at 110th Street and proceed to Broadway.

(see Sites + Parks)

6 The West End

After dinner, head over to this old stand-by for Columbia students—indeed, it's always been a favorite nightspot—perhaps because of its proximity to the main campus and its versatility as bar, restaurant, theater, and concert hall.

(see Restaurant section)

{cheap thrills}

Opera Night at Caffé Taci
Friday nights are a raucous good time as opera singers, often students from nearby Manhattan School of Music, raise their voices amongst late-night diners, bar dwellers, and coffee sippers.
(see Restaurant section)

Free Folk Music and Popcorn
The Postcrypt coffeehouse at Columbia University's St. Paul's Chapel offers free live folk music and popcorn every Thurs. night beginning at 9pm.
(see Sites + Parks)

Peacock-Watching at St. John the Divine
Just about the most unexpected phenomenon in Morningside Heights could very well be a glimpse of these exotic birds strutting and sunning amongst the foliage of the children's sculpture park.
(see Sites + Parks)

In the collective imagination, Harlem has two identities: its glorious heritage as the intellectual, political, spiritual, and artistic capital of black America, and its tragic recent history as a community besieged by poverty, crime, drugs, racism, and political disempowerment. In truth, Harlem accommodates not only these images, but also many in between. Absorbing not only the black populations for which it is most famous but also increasing numbers of Cubans and Dominicans, trying to balance the needs of the upwardly mobile with the realities of deeply rooted poverty, Harlem is undergoing radical, and in some cases painful, economical and cultural transformations.

The largest neighborhood in all of Manhattan, stretching from the Hudson River and West Harlem to Spanish Harlem and the East River, Harlem's diversity is inscribed in its buildings and on its streets. Many of the area's row houses and brownstones are beautifully restored and pristinely kept, but others are derelict and abandoned. Twelfth-generation descendants of slaves mingle with first-generation immigrants in both housing projects and historic, genteel brownstones along Striver's Row, Hamilton Heights, and Sugar Hill. Upscale restaurants, supper clubs, boutiques, and other small businesses are sprouting up amidst fast-food joints, flea markets, thrift stores, bodegas, and lush public gardens that function as neighborhood gathering places.

Racism and the economic and political disenfranchisement which generally accompany bigotry have reinforced physical and mental boundaries, rendering Harlem a city unto itself. Many Harlemites lament that the closest many tourists and even native New Yorkers dare to come to their community is to admire the panoramic view from the other side of that seemingly impassable threshold of Morningside Park.

Fortunately, through the efforts both of the city and of its native sons and daughters, Harlem is currently experiencing an economic and social resurgence, as successful locals return to rebuild it. Harlem's club scene in particular is experiencing a renaissance the likes of which it hasn't seen since the '50s. Night-crawlers will relish Harlem's jazz and supper clubs, such as Showman's and the Lenox Lounge.

Regardless of the attractions Harlem may boast, it is first and foremost a place where people live. In a neighborhood where people are truly neighborly, the words of one of Harlem's own, Langston Hughes reverberate in the hearts of many: "Harlem is a place where I like to eat, sleep, drink, and be in love. I like to work, read, learn, and understand life."

Name: Ted Williams
Age: 70
Occupation: Retired doorman, blues guitarist, and singer

Q: How long have you lived in New York?
A: Twenty years, while I'm not on tour.
Q: What do you like about Harlem?
A: Good people, good lively atmosphere.
Q: What about New York in general?
A: That it's all kinds of people mixed together.
Q: What's your favorite place in Harlem?
A: I love the Apollo Theatre.
Q: Where in Harlem do you live?
A: On 129th Street and Malcolm X Boulevard.
Q: What's your favorite thing about living here?
A: All the good friends I've met playing delta blues.

local color

Bluesman Ted Williams

history

Mosque of Islam

In 1925, when Alain Locke edited *The New Negro*, an anthology of poetry and prose by up-and-coming black artists, he wrote, "I believe that the Negro's advantages and opportunities are greater in Harlem than in any other place in the country, and that Harlem will become the intellectual, cultural, and the financial center for Negroes of the United States, and will exert a vital influence upon all Negro peoples. The Harlem Renaissance of the late 1920s proved Locke correct, but Harlem's population in the early part of that decade was by no means entirely black. The area was originally settled by the Dutch, who named it Nieuw Haarlem since it was so far from the settled areas of New York. Many immigrants from Ireland and Germany settled around 125th Street. As more and more blacks moved into the area, however, whites began to leave. The combined effect of white flight and black migration from the south helped solidify the development of black Harlem.

This new concentration of blacks spurred the Harlem Renaissance as many wealthy Harlemites began entertaining and organizing literary and social clubs. At these gatherings, authors and poets such as Countee Cullen, Langston Hughes, and Zora Neale Hurston read from their works, and locals discussed politics and arts.

The Depression sent the area into decline, and racial tensions erupted in several large-scale riots. Today, business and rebuilding efforts from within the community are helping restore Harlem to its former glory and prominent members of the black community live in the area. Perhaps that's why Nelson Mandela called Harlem, "the capital of the black world."

harlem 113

Abyssinian Baptist Church
Pastor Adam Clayton Powell, Sr. built this church in 1921 to serve the needs of the growing numbers of blacks settling on the Upper West Side. The church is named for its first worshipers, Abyssinian merchants who wanted to maintain their connection with Africa. The congregation has grown to over 4,000 to date and is known for its community involvement.
132 West 138th St. (bet. A.C. Powell and Malcolm X), 862-7474, ❷❸ *to 135th St.*

Hamilton Grange
When Alexander Hamilton commissioned this house from one of City Hall's architects, John McComb Jr., the location was far removed from the the heart of New York. Today, it serves as a public museum operating under the auspices of the National Park Service in the heart of Hamilton Heights.
Convent Ave. at 141st St., 283-5154,
Ⓐ❸ⒸⒹ *to 145th St.*

Jackie Robinson Park
Oak-lined walkways, an Olympic-sized pool, bandshells, and pick-up basketball make this oasis in Harlem's St. Nicholas district one of the area's best-equipped parks. Originally known as Colonial Park, in 1978 it was renamed after the baseball legend.
145th to 152nd Sts. (bet. Edgecombe and Bradhurst), 234-9207, Ⓐ❸ⒸⒹ *to 145th St.*

Langston Hughes House
Writers have inherited the former home of this Harlem Renaissance poet; his memory is kept alive through regular readings. Tours by appointment.
20 East 127th St. (bet. Madison and Fifth Aves.), 862-9561, Suggested Admission $3,
❷❸ *to 125th St.*

Marcus Garvey Park
The "Back to Africa" spokesman and noted civil rights leader was honored by the 1973 renaming of Mt. Morris Park. The park boasts an iron frame belltower built in 1956, as well as a manmade bed of rocks in the center of the park which offers one of the city's best vistas.
120th to 124th Sts. (bet. Fifth and Madison Aves.), 410-2818, ❷❸ *to 125th St.*

Riverbank Park
Uptown's sprawling athletic facility is free and open to the public; swim, run laps around the outdoor track, or take in a soothing view of the Hudson from the high terrace. Just $19 buys a season-long permit for the tennis courts.
679 Riverside Drive (bet. 137th and 145th Sts.), 694-3600, 694-6645 for permits, ❶❾ *to 145th St.*

Sugar Hill
By 1919, this area supported a wealthy enclave among its sizable working-class and middle-class contingents and was dubbed Sugar Hill to reflect the "sweet life" of its residents. W.E.B. Du Bois and Thurgood Marshall resided at this area's most well-known address, 409 Edgecombe Avenue, which has since been designated a landmark.
135 to 155th Sts. (bet. Edgecombe and St. Nicholas),
Ⓐ❸ⒸⒹ *to 145th St.*

Trinity Cemetery and Church of the Intercession
Once part of John J. Audubon's farm, the gentle hill cresting at Amsterdam Avenue holds the rural cemetery of the Financial District's Trinity Church. The church, boasting 13th-century glass windowpanes, overlooks the Hudson.
Riverside Dr. to Amsterdam Ave. (bet. 153rd and 155th Sts.), 368-1600, Ⓐ❸Ⓒ *to 155th St.,* ❶ *to 157th St.*

Victory Outreach Church
Former drug-addict and gang-member-turned-pastor Tony Valenzuela directs this nondenominational church, whose main goal is help the downtrodden.
2156 Second Avenue (bet. 110th and 111th Sts.), 987-3025, ❻ *to 110th St.*

Malcolm Shabazz Masjid (Mosque of Islam)
Founded by Malcolm X in the 1950s, this silver-domed mosque has become the country's most renowned Black Muslim place of worship.
102 West 116th St. (bet. A.C. Powell and Malcolm X), 662-2200, ❷❸ *to 116th St.*

114 harlem

5 Sugar Hill

Take a stroll down Convent Avenue. The stretch between 145th Street and the City College campus on 137th is lined with beautiful, historic brownstones.

(see Sites + Parks)

6

Sylvia's

No visit to Harlem is complete without a meal from this legendary soul kitchen. Bask in the history of the place while you tuck into your fried chicken and collard greens.

(see Restaurant section)

Lenox Lounge **7**

In the evening, catch Harlem's legendary jazz at this mainstay of musical culture.

(see Nightlife section)

The historic Abyssinian Baptist Church

Most Money Behind Glass
The American Numismatic Society

So much money, so little time. The Society's permanent collection consists of over one million coins, medals and paper monies, exhibited for the public to drool over. For the more scholarly, a 100,000-volume reference library is also available for public use. It's not your money they'll be displaying: admission and library use is free of charge.
Broadway and 155th St., 234-3130, Tues. through Sat. 9am-4:30pm, ❶ to 157th St.

washington heights

Rich contrasts abound in Washington Heights: between the tranquility of the Cloisters or the still-wild inner recesses of Inwood Hill Park. The main shopping districts on Dyckman, 181st, and 207th Streets offer a shopper's paradise. Washington Heights situates itself somewhere between the neoclassical reserve of Audubon Terrace and the karaoke chaos at Coogan's Bar, the city's only Latin-Irish hangout.

August educational institutions, Yeshiva University and Columbia-Presbyterian Medical Center, tower over some of the city's poorest blocks of tenement while faith healers practice out of the imposing projects along the Harlem River, and locals in their finery flock to the area's churches every Sunday.

Rapidly changing demographics and diverse cultures have combined to produce an odd but refreshing mix in the uppermost part of Manhattan, where the island narrows and the parks converge to culminate in the wilderness of Inwood Hill Park. Since the extension uptown of the old IRT and BMT subway lines in the early part of this century, the neighborhood has housed mostly immigrants, originally Irish and Jewish and now predominantly Hispanic, with more changes on the way.

In addition to its cultural diversity Washington Heights offers an alternative to downtown's overpriced aggressive urbanity. On summer evenings, local parks provide welcome relief from the hot streets. Students, artists, musicians and families are discovering Washington Heights, lured by airy, cheaper apartments, lush parks, cultural institutions and the neighborhood's affable, easy-going mien. As one happy resident puts it, "Why live in a closet downtown when up here you can buy into a co-op for the same price?"

sites + parks

Baker Field
After student rioters in the '60s effectively canceled plans for a massive recreational facility in Morningside Park, Columbia built here. Now that C.U. football has ended decades of losing, crowds are back. The complex also includes tennis courts and a baseball diamond, located in the midst of a neighborhood of beautiful brownstones.
Broadway at 218th St., 942-0431, ❶❾ to 215th St.

Dyckman Street Marina
Self-described "boat bum" John Boldt has toiled for five years to save money for a marina at the western end of Dyckman Street, the only point above 145th Street where river access isn't blocked. This is one of the latest steps in recent revitalization plans for the waterfront. The marina development has sparked a clean-up movement.
Dyckman St. on the Hudson River, ❶ to Dyckman 200 St.

George Washington Bridge
Othmar H. Ammann's original design called for granite sheathing, but the onset of the Depression forced him to leave it out. Le Corbusier called it the most beautiful bridge in the world.
Ⓐ to 175th St.

Fort Tryon Park
Home to the Cloisters, the entire park sparkles with the sheen of maintenance: well-manicured flower beds, shady hilltops, and winding paths all make the park ideal for picnicking.
Entrances at 191st and 200th Sts., 360-8111, Ⓐ to 190th St., M4 directly to Cloisters

Inwood Hill Park
This uptown expanse of woodland boasts cross-country ski trails, caves that were once inhabited by a local tribe, and the island's last remnant of primeval forest. Park Rangers organize tours of the caves during the summer; safety concerns dictate that you not explore them alone.
Entrance at 207th St. and Seaman Ave. 360-8111, Ⓐ to 207th St.

history

Until the turn of the century, the region of Washington Heights was still largely undeveloped countryside dotted with wealthy estates boasting spectacular views. The situation changed in 1904 with the arrival of the IRT subway line, which within two years, had reached the tip of Manhattan and points north.

This development led to a sharp class divide along Broadway, with poorer residents to the south and east segregated from more prosperous communities to the north and west. Many Greeks and Irish settled there and were soon joined by an influx of Jews that increased as refugees fled Germany. Quick population shifts resulted in ethnic tensions; right-wing groups and gangs vandalized synagogues and assaulted young Jews during the '30s and '40s, and many immigrants became disenchanted with a neighborhood that was supposed to offer escape from foreign persecution. By the '60s, the area was largely abandoned by the Irish and Jewish settlers and became home to a predominantly black, Puerto Rican, and Cuban population. The 1965 assassination of Malcolm X in the Audubon Ballroom was simultaneously a reminder of earlier conflict, and a harbinger of the crime wave that was to hit in the '80s.

The immigrant population continued to change, with Dominicans coming to outnumber other residents; by 1990, there were more Dominicans in Washington Heights than in any other U.S. community. District lines were eventually redrawn to offer residents better government representation, and in 1991, Guillermo Linares became the country's first elected official of Dominican descent.

washington heights 119

A Saturday in Washington Heights

1 Fort Tryon Cafe

Delicious pastries, divine coffee and heavenly soups are standard fare at this charming cafe conviently located near the Cloisters

(see Restaurant section)

2 Cloisters

Enjoy the art and atmosphere at one of the city's most peaceful (and medieval) spots. Why go out for lunch when the Cloister's lush lawns beg for a picnic?

(see Sites + Parks)

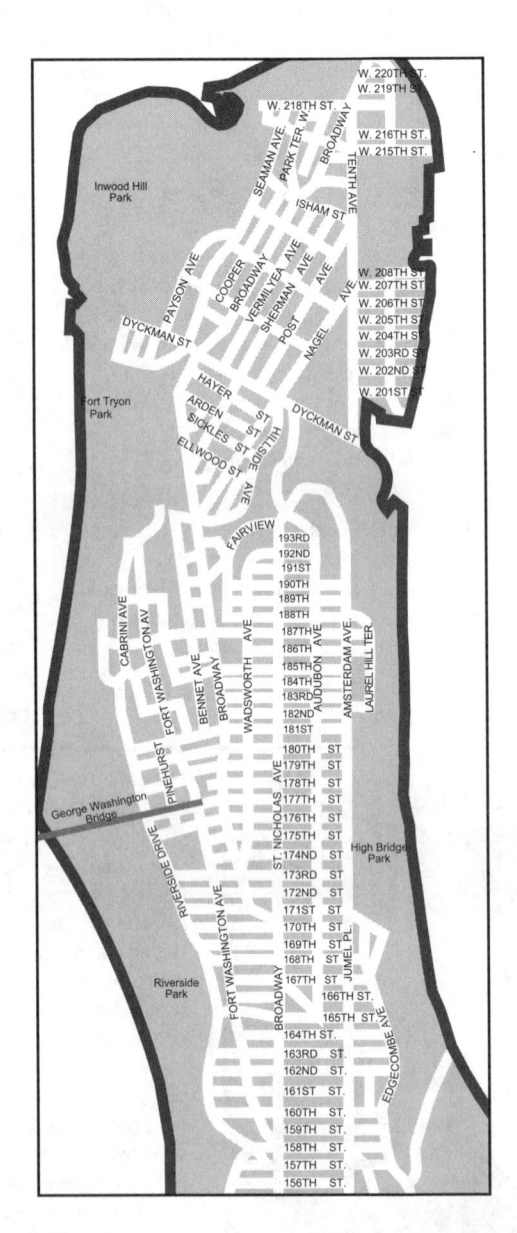

Most Medieval Experience
Cloisters
Standing in front of the world-famous Unicorn Tapestries in a hallway of cool gray stone, you'd never know you're almost in the 21st century.
(see Sites + Parks)

Most Fly Club Uptown
Club Las Vegas
NY's hottest Hispanic disco, where a bottle of Puerto Rican Rum can set you back $80.
179 Dyckman St. (bet. Sherman and Vermilyea), 942-1516, Cash Only, ❶ ❾ to Dyckman St.

Most Delicious Vegetable Cake
Carrot Top Cafe
Their superior carrot cake makes it easy to follow Mom's advice and eat all your vegetables.
3931 Broadway (bet. 164th and 165th Sts.), 927-4800, MC, V, AmEx, ❶ ❾ to 168th St.

120 washington heights

3 George Washington Bridge

Follow the sun toward Jersey and watch the tugboats steaming along the Hudson River. After your leisurely afternoon, a walk across "the most beautiful bridge in the world" will work up an appetite and prepare you for venturing back into modernity.

(see Sites + Parks)

4 Hoppin' Jalapeños

Shuttle back to the 20th century with dinner at this Cal-Mex kitchen. After a few margaritas, the Cloisters will seem like ancient history.

(see Restaurant section)

View of George Washington Bridge

Ropa
If you're patient enough to sort through acres of vintage clothes, you'll leave with some of the best deals in the city.
(see Shopping section)

99¢ World
A subway token uptown costs more than anything you'll find at this well-stocked enclave of snacks and household items. Nothing over a dollar (plus tax). 655 West 181st St. (bet. Broadway and St. Nicholas Ave.), 981-1064, Cash Only, ❶❾Ⓐ to 181st St.

George Washington Bridge
With a bike or a pair of good walking shoes, crossing the Hudson from way up high guarantees a thrill for free.
(see Sites + Parks)

washington heights 121

bronx

The Bronx is a borough defined by contrasts. With acres of parkland, what many outsiders envision as a concrete desert is in fact New York's second-greenest borough. Even with the overlooked prevalence of flora, the South Bronx represents the closest thing to the asphalt jungle Hollywood often portrays.

In contrast to the economic hardships of the South Bronx lies Riverdale, tucked away west of Van Cortlandt Park. It is one of New York's richest areas: opulent mansions line the streets of Fieldston and Riverdale, which is also home to Manhattan College and Mount St. Vincent.

Southeast of Riverdale, the Fordham area is geographically and demographically the center which holds the Bronx together: Latino, African-American, and Afro-Caribbean cultures are found here, allowing merengue mixes with hip-hop to provide the soundtrack for the area's cultural convergence. Add a few Fordham students from Long Island and the mix is complete.

Caribbean rhythms dominate the Williamsbridge and Woodlawn sections of the Bronx, giving visitors urban island flavor in a middle/working-class community directly adjacent to Westchester's Mount Vernon.

Other notable areas include Belmont's Little Italy, whose Italian authenticity remains relatively unscathed due to the lack of tourists that visit. Here you'll find bakeries, butcher shops, restaurants and produce markets concentrated on Arthur Avenue between Fordham Road and 183rd Street and on 187th Street between Third Avenue and Southern Boulevard.

Additional neighborhoods that people might view as mere appendages are in fact important community sites. Co-op city (a.k.a. "the sinking city" by the media and citizens due to its arguably precarious sea-side positioning) contains what is becoming one of the biggest (and only) malls to hit the Bronx: Bay Plaza Shopping Center. "It's so nice not to take a delay-laden train ride into Manhattan to get what I need", says Bronx resident and teacher Carmen Ferguson.

City Island, at one of the Bronx' northeastern extremes, offers maritime aesthetics with a small-town feel, proclaiming itself on advertisements as "A little bit of New England in New York City." If you came to "rumble," you might be disappointed. Popular image aside, the Bronx is as filled with different faces like any other borough.

Name: Olga Nicole Grant
Age: 23
Occupation: student

Q: How long have you lived in the Parkchester section of the Bronx?
A: 13 years (I emigrated from Jamaica.)
Q: Is the Bronx as tough a neighborhood as a lot of people think it is?
A: It depends on which neighborhood you go to. There are some beautiful places in the Bronx, like Pelham Bay, Morris Park, Pelham Parkway . . .
Q: How do you rate Parkchester on the beauty scale?
A: Parkchester is better than a lot of other Bronx areas. I've seen some changes for the worse, but lately it seems as if they're doing some revitalization. New stores are coming in, management tries to keep the place clean, renovations are always being done.
Q: As an immigrant, were there any particularly memorable issues you faced in your 13 years here?
A: I wasn't learning anything. I didn't learn a damn thing for my first three years in the country. The types of math and English being taught were things that I had already learned in third grade back in Jamaica, yet schools here were just doing these things in sixth grade.
Q: Is there a noticeable Caribbean community in Parkchester?

local color

Local street vendor

A: Yes, there has been an increase in Caribbean and Latino people. I hear the accents becoming more diversified. Lots of people from India here as well.

history

The Bronx is the only borough named after a person: Jonas Bronck, a Swedish sailor who cleared 500 acres and built a farmhouse. By 1700, Bronck's farm was destroyed and most of the land was split between four large manors: Pelham, Morrisania, Fordham, and Phillipsburg.

The Bronx became famous for its landscaping and attractions. In the late 19th century, the Grand Concourse was built, modeled after tree-lined French boulevards. In 1891, the New York Botanical Gardens opened, followed by the Bronx Zoo; at 2764 acres, Pelham Park is still the city's largest oasis.

The borough was consolidated into New York City in 1898, and immigrants flocked there after 1904, when the first subway connecting the Bronx with Manhattan was completed. Droves of Yugoslavians, Armenians, and Italians arrived, as well as many Jews from central and eastern Europe. Business in the borough took off, with the Hub and Fordham Road becoming major shopping centers. Yankee Stadium was opened in 1923 and the Bronx Bombers soon became the world's most famous baseball team.

After World War II, wealthier residents moved to luxury apartments or toward the suburbs in Westchester. An influx of poor people, displaced by urban renewal in Manhattan, moved to the southern neighborhoods, and poverty grew. While other parts of the Bronx continued to prosper as residential communities, the South Bronx declined. The recent announcement that the Yankees may leave does not bode well for that part of the borough. However a 10-year billion-dollar program to build low-income housing has recently been instituted by the city, so hopefully the area will rebound.

Bronx Zoo/Wildlife Conservation Park
Four thousand animals observe visitors with an air of profound boredom as members of the earth's single most absurd species whistle, dance, and gesticulate. Stone monuments and naturalistic landscaping contribute to the theme-park atmosphere. The monorail brings you within feet of a red panda or a tapir, with nothing between you and them. Many exhibits are individually ticketed, even on "free" Wednesdays, so be prepared to spend $7 or $8 per person over the regular price of admission.
Bronx River Parkway and Fordham Road, (718) 367-1010, Admission $7.75 regular, $4 children and seniors, free on Wednesdays, &,
❷ *to Pelham Parkway Station*

City Island
This former fishing village is still largely residential, housing a large portion of the city's small boat population and shipyards, bait-and-tackle shops, and restaurants like Johnny's Reefer and Sammy's Fish Box. From Manhattan, it's a trek: allow an hour and a half if traveling by public transportation.
❻ *to Pelham Bay Station, then transfer to* **Bx29**

Edgar Allan Poe Cottage
Situated on little more than a median strip, this tiny cottage where the godfather of gloom lived out the last years of his life and penned "Annabel Lee" and "The Bells" will nonetheless delight Poe admirers. Open only on weekends; the tour includes a video presentation.
Grand Concourse and East Kingsbridge Road, (718) 881-8900, Admission $2; ❹ *to Kingsbridge Road*

Bronx Museum of the Arts
True to its slogan, "It's more than just a museum," the space serves not only as a site for visual arts exhibitions, but also as a performance space, an artists' forum and a center for "art making workshops." Its commitment to multicultural programming is evident in its diverse array of shows and weekly events.
1040 Grand Concourse at 165th St., (718) 681-6000, Suggested Donation $3 adults, $2 students, $1 seniors, children under 12 free with an adult;
❹❺❻ *to 161st St.*

Fordham University
Security is taken very seriously at the oasis of gray stone and abundant green grass of the Rose Hill campus, but visitors are cheerfully given clearance to stroll past Keating Hall and other landmarks. The stained glass in the austere University Chapel, bequeathed by Louis Philippe of France, was installed here because it didn't fit the windows of St. Patrick's. Fordham's basketball team plays in the Atlantic Ten and sometimes hosts powerhouses like UMass. For information on games, call (718) 817-2RAM.
Ⓓ *to Fordham Road, walk east on Fordham; for Fordham University, call 636-6000*

NY Botanical Gardens
New York's largest and most magnificent gardens include both cultivated exhibits and 40 acres of pristine forest. An extensive botanical library is available to the public, and classes, sales, and events fill the calendar year-round. Weekdays afford remarkable quiet and solitude. The Garden Cafe offers sandwiches and snacks, but visitors are welcome to bring a picnic basket.
200th St. and Southern Blvd., (718) 817-8705, Passport ticket which includes tram tour is $10 for adults, $7.50 for seniors and students, $2 for children 2 to 12, Admission Free for everyone on Wednesdays and Saturday mornings 10am to noon; Ⓓ❹ *to Bedford Park Blvd., then* **Bx26** *to Gardens; on-site parking $4*

Van Cortlandt Park
The Bronx's answer to Central Park, "Vannie" is overwhelmingly huge, occupying 1146 acres near Riverdale which serve as a massive center for recreation, nature, and sight-seeing. The main parade ground hosts numerous soccer, softball, cricket, and football games every day but is just as nice for Frisbee and a blanket. Among the trees surrounding the perimeter are plenty of trails for nature hikes and biking, as well as one of the nation's best cross-country courses. Play a round at the Van Cortlandt Golf Course, the first municipal course in the country, ride a horse at the bridle path, visit the Van Cortlandt Historical Mansion, take a swim in the pool, stroll the gardens, and then take a nap in the grass.
(718) 430-1890; (718) 543-4595 golf course;
❶❾ *to 242nd St.*

The New York Botanical Garden

Wave Hill
This Riverdale estate and public garden is one of New York's best-kept sight-seeing secrets. Overlooking the Hudson River and the Palisades, Wave Hill offers a number of breathtaking views to inspire even the most jaded New Yorker. Within its 28 acres are meticulously manicured gardens and nature trails highlighting the estate's diverse flora. Guided walks are offered every Sunday; art and nature are celebrated year-round with concerts, nature hikes, and educational programs.
675 West 252nd St. (entrance at West 249th St. and Independence Ave.), (718) 549-3200, Admission Tuesdays, Saturdays 9-12am, and mid-November to mid-March free; Wednesday through Sunday $4 general, $2 seniors and students;
1 *to 231st St., then take the* **Bx10**

Woodlawn Cemetery
Filled with a staggering variety of trees and gargoyled mausoleums, the rolling landscape of Woodlawn Cemetery has been compared to Pere LaChaise in Paris and Stagliano in Genoa. Thanks to the trees, this resting place is also a roosting place for almost 200 different species of birds; even bald eagles have been spotted. Among the cemetary's deceased residents are Juilliard, LaGuardia, Macy, Duke Ellington, Miles Davis, and W.C. Handy.
Webster Ave. (at 233rd St.), (718) 920-0500; **4** *to the last stop, entrance on Jerome Ave.*

Yankee Stadium
"I don't know what your name is or where you come from, but you're wearing pinstripes so I love you'se--now hit the f-in' ball!" Big games fill more than half the seats in this 56,000 capacity stadium, which is remarkably clean and boasts ample restrooms and concession stands. Hot dogs go for $3 and a beer is $5. Monument Park, a gallery of Yankee greats, closes 30 minutes before game time, so go early and enjoy the park's history. Be sure to catch the Yanks at the house that Ruth built before they relocate to the house that Steinbrenner built.
River Ave. and 161st St., (718) 293-6000, tickets $6 bleachers, $8 main seating, **C D 4** *to 161st St./Yankee Stadium*

Bronx County Courthouse—The Supreme Court of New York
With the courthouse opening in 1934, a few decades rolled by before the NY Supreme Court was officially stationed here. Visitors who don't have court appointments can check individual case records via clerks' minutes, making the courthouse an invaluable tool as a primary resource.
851 Grand Concourse (at 161st St.), (718) 590-3646, **B D 4** *to 161st St./Yankee Stadium*

---

cheap *thrills*

If You Can't Beat 'Em, Join 'Em, at Clarke's
Friday nights, free hot dogs and sauerkraut; Thursday nights, the unbeatable five-dollars-for-all-you-can-drink-in-three-hours special! *(see Bars section)*

American Movie Theater
On "Bargain Mondays," all film showings are $4 per person. A great incentive for early-week movie-going. *1450 East Ave. (across from Macy's), (718) 863-4900,* **6** *to Parkchester/East 177th St.*

Bronx Museum of the Arts
With 11,000 square feet of galleries, classrooms, and an auditorium all open to the public. Special programs and technology-oriented classes are routinely offered to all ages and groups. *1040 Grand Concourse (at 165th St.), (718) 681-6000 ext. 32,* **B D 4** *to 161st St./Yankee Stadium*

A Saturday in the Bronx

1 Royal Coach Diner

Have a filling, tasty brunch in this Bronx classic.
(see Restaurant section)

2 Botanical Gardens

Bring a thermos of coffee and a newspaper to relax in the gardens, then spend a few hours perusing the gorgeous flora.
(see Sites + Parks)

riverdale area

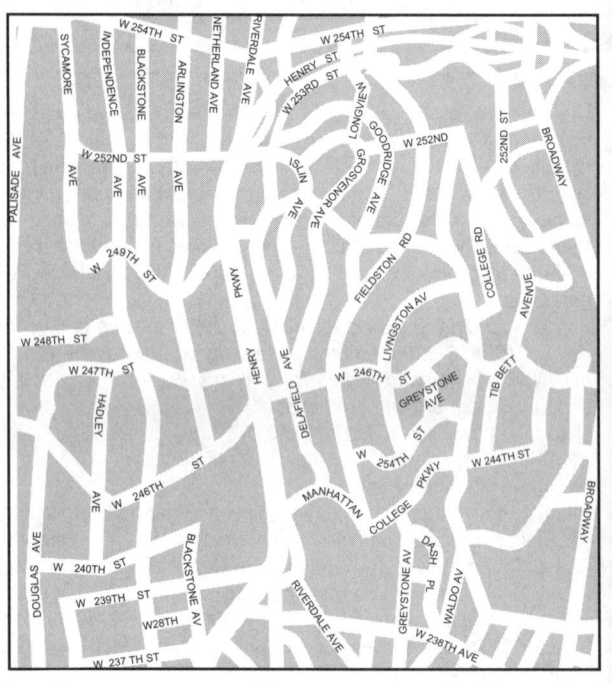

The entrance to the Botanical Gardens

3 Bronx Zoo

After you've checked out the flora, immerse yourself in New York's best fauna-watching. The world-renowned zoo tries its best to give the animals a natural habitat, but watch out for gum-spewing little kids who think it's funny to toss lollipop sticks at the seals.
(see Sites + Parks)

Most Forgiving Clothing
Bay Plaza Shopping Mall
An outdoor retail arena whose female clothing shops are geared toward plus-sized women
Bartow Ave. in Co-op City, ❷❺ *to Gun Hill Road, then Bx28 to Bay Plaza*

Most Jamaican Beef Patties in One Place
The Northeast Bronx
Referred to as "Little Jamaica," the neighborhood's vibe is heavily influenced by the aesthetics of island culture; "Yankees" are still welcome.

4 Yankees Game

Root, root, root for the Yankees in one of their last years at home in the Bronx.

(see Sites + Parks)

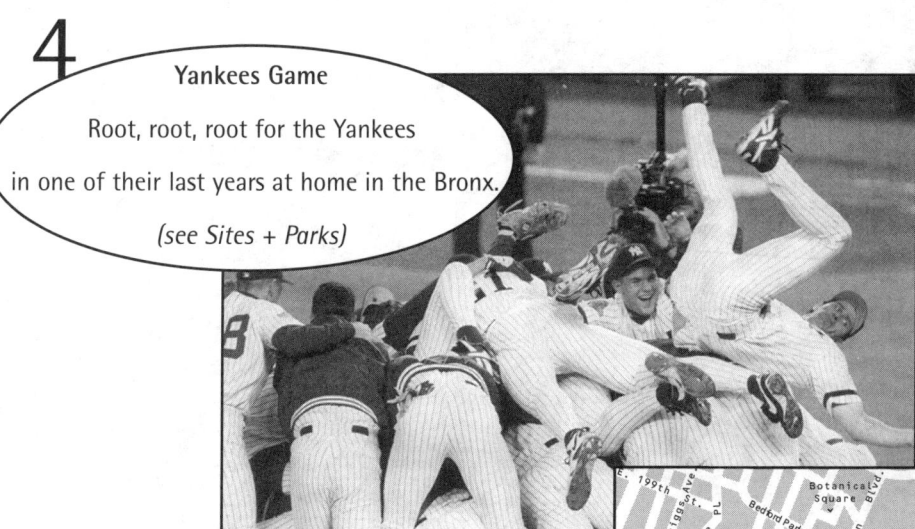

5 Little Italy, Edigio's

Walk around the Bronx's authentic Little Italy, then celebrate the Yankees' win or console yourself for their loss with dinner and drinks at this authentic Italian restaurant.

(see Restaurant section)

fordham area

Most Authentic Italian Neighborhood
Italian Belmont
The Bronx's Old World enclave is peppered with music stores, bakeries, markets, and restaurants. Unlike Manhattan's Little Italy, lots of Italians still live here
C D *to Fordham Rd., walk east on Fordham Rd. to Arthur Ave.*

Most Shopping on one Road
Fordham One Road
Nothing but stores of all types down ten lengthy blocks. Something for everybody
Fordham Rd. 9 (bet. Jerome and Webster), **4 B D** *to Fordham Rd.*

bronx 127

Queens

The most ethnically diverse part of New York City, and possibly of the world, Queens boasts residents belonging to 100 ethnic groups who speak over 120 languages in all. Enclaves still house immigrants who bring with them the most vibrant aspects of their homelands, many of whose children choose to remain in Queens. Forest Hills, Kew Gardens, and the Rockaways have long been predominantly Italian and Jewish, while Woodside and Long Island City harbor Irish; Astoria constitutes a little Greece, Jamaica and Elmhurst boast the borough's largest black population, and Jackson Heights supports communities of both Latin Americans and South Asians.

It is fitting, then, that the borough acts as a gateway to New York for the rest of the world. With two major airports, the Brooklyn-Queens Expressway, and the termination of the A, B, E, F, G, J, M, N, Q, R, Z, and #7 subway lines; virtually every resident of New York has visited Queens on one of these means of transportation. Although Queens lies among all the airplanes, highway and subway lines, Queens life offers a less hectic pace and a more family oriented environment than Manhattan.

The common ground shared by the borough's residents is their middle- and working-class status; Queens residents affirm it is a reasonably inexpensive and pleasant place to live, work, and play. They mix freely at Shea Stadium to cheer on the Mets, picnic in Flushing Meadow Park, bargain shop on Steinway Avenue, or enjoy the nightlife on Queens Boulevard. Queens boasts the comforts of suburbia while retaining an urban consciousness; college student and long-time Rosedale resident Latressa Fulton proclaims, "I simply love it here. I can't imagine ever living anywhere else!"

sites + parks

Bowne House
Historic home of John Bowne, whose trial for holding Quaker meetings and whose subsequent acquittal helped establish religious freedom in America. The oldest building in Queens, it dates back to 1661.
37-01 Bowne St., Flushing, (718) 359-0528, Admission $4 adults, $3 seniors, $2 students/children; 7 to Main St., walk two blocks east to Bowne, then one block north

Cunningham Park
Open seven days a week from 6am to sunset, this park boasts two bocce courts, 25 baseball fields, 20 tennis courts, bike paths, a running path, and two soccer fields. Also a popular site for picnics and summer concerts.
196-00 Union Turnpike, (718) 217-6452, F R to 179th St., left at Midland Parkway, left on 188th St., right on Union Turnpike

Kaufman-Astoria Studios
Valentino, the Marx Brothers, and Paul Robeson have all made films at this popular studio, which has been at the heart of New York's movie industry for years. No tours are offered.
34-12 36th St. (bet. 34th and 35th Aves.), (718) 392-5600, R to Steinway St.

King Manor
Home of Rufus King, delegate to the Constitutional Convention. The oldest house in southeast Queens has been restored to reflect the King family's tenancy in the early 19th century. Visitors can tour King's library and read pages from his diary, account books, and letters; guided tours are available in English and Spanish. Exhibit galleries are devoted to local history and to village life in Jamaica during the early 1800s.
King Park/Jamaica Ave. (bet. 150th and 153rd Sts.), (718) 206-0547, Admission $2 for adults, $1 for children, Cash Only, E J Z to Jamaica Center

Weeping Beech Tree
Created in 1847 by Samuel Parsons, this neatly landscaped park, located in a residential section of Flushing, is a New York City "living landmark."
143-35 37th Ave. (bet. Parsons and Bowne), (718) 939-0647, 7 to Main St.

World's Fair Ice Skating Rink
Near the Unisphere at Flushing Meadow Park, this is a popular attraction for kids of all ages. Great skating music, but the snack bar and vending machine food are a bit pricey. Open Oct. - March.
Flushing Meadow Park, (718) 271-1996, 7 to 111th St., then Q58

history

When Queens was consolidated into New York in 1898, much of it was still fenced off into farms, and in the eastern section of Queens, there was little desire to become a part of any city, much less one of the largest in the world. A nonbinding referendum introduced to voters in 1984 found Flushing, Hempstead, and other outlying areas solidly opposed to consolidation. This lack of a distinct borough community was mitigated by the secession of far eastern areas toward Nassau County as well as increasing urbanization, much of the original identity crisis remains today—neatly symbolized by Northern Boulevard, laid over old country pathways which led to once-rural eastern areas of Long Island. By the '20s and '30s, Queens was beginning to develop its current character, with tree-lined rows of modest brick and wood-frame houses.

Queens was well on its way to development, but it was the 1939 World's Fair that solidified its role as New York's primary locale for recreation, arenas, and beautiful parks. Preparation for the Fair converted Flushing Meadows/Corona Park from a dumpsite to the city's second largest landscaped recreation area. LaGuardia Airport and bridges were built, streets were widened, and sports stadiums were constructed.

More sprawling and peaceful than Manhattan, Queens has become the borough of choice for immigrants since the '60s, a place where newcomers can solidly establish themselves an arm's length from big-city pressures. In 1990, first-generation immigrants made up more than one-third of the two-million plus population of Queens, the greatest percentage in the five boroughs. Queens is also the most ethnically diverse borough; although certain neighborhoods are identified with predominant ethnic groups, the extent to which these areas interact and overlap demonstrates that diversity itself acts as the borough's unifying force.

Subway Railing

A Saturday in Queens

astoria area

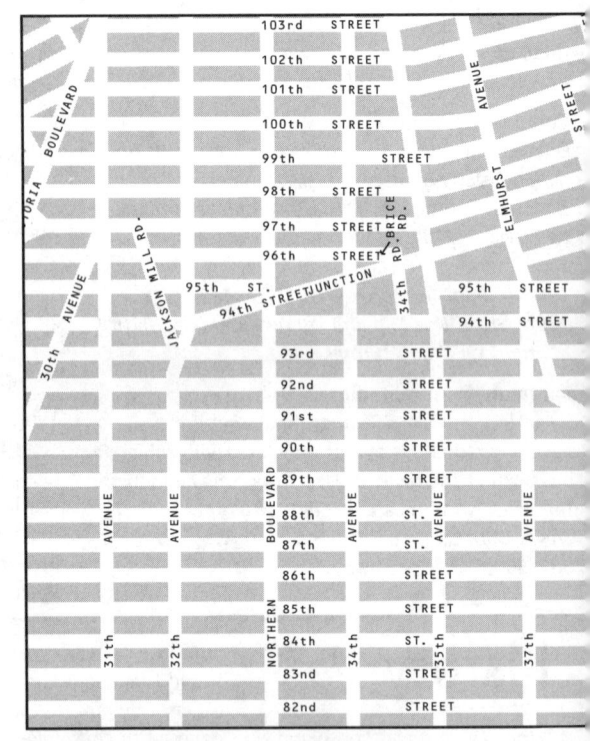

1 Bagels + Cream Cafe

Stop in for a morning meal of pastries, bagels and coffee, or try one of the inexpensive breakfast specials.

(see Cafe section)

2 Long Island City Art Loop

Take your pick of film, sculpture, performance art, painting, theater, or gardens; this neighborhood in western Queens is jam-packed with a diversity of quality art.

(see Sites + Parks)

The Socrates Sculpture Park
Large-scale outdoor sculptures by artists from all over the world are free as well as public concerts, performance art, etc.
B'way (at Vernon), Long Island City, (718) 956-1819, open 10am-sunset year-round, N to Broadway

The Unisphere
Created for the 1964 World's Fair, the Unisphere is an impressive model of our planet; its fountains provide welcome relief on a hot day.
Flushing Meadows/Corona Park, 7 to Willets Point

Ravenswood Theatre
Mainstage tickets are $7, but staged readings and various other events are free at this experimental theater in the heart of Queens' art district.
42-16 West St., L. I. City, 794-9070, Free pkng; 7 N to Queensboro Plaza

130 queens

{cheap thrills}

3 Lunch on Steinway Street

Take a break for lunch in Astoria, just northeast of Long Island City; here Steinway Street turns into a veritable global village of ethnic restaurants. Try Egyptian, Greek, Colombian, or Thai, to name just a few, and then return to the art loop if you didn't get your fill.

(see Sites + Parks)

4 View from 44th Drive

Watch the sun set over Manhattan (or between its skyscrapers) and be sure to turn around and see Queens' windows afire with reflections of the setting sun.

(see Sites + Parks)

jackson heights area

5 Jackson Diner

Replenish yourself with a dinner of delicious Indian food at this famous diner; no visit to Queens is complete without this culinary experience.

(see Restaurant section)

Most Graffiti in One Place
"The Fun Factory"
Unofficial gallery stop for those in the know; if you have trouble finding it, look for the yellow line leading there or ask across the street at P.S. 1.
Jackson Ave., L. I. City, **EF** to 23rd St./ Ely Ave., walk 2 blocks to P.S. 1 at 21st St./46th Ave., it's across the street

Most Social Action in a Library
Queens Borough Public Library/Main Branch
Libraries aren't just for reading anymore; come see the minisized art gallery or participate in a range of community-action programs. Makes you wish your old library was as socially conscious.
89-11 Merrick Blvd. (bet. 89th and 90th Sts), (718) 990-0767 or (718) 990-0768, Free, **EJZ** to Jamaica/Sutphin Blvd.

queens 131

brooklyn

Although many New Yorkers think Brooklyn has gone west with the Dodgers, the "County of Kings" is taking its place atop the city's royalty. The combination of parks, arts, and cheap(er) apartments makes Brooklyn much more than the former home of Ebbets Field.

Summing up its residents is as easy as summing up a party of United Nations delegates. While the Italian stick-balling areas depicted in film do exist, Brooklyn is ethnically and economically diverse. Brooklyn Heights, made famous by Walt Whitman has stunning views of the Manhattan skyline. Head east through the Hills (Cobble and Borm) and find the beautifully restored neighborhoods of Fort Greene and Clinton Hill, where handsome town houses are selling for one-third the price of those in the West 80s in Manhattan. Fort Greene, recently dubbed "the Black East Village," is home to the Brooklyn Academy of Music (BAM) which, with its renovated cafe and terrific schedule of symphony, dance, or opera has helped put Brooklyn back on the map.

Park Slope, long a melting pot of artists and businessmen of all colors, now is a bastion for the up and coming, all of whom seem to have a toddler in one hand, a leash to dog in the other. Its bistros, cafes, and bakeries, as well as its proximity to Prospect Park, the Brooklyn Botanical Gardens, and the Brooklyn Museum of Art, make the surge of the young and successful understandable.

Head to Williamsburg to find a burgeoning artsy enclave. But be forewarned—the word on this newest Bohemia is definitely out; rents are rising.

For those unbearable New York Augusts, Brooklyn is home to the City's longest shoreline this side of the Verrazano Narrows bridge. Pick up a few 'dogs at famous Nathan's on the Coney Island boardwalk, while trying to spot Woody Allen's alleged childhood home under the roller coaster. In addition to swimming, Brighton Beach features a collection of outrageous Russian dinner theaters.

Yellow cabs are scarce in Brooklyn, but car services are just a phone call away and aren't more expensive. Getting around this borough takes time. It may take months to make it up to Greenpoint for pierogi but it's worth the exploration. One old-timer recently exclaimed: "I don't get why anyone goes to that other borough— what's it called?—ya know, where the Giants used to play?

132 brooklyn

Name: Alex Socarides
Age: 23
Occupation: Graduate student/Freelance magazine researcher

Q: How long have you lied in Brooklyn?
A: I've lived in the city all my life, but I'm new to Brooklyn.
Q: What made you leave Manhattan?
A: The rats on my old block rallied against me and drove me out.
Q: What are your first impressions of Brooklyn?
A: I love it! I can't wait to go to a Dodgers game!
Q: Umm...right. So what do you do for fun out here?
A: It's low-key, but I like that. I jog, write, eat, sleep, go to parties. I'm only 15 minutes from the East Village, closer than I used to be on the Upper East Side or in Chelsea. It's not like this in Staten Island!

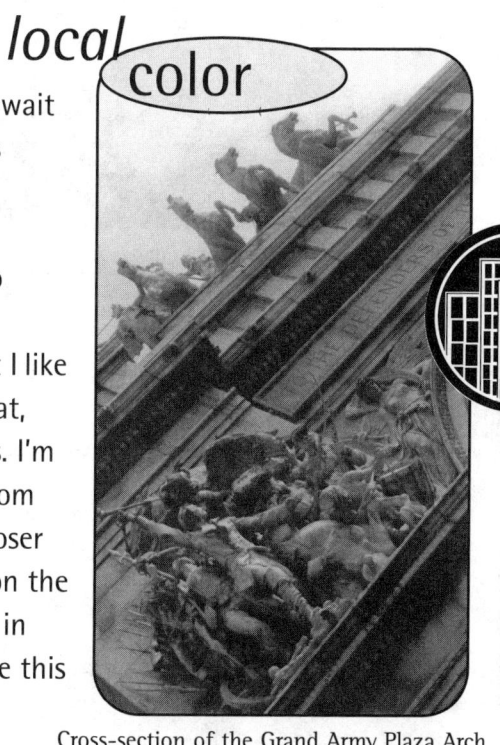

local color

Cross-section of the Grand Army Plaza Arch

history

Like Manhattan, the borough of Brooklyn was originally settled by Dutch explorers. When they purchased land from the Canarsie natives and linked together three villages in 1642, the new community called itself "Breukelen" or "Broken Land."

Brooklyn remained rural until the 1800s, when large numbers of immigrants began to settle in the area. By 1814, Robert Fulton's steamboat service established regular transportation to Manhattan and helped develop stronger commercial links between the two island communities. In 1833, Brooklyn was asked to join New York, but refused and incorporated itself as a separate city the next year. It remained an independent city even after the opening of the Brooklyn Bridge in 1883, an event which altered Brooklyn's social and economic geography more than any other. Brooklyn became a borough of Greater New York in 1898, a decision called "The Great Mistake" by writer Pete Hamill.

Brooklyn remains New York's most populous borough and maintains its own flavor and symbolic autonomy. Brooklyn's sense of self has nonetheless been subject to many vicissitudes, exemplified by the fate of the Dodgers, who won the World Series for the first time ever in 1955 and moved to Los Angeles two years later. Currently bereft of a comparable public icon, Brooklyn is most fondly thought of as a hometown by the millions who have grown up here.

brooklyn 133

movies + books

Goodfellas, 1990
In Martin Scorcese's depiction of real-life mobster Henry Hill, several key scenes take place at the Bamboo Lounge in Canarsie.

Do the Right Thing, 1989
Set in the Bedford-Stuyvesant neighborhood, on "the hottest day of the summer". Spike Lee stars as Mookie, the pizza deliveryman who wears Jackie Robinson's old Brooklyn Dodgers jersey as he makes his rounds.

Radio Days, 1985
Woody Allen's charming, episodic account of growing up in Coney Island, in a house which rattled and shook every time the roller coaster passed by.

A Tree Grows in Brooklyn, 1943
A tale of growing up in Williamsburg, by Betty Smith.

The Boys of Summer, 1970
Roger Kahn's classic then-and-now report on the Brooklyn Dodgers of the 1950s remains the best book written about the borough's beloved team, and what it meant to their fans.

sites

Brooklyn Heights Promenade
Playgrounds, room for rollerblading, and benches draw crowds of all ages, but the main attraction is the stunning view of the Manhattan Skyline.
Montague Terrace, M N R to Court St., 2 3 to Clark St.

Brooklyn Bridge
Bike, blade, or walk across the bridge on the well-maintained pedestrian path high above the traffic; the spectacular views of the downtown skyline never fail to stun both visitors and New Yorkers alike.
2 3 to Clark St., A C to High St.

Coney Island Boardwalk
The quintessential getaway by the shore. A stroll down the famous boardwalk presents a stunning view of the Atlantic shore and visions of scantily clad women in heels, Speedo-sporting men, wizened old Russian card-players, and shrieking children waving corn dogs. Walk out onto the pier, where fishermen haul in ocean fish and spiny crabs; the beach is passable, but trash mars the effect on busier days.
B D F to Stillwell Ave./Coney Island

Astroland Park
Thrills and amusements abound at this colorful amusement park, boasting kiddie rides and heart-stopping action for adults. Foremost among these thrills is Astroland's famous Cyclone roller coaster, not for the faint of heart.
Surf Avenue and West 8th Street, (718) 372-0275, (718) 265-2100 (information), adult rides $4, kiddie rides $1.75, 10 rides $15, B D F to Stillwell Ave./Coney Island

New York Aquarium
Various exhibits and habitats present marine life in both indoor tanks and outdoor pools. Replicas of an ocean habitat, the Gulf Stream, and the rocky Pacific seacoast house wildlife ranging from penguins to sea otters.
D F to West 8th St./New York Aquarium

Marine Park
With a playground, lush and grassy fields, and facilities for baseball, basketball, and tennis, Marine Park is an ideal place for picnics, gatherings, and field events.
Fillmore and Avenue U, D to Avenue U, B3 to Marine Park

Deep-Sea Fishing
Party-fishing boats offer four-hour excursions to troll for bluefish, flounder, and mackerel. Boats leave hourly, from 6am to 1pm. Call a specific boat to iron out the details about equipment and facilities.
Emmons Ave. (bet. Ocean and Bedford Aves.), Pastime Princess (718) 252-4398, Sea Star (718) 625-6857, **B D F** *to Stillwell Ave./Coney Island*

Floyd Bennett Airfield
Now that the air traffic doesn't come through, this spacious airfield is used mostly for biking and blading. The hangar has become an exhibition hall, and visitors can golf, mini-golf, and use batting cages at the nearby Gateway National Recreation Area.
At Gateway National Recreation Area, (718) 338-3799, **D** *to Avenue U,* **B3** *to Marine Park,* &

Prospect Park
Brooklyn's expansive central park borders many different neighborhoods whose residents fill the park for cookouts, sports, fishing, and tailgating; there are also secluded meadows for quiet reflection and picnicking. In June, the "Celebrate Brooklyn" festival holds weekend events in the Prospect Park bandshell, where a $3 "contribution" grants admission to concerts by the likes of David Murray, Dee Dee Bridgewater, Allen Toussaint, and Don Bryan.
From Grand Army Plaza to Fort Hamilton Parkway, (718) 965-8950, **2 3** *to Grand Army Plaza,* &

Botanic Gardens
Unwind after a busy day of sightseeing at one of the many gardens situated on the 52 acres, including the Shakespeare and Conservatory Garden, the Japanese Garden, the Pond Garden, and Celebrity Park's Herb Garden.
Entrances at Flatbush Ave. and Empire Blvd. and at Washington Ave. and Eastern Parkway, (718) 622-4433, Admission $3, **2 3** *to Eastern Parkway*

Fort Greene Park
A trip through this park is both relaxing and historical. Visitors can view Martyr's Monument, designed by Stanford White and dedicated to Continental soldiers on British prison ships in Wallabout Bay.
Myrtle and DeKalb Aves, and St. Edwards and Cumberland Streets, Admission Free, **D M N Q R** *to DeKalb Ave.*

---

cheap *thrills*

Park Slope Adventure
Put on some comfy shoes and stroll down Park Slope's beautiful tree- and brownstone-lined streets.
2 3 to Grand Army Plaza

Gallery Hop
Williamsburg and Red Hook are burgeoning artists' neighborhoods with funky galleries to explore with cute cafes for replenishment.
(see Arts section)

Promenade on the Promenade
A great place to take a date. Arrive at sunset to watch the lights go up over Manhattan.
2 3 to Clark St.

Brooklyn Moon Cafe
Grab a coffee and people-watch in this local hangout for Fort Greene artsy types.
2 3 4 5 D N Q R to Atlantic Ave.

A Saturday in Brooklyn

1 New Prospect Cafe
One of the best brunches in Brooklyn, it's also becoming one of the most popular. The food, service, and proximity to Park Slope make it well worthwhile.
(see Restaurant section)

2 Brooklyn Museum of Art
A short stroll to burn off brunch will whirl you to one of New York's best-kept secrets which probably wishes it weren't. A wonderfully curated institution with exhibitions ranging from Monet's Mediterranean to the Romanov's diamonds.
(see Sites + Parks)

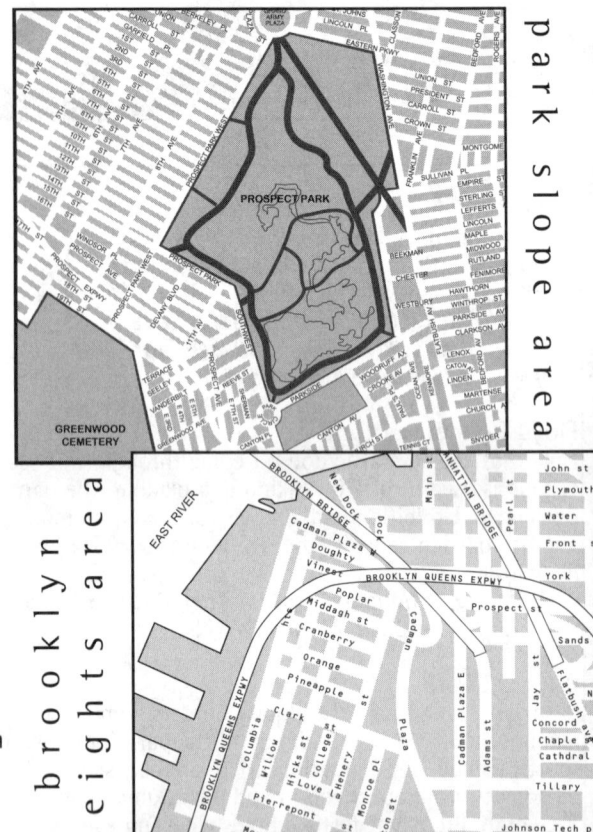

3 Seventh Avenue
An easy walk from the Museum. Many attribute Brooklyn's loss of grit to this stretch of family-friendly boutiques and coffee shops but all those toddlers out for a stroll with mom, dad, or nanny are sure adorable!

Most Strollers On Parade
Seventh Avenue in Park Slope
These upscale blocks are perfect for checking out the babes, especially in spring, when "four-wheelers" are so prominent the sidewalks could use a passing lane.
Seventh Ave. (bet. Flatbush Ave. and 2nd St.), **D Q** to Seventh Ave.

Most Old-School Brooklyn
Coney Island
The boardwalk and beaches of Coney Island are truer to more people's image of classic Brooklyn than anyplace else, and remain a fun, cheap getaway.
Coney Island, **B D F N**
to the end of the line

136 brooklyn

Prospect Park 4

Just as integral a part of Brooklyn as Central Park is to Manhattan, and just as social too. You could easily spend your whole day here or in the adjoining Botanical Garden.
(see Sites + Parks)

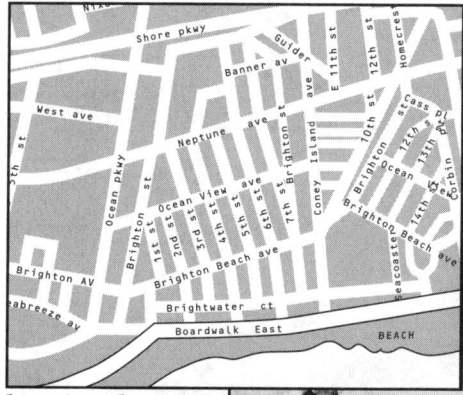

brighton beach area

Tom's 5

The cutest, friendliest, egg-creamiest; Tom's is just northeast of the park and absolutely charming. Say hi to Gus for us!
(see Restaurant section)

6 Coney Island

Spend the afternoon on the shore which is just a MetroCard swipe away. As a cultural landmark, Coney Island's significance can't be overstated, nor can you make the trip out too many times.
(see Sites + Parks)

Most Funky Nightspot
Brooklyn Mod
Since Fort Greene has recently been dubbed the "black East Village" it only makes sense that Brooklyn's hottest bar/lounge should be in this up-and-coming neighborhood.
271 Adelphi St. (at DeKalb Ave.) 718-522-1669,
6pm-4am, ❷❸❹❺ D Q *to Atlantic Ave.*

staten island

Combining the excitement of city life with the tranquillity of the suburban experience, Staten Island is the city's smallest and quietest outer borough which most New Yorkers neglect. With a plethora of fine restaurants, shopping areas, and historical sites, its residents consider it one of New York's best-kept secrets, although it's home to over 400,000 people.

Many neighborhoods on the south shore of the island, are predominantly Italian, while most of the older neighborhoods on the north shore have relatively diverse populations. A population of this size encompasses a wide scope of interests. Among the offerings for Staten Islanders and visitors are the Staten Island Mall and many cultural institutions that feature performances by the Staten Island Ballet Company and the Staten Island Symphony.

The island was won by Manhattan in a boat race sponsored by the Duke of York in 1687, and has had a difficult relationship with New York City ever since.

Separated from Manhattan by the New York Harbor and the only borough not accessible by subway, Staten Island has maintained its own distinctive character, which has led to a long and intermittent fight for secession from the city by some residents. The situation has been exacerbated by the infamous Fresh Kills Landfill, New York's garbage dump until 2001, when the city will, supposedly, stop dumping. Staten Islanders will, no doubt, raise a stink of their own and demand that Manhattan will keep its promise as their community enters the new millenium.

For many residents, Staten Island's divergence from the rest of the city and its residential character are the reasons they choose to live there. Like its neighbors to the north, Staten Island has its share of museums, historical sites and public spaces; though, unlike Manhattan, it can also claim the ups and downs of suburban culture, where communities are small, strip-malls line the main boulevard, and no one is a stranger for long.

sites + parks

Alice Austen House
This ivy-covered Victorian cottage called Clear Comfort was home to Alice Austen, the Emily Dickinson of turn-of-the-century photography. Although Austen took more than 8000 photographs of daily life from 1884-1934, she went undiscovered most of her life and died in poverty in 1952. The view from the gently sloping hill in Austen's backyard is breathtaking.
2 Hylan Blvd., (718) 816-4506, **S51**

Snug Harbor Cultural Center
This National Landmark is one of the city's great quiet retreats, with historical buildings, gardens, and exhibition sites. The New House Center for Contemporary Art is an exhibition space and concert hall which hosts various art shows, performances, and flea markets. The Staten Island Botanical Garden contains butterfly gardens, a bonsai collection, and a fragrance garden. Gardens are open from 9am 'til dusk and admission is free for everything but special events.
1000 Richmond Terrace, (718) 448-2500, **S40**

Richmondtown Restoration
Staten Island's own version of Historic Williamsburg, this indoor and outdoor exhibit documents local history and includes, among other historic buildings, the oldest surviving elementary school in America. Volunteers dressed in 18th-century costume re-enact everything from candle-making to declarations of war.
441 Clarke Ave., (718) 351-1611, **S74**

South Beach
The fourth longest boardwalk in the country is always packed with cyclists, but this is primarily a bathing beach for families and other sun worshipers admiring the great view of the Verrazano Narrows Bridge.
S51

Jacques Marchais Center of Tibetan Art
Housed in a two-story stone building resembling a Buddhist mountain temple and set in a terraced garden overlooking New York Bay, the center features a permanent collection of Tibetan and other Buddhist art and ethnography. Notable past visitors include the Dalai Lama, who came in 1991.
338 Lighthouse Ave., Wednesday through Sunday 1-5pm, (718) 987-3500, **S70**

---

history

Henry Hudson gave Staaten Eylandt its original name in 1609, when he sailed into the bay which now bears his name. In 1639, the Dutch opened Staten Island to colonization, but the area remained difficult to settle due to conflicts with native inhabitants; there were constant wars between Native Americans and the Dutch. The colony of Oude Dorp stabilized in 1661, but Staten Island became a province of New Jersey after the British took control of New York in 1664. The island was then known as Richmond County, after the Duke of Richmond, a son of Charles II, until Manhattan won it back in a sailing race in the Lower Bay at the end of the 17th century.

Even after becoming part of New York, Staten Island was reachable only by private boat and remained largely a secluded place for fishing and farming until 1713, when a public ferry began carrying passengers to and from Manhattan and continues to do so today.

But Staten Island's independent streak has persisted even since it joined New York City in 1898 and saw the 1964 construction of the Verrazano Narrows bridge, which connects it to Brooklyn. Fed up with garbage dumps filled largely with trash from elsewhere, the citizens of Richmond voted in 1993, albeit unsuccessfully, to secede from New York City.

Scenic Fresh Kills Landfill

staten island 139

A Saturday in Staten Island

1 Snug Harbor
Stroll among the flowers and butterflies in the Botanical Gardens, peruse the art in the exhibition space, visit the past in the historical buildings, then eat a picnic lunch on one of the beautiful lawns.
(see *Sites + Parks*)

2 Jacques Marchais Center of Tibetan Art
Whether spiritual or aesthetic, a pilgrimage to this Buddhist Center will center your soul.
(see *Sites + Parks*)

3 Basilio Inn
Change gears from Tibetan art to Tuscan food at this 19th-century stable which is now an incomparable place for a Staten Island dinner.
(see *Restaurant section*)

4 South Beach
Relax on the boardwalk with an ice cream cone and watch the sunset and night fall.
(see *Sites + Parks*)

5 Staten Island Ferry
Wind up your day with a gorgeous view of the Harbor and the lit-up Lady of Liberty as Manhattan's golden towers loom ever-larger ahead.
(see *Cheap Thrills*)

Most Expensive Toll Plaza in NYC
Verrazano Narrows Bridge
At an outrageous $7 a car, you'd do better to take the ferry to Staten Island.

Most Famous Ices
Ralph's Ices
From the traditional lemon to more exotic flavors like honeydew, these ices are the perfect warm weather treat.
501 Port Richmond Ave., 718-273-3675, ①⑨ to South Ferry, Staten Island Ferry to S44

{cheap *thrill*}

The Ferry
Forget the Circle Line; the Staten Island Ferry is now absolutely free and also boasts excellent musicians below deck.
Docks at the foot of Whitehall St., 806-6940, ①⑨ to South Ferry, ④⑤ to Bowling Green, or ⓃⓇ to Whitehall St.

140 staten island

SHOPPING

NYC shopping ⟶ 142

interviews:
supermodel roshumba williams.144
jewelry-maker stewart wilson.144

store listings:
art supply.147
clothing.147
computing.153
cosmetics.154
department stores.154
gifts.155

grocery.156
housewares.159
music.160
shoes.162
sports.163
miscellaneous.164

shopping

Navigating the consumer playground of Manhattan without blowing your wad in the process is an acquired skill. The average new New Yorker is typically so wowed by the selection, the novelties, the truly absurd that she or he loses all perspective. One wide-eyed newcomer reports purchasing a pair of key lime platform moon boots just because she mistook shock value for style, not an uncommon mistake among those eager to crash into New York's crazy fashion scene. However, if all you have to go with them is a pair of J. Crew chinos and a couple of lambswool sweaters, the purchase is a bit premature. Take advantage of street fairs and thrift stores for casual pieces, funky coats, and splurge every once in awhile in a high-end downtown boutique.

SoHo and the stretch up Broadway to 8th Street is a dependable first-stop for browsing; you can hit funkier outfitters like Patricia Field's and Antique Boutique, as well as boutiques like Cynthia Rowley and Todd Oldham. The streets of the East Village, especially those between Second Avenue and Avenue A, yield numerous vintage stores as well as great little shops started by young, trendy designers.

Try the mythical Madison or Fifth Avenues for window-shopping, though uniformed doormen and stifled ambiance will encourage you to remain on the outside looking in. The Upper West Side in the 70s along Columbus Avenue boasts a number of boutiques and restaurants that cater to the area's gainfully employed, thirtysomething crowd.

Flea Markets and Street Fairs

On any given weekend, Manhattan streets are closed off to traffic and empty lots are filled with vendors who create a bazaar-like atmosphere, drawing everyone from neighborhood residents out for a stroll to hardcore hagglers perusing the wares. Offerings vary greatly, with the selection depending largely on the style of the individual market. Nomadic neighborhood street fairs stop in most neighborhoods and tend to have a wide variety of merchants offering new merchandise such as handmade crafts and clothing as well as inexpensive commercially produced items, wearable imports, and of course, plenty of food. To find street fairs, be on the lookout for fliers around the neighborhood or check out the Bulletin Board section on the back of *The Village Voice* where they're often listed.

Flea markets, on the other hand, are more established institutions and operate at the same location every weekend. They tend to fall into one of two categories: the first brings the atmosphere of a cheap and trendy clothing outlet into an open air setting, like at the daily market on the corner of Spring and Wooster Streets in SoHo, or at the Saturday and Sunday set-up on Broadway at West 4th Street. The second more closely approximates a church rummage sale with various tables and racks displaying antiques, some of the best vintage clothing around, and a fair share of plain old junk. Three of the best are found downtown in Chelsea on Sixth Avenue between 25th and 26th Streets, in SoHo on Grand Street, and in the East Village on Avenue A at the corner of 11th Street. All three are very popular, so try to get there early for the best selection and remember that almost all of the prices are negotiable, so don't be afraid to haggle.

Designer Deals

Getting your hands on designer pieces before they sell out can be tough; waiting lists begin immediately after the shows, and fashion fanatics go so far as to bribe salespeople for first dibs on new stock. For the average college student, the problem is not how to score Marc Jacobs' hot new sweater; it's how to score the sweater for a decent price before it's so shop-worn that it's beyond hope.

All department stores have end-of-the-year sales of course, the trick being to gamble on that last markdown. Barney's has a twice-yearly warehouse sale, but don't believe the hype. Bad lighting and lack of dressing rooms do not automatically signify bargains. The salespeople supposedly hide all the good stuff for their friends anyhow.

The real scores are at designer sample sales. *New York Magazine* runs a weekly column called "Sales and Bargains", which often includes showroom sales, and TimeOut New York has a similar column called "Shoptalk." True fanatics turn to the *S&B Report* (683-7612, $49/year), the definitive source of designer showroom info. for insider tips. If that's not enough, opt for the preferred subscription which entails week ly updates via fax.

The last option for name-brand junkies is the much-vaunted Century 21 and Loehmann's. Somewhat of a circus-like atmosphere, but worth sifting through since there are tons of good finds. Also, the Moe Ginsburg store in Gramercy is a reasonable outlet for men's dress clothes and shoes that strives for classy ambiance mixed with bargain basement enthusiasm. *(See Shopping for more information.)*

Thrift Shopping

A huge rift in the world of secondhand clothing sales exists between vintage stores and thrift stores. Vintage represents the clothes that have been sorted to separate the junk and then slapped with hefty price tags; this is the type found in most of the well-traversed shopping areas of Manhattan, and includes notable outposts like the deceptively named Cheap Jack's and Andy's Chee-Pees. Thrift, on the other hand, encompasses the whole range of castoffs—from garbage to gems—and generally entails sorting through plenty of racks and bins full of the former before discovering any of the latter. But once the great finds come to light, the search process is rendered worthwhile by dirt cheap prices.

For the willing and bargain-hungry, there's still another barrier in the path to thrift store heaven: actually finding thrift stores. Head for the city's fringes—the far reaches of uptown Manhattan and the outer boroughs. Up in Washington Heights lies Ropa 203, a warehouse that sells piles of clothes by the pound; Harlem secondhand stores can be goldmines, since downtown vintage buyers rarely glean the finest stuff.

Moving beyond Manhattan, a trip out to Queens yields Salvation Army thrift stores (try the Astoria branch) that are full of quirky retro that's neither picked-over nor overpriced. Further south, in the Williamsburg and Greenpoint sections of Brooklyn are two local institutions: Domsey's has a couple of warehouses overflowing with everything from sweaters to pleather as well as a funky shoe selection; its neighbor to the north, Pop's, is smaller but contains the best selection of jeans and workwear around.

roshumba williams

Supermodel Roshumba Williams has been at the top of the fashion world since 1987 when the renowned designer Yves Saint Laurent immediately recognized her unique beauty and launched her career. Not only has she appeared on the runways of countless top designers and in the advertisements of many major advertisers, Roshumba has also established herself as a film and television presence. She's hosted television shows and special events, and recently appeared in Woody Allen's new film Celebrity. *Also, Roshumba is the 1998 host of the Elite Model look for which she will be appearing in major cities throughout the US. We spoke with Roshumba, a New York resident for the past eight years, about her life as a supermodel in the city.*

Q: You went straight from your hometown of Chicago to Paris to model. When you moved to New York, what was your first impression?

Stewart Wilson's jewelry has been purchased by the Folk Art Museum and the Craft Museum, and is on display at the Brooklyn Museum, the Whitney Museum, and galleries throughout the city. His pieces are sold at the Enchanted Forest (85 Mercer St., 925-6677.)

Q: How should one describe you? As an artist/jewelry maker?
A: Artist. Jewelry maker... you know, my jewelry is really my art. The Personas are little sculptures, and I commit everything I can to making them. Sometimes some are more successful than others, just like human beings are. I think they're all kind of wonderful, because they are what they are. Some are more humorous, and some are more beautiful, but they are all themselves.

Q: How did you start making the Personas?
A: In 1979 I was going through a rough transition. I got kicked out of my place in TriBeCa because developers were moving in, and ended up staying at my brother's place in Brooklyn. I didn't know what I was going to do next—and, to take my mind off of things, I began wrapping. The first figures were made of metal, and they were kind of crude, but it felt good making them. I have a record of every one I've made--over 30,000 now.

Q: How did you start marketing them?
A: I didn't know where I was going with these things. Some of my friends thought I was nuts. I was an up-coming artist/painter, and I was willing to put that aside. The first ones I took were to Fiorucci—it was the hippest shop in NY, in 1979. They ordered two dozen, and I went home and made them. I went to a few more stores, and they all loved them. Then I did a trade show at the NY Coliseum, and I got a little tiny booth against a wall, which I made really fun. I got orders from all over the country! And it just kept on going.

144 shopping

A: Well, I flew on the Concorde from Paris to New York in August. It was hot. It smelled. There were homeless people everywhere. I hated it.

Q: Understandable after spending years in Paris. When did your opinion change?
A: It happened slowly, but I eventually recognized the great energy New York has. You can actually have a life here. Besides I gotta have a slice every now and then.

Q: Where do you go to shop?
A: I love SoHo, especially the new SoHo with all the wonderful stores. Of course there's 57th Street where I go for designer things. When I'm feeling more like doing some vintage shopping, I go to the East Village.

Q: Do you have any favorite place to hang out?
A: I get bored very easily so I like to do different things. I go to my yoga classes and have my wheatgrass juice, but I also like to occasionally go out to a club. I like intimate parties, but I also like premieres and openings because I know all the people and, after all, there's plenty of free champagne. Also, I love the culture in New York, the museums, but I also like going to the zoo in Central Park.

Q: So, what's next?
A: Right now I'm an on-air correspondent for VH1, doing projects like Rock Across America where I get to visit the hottest music festivals. And there is my part in the Woody Allen movie. I mean, even if I never do another film again I can say that I worked with Woody Allen! Doesn't get much better than that.

Q: Do you want to do more film?
A: I want to be the next Jackie Brown or a Bond girl. I'm already taking karate and I can kick ass!

Q: Have you enjoyed your career as a model?
A: Sure. What other industry do women get to make this much money, have this much power, and be fabulous!

Q: What do you make besides the Persona Men? I know I've also seen pens you've wrapped in suede and gilt.
A: I started with the people, and then I started making horses. Then I began making exotic animals—kangaroos, giraffes, and camels. I also started making these weird intellectual crocodiles who would have things in their mouths. What happens is you do the trade show, and people come into your booth and they sort of play in there, they have fun.

Q: Have you ever become so attached to a piece that you couldn't sell it?
A: I try not to, but I've skimmed off a few. When I first started making them I was saying, "Okay, I can keep 10 percent of everything I make"—but as it turned out, I eventually let them go.

personas
by
stewart
wilson

shopping 145

NYC shopping districts

While clothing shopping in New York usually entails a trip to some neighborhood as funky and interesting as the product, there are many out of the way areas that house groups of trade stores that belong to one particular industry where you can find amazing bargains. Even if you're not shopping, it's still fun to check out the windows of some of these neighborhood stores, or step in and watch the pros at work.

Restaurant Equipment:
Need a large-capacity salad shredder? Formica bar stools? No-frills wholesalers of restaurant equipment line the Bowery just above and just below Houston, where saloons and flophouses once catered to Skid Row.

Arcade Games:
Equally impractical for your average dorm room but still fun to browse, shops selling pinball machines and arcade games line Tenth Avenue north of 42nd St.

Antiques:
Wholesale antique dealers are most prevalent on University Place, and the "wholesale only" signs propped in windows are an arbitrary indication of the actual policies. For more antiques, with some vintage vinyl thrown in, try Bond Street off of Broadway, and Lafayette from Bond to Spring, though beware that not much comes cheaply.

Garment District:
Running between 30th and 40th Streets between Seventh Avenue and Broadway is the granddaddy of all of the city's districts, home of New York's famous fashion industry. It's also home to the infamous "sample sales," where designers sell "samples" for cut-rate prices. You can also find great deals on fabric, buttons, and other accoutrements. There is an additional strip for fabric sales on Broadway above and below Canal Street.

Costume Jewelry:
If your budget does not accommodate fine jewelry, check out the costume jewelry district on Broadway between 27th and 28th Streets; don't be intimidated by the Wholesale Only signs since the minimum sale may be quite low.

---

a girl's best friend

Flowers and Plants:
Everything from fillers for window boxes to candidates for the roof garden are available cheaply on Sixth Avenue near 25th Street. Get there early for the best quality and enjoy that dewy fragrance so absent in New York's dusty dawns.

Shoes:
Eighth Street between Broadway and Sixth Avenue is the first stop for footwear for savvy New Yorkers. Prices are still competitive across the board, with a selection that favors mid- to high-quality Italian leather and supertrendy platforms in all materials and shapes.

Electronics:
Guarantees are spotty but the service always enthusiastic at the many storefronts selling electronics along Canal Street near Broadway; remember to try before you buy.

Diamond:
Still going strong, this legendary strip of 47th Street between Fifth and Sixth Avenues is the prime locale for haggling in the city. Arm yourself with knowledge beforehand to make educated bids.

ART SUPPLY

Lee's Art Shop
Paints and brushes are just the beginning at this valuable resource for artists who work in all mediums. Drafting supplies, silk screens, a good selection of pens and stationary, and a framing service. *220 West 57th St. (bet. Seventh Ave. and Broadway), 247-0110, MC, V, Am Ex, ❶❷❸❹❶❼ to 59th/Columbus Circle ♿*

Pearl Paint
A labyrinthine motherlode of supplies for all media, these four crowded floors offer one-stop shopping for students and pros; staff members will assist you in investigating nooks and crannies. The crotchety warehouse elevator serves as a reminder of the gritty conditions that once characterized everything below Canal Street. *308 Canal St. (bet. Church St. and Broadway), 431-7932, AmEx, D, ❶❻ to Canal St.*

Sam Flax
Whether in search of gouache, canvas, or some stylish wrapping paper, shoppers will find it all at this well-staffed store. Check out the sale section in back for some good furniture bargains as well. *20th St. (bet. Fifth and Sixth Aves.), 620-3038, MC, V, AmEx ❻ to 23rd Street ♿*

CLOTHING

Basics:
Diesel
Two stories worth of youth culture in all its incarnations: pump your well-toned system full of caffeine with a visit to the cappuccino bar before ravaging the aisles of shoes, underwear, outerwear, and accessories. Afterwards hit the steel-floored dance floor on the mezzanine, where a properly Diesel-attired DJ spins. *770 Lexington Ave. (at 60th St.), 308-0055, MC, V, AmEx, D, Diners, ❹❺❻ to 59th St.*

Original Levi's Store
Everything you always wanted to know about denim, and more. Much more. Customers are limited to buying six pairs of jeans at once, presumably to prevent large, black-market shipments to places like Eastern Europe, where they can go for over $100. *750 Lexington Ave. (bet. 59th and 60th Sts.), 826-5957, MC, V, AmEx, D, ❹❺❻ to 59th St. ♿*

J. Crew
Aging preps with money burning through their silk-lined pockets feel at home amid the classically elegant fitted suits and $18 tees. The many varieties make for great khaki hunting. *91 Fifth Ave. (at 16th St.), 255-4848, MC, V, AmEx, ❶❽❻❹❺❻ to Union Square. Many, many other locations*

Von's School of Hard Knocks
Five years ago a father-and-son sneaker and men's sportswear business spawned the School of Hard Knocks, a men's line with a large hip-hop influence. Everything from jackets and caps, to sneakers and knapsacks can be had for relatively low prices; women's and children's lines will be introduced in the fall. *106-11 Northern Blvd. (bet. 106th and 107th Sts.)., (718) 898-1113, MC, V, AmEx, D, ❼ to Northern Boulevard*

Bargain:
Burlington Coat Factory
Why pay more? With five floors of discount coats, suits, shirts and casual sportswear, you're sure to find what you need at the right price. *45 Park Pl. (bet. Church St. & West Broadway) 571-2630 MC, V, AmEx, ❷❸ to Park Pl.*

Also at:
116 West 23rd St. (at Sixth Ave.), 229-1300, MC, V, AmEx, D, ❻ to 23rd St.

Century 21
Determined shoppers will find designer items for as much as 80 percent off; the other departments attract a slightly less bloodthirsty crowd. Don't go wearing bulky clothing, as there are no dressing rooms and it's standard to try things on over what you're wearing. *23 Cortlandt St. (bet. Broadway and Church St.), 227-9092, MC, V, AmEx, ❶❻ to Cortlandt St.*

The Clothes-Out Connection
It will take diligence and a sharp eye to eke out the bargains in this garage sale of a store, but the rewards are great. Men's and women's designer clothes for prices even the poorest student can afford. Shoes, accessories, and odds and ends, such as fabric paint, are also available. *89 Chambers St. (bet. Church St. and Broadway), 571-0022, V, MC, ❶❷❸❾ to Chambers St.*

Conway Stores
Mandatory stop-over for bargain hunters everywhere. Shoppers flock here for the incredible prices: expect to get a really big bang for your buck. Words of caution: take heed of the weekend mobs and of items that are listed as slightly irregular (i.e., underwear). *340 East Fordham Rd., (718) 563-1260, MC, AmEx, D, V, ❽❹ to Fordham Rd.*

Daffy's
For more reasonable prices than most department stores, this heavily advertised pit stop for savvy shoppers sells clothes, shoes, lingerie, and accessories, usually by lesser known European designers. During clearance sales, some items are slashed to fewer than five dollars. *111 Fifth Ave. (at 18th St.), 529-4477, MC, V, D, ❶❶❶❹❺❻ to Union Square*

Dee & Dee
Bargains galore. Everything from holiday decorations and housewares to $3 tank tops and $10 polar fleece jackets fill the racks and shelves of this cut-price warehouse. Even if you don't really need anything, with deals like this it's hard to walk away empty-handed. *97 Chambers St. (bet. Church St. and Broadway), 233-3830, MC, V, ❶❸ to Chambers St.*

Filene's Basement
This bargain staple superstore carries Calvin Klein, Perry Ellis, Kenar, and other designer names, and is worth a look for shoes, lingerie, coats, suits, and evening wear. Check out

shopping 147

the occasional clearance sales where many prices are slashed to below $5. *620 Sixth Ave. (bet. 18th and 19th Sts.), 620-3100, MC, V, AmEx, D, ❶❾ to 18th St.*
Also at:
222 Broadway (at 79th St.), 873-8000, MC, V, AmEx, ❶❾ to 79th St. &

Loehmann's
As legendary as Century 21 in designer junkie circles. The Queens outpost rewards the shopper who makes the trek: lots of big-name labels, and high stock turnover justify frequent trips. *107 Seventh Ave. (bet 16th and 17th Sts.) 352-0856, MC, V, D, ❶❾ to 18th St.*
Also at:
60-66 99th St., (718) 271-4000, MC, V, D, ❻❼ to 63rd Drive/Rego Park

Moe Ginsburg
"The final resting ground for the residuals... priced at down-and-dirty deep discount," claims Paul Ginsburg, the president of this monster menswear outlet, newly arrived in Gramercy's cast-iron district. Over 10 thousand square feet of suits, overcoats, sportswear, formal accessories, and shoes, with suppliers from both Italy and the nearby Garment District. A good option if you just got that internship at Goldman Sachs. *162 Fifth Ave. (at 21st St.), 242-3482, MC, V, AmEx, ❻❼ to 23rd St.*

Price Mart
If Rite-Aid sold clothes, it might resemble this large bargain-bazaar. Toiletries and health/hygiene products are sold upstairs, while downstairs is dominated by female fashion. Most spring and summer items below $10. *165-24 Jamaica Ave. (bet. 165th and Merrick Sts.), (718) 526-7634, MC, AmEx, D, V, ❸❻❼ to Jamaica/Sutphin Blvd.*

Ropa 203
Clothes get weighed by the pound at this uptown thrift store that can pull 'em in. "Everybody loves it," says one stylishly dressed Columbia student who shops there regularly. Be prepared for the warehouse setting. *3775 Tenth Ave. (at 203rd St.), 567-1565, Cash Only, ❶❾ to Dyckman St.*

Starlight Fashion
Not everything is exactly "fashion" at this amazingly inexpensive clothing store, but the low prices make sifting through the women's section worth it. *158 West 125th St. (at Lenox Ave), 666-4592, MC, V, AmEx, D, ❷❸ to 125th St.* &

Steven Alan Outlet
The same coveted labels as his SoHo clothing store, but at half the price. Expect good deals on brands like Rebecca Danenberg, Pixie Yates, and Tocca. *330 East 11th St. (bet. First and Second Aves.), 982-2881, ❻ to Astor Pl., ❻❼ to 8th St.*

Sugar Hill Thrift Shop
Hiring disadvantaged residents of Harlem and Washington Heights, this excellent option for high-quality vintage clothing and used household merchandise, books, and jewelry has a purpose besides reaping a profit. The stock is continually replenished, and the store gladly accepts donations. *409 West 145th St. (bet. Convent and St. Nicholas Aves.), 281-2396, Cash Only, ❶❷❸❹ to 145th St.*

Syms
Up-and-coming Wall Street types buy discounted conservative clothing and luggage at this seven-story standard. Women will also find a selection of better casual wear. *42 Trinity Pl. (at Rector St.), 797-1199, MC, V, AmEx, D, ❻❼❶❾ to Rector St.*

Ten's the Limit
All the funk you'd ever want for just $10 per item. Have fun! *166 West 125th St. (at A.C. Powell Blvd.), 316-4272, Cash Only, ❶❷❸ ❹❷❸ to 125th St.*

World Financial Center
Palm trees in New York bespeak New Jersey creeping east. At the center of this mall-like complex of over 40 upscale stores and restaurants, including Anne Klein and Barneys, is the Winter Garden Atrium (home to these palm trees) which doubles as a performance space. *West St. (bet. Liberty and Vesey Sts.), 945-0505, payments accepted vary with establishment, ❶❾ to Cortlandt St., ❻❼ to World Trade Center* &

Designer:
agnès b.
Among the finest in classic women's wear, with the touch that makes you feel timelessly classic like Ingrid Bergman. Beware even touching the fabrics. *116 Prince St. (bet. Wooster and Greene Sts.), 925-4649, MC, V, AmEx, ❻❼ to Prince St.*

Anna Sui
Rock-n-roll style meets the runway and boutique world in this small designer outpost. Leather pants hang alongside sequined camouflage dresses and the atmosphere is relaxed enough to allow for trying it all on without feeling conspicuous. It's expensive, but end-of-season markdowns are often cheap enough for a reasonable and well-deserved splurge. *113 Greene St. (bet. Spring and Prince Sts.), 941-8406, MC, V, AmEx, Diners, ❻❼ to Prince St.*

Bally
One of the best-known and best-reputed leather companies in the world, this Swiss tannery sells a vast selection of high-quality leather shoes, bags, belts, and other accessories. *628 Madison Ave (at 59th St.), 751-9082, MC, V, AmEx, ❹❺❻ to 59th St., ❻❼ to Lexington Ave.* &

Calvin Klein
Pay tribute to the commercial master who made a young American public hunger for androgyny, kiddie-porn, and denim trashiness. The megastore boasts roomfuls of classically styled furniture and home accessories alongside a full staff of the most predictably trendy, long-limbed photo-session specimens come to life. *694 Madison Ave. (at East 60th St.), 292-9000, AmEx, D, ❹❺❻ to 59th St*

148 shopping

Chanel
Coco would be proud. Complete with uniformed doorman, this sparkling shrine to simple elegance with a flair, sells clothing, jewelry, shoes, accessories, and of course, perfume.
15 East 57th St. (bet. Fifth and Madison Aves.), 355-5050, MC, V, AmEx, Diners, ❸❻ to 57th St.

Comme de Garçons
Even if it were anywhere near affordable, high fashion of this variety can't be worn too often. For instance, a recent collection featured women's pieces that added lumps to the body in odd places. But for designer-wannabes and others who love to see the cutting edge up close and personal, this is the place.
116 Wooster St. (bet. Prince and Spring Sts.), 941-0277, MC, V, AmEx, D, ❻❺ to Spring St.

Dolce & Gabanna
New to SoHo, this store was long-awaited and will probably become even more popular than its Broadway predecessor. Unfortunately prices haven't gone down, but we're talking about the best names in fashion here.
West Broadway (bet. Houston and Prince Sts.), 966-2868, ❸❹❻❹ to Broadway/Lafayette St.

Emporio Armani
Cleanly cut casual suits that are a bit more accessible price-wise than Armani's main line. Just about everything looks classy in the renovated Stanford White building.
110 Fifth Ave. (at 16th St.), 727-3240, MC, V, AmEx, ❶❷❸❹❺❻ to Union Sq.

Givenchy
Audrey Hepburn and Givenchy helped make each other even more famous back in their heyday; designs are still very French and very shi-shi, though there's probably no movie star today that could carry them off like Hepburn.
954 Madison Ave. (at 75th St.), 772-1040, MC, V, AmEx, D, ❻ to 77th St.

Hanae Mori
Vibrantly colorful and irreverently patterned, the shop's collection of women's fashion is among the most cutting edge in contemporary design. Dazzle the senses even further with an eyeful of the storefront's striking stucco front and off-center chrome cylinder, designed in 1969 by Hans Hollein.
27 East 79th St. (bet. Madison and Fifth Aves.), 472-2352, MC, V, AmEx, ❻ to 77th St.

Miu Miu
More affordable than the first line (although that's not saying much), Prada's second breakthrough strikes a more contemporary look and is geared toward a younger crowd.
100 Prince St. (bet. Mercer and Greene Sts.), 334-5156, MC, V, AmEx, ❻❹ to Prince St.

Polo/Ralph Lauren
After a $14 million facelift, the old Rhinelander mansion is now home to Ralph's flagship palace. Plenty of safari gear and other throwbacks to British colonialism, and decor to match: worn leather chairs, warm wood paneling, and the scent of eau de Polo drifting through the air. Homeboys shop at Polo Sport across the street.
867 Madison Ave (at 72nd St.), 606-2100, MC, V, AmEx, ❻ to 77th St.

Todd Oldham
He's one of America's hottest young designers and for good reason. The collections found here key into the young and fresh end of fashion with lots of color, prints, denim and other un-stodgey stuff. Buy if you can afford it, otherwise browse to get a good idea of where to focus thrift-shopping efforts.
123 Wooster St. (bet. Spring and Prince Sts.), 219-3531, MC, V, AmEx, ❻❹ to Prince St.

TSE Cashmere
If you like cashmere you'll love these modern clothes in your favorite weave. With modern styles in classic cashmere, this is the best spot for young cashmere-o-philes. With wool and cashmere blends as well, come for suits, jackets, and other must-haves. Don't miss the goat's-hair blankets and the soft-as-a-baby's-bottom baby duds.
38 Greene St. (at Grand St.), 319-8284, ❻❹ to Prince St., ❻❺ to Spring St.

Valentino
Haute couture for those who can afford it. By appointment if necessary.
749 Madison Ave. (at 65th), 772-6969, MC, V, AmEx, D, ❹ to 63rd St.

Yohji Yamamoto
Two beautifully poised mannequin's carry Yammamoto's evening wear at the entrance. Favoring deep colors, and material that's thin and luxuriously light, as your wallet will be after a purchase here. Definitely one of the up-and-coming designers of the 21st century.
Grand St. (at Mercer St.), 966-9066, MC, V, AmEx, ❻❹❻ to Canal St.

Yves Saint Laurent
All the latest in YSL designs for both men and women, though the "latest" never deviates much from the signature, tireless elegance. In this case, dress up to shop- or even to window shop.
859 Madison Ave. (bet. 70th and 71st Sts.), 517-7400, MC, V, AmEx, D, ❹❺❻ to 68th St.

Zegna Corporation
Although Zegna may be less well-known than Armani or Boss, his suits are certainly among the finest.
743 Fifth Ave. (bet. 57th and 58th), 421-4488, MC, V, AmEx, Diners, ❻❹ to 57th St.

Trendy:
555 Soul/Strictly For Da Ladies
Six years ago, designer Camella Ehlke gave the hip-hop crowd something that was finally funky enough for them to wear; T-shirts and baseball caps jazzed up with some of the downtown vibe. Chic sportswear for women came along last year.
290 Lafayette St. (bet. Houston and Prince Sts.), 431-2404, MC, V, AmEx, D, ❸❹❻❹ to Houston St. or ❻❹ to Prince St.

shopping 149

99X

This two-level boutique sells some of the hippest threads in the city, with the usual high prices. Downstairs is mostly club apparel such as leather pants, itty-bitty skirts, and baby tees. Upstairs carries an extensive selection of skinhead gear.
84 East 10th St. (bet. Third and Fourth Aves.), 460-8599, MC, V, AmEx, D, Diners, 6 to Astor, NR to Union Sq.

About Time Shoes and Clothing

An upscale, pricey boutique featuring elaborate, dressy dresses and some simple, filmy throw-ons; most everything is quality and handmade.
13/15 Prince St. (at Elizabeth St.), 941-0966, MC, V, AmEx, NR to Prince St.

Anthropologie

The grown-up Urban Outfitters. Created by the same people, with a similar variety of housewares and clothing for men and women, the bent here is more stylish than trendy, with lots of classic and basic pieces that are of high quality, but prohibitively priced at around $70 and up. The clearance racks generally yield some good finds though, and sometimes paying full price isn't so bad, since the clothes are unlikely to either fall apart or go out of style quickly.
375 Broadway (bet. Spring and Broome Sts.), 343-7070, MC, V, AmEx, D, NR to Prince St.

Antique Boutique

This trendy and lively Broadway institution shouts New York at very high prices. Newer, teenage-oriented designer brands take up most of the upstairs, while downstairs is devoted to top-notch vintage coats, shirts, and jeans; clothing in the very back room is sold by the pound.
712 Broadway (at Washington Pl.), 460-8830, MC, V, AmEx, D, Diners, NR to 8th St.

APC

Clothes so simple and perfect that you simultaneously wonder why they cost so much and how you've lived without them for so long. Classics like jeans and button-down shirts hover around the $100 range, which may seem ridiculous at first, but clasp the credit cards tightly because it's hard to resist such flawless incarnations of old standards at any price.
131 Mercer St. (bet. Prince and Spring Sts.), 966-9685, M, V, AmEx, NR to Prince St.

Atrium

Familiar designer brands at mind-numbingly incredible prices for the student-budgeted shopper. It doesn't cost a penny to browse through the racks of Ralph Lauren, Donna Karan, and Calvin Klein designs, however, before skipping over to a thrift store to snag the bargain-priced originals that inspired their collections.
644 Broadway (at Bleecker St.), 473-9200, NR to 8th St., MC, V, AmEx, D, 6 to Bleecker St., BDFQ to Broadway/Lafayette St.

Betsey Johnson

In-your-face girly chic means Betsey's not afraid to flaunt lace alongside faux leather, or pair zebra stripes with fuchsia fishnets. Straightforward, sexy slip dresses are surprisingly affordable on sale. The store itself looks like some funky teenagers took a paintbrush to mom's boudoir.
138 Wooster St. (bet. Prince and Houston Sts.), 995-5048, MC, V, AmEx, NR to Prince St.

Blue

If Cinderella was set in modern-day downtown NYC, then her gown surely would have come from here. This shop offers one-of-a kind fancy dresses that fall somewhere between little girl fairy-tale fantasy and grown up chic. Definitely worth a look if there's an upcoming ball you want to be the belle of.
125 St. Mark's Pl. (bet. First Ave. and Avenue A), MC, V, AmEx, 6 to Astor Pl.ace

Calypso

Fun and funkily printed fabrics abound in this new clothing boutique which attempts to bring an international-island aesthetic to Little Italy. While the inspiration for the clothing styles may be other-wordly, though, the prices all-too-closely mirror those of fashion boutiques only blocks away in SoHo. Paradise doesn't come cheap, after all, for the true fashion elite.
280 Mott St. (bet. Prince and Houston Sts.), 965-0990, MC, V, AmEx, NR to Prince St.

Cynthia Rowley

Classic and simple designs, executed in extraordinary fabrics. The prices are relatively low for such an established designer, and much of the clothing comes in mix-and-match pieces, making it easy to achieve the look by integrating a splurge into your existing wardrobe.
112 Wooster St. (bet. Spring and Prince Sts.), 334-1144, MC, V, AmEx, NR to Prince St.

Czarina

Only enter with a full wallet and a penchant for baggy linens of the consciously bohemian variety. Morningside's only boutique, though the only thing useful to students is the expert seamstress.
2876 Broadway (bet. 112th and 113th Sts.), MC, V, AmEx, 19 to 116th St.

Dr. Jay's

Hip-hop heads of all flavas gather to purchase—or at least peruse—the latest styles of oversized ruffneck wear. Get your Fubu, Pelle Pelle, and Mecca all at the same time, while watching your wallet noticeably dwindle in thickness. Don't sleep on the occasional bargains. Two levels of hard-core trappings at both locations.
215 East Fordham Rd., (718) 220-3354, MC, V, D, AmEx, D to Fordham Rd. Also At *410 Westchester Ave., (718) 993-8008, MC, AmEx, D, V, 25 to Third Ave/149th St.*

Fab 208

The usual jeans, T-shirts, and tanks, all used, but unusually well-ordered. There's also an everything-for-$5 outlet down the street at number 117.
77 East 7th St.(bet. First and Second Aves.), 673-7581, MC, V, AmEx, 6 to Astor Pl.

150 shopping

French Connection

Modish store deftly blending '70s and '80s retro and classic clean lines to produce well-tailored but pricey clothes suitable for work and play. Seasonal sales yield bargains on silk weaves, linen, and slinky, quasi-Parisian dresses.
700 Broadway (at West 4th St.), 473-4486, MC, V, AmEx, D, ❶❷ *to 8th St.* ♿

Hyper Reality

Formerly an upscale boutique for those with lots of disposable income, the new incarnation is a downtown sample sale. It's a place to score new garb from names like John Bartlett, Rebecca Danenberg, Stephanie Plassier, and Kanae & Onyx at bargain prices. Join the mailing list or just stop by and take a gander at the affordable (yet still hip and trendy) new look. Or visit its sister store, appropriately named Downtown Sample Sale, located at 212 West 35th Street.
204 Seventh Ave. (bet. 21st and 22nd Sts.), 620-8180, MC, V, AmEx, ❶❷ *to 23rd St.*

INA

This designer consignment store features a big selection of men and women's clothing from current collections to designer vintage. First-time shoppers fast become regulars to the cozy neighborhood store. Find designer items by Prada, Helmut Lang, Agnès B. and Joseph at a 1/4 to 1/2 the price. Visit their Website at: www.citysearch.com/ina
21 Prince St. (bet. Mott and Elizabeth Sts.), 334-9048, MC, V, AmEx ATM, ❶❷ *to Prince St. or* ❻ *to Spring St.*

Label

Innovative designs line either side of this narrow hallway of a shop. The feel is revolutionary with their own signature merchandise sporting silk screens of hand grenades and Patty Hearst, a color scheme that leans toward paramilitary olives, khakis and blues and style that seems downright anarchic when compared to more established designers.
265 Lafayette St. (bet Prince and Spring), 966-7736, MC, V, AmEx, ❶❷❹❺❻ *to Spring St.*

Liquid Sky

Extremely trendy T-shirts and other merchandise made from mysterious synthetics, all featuring the telltale robot logo, the Polo alligator of the skate-rat and club-kid crowd. A sheet of falling water graces the window and the resident DJ spins raver tunes.
241 Lafayette St. (bet. Prince and Spring Sts.), 343-0532, MC, V, AmEx, ❻ *to Bleecker St.*

Living Doll

Plenty of throwbacks to the "80s chic" pioneered by Madonna at fair prices, perfect for young SoHo migrants on the east side of Broadway.
49 Prince St. (bet. Lafayette and Mulberry Sts.), 966-5494, MC, V, AmEx, ❶❷ *to Prince St.*

Lord of the Fleas

So popular that they're currently operating several outlets within spitting distance of each other. This is the place to go to add a few trendy pieces to your existing wardrobe or to find something appropriate for a night of club-hopping. The prices and quality are both generally pretty low which is ideal for stuff that's in now but probably won't be next year.
305 East 9th St. (bet. First and Second Aves.). 260-9130, MC, V, AmEx, D, ❻ *to Astor Pl., two other locations, Downtown and Upper West Side*

Love NYC

Designer Rose Baron dresses playful young women in style. Camisoles, capris, and peasant tops all made from versatile materials make up the well-priced line. A busy and popular place, it appeals to locals and tourists alike.
214 Sullivan St. (bet. Bleecker and West 3rd St.), 473-2251, ❶❷❸ ❹❺❻ *to West 4th St./Washington Square*

Mara the Cat

Sparkling dresses and other semifancy, sophisticated women's clothes set the tone at this tiny boutique.
406 East 9th St. (at First Ave.), 614-0331, MC, V, AmEx, D, ❻ *to Astor Pl.* ♿

Max + Roebling

Showcase for some of New York's hippest young designers, including Cake and Living Doll, with prices that even Williamsburg's starving artists can swing.
189 Bedford Ave. (bet. North 6th and North 7th Sts.), (718) 387-0045, MC, V, AmEx, D, Diners, ❶ *to Bedford Ave.*

Meghan Kinney

Just finding this tiny side-street store makes you feel privy to some sort of secret; while Kinney has been executing her clean, just-short-of-being-overly-trendy designs for years, she's still a relative unknown. Gunmetal synthetics and sleek, sexy dresses are several of her trademarks.
312 East 9th St. (bet. First and Second Aves.), 260-6329, ❻ *to Astor Pl.*

Mister Roger

"Italian styles for men" is the only way to view this small boutique. Prices are steep, but the establishment has managed to maintain a beautiful day in the neighborhood, having been around for almost ten years.
565 West 181st St. (bet. St. Nicholas and Audobon Aves.), 795-1774, MC, AmEx, D, V, ❶❾ ❿ *to 181st St.*

MONY

Brightly lit fashion outlet serves as singular female counterpart to Dr. Jays. The store's general layout and emphasis on designer labels with a street edge gives off an East Village feel. Make sure to check out the still-stylish reduced price items.
250 West 125th St. (bet. Adam Clayton Powell, Jr. Blvd. and Eighth Ave.), 665-2606, MC, AmEx, D, V, ❶❷❸❹❺ *to 125th St.*

Oriental Dress Company

Step inside and you'll be greeted by bolt after bolt of colorful silk brocade. The tailor will custom-make you a Chinese dress that fits like a glove for between $100-$250, depending on the type of silk you select. This service is a rarity in the U.S.—custom tailors are usually available only in China and Hong Kong.
38 Mott St. (at Pell St.), 349-0818, Cash Only, ❶❷❸ *to Grand St.*

shopping 151

Patricia Field's
Revel in the fuzzy fuchsia carpet, thick as grass, the lime-green metallic hot pants, and black beehive wigs at this double-storied commercial playland for NYU students planning their weekends. They flock here for the shiniest, boldest, most daring, iridescent, and indulgent club gear on the market, including wigs, polyester, leather, vinyl, leopard print, glitter, and even cosmetics designed for those who like to pump up the volume and deflate their wallets.
10 East 8th St. (bet. Fifth Ave. and University Pl.), 254-1699, MC, V, AmEx, D, ❽❾ to 8th St.

Phat Farm
A hip-hop house of style, where extra-large is the size of choice and clothing's executed well enough to earn the Farm its SoHo digs.
129 Prince St. (bet. West Broadway and Wooster St.), 533-7428, MC, V, AmEx, ❽❾ to Prince St. ♿

Shine
This place is very picky about what they take in, so you're sure to find a lot of moderately priced, trendy stuff in great condition. There are plenty of antique slip dresses and skirts in every color starting at $24, plus polyester shirts, dresses and shoes. Patiently shift through the small selection and you will go home in style.
159 1/2 Ludlow St. (bet. Stanton and Rivington Sts.), 539-1761, V, MC, D, ❼ to Second Ave.

Smylonylon
Old, long-warehoused '70s leftovers and tacky/trendy cheap synthetic clothes find both a market and a mark-up inside this ornate Lafayettte storefront. Fans range from ultra-hip club kids to funky designers seeking inspiration in the shimmering sea of lycra.
222 Lafayette St. (bet. Spring and Broome Sts.), MC, V, AmEx, D, ❻ to Spring St.

Stüssy
Skater-surfer gear with a west-coast feel endures here. It's still cool to have a T-shirt that reads "Stussy" so go ahead and invest.
104 Prince St. (bet. Mercer and Greene Sts.), 274-8855, MC, V, AmEx, ❽❾ to Prince St. ♿

TG-170
The most sophisticated of the small boutiques on the Ludlow strip features simple dresses, skirts, and tops in subtle but fashionably retro designs, as well as phat Freitag bags and wallets; gentrification hasn't hit the relatively cheap prices yet.
170 Ludlow St. (bet. Houston and Stanton Sts.), 995-8660, MC, V, AmEx, ❼ to Second Ave.nue ♿

Urban Outfitters
This hipster playground for the post-mall generation packs its industrial-esque interior with racks of multicolored, funky kid fashion, suitable for an array of day or evening urban outings. Weave through aisles of vintage clothing, sassy sundresses, and trendy housewares while swaying to the smooth rhythms of ambient music played in the background.
374 Sixth Ave. (at Waverly Pl.), 677-9350, MC, V, AmEx, ❶❷❸❹❺❻❼ to
West 4th St.
Also at
127 East 59th St. (bet. Park and Lexington Aves.), MC, V, AmEx, ❹❺❻❽❾ to 59th St.

Wu Wear
Wu-tang Clan, the premier rap group of Staten Island, have placed themselves on the fashion map with their own offerings of active menswear. View the platinum albums of Ol' Dirty Bastard and Method Man alongside brightly hued jackets and oversized denim. Prices are moderate, at least for designer labels.
61A Victory Blvd. (at Montgomery), (718) 720-9043, MC, AmEx, D, V, ❶❾ to South Ferry, ❽❾ to Whitehall St./ South Ferry, then take Staten Island Ferry, then take S67, S61, or S48 to Montgomery

X-Large
One stop shopping for homeboy staples like baggy designer jeans, jackets, T-shirts, baseball caps, and sneakers, mostly from the store label, are sold at this small boutique, which is owned in part by Beastie Boy Mike D.
267 Lafayette (bet. Prince and Spring Sts.), 334-4480, MC, V, AmEx, ❻❽❾ to Broadway/Lafayette, ❽❾ to Prince St. ♿

Vintage:
Alice Underground
Behind the hippie-ish exterior is one of Manhattan's biggest and best vintage stores. Skip the bargain bins as there's usually a good reason why the items are being unloaded for so cheap, and shell out a little more for pants and jackets off the racks, where the finds can range from the fabulously unique to solid standards. An excellent selection of winter coats.
481 Broadway (bet. Grand and Broome Sts.), 431-9067, MC, V, AmEx, ❽❾ to Prince St. ♿

Andy's Chee-Pees
Don't expect the store to live up to its name. Despite its extensive collection of vintage apparel, it hardly offers bargains, and caters more to French Connection shoppers who wander across the street, than to retro diehards. Worth a look.
691 Broadway (at West 4th St.), 420-5980, MC, V, ❽❾ to 8th St.
16 West 8th St. (bet. Fifth and Sixth Aves.)

Annex Antique Fair & Flea Market
This weekend market is too fashionable for true bargains, but it's still the best and biggest in town. The good stuff is often snapped up before dawn, but as the day wears on, the bargaining begins to favor the buyer. The main market has spawned smaller versions in nearby garages, creating an urban yard-sale effect.
Sixth Ave. (bet. 25th and 26th Sts.), Cash Only, ❶❾ to 28th St. ♿

Beacon's Closet
Many of the hipsters of Williamsburg are avid thrift shoppers and this is the neighborhood outlet for such diversions. A wide assortment of used clothing fills the racks and it doesn't take too much hunting to find something really nice like a suede jacket or a pair of perfectly worn boot-cut Wranglers. The prices tend

152 shopping

to be a little expensive for Brooklyn, but are still about one-third what you'd pay in Manhattan. Plus, they'll buy your unwanted clothes or take them in trade.
110 Bedford Ave. (at North 11th St.), (718) 486-0816, MC, V, AmEx, Diners, ❶ to Bedford Ave.

Canal Jean Co. Inc.
With its well-known checkered flag visible blocks away, this multi-level specialty in discount brand names (such as Levis) carries more than enough merchandise to satisfy the picky shopper. Calvin Klein underwear, Lip Gloss Dresses, and plenty of vintage clothes and jeans crowd the place. Check out the huge, overwhelming downstairs selection of used clothes.
504 Broadway (bet. Spring and Broome Sts.), 226-1130, MC, V, AmEx, D, Diners, ❶❷ to Prince St.

Cheap Jack's
Don't be fooled by the name of this groovy vintage store because the place is anything but cheap. Browse through the vast selection of plain and Hawaiian-style shirts, one-of-a-kind coats, and '60s- and '70s-style dresses on the first floor, and then head downstairs where myriads of jeans reside. Clothes are very expensive, but patience and a keen eye may lead to a heavenly bargain.
841 Broadway (bet. 13th and 14th Sts.), 777-9564, MC, V, AmEx, ❶❷❸ ❹❺❻ to Union Sq.

Cherry
All the vintage clothing from the '30s to early '80s, is "classy," "elegant," "sexy," and "far out." There

is a heavy emphasis on '60s and '70s minimalist styles from swimsuits to night-wear, plus designer pieces by Rudi Gernreich (a radical '60s designer), Gucci, and Bob Mackie. You can also find "space-age biomorphic design" furniture and home accessories such as lamps, phones, speakers, and sculpture.
185 Orchard St. (Bet. Houston and Stanton Sts.), 358-7131, MC, V, AmEx, D, ❻ to Second Avenue

Church Street Surplus
The place for all of your funky army navy needs, there's also a large selection of vintage clothing.
327 Church St., (bet. Canal and White Sts.) 226-5280, MC, V, AmEx, D, ❶❷❸❹❺ to Canal St.

Domsey's
This king of Brooklyn thrif shopping sells used clothing bu the piece, but the sheer size of the selection coupled with low prices continue to make it worth a trip down to Williamsburg. Check out their excellent shoe selection and "downstairs" separtment where housewears and cosmetics can be found at warehouse prices.
431 Kent Ave. (bet. South 9th and South 10th Sts.) (718)384-6000, Cash Only, ❶❷❸ to Marcy Ave.

Manny's Closet
Opposite the Fashion Institute of Technology, the rainbow assortment of plastic party wear here is appropriately located.
275 Seventh Ave. (bet. 25th and 26th Sts.), 463-8203, MC, V, AmEx, ❶❷ to 28th St.

Metropolis
Ideal thrift shopping that's close as it gets to fool-proof while maintaining reasonable prices. Large stock of whatever's trendy at the moment and more unique items that won't leave you looking like a fashion victim.
96 Avenue B (bet. 6th and 7th Sts.), 477-3941, ❶ to Second Avenue

Rose Is Vintage
The quirky stock is a joy to behold, though browsing takes a little more commitment, since clothes vary largely in quality and the turnover is high.
96 East 7th St. (at First Ave.), 533-8550, Cash Only, ❻ to Astor Pl.

The Salvation Army Thrift Store
All the great bargains one would expect form a true thrift store. Many of the real bargains are hidden though, so allow ample time to search for that just right item
34-02 Steinway St. (at 34th Ave.), Long Island City, (718) 472-2414, Cash Only, ❶❷ to Steinway St.

Screaming Mimi
One of the sassiest vintage boutiques, fashion here ranges from creative to indulgent; lots of cords, bellbottoms, funky prints, and slinky lingerie. Everything is in excellent shape, having been hand-selected, and old shoes and purses help ensure your accessories match your outfit.
382 Lafayette (bet. 4th and Great Jones Sts.), 677-6464, MC, V, AmEx, D, Diners, ❻ to Astor Pl., ❶❷ to 8th St.

Stella Dallas
Small, unpretentious boutique boasts a choice selection of vintage clothing from the 1930s to 1950s at somewhat more contemporary process.
218 Thompson St. (bet. Bleecker and West 3rd Sts.), 674-0447, MC, V, AmEx, ❶❷ to 8th St., ❶❷❸❹❺❻❼ to West 4th Street

Ugly Luggage
An interesting smattering of vintage clothes, furniture, and housewares along with the funky old suitcases that give the place its name fill about three-quarters of this hole-in-the-wall. The rest is reserved for their usedbook selection, which resembles a yard sale at the home of a voracious but indiscriminate reader, offering everything from laughable self-help books to hardback literature to trashy pulp fiction at prices cheap enough to make it hard not to take something home.
214 Bedford Ave. (bet. North 5th and North 6th Sts.), MC, V, AmEx, ❶ to Bedford Ave.

COMPUTING

Excel Computer and Software
All sorts of hardware (and software) is sold at this Silicon Alley resource amid other space-age must-haves like cellular phones and beepers.
401 Park Avenue South (at 28th St.), 684-6930, MC, V, AmEx, ❻ to 28th St.

Datavision
Mac owners should stop here first when in need of a spare part or assistance. The two-level store is a bit difficult to navigate, but

shopping 153

the ubiquitous staff is happy to help with even the most far-out requests. They will order parts not in stock.
445 Fifth Ave. (bet. 39th and 40th Sts.), 689-1111, MC, V, AmEx, Diners, D, ❹❺❻ to Grand Central

COSMETICS

Face Stockholm Ltd.
With MAC right up the street, the situation seems too close for comfort, though this England-based company excels at the basics. Personal attention is easy to come by within the airy boutique; the $8 nail polish selection makes you wish you had more fingers.
110 Prince St. (at Greene St.), 334-3900, MC, V, AmEx, ❶❷ to Prince St. ♿

Kiehl's
The friendly staff starts unloading free samples on you once you demonstrate interest. Since 1851, this family-owned body care company has been selling top-quality lotions, shampoos, cosmetics, and soaps in utilitarian packaging. Ingredients are all-natural, and excellent personal service make premium prices worth the investment.
109 Third Ave. (bet. 13th and 14th Sts.), 677-3171, MC, V, AmEx, D, Diners, ❶ to Third Ave. ♿

MAC Cosmetics
Makeup straight from Canada and cruelty-free to boot., SoHoites and daytime shoppers are more than willing to pay the price for the name and the creamy and metallic signature look. Drag queen Lady Bunny used to give consultations here.
113 Spring St. (at Mercer St.), 334-4641, MC, V, AmEx, D, ❶❷to Prince St.

Manic Panic
Feel like going a little crazy? This store's got everything you'll need—hair dyes, face paints and glitter, glitter, glitter.
62 White St. (bet. Church St. and Broadway) 941-0656, MC, V, AmEx, ❶❷ to Canal St.

USA Beauty Corp.
A tiny cosmetic boutique offers a decadent selection of Asian beauty products, including creations by Shiseido, the ultra-hip Japanese company.
6 Elizabeth St. (bet. Baxter and Canal Sts.), ❶❷ to Canal St., MC, V, ❶❷❸❹ to Grand St.

DEPARTMENT STORES:

Barney's
Power dressers, and those looking for something more elegant, put dents in their substantial bank accounts at this airy, beautiful legend, which still holds its head high despite the recent Chelsea-branch closure. Head to the top floor for the lowest prices and most casual wear.
660 Madison Ave. (at 61st St.), 826-8900, MC, V, AmEx, ❶❷ to Fifth Ave. ♿

Bergdorf Goodman
Tour the museum-quality merchandise worthy of its chandelier and marble surroundings in this home of high fashion. To actually purchase something, leave the clientele of wealthy Upper East Siders behind and travel to the fifth floor where less expensive (though still somewhat pricey) sportswear abounds. All cash and credit card transactions occur in a "back room"

whose doors blend with the walls. Window displays here are among Fifth Avenue's finest.
754 Fifth Ave. (at 58th St.), 753-7300, MC, V, AmEx, D, ❶❷ to Fifth Avenue

Bergdorf Goodman for Men
One of the few department stores that gives expert attention to men, this elegant standard shows awareness of its worth in its prices. If not to buy something, go for the amusement of seeing reluctant young boys with Roman numerals attached to their names getting fully outfitted.
745 Fifth Ave. (at 58th St.), 753-7300, MC, V, AmEx, D, ❶❷ to Fifth Avenue

Bloomingdale's
Although the trademark perfume arcade is usually a zoo, the upper floors are open, bright, and filled with helpful salespeople eager to successfully match people with outfits bearing three-digit price tags.
1000 Third Ave. (bet. 59th and 60th Sts.), 705-2000, MC, V, AmEx, ❶❷❸❹❺❻ to 59th St. and Lexington Avenue ♿

Green Acres Mall
Casual-wear reigns at this retail conglomerate that is technically in Nassau County. A couple of major department stores (Sears and Macy's) are thrown in to complement the smaller-scaled shops. Sunrise Highway (bet. Mill Rd. and Hook Creek Blvd.), (516) 561-1157, ❶❷ to Jamaica/Sutphin Blvd., then Q5 to Green Acres Mall

Henri Bendel
Absolutely the plushest shopping experience around; artist Marie-Paulle Pelle's elegant staircase winds its way up through the many-storied townhouse, and designer James Mansour maintains the splendor of Bendel's original boutiques while incorporating modern accents. Same type of clothing as Bergdorf's or Saks, but somehow classier.
714 Fifth Ave. (at 56th St.), 247-1100, MC, V, AmEx, D, ❹❺❻❶❷ to 56th Street

Macy's
"The Largest Store in the World" often resembles the chaos of the Thanksgiving Day parade they sponsor, especially after work and around Christmas. Most items are lower priced than other department stores, but the service and bathrooms reflect this reduction.
34th St. (at Broadway), 695-440, MC, V, AmEx, ❶❷❸❹❺❻ to 34th/Herald Square ♿

Macy's
Parkchester inhabitants do not take this micro-version of the world's largest store for granted. Hours and attitude are pleasantly divergent from Manhattan's faster-paced main location.
1441 Metropolitan Ave., (718) 828-7000, MC, AmEx, V, D, ❻ to Parkchester/East 177th St.

Macy's
Unbeknownst to many, a five-story Macy's is tucked away on the Fulton pedestrian mall. Though not as vast as its famous Herald Square cousin, it does boast a large men's and women's section, plus a

floor devoted to home furnishings.
420 Fulton St. (bet. Hoyt and Elm Sts.), (718) 875-7200, MC, V, AmEx, ❷❸ *to Hoyt St.*

Manhattan Mall
A mall! In Manhattan! Its dominating presence highlighted in glass and neon incites feelings of either veneration or loathing. Billed as having the "Largest food court in New York City!" and with Sterns as its anchor store, how could it not incite strong emotions?
33rd St. and Sixth Ave., payments vary with establishment, ❻❼❽❾❿⓫ *to 34th St./Herald Square* &

Mart 125
Enclosed, but far too interesting to feel like a mall, this neighborhood staple sells African dress, crafts, cosmetics, and accessories. The food court upstairs offers good, reasonably priced soul food.
260 West 125th St. (bet. A.C. Powell and Frederick Douglass Blvds.), 316-3340, payments accepted vary with vendor; ❶❾ *to 125th St.* &

Pearl River Mart
Sort of like a Chinese Woolworth, this two-floored department store stocks everything its American counterpart does, with a twist: bamboo mats, bedding supplies, electronics, video rentals, a minigrocery section, and traditional cookware.
277 Canal St. (at Broadway), 431-4770, MC, V, AmEx, ❶❷ *to Canal St.* &

Saks Fifth Avenue
This classy store makes for great, if somewhat dizzying, browsing. Window displays make the Fifth Avenue promenade a bit more exciting; Salvador Dali reputedly crashed his car into one of them after artists didn't execute his design well enough.
611 Fifth Ave. (bet. 49th and 50th Sts.), 753-4000, MC, V, AmEx, D, Diners, ❶❷❸❹ *to 47th-50th St./Rockefeller Center* &

Staten Island Mall
Truly massive shopping centers are rare in New York City, perhaps making this overwhelmingly vast retail arena a necessary part of Staten Island's business pool. Most stores fall into the category of standard mall fare, making the unusual unwelcome.
2655 Richmond Ave., (718) 761-6800, ❶❾ *to South Ferry,* ❶❷ *to Whitehall St./South Ferry, take Staten Island Ferry, then take* S61 *or* S44 *(scenic route) to mall*

GIFTS

Balaman Gallery
Unique American trinkets, from classically traditional wooden toys to refined wine bottle holders reinvented to keep the leisure hours of uptown residents necessarily well-occupied at home.
1031 Lexington Ave. (at 74th St.), 472-8366, MC, V, AmEx, ❻❼ *to 77th St.*

Burlington Antique Toys
Toy soldiers and other war miniatures for the collector and fanatic, though there's not much here you'd actually want to play with.
1082 Madison Ave. (bet. 81st and 82nd Sts.), 861-9708, MC, V, AmEx, ❻ &

Card-o-Mat
This card-filled cubbyhole can come up with a sentimental rhyme or a witty remark for any occasion. Don't miss the "Mr. Bean" fill-in-the-blank birthday cards.
2884 Broadway (at 112th St.), 663-2085, MC, V, ❶❾ *to 110th St.* &

Dö Kham
Handcrafted Tibetan housewares, gifts, and trinkets for selling at prices that are prone to upset the spiritual balance of even the most calm.
51 Prince St., 966-2404, ❶❷ *to Prince St.*

E. Rossi & Co.
The king of random Little Italy souvenir shops. Dust-covered merchandise, from huge neon plastic piggy banks to Pope keychains, clutter the store.
191 Grand St. (at Mulberry St.), 966-6640, MC, V, ❶❷❸ *to Grand St.*

Exit 9
A great gift selection no matter whom you need to buy for. There are lovely candle holders and picture frames for tame tastes, funky knickknacks and odd books for strange tastes, and a selection of flasks, cigarette cases, and lighters for self-destructive tastes. Simply categorize your friends and family and never worry about shopping for them again.
64 Avenue A (bet. 4th and 5th Sts.), 228-0145, MC, V, AmEx, D, ❻ *to Second Ave.*

C·A·R·D·O·M·A·T

2884 Broadway at 112th Street
212-663-2085

"Simply the best"

as seen in N.Y. Magazine

Unique selection of cards, stationary, special gifts for special people

WE PROCESS AND SELL FILM

shopping 155

Forzano Italian Imports
Aging and sun-stained souvenirs that may have actually been imported when the store first opened. Pick between large selections of Italian records, cookbooks, and 1970s greeting cards which were apparently passed over before their shelf life expired.
128 Mulberry St. (at Hester St.), 925-2525, MC, V, AmEx, D, Diners, ❶❿❷❻ to Canal St.

Gates of Marrakesh
Handmade Moroccan lamps, tapestries, cups, and other miscellaneous items at decent prices. Henna painting every Saturday and Sunday from 11am-7pm. Call for an appointment.
8 Prince St. (bet. Bowery and Elizabeth St.), 925-4104, MC, V, AmEx, ❻❻ to Prince St.

Little Ricky's
Magic water flowers, giant eyeballs, Betty Boop ring watches, penis pasta, fake tattoos... all the junk you could possibly need can be found at this entertaining and quirky gift store.
49-1/2 First Ave. (at 3rd St.), 505-6467, MC, V, AmEx, Diners, ❻ to Second Avenue

Museum of Modern Art Design Store
After finishing at the MoMA, browse through this delightful potpourri of slickly designed domestic items. Lamps, chairs, kitchen items, games—it feels like a toy store for adults.
44 West 53rd St. (bet. Fifth and Sixth Aves.), 767-1050, MC, V, AmEx, ❻❻ to Fifth Ave.

NBC Studio Gift Store
"ER" doctor's aprons, "Frasier" mugs, and teddy bears sporting "Seinfeld" T-shirts can be found at this network memorabilia shop.
50 Rockefeller Center (at 49th St. and Sixth Ave.), 664-4444, MC, V, AmEx, D, ❻❿❻❻ to 42nd St.

Our Name is Mud
Paint your own pottery at this cool little store. Up front is a gallery with finished "functional" pieces like mugs, vases, planters, frames and pitchers in bright colors. After a little instruction you can move to the back, pick your own unfinished piece and, for $5 per 1/2 hour, paint it yourself; perfect for private parties, bridal showers, and birthdays. They also offer nine week hand-building courses for $215. Thursdays from 5-10pm is adult night (no kids allowed) where you can bring in your own wine or beer and paint till you drop. (Call for other locations.)
59 Greenwich Ave. (at Seventh Ave.) 647-7899, MC, V, AmEx, ❶❾❷❸ to 14th St.

St. John the Divine Gift Shop
Everything from cathedral paraphernalia to weird souvenirs. Find fascinating gifts for all ages or read up on mysticism and ecology. A complete collection by Madeleine L'Engle, the writer in residence, also graces the store. The perfect gift shop.
Cathedral of St. John the Divine (112th St. and Amsterdam Ave.), 222-7200, MC, V, AmEx, D, ❶❾ to 110th St.

The Sharper Image
Should be named "insanely expensive gadgets you don't need," this store specializes in items for rich, bored people. Pick up a nose-hair trimmer for daddy. Most people treat the store like a museum, browsing and leaving empty-handed. Try the massage chair; it'll relax you after a hard day.
89 Fulton St. (Pier 17, South St. Seaport), 693-0477, MC, V, AmEx, Diners, ❷❸ to Fulton St.

Whitney Museum Store
Postcards, doo-dads, and other art-inspired objects make shopping here, especially for gifts, a fun time. After a visit to the museum drop by the "store next door."
943 Madison Ave. (bet. 74th and 75th Sts.), 606-0200, ❹❺❻ to 77th St.

The Windmill Shoppe
Greeting cards typically fall into one of two categories: mortifyingly tacky or cheesy. The Windmill tries hard to stock something a bit different, and often succeeds.
131 Seventh Ave. (bet. Carroll and Garfield Sts.), (718) 857-7223, Cash Only, ❻❼ to Seventh Ave., ❷❸ to Bergen St.

Wind Water
Though not much in this hip knickknack shop is actually made out of plastic, it still serves a purpose as one-stop birthday shopping; jewelry, cards, books, bath items, and the like.
2115 Broadway (at 74th), 362-1000, MC, V, AmEx, ❶❷❸❾ to 72nd St.

GROCERY

A.L. Bazzini
Primarily nut importers, the shop offers a huge variety of them for sale alongside dried fruits and other specialty items, including gift baskets. For cheap fun, stop by for a look around and treat yourself to an ice cream cone.
91 East 3rd St. (bet. First and Second Aves.), 260-8729, MC, V, AmEx, D, ❻ to Second Ave.

Alleva Dairy, Inc.
Third-generation owner, Bob Alleva, serves up hot and cold sandwiches for under $5, authentic enough to keep the idea of Little Italy respectable. Mozzarella is made fresh daily at the oldest Italian cheese store in America.
188 Grand St. (at Mulberry St.), 226-7990, MC, V, AmEx, ❻❻ to Prince St.

Balducci's
A shrine to the art of fine dining which provides all manner of gourmet foods, from produce to baked goods, to specialized deli entrées, dinners, and sandwiches. Join the downtown elite and indulge in one of the delicacies.
424 Sixth Ave. (at 9th St.), 673-2600, MC, V, AmEx, ❶❷❸❹❺❻ to West 4th Street

Blanche's Organic Take-Away
A menu loaded with macro goodies and vegan specialties is not all this corner nook has to offer. Pro-veggie paraphernalia lines the wall and fresh juices and shakes are made to stay, or to go.
972 Lexington Ave. (at 71st St.), 717-1923, ❹❺❻ to 68th. St.

156 shopping

Bonté
Patisserie with tarts, cakes, cookies, and scrumptious Parisian-style coffee eclairs, among other guilty pleasures. Orders are welcome.
1316 Third Ave. (bet. 74th and 75th Sts.), 535-2360, Cash Only, 6 *to 77th St.* &

Brooklyn Brewery
New York's closest approximation to a hometown beer is brewed here, and on weekends they open the place up. That means free brewery tours, beer tastings and merchandise for sale. The hats and T-shirts make excellent gifts for any beer lover on your list. They've recently begun using the space as a gallery and performance space as well, making this a perfect day of cheap fun for a variety of different tastes.
North 11th St., Brooklyn (bet. Barry and Wyeth Sts.), (718) 486-7422, MC, V, AmEx, L *to Bedford Ave.nue*

Chinatown Ice Cream Factory
Try flavors like lychee, papaya, almond cookie, and ginger which you won't find in any other ice cream shop in NY; as creamy as they are exotic.
65 Bayard St. (bet. Mott and ElizabethSts.), 608-4170, Cash Only J M N R Z *to Canal St.*

Citarella
Well-known for its amazingly fresh seafood, which includes octopus, sword fish, and other hard-to-find specialties, this clean, bright, meat and fish deli supplies many of the area restaurants.
2135 Broadway (at 75th St.), 874-0383, MC, V, AmEx, 1 2 3 9 *to 72nd Street* &

Confucious Plaza Vendors
Be prepared to wait in long lines for up to twenty minutes at this outdoor market where fresh produce is sold in bulk poundage. Nowhere else, though, could you get two pounds of specialty mushrooms for only $1, or three pounds of broccoli for $1.50.
Bowery (at Division St.), Cash Only, B D Q *to Grand St.*

The Damascus Bread & Pastry Shop Ltd.
The hands-down best pita bread in Brooklyn, which has caught on recently in Manhattan supermarkets. But why not buy it fresh here, where a six-pack goes for 55¢, and other staff-of-life items are equally cheap.
195 Atlantic Ave., (718) 625-7070, V, AmEx, 2 3 *to Borough Hall/Court St.*

D&G Bakery
If you're looking for fresh, thick-crusted Italian bread, this is the place to find it. They've been baking bread daily here since 1963. The earlier you get here the better as they often run out by closing time at 2pm.
45 Spring St. (Mulberry St.) 925-1947, Cash Only, 6 *to Spring St.*

Dean & Deluca
One of New York's most revered specialty food stores, the Zabars of downtown. Stop by for a caffeine break at the stand-up espresso bar, pick up some pate for your next dinner party, and ogle the produce section, full of fruits and vegetables suitable for a still-life masterpiece. They also offer specialty breads, meats, cheeses, desserts, and quality packaged foods. If you have to bring a special addition to a dinner or an impressive hostess gift, come here.
560 Broadway (at Prince St.), MC, V, AmEx, D, N R *to Prince St.,* 6 *to Spring St.*

Di Palos' Fine Foods
Has everything you'll need when you're planning an Italian feast. The guys who work here are charming and will help you choose the ingredients: fresh mozzarella, sun-dried tomatoes, sausages, bread etc. for what is sure to be an unforgettable meal.
206 Grand St. (at Mott St.) 226-1033, MC, V, AmEx, 6 *to Spring St.*

Dynasty Supermarket
One of Chinatown's largest supermarkets, boasting a full herb and medicine counter, an in-house butcher and fishmonger, a beef-jerky bar, and best of all, weekly sales.
68 Elizabeth St. (at Hester St.), 966-4943, MC, V, N R *to Prince St.,* B D Q *to Grand St.*

Economy Candy
Calling itself a "nosher's" paradise on the Lower East Side, this is the best discount store in the city for penny candy, imported chocolates, nuts, and sweets, and gourmet savories like mustards, chutney, tea, and spices. Try their dense, chewy, pistachio-laden Turkish delight, the most authentic this side of Byzantium.
108 Rivington St. (bet. Essex and Ludlow Sts.), 254-1832, MC, V, AmEx, F J *to Delancey St.* &

Elk Candy
Resist, if possible, the urge not to eat the cute, stylized candies crafted at this Yorkville landmark, renowned for more than sixty years for its marvelous marzipan.
240 East 86th (bet. Second and Third Aves.), 650-1177, V, MC, AmEx, 4 5 6 *to 86th St.*

Fairway
"Like no other market" reads the awning, and this is indeed the most popular, largest, and lowest-priced produce and gourmet market on the west side. A full deli counter offers prepared hot and cold dishes, the cheese department stocks an array of imports, and the bakery sells over a million bagels every year.
2328 Twelfth Ave. (at 133rd St.), 234-3883, 1 9 *to 125th. St.*

Garden of Eden Farmers Market
Fresh produce and gourmet foods are a welcome alternative to the corner store's offerings. Be prepared to pay for the quality however.
162 West 23rd St. (bet. Sixth and Seventh Aves.), 675-6300, MC, V, AmEx, 1 9 *to 23rd St.* &

Hong Kong Supermarket
In a slightly quieter corner of Chinatown, this supermarket carries a wide selection of Hong Kong and Taiwanese ex-pat foodstuffs. Indulge your sweet tooth with selections from the huge candy aisle, heavily stocked with fruit tablets, candies and jellies.
109 Broadway (at Allen St.), 227-3388/349-0607, MC, V, F *to East Broadway*

shopping 157

Italian Food Center
A grocery store saturated with the scents of Italian cheeses, coffees, and roasting garlic. Breads and sausages made fresh on the premises, combined with other foodstuffs, make for a scrumptious dinner. Don't miss the bruschetta baked with tomatoes, olive oil, garlic, and herbs.
186 Grand St. (at Mulberry St.), 925-2954, MC, V, AmEx, ❶❷ to Prince St.

Jamaica Market
While Harlem has Mart 125, Queens denizens can take pride in their own enclosed gathering of vendors and food stops. Tables for the lunch set are centered among booths that have everything from produce to picture frames. Also hosts to special events, such as stand-up comedy acts during evening hours.
90-40 160th St. (bet. Jamaica and Nintieth Aves.), (718) 291-0282, Alternate Entrance at 159-15 Jamaica Ave., (718), ❶❷❸ to Jamaica/Sutphin Blvd

Kam Kuo Food Corp.
A wide range of groceries and dry goods, including a wide selection of Chinese and Japanese candies and snacks. Herbs, roots, sauces, and a small selection of greens are available as well as ceramics and utensils.
7 Mott St. (at Divison St.), 349-3097, MC, V, ❶❷ to Canal St., ❶❷❸ to Grand Street

La Maison du Chocolat
As one might guess, chocolate is this store's specialty, and it comes in many shapes and sizes, none of which even approach being healthy or veer far from being absolutely divine.
25 East 73rd St., 744-7117, MC, V, AmEx, D, ❻ to 77th Street

La Piccola Cucina
Cramped little Italian grocery offers fresh pastas and delectable sauces that are well worth the splurge, as well as sandwiches and prepared (less-than-authentic) tiramisu.
2770 Broadway (bet. 106th and 107th Sts.), Cash Only, ❶❾ to 103rd St.

M. Rohrs Fine Teas & Coffee
Satiating the ever-fluctuating caffeine addictions of locals for over 100 years with its wide selection of refined tea leaves and coffee beans. Wooden counters and aged tea canisters with beveled mirrors also retain the shops original, old-world charm, an anomaly among slick new coffee bars.
303 East 85th St. (bet First and Second Aves.), 396-4456, MC, V, ❹❺❻ to 88th St.

McNulty's Tea and Coffee
Hear the soothing staccato of coffee beans cascading into brass scales in this dark, woodsy specialty shop, which boasts over 250 varieties of tea and coffee. Prices are competitive, ranging from $9 to $30 per pound. Mail order is available for far-flung java lovers.
109 Christopher St. (bet. Bleecker and Hudson Sts.), 242-5351, MC, V, AmEx, ❶❾ to Christopher St.

Mondel Chocolates
Florence Mondel has been catering to Morningside Heights chocoholics for more than 50 years. Her modest store is filled with homemade fudge and marzipan, as well as a dozen different kinds of truffles.
2913 Broadway (at 199th St.), 864-2111, V, MC, AmEx, ❶❾ to 116th St.

Mott Street
Chinatown's version of a mall, Mott Street is packed with tiny stores carrying everything from battery-operated bath toys to medicinal herbs. Stores usually sprawl out onto the sidewalks, with enthusiastic salespersons hawking their wares. Several dress stores are also hidden in shops beneath sidewalk level.
Mott St. (bet. Grand and Worth Sts.), Cash Only, ❶❷❸ to Grand St.

Piemonte Ravioli Company
When Ronzoni just won't do—this retail store sells every kind of homemade pasta and ravioli.
190 Grand St. (bet. Mott and Mulberry Sts.), 226-0475, MC, V, AmEx, ❻ to Spring St.

Porto Rico Importing Co.
Skip Starbucks and head instead to this downtown caffeine pit stop, where a wide variety of imported and specialty flavored coffee beans are sold by the pound.
201 Bleeker St. (bet. Sixth Ave and MacDougal St.), 477-5421, MC, V, ❶❷❸ ❹❺❻ to West 4th St.

Sea Grape Wines and Spirits
Boasts a very solid selection of French and Californian wines, with a friendly, helpful staff willing to give advice.
512 Hudson St. (bet. Christopher and 10th Sts.), 463-7688, MC, V, AmEx, ❶❾ to Christopher St.

Tamarind Seed Health Food
All the vitamins you'll ever need and rare vegetarian delights like veggie-bacon burgers. Both the salad and juice bars are the best in the neighborhood; you end up paying for quality, so stick to a grocery store for the basics.
2935 Broadway (bet. 114th and 115th Sts.), 864-3360, MC, V, AmEx, ❶❾ to 116th St.

Taylor's
One of the best things about life in the West Village. A fabulous selection of pastries, cakes, and other deserts, as well as soups and sandwiches. The scones can be amazing, but get there early in the morning, or your choices will be limited.
523 Hudson St. (bet. 10th and Charles Sts.), 378-2890, Cash Only, ❶❾ to Christopher St.

Ten Ren Tea and Ginseng Co., Inc.
Experience the art and healthfulness of an ancient art with a free, fresh-brewed cup of green tea. Sign up for free courses to learn about the history, art and brewing techniques of this age-old Chinese tradition.
75 Mott St. (near Canal St.), 349-2286, MC, V, AmEx, ❶❷❸ to Grand St.

Vendors at the Triangle at Canal and Baxter Streets

For fresh Chinese produce and tofu, the informal greenmarket squeezed onto this tiny concrete island will supply you with anything you need. Noodles and fresh juices are also occasionally sold. Vendors may not speak much English, so make sure your finger-counting skills are still in shape. *The triangle at the intersection of Canal, Baxter, and Centre Sts., Cash Only, NR to Canal, 6JM to Grand St.*

The Vinegar Factory

An ex-mustard and vinegar factory converted into a gourmet food warehouse with retail prices. Exotic imports such as Austrian ginger ice cream and white hot-chocolate mix from Belgium beckon from between stacks of fresh produce and gourmet delights prepared from recycled restaurant foods, gone unsold. *431 East 91st St. (bet. York and First Aves.), 987-0885, MC, V, AmEx, D, 456 to 86th St.*

Washington Market Park

An open-air farmer's market resplendent with produce, flowers, baked goods, and other delicious items. Organic items are also aplenty, as are the real-life farmers, who haul their wares from New Jersey and upstate New York. Open Saturdays, 8am-5pm, rain or shine. *Greenwich St. (at Reade St.), Cash Only, 239 to Chambers St.*

William Greenberg Jr. Desserts

A cute store with delicious desserts and service with a smile. To compensate for expense, they provide the best strawberry shortcake in the city and great black-and-white cookies. *1100 Madison Ave. (bet. 82nd and 83rd Sts.), 861-1340, MC, V, AmEx, D, 456 to 86th St.*

Zabar's

A name with impressive cachet in uptown circles, this longtime Upper West Side institution is the prime source for gourmet meats, cheese, breads, and produce. Upstairs is an equally well-stocked kitchenware department featuring at least 30 kinds of whisks. The store can get shoulder-to-shoulder crowded on the weekends and during the holidays. *2245 Broadway (at 80th St.), 787-2000, MC, V, AmEx, 19 to 79th St.*

HOUSEWARES

ABC Carpet and Home

Expect to find ample mother/daughter pairs ooh-ing and aah-ing their way through six floors of housewares, antiques, and knickknacks. Although fairly expensive, the store is worth a visit for its creative window displays and extraordinary finds such as a ten-foot tall gilded bird cage. The Parlour Café on the ground floor allows weary shoppers to lounge and lunch on the furniture that they can't afford to buy. *881 and 888 Broadway (at 19th St.), 473-3000, MC, V, AmEx, LNR456 to Union Square*

Atomic Passion

A fine selection of '50s artifacts that tread the thin line between antique and kitsch can be found here. The prices tend to be steep for bigger items like furniture or stuffed-and-mounted fish, but the smaller knickknacks are often cheap enough to take home and it's always fun to look. *430 East 9th St. (bet. First Ave. and Avenue A), 533-0718, MC, V, AmEx, 6 to Astor Pl., NR to 8th St.*

Depression Modern

Plush, beautiful furniture and housewares in retro styles make for great browsing, test-sitting, and daydreaming of a perfectly decorated home for anyone who longs for the era of their grandparents. It's all very expensive, but the people who run it are amiable and tolerant of browsers. *150 Sullivan St., 982-5699, Cash Only, 19 to Houston St.*

Dom

Need some inflatable furniture for your dorm room? Have a fondness for housewares made of neon-colored plastic? All that and plenty more for the home at this trendy decorator hot spot, as well as sundry other junk, from pens to pillboxes. Most of it is inexpensive and equally suitable for gift-giving or feeding your personal flair for home decorating. *382 West Broadway (bet. Spring and Broome Sts.), 334-5580, MC, V, AmEx, CE to Spring St., NR to Prince St.*

Fish's Eddy

This shop sells overstocks of commercial dishes and glasses, often bearing the logos of the restaurants or institutions from whence they came. Prices average about $10 for a dinner plate, but check the stacks along the walls for loose items priced below $5. *889 Broadway (at 19th St.), 420-9020, MC, V, AmEx, LNR456 to Union Square*

Also at:

2176 Broadway (at 77th St.), 873-8819, MC, V, AmEx, 19 to 79th St.

Glaubers

Shopper's hearts will shine as the golden glow of decorative items for the home dazzles the eyes. Old-style centerpieces can be bought for the parents while friends might enjoy the cute miniclocks and figure-laden picture frames. *560 West 181st St. (bet. St. Nicholas and Audobon Aves.), 927-5566, MC, AmEx, D, V, 19A to 181st St.*

Goodwill Superstore

Merchandise is in good condition and, of course, cheap. A little bit of pickiness can yield some exemplary results. *514 West 181st St. (bet. Audobon and Amsterdam Aves.), 923-7910, MC, AmEx, D, V, 19 to 181st St.*

Just Bulbs

The name really says it all. Find every variety of light bulb imaginable, including those for decoration, gifts, and specific holidays. *936 Broadway (bet. 21st and 22nd Sts.), 228-7820, MC, V, AmEx, D, Diners, NR to 23rd St.*

Manhattan Futon

Fair prices and a helpful staff compensate for the

shopping 159

small selection of various sized futons.
927 Broadway (bet. 21st and 22nd Sts.), 777-6413, MC, V, AmEx, D, ⓝⓡ to 23rd St.

McRae Furniture
Like a bazaar, the quality of this antique store's wares varies from piece to piece, credit is looked upon with suspicion, and no price is ever concrete—haggling is allowed. They buy furniture, also.
2 East 125th St. (bet. Fifth and Madison Aves.), 534-8404, Cash Only, ②③ to 125th St.

Mood Indigo
This is the first stop on the way to becoming a full-fledged member of cocktail culture. The whole idea is putting some classy retro style back into drinking, and martinis out of a plastic cup *simply* will not do. Fortunately, here they offer tons of authentic and unique glasses and accessories from the original cocktail era to choose from. It's all a little expensive, but think of it as investing in some valuable antiques.
181 Prince St. (bet. Thompson and Sullivan Sts.), MC, V, AmEx, ⓝⓡ to Prince St., ①⑨ to Houston Street

Pottery Barn
This chain apartment-and-home decorating store sells everything from colorful throw rugs to velvet and canvas wing chairs and sofas, all very stylish and (almos)t affordable for those with modest incomes.
1451 Second Ave. (near 76th St.), 988-4228, V, MC, AmEx, D, ⓺ to 77th St.

Urban Archaeology
The stock is sold both wholesale and retail at this furniture store, which houses a collection of architectural ornaments, artifacts, and lighting fixtures in the kitschy retro vein in what was once a four-story candy factory.
285 Lafayette St. (bet. Prince and Houston Sts.), 431-6969, ⓝⓡ to Prince St.

White Trash
From shiny silver toasters to impressively tacky glassware sets, your own grandmother probably got rid of '50s and '60s junk like this twenty years ago. Nevertheless, it's all hip again and the prices aren't too inflated to be a reasonable and interesting alternative to outfitting your home in Lechters standards. Also good for finding unique gifts.
304 East 5th St. (bet. First and Second Aves.), 598-5956, MC, V, ⓕ to Second Ave., ⓺ to Astor Pl.

Williams-Sonoma Outlet Center
Houseware standards from Pottery Barn, Gardener's Eden, Chambers, and Hold Everything at cut-rate prices fill the shelves at this warehouse. Real bargains on basics like plates and silverware, and some occasional furniture or decorating finds from Pottery Barn stock.
231 Tenth Ave. (bet. 23rd and 24th Sts.), 206-8118, MC, V, AmEx, D, ⓒⓔ to 23rd St.

MUSIC

Bleecker Bob's
Enough old school, punk, New York hard-core, and new wave records and CDs to find an old pressing of Stranglers or Television records. This refreshingly ugly music warehouse is a prime locale for trashy rock-n-roll, but offers next to nothing this side of 1985.
118 West 3rd St. (bet. Sixth Ave. and MacDougal St.), 475-9677, MC, V, ($25 minimum) ⓐⓑⓒⓓⓕⓠ to West 4th St.

Bleecker Street Records
The best selection of oldies and crooners from the 50s. It can be pricey, but isn't Frank worth the price?
239 Bleecker (at Sixth Ave.), 255-7899, MC, V, Am Ex, ⓐⓑⓒⓓⓔⓕⓠ to West 4th St.

Chelsea Second Hand Guitars
Just window shopping is enough to make Eddie Van Halen drool. Strats, Les Pauls, Fenders, just name it. "Anything you're looking for, we can find through our network," boasts the dude at the counter. Go in and try one on for size. Vintage guitars for the finger-picking connoisseur.
220 West 23rd St. (bet. Seventh and Eighth Aves.), 675-4993, Cash Only, ①⑨ to 23rd St.

Colony
One of the best resources for everything from CDs to sheet music. The staff will order esoteric titles, and those still trying to carry on their love affair with vinyl will happily find a decent selection of records in the same room as such memorabilia as signed guitars.
1619 Broadway (at 49th St.), 265-2050, MC, V, AmEx, D, ⓝⓡ to 49th St. or ①⑨ to 50th St.

Dance Tracks
Domestic house and acid jazz, as well as remarkably cheap Euro imports. Classic dance cuts for collectors to catch up on.
91 East 3rd St. (at First Ave.), 260-8729, ⓕ to Second Avenue

Disc-o-Rama
Behind the unassuming storefront lies a deceptively large and varied stock, with jazz, rock, world, rap, country and western, R&B, and more. Stock arrangement is somewhat haphazard and cluttered, but a little diligent searching will most likely yield a well-priced find. The staff isn't particularly helpful, but since the top thirty CDs in every genre are always $9.99, deals are easy to find.
186 West 4th St. (bet. Sixth and Seventh Aves.), 206-8417, MC, V, ⓝⓡ to 8th St.

Earwax
Genres ranging from the typical rock-n-roll and jazz, to space-age ambient and electronic music are well-represented here in the selection of both new and used CDs. The selection is both much larger and more comprehensive than you'd ever expect, considering its small size and Brooklyn location. They also offer an extensive assortment of vinyl that brings in serious record-hounds.
204 Bedford Ave., (718) 218-9608, MC, V, AmEx, D, Diners, ⓛ to Bedford Ave.

Fat Beats
Indispensable for hip-hop fans, this well-stocked shop also doesn't do too badly in the acid jazz and reggae departments either. Secondhand bins are an

amazing source of classics. *406 Sixth Ave. (bet. 8th and 9th Sts.), 673-3883, MC, V, Am Ex, ⓝⓡ to 8th St., ⓖ to Astor Pl.*

Generation Records
Punk, whether major-label and indie, with many bootlegs. *210 Thompson St. (bet. 3rd and Bleecker Sts.), 254-1100, MC, V, ⓐⓑⓒⓓ ⓔⓕⓞ to West 4th St.*

Harlem Mine Records
African music is well-represented, in addition to hip hop, R&B, and reggae. *17 West 125th St. (bet. Fifth and Lenox Aves.), 369-9706, Cash Only, ⓶⓷ to 125th St.* ♿

HMV
The neighborhood's other music superstore offers plenty of variety, including a good selection of hip hop, and frequent sales on top titles. *2081 Broadway (at 72nd St.), 721-5900, MC, V, AmEx, D, ⓵⓶⓷⓽ to 72nd St.* ♿

J&R Music World
Covering an entire block and soaring into the sky, this store carries everything in video, audio, music, and computers. The sales staff is a mix of experts and used car dealers, so ask for a lot of different opinions before you buy anything. Everything is on display, so customers can fiddle to their hearts' content. *23 Park Row (bet. Beekman and Ann Sts.), 238-9000, MC, V, AmEx, D, ⓶⓷ to Park Pl., ⓸⓹⓺ to City Hall*

Matt Umanov Guitars
Anyone in a band knows this long-time Village institution. Acoustic and electric instruments at reasonable prices, as well as a knowledgeable staff. *273 Bleecker St. (bet. Sixth and Seventh Aves.), 675-2157, MC, V, AmEx, D, ⓐⓑⓒⓓⓕⓞ to W. 4th St.*

Midnight Records
Calling all spinners, DJs, jazz heads. Remember those large round disks with deep grooves in them? This dealer of vinyl, with both old and new collectibles, is living proof that albums have not completely gone the way of the dinosaur. Check out their virtual site at www.midnightrecords.com. *263 West 23rd St. (bet. Seventh and Eighth Aves.), 675-2768, MC, V, AmEx, D, ⓵⓽ to 23rd St.*

Mondo Kim's
The sheer size and breadth of the selection, that goes far beyond the world of big name pop stars, is namely what recommends this alternative and indie megastore. The used selection is equally good, and their used CD policy a steal-they'll exchange your old stuff, if it's not damaged, straight across for any other used CD. *6 St. Mark's Pl. (at Third Ave.), 505-0311, MC, V, AmEx, ⓝⓡ to 8th St., ⓖ to Astor Pl.* ♿

The Music Factory
The latest in contemporary music including hip-hop, gospel, jazz, reggae and soul. Many artists often do in-store signings or performances here to promote their material. Cassettes, vinyl, CD's, and even videotapes are available at very affordable prices at this local DJ hang-out. *162-01 Jamaica Ave. (at 162nd St.), Jamaica, (718) 291-3135, MC, V, AmEx, D, ⓔ to Jamaica Cntr.* ♿

Norman's Sound and Vision Too
A 10 percent discount to students with IDs makes this one of the best used CDs bargains. While this location rocks 'n' rolls a bit heavier than its older sibling in Cooper Square, there's still a sizable jazz selection for the collecting buff. *228 Seventh Ave. (bet. 23rd and 24th Sts.) 255-0076, MC, V, ⓵⓽ to 23rd St.*

Other Music
Well-deserved haven for indie-rock lovers which also offers a full selection of ambient, kraut rock, psychedelia, and noise. Keep an eye out for special in-store performances (arranged by owners and ex-Kim's Underground-ers Chris Vanderloo, Josh Madell, and Jeff Gibson), which have already featured Yo La Tengo and Jowe Head. *15 East 4th St. (bet. Broadway and Lafayette Sts.), 477-8150, MC, V, AmEx, ⓝⓡ to 8th St., ⓖ to Astor Pl.*

Poor Richard's Flip A Disc
Great deals on CDs, both current and obscure. Just be prepared to shop in the rain since his locations are all outside. Cash only. *113th and Broadway, ⓵⓽ to 110th St.*
Also at:
61st St. and Fifth Ave, ⓝⓡ to Fifth Ave.
And
58th St. and Eighth Ave., ⓵⓽ to Columbus Circle

GREAT CD PRICES

"Poor Richard's Flip-a-Disc, a New York Tradition"

Poor Richard's Flip-a-Disc

NEW - USED   BUY - SELL

Five Landmark Locations:

Open 11-7 Mon-Fri   Open 11-7 every day

Columbus Circle   **Central Park**
58th & 8th Ave.   61st & 5th Ave.

113th & Broadway   **The Tramway**
N.E. Corner across from   59th & 2nd Ave.
McBain Hall

112th & Broadway
Next to Tom's Restaurant

Phone: (212) 932-9389
Fax: (212) 932-7538

shopping 161

Rebel
A decent selection of mainstream and alternative, as well as other kinds of music paraphernalia.
319 Bleecker St.(bet. Christopher and Grove Sts.), 989-0770, MC, V, ❶❾ to Christopher St. ♿

The Record Shack
Supplying music for the block, rap, and reggae emanate from this loud, crowded, but fairly priced shop, which specializes in reggae.
274 West 125th St. (bet. A.C. Powell and Frederick Douglass Blvds.), 866-1600, MC, V, AmEx, D, ❷❸❻❿ to 125th St. ♿

Route 66 Records
A lot of heavy stuff, but not necessarily great quality. Plenty of T-shirts, posters, etc.
99 MacDougal St. (bet West 3rd and Bleecker St.s.), 533-2345, MC, V, AmEx, ❶❷❸❹❺❻ to West 4th St.

Sam Ash
Ever want to DJ? Sprawling along 48th Street, these four music shops fulfill almost every music-making need, selling acoustic instruments, recording equipment, MIDI systems, computers and software, DJ equipment, lighting, sheet music, and other items. The staff knows its stuff, and all locations (except for #163) rent and repair instruments and equipment.
155, 160, 159, and 163 West 48th St. (bet. Sixth and Seventh Aves.), 719-2299, MC, V, AmEx, ❶❷ to 49th St. or ❸❹❺ to 47-50 St./Rockefeller Center

Second Coming Records
All genres are here, but plan on investing time in browsing since the quality is inconsistent.
231 Sullivan St. (bet. Bleecker and West 3rd Sts.), 228-1313, MC, V, ❶❷❸❹❺❻ to West 4th St.

TMC Asian Music
What's the Chinese pop equivalent of Mariah Carey? Huge selection of the most current popular music of Asia, not to mention the impressive array of Chinese oldies, LP's for karaoke diehards and American/Chinese blockbuster smashes, Japanese animation, ceramic toys, and oversized cloth posters of Asian teen idols that sell out in the blink of an eye.
151 Canal St. (at Bowery), 226-6696, Cash Only, ❶❷❸ to Grand St.

Tower Clearance Annex
A sale outlet for leftovers of all kinds (including 49¢ paperback rejects); the diligent classical fan will be rewarded, though those in search of other genres will be frustrated.
20 East 4th St. (at Lafayette St.), 228-7317, MC, V, AmEx, D, Diners, ❻ to Astor Pl. ♿

Tower Records
New York's first music superstore has been surpassed in size by many others, but still has a strong selection-although it can be hard to find major rock titles here, oddly enough.
692 Broadway (at 4th St.), 505-1500, MC, V, AmEx, ❶❷ to 8th St., ❻ to Astor Place

Also at
2107 Broadway (at 66th St.), 799-2500, MC, V, AmEx, D, ❶❾ to 66th St.

Venus Records
A goldmine for used CDs. There's lots of strange stuff you might have been unable to find new elsewhere already on the rack at used prices. Also a small imports and other rarities for megafans, and a downstairs full of old vinyl where the hard-core record buffs hang out.
13 St. Mark's Pl. (bet. Second and Third Aves.), 598-4459, MC, V, AmEx, D, ❶❷ to 8th St., ❻ to Astor Place

Vinylmania
Specializing in house music and imports. You can listen before you buy.
60 Carmine St. (bet. Seventh Ave. and Bleeker St.), 924-3309, MC, V, AmEx, ❶❷❸❹❺❻ to West 4th St., ❶❾ to Houston St.

Virgin Megastore
Redefining the idea of the megastore, this flashy three-level entertainment complex boasts movie theaters, over one thousand listening booths, and a wide selection of videos, laser discs, and CD-Roms.
1540 Broadway (bet. 45th and 46th Sts.), 921-1020, MC, V, AmEx, D, ❶❷❸❹❺❻❼❽❾ to Times Square

SHOES

Anbar Shoe Steal
The southeastern corner of TriBeCa is a bargain shoppers paradise, and this is by far the best outlet for great shoe deals. Quality, name brand footwear goes for close-out prices and the selection is remarkably good, especially for those seeking sizes other than a seven or eight. Perfect for finding cheap and stylish accessories to match an end-of season clothes purchase in an unusual color.
60 Reed St. (bet. Church St. and Broadway), 227-0253, MC, V, AmEx, D, ❶❷❸❹❺ to Chambers Street ♿

Cole Haan
Shoes of the finest materials and nicest design are available in this Upper East Side foot haven. The store utilizes its space so as to display the merchandise (including other leather goods), quite well.
667 Madison Ave. (at 61st St.), 421-8440, MC, V, AmEx, D, ❹❺❻ to 59th St., ❶❷ to Lexington Ave. ♿

Hester Street Shoe Outlet
Carrying women's shoes starting at size 5, this store specializes in platforms and strappy sandals at excellent prices. Accessories and a sundry of random items are also sold.
188 Hester St. (near Mulberry St.), 965-0244, Cash Only, ❶❷ to Canal St.

John Fluevog
Possibly the hippest source of shoes in the city, a Fluevog can be spotted a mile away. Chunky platforms, combat-quality boots, and funky, offbeat colors are all well-represented; end-of-the-season sales can yield amazing bargains on the otherwise expensive footwear, usually priced at around $100.
104 Prince St. (at Mercer St.), 431-4484, MC, V, AmEx, D, ❶❷ to Prince St. or ❸❹❺ to Broadway/Lafayette St. ♿

162 shopping

Sacco

Trendy, retro, classic: this chic shop carries it all. Make this store your first stop for well-made, eclectic women's footwear. Shoes tend to be dressy and relatively expensive, but there are always sale selections. Clearances offer an additional 20 percent off the sale price.
Broadway (at 75th St.), 799-5229, MC, V, AmEx, D, ❶❾ to 72nd St.

Sigerson Morrison

Classic and conservative shoes ranging from sandals to career footwear.
242 Mott St. (bet. Prince and Houston Sts.), 219-3893, MC, V, AmEx, ❿❼ to Prince St. or ❷❹❺❻ to Broadway/Lafayette

Steve Madden

Theres no live entertainment with the shop owner singing tunes as in the downtown shop, but its uptown counterpart promises similarly designed shelves faithfully stocked with the same fashionably designed footwear for those with a strictly urban sensibility.
152 86th St. (bet. Lexington and Third Aves.), MC, V, D, AmEx, ❹❺❻ to 86th St.

Steven Madden Shoes

This well-known designer sports trendy, extremely wearable black and brown leather shoes and purses. The store is always crowded; merchandise changes, though the style is.
540 Broadway (bet. Prince and Spring Sts.), 343-1800, MC, V, AmEx, ❿❼ to Prince St., ❷❹❺❻ to Broadway/Lafayette, also on the Upper East Side.

Trash and Vaudeville

Once this split-level store defined a look that made New York famous. Now merchandise appears trashy and punkish, but the shoe and boot selection in the back is still one of the best in town.
4 St. Mark's Pl. (bet. Second and Third Aves.), 982-3590, MC, V, AmEx, D, ❻ to Astor Pl.

SPORTS

Bicycle Habitat

If the quality of a bike store can be determined by counting the number of customers' bikes that are chained outside, then this is one of the best in the city. The customers here are serious about their bikes and the same people can be found day after day hanging around checking out new models, picking up parts or just discussing their obsession. This all adds up to the fact that they know what they're doing, so if you're seeking some serious advice, this is the place.
244 Lafayette St. (bet. Prince and Spring Sts.), MC, V, AmEx, ❿❼ to Prince St.

Big City Kites Co.

Kites in all shapes and sizes, from the standard diamond shape to more
(bet. A. C. Powell and Frederick Douglass Blvds.), 866-1600, MC, V, AmEx, D, ❷❸❹❹ to 125th St.

Blades Boards & Skates

A friendly and oh-so-helpful staff which would readily join their skate boarding patrons at one of Astor Place's wheels-only congregations on a lunch break. Slick new styles of roller blades, skates, and skater gear also available

at the standard, not-so-unconventionally commercial prices.
659 Broadway (bet. Bleecker and Great Jones Sts.), 477-7350, MC, V, AmEx, D, ❿❼ to 8th St.

Body Strength Fitness

Want a hard body and a calm mind? This is the place. BSF offers free weights, personal training, aerobic classes, as well as massage, energy healing, and aromatherapy. Speak with them about customizing a workout plan to suit your needs.
250 West 106th at Broadway, 316-3338, V, MC, AmEx, ❶❾ to 103rd St.

Gotham Bikes

A good place to go for those looking for a to buy a bike without having to deal with being intimidated by a staff of bike maniacs looking to show off their knowledge. The selection is good and the staff is helpful without trying to push an Italian racing model when you just want something cheap to ride through the park. They also offer bike rentals.
116 West Broadway (bet. Duane and Reade Sts.), MC, V, AmEx, ❷❸❹❶❾ to Chambers St.

Paragon

Whether the game is badminton, snowboarding, or basketball, this sports superstore is sure to have the right gear. The shoe department often has better deals than the athletic footwear chains, but be prepared to navigate some mean crowds.
867 Broadway (at 18th St.), 255-8036, MC, V, AmEx, ❶❾ to 18th St.

SPECIALTY

Anime Crash

Mecca of Asian pop culture which specializes in Japanimation and Hong Kong Action videos, comics, books, magazines, and general kitsch. A wide selection of Sanrio merchandise and Japanese model kits of everything from robots to bizarre, futuristic dolls.
13 East 4th St. (bet. Broadway and Lafayette St.), 254-4670, MC, V, AmEx, D, Diners, ❻ to Astor Place

Aphrodisia

Herbs, spices, and a variety of teas intended to rejuvenate mind and body.
264 Bleecker St. (bet. Cornelia and Jones Sts.), 989-6440, MC, V, AmEx, ❶❷❸❹❺❻ to West 4th St.

The Big Cigar Co.

Fragrant tobacco lures the cigar-smoker into the store to gaze at the collection of fine smokes.
193A Grand St. (at Mulberry St.), 966-9122, MC, V, AmEx, Diners, ❶❷❹ to Grand St.

Capitol Fishing Tackle

Rounding out an eclectic mix of stores on this block, this emporium specializes in everything an angler would ever want or need: rods, hook, tackle, etc. No chance of blending in with the loyal clientele of piscine nimrods unless you're one of them.
23rd St. (bet. Seventh and Eighth Aves.), MC, V, AmEx, D, ❶❾ to 23rd St.

shopping 163

The Coliseum
Seekers of gold chains, earrings, and rings will be dazzled by the number of merchants on the first floor of this double-tiered mart. Negotiations on jewelry prices are routine. Upstairs contains shops dedicated to scents, sneakers, and urban gear for da' youth. Relatively affordable.
Jamaica Ave. (at 165th St.), Credit accepted at some venues, ❸ to Jamaica Ave.

Condomania
Self-explanatory; prophylactics of all shapes, sizes, and flavors. Merely browsing here can be an amusing experience.
351 Bleecker St. (bet. Christopher and W. 4th Sts.), 691-9442, MC, V, AmEx,❶❾ to Christopher Street

Cut & Dried
Madi Heller and her husband Felix Blume sell striking bouquets and topiaries made from carefully selected and dried flowers from Europe.
968 Lexington Ave. (bet. 70th & 71st Sts.), 772-7701, V, MC, AmEx, ❻ to 68th St.

Fabbricatore Jewelry Design
Just discovering this tiny treasure makes you feel privy to some sort of secret; Frank Fabbricatore's gorgeous wedding bands, engagement rings, and bridal gifts are the most sought after baubles in the city.
29 John St. #805 (bet. Broadway and Nassau Sts.), 513-1391, Cash or Check Only, ❷❸❹❺❻❼ to Fulton St. ❹❻ to Broadway/Nassau St.

The Fountain Pen Hospital
Pens from $1 to $2,000 are on display for your prying eyes. Whether you want a regular old Bic or a gourmet Mont Blanc, the knowledgeable staff will be at your beck and call to help you choose. The sale and repair of antique and limited-edition pens are also specialties.
10 Warren St., 964-0580, AmEx, MC, V, D, Diners, ❶❷❸❹ to Chambers St.

MISCELLANEOUS

Good Field Trading
Squeeze through the narrow aisle to find a varied selection of pens, stationery products, Chinese greeting cards, magazines, and writing tablets. The requisite smattering of Sanrio products as well.
74 Mott St. (bet. Canal and Baxter Sts.), MC, V, ❻❼ to Canal St.

The Great American Backrub
No appointment necessary at this now-ubiquitous chain. Just walk in and treat yourself to one of life's most enjoyable experiences. The certified staff is friendly and their expert hands will knead all the tension away. Check out their line of healthy back products.
2068 Broadway (at 71st St.), 501-7884, V, MC, AmEx, ❶❷❸❹ to 72nd Street ♿

House of a Million Earrings
Ethnic-inspired clothing, posters, paintings, crafts and books. Hand-made jewelry, incense and greeting cards are also for sale at this family-owned business. Great place for gifts.
169-17 Jamaica Ave. (at 169th St.), (718) 297-7950, MC, V, AmEx, D, ❸ to Jamaica Center/Parsons/Archer Ave.

Jerry Ohlinger's Movie Mania
Shoeboxes of old publicity shots, movie stills, posters, and playbills crowd this treasure trove of memorabilia for avid film buffs; color stills go for around $3.50. Don't miss the autographed pics of Orson Welles and Montgomery Clift by the door.
242 West 14th St. (bet. Seventh and Eighth), 989-0869, MC, V, AmEx, D, ❶❾ to 14th St.

Just Jake
TriBeCa is full of pampered children, so it only makes sense that the stores catering to their needs are rather extraordinary. Here, they offer *A selection of children's books nearly as large as a small adult bookstore with choices for various age groups, along with lots of well-made and interesting educational toys. Fun enough to intrigue children and responsible enough to impress their parents.
40 Hudson St. (at Duane St.), 267-1716, MC, V, AmEx, D, ❶❷❸❹ to Chambers St. ♿

K.C.C. International Trading
Sanrio lovers indulge their cravings for animated Japanese characters frolicking over stationery, pencils, wallets, notepads, and more.
6A Elizabeth St. (at Canal St.), 964-8728, MC, V, ❻ to Canal St.

Kam Wo Trading Co.
Drawers of medicine line the walls in this apothecary shop, smelling thickly of herbs. Specialty medicinal cookware and a library of health books written by the boss himself, Dr. Leung. Herbs, weighed out on handscales and wrapped in white rice-paper envelopes, will cure any ailment.
211 Grand St. (near Elizabeth St.), 966-6370, MC, V, ❼❽ to Canal St. ♿

Kate's Paperie
Sheaves of fanciful wrapping paper and reams of stationery fill every nook of this location, augmented by paper-related merchandise ranging from kites to hatboxes to desks.
561 Broadway (at Prince St.), 941-9816, MC, V, AmEx, ❼❽ to Prince St.

Mariposa
New-age music and massive wall displays strive to

Hartley Chemists
FULL LINE DRUG STORE
MAJOR PRESCRIPTION PLANS ACCEPTED
1219 Amsterdam Ave.   (Cor 120th St.), New York, NY 10027

Syed N. Rahman, M.S., R.Ph.

PHONE (212) 749-8480
FAX (212) 316-6592

164 shopping

put this beautiful boutique's butterfly wares into naturalistic context; lepidopterists can check out the carefully mounted winged specimens in their infinite variety behind clear Plexiglas frames.
South St. Seaport Pier 17, 233-3221, MC, V, AmEx, ❶❿❷❸❹❺ to Fulton Street

Maxilla and Mandible
Literally filled to the rafters with perfect seashells, fossilized trilobites from exotic locales, authentic antlers and skulls, and insects preserved in amber.
451 Columbus Ave. (at 82nd St.), 724-6173, MC, V, AmEx, ❶❾ to 79th St.

New York Public Library Shop
All manner of trinkets and souvenirs for bibliophiles and the merely literate alike; they also have a wide selection of writing journals. Open during library hours.
Fifth Ave. (bet. 40th and 42nd Sts.), 930-0641, (located on the first floor of the library), MC, V, AmEx, ❶❼❽❶❷ ❸❼❾ to 42nd St.

116th Street Market
Labrynthine paths between merchandise-filled tents guide visitors to a wide assortment of goodies in this outdoor shopping area. Visitors can see solemn, traditional sculptures stare out at rows upon rows of contemporary bootlegged cassette vendors. The perfect place to find African-print cloth/wraps.
116th St. and Malcolm X Blvd. (at Lenox Ave.), Cash Only, ❷❸ to 116th St.

Paris Images Inc.
Art photos of the Robert Doisneau school and a large collection of fine art reproductions for about $20 per poster; though, if you have money to burn, they've got fine art prints, whose prices run into the thousands. Open past midnight for late-night browsing after a healthy dose of caffination at one of the nearby Bleecker Street cafes.
170 Bleecker St. (at Sullivan St.), 473-7552, MC, V, AmEx, ❶❷❸❹❺ to West 4th Street

Phoenix Import
A tiny tourist shop with plenty of jade figurines, fisherman bamboo hats and countless other props characteristic of China's countryside.
51 Mott St. (near Canal St.), 608-6670, MC, V, ❶❷ to Canal St.

Pier 17
Three levels of somewhat overpriced tourist shops may not seem like anything special, but at least you can get some great views of the Brooklyn Bridge from the top floor. Also a good place to bring Aunt Martha from Ohio.
South St. (at Fulton St.), ❹❺❻ to Brooklyn Bridge/City Hall

The Pink Pussycat
A Village landmark. All manner of erotica, from lingerie and clothing to, well, other things designed to aid your love life.
167 West 4th St. (bet. Sixth and Seventh Aves.), 243-0077, MC, V, AmEx, ❶❷❸❹❺ to W.4th St., ❶❾ to Christopher St.

The Plant Shed
It's a regular jungle inside this gardening center, which offers many different kinds of ferns, flowering shrubs, and other plants. The helpful staff can recommend which plants would best suit your lifestyle, and which would thrive in your home.
209 West 96th St. (bet. Broadway and Amsterdam Ave.), 662-4400, V, MC, AmEx, ❶❾❷❸ to 96th St.

Postermat
From Elvis movie posters to Betty Boop ice buckets, dorm essentials abound here, with movie, music, and photography posters priced at $10-$25. There's also an extensive collection of T-shirts replete with indie logos and pop-culture icons. Round out your kitsch trip with cards, candles, toys, and candy.
37 West 8th St. (bet. Fifth and Sixth Aves.), 982-2946/228-4027, MC, V, AmEx, D ❶❷❸❹❺❻ to West 4th St.

Progressive Unlimited
This tiny but well-stocked enclave near Harlem's primary artery maintains an Afro-centric twist; its single aisle has everything from carved picture frames to black-authored literature to brightly hued regalia. Experienced locktician also available by appointment.
14 East 125th St. (bet. Madison and Fifth Aves.), 427-7084, ❷❸❹❺❻ to 125th St.

The Russian Bathhouse
For just $20 you can enjoy a whole day in four kinds of high-temp, low-humidity Russian and Turkish steam rooms, including an aromatherapy room. One hour massages are offered for $45, and 1/2 hour massages are $30. Monday, Tuesday and Friday are coed days, Saturday and Wednesday are female only, and Thursday and Sunday are for men only, and they are open every day until 10pm. The Russian Bathhouse was established 105 years ago by immigrants, and has a real historic feel.
268 East 10th St. (Bet. First Ave. and Ave. A), 505-0665, MC, V, D, AmEx, ❶ to First Ave., ❻ to Astor Place

Tents & Trails
Manhattan's low-key place for gearheads. If you're sick of battling it out in E.M.S. and Paragon Sports, this outdoor clothing and equipment store is the place for you. The prices are the best in town.
21 Park Pl. (bet. Church St. and Broadway) 227-1760, MC, V, AmEx, ❷❸ to Park Place

Urban Bird
If you can stand the squawking, visiting this cramped bird shop, chock full of flamboyantly colored parrots, cockatoos, and other tropical birds, is like a free trip to the zoo. If you happen to have a bird, they stock everything you may need for it.
177 West Broadway (bet. Worth and Leonard Sts.), 219-3010, MC, V, AmEx, D, Diners, ❶❾ to Franklin St.

Vendors along Canal Street
When you're looking for a Prada knock-off for mom or a cheap pair of shades for yourself, this is the place to go. Prices are always negotiable, no

shopping 165

matter how intimidating the vendor appears. If Mom wants that bag to be a Donna Karan instead, no problem—most stands will change the label for you in a jiffy.
Canal St. (bet. Broadway and Elizabeth St.), Cash Only, ❻❽❿ to Grand St.

Village Chess Shop
Play chess from noon to midnight with fellow experts, or indulge a passion by purchasing game sets made from materials ranging from nuts and bolts of ivory and onyx.
230 Thompson St. (bet. Third Ave. and Bleecker.), 475-9580, MC, V, AmEx, ❶❷❸ ❹❺❻❼to West 4th St.

Wa Fun Company
Well-stocked with Chinese silks, soaps, weaponry, and other goodies, this tiny sliver of a store offers very reasonable prices and good service. The silk robes and Mandarin shirts are a particularly good buy. Be forewarned: there are no dressing rooms, so the store clerk will size you up.
43A Mott St., no phone, Cash Only, ❻❽❿ to Grand Street

Walking Dogs
Stationed next-door to the more widely known Wu Wear (both establishments are owned by the rap group), fun frocks for both sexes are folded and hung neatly in a small but roomy space. "A party ain't a party" without some of these cute outfits, proving that Staten Islanders know where to go to get hooked up for a good time.
61B Victory Blvd. (at Montgomery), (718) 815-7100, MC, AmEx, D, V, ❶❾ to South Ferry, ❿❿to Whitehall St./South Ferry,

then take Staten Island Ferry, then S67, S61, or S48 to Montgomery

West 4th Street Flea Market
Squeeze through the traffic of weekend out-of-towners who swarm the outdoor market, in search of hand-crafted jewelry (which all looks suspiciously similar), trinkets, tourist and metalhead T-shirts, and cheap, trendy clothing executed in a variety of polychromatic synthetics.
Broadway at West 4th St. (next to Tower Records), Cash Only, ❿❿ to 8th St.

Wow Comics
Those who can't always make it to Manhattan's larger comic stores take heart in this comfortable mainstay. New and old releases from a variety of both mainstream and independent companies are sold alongside baseball cards, action figurines, and other memorabilia.
2084 White Plains Rd. (at Pelham Parkway), (718) 829-0461, ❷ to Pelham Parkway.

Zambezi Gallery & Boutique
Masks, sculptures, ebony carvings, decorative plates, exotic clothing, and photographs are all for sale at reasonable prices in this local shop. There are frequent book signings, poetry readings and other cultural events on the premises as well.
149-41 Francis Lewis Blvd. (at 258th St.), Rosedale, (718) 276-1984, MC, V, AmEx, D, Q85 Bus toFrancis Lewis Blvd

INDEX BY NEIGHBORHOOD

BROOKLYN
Brooklyn Brewery
Conway Stores
Dr. Jay's
Earwax
Macy's
Max and Roebling
Tarizan West
The Windmill Shoppe

BRONX
Dr. Jay's

CHELSEA
Annex Antique Fair and Flea Market
Burlington Coat Factory
Capitol Fishing Tackle
Chelsea Second Hand Guitars
Filene's Basement
Garden of Eden Farmer's Market
HyperReality
Just Bulbs
Loehmann's
Manhattan Futon
Manny's Closet
Midnight Records
Norman's Sound and Vision Too
Williams-Sonoma Outlet Center

CHINATOWN
Chinatown Ice Cream Factory
Church Street Surplus
Confucious Plaza Vendors
Dynasty Supermarket
Fresh Tofu Vendors
Good Field Trading
Hong Kong Supermarket
K.C.C. International Trading
Kam Kuo Food Corp.
Kam Wo Trading Co.
Mott Street
Mott Street Vendors
Oriental Dress Company
Pearl River Mart
Phoenix Import
Ten Ren Tea and Ginseng Co. Inc.
TMC Asian Music
Usa Beauty Corp.
Vendors along Canal Street
Vendors at the Triangle at Canal and Baxter Streets
Wa Fun Company

EAST VILLAGE
99X
Anime Crash
Antique Boutique
Atomic Passion
Atrium
Blue
Cheap Jack's
Cherry
Dance Tracks
Exit 9
Fab 208
Fat Beat
Halo
Kiehl's
Little Ricky's
Lord of the Fleas
Mara the Cat
Meghan Kinney
Metropolis
Mondo Kim's
Other Music
Rose is Vintage
Screaming Mimi
Shine
Steven Madden Shoes
Steven Alan Outlet
Tower Clearance Annex
Tower Records
Trash and Vaudeville
Urban Outfitters
Venus Records
White Trash
X-Girl
X-Large

FINANCIAL DISTRICT
Century 21
Fabbricatore Jewelry Design
J&R Music World
J. Crew
Mariposa
Pier 17
The Sharper Image
Syms
Tents and Trails
World Financial Center

GRAMERCY
ABC Carpet and Home
Daffy's
Disc-O-Rama Annex
Emporio Armani
Excel Computer and Software
Fish's Eddy
J. Crew
Just Bulbs
Manhattan Futon

166 shopping

Moe Ginsburg
Paragon
Sam Flax

GREENWICH VILLAGE
Andy's Chee-Pees
Aphrodisia
Balducci's
Bleeker Bob's
Bleeker Street Records
Condomania
Disc-O-Rama
French Connection
Generation Records
Jerry Ohlinger's Movie Mania
Love NYC
Manic Panic
Matt Umanov Guitars
McNulty's Tea and Coffe
Our Name's Mudd
Paris Images Inc.
Patricia Field's
The Pink Pussycat
Porto Rico Importing Co.
Postermat
Rebel Rebel
Route 66 Records
Sea Grape Wines and Spirits
Second Coming Records
Stella Dallas
Taylor's
Urban Outfitters
Village Chess Shop
Vinylmania
West 4th Flea Market

HARLEM
116th Street Market
Fairway
Harlem Mine Record Mart 125
McRae Furniture
MONY
Progressive Unlimited
The Record Shack
Ropa 203
Starlight Fashion
Sugar Hill Thrift Shop
Ten's the Limit

LITTLE ITALY
About Time Shoes and Clothing
Alleva Dairy Inc.
Calypso
Di Palos'
Do Kham
E. Rossi and Co.
Forzano Italian Imports
Gates of Marrakesh
Hester Street Shoe Outlet

Ina
Italian Food Center
Living Doll
Piemonte Ravioli Company
The Big Cigar Co.

LOWER EAST SIDE
420 Inc.
555 Soul /Strictly for Da Ladies
Economy Candy
The Russian Bathhouse
TG-170

MIDTOWN
Colony
Daffy's
Datavision
Lee Art's Shop
Macy's
Manhattan Mall
Museum of Modern Art Design Store
NBC Studio Gift Store
New York Public Library Shop
Sam Ash
Urban Outfitters
Virgin Megastore

MORNINGSIDE HEIGHTS
Body Strength Fitness
Card-O-Mat
Czarina
La Piccola Cucina
Mondel Chocolates
Movie Place
The Plant Shed
Samad's Gourmet
Tamarind Seed Health Food

QUEENS
The Coliseum
Green Acres Mall
House of a Million Earrings
Jamaica Market
Loehmann's
Macy's
The Music Factory
Price Mart
The Salvation Army Thrift Store
Von's/School of Hard Knocks
Zambezi Gallery and Boutique

SOHO
A.L. Bazzini
agnes b.
Alice Underground
Anna Sui
Anthropologie
APC
Betsey Johnson
Bicycle Habitat
Canal Jean Co. Inc
Comme de Garcons
Cynthia Rowley
D & G Bakery
Dean and Deluca
Depression Modern
Dolce and Gabanna
Dom
Face Stockholm Ltd.
John Fluevog
Kate's Paperie
Label
Liquid Sky
MAC Cosmetics
Miu Miu
Mood Indigo
Phat Farm
Sigerson Morrison
Smylonylon
Stussy
Todd Oldham
TSE Cashmere
Urban Archaeology
Yohji Yammamoto

STATEN ISLAND
Staten Island Mall
Walking Dogs
Wu Wear

TRIBECA
Anbar Shoe Steal
The Clothes-Out Connection
Dee and Dee
The Fountain Pen Hospital
Gotham Bikes
Just Jake
Pearl Paint
Urban Bird
Washington Market Park

UPPER EAST SIDE
Balaman Gallery
Bally
Barney's
Bell-Bates
Bergdorf Goodman
Bergdorf Goodman for Men
Big City Kites Co.
Blanche's Organic Take-

Away
Bloomingdale's
Bonte
Burlington Antique Toys
Calvin Klein
Chanel
Cole Haan
Cut and Dried
Diesel
Givenchy
Hanae Mori
Henri Bendel
HMV
La Maison du Chocolat
Mr. Rohrs Fine Teas and Coffee
Original Levi's Store
Polo/Ralph Lauren
Pottery Barn
Saks Fifth Avenue
The Sharper Image
Steve Madden
Urban Outfitters
Valentino
The Vinegar Factory
Whitney Museum Store
William Greenburg, Jr. Desserts
Yves Saint-Laurent
Zegna Corporation

UPPER WEST SIDE
Citarella
Elk Candy
Fairway
Filene's Basement
Fish's Eddy
The Great American Back Rub
HMV
Kenneth Cole
Lee's Art Shop
Lord of the Fleas
Maxilla and Mandible
Sacco
Tower Records
Wind Water
Zabar's

WASHINGTON HEIGHTS
Glaubers
Goodwill Superstore
Mister Roger

shopping 167

BAM
Brooklyn Academy of Music

Next Wave Festival
Theater / Opera / Dance
Brooklyn Philharmonic

Student
Tickets Just $7.50!
Rush

For info call 718.636.4100 ext 5
www.bam.org

arts

visual arts ←············ 169
performing arts ------→ *189*
literature ←················→ **205**
film + television   221

visual arts

NYC visual arts scene.171
museums+galleries listings.178
cultural institutes+societies.186
index by neighborhood.188

visual arts

From the bright landscapes of Jacob Lawrence to the stark minimalism of Jacob Kline, from Alfred Stieglitz' clean urban angles to the sprawling graffiti of counter-culture phenomenon Jean-Michel Basquiat, New York has fostered the cutting edge of the art world for decades. While artists like multimedia pioneer Bill Viola and celestial abstractionist Ross Bleckner enjoy one-man shows at the Guggenheim, and in swank 57th Street galleries like Mary Boone's, the proverbial struggling artist starts from scratch at galleries like the Lower East Side's Esso, where Parsons, School of Visual Arts, and Pratt grads explore the aftermath of pop art; at burgeoning BoHo paradise Pierogi 2000; and on the walls and sidewalks of the East Village and SoHo, where street-level graffiti artists turn pocked cement into canvas.

Like struggling actors, struggling artists have day jobs; they work in spaces which betray their pursuits, like at Limbo, a perennially popular Avenue A coffeehouse whose rotating installations come across as either pretentious or promising. The Anchorage, a space which opens up beneath the Brooklyn Bridge in the summer, displays intriguing and provocative pieces on its sweeping brick walls and archways. Neophytes should begin with a copy of the *Gallery Guide*, free in most showrooms, to become familiar with what the city has to offer.

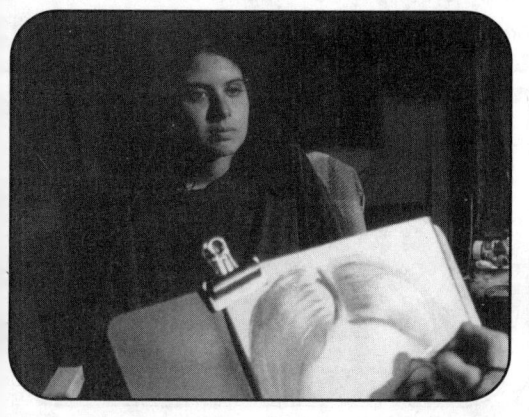

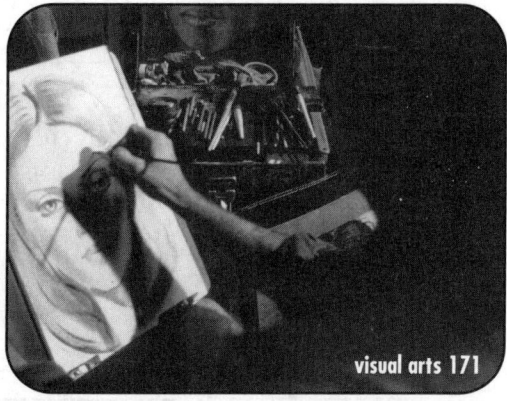

Rising rents have caused many galleries to flee SoHo for Chelsea, the Lower East Side, and Williamsburg, Brooklyn, although there are still devoted daytrippers who crowd into the cast-iron buildings that are central to the art world. Don't be intimidated by stodgy guards or uppity desk clerks; if you can't get up the nerve, try starting at low-key spots like Wooster Street's The Drawing Center and Broadway's Exit Art, or get your feet wet at one of the city's excellent museums, which consistently launch forward-thinking, provocative exhibits that keep abreast of national and international trends. The ambitious and defiant curators of the Whitney's Biennial, a show occurring in summers of odd-numbered years, never fail to provoke critical and public outcry with their unveilings. Once you've raised your confidence level, try crashing a well-attended white wine reception (uptown on 57th Street between Madison and Park Avenues, downtown along West Broadway or Prince Street in SoHo) for some insight into the gossip, intrigue, and sordid details of the city's art world.

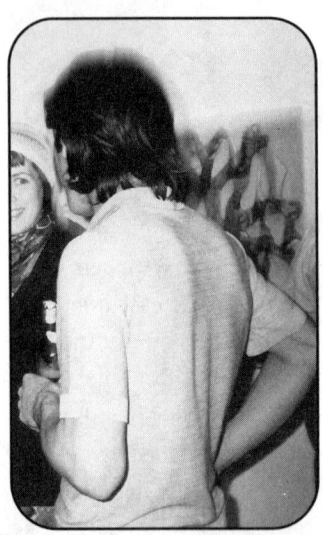

Artists in New York History

New York's influence on the course of 20th-century art reflects the same rhythm of modulation and progress that characterizes most of the city's history. Beginning with the Ashcan School shortly after the turn of the century, New York has emerged as an artistic laboratory in which experimentation is the norm and deviation is embraced.

Exchanging the 19th-century's "art-for-art's-sake" sensibilities for what one leader of the movement called "art for life," members of the Ashcan School grew dissatisfied with the academic elitism of contemporary artists. They painted what they saw around them, favoring a Bowery street urchin as a subject over a nude in a studio. Celebrating the vitality that the city provided them, Ashcan artists Maurice Prendergast and George Lukes helped unmoor 20th-century art from its neoclassical foundations.

Working concurrently, the Photo-Secession group was determined to firmly establish photography, an upstart among the fine arts. Alfred Steiglitz and his cohorts also embraced other experimental artists looking for "legitimacy." Opening the seminal 291 Gallery in 1905, he organized exhibitions responsible for introducing America to the works of many of Europe's avant-garde with shows featuring Picasso, Braque, and Picabia: the United States' first encounter with cubism.

The onset of World War I brought many European artists to New York. Picabia and Marcel Duchamp met Man Ray and launched the

New York Galleries are the most exciting places to see new artwork.

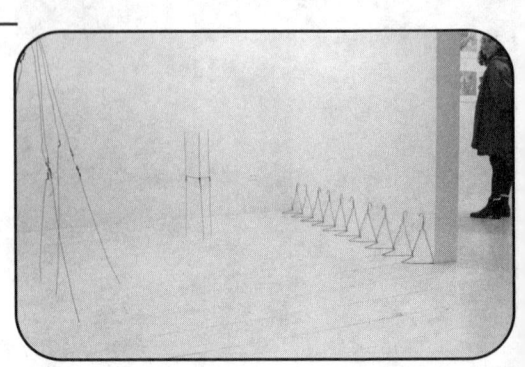

172 visual arts

CROSS-SECTION OF SOHO

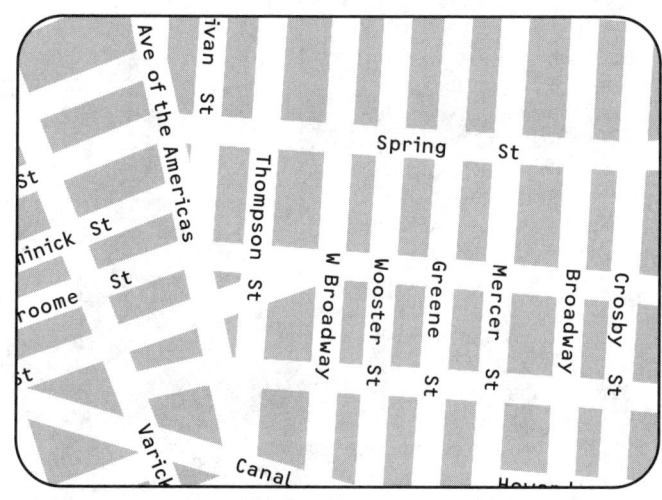

SoHo has more galleries than any other NY area

city's Dada movement. Commenting obliquely on the nonsense of "the human condition," New York's Dadaists mocked both the establishment and the avant-garde. When the United States entered the war, the group disbanded temporarily as its expatriate constituents fled to different parts of the world. The group reconvened in Paris in 1921.

As New York established itself as a "vertical city," skyscrapers and other urban novelties became subjects for a new group of urban artists. Inspired by the grid street-plan and the sea of rectangular forms, Dutch painter Piet Mondrian perfected his aesthetic of right angles. The Precisionists emerged in the 1920s, enchanted with the city's buildings, bridges, waterfronts, and warehouses, and aimed for a new, objective portrayal. Borrowing from the Cubist vocabulary of planarism and basic geography, the Precisionists were regarded by many critics as regressive. Nonetheless, the works of these artists, emergent through World War II, remain among the most stirring representations of the city and its structures.

After Paris fell to Germany in 1940, New York hosted an influx of European avant-guard artists making the city the world's undisputed artistic capital. The influence of émigré artists, such as Mondrian, Fernand Leger, and Max Ernst precipitated an infusion of freedom and expressionism in American art, though their work had been foreshadowed in the homegrown organization American Abstract Artists, which formed in 1936 and included more obscure artists like George L.K. Morris.

Abandoning most things mimetic, the aptly dubbed Abstract Expressionists appended Freud's notion of the subconscious to Surrealism's notion of human-as-automaton and threw in concepts prevalent in mythology and Native American traditions as well. This amalgam, a kind of automatic art analogous to stream-of-consciousness writing, is one popular rationale which would explain the work of Jackson Pollack, Willem De Kooning, and Mark Rothko, whose emphasis on the artistic process led one critic to dub their style "action painting." The movement's first significant museum recognition was not until an immensely popular 1958 exhibit, which eventually traveled to Europe. Other important members of what came to be known as the New York School included Clyfford Still, Robert Motherwell, Lee Krasner, Franz Kline, Elaine de Kooning, and Arshile Gorky. America's artistic dominance following the New York School's success led to the

in the *public* eye

Often obscured, overlooked, or dismissed with mild bewilderment, pieces of public sculpture pepper the city; with a little research, it's possible to make sense of the more abstract pieces.

The artistic trends of the '50s and '60s are evident in Isamu Noguchi's "Sunken Garden" sculpture, constructed with granite, glass, and stone in 1961, at the forecourt of One Chase Manhattan Plaza. Lying adjacent to the ground floor's banking area and visible from the street-level plaza above, the sculpture was inspired by the raked patterns of Japanese rock gardens from the Uji River in Kyoto.

In the '70s, Jean Dubuffet's whimsical "Group of Four Trees" was added to the plaza, pairing its synthetic aluminum and fiberglass frame with the natural stones of Noguchi's piece.

In the mid-'60s at Lincoln Center, sculptures were chosen to represent the urban redevelopment programs which were reshaping the city, and city beautification through sculpture placement was also taking place around the same time downtown, with the Parks Department's ambitious program called "Sculpture in Environment." Twenty-nine contemporary sculptures were placed throughout Manhattan, including Astor Place's familiar tilted steel black box, which formally goes by the name "Alamo" but is usually referred to as The Cube. The piece, designed by Bernard Rosenthal in 1967, was one of the first abstract sculptures on city property and has since served as a hangout for prepubescent skateboarders.

A few blocks southwest, in the court between the three towers of the residential complex at New York University Towers, Picasso's 1968 "Bust of Sylvette" is a towering presence between Mercer and LaGuardia Place. Critics complain that the piece exemplifies the problems inherent in enlarging a small piece to monumental scale, but that doesn't mitigate local resident's pride in having the 20th-century master's work grace their otherwise empty courtyard.

founding of an unprecedented number of galleries.

In the '60s, Abstraction gave way to pop art. Presaged by Jasper Johns and Robert Rauschenberg in the '50s, who tampered with images from popular culture, this new wave of artists attempted to elevate the residue of American life to a fine aesthetic, blurring the distinction between high art and kitsch. Andy Warhol, Roy Lichtenstein, and Claes Oldenburg, among others, distilled Abstract Expressionism's esoteric and cerebral qualities into its popular and visceral derivatives.

Supplemented in the late '60s by the understated subtlety of conceptual art and minimalism, New York's scene became the art world's hotbed of innovation, variety, and nontraditional aesthetics. Whereas, for instance, Warhol's concept of American life focused on its predominantly wild consumer culture, artists like Robert Morris contested that vision with more elemental works. At the same time, other artists were developing their own styles; Helen Frankenthaler used broad strokes of thin paint to create canvases that were ethereal and haunting; Frank Stella and Robert Ryman

174 visual arts

used geometry to produce stark works in the shape of protractors; May Stevens and Nancy Spero took their cues from the liberalism of the '70s to critique sexism, racism, and imperialism.

Performance art, which became popular in the '70s, added a more immediate sense of interaction between viewer and artist to the mix. To better suit these "dialogues," large exhibitions slowly gave way to more intimate galleries and performance spaces.

Many contemporary city artists continue to challenge mainstream culture with controversial works infused with a political consciousness. The photographic images of Robert Mapplethorpe, who attended the Pratt Institute during the late '60s, were well-known for their explicitly homoerotic portraits of male nudes and incited a furor when they were included in a federally funded exhibit. Painter Keith Haring, who studied at the School of Visual Arts in the '80s and was supported by Andy Warhol, adopted a decidedly more self-conscious political voice with his works, which even after his death continue to promote federal support for the arts and AIDS research, and to encourage public awareness. Everything from book bags to sweatshirts emblazoned with his designs are sold at his downtown store, the Pop Shop, on Lafayette Street.

The same energy that has allowed New York's art scene to re-energize areas once considered "uninteresting" and "tired," words used to describe SoHo of the late '60s and early '70s, and TriBeCa in the mid-'70s, continues to inspire progress and change. New York's catalog of 20th-century art is uniquely dynamic and has earned the city a seminal role in the current direction of Western art.

brooklyn galleries

Looking for a change from the museums and galleries of Manhattan? Brooklyn boasts a thriving art gallery/museum culture. If you're into big museums, check out mainstays like the Brooklyn Museum of Art, where the permanent collection includes Egyptian and ancient Middle Eastern art, arts of Africa, the Pacific, the Americas, and Asia, as well as photography. The Brooklyn Historical Society offers a detailed and fascinating look into Brooklyn's history, including permanent exhibits on the Brooklyn Bridge, Coney Island, the Brooklyn Navy Yard, and the Brooklyn Dodgers. If you have a penchant for galleries, Williamsburg is a veritable gold mine. This charming, funky neighborhood is home to many galleries, with something for almost any art lover's palate. Moments Art, a nonprofit gallery, is constantly changing and expanding its repertoire, most recently including a series of interviews with independent and avant-garde filmmakers. Owned and operated by artists, Salon 75 and Feed strive to, in the words of one of the curators, put on shows that cross the great divide between artmaking and curating. Pierogi 2000 is one of Williamsburg's most popular galleries, featuring the works of well known artists like Lawrence Weiner and Fred Tomaselli in addition to works by lesser known artists. Work here costs a fraction of what they cost in Manhattan. Four Walls, which has made its home in Williamsburg since 1931, has made the neighborhood art-friendly by incorporating writers, artists, and filmmakers into curating.

the roots of museum culture

New Yorkers take their city's immersion in art for granted—but those new to the city will note that this is taking a lot for granted: The museums are excellent; the galleries exciting and diverse; the breadth of the collections astonishing. Avoid museum burnout by staggering visits, and by selecting museums of different sizes and focus. Most of the major museums now have good—if pricey—cafes, which serve as a perfect way of restoring energy without retreating back onto the streets.

Museums, like everything else in New York, are not cheap. But for the impoverished and the flexible, there's usually a way around entrance fees at the major museums. The Metropolitan Museum, MoMA, and the Whitney offer free entry to the public one night a week, usually a weekend night. While museums throughout the city cater to a wide variety of tastes, these three institutions pave the way. Stroll around and be thankful for those great 19th-century robber-barons—most of the collections in the major museums were formerly private.

The Metropolitan has benefited from sizable bequests from railroad tycoon Jacob Rogers, as well as from W.C. Bryant, and J.P. Morgan. Founded in 1870, additions were made in 1909 by McKim, Mead, and White. By 1929, other substantial additions included gifts made by John D. Rockefeller and Louisine Havemeyer. Content to revel in the elitist connotation which high art carries, the Met's collection reflects none of the dynamism of the contemporary art scene; indeed, the museum balked at Gertrude Vanderbilt Whitney's 1930 offer of her collection of American paintings and the funding to build a wing for it. Since World War II, however, the museum's attitude has been decidedly more open-minded, seeking to exhibit a wider range of art; the Met has since presented more broad-based shows, as well as educational and community programs. Today, with more than a million pieces, the Met is the largest art museum in the western hemisphere. The museum functions on a pay-as-you-wish basis, suggesting, but not enforcing, a donation of $8 for adults. Summers, the roof garden offers museum-goers cocktails and a spectacular view of the midtown skyline.

Unlike the Met, which was funded as a result of a $500,000 tax levied by the city, the Whitney began as one family's private enterprise; perhaps as a result, the autonomous Whitney has proven tolerant of all genres of American art. Originally housed in four town houses on 8th Street, the Whitney Museum of American Art committed itself to the promotion of the works of living artists overlooked by other galleries and museums. By 1932, the first of the Whitney's Biennial Exhibitions quickly established the museum as the vanguard showcase of contemporary American painting. A cultural incubator for many American movements, including Abstract Expressionism and Pop Art, the museum provided an arena in which artists excluded from the mainstream could be celebrated. Equally as important as the breadth of its collection is the contribution the museum has made to the scholarship and legitimization of American art. Due to its enormous appeal, the museum has moved twice in order to accommodate its popularity and the expansion of its collection. With parts of this collection now on display at its downtown branch and in the

176 visual arts

lobbies of some of the city's most populous corporate spaces, like the Philip Morris Office Building, the Equitable Center, and the Federal Reserve Plaza, the Whitney encourages prominent presentation of and high regard for American art. Admission is free on Thursdays from 6-8pm.

The Museum of Modern Art is the third of New York's triumvirate of museum powerhouses. Abby Rockefeller established the museum in 1929 with a modest gift of eight prints and one drawing. Shortly thereafter, a generous gift from the wife of Colorado Senator Simon Guggenheim enabled Rockefeller to expand the collection considerably. The MoMA now owns more than 100,000 pieces. Committed from its inception to presenting the visual arts in all its various forms, the museum is responsible for introducing much of the European avant-garde to America. In addition to the traditional visual arts of painting and sculpture, the MoMA also features furniture design and architecture, prints and illustrated books, and photography; the museum's film and video archives, self-described as "the strongest international film collection in the United States," contain all extant negatives from the Biograph and Edison companies. Apart from the permanent collection, the MoMA runs a special exhibit which changes every few weeks and costs extra to view. During the summer, visitors can enjoy the outdoor sculpture garden featuring works by Rodin; weekend evenings, MoMA hosts the Summer Garden concert series. Entrance is free on Friday evenings.

Keep in mind that these are only three of the city's 40-plus museums; the Solomon Guggenheim Museum, the Cooper-Hewitt, and the Jewish Museum, among others, can be equally rewarding. In Brooklyn, the often-neglected jewel, the Brooklyn Museum, houses an enormous world-class permanent collection and changing exhibits. Living history museums, whose situation in a historic house lends them a more naturalistic feeling, are tucked away in unassuming corners of the city, from the Theodore Roosevelt birthplace in Gramercy to the reputedly haunted Morris-Jumel Mansion in Washington Heights; the Frick Collection, although it displays works of art in a museum fashion, is set up as a house, as opposed to the sterile white-washed look of most city display museums. Most museums run special tours and the larger ones often sponsor lectures and movie screenings; call or stop by for a schedule and information about becoming a member. After all, without the support of their patrons, many museums would go under.

visual arts 177

MUSEUMS

A

Abigail Adams Smith Museum

John Quincy Adams' daughter wanted to replicate Mount Vernon here, but ended up with this 1799 carriage house. Formerly a hotel with offices for Standard Oil, the museum displays Colonial American memorabilia from the 1820s-40s in reconstructed rooms, which include a tavern, kitchen, bedroom, and several parlors. There are lectures regularly, along with live music and an outdoor cafe open during the summer months.
421 East 61st St. (bet. First and York Aves.), 838-6878, Admission: $3, $2 (students) Tuesday-Sunday, 11am-4pm, ❹❺❻ to 59th St., ⓃⓇ to Lexington Ave.

African American Wax Museum

Nelson Mandela and Magic Johnson, together at last in life-size wax sculpture. Opened in 1989 by fashion designer and innovative artist Raven Chanticleer, the museum allows tours by appointment only, lending an intimacy to the experience.
316 West 115th St. (bet. Manhattan and Frederick Douglass Aves.), 678-7818, Cash Only, Suggested Donation $10, $5 (students), Tours: Tuesday-Sunday, 1pm-6pm, ⒷⒸ to 116th St.

Alternative Museum

Founded and operated by artists, this strikingly introspective nonprofit organization features a range of works that compel viewers to examine the relationship between society and art.
594 Broadway, Suite 402 (bet. Houston and Prince Sts.), 966-4444, Admission: $3 suggested, ⓃⓇ to Prince St.

American Craft Museum

Utilitarian, 20th-century American art, from chairs to teapots, finds a home in this magnificent space. Exhibits in the past have included textiles and intricate weavings.
40 West 53rd St. (bet. Fifth and Sixth Aves.), 956-3535, Admission: $5, $2.50 (students), Tuesday, 10am-8pm, Wednesday-Sunday 10am-5pm, ⒺⒻ to Fifth Ave.

American Museum of Moving Image

"One has the sense of being transported from the everyday world straight to the set of a modern-day Oz," wrote Stephen Holden in the *New York Times*, referring to "Behind the Scenes," one of the permanent exhibits at this museum devoted to the art, history, technique, and technology of the visual media and its influence on culture and society. Housed in the old Paramount Studios at the heart of Queens' old movie district, the museum is a treasure trove of movie memorabilia from the '30s and 40's. Regular film series at the Riklis Theater screen over 500 movies a year, which are free with admission.
35th Ave. (at 36th St.), (718) 784-4520, Admission: $4-$8, Tuesday-Friday, 12pm-4pm, Saturday-Sunday, 12pm-6pm, ⓃⒼⓇ to Steinway St.

American Museum of Natural History

A taxidermist's paradise and proud owner of a fantastic new wing packed with dinosaurs. The museum also houses a Hall of Human Evolution and Biology, chronicling human development from ape to homo sapiens. Eat lunch under the whale.
79th St. and Central Park West, 769-5100, Admission: $7, $5 (students), Monday-Thursday, 10am-5:45pm, Saturday-Sunday, 10am-8:45pm, ⒷⒸ to 81st St.

Asia Society

America's preeminent organization celebrates Asian cultural awareness with notable film series, lectures, and an art collection featuring sculpture, paintings, ceramics, prints and bronzes from across Asia. Prominent authors and public leaders speak regularly here; other programs for the public include dance performances, well-attended art exhibits usually gathered from private collections, and receptions involving community and professional organizations.
725 Park Avenue (at 70th St.), 288-6400, MC, V, AmEx, ❻ to 68th St.

Asian American Arts Center

As the name suggests, Asian-American artists have top billing at this thriving community arts center, which supports activities ranging from traditional dance performances to the journal on contemporary Asian-American artists, Arts Spiral. In February, the Asia Folk Arts Festival brings traditional arts produced both in the States and abroad for display.
26 Bowery (at Bayard St.), 233-2154, ❻ to Grand St., ⓃⓇ to Canal St.

B

Black Fashion Museum

Both a school and museum of African and black American design and memorabilia since 1979; visits are by appointment only.
155 West 126th St. (bet. A.C. Powell and Malcolm X Aves.), Admission: $1.50, $1 (students), ⒶⒷⒸⒹ❷❸ to 125th St.

Bronx Museum of the Arts

Representing the urban experience through photography, sculpture, painting, and mixed-media, this community museum pays special attention to the African, Asian, and Latino heritage that define the Bronx. Shows change every three months.
1040 Grand Concourse (at 165th St.), (718) 681-6000, Admission: $3, $2 (students), Wednesday, 3pm-9pm; Thursday-Friday, 10am-5pm; Saturday-Sunday, 1pm-6pm, ⒸⒹ❹ to 167th St.

The Brooklyn Museum

A world-class museum with strong permanent collections and impressive special exhibitions. The American paintings are excellent, the Egyptian Wing is outstanding, and there's a lovely sculpture garden as well. Located next to the botanical garden, it's a great way to get away from it all while remaining in the City.
1200 Eastern Parkway (at Washington Ave.), next to Prospect Park, (718) 638-5000, Suggested admission: $4, $2 (students), ❷❸ to Eastern Parkway

178 visual arts

C

Casa Italiana
The former home of General Winfield Scott, hero of the Mexican-American War and Chief-of-Staff of the U.S. Army in the 1850s. Call for information about free lectures, films, and art exhibits that focus on Italian culture.
24 West 12th St. (bet. Fifth and Sixth Aves.), 998-8730, ❶❷❸ *❷❸❾ to 14th St.*

Casa Italiana
Ubiquitous in the press though nowhere to be found on campus, intellectual Umberto Eco is a scholar in residence at this recently remodeled institution at Columbia, where lectures and events concerned with Italian culture are hosted regularly in the center's mock High Renaissance auditorium.
1161 Amsterdam Ave. (at 118th St.), 854-2306, ❶❾ *to 116th St.*

Children's Museum of Manhattan
Apartment-bred kids get a taste of nature in the Urban Tree House, see what makes TV tick at the Time Warner Media Center, and read about the life and works of Dr. Seuss at this creative, interactive museum for children of all ages. Lots of wild water fun when the gets hot.
212 West 83rd St. (bet. Broadway and Amsterdam Aves.), 721-1234, Admission: $5, Monday, Wednesday, Thursday, 1:30pm-5:30pm, Friday-Sunday, 10am-5pm, ❶❾ *to 86th St.*

The Cloisters
A smorgasbord of old-style European glories, not to mention the finest picnicking in the city. The Met has their famed medieval collection here, including the breathtaking Unicorn tapestries, and medieval-themed readings and concerts keep hobbyists and scholars busy. The Cloisters themselves are a collection of European chapels and buildings in the Gothic and Romantic styles disassembled and shipped overseas stone by stone by John D. Rockefeller and George Barnard, then reassembled way uptown.
Fort Tyon Park, 923-3700, Sugg. admission (cash only): $7.50, $3 (students), MC, V, AmEx, Diners, D at the gift shop, ❶ *to 190th St., M4 to Cloisters*

The Cooper-Hewitt Museum
The Smithsonian's National Museum of Design utilizes its 11,000 square feet to present landmark historic pieces as well as pioneering contemporary designs. Attention is paid to both the one-of-a-kind and the mass-produced. The building, once the Carnegie Mansion, boasts an eye-catching ceiling and an intricate staircase. Come free between 5pm and 9pm on Tuesdays.
Two East 91st St. (at Fifth Ave.), 860-6868, Admission: $3, $1.50 (students), Tuesday, 10am-9pm, Wednesday-Saturday, 10am-5pm, Sunday, 12pm-5pm, ❹❺❻ *to 86th St.*

Czech Center
Exhibits on Czech culture and contemporary art; one recent show included photographs taken by blind children.
1109 Madison Ave. (at 83rd St.), 288-0830, Cash Only, ❹❺❻ *to 86th St.*

D

Deutsches Haus
Lecture series by scholars and cultural emissaries, readings by visiting German language authors, and a beautiful gallery space and library with an extensive periodical section are all open to the public. The NYU community enjoys a free film series showcasing everything from Weimar cinema to the contemporary work of artists like Wim Wenders. Ten week German language programs cost $300-400.
42 Washington Place (bet. University Pl. and Fifth Ave.), 998-8660, MC, V, ❶❷ *to 8th St.*

The Drawing Center
This nonprofit organization has an extensive collection of works on paper, including lots of drawings by a variety of new and established artists. The operation has been so successful that a second space recently opened across the street.
35 Wooster St. (bet. Grand and Broome Sts.), 219-2166, Cash and Check Only, ❶❷❸❾ *to Canal St.*

Dyckman Farmhouse Museum
A museum of 18th-century farmhouse life, located in one of Manhattan's oldest residences, reminds urbanites that the city did not simply spring from the soil full-grown. Period furnishings and quiet gardens maintain the mood. Benches out front are ideal for catching rays or hanging out with the area's elderly population (and no, none of them actually lived here).
4881 Broadway (at 204th St.), 304-9422, Donations accepted, Cash Only, ❶ *to 207th St.*

E

El Museo del Barrio
Originally a project in an East Harlem classroom, the sole American museum of Puerto Rican arts and culture has graduated to Museum Mile. Nearly 8000 objects span over 800 years of history; the museum recently added more gallery space and celebrated its twenty-fifth anniversary.
1230 5th Ave. (at 104th St.), 831-7272, Admission: $4, $2 (students), Wed.-Sun., 11am-5pm, ❻ *to 103rd St.*

F

Fashion Institute of Technology
Exhibits feature famously fabulous designers, as well as work by talented FIT students.
227 West 27th St. (at Seventh Ave.), 760-7700, Admission Free, ❶❾ *to 28th St.*

FIRE Museum
If a field trip to the fire station is a favorite childhood memory, don't miss this chance to relive it. The collection, housed in a renovated Beaux-Arts style firehouse from 1904, is the country's largest; it's full of all standard firehouse trappings, old engines and pump cars, and plenty of intriguing New York City fire history.
278 Spring St. (bet. Houston and Varick Sts.), 691-1303, Admission: $3.50 (kids), Tues.-Sat., 10am-4pm, MC, V, AmEx, ❶❸❺ *to Spring St.*

visual arts 179

Floral Park

Dating back to 1772, this farm covers 52 acres of land and is the only working farm of its era that has been restored and reopened to the public. Open year-round Monday-Friday.
73-50 Little Neck Parkway, (718) 347-3276, Admission free, Monday-Friday, 9am-5pm, Saturday-Sunday, 10am-5pm, ❸❻ to Union Turnpike Kew Gardens

Fraunces Tavern Museum

George Washington gave his farewell address to his troops at this Georgian mansion, which was home to the Departments of Foreign Affairs, Treasury, and War during New York's brief spell as a capital city. Now the museum specializes in American history and culture of the 18th and 19th centuries, with plenty of period rooms in which to play pretend.
54 Pearl St. (at Broad St.), 425-1778, Admission: $2.50, $1(students), Monday-Friday 10am-4:45pm, Saturday, 12pm-4pm, ❶❾ to South Ferry, ❹❺ to Bowling Green

Frick Collection

Steel kingpin Henry Clay Frick built this mansion with his fine art collection and a future museum in mind. The museum's been realized and now offers a rare chance to view masterpieces displayed in a residential setting. Highlights include portraits by El Greco, Rembrandt, and Renoir, and waterscapes by Turner. One of the most soothing spots in the city is the sun-lit, virtually soundproof indoor courtyard with marble benches and a drizzling fountain. The mail-in procedure for free tickets to Sunday concerts is an ordeal, but no tickets are required to listen in from the courtyard.
One East 70th St. (at Fifth Ave.), 288-0700, Admission: $5, $3 (students), Tuesday-Saturday, 10am-6pm, Sunday, 1pm-6pm, ❻ to 68th St. ♿

G

Guggenheim SoHo

An ENEL virtual reality gallery and an electronic reading room with CD-ROMs are several of the ultramodern highlights of this downtown counterpart to its Museum Mile heavyweight, which opened in 1992. Though the architecture is hardly Frank Lloyd Wright, the SoHo building, designed by Arata Isozaki, is airy and conducive to the curators' ambitious programs, which re-examine 20th century innovators like Max Beckmann and showcase contemporary stars like media artist Bill Viola. Come Sundays at 2pm for a free tour of the collection.
575 Broadway (at Prince St.), 423-3500, Admission: $6, $4 (students), ❻❻ to Prince St.

H

Hayden Planetarium

What is a black hole? Does Planet X exist? Find out at "The 20 Most Asked Questions About the Universe And the Answers," just one of the programs at the astronomy department in the domed building adjacent to the Museum of National History. Weekends find a youngish crowd at the ever-popular 3-D laser light shows; Pink Floyd is an old standby, while the more recent show featuring Nirvana and friends from Seattle ("Laser Grunge") rocks a little harder.
80th St. (bet. Columbus Ave.and Central Park West), 769-5900, Admission: $5, $3 (students), $8.50 for laser shows, October-June, Monday-Friday, 12:30pm-4:45pm, Saturday-Sunday, 10am-5:45pm, July-September, weekends 12pm-4:45pm, ❻❻ to 81st St. ♿

I

International Center for Photography

Founded in 1974, one of the youngest members of Museum Mile showcases over 45,000 photographs and serves as a learning center for budding photographers of all levels of expertise.
1130 Fifth Ave. (at 94th St.), 860-1777, Tuesday, 11am-8pm, Wednesday-Sunday, 11am-6pm, ❻ to 96th St.

Islamic Cultural Center and Mosque

The city's central mosque holds prayer and studies on Sundays, as well as free courses for women on Saturdays on religion and the Arabic language
97th St. (bet. First and Second Aves.), 732-5234, ❻ to 96th St.

The Isamu Noguchi Garden Museum

More than 300 works in granite, steel and marble, including the famous Akari paper light sculptures by Isamu Noguchi, who also designed the twelve galleries and the outdoor sculpture garden. Open April to October.
32-37 Vernon Boulevard, (718) 204-7088, Cash Only, Admission $4, $2 (students), Wednesday, Saturday, Sunday, 11am-6pm, shuttle runs from 70th St. and Park Avenue on weekends

J

Jewish Museum

The country's largest collection of Judaica, housed in an imperious French Renaissance structure, boasts over 14,000 works in the permanent collection. Works detail the Jewish experience throughout history and feature archeological pieces, ceremonial objects, modern masterpieces by Marc Chagall and Frank Stella, and even an interactive computer program based on the Talmud. The first two floors host temporary installations and exhibits. Admission is free Tuesdays 5pm-8pm.
1109 Fifth Ave. (at 92nd St.), 423-3200, Admission: $7, $5 (students), Sunday, Monday, Wednesday, Thursday: 11am-5:45pm, ❻ to 96th St.

K

King Juan Carlos I Center

King Juan Carlos the First himself showed up along with Queen Sophia and Hillary Clinton to inaugurate the new hub of Spanish culture in the city. Housed in architect Stanford White's historic 19th century Renaissance-style Judson Hall, the center encourages the study of Spain and the rest of the Spanish-speaking world through lectures, colloquia, and conferences

180 visual arts

with scholars and dignitaries.
53 Washington Square South (Thompson St. and 6th Ave.), 998-3650, ABCDEF Q to West 4th St.

L

Lower East Side Tenement Museum

Chronicling an era when these streets were the most densely packed in the world, this museum, founded in 1988, is the first attempt the city has made at preserving a tenement. Like most tenements, the building predated existing housing laws; this one dates from 1863. Bedrooms were typically eight square feet, most apartments' largest rooms were a mere twelve by eleven feet, and tenants had no running water, flush toilets, or electric lights. Most rooms even lacked windows. Founders Ruth J. Abram and Anita Jacobson strive to recreate the conditions in this progressive attempt at reclaiming an often overlooked chunk of the city's history.
97 Orchard Street (bet. Broome and Delancey Sts.), 431-9233, MC, V, AmEx, Admission $6 for walking tour, $6 for tenement tour, $2 for slide and video shows, F to Delancey St.

M

The Metropolitan Museum of Art

Where to begin? The Met seems to be as big and sprawling as the city itself, and similarly the trick is finding the hidden (or not so hidden) treasures. Favorites include the spectacular Temple of Dendur, the American Wing Garden Court, the medieval section, and in the summer, the Roof Garden where an older crowd sips white wine and ponders the sculpture (out loud). Don't try to do too much, or to follow a strict plan, since this is the best place to get lost in New York City.
Fifth Avenue (bet. 79th and 84th Sts.), Suggested admission: $8, $5 (students), Tuesday-Thursday, 9:15am-5:45pm, Friday-Saturday, 9:15am-8:45pm, 6 to 86th St.

Morris-Jumel Mansion

Down from the remaining farmhouse is the area's extant Georgian mansion, where Washington kept his troops during the Revolution. A choice exhibit displays the obit of Vice President Aaron Burr's wife Elise Jumel, whose early life as a "lady of the night" once scandalized New York society.
160th St. and Edgecombe Ave., 923-8008, Admission: $3, Cash Only, BC to 163rd St.

The Museum for African Art

Exhibits seeking to facilitate a greater understanding of African art change twice a year at this two-floor showcase, one of two of its kind in the country. Complex exhibits often incorporate elements of folk art, sculpture, and more conventional mediums to examine pervasive concepts in the tradition. Past exhibits include "Secrecy: African Art That Conceals and Reveals," and "Face of the Gods: Art and Altars of the Black Atlantic World." Film and video presentations, performance art, and interactive, hands-on workshops take place in the newly opened Educational Department.
593 Broadway (bet. Houston and Prince Sts.), 966-1313, Admission: $4, $2 (students), Wed., Thurs., and Sun., 11am-6pm, Fri.-Sat., 11am-8pm, NR to Prince St.

Museum of African American History and Arts

Minority artists of all genres, both well-known and relatively obscure, display their work here. Also known as the Adam Clayton Powell, Jr. Gallery. Viewings must be scheduled in advance.
163 West 125th St., 2nd Floor (bet. A.C. Powell and Malcolm X Aves.), 873-5040, Admission free, Wed.-Sun., 11am-5pm 6 to 103rd St.

Museum of American Folk Art

A compact venue which explodes the stereotype of folk art with exhibits ranging from portraits to weathervanes to pottery. Some displays are thematic, while others are based around the personal holdings of prominent collectors.
Two Lincoln Square (at Columbus Ave. and 66th St.), 977-7298, Suggested admission: $3, Tuesday-Sunday, 11:30am-7:30pm, 1 9 to 66th St.

Museum of American Illustrators

View the work of key illustrators like Norman Rockwell and N.C. Wyeth at the home of the elite Society of Illustrators, which claims a long history of service to none other than the United States Army. Educational opportunities include sketch classes and lectures.
128 East 63rd St. (bet. Park and Lexington Aves.), 838-2560, 456 to 59th St., NR to Lexington Ave.

Museum of Modern Art

Toeing a precarious line between avant-garde and establishment, this New York institution holds the world's most comprehensive collection of 19th and 20th century art, ranging from paintings to sculpture to photographs and beyond. Take a break amidst the Rodin sculptures in the outdoor garden. Admission is free on Thursday nights, along with free jazz in the café.
11 West 53rd St. (bet. Fifth and Sixth Aves.), 708-9400, Admission: $8.50, $5.50 (students), EF to Fifth Ave.

Museum of Television and Radio

Watch TV all day and still feel cultured. Computer consoles and viewing cubicles access tens of thousands of programs (and you thought cable was overwhelming), though if your tastes are way obscure, you should order ahead of time. A nostalgic display of Kermit the Frog and friends is worth the trip alone.
25 West 52nd St. (bet. Fifth and Sixth Aves.), 621-6800, Admission: $6, $4 (students), BDFQ to Rockefeller Center

Museum of the City of New York

In light of its ego, it's fitting that New York was the first city to get its own museum. Exhibits glorify New York's vast history, and include pho-

visual arts 181

tographs, furniture, costumes, and toys. The Sunay concert series and the Big Apple Film make the trip worthwhile.
1220 Fifth Ave. (bet. 103rd and 104th Sts.), 534-1672, Suggested admission: $5, $4 (students), Cash Only for Admission, MC, V, AmEx for Gift Shop, Wednesday-Saturday, 10am-5pm, ❻ *to 103rd St.*

N

National Academy of Design

Founded in 1825 to promote the art of design in America through painting, sculpture, architecture, and engraving, the academy still strives to meet its same purpose through training young artists and serving as a fraternal organization for other distinguished American artists. Its permanent exhibit features works by such 19th-century masters as Winslow Homer, John Singer Sargent, and Thomas Eakins, and such contemporary artists as Robert Rauschenberg, Isabel Bishop, and Phillip Johnson.
1083 Fifth Ave. (bet. 89th and 90th Sts.), 369-4880, Admission: $3.50, $2 (students), Wednesday-Sunday, 12pm-5pm, Friday, 12pm-8pm, ❹❺❻ *to 86th St.* &

New York Hall of Science

While designed primarily for kids, this playground of hands-on exhibits appeals to the science nut in everyone. The newly expanded exhibition hall boasts a Technology Gallery, with access to the Internet and a wide range of CD-ROMs. Who can

resist entering the Realm of the Atom or the World of the Microbes? Wednesdays and Thursdays are free 3pm-5pm.
47-01 111th Street, Flushing Meadow Park, (718) 699-0005, Wed.-Sun., 9:30am-5pm, Admission: $3-$4.50, Free Monday, Wednesday, Thursday, 2pm-5pm, ❼ *to 111th St.* &

The New York City Transit Museum

While you may consider the turnstiles in working stations antique, the originals are really housed in this authentic 1930s subway station. Vintage subway maps and mosaics comprise the permanent collection, along with exhibitions chronicling the development of rapid transit. Tag along with a school group for a field trip to somewhere great like the Metro-North car-repair facility.
130 Livingston (bet. Boerum Place and Schermerhorn), (718) 330-3060, Admission: $3, $1.50 (students), Tues.-Fri., 10am-4pm, Sat.-Sun., 12pm-5pm, ❷❸ *to Borough Hall* &

New York Unearthed

Archeology and New York may seem like strange bedfellows, but this smallish museum does the juxtaposition justice; artifacts along the lines of cannon balls and bones, as well as excavation finds, are on display. The Lower Gallery offers the chance to watch conservationists working busily behind glass. Take the New York Systems elevator down for a simulated dig. And you thought this city was just built on top of a bunch of garbage.
17 State St. (at Water St.),

748-8628, Admission free, ❶❾ *to South Ferry* &

Nicholas Roerich Museum

Discreetly hidden among a row of brownstones, this museum honors Nicholas Roerich, the artist who designed an international peace symbol during World War II.
107th St. (bet. Broadway and Riverside), 864-7752, Suggested contribution, ❶❾ *to 110th St.*

P

Pierpont Morgan Library

The country's largest collection of Mesopotamian cylinder seals now rests where J.P. Morgan used to pad about in slippers, though the appeal of this library and museum is much more broad-based. For a minimal fee, students can peek at the Renaissance-focused collections of the rare book library; call ahead to use the reading room.
29 East 36th St.at Madison Ave., 685-0008 or 685-0610, ❻ *to 33rd St.* &

Police Academy Museum

Ever really wanted to see Al Capone's machine gun? Other police memorabilia and crime-related items are also on exhibit.
235 East 20th St. (bet. Second and Third Aves.), 2nd Fl., 477-9753, Admission free, ❻ *to 23rd St.*

Q

Queens Museum of Art

The must-see exhibit of this small museum, which is located right opposite the Unisphere and housed

in the original U.N., is the scale model, the largest of its kind, of New York City. Half-price admission for students.
Flushing Meadows/Corona Park, (718) 592-2405, Admission: $3, Wednesday-Friday, 10am-5pm; Saturday-Sunday, 12pm-5pm, ❼ *to Willets Point/Shea Stadium*

S

Solomon R. Guggenheim Museum

It's now hard to imagine upper Fifth Avenue, without Frank Lloyd Wright's famous spiral of a building, home to one of the most remarkable 20th-century art collections in the world. The controversial new addition, a rectangular tower, was opened in 1992 and houses the permanent collection; special exhibits still wind their way down interior ramps. This may not be the best way to view art, but it's surely the most distinctive. Friday evenings are freebies.
1071 Fifth Avenue (bet. 88th and 89th Sts.), 360-3500, Admission: $10, $7 (students), Sunday-Wednesday, 10am-6pm, Friday-Saturday, 10am-8pm, ❹❺❻ *to 86th St.* &

Sotheby's

Don your most expensive dress and pretend you're an heiress at a viewing at Manhattan's other leading auction house; collectibles sold here range from rare coins, jewels, and vintage wine to decorative and fine arts. Admission is free, but the glossy catalog will set you back about 20 bucks.
1334 York Avenue (at 72nd St.), 606-7000, MC,

182 visual arts

V, 6 to 68th St., B Q to Lexington Ave.

Studio Museum in Harlem

From its origins as a rented loft in 1967, this museum has burgeoned into one of the most innovative focusing on arts from Africa and Black America. The artists-in-residence program gives emerging artists gallery space, and the Cooperative School Program puts professional artists in Harlem schools.
144 West 125th St. (bet. A.C. Powell and Malcolm X), Admission: $5, $3 (students), Wednesday-Friday, 10am-5pm, Saturday-Sunday, 1pm-6pm, A B C D 2
3 to 125th St.

W

The Whitney Museum of American Art

A motherlode of American avant-garde and post-modern art. Lively, provocative shows are the rule here, including the ever-controversial Biennial, an exhibit of contemporary works held in odd-numbered years that never fails to rile the critics.
945 Madison Ave. (at 75th St.), 570-3676, Admission: $8, $6 (students), Wednesday, Friday, Saturday-Sunday, 11am-6pm, Thursday, 1-8pm, 6 to 77th St.

Y

Yeshiva University Museum

In the eastern reaches of Washington Heights, the country's oldest Jewish institution of higher learning regularly holds exhibits on both historical and contemporary Jewish themes, such as "The Emergence of the Synagogue in the Ancient World."
2520 Amsterdam Ave. (bet. 185th and 186th Sts.), 960-5390, Admission: $3, $2 (students), Cash Only, 1 9 to 181st St.

GALLERIES

A

Acquavella

Uptown gallery hoppers never overlook this motherlode of 19th and 20th century European masters and postwar European and American pieces.
18 East 79th St. (bet. Madison and Fifth Aves.), 734-6300, Cash Only, 6 to 77th St.

Apex

Off the beaten path of art with a fresh perspective, this is one of the best places to find innovative work; appreciating it comes easily also, since the staffers are far less aloof than most of their SoHo counterparts. Shows tend to feature a combination of efforts by a few different artists and include both painting and sculpture.
291 Church Street (bet. Walker and White Sts.), 431-5270, 1 9 to Franklin St.

Artist's Space

A testing ground where new artists get the chance to cut their teeth, pay their dues, and show their stuff to the gallery world. Shows generally focus on a central theme and contain several new artists with work that fits in. Check out up-and-coming talent in its larval stages.
38 Greene Street (bet. Grand and Broome Sts.), 226-3970, N R 1 9 C E to Canal St., F to Lafayette St.

B

Barbara Gladstone

This enormous space has tall ceilings and two levels displaying contemporary and modern art in various media, including rotating painting, sculpture, video installations, and photography.
515 West 24th St. (bet. Tenth and Eleventh Aves.), 206-9300, C E to 23rd St.

Basilico

One-person shows are the standard at this sprawling showroom where promising newcomers attempt to prove themselves. Pieces are displayed in an unusually manageable fashion.
26 Wooster St. (bet. Grand and Canal Sts.), 966-1831, Cash Only, A C E N R to Canal St.

C

Christie's

Scope out the goods at the free public viewing five days before the auction at this New York branch of the London legend; 19th and 20th century European art, traditionally favored here, are still strong suits.
502 Park Avenue (at 59th St.), 546-1007, Cash and Checks Only, 4 5 6 to 59th St.

D

Danese

If artists were incomes (a rather germane comparison for 57th Street too), those featured here would be upper-middle class; some risks but some more established stuff also to keep it safe. Columbia's generous student bartenders typically tend the wine bar, so a little looksee at openings could be rewarding.
41 East 57th Street, (bet. Madison and Park Aves.), 223-2227, Cash Only, B Q to 57th St., 4 5 6 to Lexington Ave.

David Zwirner

A good place for good art. Whatever the well-known featured artist displays, it's done to near perfection, to the delight of critics and other viewers. Even if the style isn't something you find particularly inspiring, the high level of technique demonstrated is easy to admire.
43 Greene Street (bet. Grand and Broome Sts.), 966-9074, Cash Only, 6 to Canal St.

Dia Center for the Arts

Dia opened its main exhibition facility in a four-story renovated warehouse in 1987, dedicating it to large-scale, long-term exhibitions, offering artists the opportunity to develop new work or a focused presentation of work on a full floor of the building.
548 West 22nd Street, 989-5566, Admission: $4, $2 (members, students, and seniors), 1 9 C E to 23rd St.

E

Esso

If there is a mien that suggests I-just-became-legal at a drinking establishment, then the artistic counterpart that suggests I-just-finished-art-school

visual arts 183

reigns at this funky downtown space, where pop art is reworked for a generation that grew up on the Smurfs and Atari.
191 Chrystie St., 6th Fl., (bet Rivington and Stanton Sts.), 714-8192, Cash Only, F to Second Ave.

Exit Art
A huge upstairs loft space, complete with a cafe made for lingering when gallery hopping becomes tiresome, and a shop filled with art trinkets. Never stodgy, themed group shows are favored; past innovations include having the artists move their studios into the gallery and an exhibit of art/paraphernalia from social protest movements. Openings here should not be missed.
548 Broadway (bet. Prince and Spring Sts.), 966-7745, Donation requested, MC, V, AmEx, N R to Prince St., 4 5 6 to Spring St.

G

Gagosian
A vast gallery filled by established artists who are often eager to take advantage of the space. As such, large paintings, three-dimensional pieces, and sculpture often come into play, and the results can be more absorbing than a similar show executed in a smaller area. Even when the physical potential isn't utilized, the art is usually worth checking out.
136 Wooster St. (bet Prince and Houston Sts.), 228-2828, Cash Only, N R 6 to Prince St.

Greene Naftali Gallery
A western exposure bathes the space in natural light. Works are contemporary and tend to be experimental; genres range from sculpture and painting to multimedia exhibits.
526 West 26th St., Eighth Floor (bet. Tenth and Eleventh Aves.), 463-7770, C E to 23rd St.

Grey Art Gallery
Both foreign and domestic contemporary artists display their work at this offbeat gallery on New York University's main campus.
100 Washington Square East (at Waverly Pl.), 998-6780, donation suggested, N R to 8th St.

J

Jack Tilton
The artists shown here are respected, but not necessarily for producing expected conventional pieces. Often, the stuff on display requires a second look to see what's really going on. On closer examination, a recent collection of Fred Tomaselli's paintings focusing on birds, leaves, and butterflies proved to be elaborate mosaics made up of pills.
49 Greene St., 941-1775, Cash Only, A C E to Canal St.

Jessica Fredericks Gallery
Housed in a brownstone-like building, this smallish space consists of one main viewing room showcasing established and emerging artists.
504 West 22nd Street, Ground Floor (bet. Tenth and Eleventh Aves.), 633-6555, Cash Only, C E to 23rd St.

Jim Deitsch Projects
The small entryway here gives way to big-time modern art inside. Don't pass up the chance to experience anything from relatively tame nontraditional sculpture installations to a Russian performance artist living inside a doghouse within the gallery and getting confrontational with visitors, just two of the recent offerings.
76 Grand Street (bet. Wooster and Greene Sts.), 343-7300, Cash Only, N R to Canal St.

K

Knoedler Gallery
Not to be missed by art historians or art historians in-the-making, the oldest New York-based art gallery, established in 1846, exhibits such modern greats as Nancy Graves, Robert Motherwell, Frank Stella, and Robert Rauschenberg.
19 East 70th St. (bet Madison and Fifth Aves.), 794-0550, 6 to 68th St.

L

Leo Castelli
Don't want to take a risk? The next best thing to playing it safe at a big museum is found here. The art is all by people who have made a name for themselves, either in the art world or the culture at large. Back in 1958 Castelli hand-picked Jasper Johns for a one-man show, thus launching pop art and minimalism. They even show some Picassos here.
420 West Broadway, 431-5160, Cash Only, N R to Prince St.

Linda Kirkland Gallery
Modest in size, but not in vision: the gallery's focus "will be to exhibit art that combines a conceptual bent with a sensual visual form."
504 West 22nd St., Third Floor, (bet. Tenth and Eleventh Aves.), 627-3930, Cash and Checks Only, C E to 23rd St.

M

Mary Boone Gallery
This longtime SoHo staple recently headed for greener grass up north; an elegant address on Fifth Avenue, though the many of the same artists, among them Ross Bleckner, who had a solo show at the Guggenheim a couple of years back, came along for the ride.
754 Fifth, Fourth Floor (bet. 57th and 58th Sts.), 752-2929, Cash Only, N R to Fifth Ave.

Metro Pictures
Three separate rooms here allow for three simultaneous exhibits. Sneak a peek at the main room through the large windows facing 24th Street.
519 West 24th St. (bet. Tenth and Eleventh Aves.), 206-7100, Cash Only, C E to 23rd St.

Miriam and Ira D. Wallach Art Gallery
Columbia's resident gallery presents traveling exhibitions throughout the year, curated by profs and students who ensure an academic tilt to the line-up. Lectures and receptions are often sponsored in conjunction with exhibits.
Columbia University, Schermerhorn Hall Eighth Floor, (116th Street and

184 visual arts

Broadway), 854-7288, ❶❾ to 116th St.

Momenta Art
The neighborhood's most grown-up gallery, still floating beyond the orbit of the conventional. The focus is on group shows featuring works by many artists reflecting a central, provocative theme, and the execution ranges from competent to brilliant. Well worth the trip for anyone looking for something beyond the SoHo scene.
72 Berry Street (bet. Ninth and Tenth Sts.), (718) 218-8058, Cash Only, ❶ to Bedford Ave.

N

New World Art Center
This "New Renaissance" gallery has an ambitious agenda, as it seeks to unite fine, graphic, literary, film, video, photographic, designing, and performing artists under one roof. The splintered focus keeps exhibits changing monthly.
250 Lafayette St. (bet. Prince and Spring Sts.), 941-9296, MC, V, AmEx, D, ❻ to Spring St., ❶❷ to Prince St., ❶❷❸❹ to Broadway/Lafayette St.

P

Pace Wildenstein Gallery, Midtown
An old hand at this art thing, this multilevel space hosts somewhat famous names, like Alexander Calder and Chuck Close.
32 East 57th Street (at Madison Ave.), 977-7160, ❶❷ to Fifth Ave., Cash Only, ❻ to Bleecker St.

Pace Wildenstein Gallery, SoHo
A Manhattan art world standard with several outlets throughout the city, the SoHo branch is a testament to the quality that sustains its popularity. Housed in a large and accessible street level space, they offer solo shows by some fine established artists not yet past their prime, such as Elizabeth Murray.
142 Greene Street (bet. Houston and Prince Sts.), 431-9224, ❶❷❸❹ to Broadway/Lafayette St.

Paula Cooper Gallery
You'll have to squint to read the lettering at this gallery's entrance on the south side of the street. Woodwork in the two rooms resembles a cross between a barn and a church; tall ceilings in the back room allow for massive installments. Natural light filters through fogged windows.
534 West 21st Street (bet. Tenth and Eleventh Aves.), 255-1105, Cash Only, ❶❷ to 23rd St.

Peter Blum
Generally on the beaten path in terms of content, with frequent swerves to the odd and obscure. In addition to paintings and sculpture by known artists, architectural sketches, non-Western archeological artifacts, and more have been known to make an appearance in this large, rectangular room.
99 Wooster Street, 343-0441, Cash and Check Only, ❶❷❸ to Spring St.

Phyllis Kind
Since the work of established white male artists still constitutes the majority of what makes it into serious galleries, this deceptively large space often contains shows that challenge this order. Artists like Betty Saar-who are African-American, female and from other underrepresented groups-regularly produce some of the most thought-provoking installations you're likely to see.
136 Greene St., 925-1200, MC, V, AmEx, D, ❶❷❸ to Broadway/Lafayette St., ❶❷ to Prince St.

Pierogi 2000
The name reflects the way the traditional Polish flavor of the community melds with the influx of forward-focused artists and others, and like most Williamsburg galleries, the art here is a far outside of the mainstream as the location. The gallery serves as everything from an outlet for resurrections of art treasures unseen for years to a center for lots of the neighborhood's resident artists, many of whom can be found hanging out on its stoop.
167 North 9th Street (bet. Bedford and Driggs Aves.), (718) 599-2144, Cash Only, ❶ to Bedford Ave.

PostMasters
A challenge to much of what's taken for granted in the art world shows up regularly here. Shows have included artists working together as a team to produce installations of seemingly ordinary scenes from everyday life, and work questioning directly the idea of art-as-business.
80 Greene Street, 941-5711, Cash Only, ❶❷ to Prince St.

PPOW
Started in the 80's in the East Village by two women, this gallery moved here after developing an excellent reputation. The two rooms generally each contain work by a different artist. Women artists are well represented here, as are others with perspectives that don't fit into the old standards so well, like those of the late well-known AIDS-chronicler David Wojnarowicz, whose estate they own.
532 Broadway (bet. Prince and Spring Sts.), 941-8642, Cash Only, ❶❷ to Prince St.

R

Ronald Feldman
Artists with enough talent to land them safely on the winning side execute interesting ideas that could easily fall on either side of the thin line dividing successes and failures. A recent show by Roxy Paine consisted of 2,200 handmade mushrooms, each unique, displayed so that they appeared to be sprouting from the floor. Wacky indeed, and it received rave reviews.
31 Mercer St. (bet. Grand and Canal Sts.), 226-3232, Cash Only, ❶❷ to Canal St.

S

Salander-O'Reilly Galleries
20th century Modernist American painters of the Stieglitz group are exhibited alongside a new generation of similarly daring, young artists.
20 East 79th St. (bet. Madison and Fifth Aves.), 879-6606, Cash Only (catalogues), ❻ to 77th St.

visual arts 185

SoHo Photo Gallery
One of the most well-established photography galleries in town, with shows highlighting many different styles. Additionally, they offer a lot of classes to the public to educate on the history and work of various photographers and to help people learn and improve artistic skills. Call for schedule information.
15 White St. (bet. 6th St. and West Broadway), 226-8571, Cash Only, ❶❾ to Franklin St.

Staley-Wise
Love photography? Sorting through the array of different styles that get thrown together based on the fact that they all somehow involve using a camera and film as media can be daunting. This is the place for those who love the glamour aspect of photography, featuring work ranging from old classic Life magazine-style celeb photos to work by today's most prominent fashion photographers. The attitude that commercial success is validation rather than a sign of selling out is prominent here.
560 Broadway (at Prince St.), 966-6223, and 47 Mercer Street, 334-3704, MC, V, ❿❻ to Prince St. ♿

Storefront for Art and Architecture
This unique international gallery favors abstract works, and often organizes shows along geographical themes. The name is derived from the gallery's unique facade.
97 Kenmare Street (bet. Mulberry and Lafayette Sts.), 431-5795, Only open from March to November, ❻ to Spring St.

T

303 Gallery
An intimate gallery on a single floor exhibits contemporary work in many different media.
525 West 22nd St. (bet. Tenth and Eleventh Aves.), 255-1121, Cash Only, ❻❼ to 23rd St. ♿

W

William Secord Gallery
While the occasional feline or barnyard theme sneaks in, this anomalous uptown gallery is known for its carefully (and very seriously) curated and meticulously selected dog art. True canine addicts not fully satiated by this gallery alone need not distress: a similar showcase, the Dog Museum, once directed by Secord as well, exists in St. Louis.
52 East 76th Street, Third Floor (bet. Park and Madison Aves.), 249-0075, MC, V, AmEx, ❻ to 77th St.

Wooster Gardens
This upstairs gallery is a stomping ground for those whose work is "legitimate" (nothing too scary or strange) but whose race, gender, or choice of medium has placed them just outside of the mainstream. A good starting place for when growing art savvy demands a move but not a leap beyond the big names.
558 Broadway (at Prince St.), 941-6210, Cash Only, ❿❻ to Prince St. ♿

Cultural Institutions and Societies

A

Alliance Française
Brush up on the language of love at Tuesday's $5.50 screenings of French flicks; dance classes and more than 200 language courses are also available. Members enjoy free films, culinary and wine tastings, travel seminars, art excursions, discounts on French performances around the city, and the use of the multimedia library.
22 East 60th Street (bet. Madison and Park Aves.), 355-6100, MC, V, AmEx, ❿❻ to Lexington Ave. ♿

The American Academy of Arts and Letters
Recent initiates, Oliver Sacks and Elie Wiesel, attest to the prestige of this exclusive society created to honor American artists, writers, and composers for their accomplishments. Check out samples of honorees' works inside the gallery. For a good look at the neighboring Trinity Church Cemetery, stop by the South Gallery.
633 W. Broadway (at 155th St.) 368-5900, Admission Free, ❶❾ to 157th St.

American Ballet Theatre
Drop-in classes to the tune of 12 dollars a pop ($110 buys ten classes) for aspiring prima donnas at one of the country's premier studios. Alaine Haubert and Diana Cartier teach regularly, though guest instructors from the ABT Artistic Staff occasionally fill in. Advanced dancers should stop by at 10am during the week, while intermediates will be best served by the 6pm weekday classes.
890 Broadway, Third Floor (at 19th St.), 477-3030, Cash Only, , ❶ to Union Square ♿

American Folk Art Institute
Classes and workshops are offered in all manners of media. Lectures and other panels are also held here.
2 Lincoln Square (at Columbus bet. 65th and 66th Sts.), 977-7170, ❶❾ to 66th St./Lincoln Centr. ♿

The American Numismatic Society
If you had one of those penny books as a kid, this is your chance to see what you may have had if you'd only stuck with it. Numismatics, the study of coins and medals, has been practiced in these hallowed halls since 1858, and their library maintains over 70 thousand volumes. Other pursuits include a fellowship program for grad students and museum professionals, publishing monographs and journals, and running the annual conference on coinage in America.
Audubon Terrace, Broadway at (155th St.), 234-3130, Admission free, ❶❾ to 157th St. ♿

Americas Society
Inter-American policy issues come up for debate at the conferences and study groups organized by the Society's Western Hemisphere Department;

186 visual arts

the Cultural Affairs department offers an extensive arts library, lectures in conjunction with special exhibits, and concerts with receptions for the white wine crowd.
680 Park Avenue (at 68th St.), 249-8950, Cash Only, ❻ to 68th St. ♿

Asia Society

America's preeminent organization celebrates Asian cultural awareness with notable film series, lectures, and an art collection featuring sculpture, paintings, ceramics, prints and bronzes from across Asia. Prominent authors and public leaders speak regularly here; other programs for the public include dance performances, well-attended art exhibits usually gathered from private collections, and receptions involving community and professional organizations.
725 Park Avenue (at 70th St.), 288-6400, MC, V, AmEx, ❻ to 68th St. ♿

B

Ballet Academy East

Itching to test those dancing shoes? Drop in here and for 11 dollars you can sample one of the jazz, ballet, or tap classes.
1651 Third Avenue (bet. 92nd and 93rd Sts.), 410-9140, MC, V, AmEx, ❻ to 96th St.

Bronfman Jewish Center

In a townhouse built for Lockwood de Forest, a wealthy exporter, the center presents free lectures focusing on Jewish religious concerns and Israeli politics for an almost exclusive NYU audience. De Forest founded workshops in India to revive the art of woodworking, so the center is replete with the fruits of his labor-original, intricately-carved teak wood imported from India.
7 East 10th St. (bet. University and Fifth Aves.), 998-4114, ❶❷❸❹❺❻ to Union Square ♿

C

China Institute

America's oldest bicultural organization focusing on China promotes awareness of Chinese culture, history, language, and arts through semester-long classes in Mandarin, Cantonese, Tai Chi, calligraphy, cooking, and painting. Seminars, lecture series, and film screenings with Chinese and Chinese-American themes are also regularly scheduled.
125 East 65th St. (bet. Lexington and Park Aves.), 744-8181, MC, V, AmEx, Admission: $5, ❻ to 68th St.

I

Istituto Italiano di Cultura

The Italian consulate operates this center for the dissemination of the country's culture; concerts, exhibits and lectures occur frequently, or just swing by to flip through Italian mags for some insight into the haute couture.
686 Park Ave. (bet. 68th and 69th Sts.), 879-4242, ❻ to 68th St.

J

Japan Society

An all-purpose center of Japanese art and culture, located appropriately enough in Japan House, with exhibitions on the second floor and a stone-lined pool garden on the first floor, complete with bamboo shafts.
333 East 47th St. (bet. First and Second Aves.), 832-1155, MC, V, AmEx, ❹❺❻ to 51st St. ♿

L

La Maison Française

The epicenter of Francophone and Francophile life at New York University. Call for information about free lectures, usually in French, along with conferences and exhibitions which are presented in the center's historic 19th century carriage house.
16 Washington Pl. (bet. Fifth Ave. and University Place), 998-8750, ❶❷ to 8th St.

N

New York Historical Society

An imposing building across from the park houses both a library and a museum with a wealth of information and images of New York up to the turn-of-the-century. The museum also features a permanent installation of 19th century paintings.
2 West 77th (at Central Park West), 873-3400, Admission: $5, $3 (students), ❶❷ to 81st St. ♿

New York Library Society

George Washington, James Fenimore Cooper, Henry Thoreau, and Herman Melville all frequented the oldest circulating library in New York, founded in 1754. Nowadays you'll have to fork over 90 bucks ($135 for non-students) for the privilege of perusing literature in the luxurious reading rooms. Non-members are accommodated in the ground floor's reference room.
53 East 79th St. (bet. Madison and Park Aves.), 288-6900, Cash Only, ❻ to 77th St.

New York Zendo Shobo-ji

New Yorkers looking to escape urban chaos seek out this serene temple, complete with rock gardens, instructions on correct breathing, meditation, posture, etiquette, and Oriental floor cushions. Hard-core enthusiasts can partake of a purer experience on one of the weekend retreats held at an affiliated monastery in the Catskills.
222 East 67th Street (bet. Second and Third Aves.), 861-3333, $10 per session, $40 membership for a month, Cash Only, ❻ to 68th St.

92nd Street Y

One of New York's most valuable cultural resources serves as an umbrella for a multitude of classes, workshops, and speaking and reading series. The reading series is by far the city's most star-studded, consistently drawing the finest poets and authors, both national and international, established and emerging; tickets run around $5-$7 for students.
1395 Lexington Avenue (at 92nd St.), 996-1100, MC, V, AmEx, ❹❺❻ to 86th St. ♿

S

Schomburg Center for Research in Black Culture

The Center was founded in 1925 to showcase scholar and historian Arturo

visual arts 187

Alfonso Schomburg's personal collection of 10,000 items, documenting the development of Black history worldwide. Priceless volumes, manuscripts, paintings, photographs, and newspapers are among the five million articles housed here. Film screenings and live performances occur regularly.
515 Malcolm X Boulevard (at 135th St.), 491-2200, Admission Free, Monday-Wednesday, 12pm-8pm, Thursday-Saturday, 10am-6pm, ⒶⒸⒺ to 135th St. ♿

The Spanish Institute

Exhibitions, events, and lectures acquaint visitors with Spanish culture. Semester-long language classes include the perks of access to both the reference collection and reading room with current publications.
684 Park Ave. (bet. 68th and 69th Sts.), 628-0420, $50 per membership, $15 for students, MC, V, AmEx, D, Diners, ⑥ to 68th St., ⒷⓆ to Lexington Ave.

INDEX BY NEIGHBORHOOD

BRONX
Bronx Museum of the Arts

BROOKLYN
The Brooklyn Museum
Momenta Art
The New York City Transit Museum
Pierogi 2000

CHELSEA
303 Gallery

Barbara Gladstone
Dia Center for the Arts
Fashion Institute of Technology
Greene Naftali Gallery
Jessica Fredericks Gallery
Linda Kirkland Gallery
Metro Pictures
Paula Cooper

CHINATOWN
Asian American Arts Center
The Drawing Center

FINANCIAL DISTRICT
Fraunces Tavern Museum
New York Unearthed

GRAMERCY
American Ballet Theatre
Police Academy Museum

GREENWICH VILLAGE
Bronfman Jewish Center
Casa Italiana
Deutsches Haus
Grey Art Gallery
King Juan Carlos I Center
La Maison Francaise

HARLEM
African American Wax Museum
Black Fashion Museum
El Museo de Barrio
Museum of African American History and Art
Studio Museum in Harlem
Schomberg Center for Research in Black Culture

LITTLE ITALY
Storefront for Art and Architecture

LOWER EAST SIDE
Esso
Lower East Side Tenement Museum

MIDTOWN
American Craft Museum
Christie's
Danese
Japan Society

Mary Boone Gallery
Museum of Television and Radio
Pace Wildenstein Gallery
Pierpont Morgan Library

MORNINGSIDE HEIGHTS
Casa Italiana
Miriam and Ira D. Wallach Art Gallery
Nicholas Roerich Museum

QUEENS
American Museum of the Moving Image
Floral Park
The Isamu Noguchi Garden Museum
New York Hall of Science
Queens Museum of Art

SOHO
Alternative Gardens
Artist's Space
Basilio
David Zwirner
Exit Art
FIRE Museum
Gagosian
Guggenheim SoHo
Jack Tilton
Jim Deitsch Projects
Leo Castelli
The Museum of African Art
New World Art Center
Pace Wildenstein Gallery
Peter Blum
Phyllis Kind
PostMasters
PPOW
Ronald Feldman
SoHo Photo Gallery
Staley-Wise
Wooster Gardens

TRIBECA
Apex

UPPER EAST SIDE
Abigail Adams Smith Museum
Acquavella
Alliance Francaise
Americas Society
Asia Society

Ballet Academy East
China Institute
Cooper-Hewitt Museum
Czech Center
Frick Collection
Instituto Italiano di Cultura
International Center for Photography
Islamic Cultural Center and Mosque
Jewish Museum
Knoedler Gallery
The Metropolitan Museum of Art
Museum of American Illustrators
Museum of Modern Art
Museum of the City of New York
National Academy of Design
New York Library Society
New York Zendo Shobo-ji
92nd Street Y
Salander-O'Reilly Galleries
Solomon R. Guggenheim Museum
Sotheby's
The Spanish Institute
The Whitney Museum of American Art
William Secord Gallery

UPPER WEST SIDE
American Folk Art Institute
American Musuem of Natural History
Children's Museum of Manhattan
Hayden Planetarium
Museum of American Folk Art
New York Historical Society

WASHINGTON HEIGHTS
The American Academy of Arts and Letters
The American Numismatic Society
The Cloisters
Dyckman Farmhouse Museum
Morris-Jumel Museum
Yeshiva University Museum

188 visual arts

performing arts

NYC performing arts scene.190
interviews:
musician matt hong.193
actor/musician malik yoba.196
performance listings.198
index by type.204
index by neighborhood.204

performing arts

At the heart of New York's tourist industry lies 42nd Street, whose glittering lights and theaters on Broadway draw visitors from all over the world. However, despite the enormous amount of revenue generated by successful shows, and high ticket prices, launching a production is among the most expensive and risky of business propositions. As a result of the prohibitive fiscal pressures faced by all new productions, a thriving community has also developed away from Midtown's main drag, particularly in the downtown area which originally housed many of the major theaters, resulting in three categories of production: Broadway, Off-Broadway, and Off-Off-Broadway.

Roaring New York

While the city's professional theater was launched in 1750 with an imported production of Richard III (the first in a succession of exchanges between the British and American stages that has proved extremely fruitful both for New York and for London's West End) the New York theater scene really got its start around the turn of the century. The city's high society frequented productions by stage luminaries like Lunt and Fontanne, the Barrymores, and the Booths. Meanwhile, the "common folk" packed the city's vaudeville, variety, and minstrel theaters located along the Bowery. Vaudeville often fed Broadway during the teens and the '20s: before launching their movie careers, performers such as the Marx Brothers graced Broadway stages with their Vaudeville circuit reviews.

Edna St. Vincent Millay and her literary friends helped to launch the Provincetown Playhouse and similar avant-garde theaters in Greenwich Village. The Group Theater featured the works of playwrights such as Eugene O'Neill and Clifford Odets. O'Neill called the city home during this pre-World War I period. His Pulitzer Prize-winning drama *Anna Christie* was based upon the seedy Lower East Side nightlife and was set in the Golden Swan, the saloon frequented by the playwright himself.

The Broadway scene hit its height in the late '20s, with literally hundreds of shows opening each year. In a time of such bounty, there were certainly a few bad apples. The critics of the time, such as Robert Benchley, Dorothy Parker, and Alexander Wollcott, were never out of work. Several New York writers, playwrights, actors, and critics- including the dignitaries previouslymentioned-lunched together regularly at midtown's Algonquin Hotel. These gatherings were vicious and productive, serving as an artistic think-

190 performing arts

tank in a time of tremendous theatrical activity. George S. Kaufman (along with his myriad of writing partners, such as Moss Hart and Marc Connolly) was very active during this period, penning scores of incredible comedies, several of which were based on the exploits of this group of wits and intellectuals.

The World War II and postwar periods were also quite fruitful for New York drama, as two brilliant young playwrights came to make their mark on American theater. Tennessee Williams set new standards with works such as *A Streetcar Named Desire*, *The Glass Menagerie*, *Cat on a Hot Tin Roof*, and *Camino Real*. Brooklyn-based Arthur Miller gave us the American classics *Death of a Salesman*, *The Crucible*, and *A View from the Bridge*.

When the moon was in the seventh house . . .

Impresario Joseph Papp founded the Public Theater, producing works such as *Hair* and *A Chorus Line*. In addition, Papp founded the New York institution Shakespeare in the Park. (Papp's goal for the Public to produce all of Shakespeare's plays was posthumously met in 1997, when *Henry VIII* was presented in Central Park.) Off-Broadway and Off-Off-Broadway theaters boomed with the works of innovative new groups and artists such as the Open Theater and the Wooster Group, (which spawned monologist Spaulding Gray). In the late '70s and moving into the '80s, playwrights such as August Wilson and Wendy Wasserstein brought minority voices to Broadway. The mid-eighties saw the introduction of a genre of AIDS related plays, such as T*he Normal Heart* by Larry Kramer, and Tony Kushner's *Angels in America*.

If Godzilla could sing . . .

The eighties also ushered in the era of the uber-musical: theatrical monsters of varying quality that crushed all in their path.

These musicals (*Cats*, *The Phantom of the Opera*, and *Les Miserables*, to name a few) feature extremely high production values-so many audience members are attracted by the sheer spectacle. Sometimes the ubermusical is an electrifying experience, occasionally because the production is exciting and important, but usually because it stimulates the same part of the brain that experiences a thrilling ripple at the sight of a car crash.

Large musicals still dominate Broadway, but they have taken on a different quality from the brassy productions of the eighties. Disney's Tony Award winning *Lion King*, directed by Julie Taymor, was hailed by critics and audiences alike. *Rent*, a 90's version of *La Boheme*, crawled uptown to Broadway from Downtown's esteemed New York Theater Workshop.

performing arts 191

on, *off*, or *way off*?

It's pretty clear what someone's talking about if they mention a Broadway show. But what exactly does the phrase "Off-Off" signify? Here's a simple guide:

Broadway means the district of theaters clustered around Times Square, usually between 41st and 53rd Streets. Tickets easily cost as much as $75 a pop, and there is the chance of shelling out that much to end up witnessing the kind of empty spectacle that films provide more inexpensively. Lately, however, Broadway has been providing the kind of entertainment that these ticket prices require, and over the last few years shows like *Rent, Cabaret,* and *The Lion King* have been drawing huge crowds and enlivening the strip.

Off-Broadway originally meant theaters in Greenwich Village, the majority of which have a seating capacity of 500 or less. Lately, however, this term has come to refer to smaller theaters anywhere throughout the city. Off-Broadway shows tend to have greater literary and social importance, a wider variety in quality of the productions, and cheaper ticket prices (max. $40.)

Off-Off Broadway is a term used to refer to productions featuring actors who are nonequity, working in theaters of less than 100 seats. Here you can find exciting, daring, brilliant performances at shoestring pricing. Conversely, of course, there are the occasional painful freak-shows. Conservative theater-goers should perhaps avoid Off-Broadway; the more adventurous who take the risk will find interesting experimental theater in abundance.

R E N T

Throughout the '80s and the early '90s, Jonathan Larsen was a struggling composer living on Greenwich Street—not quite in the Village, and not quite in SoHo. To pay his bills, he worked as a waiter at the Moondance Diner and spent the rest of his time writing and composing. Optimistic and romantic, Larsen embodied the mythical image of the starving artist. He lived in a small apartment and was usually just able to make ends meet.

In the early '90s, Larsen began work on a modern-day version of the Puccini opera *La Bohéme.* Relocating the action to the East Village, Larsen spun a relevant and timely portrayal of New York bohemian life. The show tackled problems ranging from AIDS and drug abuse, to housing and unpaid utility bills. More than a vehicle for theatricalizing suffering, however, *Rent*, the resulting production, was a celebration of the lifestyle of New York artists.

Tragically, Larsen passed away on the night before the first preview. The show, however, continued and went on to become a record-breaking success story. *Rent* opened at the New York Theater Workshop on February 13, 1996. On April 29 of the same year, it opened on Broadway at the Nederlander Theater. Larsen was honored with a posthumous Pulitzer Prize for his work. In addition to the regularly priced tickets available through Ticketmaster, Rent has a standing rush ticket policy. Potential audience members huddle in front of the theater starting in the early hours of the morning in hopes of getting one of the discount $20 tickets that are made available for each performance.

gigging in NYC

Matt Hong is a saxophone player, and the leader of the Matt Hong Quartet. He has studied and taught music at the Manhattan School of Music, and at Harvard University. Now he works full-time as a jazz musician, either in his own group, with the Chuck Clark Little Big Band, or at gigs he's offered by colleagues.

Q: When did you start playing the saxophone?
A: I was about ten or twelve. It was in the family—everybody played. I was close to my cousin, and he played the trumpet, so I had to pick something else. I didn't begin studying seriously until college, though. And when I got out of school, I worked in a market/researching firm for a year-and-a-half before I really started playing.

Q: When and why did you move to NYC?
A: In '92. In the back of my mind, this was always the place to be. It is for anyone, if you want to play with the best musicians. I made the move via the Manhattan School of Music, because at the time, it was the only place you could get a Master's in Jazz. I also studied a semester at Queen's College with Jimmy Heath—he was amazing. I learned more in that semester than in all the others combined, I think.

Q: Where do you live?
A: Still up near the School of Music. I like the interaction with students, and there's performance space available. Plus, the rent is good, and there's a real neighborhood feel. Most of my time, though, is spent in the East Village because that's were the jazz clubs are.

Q: How did you start the Matt Hong Quartet?
A: Playing with friends from school. There are three main guys I play with, and we play in different situations with me leading the group. It's also fluid, it depends on who's available on a certain night, who's around. You want to play with people who have the same influences, musically.

Q: What is the hallmark sign of a bad gig?
A: You know it will be a bad gig if the guy that hired you is a bad musician. And, when I first moved here, I worked a lot of weddings—there's a lot of wedding band traditions in Westchester County—Madonna medleys with no break at all. I only do jazz weddings now. You have to make your money in lots of different ways. I know people who've done stuff you wouldn't believe for $200.

performing arts 193

dixon place

Housed in a converted loft in SoHo, Dixon Place is a haven for performance artists, multicultural performers, and other artists generally considered to be too off-center for traditional venues. Audience members enjoy a relaxed atmosphere, seated on sofas and chairs in an intimate house that holds approximately 80.

Included in each month's performance schedule are: 3 dance performances, a spoken-word performance, a science-fiction evening, a gay and lesbian reading called *Homotexts*, a new play reading, and an open performance night. Artists such as John Leguizamo, Wallace Shawn, and the Blue Man Group have performed at Dixon Place in the past; recent performances featured Reno, Peggy Shaw, and Holly Hughes. Additionally, in July, the theater hosts the only Gay and Lesbian theater festival in the city.

Dixon Place features 24 shows per month (call 219-3088 for the bimonthly calendar.) Shows begin at 8pm, with the occasional weekend performance at 10pm. The theater is located at 258 Bowery, between Prince and Houston Streets. Tickets prices range from free to $12, averaging around $10. Students and senior citizens are always half price, and TDF vouchers are accepted. Reservations are suggested.

times square

In previous years, the area surrounding 42nd Street was rather harrowing. Along with a high crime rate, the street was extremely dirty and crowded with sex shops and decrepit buildings in abundance. In the early part of this decade, however, the city began an effort to increase the presence of large businesses in what would normally be an extremely desirable area. Before long, Times Square underwent a near-magical transformation from a hot spot for muggers to a haven for tourists.

The foundation, called the Business Improvement District, an independent organization funded by the property owners of the Times Square area, began in 1992. With an annual budget of six million dollars, the BID is able to provide extraordinary services to a relatively small geographical area. The organization employs 40 unarmed security officers, connected to the NYPD by radio, who patrol Times Square at all times. Their primary function is to provide assistance to tourists and city dwellers whom have questions or concerns. In addition, the BID provides additional sanitation workers that keep the area-if not spotless-at least relatively spiffy. In addition, there have been incentives offered for business to relocate in the area. The resulting influx of places like the Disney Store, the All-Star Cafe, the Virgin Music mega-store, etc., have made Times Square feel more like an amusement park than the world-renowned slime-pit it used to be. Of course, during the annual New Year's celebration, Times Square reverts to its seedy roots, attracting pickpockets and con artists by the dozen. Folks, watch the ball drop on television.

If Broadway tickets are out of your price range, the BID is sponsoring an event on September 13th called Broadway on Broadway. The performance will feature one number from every Broadway show currently running or in previews. The performance takes place on the island between 43rd and 44th Streets. Arrive early to secure a good spot.

cheap tickets

With so many excellent and affordable Off- and Off-Off Broadway venues and so many avenues for obtaining discounted tickets to the Broadway blockbusters, why pay upwards of $60 a seat to further fatten the pocketbooks of Cameron Mackintosh and Andrew Lloyd Webber? Here are some ways to see great productions for (almost) nothing:

TKTS
This booth sells same-day tickets to Broadway shows at 25-50 percent discounts. Even the best seats are available, but come early or you'll wind up with a "partial view" spot. The wait can be long-up to an hour or so-but is usually enlivened by the delicious chaos of the surroundings.
West 47th St. at Broadway: branch in the mezzanine of 2 World Trade Center, 212-221-0013, ❶❾ *to Cortlandt St.*

Theater Development Fund
TDF is the best program for college students. A $14 annual fee pays for a spot on the mailing list for Broadway tickets for $17 or less, and TDF's "4-for-$28" voucher program gains admittance to Off-Off Broadway shows. Send a legal-size, self-addressed stamped envelope for an application and allow six to eight weeks for processing.
1501 Broadway, Room 2110, New York, NY 10036, 221-0013 (recorded information), 221-0885 (operator).

Passport to Off-Broadway
The Alliance of Resident Theaters of New York offers hot seats to Off-and Off-Off Broadway shows at a discount during the spring and fall only. Call 989-5257 to get on their mailing list.

Standing Room and Rush Tickets
Many shows offer discounts at the box office of the theater a few hours before curtain, generally balcony seats or standing room. Ushers often turn a blind eye while you sneak down to the orchestra or mezzanine and find empty seats.

Two for Ones
Many universities are part of a theater promotion program that offers students coupons known as "twofers": Two tickets to big-budget productions for the price of one. Visit your school's Student Activities office for information about the program.

Shakespeare in the Park
Productions can be uneven and the star-studded casts underwhelming and overblown, but what better way to spend a balmy summer evening than sitting under the night sky in this intimate theater-in-the-round watching the best dramas by the best writer in the Western world? Tickets are free, but regular working folks will have to take a personal day to line up at sunrise to obtain seats to the more popular shows; weekends can also be sacrificed to the cause. The bigger the stars, the longer the queue. Tickets are distributed the day of the performance beginning at 1pm at the Delacorte and Public Theaters. Show up to an hour or two early for the less-hyped productions and many, many hours early for productions like *A Midsummer's Night Dream* in which Patrick Stewart (of *Star Trek* fame) starred a few years ago.
Tuesday through Sunday June-September, Delacorte Theater, Central Park (at West 79th Street), 539-8500, ❽❻ *to 81st Street*

King's County Shakespeare Festival
The New York Shakespeare Festival's country cousin, staged in the bandshell of Brooklyn's Prospect Park. Their makeshift outdoor productions can produce haphazard, lively, boisterous fun. Named for their Brooklyn homebase, otherwise known as King's County.

performing arts 195

CityLife: Actor/Musician *Malik Yoba* and Musician *Raliegh Neal* Talk about the CityKids Foundation

The CityKids Foundation is a New York City-based organization whose mission is to help young people of diverse cultures affect positive change. Through leadership training programs and services for youth, the foundation educates, trains, and empowers people from the ages of 12 to 21 to produce valuable solutions to individual and societal problems. In addition, CityKid's repertory theater functions as the voice of the foundation, using music, drama, dance, and poetry to bring its message to millions of young people a year.

Malik Yoba and Raliegh Neal credit CityKids with giving them their start. Since his association with CityKids began in 1989, actor/musician Malik Yoba has starred as J.C. Williams on the FOXTV drama *New York Undercover*, an award-winning portrayal. He's also appeared in numerous movies including: *Cool Runnings*, *Smoke*, *Blue in the Face*, *Copland*, and *Ride*. However, music is Malik's "first love," and he recently founded Nature Boy Records, a division of Nature Boy Entertainment which is a multi-media entertainment group he runs with his mother and five siblings. Malik describes his music as "acoustic soul," a blend of R&B, reggae, hip-hop, Latin and folk music. With the release of his single, "Ain't No Sun-shine," Malik will also make his directorial debut.

Raliegh Neal, Malik's musical right-hand man, describes Nature Boy as the "urban folk experience." As a key member of Malik's musical group and his partner, Raliegh works with all the artist's on Nature Boy Records. He is also the musical director of CityKids which is where he and Malik first formed their friendship.

We caught up with Malik and Raliegh just after an informal jam session and asked them a few questions about CityKids and life in New York City.

Q: You guys have very different backgrounds. How did you come to New York?

Malik: I was born in the Bronx, the South Bronx. I was in the area recently and was taken back to when I was kid. I never thought it was a bad neighborhood, just where I lived.
Raliegh: I grew up in Reston, Virginia, in a planned community; it was like living in bubble. I knew I had to go to the real world.
Malik: New York is one of the realest places on earth, and I've been to a lot of points on this earth. You have to walk, get on the subway, see the people; you can hear five languages between just one subway stop.
Raliegh: New York is definitely the best spot in the U.S. for broadening your horizons.

Q: How did you get your start as performers?

Malik: Growing up without television. I wrote plays, made up songs, performed for friends and family.
Raliegh: My Dad's a musician; he plays many instruments and I got it from him. I was in music school and ended up getting in a band which took off. We auditioned to be Stacy Latisaw's tour band and got the gig. I toured with her for a couple years then moved to New York.

Q: What are your roles in CityKids? How did you both become involved in the Foundation?

Malik: I used to be a vice-president, and now I'm on the Board of Directors. I got involved through volunteering. CityKids has afforded me lots of opportunities, to be on television and be a musician. My life would be totally different without it.
Raliegh: I wear many hats at CityKids--musical director first. I'm also a trained facilitator in conflict resolution and group interaction. I'm a technical director, I teach music composition and theory, and I'm a big brother. When I first came to New York, I decided to volunteer at CityKids. A good friend of mine, then the musical director, left the organization so I auditioned for his job.

Q: What have been your most fulfilling moments with CityKids?

Malik: The whole experience really. CityKids shaped my relationships, my career. The way I deal with people, with the dynamics between the members of my band is from my experience at CityKids.
Raliegh: Getting a kid who'd been homeless for four years into a home was my most fulfilling moment. Another wonderful moment was playing with Herbie Hancock at a fundraiser. Afterward, I was like, "Okay, I can die right now."

Q: How do you think New York City has shaped CityKids? How has it shaped you as artists?

Raliegh: New York has made the organization possible. In the city, anyone can be anywhere in a couple hours; it's allowed accessibility to young people who can take it upon themselves to get there. They can be independent and proactive. As an artist, New York has completely widened my view of what is possible. The boundaries of my imagination have been completely blown away.

Malik: Like I said before, New York is so real; it's made me real. Everything has happened to me in the city: I've been shot; fell in love; got my first job; auditioned for my first movie.

Q: What are your plans for the future?

Malik: I just want to be proactive, productive citizen. I want to affect positive change in my community through music and film; that's what I'm doing right now and I want to keep on.
Raliegh: I want people to recognize my name and my work and have positive associations with both. I'm a solution-oriented human being. I think that's why Malik and I get along; we both want to create solutions and make a difference.

For more information about the CityKids Foundation, call 925-3320 or visit their website at: www.citykids.com

197 performing arts

A

Actor's Playhouse
Gay-and-lesbian-themed shows command the stage at this Off-Broadway space. Though the seats may be dingy and worn, and the floor may retain a stickiness from a soda that was spilled long ago, it's still the best cutting-edge queer and gay theater.
100 Seventh Avenue South (bet. Christopher and Bleecker), 691-6226, MC, V, AmEx, D, **1 9** *to Christopher St.*

The African Poetry Theater, Inc.
Fledgling poets, playwrights, directors, and actors all do shows regularly. For those in need of more structured training, various dance, drum and Shakespeare classes are available.
176-03 Jamaica Avenue (at 176th St.), (718) 523-3312, Cash Only, **F** *to 179th St.* ♿

Alvin Ailey American Dance Theater
"The dance came from the people. It should be given back to the people," this theater's namesake once said and developed the repertoire here with the uniqueness of black cultural expression in mind. Pieces are often set to music by jazz greats such as Duke Ellington and Wynton Marsalis. Works performed here include both those choreographed by Ailey himself and choreographers who shared his vision.
City Center, 131 West 55th St. (bet. Sixth and Seventh Aves.), 581-1212, MC, V, AmEx, **B D N R** *to 57th Street* ♿

Amato Opera House
Head downtown to see the divas of tomorrow paying their dues in an intimate setting. An alternative for opera lovers who lack the funds for nosebleed seats at the Met. One of Amato's goals is to foster opera appreciation by making it more accessible, so manyperformances are English translations of Italian operas.
319 Bowery St. (at East 2nd St.), 228-8200, Cash Only, **6** *to Bleecker St.*

American Ballet Theater
This dance giant, once led by legends like Lucia Chase, Oliver Smith, and Mikhail Baryshnikov, and now headed by former Principal Dancer Kevin McKenzie, continues to stage staggering performances at its home at Lincoln Center. Classical ballet had its first renaissance here, and new works have been commissioned specifically for the ballet by key composers such as Balanchine, Antony Tudor, and Agnes de Mille. The company will premiere Othello in their 1997-8 season; call for schedules.
Metropolitan Opera House, Lincoln Center (at West 64th St. and Columbus Ave.), 362-6000, MC, V, AmEx, **1 9** *to 66th/Lincoln Center* ♿

American Jewish Theater
A performance space for plays directly related to the American-Jewish experience.
307 West 26th St. (bet. Eighth and Ninth Aves.), 633-9797, **1 9** *to 28th St.*

Apollo Theater
Fostering such performers as Josephine Baker, the Supremes, and Bill Cosby since it started integrating black audiences and performers in 1935, this multi-use theater is in full swing thanks to a revival effort in the Eighties. The televised "Amateur Night" rages on Wednesdays, and comedians and children's flicks also find space here; the stage even hosted James Brown's post-prison comeback concert.
253 West 125th St. (bet. A.C. Powell and Frederick Douglas Blvd.), 222-0992, MC, V, AmEx, D, **A B C D** *to 125th St.*

B

BargeMusic
Excellent chamber music on the water in the moonlight; bring a date and get all mushy on this converted coffee barge.
Fulton Ferry Landing, Brooklyn, (718) 624-4061, Cash Only, **A C** *to High St* ♿

Bessie Schomberg Theater
Home to the Dance Theater Workshop, a non-profit organization dedicated to assisting and promoting independent artists in the community, this intimate space seats 150 people and stages cutting-edge dance and musical performances.
219 West 19th St. (bet. Seventh and Eighth Aves.), 924-0077, MC, V, AmEx, **1 9** *to 18th St.*

Black Spectrum Theater Company, Inc.
Three to five large-scale productions a year, with directors favoring socially conscious works by both emerging and established writers. Kids and teens get in on the action with their own productions.
119 Merrick Boulevard (Corner of 177th and Basley Boulevard), (718) 723-1800, Cash Only, **E** *to Parsons,* Q85 *to Merrick Boulevard* ♿

Bouwerie Lane Theater
Founded in 1973 by Eve Adamson, this old-fashioned, European-style, one-stage theater is one of the few dedicated entirely to producing classics.
330 Bowery St. (at Bond St.), 677-0060, Tickets: $24, $12 (students), MC, V, AmEx, **6** *to Bleecker St.*

Boy's Choir of Harlem
Founded in 1968, this legendary choir has evolved from a small church group to an internationally-acclaimed phenomenon, singing classical, contemporary, spiritual, and jazz music at their year-round worldwide performances.
2005 Madison Avenue (bet. 127th and 128th Sts.), 289-1815, Cash Only, **4 5 6** *to 125th St.* ♿

The Brooklyn Academy of Music
Although the Brooklyn Philharmonic has distinguished itself with its range and a repertoire that runs the gamut from European classics to selections from African-American traditions, its pet projects are clearly those rooted in the avant garde, which are best realized in BAM's provocative yearly "New Wave" festival that consistently pushes the boundaries of classical music.
30 Lafayette Avenue (at Hanson Place), (718) 636-4100 (tickets), (718) 636-4137 (Brooklyn

198 performing arts

Philharmonic), MC, V, ❷❸ to Atlantic Ave. ♿

C

Carnegie Hall
A century has passed since Tchaikovsky conducted at the inauguration, but this stage keeps abreast of musical trends in their many variations: the Beastie Boys and the Tibetan Freedom Fighters have appeared on the same stage as today's classical giants like Emanuel Ax. Jazz performers are also frequent guests. How do you get to perform here? Practice, practice, practice.
881 Seventh Avenue (at 57th St.), 247-7800, MC, V, AmEx, ❶❷❸❹❶❾ to 59th St. ♿

Castillo Theater
For the last decade, this space has served as a "cultural laboratory" for Artistic Director Fred Newman to practice Developmental Theater, a genre which is predicated on a number of post-modern philosophies but boils down to the idea of psychotherapy for performer and audience members alike. The focus is on black, Latino, gay theater, and the international avant-garde- which means you can expect anything.
500 Greenwich St. (bet. Spring and Canal Sts.), 941-5800, MC, V, AmEx, ❶❸❸ to Canal St. ♿

Catch a Rising Star
The variety club and restaurant can seat over 200 for faves like Jerry Seinfeld and Janeane Garofalo. The venue also books cabaret, stand-up, R&B, and jazz.
253 West 28th St. (bet. Seventh and Eighth Aves.),
462-2824, MC, V, AmEx, ❶❾ to 28th St.

Centerfold Coffeehouse at Church of St. Paul and St. Andrew
Poetry readings are free but hit or miss, so prepare to indulge some neophyte bards; evening jams with folk and jazz bands provide dependable, cheap weekend entertainment.
263 West 86th St. (bet. Broadway and West End), 362-3179, Admission Free, ❶❾ to 86th St.

Center for the Arts (College of Staten Island)
Many island residents ignore CSI's performance space, favoring Manhattan for theatrical pursuits. A true shame considering the 450 seat theater, 9,000 seat concert hall, and art gallery housed within the center. Past well-known acts (Shawn Colvin, Tito Puente, etc.) have graced the concert stage, allowing diverse artistic tastes to be appreciated.
2800 Victory Boulevard, (718) 982-2505, ❶❾ to South Ferry, ❽❾ to Whitehall St. - South Ferry, take Staten Island Ferry, then take S61, S62

Cherry Lane Theater
Founded in the Twenties by a literary circle headed by the poet Edna St. Vincent Millay, Cherry Lane's productions are lead by the best of the century's avant-garde and adventurous new pieces.
38 Commerce St. (bet. Bedford and Hudson Sts.), 989-2020, MC, V, AmEx, ❶❸❸❹❹ to West 4th St.

Chicago City Limits
No alcohol is served at
New York's best improv theater, but you may get a buzz from the audience participation. It's generally pricey, but Thursday's touring troupe performs for only ten bucks. Ask about student discounts.
1105 First Avenue (at 61st St.), 888-5233, Admission: $20, MC, V, AmEx, ❹❺❻ to 59th St., ❽❾ to Lexington Ave.

Circle Repertory Theater
First-rate breeding ground for New York's wealth of fresh talent who are consistently among the most outstanding of the Off-Broadway performers.
99 Seventh Avenue South (at West 4th), 691-3210, MC, V, AmEx, Tickets: $22-$30, ❶❸❸❹❹❹ to West 4th St.

Colden Center For the Performing Arts at Queens College
Classical, pop, jazz, theater, opera, and children's events weekly. Call the box office for more precise information.
65-30 Kissena Boulevard, (718) 997-3800, MC, V, AmEx, ❼ to Main St. ♿

Collective Unconscious
Every possible configuration of campy art and anti-art event takes place at this downtown performance space. The hip, tongue-in-cheek crowd doesn't take anything very seriously-especially not the art world. Popular open mike at Reverend Jen's Anti-Slam, Wednesday nights.
145 Ludlow St. (bet. Stanton and Rivington Sts.), 254-5277, Call for schedule and show times, Cash Only, ❻ to Second Avenue ♿

The Comic Strip
New York's most famous comedy theater regularly plays host to mainstream big-name performers and other crowd-pleasers. Cheapest of thrills on no-cover Mondays.
1568 Second Ave. (bet. 81st and 82nd Sts), 861-9386, MC, V, AmEx, D, Admission: $8-$12 (weekends), ❹❺❻ to 86th St.

Context Studios
"Like a kitchen with lots of different vegetation," is the somewhat convoluted definition given for this multi-media performing arts space which brings dance theater, experimental musical performances, and opera to its digs regularly. Shows usually last two to three days, but can go on for up to two weeks by popular demand.
28 Avenue A (bet. Second and Third Aves.), 505-2702, Tickets: $10, Cash Only, ❻ to Second Avenue

D

Dance Theater of Harlem
This world-renowned, neo-classical company, founded in 1969 as a school and now one of the country's most competitive, dabbles in a bit of everything: jazz, tap dance, modern ballet, and ethnic genres. Students of all ages and at all levels perform in a monthly open house, usually with accompanying performances by guest artists. Reservations necessary for large groups.
466 West 152nd St. (bet. St. Nicholas and Amsterdam Aves.), 690-2800, MC, V, AmEx, D, ❶❸❸❹ to 155th St.

performing arts 199

Dangerfield's
Join out-of-town convention-goers for new and established comic talent in the hyper-Las Vegas atmosphere of this uptown club operated under the auspices of Rodney Dangerfield.
1118 First Avenue (bet. 61st and 62nd Sts.), 593-1650, Cover: $12-$15, AmEx, ⓃⓇ❹❺❻ to 59th/Lexington Ave.

G

Grandma Sylvia's Funeral at The SoHo Playhouse
The audience is invited to get caught up in the heirs' fighting and to sample the bagel and lox Mitzvah with the actors.
15 Vandam St. (bet. Sixth and Varick Avenues), 691-1555, Tickets: $35-$55, MC, V, AmEx, ⒸⒺ to Spring Street

H

Harkness Dance Center at the 92nd St. Y
The Upper East Side's cultural mecca hosts professional performances as well informal shows of works-in-progress or new works. The dance workshops are a good reason for visiting, with programs like Argentine Tango Party, boasting Madonna's Evita coaches as instructors, and Israeli Folk Dancing classes occurring regularly. Call for schedules.
1395 Lexington Avenue (bet. 91st and 92nd Sts.), 415-5552, Tickets: $15, ❹❺❻ to 86th St.

HERE
The western end of SoHo is as underdeveloped as TriBeCa but with a funkier feel, creating the perfect atmosphere for this unconventional arts venue. Attractions include gallery shows of fine art and theater productions of new plays by younger playwrights with some fascinating stories to tell. Not as strange stylistically as what you'll find down on the Lower East Side but definitely Off-Off-Broadway.
145 Sixth Avenue (bet. Spring and Dominick Sts.), 647-0202, MC, V, AmEx, ⒸⒺ to Spring St.

I

The Irish Repertory Theatre
Intimate performance space for Irish and Irish-American plays.
132 West 22nd St. (bet. Sixth and Seventh Aves.), 727-2737, MC, V, AmEx, Ⓕ to 23rd St.

J

Jamaica Arts Center
A neo-Italian Renaissance structure built in 1898, houses a non-profit community cultural center dedicated to making all genres of the performing arts accessible to the Jamaica community.
161-04 Jamaica Avenue (at 161st St.), (718) 658-7400, Cash Only, ⒺⒿⓏ to Jamaica Center

Joseph Papp Public Theater
"A Chorus Line" started here. The beautiful red brick Italian Renaissance style building was once the Astor Library and became the permanent home of the New York Shakespeare Festival in 1967. Along with the Bard and other classics, the five stages here also host an eclectic mix of European imports, established, and up-and-coming American playwrights. New York's most venerable avant-garde theater.
425 Lafayette St. (bet. Astor Place and East 4th St.), 539-8500, MC, V, AmEx, D, ❻ to Astor Place, ⓃⓇ to 8th St.

Joyce SoHo
All professional and aspiring dancers are familiar with this branch of the Joyce, the venue of choice for seeing all genres in a setting that's not stiflingly formal. Performances are on Friday and Saturday nights with tickets available thirty minutes before curtain.
155 Mercer St. (bet. Houston and Prince Sts.), 431-9233, Cash Only, ⓃⓇ to Prince St., ❻ to Bleecker St., ⒷⒹⒻ to Broadway/Lafayette Sts.

Joyce Theater
The unlikely successor to a former porno palace, this hotbed of talent inherited a large stage and virtually clear sightlines, which create an ideal setting for performances by top touring companies from around the world. Bookings range from weekly engagements to a month-in-residence with the Feld Ballet and Margie Gillis; the Joyce often subsidizes in-theater production costs. "All Together Different" promotes the seven most promising up-and-coming companies.
175 Eighth Avenue (at 19th St.), 242-0800, MC, V, AmEx, Tickets: $18-$27, ❶❾ to 18th St.

K

The Kitchen
Located among dismal warehouses, this raw space thrives on experimental music and dance performed in a black box theater with bleachers seating about 150 and a multi-media lab with visual arts exhibitions. Check out the café theater on the second floor.
512 West 19th St. (bet.Tenth and Eleventh Aves.), 255-5793, MC, V, AmEx, ⓃⓇ to 23rd St.

L

La MaMa etc.
Four small theaters offer new and experimental dance and theater, as well as off-beat performance. The avant-garde nature of the place means shows are hit or miss, but cheap tickets make it worthwhile to test the odds.
74A East 4th St. (bet. Second Ave.and Bowery), 475-7710, MC, V, AmEx, Ⓕ to Second Ave.

Langston Hughes Community Library and Cultural Center
Year-round readings and performances, as well as a wealth of reference materials in the on-site library.
102-09 Northern Boulevard (at 102nd St.), (718) 651-1100, ❼ to 103rd St.

Lucille Lortel Theater
Cramped between the music-pumping, glittered merchandise-selling shops of Christopher St. is this supremely immodest performance space, which claims to be New Yorks foremost off-Broadway theater. A recent success for the theater has been

the acclaimed Mrs. Klein, chronicling the life and times of famed psychoanalyst Melanie Klein.
121 Christopher St. (bet. Bedford and Hudson Sts.), 924-2817, MC, V, AmEx, ❶❾ to Christopher St.

M

Manhattan School of Music
Prodigies at one of the country's most prestigious conservatories perform, usually for free. Call ahead for scheduled performances and times.
120 Claremont Avenue (at 122nd St.), 749-2802 or 749-3300, Cash Only at the Box Office, ❶❾ to 125th St. ♿

Metropolitan Opera
When the Carnegies were the nouveau riche, Old Money's monopoly on the city's theater boxes frustrated the family so much that they went and built their own opera house. Though the original Met was further downtown, its current location retains a historic stodginess. A safely classical though consistently outstanding repertory. Once again, you'll have to inherit a box, marry into it, or build your own theater.
Lincoln Center (at 66th St. and Broadway), 362-6000 (ticket sales), MC, V, AmEx, ❶❾ to 66th/Lincoln Center

Miller Theater
The student price of five bucks buys a consistently impressive line-up, from readings by poet demigods such as Pulitzer prize winners Richard Howard and Louise Glück to performances by established professionals like Yo Yo Ma and Ann Bogart's SITI

troupe. Although the stage is shallow and seating limited, the acoustics are excellent and balcony seats are intimate enough to make the microphones almost superfluous. The theater's curators also present film retrospectives featuring hard-to-find directors and actors.
Broadway and 116th St. (at Columbia University), 854-7799, Cash Only at Box Office, ❶❾ to 116th Street ♿

Minetta Lane Theater
Revues and new plays in a notably comfortable seating. Recent shows include the acclaimed docudrama *Gross Indecency-the Three Trials of Oscar Wilde*, recounting the legal ordeals that made the artist one of homosexuality's most prominent martyrs.
18 Minetta Lane (bet. Minetta Ln. and Sixth Ave.), 420-8000, MC, V, AmEx ($4 extra charge), ❶❷❸❹❺❻ to West 4th St. ♿

Minor Latham Playhouse
Once home to legends such as Duke Ellington, this student-run theater hosts productions by both Barnard and Columbia theater groups, who perform works such as the annual Greek drama (performed in the original), as well as works by student playwrights. Tickets are cheap and the seating is quite democratic.
Broadway and 119th (enter at 117th St., Barnard Campus), 854-2079, Cash Only, ❶❾ to 116th Street

Monkey Wrench Theater
Artistic Director Julia Barclay and Writer-in-Residence C.J. Hopkins developed their ideas as resident artists with Mabou Mines in 1995. Their ensemble explores "language-based techniques," -provocatively coined "symbolic innuendo" by Ms. Barclay-over an intensive rehearsal and development period. Keep an eye out for this young, ambitious, alternative repertory company.
P.O. Box 47, Gracie Station, 352-3213, located at HERE (see listing), MC, V, AmEx, ❻❺ to Spring Street

N

Nada
Home of the neo-futurists. Catch a show almost every night. Call for theater and band listings.
67 Ludlow St. (bet. Houston and Stanton Sts.), 330-8087 or 420-1466, Admission: $12, $10 (students), MC, V, AmEx, ❻ to Second Avenue

National Black Theatre
Family values are the focus at this company, founded in 1968 by Broadway star Barbara Ann Teer. Performances take place year-round, and acting workshops are also available.
2033 Fifth Avenue (bet. 125th and 126th Sts.), 722-3800, Check or money order, Tickets: $16-$22, ❷❸ to 125th St.

New York City Ballet
Founded in part by Balanchine after WWII, this top-notch company produces a

---

miller theatre
COLUMBIA UNIVERSITY
SCHOOL OF THE ARTS

"...the city's hottest hotbed for innovative programming."
- The New Yorker

A season of exhilarating performance and thought.

DANCE
THEATRE OF IDEAS
CLASSICAL MUSIC
JAZZ
THEATRE
NEW MUSIC
WORLD MUSIC
FILM
CHAMBER OPERA

miller theatre
116TH & BROADWAY
212.854.7799
WWW.COLUMBIA.EDU/
CU/ARTS/MILLER

performing arts 201

particularly breathtaking *Nutcracker* with champagne galore and lots of three-year olds made up like dolls. In residence at the $30 million New York State Theater, the ballet has the largest repertory of any company.
20 Lincoln Center, 870-5500 (box office), MC, V, AmEx, ❶❾ *to 66th/Lincoln Center* &

New York City Opera
Renews and redefines the soul of opera through stellar, innovative performances of both forgotten and familiar classics. A World Premiere Festival takes the kinds of risks which have made NYCO famous. The theater is smaller, so most seats are more attainable than at the Met and cost less, though the interior belies its origins in its mad, modern reincarnation of the Sixties and Seventies.
Lincoln Center (at 66th St. and Broadway), 870-5970, MC, V, AmEx, ❶❾ *to 66th St./Lincoln Center*

New York Philharmonic
Over a hundred virtuosos led by Kurt Masur play Western classics, with an emphasis on European standards and American innovations.
Lincoln Center, 875-5378, ❶❾ *to 66th St./Lincoln Center*

Nuyorican Poet's Cafe
Founded in 1975 as a gathering and performance space for the Spanish-speaking voices of the New York literary scene, it remains one of the most significant outlets for outsider art because of diversification and even after numerous site changes. In addition to Poetry Slams and other readings, which helped create the resurgence of poetry as an aspect of cafe culture throughout the country, a night's program often includes theater, a video presentation, or a jam session. The Nuyorican Poets have garnered enough respect for their work to sustain several published anthologies and to tour the globe performing. Don't pass up the chance to see them at home.
236 East 3rd St. (bet. Aves. B and C), 465-3167, Cash Only, ❻ *to Second Ave.*

O

The Ohio Theater
Anything goes here, since the stage is rented out to various freelance performance groups.
66 Wooster St. (bet. Spring and Broome Sts.), 966-4844, Tickets: $10-$12, Cash Only, ❶❾ *to Prince St.,* ❻❻❺ *to Spring St.* &

P

P.S. 122
This small performance space in a converted church serves as a showplace for cutting-edge dance, theater and performance art. Artists range from obscure but talented newcomers to established members of the downtown scene. Runs tend to be short and very popular, so try to get tickets in advance.
150 First Avenue (at 9th St.), 477-5288, MC, V, AmEx, ❻ *to Second Ave.*

Pearl Theater
This classic repertoire/resident company sticks to a strict pre-WWI itinerary, with conventional productions of Shakespeare, Moliere, Sophocles, and others of their ilk, as well as revived relics. Shows generally run seven weeks. Heterogenous crowd with plenty of local traffic.
80 St. Marks Place (at First Ave.), 598-9802, Tickets:never over $30, ❻ *to Astor Pl.,* ❶❻ *to 8th St.*

R

Roundabout Theater
The most consistently intelligent indigenous productions and European imports on Broadway proper.
1530 Broadway (bet. 44th and 45th Sts.), 719-9393, MC, V, AmEx, ❶❻❺❶❷❸❼❾ *to Times Square* &

S

SoHo Rep
Home for anything new and compelling, from freshly adapted literary works to personal dramas. Well known for excellent casting choices, the theater generally offers several overlapping runs from which to choose.
46 Walker St. (bet. Church and Broadway Sts.), 334-0962, Cash Only, ❶❻❺ *to Canal St.*

St. Clement's Church
A working theater for thirty-five years, this charming little church has hosted some of the best Off-Broadway theater in the city. Episcopal services are still held here Sundays and Wednesday nights. Conveniently located on Restaurant Row and around the corner from the greatest concentration of ethnic restaurants in the city.
423 West 46th St. (bet. Ninth and Tenth Aves.), 246-7277, ❶❻❺ *to 42nd St./Port Authority*

St. Marks Church in the Bowery
A quiet and beautiful cultural oasis in the bustling East Village, this century-old church is home to three excellent arts "projects," including Danspace, Poetry Project, and the Ontological Theater. Most notable is the Poetry Project, one of the only programs of its kind, offering special literary events and workshops for budding poets, a forum for both well-known and up and coming poets to read their work.
131 East 10th St. (at Second Ave.), 674-6377, Cash Only, ❻ *to Astor Pl.*

St. Paul's Chapel
LeFarge stained glass, tiled ceilings, and a 5,347-pipe organ make this the perfect niche for Thursday's midday organ concerts, between noon and 1pm. The Columbia-Barnard Chorus and Gospel Choir perform here regularly, as well as visiting musicians from violinists to vocalists.
1116 Amsterdam (at 117th St., Columbia University), 854-6625, Cash Only, ❶❾ *to 116th St.*

Stand-Up NY
Brett Butler and Dennis Leary cut their teeth here years ago and still swing by to pay their respects when in the neighborhood. The next wave of aspiring comedians hits the stage on Wednesdays for amateur night while Fridays at 11:30pm "Comedy in Colors" program, showcasing entertainers of varying ethnicities.
236 West 78th St. (bet. Amsterdam and

202 performing arts

Broadway), 595-0850, MC, V, AmEx, D, Admission: $7-$12 (Friday and Saturday), ❶❾ to 79th St.

Sullivan St. Theater
Home since 1960 to The *Fantasticks*, the longest running show in U.S. history. Don't miss the art gallery upstairs, which boasts a varied collection of Fantasticks memorabilia from around the world so extensive that it shares space with the ladies' room.
181 Sullivan St. (bet. Houston and Bleecker Sts.), 674-3838, ❹❻ ❶❷❾ *to West 4th St.*

Surf Reality
"Anything can happen here" boasts one of the regulars at this zany alternative comedy space. The tiny, makeshift stage hosts acts too silly or outrageous for the mainstream comedy circuit. New York's most bizarre performers turn out for Faceboy's Open Mike, Wednesdays, 8pm-3am, $3 to sign up and perform. Once a woman pulled an onion out of her vagina.
172 Allen St., 2nd Floor (bet. Stanton and Rivington Sts.), 673-4182, Wednesday-Sunday, two shows nightly at 8pm, 10pm, Cover Varies, ❻ *to Second Ave.*

Symphony Space
Playing host to an incredible range of talent, this spacious theater consistently offers up unique programs, often incorporating disparate genres into a unifying theme. Past line-ups include a Best Films of Our Lives (the curators' lives, which were considerably longer than most of the audience's), which paired movies like *Singing in the Rain* with Fellini's *8 1/2*. A recent program, "Golden Voices/Silver Screen," presented live cabaret and film musicals. Student memberships available.
2537 Broadway (at 95th St.), 864-1414 (program info), MC, V, AmEx, ❶❷❸❾ *to 96th St.*

T

Thalia Spanish Theater
One of New York's hottest stages for established and new Hispanic playwrights, actors, and directors. Three productions yearly, as well as three ongoing showcases in music, dance, and special events.
41-17 Greenpoint Avenue (bet. 41st and 42nd Sts.), (718) 729-3880, Cash Only, ❼ *to 40th St.*

Theatre for a New Audience
Some of the most innovative, provocative, thoughtful, and coherent productions of Shakespeare and other classics.
154 Christopher St., Suite 3D (bet. Greenwich and Washington Sts.) (Administrative offices only; venue changes regularly), 229-2819, AmEx, ❶❾ *to Christopher St.*

Theatre Off Park
A vehicle for its artistic director, this tiny production company doesn't shy away from risks, an attribute that can cut both ways.
224 Waverly Place (bet. Perry and 11th Sts.), 627-2556, ❶❷❸❹❺❻❾ *to West 4th St.*

Tony and Tina's Wedding at St. John's Church
Interactive drama as it's understood these days was born with Tony's proposal; for the past eight years the two Italian lovers have been saying "I do" and guests have been shelling out at least sixty bucks to witness the wedding, attend the reception afterwards, and generally partake of the mayhem.
81 Christopher St., 279-4200, ❶❾ *to Christopher St.*

TriBeCa Performing Arts Center
Inconspicuously housed in the main building of the Boro of Manhattan Community College, this large venue is easy to miss. That would be a shame since the programming is excellent, offering multi-cultural music, dance, theater from around the world, and urban youth-themed performances consistent with the diverse student population. The college connection means cheap student-rate tickets.
199 Chambers St. (bet. West Broadway and Church Sts.), 279-4200, MC, V, ❶❷❸❾ *to Chambers St.*

Trinity Church
Functional, historic, and aesthetic qualities make this the ideal venue for chamber music and organ recitals. Lunchtime performances are still free.
74 Trinity Place (at Broadway and Wall St.), 602-0872/0800, ❷❸ *to Wall St.*

V

Variety Arts Theater
The place to go for campy theater and a distorted dose of pop culture. Recent productions have included a new work by writer/drag queen Charles Busch and a musical based on the life of Patsy Cline. Proof that theater doesn't have to be dull, stodgy or squeaky-clean.
110 Third Avenue (bet. 13th and 14th Sts.), 239-6200, MC, V, AmEx, D, Diners, ❶❹❺❻❾ ❽ *to Union Square*

W

Warren St. Performance Loft
"We make dance as we dance it," explains Richard Bull, who heads up the dance company in-residence which bears his name. Choreographic improvisation is the company's forte; any dance enthusiast with an open mind should check out Saturday's dance series.
46 Warren St. (bet. Church and West Broadway Sts.), 732-3149, Cash Only, ❹❻ ❶❾ *to Chambers St.*

Worth St. Theater
Begun as a small-time theater company on its namesake Worth St., they've since grown into bigger digs on Laight St. and remain a testing ground for new productions that larger companies lack the freedom to attempt. A fine place to catch several one-acts that all fit into a grander theme, satisfying the urge for consistency without putting all your eggs in one basket.
13-17 Laight St., 604-4195, Cash Only, ❶❾ *to Canal St.*

performing arts 203

PERFORMANCE INDEX BY TYPE

COMEDY CLUBS
Catch a Rising Star
Chicago City Limits
The Comic Strip
Dangerfield's
Stand-Up NY
Surf Reality

THEATERS
Actor's Playhouse
American Jewish Theatre
Black Spectrum Theatre Company, Inc.
Bouwerie Lane Theater
Cherry Lane Theater
Circle Lane Theater
Circle Repertory Theater
Grandma Sylvia's Funeral at the SoHo Playhouse
Irish Repertory Theatre
Joseph Papp Public Theater
Lucille Lortel Theater
Minetta Lane Theater
Monkey Wrench Theater
National Black Theatre
Pearl Theater
Provincial Playhouse
SoHo Rep
St. Clement's Church
Sullivan Street Theater
Thalia Spanish Theater
Theater for a New Audience
Theatre Off Park
Tony and Tina's Wedding at St. John's Church
Variety Arts Theatre
Worth Street Theatre

PERFORMANCE SPACES
The African Poetry Theatre, Inc.
Castillo Theatre
Colden Center For the Performing Arts at Queens College
Collective Unconscious
Context Studios
HERE
Jamaica Arts Center
The Kitchen
La MaMa Etc.
Minor Latham Playhouse
Nada
Nuyorican Poet's Cafe
The Ohio Theater
P.S. 122
St. Marks Church in the Bowery
Symphony Space
The Synchronicity Space
TriBeCa Performing Arts Center

MUSIC VENUES
Barge Music
Boys Choir of Harlem
Carnegie Hall
Manhattan School of Music
Miller Theatre
New York Philharmonic
St. Paul's Chapel
Trinity Church

OPERA HOUSES
Amato Opera House
Metropolitan Opera
New York City Opera

DANCE THEATERS
Alvin Ailey American Dance Theatre
American Ballet Theatre
Bessie Schomberg Theatre
Dance Theatre of Harlem
Harkness Dance Center at the 92nd Street Y
Joyce SoHo
Joyce Theatre
New York City Ballet
Warren Street Performance Loft

INDEX BY NEIGHBORHOOD

BROOKLYN
Barge Music
The Brooklyn Academy of Music (BAM)

CHELSEA
American Jewish Theatre
Bessie Schomberg Theatre
Catch A Rising Star
Collective Unconsciousness
The Irish Repertory Theatre
Joyce Theater
The Kitchen

EAST VILLAGE
Amato Opera House
Context Studios
Joseph Papp Public Theater
La Mama, etc.
P.S. 122
Pearl Theater
St. Marks Church in the Bowery
Variety Arts Theatre

FINANCIAL DISTRICT
Trinity Church

GREENWICH VILLAGE
Actor's Playhouse
Boulevard Lane Theatre
Cherry Lane Theatre
Circle Repertory Theatre
Lucille Lortel Theatre
Minetta Lane Theatre
Sullivan Street Theatre
Theater for a New Audience
Theatre Off Park
Tony and Tina's Wedding at St. John's Church

HARLEM
Apollo Theater
Boy's Choir of Harlem
Dance Theatre of Harlem

LOWER EAST SIDE
Chicago City Limits
Nada
Nuyorican Poet's Cafe
Surf Reality

MIDTOWN
Alvin Ailey American Lance Theatre
Carnegie Hall
Monkey Wrench Theater
Roundabout Theatre
St. Clement's Church

MORNINGSIDE HEIGHTS
Manhattan School of Music
Miller's Theater
Minor Latham Playhouse
National Black Theatre
St. Paul's Chapel
Symphony Space

QUEENS
The African Poetry Theatre, Inc.
Black Spectrum Theatre Company, Inc.
Colden Center for the Performing Arts at Queens College
Jamaica Arts Center
Langston Hughes Community Library and Cultural Center
Thalia Spanish Theater

SOHO
Castillo Theatre
Grandma Sylvia's Funeral at the SoHo Playhouse
HERE
Joyce SoHo
The Ohio Theater

STATEN ISLAND
Center for the Arts (College of Staten Island)

TRIBECA
SoHo Rep
TriBeCa Performing Arts Center
Warren Street Performance Loft
Worth Street Theatre

UPPER EAST SIDE
Comic Strip
Dangerfield's
Harkness Dance Center at 92nd Street Y

UPPER WEST SIDE
American Ballet Theatre
Centerfold Coffeehouse
Church of St. Paul and St. Andrew
Metropolitan Opera
New York City Ballet
New York City Opera
New York City Philharmonic
Stand-Up NY

LITERATURE

NYC literature scene.206
interview with
author helen schulman.211
bookstore listings.213
index by neighborhood.218
index by type.219

literature

From the restrictive elegance of Edith Wharton's New York, through the grim realism of Nathanael West's *Miss Lonelyhearts*, to Tama Janowitz's *Slaves of New York*, through to Oscar Hijuelo's *Mr. Ives Christmas*, New York is depicted in literature as the city where your dreams can come brilliantly true and, often, how tragic that brilliance can be. Manhattan seems to increase human appetites for money, for love, for success—and writers, who work in isolation and reflection, view it all with a passionate yet cynical eye.

The uneasy relationship between writers and New York is over a century old. Wharton and Henry James had to leave their restricted society backgrounds in order to develop as artists: But invariably, their best stories came from their New York experiences.

By the turn of the century, two styles of writing came in vogue—the journalistic style represented by Dreiser's *Sister Carrie*, and later by Mencken and Hemingway. *The New Yorker* represented the second voice typified by Dorothy Parker—witty, urbane, and utterly lacking Victorian complacency.

If New York is a subject fit for ambitious writers, it is also a city of ambitious readers and thinkers. The revival of spoken word is an exciting outcome of the blending of Beat narrative and Latino immigrants cultural history. The 92nd Street YMCA offers a variety of readings and lecture series with the most fascinating writers working today. At Symphony Space, accomplished actors read published stories for live broadcast on public radio, bringing a writer's vision to life and to the rest of the country. Tiny coffee shops throughout the city and its boroughs feature weekly readings where the next generation of writers raise their voices, hoping to be heard above the hiss of an espresso maker. The Strand Bookstore and other great independent bookstores are shrines to the written word. On any day you can go in them and see New Yorkers, their heads bent over a new—or long-beloved—title, silent for once.

From Socialites to Social Agitators

Some of New York's earliest chroniclers were simply writing what they knew. Members of exclusive enclaves of high society like James and Wharton spun tales of the hypocrisies and invisible obstacles which faced even the most privileged among city-dwellers. The late 19th-century "gentleman culture" in the West Village supported a loose intelligentsia, from which Henry James emerged; his *Washington Square* details the savage yet repressed emotions of the upper-class families who came to inhabit the mansions and row houses ringing the famous park. Across town, in Gramercy, Edith Wharton commented bitterly on what it was to be female in the constricted social atmosphere of her "age of innocence."

In the wake of massive immigration and the Industrial Revolution, a group of authors and journalists who became known as "muckrakers" let their social consciousness guide them into such projects as Jacob Riis' *How the Other Half Lives*, and expose of squalid tenement conditions on the Lower East Side which led to serious attempts at housing reform, and which signaled the arrival of modernity through the introduction of the themes of alienation, mechanization, and the breakdown of tradition.

The 1841 migration of Horace Greeley's *New York Tribune* to New York presaged the city's heritage as the nerve center of the printing industry. At the end of the 1800s, Willa Cather's *McClure* joined the ranks of the muckrakers, while the *Sunday World* published fiction by O. Henry which brought the grittier side of urban life into households. After the turn of the century, these journals were joined by witticist H.L. Mencken's *Smart Set*, which brought James Joyce to the other side of the Atlantic, *Others*, which featured the poetry of Marianne Moore and William Carlos Williams, and *Crisis*, the editorship of which lured W.E.B. Du Bois from the South.

Interwar Extremes

The interwar period produced writers whose experience covered the spectrum of rebirth, excess, and breakdown. The Harlem Renaissance gathered black artists from all corners of the nation at various clubs and salons in Harlem; Langston Hughes, Countee Cullen, and Zora Neale Hurston are only a few of the writers who sang Harlem's praises, although their optimism was matched by the pessimism of Richard Wright and Ralph Ellison, whose monumental *Invisible Man* is widely recognized as one of the greatest novels of these decades. F. Scott Fitzgerald—whose forays into society ended tragically, both in fiction and life—was renowned in the '20s for his drunken exploits at the Biltmore with his talented, beautiful, unbalanced wife, Zelda. Dorothy Parker engaged in similar excesses, viewing the world with an acerbity which distanced her from those who would admire her quick wit—once, when challenged to make a joke using the word "horticul-

writer's workshop

Looking for a writer's workshop? There are a number of different options in the city, ranging from informal groups of writers who gather at coffee shops and people's apartments and critique each other's work, to more formal, structured workshops. The former are mostly found on a word-of-mouth basis, but the latter are easy to find. The most popular is the Gotham Writer's Workshop, which offers workshops in fiction, poetry, screenwriting, and a number of other genres at seven different locations in Manhattan. They even have online classes for your convenience—check out their website for pertinent info. Classes meet once a week for three hours and cost about $400 for a ten-week semester. The teachers are widely published writers and have been described as "awesome," "amazing," and "incredible." The Writer's Voice of the West Side Y offers a number of different writing workshops, including nonfiction and literary memoir in addition to a number of discussion groups. They offer one-session intensive courses, which go for $20, weekend-long courses for $190, and the typical ten-week long course rings in at $270. If you are looking for something a little more specific or culturally diverse, check out Other Countries, a black, gay and lesbian organization, and the Asian American Writers' Workshop (AAWW). Unlike its counterparts, the weekly sessions held by Other Countries are free except for a $2 fee for the space. Anyone is welcome to attend and should bring copies of their work to read at the session. This year Other Countries introduced a new, monthly workshop series, including one session titled "Changing Your Inner Underwear." Other Countries also offers a virtual workshop. The AAWW offers 6-week long workshops which cost about $125, and feature topics such as poetry writing, fiction-in-progress, how to get published, and screenwriting as well as discussion groups and book clubs.

ture," she quipped, "You can lead a whore to culture, but you can't make her think." Nathanael West wrote with a resigned bitterness and knowledge of the world, and stoically refused to follow the trend of glamorizing the jazz age—instead he focused on the mechanized lives and meaningless tragedies of the grimly aspiring professional classes.

Besides the *New Yorker*, a crop of fresh publications joined the ranks as well, called "little magazines" in order to distinguish them from more established and conservative journals; In 1920 *The Little Review* published installments of Joyce's *Ulysses*, and was fined $100 after losing an obscenity suit.

The Widening Gyre

The post-World War II founding of suburbia under the Eisenhower administration sparked the first stirrings of a new kind of animosity, one between suburb and city; the weary commuter was thrown by the incongruity between the corporate boot camp of his working day and the false tranquillity of the suburbs. John Cheever was the king of such disturbing literature, and his collected stories were topped only by his chilling novel *Bullet Park* in portraying disillusionment. A well-beloved, albeit often misinterpreted author, who wrote in a similar vein was J.D. Salinger, whose works studied the effects of blandly oppressive WASP culture on its young. *Catcher in the Rye* stands as a defining masterwork, portraying an adolescent whose perception of the world is painfully warped, due to his family's need to keep up appearances.

In the city, a growing bohemia, led by Anäis Nin and James Agee, established itself in the Village, and beckoned college students John Berryman, Allen Ginsberg, and Jack Kerouac from Columbia University into downtown's gritty world of heavy drinking and sexual liberalism. Kerouac, Ginsberg, and William S. Burroughs developed what would become the Beat aesthetic, convening in a Morningside Heights apartment and at the West End. Soon after, Ginsberg moved to the seedy East Village, renting an apart-

books + java

Bookstores with cafes are all the rage these days. Though the cafes tend to be overpriced, crowded joints, they're nice to chill out in after you've picked out a fat stack of must-reads.

If you're lonely for a the mall bookstores of your hometown, check out Borders Bookstore and Cafe in the World Trade Center. Generally impersonal but well-stocked and replete with a helpful staff, grab a stack of books and head to Border's own Cafe Espresso to browse. In the mood for something a little more funky? A Different Light, a gay bookstore in Chelsea, is loved by many for its eclectic collection ranging from gay paraphernalia to all different kinds of gay literature. The store is tiny, allowing lots of chances for meaningful brushes past other people, and the cafe offers great homemade lemonade served with a smile. If you don't feel like venturing that far, check out the Barnes and Noble nearest you. Let's face it, B + N has enough books to ensure you'll find something that interests you, their cafés are generally quite spacious, and the selection of Republic of Teas offered is excellent. The Barnes and Noble Cafe is the latest twist on the singles bar—it's the place to go if you want to exchange deep, long glances over the latest thriller and steaming cup of tea. Finally, many of the fine independent bookstores around New York are catching on to the cafe trend. In Brooklyn, the Community Bookstore on Seventh Avenue in Park Slope offers not only an excellent choice of literature, but excellent pastries to munch as you peruse their selection.

Borders Bookstore
5 World Trade Center
A Different Light
151 West 19th St. bet. Sixth and Seventh Aves.
Barnes and Noble Bookstore
2289 Broadway at 82nd St.
Community Bookstore
143 Seventh Ave. bet. Carrol and Garfield Sts.

ment on East 7th Street; Kerouac and Burroughs followed. The subculture of the decidedly rough-around-the-edges area played a major role in Burroughs' first novella, *Junkie*, Ginsberg's famous poem, "Howl," and Kerouac's *The Subterraneans*.

Writing took a radical turn in these decades as people wrote to perform. Unlike plays, these "spoken word" performances were by the author, speaking in a stylized manner and circumventing the isolating effects of writing and reading novels, and therefore achieving an intimacy that had long eluded writers and their audiences. Another young generation of writers also made the East Village their home during this period; LeRoi Jones, Diane Di Prima, and Michael McLure unleashed performance art, dance programs, and semi-scripted events called "happenings" at local hangouts like Cafe le Metro and St. Mark's Church.

Postmodern Panic

An air of heavy pretension hung over the uptown literary scene in the late '60s and early '70s, as self-conscious intellectual journals flourished, stimulated by the double impact of Marxism and feminism on the academic world. A return to the patrician salons (à la Willa Cather of the 1920s) became fashionable amongst staid and self-satisfied intellectuals, who gathered at *Paris Review* editor George Plimpton's palatial East 72nd Street mansion for highballs and conversation. The pompous affectation often characteristic of such gatherings was brilliantly skewered by Woody Allen in *Annie Hall*: In a flashback to his second marriage, he remarks to his wife, who has dragged him to such an affair, "I heard *Dissent* and *Commentary* had merged to form *Dysentery*." Although a great number of literary luminaries lived in New York during this time, they did not constitute a community per se and many of them had left the city by the end of the '70s.

In the '80s, the most prominent novels reflected the materialist feeding frenzy which took hold of the city during the economic boom of the Reagan Era: Tom Wolfe's *Bonfire of the Vanities*, and Brett Easton Ellis' *American Psycho* scathingly represent Wall Street ethics run amuck. Meanwhile, Columbia graduate and Brooklyn-based author Paul Auster marked the quieter pace of life in his New York trilogy of *City of Glass*, *Ghosts*, and *The Locked Room*, although he too grasped the runaway nature of urban decay in *In the Country of Lost Things*.

Journals continue to thrive, and writers are returning to New York City, populating sections of Brooklyn like Williamsburg. The M.F.A. programs at both Columbia and NYU have achieved a heightened popularity as academic approval is still de rigueur for those aspiring New York intellectuals, out to prove that there is no dearth of talent or new material for the city's many voracious literary buffs to devour.

spoken WORD

Spoken word can mean anything from a simple reading to an elaborate performance featuring instruments and props; the constant is the use of creative writing as the narrative thrust, the means to convey the message. This art form has recently experienced a surge of popularity as evidenced by sold-out shows, TV performances and CD sales of the spoken-word artist. If you want to check out either a reading or a full-fledged performance, there are many venues throughout the city where both budding talents and venerable members of the literati read their own work and perform the words of others.

The Unterberg Poetry Center at the 92nd Street Y (see *Performing Arts, Upper East Side*) is the Carnegie Hall of poetry, if poetry could really draw that big a crowd. Everyone from Poet Laureate Rita Dove to W.S. Merwin to Nobel-Prize winner Joseph Brodsky have read here. The city's universities, especially New York University and Columbia, also attract well-known authors. Columbia's resident performing space, Miller Theater (see *Performing Arts, Morningside Heights*), dabbles in literature and offers $5 student tickets. Though shows are few and far between, they're worth the wait: in the past few years, curators of "Theater of the Mind" have sponsored a performance by Yevtushenko, an appearance by Seamus Heany, and a tribute to John Berryman which drew Donal Justice, Richard Howard, Helen Vendler, and Louise Gluck. The Columbia Writing Department also brings big names to read on campus. NYU's Master's in Fine Arts program also draws established talent, although annual budget fluctuation dictates varying bookings, since admission is always free. Annie Dillard read to a full house there, and others of her ilk will, it is to be hoped, soon follow. For writing department readings open to the public, check the "Readings" section of the *Voice* or *NY Press*.

The line-up at KGB (see *Bars, East Village*), which has recently included Karl Kirchway and David Foster Wallace, just keeps getting better. Another downtown social scene that supports poetry is Limbo (see *Cafes, East Village*), where writers on the cusp read in the quintessential East Village intellectual ambiance. Very refined, and packed with people who love their MTV. More great downtown poetry can be found at the Nuyorican Poet's Cafe (see *Performing Arts, East Village*), long a mecca for cutting-edge talent. Performances here are never a disappointment as these are not simply readings; the theatrical elements of spoken word are emphasized as much as the poetry, and if someone starts to drag, the audience loudly lets them know it. Over in SoHo, The Drawing Center (see *Galleries, SoHo*) hosts a readings series entitled "Nightlight" which has featured writers like Sapphire and Gary Indiana; readings are held one Wednesday a month.

Elitism aside, Barnes and Noble, the enemy of independent booksellers, is a stop on every author's promotion trail and boasts some stellar guests; it's always free, although the folding chairs hardly evoke a salon atmosphere. Alliance Poets Reading Series at the Educational Alliance (197 East Broadway, 475-6200, F to East Broad-way) hosts one of the most eclectic reading series in the city and is notable for its literary nonpartisanship and willingness to feature rising stars alongside established poets. Symphony Space (see *Performing Arts, Upper West Side*) is another excellent option for series; expect the venerable theater to preserve the classics and to push the avant-garde envelope with "Selected Shorts," readings of short stories by theater and Hollywood actors. The readings are broadcast Sundays on WNYC 93.9, New York's NPR station.

Annual Festivals

Every June 16th, a ripple of excitement passes through New York's circles of literati as James Joyce fans—more precisely, fanatics—prepare to re-enact Leopold Bloom's travels through the streets of Dublin, as told in the epic novel *Ulysses*, in a celebration known as Bloomsday. Numerous societies throughout the city perform staged readings and offer commentary and papers on related topics, such as historical Dublin. Foremost among the programs is Symphony Space's "Bloomsday on Broadway," broadcast live on WNYC and culminating in Finola Flanaghan's incredible delivery of Molly Bloom's soliloquy. Downtown, St. Mark's Church also hosts a Bloomsday program.

Another annual occurrence is the Downtown Arts Festival RAW, a city-wide contest which identifies new talent. Selected writers read during the week-long festival, which will be held this year from September 10th-20th. Call 925-4200 for more info.

210 literature

The literary life

Helen Schulman is the author of a collection of stories called Not a Free Show, *and the novel* Out of Time. *She co-edited a collection of essays called* Wanting a Child, *published by Farrar, Straus, Giroux in the spring of 1998. Her new novel,* The Revisionist, *will be released in September. The* Revisionist's *opening chapter was published in* Paris Review, *and won the 1998 Pushcart Prize. Helen Schulman lives in Manhattan with her husband, Bruce, and daughter Zoë.*

Q: Tell us how your first book was published?

A: I went to a birthday party. There was a girl there who was assistant to an agent, and she had gone to high school with me. She asked me some favor—I can't remember what it was—and I did it for her, and she said, "Well, to return the favor, why don't you send me your stories?" I had three stories which she showed to her boss, and he took me on. This was the best period of my life. Eric Ashworth was my agent. He has since died of AIDS—He was a lovely, lovely man. They sold a couple of these stories to little journals--maybe they made 50¢. But when I finished graduate school, I had about ten stories for my thesis. Eric, behind my back, slipped them to a man named Lee Gurner, who was then an editor at Knopf. Lee had gone to Cornell and so had I, and some of the stories took place in Ithaca. Eric thought Lee might like them—and he bought them. They gave me another year, year and a half to finish it. I thought I was made, at that time. I thought, there go the lean years. But then my book came out, and it sold two copies. There I was, with no money and no income and no job. So I temped for the next three years, and I worked for a neurologist as an assistant. I'd get up at five, I'd write until eight, and I'd get ready and I'd go to some bank, where whoever was bossing me around was three years younger than me. Pretty demoralizing.

Q: How'd you get out of that?

A: During that time I wrote my second book, and it was just around the time of the publication of the second book that all these teaching jobs started falling in my lap. And then I did a bunch of screenplay writing after the second book, so things kind of righted themselves in a way.

Q: Have any of the screenplays been produced?

A: Not yet. I've written a few—and they've gotten close. I had one project that was set up with four different directors. Another project had a starting date and a budget—but no go.

Q: What's the difference between writing for film and writing a novel?

A: There's a huge difference. I think when you write for films you're thinking of pictures; when you write novels you're thinking words. It's a completely different thought process. I hope the two help each other—because of screenwriting I had to think a lot more of story and plotting, and I hope that's helping my fiction. I think one of the strengths I have as a screenwriter, albeit for a small, independent filmmaker, is that of being a really careful writer. So people are pleased by how carefully the pieces are written—but I could never be a big studio screenwriter. Mine are small independent projects, with European producers.

Q: Tell me about your new novel.

A: *The Revisionist*. It took me 5 years to write—I work slowly. The novel is about a man who is about to turn forty, and his wife throws him out. Mid-life crisis is an understatement. He finds himself becoming increasingly obsessed with a holocaust revisionist, one of those guys who says the holocaust never occurred. He hunts this revisionist down—and in the process of the journey, the hero/antihero begins to confront the lies his own life has been built on, the revisions in his own history.

Q: What was the original idea for *The Revisionist*?

A: I was told an anecdote about some friends of ours, a friend was coming home from work and he watched another man jogging down the street, and jog straight into my friend's house. It turned out that the person was crazy on drugs. But I thought, what a story. To come home from work and watch another man enter your house, seeming to take your place. So that's where the book begins.

helen schulman

literature 211

Literary Walking Tour

The East Village:

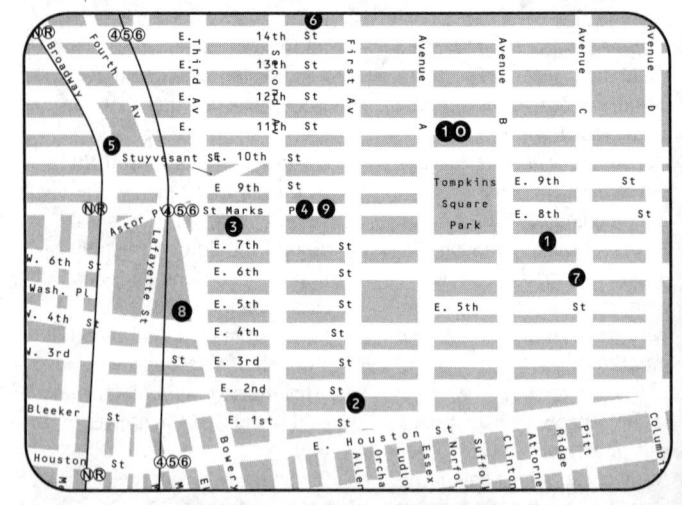

① **Allen Ginsberg** led the Beats here in 1951. He was the first of the group to move to the neighborhood.
206th East 7th Street.

② **Norman Mailer** moved to the East 50s after being assaulted by a gang at this address. Hey, he was asking for it.
39 First Avenue

③ **James Fenimore Cooper** once resided here.
6 St. Mark's Place

④ **W.H. Auden** spent his winters for twenty years in this windowless brick tenement writing on a portable typewriter.
77 St. Mark's Place

⑤ **Frank O'Hara** watched TV and fought LeRoi Jones over a glass in this apartment.
791 Broadway

⑥ **LeRoi and Hettie Jones** ran the magazine *Yugen* from their apartment.
324 East 14th Street

⑦ **Gregory Corso**, Beat writer, moved here in 1967, "right in the heart of the horror!"
Avenue C at 5th Street

⑧ **Diane Di Prima** founded *Floating Bear* magazine with LeRoi Jones and the American Theater for Poets in 1969.

31 Cooper Square
⑨ **Leon Trotsky** published *Novy Mir* while he lived here.
77 St. Mark's Place

⑩ **Jack Kerouac** had an affair here with a woman he would call Mardou Fox in *The Subterraneans* in 1953.
501 East 11th Street

Greenwich Village:

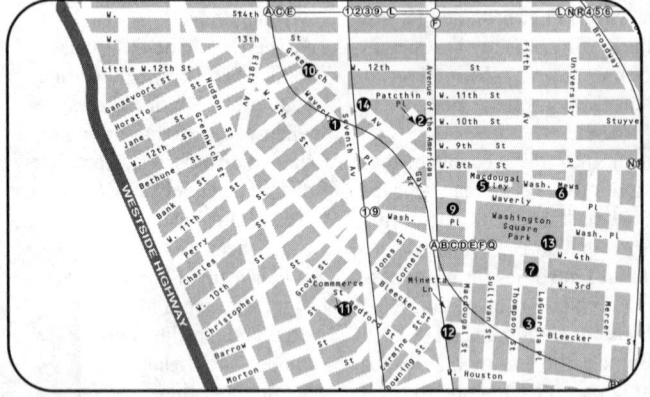

① **James Agee's** first apartment after graduating from Harvard.
38 Perry Street

② **Djuna Barnes** shared an alley with e.e. cummings.
5 Patchin Place

③ **Theodore Dreiser** paid 25¢ a night for his first apartment in New York.
Greenwich Hotel, then Mills at Thompson and Bleecker Streets

④ **Willa Cather** lived at the Grosvenor Hotel, which once stood at 35 Fifth Avenue.
Fifth Avenue at 10th Street

⑤ **Henry James'** grandmother's house. He wrote *Washington Square* about his experience there.
19 Washington Square North

⑥ **Edith Wharton** and her mother moved in after the death of her father in 1882.
7 Washington Square North

⑦ **Edgar Allen Poe** lived here when it was 85 Amity Place.
85 West 3rd Street

⑧ **Mark Twain** moved here in 1900, at the height of his success, to what was then one of the city's most fashionable neighborhoods.
14 West 10th Street

⑨ **Marta's Restaurant** was the favorite eating place of Elinor Wylie, William Rose Benét, and John Dos Passos, circa 1921.
75 Washington Place

⑩ **William Styron's** first "nice" apartment after publication of *Lie Down in Darkness*.
45 Greenwich Avenue

⑪ **Edna St. Vincent Millay** lived in this nine-and-a-half foot space after her marriage.
75 1/2 Bedford Street

⑫ **Gregory Corso** was born in this tenement and frequented the nearby San Remo Hotel.
190 Bleecker Street

⑬ **John Reed** wrote *Ten Days that Shook the World* here.
147 West 4th Street

⑭ **Edward Albee** saw the words "Who's Afraid of Virginia Woolf?" written in soap on a bathroom mirror here.
Tenth Avenue, bet. Greenwich and Waverly.

212 literature

A

A Different Light
The East Coast branch of the largest gay and lesbian specialty book vendor in the country feels refined but homey. A mellow crowd browses through great selections from kitsch to academia and partakes of the small cafe's coffee and sandwiches. The store regularly hosts lectures, musicians, and poets.
151 West 19th St. (bet. Sixth and Seventh Aves.), 989-4850, MC, V, AmEx, **1** **9** *to 18th St.* ♿

Academy Bookstore
Find used or otherwise discounted books on every subject—especially art, architecture, photography, history, and philosophy. The staff will search for out-of-print books.
10 West 18th St. (bet. Fifth and Sixth Aves.), 242-4848, MC, V, AmEx, D, **F** **L** **1** **2** **3** *to 14th Street*

Applause Theatre and Cinema Books
Scripts, books and screenplays. Perfect for the cinephile who has time to browse.
211 West 71St, 496-7511, **2** **3** **9** **1** *to 72nd St.*

Argosy Bookstore
Rare books, old maps, and lithographs fill this time warp of towering bookshelves and cluttered desks. The only real bargains here are on the outside table.
116 East 59th St. (bet. Park and Lexington Aves.), 753-4455, MC, V, AmEx, **4** **5** **6** *to 59th,* **N** **R** *to Lexington Ave.*

B

B. Dalton's
A trademark combo of extensive contemporary fiction selection and paltry intellectual offerings. Strong sports section downstairs.
396 Sixth Ave. (at 8th St.), 674-8780, MC, V, AmEx, **A** **B** **C** **D** **E** **F** **Q** *to West 4th St.*

Bank St. College Bookstore
Serving the fledgling schoolteachers of the nearby Bank St. College with an extensive selection of children's books and educational theory and planning guides. Flip through old faves like *Madeleine* and *Where the Wild Things Are.*
2879 West 112th St. (at Broadway), 678-1654, MC, V, AmEx, **1** **9** *to 110th St.* ♿

Barnes and Noble- 82nd St.
This branch was the first of the megastores in Manhattan, now dwarfed by its downtown colleagues but still a nice oasis from the chaos of Broadway. The selection is remarkable, and New York magazine has named the coffee bar on the mezzanine a major West Side singles scene, making the check-out line something of a double-entendre.
2289 Broadway (at 82nd St.), 362-8835, MC, V, AmEx, **1** **9** *to 79th St.* ♿

Also at
223-82 Bell Boulevard, (718) 224-1083, MC, V, AmEx, Diner, D, **7** *to Flushing,* **Q13 Q28** *to Bay Terrace Shopping Center*
And
1280 Lexington (bet. 86th and 87th St.), 423-9900, **4** **5** **6** *to 86th St.* ♿
33 East 17th St. (Union Square at Park Ave. South), 253-0810, **L** **N** **R** **4** **5** **6** *to Union Sq.* ♿
And
267 Seventh Avenue (bet. 5th and 6th Sts.), (718) 832-9066, **F** *to Seventh Avenue*

Beyond Words
A tiny Park Slope storefront specializing in queer, ethnic and gender studies with a selection that leaves. the "special interest" sections at the giant book chains in the dust. Offerings range from the expected academic and literary fare to magazines, comics and even a book on lesbian semi-vegetarian cookery in a comfortable and pleasant atmosphere.
186 Fifth Ave. (bet. Brooklyn and Lincoln Sts.), MC, V, AmEx, **N** **R** *to Union St.* ♿

Biography Bookshop
Muckrakers, voyeurs, and fan club presidents come to this high-ceilinged and brick-walled store for the latest on their respective celebs. Also boasts an impressive gay and lesbian section.
400 Bleecker St. (at 11th St.), 807-8655, MC, V, AmEx, **1** **9** *to Christopher St.*

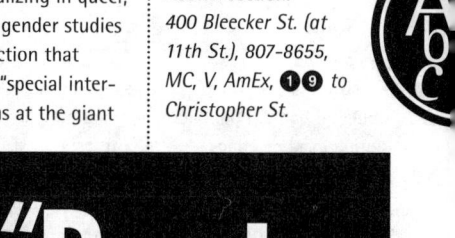

"**Best Bookstore for Kids**"
– *New York Magazine*

www.citysearch.com/nyc/bankstbooks

Bank Street Bookstore
CORNER **112TH ST. & BROADWAY** • 678-1654

40,000 titles • friendly, knowledgeable staff • gift certificates
gift wrapping • telephone orders • shipping worldwide

literature 213

Black Books Plus
African and African-American issues are the top priority at this rare find which stocks a selection spanning a number of genres.
Amsterdam Ave. and 94th St., 749-9632, MC, V, AmEx, ❶❷❸❾ to 96th St.

Blackout Books
The radical writings available here are required reading for any potential East Village resident. Browsers can educate themselves about global political uprisings, sexual liberation, or just have a good laugh with the books, newspapers, magazines, and alternative comic books. For the civic-minded, there's a bulletin board in the back noting local meetings and organizations.
50 Ave. B (bet. 3rd and 4th Sts.), 777-1967, ❻ to Second Ave.

Book Ark
Relief for those weary of superstores. Fiction offerings are solid, as is the foreign language selection.
173 West 81st St. (bet. Amsterdam and Columbus Aves.), 787-3914, MC, V, ❶❾ to 79th St.

Bookberries
Coffee table books are the specialty of this store—huge volumes loaded with pictures, especially along the lines of travel and food. A children's section is located in the rear.
983 Lexington Ave. (at 71st), 794-9400, ❹❺❻ to 68th St.

Booklink/Booklink Too
Come to either of these sister shops for quality fiction and children's books; also a sampling of intellectual and academic periodicals.
99 Seventh Ave. (bet. President and Union); Booklink Too 320 Seventh Ave. (bet. 8th and 9th Sts.), (718) 783-6067, MC, V, AmEx, ❷❸ to Seventh Ave.

C

Columbia University Bookstore
Recently transferred to a tin shed in order to facilitate the building of a new student center, the bookstore is the only option for students with one-stop shopping for all the proper accouterments of the enthusiastic student, from sweat-shirts to pennants.
Columbia Campus, entrance at Broadway and 116th St., 854-4131, MC, V, AmEx, ❶❾ to 116th St. ♿

Community Book Store and Cafe
This integral part of Park Slope's social life carries a mixture of current best-sellers and classic fiction, with a wonderful cafe and garden in the back. The owners also coax well-known authors out for readings, most recently Mary Gordon and Pete Hamill.
143 Seventh Ave. (bet. Garfield and Carroll Sts.), (718) 783-3075, MC, V, AmEx, ❷❸ to Seventh Ave.

Complete Traveller
The best store for new and out-of-print books providing information for real trips and fuel for the imagination; the prices reflect the quality and the selection. The staff is amiable, erudite, and willing to discuss anything from city politics to traveling in the sub-Sahara.
199 Madison Ave. (at 35th St.), 685-9007, MC, V, AmEx, D, Diners, ❻ to 33rd St. ♿

Crawford Doyle Booksellers
Good browsing for high-quality fiction.
1082 Madison Ave. (bet. 81st and 82nd Sts.), 288-6300, MC, V, AmEx, ❻ to 77th St.

D

Dina Magazines
Though the staff tends to frown upon browsing, try to sneak a peek at this impressive selection of periodicals, including a number of foreign magazines and newspapers.
2077 Broadway (bet. 72nd and 73rd Sts.), 875-8824, MC, V, AmEx, D, ❶❷❸❾ to 72nd St.

Double Day Book Shop
Centrally located on Fifth Avenue, this bookstore caters to more mainstream clientele, stocking their shelves with new titles, best-sellers and travel guides.
724 Fifth Ave (bet. 56th and 57th Sts.), 397-0550. ❸❷ to 57th St.

Drama Bookshop
Plays, biographies, acting/directing and writing manuals, and much more.
723 Seventh Ave.(bet. 48th and 49th St.). 2nd fl., 944-0595, ❶❾ to 50th St.

E

East-West Books
As the name suggests, the emphasis here is on introducing Western readers to the literature of the East, specializing in religious and philosophical traditions from Mahayana Buddhism to neo-Confucianism. The staff will make special orders.
78 Fifth Ave. (bet 13th and 14th), 523-5994, MC, V, AmEx, ❻❶❶❷❸❾ (Also on the Upper West Side and in Greenwich Village)

Ed's Book Exchange, Inc.
Specializing in buying and selling textbooks, both old and new.
176-27 Union Turnpike, (718) 969-7173, Q46 to St. John's University ♿

F

Fashion Design Books
Located at the heart of FIT's urban campus, this unique take on the university bookstore stocks a plethora of fashion mags, from the popular to the obscure, and art and design books. In lieu of office accessories, you'll find art and sewing supplies.
234 West 27th St., (bet. Seventh and Eighth Aves.), 633-9646, MC, V, AmEx, D, ❶❾ to 23rd St. ♿

214 literature

Forbidden Planet
Comics fans seeking everything from superheroes to the latest Eightball cruise the racks to weed out the best of the new and used selection. But the big thing here is science fiction with significant dashes of fantasy and horror.
840 Broadway (at 13th St.), 473-1576, MC, V, AmEx, D, ❶ⓁⓃⓇ❹❺❻ to Union Square

G
Gryphon
Crowded shelves of used books climbing almost to the ceiling and piled on the floor: "I'd like it more if I could actually turn around in the aisles," complains one regular. There are books here which can be found nowhere else in Manhattan; you just have to look, real hard.
2246 Broadway (bet. 80th and 81 St.), 362-0706, ❶❾ to 79th St.

H
Hacker Art Books
An eager, knowledgeable staff headed by Pierre, the Parisian owner and conversationalist extraordinaire, can help browsers wade through the initially intimidating selection. The clientele are true artlovers, not just collectors.
45 West 57th St. (bet. Fifth and Sixth Aves.), 688-7600, MC, V, AmEx, ❻ⓇⓇ to Fifth Avenue

Hotalings
Walls of magazines, including one of the city's finest selections of foreign-language periodicals.
142 West 42nd St. (bet. Sixth and Seventh Aves.), 840-1868, MC, V, AmEx, ❼ⓇⓈ❶❷❸❼❾ to Times Square

Housing Works Used Bookstore Cafe
Used books SoHo style. No dingy paperbacks with tattered covers and peculiar odors here. Instead, browse through nearly pristine coffee table art books and hardcover fiction with jackets fully intact, all at low used-book prices. There's also a coffee bar for refueling while settling on what to take home.
126 Crosby St. (bet. Houston and Prince), MC, V, AmEx, ❻ⒹⓆ to Broadway/Lafayette, ⓃⓇ to Spring Street

K
K & W Books and Stationary
One of the biggest Chinese bookstores, K & W carries Hello Kitty toys and a large selection of books in Chinese and in English on topics like martial arts, bonsai care, Buddhism, and knife throwing.
131 Bowery St., 343-0779, Cash Only, ⓃⓇ to Canal St.

Kinokuniya Bookstore
Japanese books, some in English translation, with a diverse selection of stationary and gifts.
10 West 49th St. (bet Fifth and Sixth Aves.), 765-7766, MC, V, AmEx, ($10 minimum) ❻ⒹⒻⓆ to 47-50th/ Rockefeller Center ♿

Kitchen Arts and Letters
With a fabulous selection of over 9,000 cookbooks, the definitive answer to "what's cooking?" for either the novice or the gourmand.
1435 Lexington Ave. (bet. 93rd and 94th Sts.), 876-5550, MC, V, ❹❺❻ to 92nd St.

L
Labyrinth Books
Professors and students alike applaud this recent addition to Morningside's healthy population of bookstores, made possible in part by the rare generosity of its landlord (Columbia). Relying on a strong selection of academic titles rather than coffeeshops and comfy furniture, Labyrinth is a welcome retreat for hard-core bibliophiles.
536 112th St. (bet. Broadway and Amsterdam Aves.), 865-1588, MC, V, AmEx, ❶❾ to 110th St. ♿

The Last Word
Used books in various stages of disrepair, especially those which consistently turn up in the syllabi of Columbia core curriculum classes. Bargain tables outside offer a lot of junk along with the occasional gem.
1841 Amsterdam Ave. (at 119th St.), 864-0013, Cash Only, ❶❾ to 116th St.

Lectorum Book Store
Spanish and Latin American authors whose native-language tomes are dispersed throughout the store comprise the bulk of the selection. Translations of popular titles by the likes of Stephen King and James Cavell, bibles, dictionaries, and a host of other reference books round out the selection. Check at the desk for information about lectures and readings.
137 West 14th St. (bet. Sixth and Seventh Aves.), 741-0220, MC, V, AmEx, ❶❾❷❸ to 14th St. ❻ⒹⒻⓆ to 14th St./ Sixth Ave. ♿

Liberation Book Store
One of the country's largest and best selections of books about black history and culture. Posters, calendars, and greeting cards are also available.
421 Lenox Ave. (at 131 St), 281-4615, Cash Only, ❷❸ to 135th St. ♿

Librairie de France
One-stop shopping for French émigrés and Francophiles. New York's largest French-language bookstore sells magazines upstairs and a vast assortment of literature, history, and biographies available downstairs.
610 Fifth Ave., on the Rockefeller Center Promenade, (bet. 49th and 50 St.), 581-8810, MC, V, AmEx, ❻ⒹⒻⓆ to Rockefeller Center

M
Macondo
Pick up an import from either Spain or South America here. The store caters to native speakers

literature 215

with an excellent selection of literature, plays, and poetry, although prices reflect the import status.
221 West 14th St. (bet. Seventh and Eighth Aves.), 741-3108, AmEx, **❶❷❸❾** *to 14th St.*

Manhattan Books
Mainly catering to the textbook needs of students at the nearby college; this can be a good spot to find steals on reference books like dictionaries and style guides. The real attraction is that they'll pay out a small amount of cash for almost any textbook or other academic text, so if something has proven hard to unload, give them a shot.
150 Chambers St. (bet Greenwich and West Broadway), 385-7395, MC, V, AmEx, **❶❷❸❾** *to Chambers St.* ♿

Manhattan Comics and Cards
Action figures gaze down at customers navigating the stacks of comic books; mags run the gamut of old, new, latest, and greatest. Scavenge through Sunday's half-price bins.
228 West 23rd St. (bet. Seventh and Eighth Aves.), 243-9349, MC, V, **❶❾** *or* **❸❺** *to 23rd St.*

Municipal Art Society Urban Center Books
Books on every architectural topic, from urban design to Freudian interpretations of city planning, line the walls of this cozy nook, complete with a fireplace and library ladders. Enjoy a recent purchase in the courtyard outside.
457 Madison Ave. (at 51st), 935-3592, MC, V, **❸❻** *to 53rd St.*

Murder Ink
This specialty bookstore featuring new and used mystery fiction is every sleuth wannabe's dream. Their stock includes many classic whodunits as well as novels featuring elements of espionage and suspense. A mecca for the city's true mystery buffs, this shop has frequent book-signings that draw some big names.
2486 Broadway (bet. 92nd and 93rd), 362-8905, MC, V, AmEx, **❶❷❸❾** *to 96th St.*

Also at:
1435 Lexington Ave. (at 76th St.), 517-3222, MC, V, AmEx, **❻** *to Lexington Ave. 2486 Broadway at 92nd St., 362-8905, V, MC, AmEx,* **❶❷❸** *to 96th St.* ♿

Mysterious Bookshop
Serving the city's voracious mystery readers, this store stocks both current and out-of-print books as well as a healthy number of imports from Britain.
129 West 56th St. (bet. Sixth and Seventh Aves.), 765-0900, MC, V, AmEx, **❶❷❸❹❶❾** *to 59th St.*

N

New York University Booksellers
Lines wind around the stacks during the beginning of each college semester at this academic standard. Students get no special discounts.
18 Washington Place (bet University and Greene Sts), 998-4656, MC, V, D, **❶❷** *to 8th St.*

O

Oscar Wilde Memorial Bookstore
For over twenty-five years, New York City's flagship gay bookstore has been offering books for and by gay men and women, as well as videotapes, music, magnets, T-shirts, and jewelry. Occasional readings by established authors are scheduled.
15 Christopher St. (at Sixth Ave), 255-8097, MC, V, AmEx, D, **❶❾** *to Christopher St.*

P

Papyrus
Though its hegemony was slightly infringed upon with the introduction of Labyrinth bookstore, this

---

Looking to increase your options?

Visit

Office of **C**ommunications **S**ervices

We offer:
- private lines
- digital data
- analog adapters
- cable television
- voice mail

CALL 854•6250

216 literature

smallish store stocks a little bit of everything. The literature and travel sections are excellent, as is the selection of textbooks, which often run cheaper than at Columbia Univerisity's bookstore.
2915 Broadway (at 114th St.), 222-3350, ①⑨ to 116th St.

Partners & Crime
Serving Village mystery aficionados, P&C carries a lot of current mysteries and a shelf of out-of-print books; the staff will special-order books not in stock. Call for a schedule of readings.
44 Greenwich Ave. (bet. Sixth and Seventh) 765-0900, MC, V, AmEx, ⒶⒷⒸⒹ①⑨ *to 59th St.*

Photographer's Place
New and used books from camera manuals to texts on fashion photography line the intimate wood-paneled walls of this photographer's pit stop.
133 Mercer St. (bet. Prince and Spring Sts.), 966-2356, ⓃⓇ *to Prince St.*

Posman's
Avoid coming during the beginning-of-the-semester madness in January or September, as the lines to buy books seem endless. Off-season, browse through new and used academic titles at your leisure or rifle through the bins outside for super discounts.
2955 Broadway (bet 115th and 116th Sts.), 961-1524, MC, V, AmEx, ①⑨ *to 116th st.*

Also at:
1University Place, 533-2665, MC, V, AmEx, D, ⓃⓇ *to 8th St.*

R
Rizzoli
Pop in to escape the chaos of Midtown and get lost in this dark, warm store which, like its downtown counterpart, specializes in beautiful architecture, art, design, and coffeetable books. Literature and non-fiction selection is adequate if not inspiring.
31 West 57th St. (bet. Fifth and Sixth Aves.), 759-2424, MC, V, AmEx, D, ⓃⓇ *to 57th St.*

Also at:
454 West Broadway (bet. Houston and Prince Sts.), 674-1616, MC, V, AmEx, D, ⓃⓇ *to Prince St.*

S
Science Fiction, Mysteries and More!
Literally named to the point of absurdity, this Sci-fi den is the stomping ground of those whose genre-lust creates needs even Forbidden Planet cannot satisfy. New and used paperbacks abound, along with rare editions and collectibles for the very serious. There's also lots of stuff about aliens, occult, and conspiracy theories for X-philes.
140 Chambers St., 385-8798, MC, V, AmEx, Diners, ⒶⒸⒺⓃⓇ①②③④⑤ ⑥⑨ *to Chambers St.*

See Hear
Want to buy a 'zine without getting stared down and scoffed at by the ultra-cool record store guy? Check out the largest array of homemade publications around, with lots of stuff for hardcore and indie-rock fans as well as those who just appreciate irreverent writing that doesn't answer to advertisers.
59 East 7th St. (bet. First and Second Aves.), 505-9781, MC, V, AmEx, Ⓕ *to Second Ave.*

Shakespeare & Co.
One of two locations left after the recent demise of the Upper West Side store, offering a diverse selection of books and the soul of an actual bookstore, too.
939 Lexington Ave. (bet. 68th and 69th Sts.), MC, V, AmEx, D, ⑥ *to 86th Sts.*

Also at:
716 Broadway (at Washington Place), 529-1330, MC, V, AmEx, ⓃⓇ *to 8th St.*

SoHo Books
The best sale tables around await outside this bargain book cavern, which offers everything from slightly outdated editions of Let's Go guides to slick Gen X novels for $1.98 each or three for five dollars.
351 West Broadway, MC, V, AmEx, 226-3395, Ⓐ ⒸⒺ *to Spring St.*

South St. Seaport Museum Shop
Any wannabe sailors who pride themselves on knowing how to tie knots can learn the rest from one of the many books about ships and port histories, and New York City from the colonial period to the 19th century.
12-14 Fulton St. (bet. South and Front), 748-8663, MC, V, AmEx, D, ②③ *to Fulton St.*

Spring St. Books
Housing a fairly large magazine selection, including a healthy number of literary and academic journals, this tidy, soothingly quaint shop is a welcome respite from the bevy of chic boutiques hemming it in.
169 Spring St. (bet. West Broadway and Thompson), 219-3033, ⒸⒺ *to Spring St.*

St. Mark's Books
Why go to a chain when everything you'd ever want can be found in the tall racks of this favorite excursion? Literature, sci-fi, and mystery are all strong suits. It's just cooler to shop here.
31 Third Ave. (at 9th), 260-7853, MC, V, AmEx, D, ⑥ *to Astor Place*

St. Mark's Comics
From "The X Men" to less conventional titles like "Sexy Sushi," there's enough here for any comic book connoisseur.
11 St. Marks Place (bet. Second and Third Aves.), 598-9439, MC, V, AmEx, ⓃⓇ *to 8th St.,* ⑥ *to Astor Place*

Stowell and Sons Bookstore
Narrow aisles and a certain mustiness lend an authenticity to this bookstore's monthly "Dead Poets" reading series. Check out the back alcove for used books.

literature 217

33-18 Broadway (bet. 33rd and 34th Sts.), Astoria, (718) 204-5775, MC, V, **N** to Broadway

The Strand Bookstore Inc.
Advertising "eight miles of books," The Strand is an awesome sight: two cavernous floors of bookshelves stuffed solid and tables crammed into the space in between. Browse slowly, and with the proper investment of time, you'll turn up books you never dreamed existed. 828 Broadway (at 12th St.), 473-1452, MC, V, D, AmEx, **N R** to Eighth Ave.
Also at:
25 Fulton St. (at Water St.), 732-6070, MC, V, AmEx, D, **2 3** to Fulton

Sufi Books
If there were such a thing as a typical neighborhood spiritualist bookshop, this would be TriBeCa's. The quiet atmosphere with a soft-spoken staff to match contains a wealth of Eastern religion resources and smaller sections on Judaism and Christianity to feed spiritual quests of any ilk. There's also a large space next door where meditation and yoga classes take place regularly. 227 West Broadway, 334-5212, MC, V, AmEx, **1 9** to Franklin St. &

T
Tower Video and Books
This counterpart to the Broadway Tower Records has a stellar video selection downstairs and a bookstore upstairs with notable sections in art, photography and music. Expect the same commercial atmosphere of the record store. 383 Lafayette (at 4th St.), 228-5100, **N R** to 8th, **6** to Astor Place &

U
Unity Book Center
"You say you want a revolution?" If reading about one suffices, this smallish shop chock-full of radical leftist writings is the place to go. Check out the great Marxist, African-American, and women authors who most likely didn't make your high school government class reading list. 237 West 23rd St. (bet. Seventh and Eighth Aves.), 242-2934, Cash Only, **1 9** to 23rd St. &

W
West Side Judaica
This haven of Judaica supplies music, art, decorations, and children's educational tools as well as a number of books dealing with Jewish issues. Closes at 3pm on Fridays for Shabbat and doesn't reopen until Sunday. 2412 Broadway (bet. 88th and 89th Sts.), 362-7846, MC, V, **1 9** to 86th St.

Wow Comics
Those who can't always make it to Manhattan's larger comic stores take heart in this comfortable mainstay. New and old releases from a variety of both mainstream and independent companies are sold alongside baseball cards, action figurines, and other memorabilia. 2084 White Plains Rd.(at Pelham Pkwy.), (718) 829-0461, **2** to Pelham Parkway

Z
Zakka
Insight into the world of the Japanese adolescent. Bookstore, boutiques and video palace focusing on Japanese pop culture. 510 Broome St.. 431-3961, **C E** to Spring St.

BOOKSTORE INDEX BY NEIGHBORHOOD
BRONX
Wow Comics

BROOKLYN
Community Bookstore and Cafe
Booklink/ Booklink Too
Nkiru Books

CHELSEA
A Different Light
Barnes and Noble
Fashion Design Books
Lectorum Bookstore
Maconda
Unity Book Center

CHINATOWN
K and W Books and Stationary

EAST VILLAGE
Forbidden Planet
See Hear
Shakespeare and Co.
St. Mark's Books
St. Mark's Comics
The Strand
Tower Video and Books

FINANCIAL DISTRICT
South Street Seaport Museum Shop
The Strand Bookstore

GRAMERCY
Barnes and Noble
East West Books

GREENWICH VILLAGE
Academy Bookstore
B. Dalton's
Beyond Words
Biography Bookshop
East West Books
NYU Booksellers
Oscar Wilde Memorial Bookstore
Partners and Crime
Posman's

HARLEM
Liberation Bookstore

LOWER EAST SIDE
Blackout Books

MIDTOWN
Gryphon
Hacker Art Books
Hotalings
Kinokuniya Bookstore
Librairie de France
Manhattan Comics and Cards
Municipal Art Society

218 literature

Urban Center Books
Mysterious Bookshop
Rizzoli

MORNINGSIDE HEIGHTS
Bank Street College Bookstore
Black Books Plus
Columbia University Bookstore
Labyrinth Books
The Last Word
Papyrus
Posman

QUEENS
Barnes and Noble
Stowell and Sons Bookstore

SOHO
Housing Works Used Bookstore Cafe
Photographer's Place
SoHo Books
Spring Street Books
Zakka

TRIBECA
Manhattan Books
Science Fiction, Mysteries and More!
Sufi Books

UPPER EAST SIDE
Argosy Bookstore
Barnes and Noble
Bookberries
Complete Traveler
Crawford Doyle

Booksellers
Double Day Book Shop
Drama Bookshop
Kitchen Arts and Letters
Murder Ink
Shakespeare and Co.

UPPER WEST SIDE
Applause Theatre and Cinema Books
Barnes and Noble
Book Ark
East West Books
Murder Ink
West Side Judaica

BOOKSTORE INDEX BY TYPE
ACADEMIC AND CULTURAL STUDIES
A Different Light
Beyond Words
Black Books Plus
Blackout Books
East-West Books
Labyrinth Books
Liberation Bookstore
Oscar Wilde Memorial Bookstore
Papyrus
Shakespeare and Co.
St. Marks Books
Sufi Books
Unity Book Center

ART
Fashion Design Books
Hacker Art Books
Municipal Art Society

Urban Center Books
Photographer's Place

FOREIGN LANGUAGE AND CULTURE
Agueybana Bookstore
K and W Books and Stationary
Kinokuniya Bookstore
Lectorum Bookstore
Librairie de France
Macondo
Oceanie Afrique Noire Books

GENERAL
B. Dalton's
Barnes and Noble (several locations)
Booklink/ Booklink Too
Coliseum Books
Community Book Store and Cafe
Crawford Doyle Booksellers
Rizzoli
SoHo Books
Spring Street Books
Stowell and Sons Bookstore

MAGAZINES
Bank Street College Bookstore
Biography Bookshop
Complete Traveler
Dina Magazines
Hotalings
Kitchen Arts and Letters

See Hear
Tower Video and Books

MYSTERY
Murder, Ink
Mysterious Bookshop
Partners and Crime

NEW YORK CITY
Forbidden Planet
Manhattan Comics and Cards
New York Bound Bookshop
Science Fiction, Mysteries, and More!
South St. Seaport Museum Shop
St. Marks Comics

TEXTBOOKS
Columbia University Bookstore
Ed's Book Exchange, Inc.
Manhattan Books
NYU Booksellers
Posman's

USED AND RARE
Academy Bookstore
Argosy Bookstore
Book Ark
Gryphon
Housing Works Used Bookstore Cafe
The Last Word
The Strand

literature 219

PLASTIC WALLET MAPS

New York
San Francisco
Los Angeles
Boston
Atlanta
Chicago
San Diego
Washington D.C

Our Plastic Wallet Maps Are available at:

Hagstrom
Map & Travel Center
57 W. 43rd St, bet. 5th/6th Aves.
(Full-Line Dealer)

The Civilized Traveller Stores
Barnes & Noble Bookstores
Doubleday Bookshops
B. Dalton Booksellers
Borders Books & Music
Rizzoli Bookstores
Tower Books & Records
Rand McNally
　-Map & Travel Stores
Whitney Museum
　-The Store Next Door
Guggenheim Museum Stores
Benjamin Book Stores
Avis Currency Exchange
And Other Fine Stores

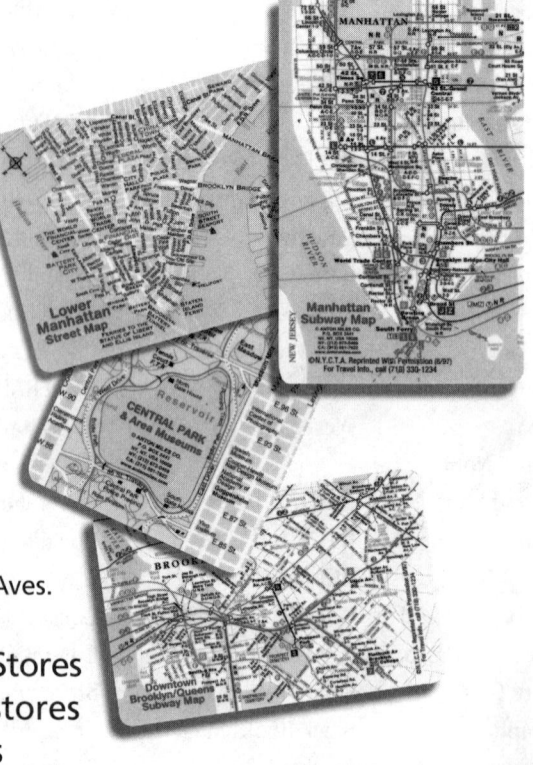

Anton Miles Co.
"The Worlds' Largest Publisher of Little Maps"

Anton Miles Co.
PO Box 3441
New York, N.Y. 10009
Tel: (212) 673-0469
Fax: (212) 673-0504
www.antonmiles.com

Visit our Web Site For Retail Locations And Product Information
www.antonmiles.com

film+tv

nyc film and tv scene.221
interview with film editor
 chris osborne.224
movie theater listings.227
index by neighborhood.229
index by type.229

film + tv

New Yorker Mae West, once said to a Hollywood studio executive, "I'm a big girl, from a big town--so don't blow smoke at me, little man." After decades of losing ground to Los Angeles as the film production capital of the country, New York is hot again in the '90s, both as a location and a production site. New Yorkers acknowledge this with a but-of-course attitude and a warning to filmmakers using their city: Don't get Hollywood on us, and don't expect any more respect than the next schmuck on the street. After all, the birthplace of film on this side of the Atlantic doesn't owe anyone anything.

At the turn of the century, budding filmmakers shot footage of the city's vaudeville and theatrical shows and other sites; even footage of buildings under construction was popular with audiences. After perpetual sunshine had drawn the studios to California, agents and executives still scanned New York stages for talent, realizing, in the late '20s, that many of the stunningly beautiful silent-screen stars had squeaky speaking voices and needed to be replaced with actors from Broadway. In the early '30s, stage diction was the rage and actors imitated the accent of the English upper-class. Straight-talking Humphrey Bogart, however, had his big break on Broadway in *The Petrified Forest*. Bogart impressed his co-star (the hugely popular Leslie Howard) so much that Howard refused to appear in the film version unless Bogart also reprised his Broadway role. Barbara Stanwyck and Joan Crawford both started out as Broadway "hoofers", giving them the gams and attitude to sustain their long careers.

In the '40s, neo-realism, film noir, and avant-garde filmmaking deepened the power and complexity of image on film. New York, with its combination of grit and glamour, was the perfect setting for noir classics like Billy Wilder's *The Lost Weekend*. In the '50's when Hollywood was focusing on teenyboppers and Technicolor, New York television and filmmakers found increasing meaning in realism. *On The Waterfront* was a revolutionary combination of method acting and on-location shooting whose stark simplicity stood out from the over-elaborate productions of the dying studio system. Realism merged with pageantry in the 1972 production of *The Godfather*, which marked the beginning of a decade of great American films, most of them reflections on the American Dream-New York style. Coppola and Pacino, Scorcese and DeNiro united to present the world with defining images of New Yorkers, images which still form an international perception of this city and its people. With hindsight, it now seems clear that, in 1986, when Spike Lee scraped together funding for his second feature-length film, *Do the Right Thing*, he was setting the stage for the surge of independent films which would revolutionize the business in the nineties. Independent films continue to provide a much needed alternative to alien-slaughtering blockbusters, while also allowing the art and business of filmmaking to be passed on to the next generation. On any given day in Manhattan (and the four boroughs), there are hundreds of films in production; from the simplest student short to a Meg Ryan/Tom Hanks film which shuts down an eight-block stretch of Columbus Avenue. Theatres like the Angelika, Lincoln Plaza, and Film Forum offer the world's best cinema- and countless organizations like The Independent Feature Project are nurturing and networking with the great filmmakers of tomorrow.

222 film and television

1893 W.K.L. Dickinson, working for Thomas Edison, invents the kinetoscope.

1894 The first kinetoscope parlor opens at 1155 Broadway. Charles E. Chinnock, a former Edison worker, shoots what is probably New York City's first moving-picture film from a roof in Brooklyn.

1896 Felix Mesguich, a Lumiére camera/projector operator, premieres his film at B.F. Keith Music Hall; Edison acquires Vitascope, launches screenings to compete with Lumiére's cinematographe.

1918 A winter coal shortage drives many production companies to California.

1930 The Worker's Film and Photo League is created to combat studio policies of showing only noncontroversial films. The group becomes the Film and Photo League in several major cities, producing a compelling feature-length documentary, *Hunger*.

1939 Ralph Steiner and Willard Van Dyke make *The City*, a documentary that captures all aspects of quotidian New York life, sometimes through hidden cameras.

1948 *The Quiet One*, shot in Harlem in documentary style, is a sensitive, moving piece of fiction about a disturbed black boy growing up in the city.

1954 Eli Kazan shoots *On The Waterfront* on the docks of Hoboken.

1956 Lionel Ragosin shoots the documentary, *On the Bowery*, chronicling the meanderings of an alcoholic who spends his time on the strip.

1966 Andy Warhol makes *Chelsea Girls*.

1968 Standish D. Lawder makes a quirky meta-documentary called *Necrology*. A single long take of average commuters on a down escalator in New York City, when played backwards, creates an effect of people rising to the top of the screen.

1973 Scorcese's release of *Mean Streets*, filmed in and around Little Italy.

1990 Due to a labor dispute, film production in the city comes to a halt as its infrastructure crumbles under a Hollywood boycott.

1991 The East Coast Council is formed to ensure profit and work to both New York City unions and Hollywood studios.

1998 The tension between New York and Hollywood heats up again, as mega-bucks McMovies from L.A. are increasingly rivaled by independent productions.

a brief history of film

Name: Chris Osborne
Age: 29
Occupation: Film Editor

Q: How did you start out?
A: Had a very good friend in the film industry. I stopped down here and helped him put a film together-what's called synching it. Months later, another film student offered me a job, and I finally started getting paid.
Q: Why did you move to NY?
A: A friend offered me a place to sleep in exchange for working on his film. First job earned me $125 a week.
Q: Did you apprentice?
A: No, I went another route. I had computer skills so I could hire myself out at $40 per hour for computer work.
Q: How did you learn editing?
A: I learned the old way, with film, as an underground on the flatbed. That's razor blades and tape and all the rest of it. I went to this great workshop, The Main Photographic workshop-specialty classes for people in the industry. You train with a pro in the field.
Q: Tell me about Sundance.
A: The film accepted was the Absolution of Anthony. Our first film was *Post Apartheid Popcorn*-that's one we did on a flatbed. Getting into Sundance, it's like certification. You can prove you're a filmmaker. Sundance itself is not a lot of fun; it's a nasty cruel world that cares not about film but about money.
Q: Is it true short film is a better calling card nowadays for newcomers?
A: There are things you can do with a short film that you can't do with a long film. There's no time for great cinematography, and as far as character development, you paint your image starkly. You either prove you can tell a story or you can't-you have nothing to hide behind.
Q: How do you get a job in film?
A: The best way to get a job in film: Don't send a resume-walk in. Say, "Hi-I'm looking for a job." Right now we're looking for assistants at the place where I work. If someone had the initiative to walk in right now, say "Hi! I want to edit!"-we'd hire them. If you want anything bad enough you will do it-that certainly holds true for me.

Chris Osborne works at Salamandra, a film and video editing company in midtown. He studied film both as an undergrad and as a graduate student. A short film of Chris' is currently showing in the international film festival scene, and appeared at Sundance in 1998.

to the budding filmmaker,

New York City is filled with auteurs-to-be who are filming low-budget projects of enormously varying quality. The good news is, despite how hot this field is now, it's surprisingly easy to break in--on a low level. All you have to do is work for free! The Independent Feature Project (465-8200) requires volunteers year-round; work a few hours and you can attend the rest of a weekend seminar or festival for free. Also, be sure to buy the publications: Screenwriter and The Independent Filmmaker are good, and Backstage is essential--film students advertise there for actors. Call them up and volunteer to do anything! Film is a hugely social business, so the more people you meet, the more chance you have of ending up with paid work.

Once you find a circle of similarly cinematically obsessed friends, chances are you'll start working the circuit. Going to film festivals is not cheap, but the arguments about the films and speakers are fierce, and again--gotta network, baby! Or, do your own thing. The Mayor's Office of Film, Theater, and Broadcasting (212-489-6710) was created to aid with such productions. Students or professionals go to the office to get special permits and even police help to accommodate filming in New York City. When you've got that short-film shot and edited, you'll have the hot calling card of the nineties. And, hopefully, you'll already have schmoozed with a few distributors--because distribution is the major challenge in this business--that is, unless your old bud L. DiCaprio agreed to appear in your film. (If that's the case-- sit back and wait for Miramax to come knockin'.)

224 film and television

There are festivals in New York to celebrate every type of film and filmmaker--it's important to keep an eye on the Times, and on what's going on at Lincoln Center and MoMA, which host the prestigious, big-name festivals. The New York Film Festival (September and October) has been celebrating American and foreign films for several decades. Tickets for this event, particularly opening and closing nights, are snapped up weeks in advance. Another hot festival, particularly as the trend for indies continues to heat up, is the New Directors, New Films series at MoMA (April). Here, industry bigwigs and idealistic film students eye one another with wary hunger. Films looking for distribution are also featured at the Independent Feature Film Market (September 18th-25th at the Angelika), sponsored by the Independent Feature Project. The IFP has been a godsend to filmmakers in New York--but the tickets at the Film Market are priced to cater to serious filmmakers, and are expensive, even with the membership discount.

Once summer arrives, films are screened at Bryant Park Free Festival (Sixth Avenue at 42nd Street) on Mondays at 8:30 pm. Bring a picnic dinner, a blanket, and a friend--sit back and watch *King Kong* or *Vertigo* under the stars. The tenth annual Gay and Lesbian Film Festival will be held June 4th-14th at the Joseph Papp Public Theatre. (For updates and info. call 254-7448.) The first week of August, enjoy air-conditioned splendor and affordable ticket prices at the Harlem Week Black Film Festival at the Adam Clayton Powell Jr. State Office Building (749-5298). Also, arts theaters like Film Forum (727-8110) and the Angelika (995-2000) have festivals of their own, year-round.

film festivals

Actors, actors, actors, actors, everywhere...

For anyone new to New York and aching for a little intelligent discourse on the state of the stage, the opportunities are endless. The rumor about New York is true: swing your arm in any direction on the average street and you will likely strike an actor. The bartender at the cool SoHo lounge, the waiter in the midtown restaurant, the clerk in the Barnes and Noble. It would be quite a challenge to go through a typical New York day and not run into a budding thespian. Many hours of pleasant and informative theatrical conversation can be had in the most unlikely of places. Display a playbill or mention a show, and you're quite likely to find yourself completely engaged in a heated debate on the merits of Arthur Miller's later work or Robert Wilson's latest production. Conversation is something actors can offer in abundance--mainly because it's free.

For reading material and theatrical information, try The Drama Bookshop, located on Seventh Avenue at 48th Street. From the outside, the shop looks like an unassuming doorway. Take the stairs up to the second floor, however, and you will find an astonishing selection of plays and theatrical books. On a normal day, the aisles are packed with actors and theatrical professionals who can share years of experience and survival skills. They can also recommend shows, materials, and coaches. To catch post-performance actors, try the West Bank Cafe on 42nd and Ninth Avenue. For the cost of a moderately priced entrée, you may spot a Broadway ingenue or meet an all-important producer. The cafe also features a basement theater. Otherwise, to find young actors on the verge, hang out in any downtown hotspot because chances are the gorgeous staff member who just delivered your order is biding his or her time, waiting to be discovered.

Free Tickets to Television Tapings

Ever wanted to find out if Letterman's jokes about the fifty-degree temperature in the Ed Sullivan Theater are well-founded? Luckily, the practice of packing theaters full of eager beavers (usually out-of-towners, who tend to be more excitable than New Yorkers) who clamor to see the stars up-close, will allow you to verify these and other rumors. If you request tickets by mail, send in your postcard well in advance of the date you want to see the show, since many tapings have six-to-twelve month waiting lists. Locals tend to get last dibs, so try to have an out-of-town friend make the request on your behalf. Stand-by seats are available for most shows for those who are willing to arrive very early and wait in line.

Geraldo Rivera--To receive tickets in advance, send a letter with a self-addressed stamped envelope. Standby tickets are distributed forty-five minutes before taping, which occurs Tuesday through Thursday at 1-4pm. *524 W. 57th St.(bet. Tenth and Eleventh Aves.), 265-8520*

Late Night with Conan O'Brien--Send a postcard requesting tickets in advance, or drop by before 9am the day of the show to try to get one of the limited same-day tickets. Taping takes place Tuesday through Friday at 5:30pm. *30 Rockefeller Plaza (bet. Fifth and Sixth Avenues) 664-4000*

Late Show with David Letterman--Drop a postcard to Dave in the mail for advanced tickets or try to snag standby tickets by waiting in line for the noon distribution. Taping takes place on Monday through Thursday at 5:30pm. *Ed Sullivan Theater, 1697 Broadway at 54th Street, 975-5853.*

Live with Regis and Kathy Lee--If you can bear the saccharine content, request tickets in advance via postcard or arrive prior to 8am for standby tickets. The show is taped on weekdays at 9am. *7 Lincoln Square (at 67th Street and Columbus Ave.), 465-1000*

Maury Povich--You can request tickets by mail or by phone. Call a day in advance to check o the availability of standby tickets. The show is taped on weekdays at 10:30am. *221 West 26th Street (bet. Seventh and Eighth Avenues), 989-3622*

Montel Williams--Phone or write for tickets for tapings at 10am, 1:30pm, and 3:30pm each Thursday and Friday. *356 West 58th Street (bet. Eighth and Ninth Avenues), 989-8880*

Rosie O'Donnell--Send a postcard requesting tickets in advance; day-of tickets are distributed at 8am. Taping takes place on weekdays at 10am. *30 Rockefeller Plaza (bet. Fifth and Sixth Avenues), 664-4000*

Sally Jesse Raphael--Tickets are available by sending a postcard in advance or showing up at least two hours before taping, which is from 1-3pm, Monday though Wednesday. *515 West 57th Street (bet. Tenth and Eleventh Avenues), 582-1722*

Saturday Night Live--Postcards requesting tickets are only accepted in August, when the annual ticket lottery is held. Standby tickets are distributed Saturdays at 9:15am for same-night tapings at 11:30pm. *30 Rockefeller Plaza (bet. Fifth and Sixth Avenues), 664-4000*

226 film and television

American Museum of the Moving Image
See Museums

Angelika Film Center
Recently taken over by City Cinemas, this independent film multiplex remains largely unchanged. The films aren't as great as they used to be and they come and go a lot more quickly, but enjoying cappuccino and gelato from the well-stocked café in the movie is still an option as is the possibility of running into celebrities like Bono or Brad Pitt. Just be careful not to mess with the sassy staff.
18 West Houston (at Mercer), 995-2000, MC, V, AmEx, **B D F Q** *to Broadway/Lafayette Sts.* &

Anthology Film Archives
Started in 1970 as a museum devoted to avant garde cinema, this institution has since become a mecca for established and aspiring artists seeking inspiration and hardened film buffs seeking things even they've never heard of. With a vast library and programming designed to showcase it, an excellent opportunity is provided to see rare foreign films, early works by now-established directors, and legendary but rarely seen stuff like Warhol flicks.
32 Second Ave. (at 2nd St.), 505-5181, Cash Only, **6** *to Bleecker,* **F** *to Second Ave.* &

Art Greenwich Village Twin
Two screens keep West Villagers well-entertained with first run films.
97 Greenwich Ave. (at 7th St.), 929-3350, MC, V, AmEx, D, Diners (call 505-2463 for credit card payments), **1 9** *to Christopher St.* &

Cinema Village
The single movie screen may have a reputation for hosting questionable flicks of the porn persuasion, but it actually accommodates a far wider array of independent films, with themes ranging from gay and lesbian to kung fu action to African Diaspora. August gets beaten to a pulp here by the two-week long Hong Kong Action film festival.
22 East 12th St. (bet. University Pl. and Fifth Ave.), 924-3363, Cash Only, **L N R 4 5 6** *to Union Square*

Cinematographe
Many quality independent and foreign films.
15 Vandam St., 675-4680, **1 9** *to Christopher St.*

Cineplex Odeon Chelsea West
333 West 23rd St. (bet. Eighth and Ninth Ave.), 989-0060, MC, V, AmEx, **C E** *to 23rd St.* &

Cineplex Waverly
Your basic two-theater movie house, which vacillates between mainstream and art films. This can lead to interesting juxtapositions, such as *Godzilla* and *The Ice Storm*.
323 Sixth Ave. (at 3rd St.), 929-8037, MC, V, AmEx, **A B C D F Q** *to West 4th St.*

City Cinemas Village East
By all indications this seems to be just another many-screened showplace for big-budget Hollywood productions, but within the nondescript exterior lies the preserved interior of the old Yiddish Theater complete with its original adornments and multi-tiered theater-style seating. So for a real treat, buy a ticket for whatever is showing in Theater Number One and get there early to check out this historical landmark.
181-189 Second Ave. (at 12th St.), 529-6799, MC, V, AmEx, **L R 4 5 6** *to Union Square*

E & R Video
Want to see *Space Jam* with Chinese subtitles? Packed with Chinese action movies and a fine selection of animated films, E & R's your man. A couple of Western titles are thrown in for variety.
82 Mulberry St. (bet. Canal and Bayard Sts.), 285-1546, **N R** *to Canal*

Film Forum
Two programs run in this classic setting. Program One has first-run independent and foreign feature films as well as some excellent documentaries. Program Two screens revivals including reissues of individual classics as well as film series featuring everything from the complete works of great, if sometimes obscure, directors to genre films, making this the place to go when nothing at the Sony megaplex seems particularly appealing.
209 West Houston St. (bet. Sixth and Varick Aves.), 727-8110, Cash Only, **1 9** *to Houston Street* &

Kim's Video and Audio
Less pedantic than their East Village counterparts, the staff here still knows what's up and has no qualms about either helping you sift though a gaggle of out-there directors, or matching your trivia on obscure Weimar actresses. Foreign film selection here also beats the East Village location's.
350 Bleecker St. (at W. 10th St.), 675-8996, MC, V, AmEx, D, Diners, **1 9** *to Christopher St.*

film & television 227

Kim's Video
The most interesting and comprehensive selection of videos in town including everything from the typical new releases to the most esoteric arthouse, foreign and genre flicks. Be forewarned, most everything is arranged by director or some odd category so come well-informed with something in mind or deal with the staff, who are knowledgeable but a little overeager to prove it.
85 Ave. A (at St. Marks Place), 529-3410, MC, V, AmEx, ❻ to Second Ave.

Lincoln Plaza Cinemas
Down the street but still in the shadow of its titan neighbor Sony, this smallish theater doesn't want to do the big-budget Hollywood schtick anyway, preferring foreign and independent film festival standouts and a few surprises.
Broadway (bet. 62nd and 63rd Sts.), 757-2280, MC, V, AmEx, ❶❾ to Lincoln Center ♿

The Movie Place
Avoid the weekend hordes at Blockbuster and that migraine-inducing light too. Comparable selection here, and more importantly, they deliver to your doorstep.
Broadway and 105th St., 864-4620, Cash Only, ❶❾ to 103rd St.

NYU's Program Board
By the students, for the students, and offered at the oh-so student-friendly rate of two dollars a pop. The theater's screen spans a minimal width and metallic fold-up chairs do little to keep viewers comfortable, but the cash saved can readily be shoved into a back pocket for extra padding.
566 La Guardia Place (bet. 3rd and 4th Sts.), 998-4999, Cash Only, ❶❷❸❹❺❻ to West 4th St.

The Paris
Highbrow European first runs and revivals show at this tony midtown movie house behind the Plaza Hotel. Very civilized.
West 58th St. (bet. Fifth and Sixth Aves.), 688-3800, ❶❷ to Fifth Ave.

Quad Cinema
As can be expected with most theaters, which run primarily independent flicks, the movie screens here are smaller here than in first-run theaters. But the film selections, which include many foreign and revival series, are so choice that screen size is the last thing considered. Tucked away from heavy street traffic on 13th St., and with only 4 screens hosting its wares, there's little chance the intimate, neighborhood appeal of this movie house will be mainstreamed any time soon.
34 West 13th St. (bet. Fifth & Sixth Aves.), 225-8800, ❶❷❸❹❺❻ to Union Square

The Screening Room
The place to catch independent and foreign film hits after they leave the Angelika/Film Forum/the Quad, or classics like Breakfast at Tiffany's shown every Sunday. The non-traditional seating makes it feel as comfy as a Blockbuster night, without the Bud Light and the remote. Diners at the restaurant next door get seated first for shows, so with a dinner-and-movie date, you can score a loveseat.
54 Varick St. (at Canal St.), 334-2100, MC, V, AmEx, ❶❷ to Canal St. ♿

Sony IMAX at Lincoln Center
By far the multiplex's coolest attraction: nature films, which were always amusing for their magnificent underwater action shots and close-ups of snouts and bug eyes have given way a bit to plot-oriented pieces (the idea of plot is used very liberally). The show on new York City's history is a crowd.
Broadway and 68th St., 336-5000, MC, V, AmEx, ❶❾ to Lincoln Center ♿

Sony Theaters Lincoln Square
Perhaps the city's glitziest theater where sweeping murals depicting stars of the Thirties and Forties and higher-than-average ticket prices try to suggest a larger-than-life cinematic experience. It's really just a lot of escalators, a screen or two the size of Kansas, and the videos playing at the concessions stand that try to prompt salivating by actually panning over the candy selection that distinguish it. The big-budget box-office hits are as predictable as ever.
Broadway and 68th St., 336-5000, MC, V, AmEx, ❶❾ to 66th St. ♿

UEE
Find out who's heating up the silver screen in Hong Kong cinema or pick up on the craze of renting the most recent soaps, beauty pageants and live concerts you didn't catch the first time around. A hundred dollars rents you forty-five UEE videos, which translates to maybe only thirty at Blockbuster.
118 Mott St., 219-0327, Cash Only, ❶❷ to Canal St. ♿

228 film and television

Walter Reade Theater/Film Society of Lincoln Center

Since 1985, the luxurious Walter Reade Theater has been the home of New York's elite film club, which screens everything from Jim Carrey to Godard, with an emphasis on the latter end of the spectrum. New Directors/New Films, in conjunction with the MoMA, has premiered work by such directors as Pedro Almodovar and Peter Greenaway, while film festivals sport titles like Rendez-vous With French Cinema Today. Overall, rich in retro and avant-garde classics, just avoid the post-film talk if you fear pretension. *70 Lincoln Center Plaza (at 65th bet. Broadway and Columbus Aves.), 875-5600, Cash Only at box office,* ❶❾ *to Lincoln Center*

Worldwide Cinemas

Inflation recently pushed the price per movie from two bucks to three, but it's still a great deal for slightly-older films. Groups of teenagers sometimes talk back to the screen. *340 West 50th St. (bet. Eighth and Ninth Aves.), 246-1583, Cash Only,* ❶❾ *to 50th St.*

The Ziegfeld Theater

This elegant, immaculate old show palace, one-time home of the Ziegfeld Follies, restores some of the glamour and sense of occasion to the typical movie-dinner date. The biggest and best screen in town on which to see blockbuster new releases and re-mastered old ones like *Vertigo*, *Lawrence of Arabia*, and the *Star Wars* trilogy. *141 West 54th St. (bet. Sixth and Seventh Aves.), 765-7600,* ❷❹❺❻ *to Rockefeller Center*

MOVIE THEATER INDEX BY NEIGHBORHOOD

CHELSEA
Cineplex Odeon Chelsea West

CHINATOWN
E & R Video
UEE

EAST VILLAGE
City Cinemas Village East
Kim's Video

GREENWICH VILLAGE
Art Greenwich Village Twin
Cinema Village
Cinematographe
Cineplex Waverly
Kim's Video and Audio
NYU's Program Board Cinema

MIDTOWN
The Paris
Worldwide Cinemas
The Ziegfeld Theater

MORNINGSIDE HEIGHTS
The Movie Place

QUEENS
American Museum of the Moving Image

SOHO
Angelika Film Center
Film Forum

TRIBECA
The Screening Room

UPPER WEST SIDE
Lincoln Plaza Cinemas
Sony IMAX at Lincoln Center
Sony Theaters Lincoln Square

MOVIE THEATER INDEX BY TYPE

ART HOUSE/REVIVAL
American Museum of the Moving Image
Anthology Film Archives
Cinema Village
Cinematographe
Film Forum
Worldwide Cinemas
The Ziegfeld Theater

NYU's Program Board
Quad Cinema
The Screening Room
Walter Reade Theater/Film Society of Lincoln Center

FIRST RUN
Angelika Film Center
Art Greenwich Village Twin
Cineplex Odeon Chelsea West
Cineplex Waverly
City Cinemas Village East
Lincoln Plaza Cinemas
The Paris
The Screening Room
Sony Theaters Lincoln Square
Worldwide Cinemas
The Ziegfeld Theater

IMAX
Sony IMAX at Lincoln Center

RENTAL
E & R Video
Kim's Video
Kim's Video and Audio
The Movie Place
UEE

film and television 229

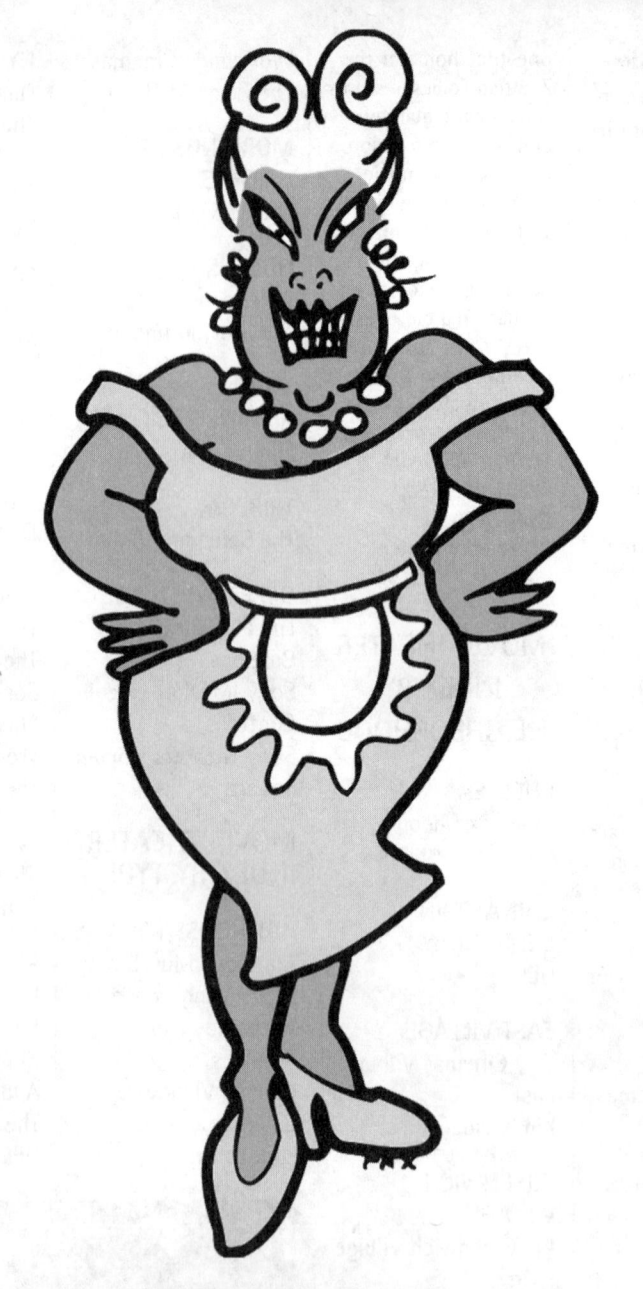

MAMA'S FOOD SHOP

200 EAST THIRD STREET. AT AVE B
TEL (212) 777-4425 FAX (212) 533-1295

StepMaMa

199 EAST THIRD STREET. AT AVE B
TEL (212) 228-2663
RESTAURANT. TAKE OUT. CATERING

restaurants +cafes

restaurants
 listings ⟷ 235
 index by cuisine ⟵⋯⋯ 264
 index by *neighborhood* ⟶ 265
cafes
 listings ⟷ 268
 index by *neighborhood* ⟶ 279

restaurants

Some of NYC's most famous hangouts

Restaurant trends in New York City can change as quickly as traffic lights. Gone are the '80s when the approach to entrees was to make them too small and beautiful to eat. A new dining era has dawned and chefs who have traditionally been preoccupied with presentation are also making sure that their customers don't leave hungry. Utilizing an ever- widening assortment of exotic ingredients like foie gras, truffles (the mushroom not the chocolate) yellow cherry tomatoes and huidlacoche (a corn fungus popular in Mexico), chefs are pushing the envelope, encouraging New Yorkers to be more adventurous with their tastebuds than ever before. But this doesn't mean that you can't still get a good steak. Plenty of chefs have stuck to the tried and true—where straight forward meat and potatoes still reign.

Because New York City is a "melting pot," it's possible to immerse yourself in different cultures simply by choosing the appropriate neighborhood restaurant to dine in. Chinatown is a lot closer than Hong Kong if you're looking for a traditional Sunday brunch of dim sum. There's no need to travel to Katmandu, when you can go to 6th Street between First and Second Avenues and dine in what is known as "Little India." And the Ukrainian Diners of the East Village still serve a mean Borscht and pierogi combo.

Which doesn't mean that you can't find a down home American meal of meatloaf and mashed potatoes. While the local diner is sure to offer reasonably priced standbys like hamburgers, milkshakes, porkchops and apple sauce, there are an increasing number of moderately priced bistros where quality can make a difference, even when it comes to comfort food.

With 10,000 restaurants to choose from, deciding what and where to eat in Manhattan can produce both anxiety and despair. Our restaurant listing will help you make an informed decision which ought to alleviate both of these symptoms.

232 restaurants

tipping

It is standard to tip your server 15 to 20 percent of the check's total. An easy way to calculate the tip is to double the sales tax which appears below the subtotal on the check. Certain restaurants will add a gratuity to the bill for parties of more than six people, so if you're with a group, it's wise to make sure your total doesn't already include the tip. There are occasions when the service is so fantastic, that even when the tip has been included you might want to give a little more. This is true for tipping in general. When it comes to showing your gratitude for a meal made perfect by the service, there are no rules that prohibit tipping a little extra. The same holds true when the service is below adequate. Although most people feel too guilty to leave anything under the standard 15 percent, if your waiter has gone out of his or her way to make your meal un-pleasant (which, unfortunately, is sometimes the case due to the number of overqualified waitstaff in many restaurants who would rather be making their living on Broadway), the tip you leave can be used to show your displeasure.

prix fixe

If you're on a student budget but don't want to deprive yourself of dining out in style every once in a while, a prix fixe meal is a great way to get some bang for your buck. Generally including an appetizer, entrée, and dessert, the prix fixe cost is almost always lower than ordering a la carte. Although prix fixe menus are offered in restaurants throughout Manhattan, they are most abundant in the Theater District, where the establishments on Restaurant Row try to lure in ticket-holding customers by promising to save them both time and money. Many prix fixe menus are only available earlier in the evening, say, before 6:30 or 7:00pm, so it's good to call ahead and find out what a restaurant's policy is.

restaurants 233

dining + entertainment

For those of you looking for a little something extra with your meal, or a good way to impress a date, here are a handful of entertaining restaurants to choose from. In some instances, the entertainment outshines the food—but you'll probably be having too good a time to notice.

The Supper Club
An excellent choice for a Friday or Saturday night of entertainment, this "throwback to a classic 1920s nightclub" is better known for its decor, music and dancing than for its food.
240 West 47th Street (between Broadway and Eighth Aves.), 921-1940.

The Ear Inn
Some of the best rock and blues bands in town have been known to jam at this gritty bar/restaurant. The pub food is surprisingly good.
326 Spring Street (between Washington and Greenwich Sts.), 226-9060.

S.O.B's
A.K.A. Sounds of Brazil. Nightly Latin bands and Caribbean floor shows accompany Latin American cuisine. If you want to get into the act, you'll have to wait until Sunday for your Tango lessons.
204 Varick Street (at Houston St.), 243-4940.

Cotton Club
Head uptown for the "Harlem experience." In the evenings the Southern American cooking is accompanied by jazz and R & B. On weekends wake up with their gospel Sunday brunch.
656 West 125th Street (between Broadway and Riverside), 663-7980.

The Algonquin Hotel
This Theater District literary landmark is not known for the excellence of its food, but rather, the quality of its cabaret.
59 West 44th Street (bet. Fifth and Sixth Aves.), 840-6800.

Lucky Cheng's
Sip Polynesian drinks and try to make conversation while leggy, female impersonators serve tuna steaks and wasabi mashed potatoes and pour candle wax on their stomachs. Despite the six-inch stilettos, the service is excellent and a night here is never dull.
(see Restaurant section)

Five Best Places to Get a Burger

The Corner Bistro
It looks like a bar, it feels like a bar (excellent jukebox selection) but the burgers might make you forget to order a drink.
331 West 4th Street (at Jane St.) 242-9502

Aggie's
Actually, hamburgers aren't the only thing that are good here. Aggies is one of the only "diners" in town where you won't be disappointed in anything on the menu.
146 West Houston St. (at MacDougal St.) 673-8994

Home
Burgers are just the beginning of fine offerings at this homey village haunt. If you want to feel like you're chilling in a little farmhouse in the country for an hour or two, this is your place. Even the ketchup is homemade.
20 Cornelia St. (bet. Bleecker + West 4th St.) 243-9579.

Elephant + Castle
It's been around for a while, but that doesn't mean you shouldn't check it out. Excellent burgers prepared just the way you like 'em.
68 Greenwich Avenue (Seventh Avenue and 11th Street) 243-5413.

Prime Burger
The old-time waiters and "classic cheeseburger decor" create the perfect burger-eating atmosphere.
5 East 51st Street (bet. Madison and Fifth Aves.) 759-4729.

A

A Taste of India II
Always trust the waiters' recommendations and you'll never be disappointed: samosas, tandooris, and curries all merit a try, and each is best polished off with a cup of spiced tea.
287 New Dorp Lane (Clawson and Edison Sts.), (718) 987-4700, MC, V, AmEx, D, Entrées: $6-$17, **S74** *to New Dorp Ln.* &

ACME
Comfort food with cleaned-up southern style. Choose from entrées like catfish and fried chicken, and be sure to accompany them with a side of heavenly skin-on mashed potatoes. By night, the place becomes packed both at the tables and around the bar with downtown twenty- and thirtysomethings making the scene.
9 Great Jones St. (bet. Broadway and Lafayette St.), MC, V, Diners, D, Entrées: $6-$15, **❻** *to Astor Pl.,* **❽❾** *to 8th St.*

Alley's End
Literally at the end of an alley on a vaguely unsavory block of Chelsea, finding this restaurant is half the fun. But only half. Prim and relaxed, this hideaway is a hidden jewel, with an interior garden and a banquet room, complete with fireplace, for larger parties. No longer undiscovered, there tends to be a crowd weekend nights, but the cute quarters and quality food are sure worthwhile.
311 West 17th St. (bet. Eighth and Ninth Aves.), 627-8899, V, MC, D, Entrées: $8-$18, **❶❸❺** *to 14th St.,* **❶❾** *to 18th St.*

Allison on Dominick
Small, intimate, and appropriately nestled away in the relatively barren western edge of SoHo, this place is truly unique. The food is flawlessly prepared upscale French Bistro fare which matches the ambiance perfectly. Ideal for a romantic dinner.
38 Dominick St. (bet. Varick and Hudson Sts.), 727-1188, **❻❶** *to Spring St.*

Alouette
Brand new to Morningside Heights is this anomaly of the neighborhood: an intimate bilevel French bistro serving up savory and inventive cuisine in a rich, warm atmosphere. Donning red velvet drapery and lace-curtained windows Alouette is a romantic option in westside dining. The prices are great in exchange for this culinary and atmospheric decadence.
2588 Broadway (bet. 97th and 98th Sts.), 222-6808, V, MC, AmEx, Diners, Entrées: $15-$18.50, **❶❾** *to 96th St.* &

Ambassador Grill
Consistently overrated, but badly needed in the gastronomically challenged area near the UN. The menu appears intriguing, but the kitchen can't always pull it off, although the desserts are unfailingly delectable. Bring good company, as service is excruciatingly slow and other diners are as staid as characters in a painfully drawn-out dinner scene in a Merchant-Ivory film.
1 UN Plaza (44th St. at First Ave.), 702-5014, MC, V, AmEx, D, Diners, Entrées: $20-$30, **❹❺** *to Grand Central*

Amin Indian Cuisine
Dinner here avoids the circus-like pitfalls of Sixth Street's outfits. Curries, kebabs, and kormas are spicy enough to satisfy natives, and will only set you back about $10. Combo platters allow for both gluttony and variety.
155 Eighth Ave. (bet. 17th and 18th Sts.), 929-7020, MC, V, AmEx, Entrées: $7-$17, **❶❸❺** *to 14th St./ Eighth Ave.* &

Amir's
Like McDonald's, this tiny oasis for falafel and honey-drenched baklava goes easy on the wallet but not always on the stomach. Eat at one of the tables under the mildly pornographic wall murals, since the tahini can get a bit unruly.
2911 Broadway (bet. 113th and 114th Sts.), 749-7500, Cash Only, Entrées: $4-$6, **❶❾** *to 116th St.* &

Amsterdam Cafe
Much of the crowd here is local and older, but students can still be seen, particularly on the weekends. Friendly neighborhood feel with a good menu of classic bar items and pastas. Their Sunday brunch for $4.95 is the best deal in the area.
1207 Amsterdam Ave. (bet. 119th and 120th Sts.), 662-6330, MC, V, AmEx Entrées: $7-$10, **❶❾** *to 116th St.* &

Andalousia
A relatively yuppie-free zone for quality North African fare; $20 buys the three-course prix-fixe that offers plenty of options, though it's just as easy to subsist on dips and light lamb dishes. Dark and understated, no liquor license means its BYOB (or BYOW) for the older, cultured Village crowd.
28 Cornelia St. (bet. Bleecker and West 4th Sts.), 929-3693, MC, V, AmEx, Entrées: $12-$20, **❶❷❸❹❺❻❼** *to West 4th St.*

Angelica Kitchen
A vegetarian's paradise as well as an introductory course for vegan-phobic carnivores, offering tangy soups, tofu and pesto sandwiches, and tofu-lime "cheesecake." Portions are generous and very moderately priced.
300 East 12th St. (bet. Second and Third Aves.), 228-2909, Entrées: $6-$12, **❻** *to Second Ave.*

Anglers and Writers
No longer home to the *Paris Review* crowd, but the soups and stews are probably better now than they were in the good old days. There will often be a wait.
420 Hudson St. (at St. Luke's), 675-0810, Cash Only, Entrées: $8-$14, **❶❾** *to Christopher St.*

Annam Brahma Restaurant
The eclectic menu's only unifying thread is that everything is prepared sans meat, meaning everything from India ratia to tofu omelets to chapatti roll-ups may grace your table. Thursdays the cooks rally around pasta for Italian day; Tuesdays put Chinese vegetarian mainstays center stage. Check out the books, tapes, and other items for sale in the back of the restaurant.
84-43 164th St. (at 85th Ave.), Jamaica, (718) 523-

restaurants 235

2600, Entrées: $4-$8, Cash Only, Ⓕ to Parsons Blvd. 🚲

Arcadia
Chef and owner Anne Rosenzweig made headlines years ago when she stormed the citadel of all-male chefs at the city's top-rated restaurants. Indulge in one of her signature dishes like corn cakes with creme fraiche and caviar or chocolate-bread pudding swimming in brandy-custard sauce, combining French technique and American heartiness.
21 East 62nd St. (bet. Madison and Fifth Aves.), 223-2900, MC, V, ❹❺❻ *to 59th St.*

Arizona 206
The name says it all. Walk through the door and it's practically Sedona, by way of Third Avenue. The rustic floors, cozy tables, and stucco alcoves all make for nice atmosphere, though dining can get cramped. Prices are fine for retired condo denizens, but students may want to wait until the parents come to town.
206 East 60th St. (at Third Ave.), 838-0440, MC, V, AmEx, D, Entrées: $20-$35, ❽❾❹❺❻ *to 59th Street/Lexington Avenue* ♿

Around the Clock
There's not much to recommend it during the day, but the late-late-night crowd qualifies as a revealing cross-section of the East Village's maladjusted. Depending on how far the hands are past midnight when you swing by, either from bleary-eyed club kids with the munchies are killing time or else the harried waitstaff is half-heartedly trying to oblige the grumpy, idiosyncratic early-morning regulars.
8 Stuyvesant St. (bet. Second and Third Aves.), 598-0402, MC, V, AmEx, D, Diners, Entrées: $8-$10, ❻ *to Astor Place,* ❽❹ *to 8th Street*

Arqua
This Northern Italian gem won't show your wallet much mercy, but the food's worth it. The room has an airy "minimalist" look which suits both the lunch time expense account crowd, as well as the trendy dinner regulars. The authentic Venetian cuisine is consistently good, especially the homemade pastas.
281 Church St. (at White St.) 334-1888, MC, V, AmEx, D, Entrées: $10-$23, ❶❾ *to Franklin St.*

Atlantis
This fish market not only supplies Morningside Heights with fish flown in daily but also, to Columbia student's delight, has an in-house sushi chef who prepares your order directly for take out, eliminating the middle man.
588 west 110th St. (bet. Broadway and Amsterdam Ave., 749-6073, MC, V, Entrées: $2.95-$8.99, ❶❾ *to 110th St.*

Aubudon Bar and Grill
Gourmet Caribbean/French fusion cuisine is right at home at this Harlem newcomer. Their barbeque and pasta dishes are also delicious and worth the trip uptown. On a historical note, the restaurant is located on the site where Malcolm X was assasinated.
3956 Bradway (at 166th St.) MC,V, AmEx, Entrées: $8-$12, 928-5200 ❶❾ *to 168th St.*

Aunt Suzie's
Pleasant and cozy the place exudes a certain bonhomie. Lovebirds, local grad students, and somewhat gainfully employed twentysomethings fill up on basic Italian dishes.
247 Fifth Ave. (at Union St.), (718) 788-3377, V,

MC, AmEx, Entrées:$8-$12, ❽❹ *to Union St.*

B

Babylon
Even on a slow day, expect to wait a bit while dread-locked owner Damon Gordon prepares your Mediterranean style veggie meal in his one-man kitchen set-up. No worries though: the sunny '70s vibe is conducive to chilling for hours with pen and paper in hand, and Gordon will kindly refill your mug a bunch of times, before your leek quiche emerges from the steamer, fluffy, with a flaky, buttery crust.
237 Eldridge St. (bet. Houston and Stanton Sts.), 505-7546, Cash Only, Entrées: $4-$7, Ⓕ *to Second Ave.* ↩

Bachue
This vegan breakfast, lunch, and dinner place hase large store-front windows which ensure most of the tables are well-lit. The restaurant is a rare treat: one of the few places in the city where you can order delicious (egg-less) pancakes and waffles as well as a fine selection of bean, pasta, seitan, tempeh, tofu, and vegetable dishes.
36 West 21st St. (between Fifth and Sixth Avenues),

ATLANTIS SEAFOOD

fresh fish
fried
steamed
sushi

"Fresh Daily Guaranteed"

lunch & dinner
take out
free delivery

558 West 110th Street
bet. Tenth and Eleventh Aves.
Tel: (212)749-6073

WKCR DJ Matt Matlack and the *Seinfeld*-hating "Soup Nazi"

236 restaurants

229-0870, V, MC, AmEx, D, Entrées: $5-$13, ❶❾ to 21st St. ♿

Balthazar

Open less than a year, this SoHo gem already has a reservation line and a ten minute wait. Onlookers rave about the lofty bistro decor and surprisingly arrogant-free staff. The authentic French brassiere "looks just like Paris," with music to match.
80 Spring St. (bet. Broadway and Lafayette St.), 965-1414, V, MC, AmEx, Average Entrée: $20, ❻❼❻ to Spring St.

Baluchi's

Named after Pakistan's Balochistan, this bonafide Indian restaurant does justice to the sultry opulence for which the region is known, with exquisite brass cups and ornately decorated walls. Numerous options will satisfy vegetarians, including "aloo chole, pallak paneer," and "Basmati" rice.
193 Spring St. (bet. Thompson and Sullivan Sts.), 226-2828, MC, V, AmEx, Diners, Entrées: $10-$30, ❶❻❼❻ to Spring St.

Basilio Inn

Housed in a 19th-century stable imbued with a Tuscan rustic flavor, the Inn serves up incredible Italian—the red snapper Livornese is divine—the likes of which Manhattanites have never seen. Prices reflect the Island's low rent and low pretension.
2-6 Gainsville Court, (718) 447-9292, MC, V, AmEx, Entrées: $9-$12, ❶❾ to South Ferry to Staten Island, then the bus to S. Beach

BBQs

Eden for budget-constrained carnivores. The decor is trite and the breadth of the menu is confined to the obvious, but where do fall-off-the-bone tender meat with satisfyingly greasy fries sell for less than the price of a couple of Happy Meals? The only things missing from the Southern cookout ambiance are the horseflies.
21 University Pl. (at 8th St.), 674-4450, MC, V, AmEx, ❶❻ to 8th St.

Bendix Diner

Whether it's because of the motto's invitation to "get fat" or because of the subsequent surprise of a health-conscious menu, patrons have been congregating at this casual hotspot in such numbers that owners have been forced to expand. Greasy spoon prices mean the American-Thai fusion dishes leave no room for guilt.
219 Eighth Ave. (at 21st St.), 366-0560, MC, V, D, Entrées: $6-$8, ❶❻ to 23rd St. ♿ 🚲

Bistro Margot

A French treasure hidden in Little Italy, gourmet enough to satisfy the upper-crust, older patrons who don't mind the bloated pricing. The preponderance of two-person tables and the seductive lighting emphasize its viability as a date restaurant.
26 Prince St. (at Mott St.), 274-1027, Cash Only, Entrées: $8-$20, ❻ to Spring St., ❻❻❻ to Broadway/Lafayette St. ♿

Bo Ky

Seafood variations served over rice and noodles are the staple of the Cantonese menu. The central location attracts both tourists and locals on lunch break; efficient service moves patrons in out in a hurry.
80 Bayard St. (at Mott St.), 406-2292, Cash Only, Entrées: $6-$12, ❶❻❶❻❻ to Canal St.

Boca Chica

Great for anyone who likes to have fun as part of the deal when paying to eat out. The atmosphere is decidedly festive and colorful, a perfect match to the South American and Caribbean food they serve. Best bets are the menu choices with pork or seafood, staples of the cuisine that you've probably never tasted like this before, which should be washed down with one of their exotic margaritas. Live music and dancing are occasionally offered, call ahead for details.
13 First Ave. (bet. 1st. and 2nd Sts.), 473-0108, MC, V, ❻❻❻ to 86th St. ♿

Bodega

An upscale diner that caters equally to neighborhood dwellers and office types on days when there's no business lunching to be done. The atmosphere is clean, colorful and efficient, well-suited to the eclectic menu which has all sorts of quick and interesting choices like fried-egg sandwiches and their foccacia that's great topped with almost anything.
136 West Broadway (bet. Duane and Thomas Sts.), 285-1155, MC, V, AmEx, D, Entrées: $7-$13,

❶❷❸❾ to Chambers St., ❹❺❻ to City Hall ♿

Bolo

Food Network favorite Bobby Flay's version of "Fantasy Spanish" cuisine doesn't miss a beat at this relaxed Flatiron restaurant. Passion fruit sangria, rabbit on roasted pea risotto, and sautéed wild mushrooms with chile oil are only a few of Mr. Flay's playful gastronomic creations. A comprehensive selection of fine wines and ports are perfect complements to a meal that is the stuff dreams are made of.
23 East 22 St., 228-2200, MC, V, AmEx, Entrées: $25-$30, ❻❻ to 23rd St. ↩ (at bar)

Boulevard

A fun family restaurant with Sesame Street-style murals and all-you-can-eat specials every night: screaming babies covered in mashed potatoes, platefuls of enormous dinosaur ribs, and the Maryland crab cake blue-plate special are all part of the charm. You'll have to request the aptly named "Liquid Hell" barbecue sauce, which is kept hidden in back.
2398 Broadway (at 88th St.), 874-7400, M, V, AmEx, Entrées: $7-$15, ❶❾ to 86th St.

Bouley Bakery

Reserve well in advance for what many consider to be "the perfect meal." The white walls, curved ceiling and green stone floors, all work to create an ambiance that is both elegant and casual. Bouley Bakery maintains the Bouley reputation for excellence by using the

restaurants 237

finest regional ingredients, and taking great care with each meal that is served. The waitstaff will help you order so sit back and relax. *120 West Broadway (between Duane and Reade Sts.) 964-2525, MC, V, AmEx, Prix fixe lunch: $35, nine-course tasting menu at dinner: $75 per person,* ❶❾ *to Franklin St.*

Bright Food Shop

Tortillas join forces with the likes of egg rolls in creating a successful hybrid menu at this simple, almost quaint eatery which proclaims itself the place where "The Southwest meets the Far East." Not a bad date place—the name belies the low ambient lighting at night. *216 Eighth Ave. (at 21st St.), 243-4433, Entrées: $6.50-$14, Cash Only,* ❹❻ *to 23rd St.* ♿

Bryant Park Grill

Nestled up against the backside of the Humanities library, a restaurant would be hard-pressed to be more picturesque, especially in Spring, when Bryant Park assumes its full majesty. The food is tasty, if pricey, and the after-work bar and dinner scene at the Grill and its outdoor cafe buzzes with "suits" letting loose. Brunch is excellent. *25 West 40th St. (bet. Fifth and Sixth Aves.), 840-6500, V, MC, AmEx, Entrées: $12-$18,* ❸❹❺❻ *to 42nd St.* 🚇

Bubby's

Forego the fancily named sandwiches, which don't merit their prices, in favor of the sturdier main fare, like quesadillas served with great salsa. Gorgeous ceiling-high windows afford people-watching and the wooden floor and benches evoke the comfort level of an unpretentious, rather rustic cafe. Great Sunday brunch. *120 Hudson St. (at North Moore St.), 219-0666, MC, V, AmEx, Entrées: $7-$15,* ❶❾ *to Franklin St.* ♿

Burritoville

One of best burrito places in the city is also one of the more reasonably priced. It's a perfect choice for a nutritious, satisfying meal on the run. Their policy forbids the use of lard, pork, and preservatives, and they press their own tortillas, five different flavors, fresh every day. Vegetarians will appreciate the many flesh-free selections, especially the Route 66 Burrito, but any burrito can be ordered with tofu sour cream and soy cheese. Nine locations throughout Manhattan, consult yellow pages, *V, MC, AmEx, Entrées: $6-$8, Free Delivery,* ♿

C

Cafe Roma Pizzeria

Enjoy a quick, delicious slice of falafel at this run-of-mill pizzeria. *175 West 91st St. (at Amsterdam Ave.), 875-8972, Entrées: $2-$15 (for a pie), MC, V,* ❶❷❸❾ *to 96th St.* ♿

Cal's

A striking open loft space gives you ample elbow room and surprising privacy while dining, yielding an unusually relaxed atmosphere for this trendy neighborhood. In general, the food is quite good, and the risotto is a standout, as is the waitstaff. *55 West 21st St. (bet. Fifth and Sixth Aves.), 929-0740, V, MC, AmEx, Entrées: $10-$15,* ❻❽❾ *to 23rd St.* 🚇

Camille's

Named after the owner's mother, this cozy Columbia magnet is reliably good. Pizzas are a bargain at $4.25, and the hearty pasta dishes are topped with light and flavorful sauce. It's difficult to eat this well for less money; breakfast is a particularly cheap alternative to bacon 'n egg greaseballs at area diners. *1135 Amsterdam Ave. (at 116th St.), 749-2428, MC, V, Entrées: $3.15-$7,* ❶❾ *to 116th St.*

Candy Bar and Grill

Currently on the A-list for stylish, late-night dining, this vibrant bar and restaurant, famous for its mile-long cocktail menu, attracts a boisterous and amiable, largely gay crowd for sizable helpings of tasty basics, as well as eclectic ethnic entrées: Mom's meatloaf with red bliss mashed potatoes tops the American portion of the menu followed by the more exotic Cornish hen Moroccan-style served with dried apricot and toasted-almond couscous. For starters or smaller appetites, try the ginger-chicken satay or the grilled portabello shrooms with the sundried-tomato coulis. *131 Eighth Ave. (bet. 16th and 17th Sts.), 229-9702, MC, V, D, Diners, Entrées: $7-$15,* ❹❻❺❻ *to 14th St./Eighth Ave.* ♿ 🚇

Camille's
Ristorante Italiano

"Home-cooked Italian Food at Student Prices"

Breakfast	Brunch	Lunch	Dinner

Hand-tossed pizzas $4.25
Brunch Specials $3.95
Pasta Specials $6.95

Focaccia bread, cookies, and cakes baked fresh daily

Lunch Specials $3.15-$5 Prepared fresh daily

1135 Amsterdam Avenue • 749-2428
Across from Columbia's 116th and Amsterdam Gates

Che' Bella Pizza
Pizza Pasta

- Homemade Italian Dishes
- Juice Bar (Veggie or Fruit Juices)
- Lunch and Dinner Specials
- Free Delivery

1215 Amsterdam (Bet.119&120)
212-864-7300

Canton
Prices, food quality, service, and decor are all a step above the typical Chinatown eatery. Specializing in seafood dishes and other Cantonese cuisine, always ask the waiter for recommendations, since the English version of the menu is only partial.
45 Division St., 226-4441, Cash Only, Entrées: $7-$18, ❻❿❼ to Grand St.

Carmichael's
Wizened locals fill up on soul food after Sunday's sermon at this slightly derelict, though entirely cozy neighborhood favorite. The fried chicken is amazing!
117-08 Guy R. Brewer Boulevard (at 118th Ave.), (718) 723-6908, Cash Only, Entrées: $6-$10, ❸ to Parsons/Archer.

Carmine's
Come with a group of friends and order up a storm of family-style Italian-inspired dishes. The immense popularity of this enormous dark-wood institution virtually mandates a stop at the lovely bar characteristic of New York's old-school restaurants, since there's always a wait; only parties of six or more can reserve a table in advance. A small annex serves take-out.
2450 Broadway (bet. 90th and 91st Sts.), 362-2200, MC, V, AmEx, Entrées: $8-$18, ❶❾ to 86th St.

Castillo de Jagua
A homely but decent Dominican dive in the heart of Loisaida, this place pleases with beans and yellow rice, fried plantains, cafe con leche, and fresh-squeezed O.J. to the beat of loud salsa music.
113 Rivington St. (bet. Ludlow and Essex Sts.), 982-6412, Cash Only, ❻❼❽❷ to Delancey St.

Chanterelle
One of the city's most high-brow restaurants, serving elegant cuisine in a lovely high-ceilinged dining room. The prix-fixe brunch is superb, and the most affordable option.
2 Harrison St. (at Hudson St.), 966-6960, Prix Fixe: $35, ❶❾ to Franklin St.

Chi-Chi Steak
This mother-and-daughter team lets their exotic decor-lush tropical plants and omnipresent mirrors-influence the preparation of the Thai cuisine. Indonesian rice bags come plumped like little cushions, but luscious entrées: like coconut chicken soup and warm sticky rice dessert with custard stand on their culinary merit alone. Drawbacks? What started out as a little indulgence turns into full-fledged gluttony after you see the reasonable prices.
135 Christopher St. (bet. Hudson and Greenwich Sts.), 462-0027, MC, V, AmEx, D, Entrées: $7-$14, ❶❾ to Christopher St.

Che Bella
Pizza pizza pizza! This neighborhood favorite has been serving the Morningside Heights community for years with their wonderful cheesy pizzas and fresh sandwiches. Stop in for a slice and mingle with locals and Columbia students alike.
1215 Amsterdam Ave. (bet. 120th and 119th Sts.), 864-7300, Cash Only, ❶❾ to 116th St.

China Shalom II
As opposed to eating at most Chinese joints, you won't be hungry an hour after dining at this popular restaurant filled with large boisterous groups of families visiting their mensches.
686 Columbus Ave. (bet. 93rd and 94th Sts.), 662-9676, V, MC, Entrées: $8-$16, ❶❷❸❾ to 96th St.

Chinatown Ice Cream Factory
If chocolate and vanilla make you sigh with boredom, this tiny cafe will satiate even your jaded taste buds. Lick away at flavors such as red bean, green tea, taro, and lychee. The ginger is not to be missed.
65 Bayard St. (bet. Mott and Elizabeth Sts.), 608-4170, Cash Only, Ice Cream $1.50-$3.50, ❻❿❼ to Grand St.

City Crab and Seafood Co.
Big, brash and bustling, this urbane seafood house just steps from Union Square is a mainstay for the area's white-collar crowd. The giant oyster bar is quite a scene after work; it's trendy and gimmicky, but it certainly works well.
235 Park Ave. South (at 19th St.), 529-3800, MC, V, AmEx, D, Entrées: $10-$20, ❿❼ to Union Sq.

Clementine
Chic SoHoites meet uptown yuppies for meticulously prepared fare at this noteworthy newcomer. The rock water garden complements an unfaltering wine list, to-die-for deserts, and imaginative comfort food. Innovation extends to the drink and cigarette menu, where Clementine mimosas and the like offer a taste of what's to come.
One Fifth Ave. (at 8th St.), 253-0003, MC, V, AmEx, D, Diners, Entrées: $14-$24, ❻ to Astor Pl.

Columbia Cottage
Copious carafes of dicey free wine, along with a magnanimous carding policy, draw locals and undergrads like moths to a light. Ample portions of hit-or-miss Szechuan-sesame tofu and chicken with black pepper are consistently good. Keeping everyone well-fed, and with a tolerant waitstaff who usually won't cut off the wine unless you start singing along to the Muzak.
1034 Amsterdam Ave. (at 111th St.), 662-1800, MC, V, AmEx, D, Diners, Entrées: $5-$12, ❶❾ to 110th St.

Coogan's Restaurant
Latinos and Irish congregate at this upscale pub to partake of classics such as shell steak, shrimp scampi, French onion soup, and roast beef au jus. Karaoke nights on Tuesdays and Saturdays enhance the eclecticism of this popular local hangout, just down the street from the Columbia Presbyterian Medical Center.
4015 Broadway (at 169th St.), 928-1234, MC, V, AmEx, Entrées: $9-$17, ❹❽❸❶❾ to 168th St.

Copeland's
A rich and varied menu offers everything from braised oxtails and gumbo to grain-fed catfish and shrimp Creole. The atmosphere is for serious eating;

Cowgirl HALL OF FAME BAR·B·Q

every wednesday night 6 - 10 PM

LIVE COUNTRY MUSIC AND ALL-U-CAN EAT:
- FRIED CATFISH
- CAJUN CHICKEN
- MASHED POTATOES
- COLLARD GREENS
- COLESLAW
- BISCUITS
- TOSSED SALAD
- PICKLES
- ONIONS

only $10.95

served up country style

519 Hudson Street, NYC at 10th Street
Tel: 212-633-1133

Sunday's gospel brunch is among the neighborhood's finest.
547 West 145th St. (bet. Broadway and Amsterdam Ave.), 234-2357, MC, V, AmEx, D, Entrées: $9-$25, ❶❾ *to 145th St.* ♿

Corner Bistro
Locals lament the marathon waits at this immensely popular burger-and-beer joint, but they still throng here in to see and be seen despite the slow service. It's the prime territory to see and be seen: the basic, effortlessly funky version of the neighborhood haunt made palatable to yuppie Villagers by virtue of its enduring cachet and steady stream of televised college basketball games. Tables long ago claimed by penknives crowd the middle, though an intimate space does open up in back.
331 West 4th St. (at West 12th, Jane St., and Eighth Ave.), 242-9502, Cash Only, Entrées: $7-$12, ❶Ⓐ*Ⓒ*Ⓔ *to West 4th St.*

Cotton Club
During the legendary gospel brunches, diners in their Sunday best chow on basics like fried chicken, yams, and corn bread at this slightly dried-up but still entertaining granddaddy of Harlem glamour. Call for seating times or to make reservations.
656 West 125th St. (bet. Broadway and Riverside Ave.), 663-7980, MC, V, Entrées: $25, ❶❾ *to 125th St.* ♿

Cowgirl Hall of Fame
Before riot-grrrls there were cowgirls and at this Greenwhich Village fave owner Sherry Delameter won't let gringos forget. Come for the history lesson and eclectic Southern dishes like eggplant fitters and Frito pie. Yeehaw!
519 Hudson St, (at 10th St.), 633-1133, MC, V AmEx, Entrées: $8-$15, ❶❾ *to Sheridan Square*

Crystal Fountain
Perfect for a power lunch or a ladies' brunch, either served with a stunning view of 42nd Street. Plenty of windows and sunshine complete the luxurious Crystal Room experience.
Grand Hyatt Hotel, Park Ave. (at Grand Central Station), 850-5998, ❹❺❻Ⓢ❼ *to Grand Central Station.*

Cucina Della Nonna
The scent of fresh basil wafts from the open kitchen as young, sophisticated diners sample seasonal specials and standards like fusilli with tender eggplant and tangy Caesar salad; the owner personally keeps an eye on the comfort level of this delightful option for cleanly executed pastas and salads. Portions are just right
104 Grand St. (at Mercer St.), 925-5488, MC, V, D, Entrées: $13-$18, ⓃⓇ *to Prince St.* ♿

Cucina Di Pesce
A few outdoor tables in front satisfy those who need to segregate themselves from the city's late-night energy while they eat. Otherwise step downstairs and wait at the packed bar with the rest of the after-work crowd. Italian soccer games play on the TV above the bar, but no one seems interested. Instead they are stuffing their faces at the free mussel buffet and talking above the lively music beat; this place sets the night off to a roaring start. The bargain basement seafood dazzles and the service is incredible. For a more serene dinning experience try the trellised garden out back.
87 East 4th St. (bet. Second and Third Aves.), 260-6800, Cash Only, Entrées: $6.95-$10.95, Ⓕ *to Second Ave.* ♿ 🚲

Cucina
One of the best restaurants in New York and it's not even in Manhattan. Everything's great here, but the risotto is what people rave about. The antipasto is the best this side of Tuscany and the wine and desert menus are superb. Plus there's valet parking! In a word: perfect.
256 Fifth Ave. (bet. Garfield and Carroll Sts.), (718) 230-0711, V, MC, AmEx, DC, Entrées: $18-$25, ⓂⓃⓇ *to Union St.*

D

Da Nico
After a mere four years of upholding the honor of Little Italy, this romantic, glass-and-marble-accented hideaway has gained a loyal, diverse clientele including Johnny Depp. Kick off the meal with a crisp Caesar salad and dense focaccia, then move on to favorites like penne ala vodka and lobster fra' diavolo.
164 Mulberry St. (bet. Grand and Broome Sts.),

240 restaurants

343-1212, MC, V, AmEx, D, Diners, Entrées: $9-$17 ❶Ⓜ❷❹❺❻ to Canal Street. &

Daily Soup
Office workers visit this little specialty shop for soups reminiscent of home. Cup sizes range from medium (typically $5.95) to extra large (up to $14.95) and the menu covers most of the bases, including vegetarian, seafood, and an assortment of chicken soups; the gazpacho is a must. Join those who can afford a little time away from the desk at the counter seating.
21 West 41st St. (bet. Fifth and Madison Aves.), 953-7687, Cash Only, Soup: $6-$15, ❹❺❻ *to Grand Central.*

Dallas BBQ
The old expression "don't eat more than you can lift" is sound advice at this large, informal ribs 'n chicken extravaganza, where monstrous portions are rendered even more unmanageable by irresistible cornbread. Top it all off with their infamous, huge margaritas.
27 West 72nd St. (bet. Columbus Ave. and Central Park West), 873-2004, MC, V, AmEx, Entrées: $4-$8, ❽Ⓒ *to 72nd St., Also in Greenwich Village, East Village*

Dante Restaurant
Mature crowds of businessmen and nearby St. John's University professors and athletes visit this dimly lit Italian bistro and bar.
168-12 Union Turnpike, (718) 380-3340, Lunch Entrées: $7-$13.25, V, MC, AmEx, Q30/Q46 *to Union Turnpike,* & ⇌

Deli Kasbah
Orthodox patrons fill the dining room, while takeout satisfies folks of all faiths with amazingly fresh meats and stellar entrées: like the jumbo pastrami burger. The menu has a Middle Eastern slant, with lots of hummous, babaganoush, and falafel; all three can be sampled in the special Kasbah Combination.
251 West 85th St. (bet. Broadway and West End Ave.), 496-1500, MC, V, D, Entrée: $8-$20, ❶❾ *to 86th Street*

Desperados
Tex-Mex comes to Morningside Heights. This newcomer boasts both tasty chicken and steak burritos and tacos as well as heart-healthy vegetarian alternatives bursting with freshness. Perfect for satisfying late-night cravings with almost instantaneous delivery.
996 Amsterdam Ave. (bet.109th and 110th Sts.), 531-8200, Cash Only, Entrées: $4-$7, ❶❾ *to 110th St.*

Dish of Salt
Giant wooden parrots and colorful banners cater to the exotica stereotype, but the greasy and decidedly Americanized Chinese food is safe enough for the after-work and pre-theater crowds.
133 West 47th St. (bet. Sixth and Seventh Aves.), 921-4242, MC, V, AmEx, Entrées: $18-$27, ❶❷ *to 49th St.* &

Dix et Sept
The kind of place that upscale Village types frequent to feel sophisticated and Parisian; bistro fare is well-done though not particularly authentic or inventive—case in point: steak frites are one of the highlights. The posturing at the bar appears just subtle enough to not seem practiced.
181 West 10th St. (at Seventh Ave.), 645-8023, MC, V, AmEx, D, Diners, Entrées: $17-$23, ❶❷❸❹❺❻❼ *to West 4th Street*

Dojo
American- and Japanese-influenced dishes here only really please fans of macrobiotic fare. The dirt-cheap prices and a frisky social scene are enough lure NYU undergrads away from their meal-plan fare.
14 West 4th St. (bet. Mercer St. and Broadway), 505-8934, MC, V, D, Entrées:$5-$10, ❶❷ *to 8th St.,* ❻ *to Bleeker St.* &

Dok Suni's
Korean home-cooking finds its way into the cultural melee of the East Village, demurely screened by lace curtains, low lighting, and trendy overtones; the homemade noodles and their bevy of spicy complements have earned quite a following among locals.
119 First Ave. (at 7th St.), 477-9506, Cash Only, Entrées: $8-$14, ❻ *to Astor,* ❶❷ *to 8th St.* &

Don Giovanni
For a slice of the neighborhood, sit outside at a table at enjoy a pie at Don Giovanni. Made in a brick oven, with thin crust, fresh mozzarella, and a sweet tomato sauce, this pizza is bound to please. Be forewarned that delivery takes at least an hour.
358 West 44th St. (bet. Eighth and Ninth Aves.), 581-4939, MC, V, AmEx, Entrées:$6.95-$13 (large pie), ❶Ⓒ❸ *to 42nd St.* & ⊛

Donald Sacks
Sandwiches, soups and salads make this workaday eatery pleasant enough for a quick lunch, though Fridays after work it resembles the trading floor. Sit "outside" in the large, airy courtyard of the World Financial Center.
220 Vesey St. (3 World Financial Center, Winter Garden), 619-4600, MC, V, AmEx, D, Diners, Entrées: $7-$17, ❶❾ *to Cortland,* ❷❸ *to Chambers St.* & ⇌

Duke's
The sign outside—"Get in Here and Eat"—just about

Desperado's N.Y.C.
996 Amsterdam Ave. (between 109th & 110th St.)
tex-mex-cal cuisine
212.531.8200
Fast · Free · Delivery (minimum $7.50)
HOURS:
Open 24 hours
Takeout and Delivery Only   Catering available
Inquire about group rates

restaurants 241

sums it up. Clearly not for the calorie-conscious, this bastion of beef brisket and barbecue sauce caters to everyone's inner Southerner; the meal's necessary epilogue, a hefty slice of pecan pie, similarly finds the inner glutton. *99 East 19th St. (bet. Park Ave. and Irving Pl.), 260-2922, MC, V, AmEx, Diners, Entrées: $7-$11,* ❶ ❷ ❸ ❹ ❺ ❻ *to Union Sq.*

Dynasty
With recent renovations and a revised menu, this neighborhood standard has managed to shake the epithet "Die Nasty" and establish a loyal clientele. The restaurant is hardly luxurious, but its "upscale" status indicates higher prices than at other Asian options in the area. *2836 Broadway (at 110th St.), 665-6455, MC, V, AmEx, Entrées: $6-$12,* ❶ ❾ *to 110th St.*

E

East
Sushi addiction finally is made affordable at this small, boxy side-street staple for neighborhood fans of Japanese cuisine; sushi may be more elaborate elsewhere, but not at these prices. Other crowd-pleasers like chicken teriyaki are equally tasty and cheap, and while service may lag a bit, dishes are well worth the wait. *9 Barrow St. (bet. West 4th St. and Seventh Ave. South), 929-3353, MC, V, AmEx, D, Diners, Entrées: $2.75-$6.50,* ❶ ❷ ❸ ❹ ❺ ❻ ❼ *to West 4th St.*

El Cid Tapas
Fit for Picasso, this tiny secret features the most authentic tapas this side of Barcelona. Go with a group and split a pitcher of white or red sangria, and fight over the last bite of marinated quail, seafood salad, or, their specialty, braised sweetbreads in garlic sauce. Come early on weekends. *322 West 15th St. (bet. Eighth and Ninth Aves.), 929-9332, MC, V, Entrées: $4-$8,* ❶ ❷ *to 14th St.*

El Nuevo Sambuca Restaurant
Mirrored pillars and a loomingly dark piano room serve as an appropriately classy backdrop to an "international" culinary selection. Daytime and evening hours strongly differ in mood and cuisine. *4199 Broadway (at 181st St.), 795-4744, MC, AmEx, V, D, Entrées: $1.50-$20,* ❶ ❷ ❾ *to 181st St.*

El Pollo
All hail Peru's favorite bird—the chicken—at one of the city's very few Peruvian kitchens. Order the "pollo" in whole, half, or quarter portions and expect it to be spicy and succulent. Don't pass up the Andean peasant staples-the "mote" (Peruvian corn) and the "papas rellenas" (stuffed potatoes) are two of the country's crowning culinary achievements. *1746 First Ave. (bet. 90th and 91st Sts.), 966-7810, MC, V,* ❹ ❺ ❻ *to 86th St.*

El Sitio II
Set the mood for truck-stop romance with your table's jukebox, although deals like the bandejas completas—a massive serving of meat, rice, beans, plantains, and croquettes—aren't among the wisest first-date choices, but getting a little tipsy on the sangria is part of the fun. *35-55 31st St., Long Island City, (718) 278-7694, MC, V, AmEx, Entrées: $7-$13,* ❼ *to 36th Ave.*

El Teddy's
Known for its crazy, amusement-park facade, this TriBeCa favorite specializes in Tex-Mex cuisine and legendary margaritas. Bar scene is mostly Wall Streeters during the week, and neighborhood types, though it definitely picks up with a rather shi-shi crowd later in the night. *219 West Broadway (bet. White and Franklin Sts.), 941-7070, MC, V, AmEx, D, Diners, Dinner: $15-$19,* ❶ ❾ *to Franklin St.,* ❶ ❷ ❸ *to Canal St.*

Elaine's
A magnet for A-list hometown celebs oft-featured in gossip columns. This popular hangout serves up standard American fare; quality blows hot and cold (mostly cold), but coming here for the food is like living in New York for the weather: it just shouldn't be a priority. Regulars include Woody Allen, Barbara Walters, and George Plimpton; Pat Reilly also frequented this chic dining room. *1703 Second Ave. (bet. 88th and 89th Sts.), 534-8103, MC, V, AmEx, D, Diners, Entrées: $15-$25,* ❹ ❺ ❻ *to 86th St.*

Empire Diner
Featured in Woody Allen's opening montage of *Manhattan*, this 24-hour eatery boasts an upscale diner menu, complemented by a jazz pianist. It's a great club-hopping pit

---

open late since 1996

Empire Szechuan Gourmet

Exotic Chinese & Japanese Cuisine

- 2574 Broadway at 97th st.   212-663-6004
- 2642 Broadway at 100th st.   212-662-9404
- 193 Columbus Ave. bet. 68th and 69th sts. (Lincoln Center)   212-496-8778
- 15 Greenwich Ave. at 10th st.   212-691-1535

A Taste of China (Classic & Innovative)
A Taste of Japan (With Creative Sushi Bar)
Hong Kong Seafood & Grill
Authentic Vegetarian Menu
Exotic Chef Specialties
Cantonese Noodle Soup
Soft Shell Crab
Fresh Live Lobster
Fresh Asparagus

50% off Fresh Sushi & Maki

THE BEST DIM SUM IN TOWN DAILY
LARGE VARIETY ON SAT. + SUN. 10:30-3:30
*only at 2574 Broadway

superb party & catering take out and free delivery
Open 7 Days a Week
10:30 am - 2 am

stop; staying up for prix-fixe brunch is well worth the sleep deprivation. Don't go a la carte, as the prices soar.
210 Tenth Ave. (at 22nd St.), 243-2736, MC, V, AmEx, Entrées: $5-$18, C E to 23rd St.

Empire Szechuan
Chinese, Thai, and Japanese cuisine all under one roof at reasonable prices. A neighborhood favorite for their quick service and the variety of their menu. Fresh orange slices after dinner are a special perk.
2574 Broadway, (at 96th St.), 663-6004, MC, V, Entrées: $7-$11, 1 9 2 3 to 96th St.

Ernie's
The food would be called American in Italy, but heaping portions and Rolaids-demanding sauces draw lovers of hearty, straightforward pasta to this preperformance spot. Seldom crammed to its cavernous capacity, it's ideal for large parties, and the waitstaff mixes the practiced professionalism of long-suffering actors with the candor of Little Italy boys. Fabulous tartuffo and cappuccino for dessert.
2150 Broadway (bet. 75th and 76th Sts.), 496-1588, MC, V, AmEx, D, Entrées: $9-$20, 1 9 to 79th St.

F

Famiglia's
Come for the photos of celebrities on the wall, the jocular service, and the delicious and greasy pizza. The 'hood's finest garlic twists and the pizza's garlicky tomato sauce will keep the vampires away.
2859 Broadway (at 111th St.), 865-1234, Cash Only, Entrées: $3-$5, 1 9 to 110th St.

Fanelli's
One of the last remnants from pregentrification SoHo. Everything about this place is unpretentious, from the spare decor to the sturdy pub-style food, which is what keeps it going strong as an alternative all the other too chic and trendy restaurants in the neighborhood. Be prepared to wait, on weekend nights they're often packed for hours.
94 Prince St. (bet. Prince and Mercer Sts.), 226-9412, MC, V, AmEx, N R 4 5 6 to Prince St.

Fiesta Mexicana
Perhaps the quality of the food is best gauged by the crowds of Mexican-Americans who come here for an evening out. The guacamole fresco, prepared from scratch at your table, is absolutely superb. Just when it seems it can't get any better, the smart waitstaff comes around proffering free shots of blue tequila just before you pay the bill. ¡Viva Mexico!
2823 Broadway (at 109th St.), 662-2535, MC, V, AmEx, Entrées: $8-$15, 1 9 to 110th St.

First
Sip a martini or smoke a cigar at the bar in this hip late-night dining spot. The stainless steel and faded brick interior provides an atmosphere as eclectic and cosmopolitan as the food. A little bit of everything can be found here: American, French, Italian, pan-Asian, and chef Sam DeMarco gives it all a unique twist.
87 First Ave. (bet 5th and 6th Sts.), 674-3823, MC, V, AmEx, Entrées: $18, F to Second Ave.

The Flame
Better known as a neighborhood icon than for its food, The Flame nonetheless ably serves up the expected diner menu, from omelets to burgers to gyros. The business crowd converges around 1pm for lunch, but otherwise there is ample seating and rarely (if ever) a wait. A good place to chat without having to fork over lots of dough.
893 Ninth Ave. (at 58th St.), 765-7962, V, MC, AmEx, D, Entrées: $4-$10, A B C D 9 to Columbus Circle

Florent
Fanciful bistro fare is available at all hours for a sophisticated and slightly affected mixed gay and straight crowd in the newly-hip Meat-Packing District. Housed in an old diner, the space is cool and understated; dishes are gourmet rustic.
69 Gansevoort St., 989-5779, Cash Only, Entrées: $5-$15, A C E L to 14th St./Eighth Ave.

Fraunces Tavern
If your parents happen to be history buffs, take them here. Marvel at the spot where George Washington bid farewell to his troops in 1783 before feasting on cornish hen, crabcakes, and mousse. The effect of the dark-wood paneling and enormous leather chairs can be either cozy or enervating, depending on how busy the place is.
54 Pearl St. (at Broad St.), 269-0144, MC, V, AmEx, Diners, D, Entrées: $12-$21, J M Z to Broad St.

Friend of a Farmer
Only in Gramercy could you find a Vermont smugness more convincing than anything you'd ever find in the Green Mountain State itself. While dinner is hearty and well-prepared, featuring stick-to-your-ribs specialties like sheppard's and chicken pot pies, the crowded brunch is the best feature. Another plus is that you've possibly seen similar prices in Montpelier.
77 Irving Pl. (bet. 17th and 18th Sts.), 477-2188, V, MC, AmEx, Entrées: $8-$14, 4 5 6 N R to Union Sq.

Frutti Di Mare
Much nicer than you'd expect at these prices. The menu has good versions of all the usual Italian standards along with a number of delicious seafood specialties that give the place its name. The service is extraordinarily attentive, and touches like cloth napkins and candlelight help create the ambiance that makes this a great place for a romantic dinner that won't break the bank.
84 East 4th St. (at Second Ave.), 979-2034, Cash Only, Entrées: $7-$11, F to Second Ave.

G

Gabriel's
Perhaps the crème de la crème of the bevy of restaurants around Lincoln Center, the combination of casual and class here is just about perfect. Beautiful decor, an astonishing, seasonal menu

restaurants 243

(order the delectable butternut squash ravioli if it's on the menu!), and a refined yet informal staff all account for why this is one of New York's hottest spots for dinner. Come after 7:30pm to avoid the preconcert crowd.
11 West 60th St. (bet. Broadway and Columbus Ave.), 956-4600, V, MC, AmEx, Entrées: $16-$22, ❶❷❸❹❶❾ *to Columbus Circle.*

Galaxy
This dark, cozy, Irving Plaza neighbor has a ceiling spattered with twinkling stars and swirling blue planets. After sampling their hemp-infused dishes like "hemp-Szechuan spice tunaLoin medallions" or "hemp garden burger", you might feel like you're dining on cloud nine. For your non-culinary needs, they also sell a complete line of hemp products from hemp lip balm to Hemp Pedaler Chain Lube.
15 Irving Place (at 15th St.), 777-3631, MC, V, Entrées: $8-10, ❶❷❸❹❺❻❼ *to Union Sq.*

The Garage
Suburban Steakhouse meets Greenwich Village panache at this sprawling multi-leveled village favorite. Its famous Sunday jazz brunch offers both top-notch music and a mean eggs benedict. During the week, come for the music but stay for the unforgettable mussels provencal, or their hearty sandwiches and raw bar.
99 Seventh Ave. South (at Grove St.), 337-0806, MC, V, AmEx, Entrées: $8-$15, ❶❾ *to Christopher St.*

Gascogne
Feast on sumptuously prepared food while sipping cognac and surreptitiously loosening your belt a notch. Creative fowl like duck, quail, wild boar, and rabbit all grace the menu, as does everyone's favorite French innovation, escargot. If the weather proves as good as the food, take a seat in the exquisite back garden, though indoors is amazingly atmospheric as well. As close to royalty as the bourgeoisie can get.
158 Eighth Ave. (bet. 17th and 18th Sts.), 675-6564, Reservations recommended, MC, V, AmEx, Entrées: $18-$21, Prix Fixe: $25, ❶❸ *to 14th St.*

Ginger Ty
Impressive decor and pleasant service mandate at least one visit. An entire menu of suprisingly affordable cuisine tempts you back for more. The "lunch boxes," for takeout or delivery only, are a particularly good deal; a full vegetarian menu is also available.
363 Greenwich St. (bet. Franklin and Harrison Sts.), 925-7440, Cash Only, Entrées: $8-$16, ❶❾ *to Franklin St.*

Golden Rule Diner
The neighborhood's best diner is ideal after a rough night in the local Irish pubs, with lighting that won't induce migraines. Deals are standard diner, and include seafood and Greek dishes.
4959 Broadway (bet. 207th and 211th Sts.), 942-8840, Cash Only, Entrées: $4-$10, ❶❾ *to 207th St.*

Golden Unicorn
More sanitized and polished than most Chinatown dim sum houses, this chandeliered, temperature-controlled restaurant has become especially popular among tourists and local businessmen hosting lunch meeting. Delicious dim sum is served Hong-Kong style, stacked on metal carts piloted by vigorous employees.
18 East Broadway (at Catherine St.), 941-0911, MC, V, AmEx, Diners, D, ❶❷❸ *to Grand St.*

Gotham Bar and Grill
Architectually brilliant entrées like pyramidal crabcakes, betray the hand of one of the city's finest gourmets, Alfred Portale, and his kitchen team of all-star chefs, who've made Gotham's New American a staple for New York connoisseurs. Entrées bypass typical meats for rabbit, pheasant, and a couple so rare they're probably endangered. Sample it all with a $19.97 prix-fixe lunch in the spacious, angular dinning room.
12 East 12th St. (bet. Fifth Ave. and University Pl.), 620-4020, MC, V, AmEx, Diners, Entrées: $25-$35, ❶❷❸❹❺❻ *to Union Square.*

Gramercy Tavern
Don't be fooled by the rustic decor: prices reflect the all-star clientele at this hot-spot for hobnobbing and networking. Stargazers may be willing to pay the price for a chance at sharing lunch with Johnny Depp.
42 East 20th St., 477-0777, MC, V, AmEx, Diners, *Entrées: $18-$25 ,* ❻❽❾ *to 23rd St.*

The Grand Deli
Enjoy both deli and Chinese while you schoomze at this classic Lower East Side spot.
399 Grand St. (near Clinton St.), 477-5200, AmEx, V, MC, D, Entrées: $8-$18, ❶❷❸❹❾ *to Canal St.*

Grand Luncheonette
Owner Fred Hakim has been dishing up "all-beef patties and franks" and fluorescent orangeade at this old-fashioned Times Square lunch counter for over thirty years. This relic has miraculously eluded the spurious cleansing efforts of the Urban Development Commission. The Formica and vinyl decor hasn't changed, and neither have the prices: a burger and drink will set you back about $2. Open 10am to 10pm, seven days per week.
229 West 42nd St. (bet. Seventh and Eighth Aves.), Unlisted number, Cash Only, ❶❷❸❹❼ ❶❷❸ *to Times Sq.*

The Grange Hall
The coziest corner in the West Village is home to one of its very finest restaurants. One of Uma Thurman's known haunts, this classy outpost of European refinement and American-style roasts and chicken dishes displays excellent taste without being ostentatious.
50 Commerce St. (bet. Bedford and Hudson Sts.), 924-5246, AmEx, Entrées: $12-$25, ❶❷❸❹❺❻ ❶❷ *to West 4th St.*

244 restaurants

Granville Restaurant/Lounge
Depending on the hour, the scene at this dark wood and leather-laden newcomer is set either by professionals or beautiful people. Dress accordingly and practice some posing in the upstairs cigar lounge.
40 East 20th St. (bet. Broadway and Park Ave. South), 253-9088, MC, V, AmEx, Diners, Transmedia, Entrées: $18–$25, **N R 6** *to 23rd St.*

Grapino's
A gem tucked away on a quiet block, this dark and distinguished cucina is an oasis in the thick of corporate New York. The pastas are superb, the wine reasonably priced, and the waiters cheerful, knowledgeable, and discreet. A great alternative to the pretheater hubbub of on the west side.
38 West 39th St. (bet. Fifth and Sixth Aves.), 398-0350, V, MC, AmEx, **B D F Q** *to 42nd St.*

H

Habib's Place
Sorting through downtown falafel joints can be a tough task and its not uncommon to get food poisoning along the way. No worries here though, they have the kind of falafel that made you want falafel in the first place, along with lots of other Middle Eastern specialties. The atmosphere is as friendly as you'll find anywhere and there's often live jazz.
1438 East 9th St., (bet. First Ave. and Ave. A), 979-2243, Cash Only, Entrées: $3–$12, **N R** *to 8th St.*

Hangawi
A perfect choice for any occasion, Midtown's supreme Korean vegetarian restaurant is easily one of the wonders of fine New York dining. Guests remove their shoes at the door and are transported by relaxing music and innovative, delicious cuisine into a state of utter bliss. First-timers should select from the prix fixe menu as it offers an unforgettable multicourse culinary experience.
12 East 32nd St., 213-0077, V, MC, AmEx, D, Prix Fixe Dinner: $28–$33, A la Carte: $4–$17, **1 9 N R** *to 34th St.,* **6** *to 33rd St.*

Harry's at Hanover Square
When you're in the mood for suits, cigars and meat, this Wall Street hangout is the place for you. Order a martini and peruse the great wine list as you'll no doubt be ordering one of Harry's excellent steaks. Not known for it's feminine touches, this is not the place for "ladies who lunch."
1 Hanover Sq. (bet. Pearl and Stone Sts.), 425-3412, MC, V, AmEx, Diners, D, Entrées: $12–$25, **J M Z 2 3 4 5** *to Broadway/Nassau St.*

Healthy Henrietta's
Bulky macrobiotic burritos recommend this charming BoHo outpost, where the food comes straight from the earth and the slight twang of an acoustic guitar sounds as Manhattan's urbanity is just a twinkle on the horizon.
60 Henry Street, (718) 858-8478, AmEx, Entrées: $6–$12

Home
The name conjures up the American iconography of mom and apple pie, but despite the low pretension and familiar line-up of potato hash and chocolate pudding, this refined Village eatery is a bit too urbane to qualify as a suburban transplant. Chefs may not infuse the catfish with mom's love, but they are committed to resisting the strong French trends in new American cuisine, instead steering culinary attention toward hometown faves.
20 Cornelia St. (bet. Bleeker and West 4th Sts.), 243-9579, AmEx, Entrées: $13–$17, **A B C D E F Q** *to West 4th St.*

Hoppin' Jalapeños
Traces of its former resident, an Irish pub, are nowhere to be found in this bustling Inwood Cal-Mex kitchen. Traditional Mexican fare such as "enchiladas molé poblano" are served alongside Americanized versions of chicken fajitas and potent margaritas. On most nights locals crowd the bar to watch sports.
597 West 207th St. (bet. Broadway and Vermilyea Sts.), 569-5069, MC, V, AmEx, Entrées: $6–$13, **A** *to 207th St.*

House of Seafood
This bright, utilitarian fast food joint serves very fresh, very tasty, very cheap deep-fried and steamed shrimp, scallops, and crabs to a neighborhood crowd. Best eaten standing at the counter from the greasy paper bag.
2349 Frederick Douglass Blvd. (at 126th St.) 531-0405, Cash Only, Entrées: $4–$14, **A B C D** *to 125th St.*

House of Vegetarian
The chefs here can trick even hard-core carnivores with their meatless renditions of duck, chicken, and pork dishes that taste just like the real things. Even vegans can indulge without the guilt.
68 Mott (bet. Canal and Bayard Sts.), 226-6572, Cash Only, Entrées: $6–$10, **J M N R Z** *to Canal St.*

Howard Johnson's Restaurant
The food is gratuitously bad, but the orange and teal Formica and imitation wood paneling merit the indigestion. The city's only extant HoJo's, opened in 1950, attracts a motley crew of tourists, punks, and Times Square denizens for baskets o' nachos 'n' fries and flat cola into the wee hours.
1551 Broadway (at 46th St.), 354-1445, MC, V, AmEx, Diners, **N R S 1 2 3 7 9** *to Times Sq.*

HSF
Count on this ever-popular dim sum house, which claims to have been among the first in Chinatown to offer a full menu of dim sum dishes, to be packed and loyal locals.
46 Bowery (bet. Canal and Bayard St.), 374-1319, MC, V, AmEx, Diners, D, $2–$3.50 per piece, **J M Z N R 6** *to Canal St.*

Hudson River Club
Advertising that this Wall Street-professional haven "specializes in food from

restaurants 245

the Hudson" might not seem too smart, but the seasonal seafood masterpieces are delectable. Gorge on artfully prepared shellfish while Lady Liberty gazes stolidly in the distance.
4 World Financial Center, 250 Vesey St. (bet. West St. and North End), 786-1500, MC, V, AmEx, D, Diners, Entrées: $28-$36, ❶❾ to Cortlandt St. or ❸❹❺ to World Trade Cntr.

I

Indigo
Creative cuisine and impeccable presentation make this tucked-away gem a find. With chef Scott Bryan from Luma, this excellent but unpretentious French-American bistro also has reasonable prices. Votive candles set a subtle indigo mood and the coat check gives everyone a little more room. Try the sorbet for dessert and understand why the next table called it 'orgasmic.'
142 West 10th St. (bet. Greenwich Ave. and Waverly Pl.), 691-7757, AmEx, Average Entrée: $15, ❶❾ to Christopher St.

J

Jake's Steakhouse
New York meets the Wild West, though the decor, service, and style is pure Gotham, right down to the menus plastered with photographs of cows grazing in front of the World Trade Center. Pastas are an option, but only a true carnivore can appreciate the Jake's experience: thick burgers and other slabs of beef guaranteed to satiate the most ravenous urban cowboy.
1155 Third Ave. (at 68th St.), 879-9888, MC, V, AmEx, D, Diners, Entrées: $13-$30, ❻ to 68th Street

Jamaican Hot Pot
Enjoy authentic Caribbean renditions of jerk chicken and spicy island sauces at this hole-in-the-wall local hangout. Order some Sorrel, a cool beverage made from a Jamaican flower and doused with rum and ginger, to complete the experience.
2260 A.C. Powell, Jr. Blvd. (at 133rd St.), 491-5270, MC, V, AmEx, D, Entrées: $9-$17, ❷❸ to 135th St.

Jean's Restaurant
The utilitarian façade is all part of the no-frills approach to authentic Caribbean favorites: the stellar roti and curry goat may qualify as the borough's best. Swing by and grab take-out for the perfect midday picnic.
188-36 Linden Boulevard (at Farmers), (718) 525-3069, MC, V, AmEx, D, Diners, Entrées: $7-$10, ❻ to Jamaica, Q4 to Linden, or ❸❿❿ to Parsons/Archer St.

Jerusalem II
The most popular Kosher Pizza joint in Manhattan. Lots of students from the nearby Stern College for Women drop by for a slice, as do Jewish office workers or tourists heading out to a Broadway show. Delivery is available to almost anyone anywhere in the world.
1375 Broadway (bet. 37th and 38th Sts.), 696-0942, MC, V, Entrées: $2-$8, ❶❷❸❾ to 34th St.

Jim McMullen
The pot pies are the stuff legends are made of, and deservedly so, at this old-school New York hangout, one of the plushest neighborhood pubs around. The burgers and other mainstream fare, however, are hardly worth the trip.
1341 Third Ave. (bet. 76th and 77th Sts.), 861-4700, MC, V, AmEx, Diners, Entrées: $10-$22, ❻ to 77th St.

Jimmy's Bronx Café
After just four years in the Bronx, this "Latin Restaurant and Entertainment Complex" has become the nucleus for nightlife in the borough's Latino community. Upstairs, seafood is served into the wee hours as patrons watch boxing and baseball on the large TVs. Downstairs, the dance floor resembles a hotel ballroom, built for high capacity. As at other Latin clubs, there's no such thing as overdressing, though casual seems prevalent. Thurs. feature free salsa lessons 8-9pm.
281 West Fordham Rd. (at Major Deegan Expwy), (718) 329-2000, MC, V, AmEx, D, Diners, Entrées: $8-$40, ❶❾ to 207th St.

Joe Allen
Upscale thespians, including bonafide Broadway celebs in search of some postperformance relaxation, come to this dark and elegant but unpretentious eatery to fill up on gourmet meatloaf and banana cream pie. Fifteen percent of every check goes to Broadway Cares/Equity Fights AIDS.
326 West 46 St. (bet. Eighth and Ninth Aves.), 581-6464, MC, V, Entrées: $10-$20, ❹❸❺ to 42nd St.

Joe's Shanghai
Tourists, locals, and suburban Chinese flock here for the juicy crabmeat buns for which Joe's is deservedly famous. Friendly service and the savory quality of the rest of the fare keeps customers coming back for more.
9 Pell St. (bet. Bowery and Mott St.), 233-888, Cash Only, Entrées: $9-$20, ❻ to Canal St.

John's of Bleecker Street
This thin, coal-oven-baked pizza is preceded by its well-deserved reputation. A good place for groups to hang out. No slices—only whole pies, the mark of an excellent pizzeria.
278 Bleecker St. (bet. Sixth and Seventh Aves.), 243-1680, Cash Only, Entrées: $12, ❶❸❹❺❻❼❽ to West 4th St.

Josephina
Indulge with a clear conscience at this upscale Lincoln Center establishment boasting a genuinely obliging waitstaff and understated elegance. Partake of wasabi mashed potatoes and macadamia-crusted chicken breast and save room for desserts like crumbly crusted seasonal fruit pies topped off with homemade soy ice cream. Beans, grains, and flours are all organic, and meats and poultry are free-range. Dairy-free options are clearly marked on the menu.
1900 Broadway (bet. 63rd and 64th Sts.), 799-1000, MC, V, AmEx, Diners,

Entrées: $12.50-$22, **1 9** to 66th St.

Junior's
Sample "New York's Best Cheesecake" (don't confuse it with the cheese pie!) or just about anything else you can imagine at this monster diner/bar, open till 2pm. Busy bar, with eclectic group of patrons. Speedy service, but sometimes a wait for a table on weekends.
386 Flatbush Ave. (at DeKalb Ave.), (718) 852-5257, V, MC, AmEx, D, Entrées: $6-$15, **D M N Q R** *to DeKalb Ave.*

K

Kate's Joint
If the idea of barbecue evokes images of pigs roasting on a spit or giant racks of beef ribs, think again. "Vegetarian barbecue" here means everything from faux versions of fleshy favorites to revved up vegetable dishes to excellent meatless chili. At times the crowd of devoted East Village types packs the hip little eating area to the gills, which means occasional annoying but worthwhile waits. Try the garlic fries.
58 Avenue B (bet 4th and 5th Sts.), 777-7059, MC, V, AmEx, Entrées: around $9, **F** *to Second Ave.*

Katz's Delicatessen
Steaming pastrami and corned beef sandwiches and other artery-clogging delicacies await at this cavernous, superior delicatessen, where yellowing paint and curling posters exhorting patrons to "Send a salami to your boy in the army" prove that nothing much has changed here in about fifty years. A dollar tip to one of the gruff, portly attendants behind the encounter will beget a sandwich big enough to feed a family of five.
205 East Houston St. (at Ludlow St.), 254-2246, MC, V, AmEx, ($20 minimum), Entrées: $5-$9 , **F** *to Second Ave.*

Keen's Chophouse
New York's only haunted restaurant sports a suit of armor, stained glass windows, and thousands of Victorian clay pipes dangling from its low oak rafters. Opened in 1885, this dark, handsome, atmospheric chophouse looks and feels like an old boys' smoking room, with a corporate male clientele and a macho menu of steaks, chops, and oysters to match. The ghost, however, is Lillie Langtry, who has been frequenting this spot in flesh and in spirit since its heyday as a theatrical hangout at the end of the 19th century.
72 West 36th St. (bet. Fifth and Sixth Aves.), 947-3636, MC, V, AmEx, **B D F N Q R** *to 34th St.*

Kin Khao
Don't be surprised to see a budding supermodel sitting down the bench from you here, this place is very trendy. However, the atmosphere isn't prohibitive to normal people and once you get inside, the waitstaff is unpretentious and the decor is beautiful and comfortable. The food is Thai, and the quality isn't all that consistent, to be safe stick to one of the noodle dishes that are almost always delectable.
171 Spring St. (bet West Broadway and Thompson Sts.), 966-3939, Entrées: $11-$18, **F** *to Second Ave.*

Kitchen Club
Has been voted the "best dinner for two under $100 in Manhattan." Serving up Continental cuisine with an Asian twist, this "friendly little place" has an eccentric feel to it. The turquoise curtains, huge checkered tile floor, and French doors which open out onto the street may have something to do with the atmosphere.
30 Prince St. (at Mott) 274-0025, Cash Only, **N R** *to Prince St.,* **6** *to Spring St.*

Koronet's
Thousands of hungry students over the years have found nourishment (or at least calories) in the giant, doughy slabs served at this greasy spoon. Folding it in half will make eating more manageable, though as the mirrored wall at the counter seating will reveal, there's really no polite way to chow through an entire slice.
2848 Broadway (bet. 110th and 111th Sts.), 222-1566, Cash Only, Entrées: $2-$6, **1 9** *to 110th St.*

Kosher Delight
Burger King for Orthodox Jews. This is one of the city's fast-food restaurants, serving juicy hamburgers, hot dogs, and chicken cutlet sandwiches. Kosher meat at these prices is impossible to come by anywhere else.
1365 Broadway (bet. 36th and 37th Sts.), 563-3366, **1 2 3 9** *to 34th St.,*
Also at
1156 Sixth Ave. (at 45th St.), 869-6699, MC, V, AmEx, Entrées: $2-$11 **4 5 6** *to 42nd St.*

KPNY
Chef Ken Lammer's "Eclectic Body Food" might prove to those who don't already know: healthy food can be as amiable to the palate as burgers and fries. The inventive, organic menu caters to both vegetarians and meat-eaters alike. Earth-tones, fruit and vegetable stills, and warm lighting complete the casual atmosphere.
557 Hudson St. (bet. Perry and West 11th St.), 627-3092, MC, V, AmEx, Entrées: $10-18, **1 9** *to Christopher St.*

L

L'Express
"Faux but fabulous" describes both the clientele and the food. Open 24 hours, this moderately priced attempt at a bistro is welcomed by hip twentysomethings starved for cheap eats in this pricey area.
249 Park Ave. South (at 20th St.), 254-5858, MC, V, AmEx, Entrées: $8-$18, **6** *to 23rd St.*

La Jumelle Inc.
Trendy French cuisine in lower SoHo, with a smoky bistro ambiance; classic French onion soup and salmon dishes are among some of the best menu options.
55 Grand St. (at West Broadway), 941-9651, MC, V, Entrées: $12-$16, **B D Q** *to Grand St.*

La Poeme
Inside the antique-laden dining room of chef Martine Arbitol's daytime home, aging poets and artists chatter while seat-

restaurants 247

ed around a taffeta-covered table crowded with platters of steaming seafood. The Arbitol famly's silver husky pads his way across the floor toward the kitchen while Martine leaves her stove momentarily to ask customers how they're enjoying the hearty, French and Corsican influenced dishes.
14 Prince St. (at Elizabeth St.), 941-1106, Cash Only, Entrées: $10-$15, ❶❸ *to Prince St.*

Lanza's
Solid authentic Italian food without any gimmicks or fancy perversions. The clientele is large and loyal, filling the restaurant nightly for both the classy old-style ambiance and superior food at bargain prices. Thankfully it's neither trendy nor cutting-edge.
168 First Ave. (bet. 10th and 11th Sts.), 674-7014, MC, V, AmEx, Diners, Entrées: $13-$17, ❶❷❸❹❺❻ *to Union Square.* &

Layla
For an authentic Mediterranean or Middle Eastern dining experience, look elsewhere. But for authentic food from a trendy restaurant with beautiful decor, this is as good as it gets. The menu is a mix of standards like tabouleh and new creations centered around fish and lamb, classic staples of the regions' cuisine. Even when the food isn't incredible, the beautiful setting is enough to compensate.
211 West Broadway (at Franklin St.), 431-0700, MC, V, AmEx, Entrées: $17-$25, ❶❷ *to Franklin St.*

Le Bilboque
Chain-smoking Euro-trash trail crowds of beautiful people into this permissive French restaurant, currently boasting some of the hippest new lounging turf. The models can't appreciate the menu, but don't let that stop you from taking advantage of the well-executed bistro fare.
25 East 63rd St. (bet. Madison and Park Aves.), 751-3036, MC, V, AmEx, 456 to 59th St., ❻❹ *to Lexington Ave.*

Le Grenier
The cuisine at this popular neighborhood spot is straight from the Ivory Coast, to which the locals in African garb and the outbursts in French attest. Indeed, patrons are assured of authentic West African dishes like jolof rice and suppu kavjan.
2264 Frederick Douglass Blvd, (bet. 121st and 122nd Sts.), 666-0653, MC, V, AmEx, D, $10-$12, ❶❷❸❹ *to 125th St.* &

Le Roy's Restaurant and Coffee Shop
Organic vegetarian health food is served here in addition to classics such as meatloaf and hearty sandwiches. Prices for the veggie items are a bit steep, but the talented cooks (and homey atmosphere) is worth the extra bucks.
247 West Broadway (at Sixth Ave.), 966-3370, Cash Only, Entrées: $2.50-$8, ❶❷ *to Franklin St.*

Lemon
Spend a romantic summer evening watching crowds meander down Park Avenue South while the moonlight streams through large windows. Thirtysomethings crowd the bar area but the restaurant doesn't take its popularity too seriously, maintaining a soothing atmosphere and a light menu. Great brunch.
230 Park Ave. South (bet. 18th and 19th Sts.), 614-1200, MC, V, AmEx, D, Entrées: $12-$22, ❶❷❸❹❺❻ *to Union Square.* &

Lemongrass Grill
Straw baskets and a thatched-roof bar strive to create a little Vietnam in Manhattan. Beef with ginger is excellent, and there are five locations throughout the city.
2534 Broadway (bet. 94th and 95th Sts.), 666-0888, MC, V, AmEx, Entrées: $8-$16, ❷❸❾ *to 96th St.* &

Les Halles
Authentically Parisian, down to the boucherie by the front door, this bustling brasserie is well-known for its memorable steak frites and onion soup. Cramped tables mean people-watching and eavesdropping are favored diversions.
411 Park Ave. South (bet. 28th and 29th Sts.), 679-4111, MC, V, AmEx, D, Entrées: $14-$25, ❹❺❻ *to 28th St.* &

Lexington Candy Shoppe Luncheonette
Its antique malt-mix dispenser and shake machine have been churning since 1925, making a meal at this old-fashioned soda fountain and diner a historical event. Pay homage by ordering one of the burgers sizzling on a small griddle and a complicated dairy concoctions.
1226 Lexington Ave. (at 83rd St.), 288-0057, Cash Only, Entrées: $5.50-$7.50, ❹❺❻ *to 86th St.* &

Lincoln Tavern
The blue-checked tablecloths and elegant wood bespeak pampered rustic, though Lincoln Center, visible at an angle through the gorgeous wall of windows facing the Street, and the vaguely upscale crowd belie this local favorite's urban setting. Deviations like a delectable goat cheese ravioli get tossed in with classics of the steak variety; salads are simple yet flavorful, as are the down-home, oven-warm rolls which accompany each meal.
51 West 64th St. (at Broadway), MC, V, AmEx, Diners, Entrées: $10-$23, ❶❾ *to 66th St.* &

Londel's
Owner Londel Davis greets customers at the door of his sophisticated new Sugar Hill supperclub, a harbinger of gentrification in this quickly changing neighborhood. Harlem's hottest restaurant serves delicious, painstakingly prepared Southern food like smothered pork chops and pan-seared red snapper to the neighborhood's most upwardly mobile. Sunday brunch draws a crowd, as do the live jazz and blues acts Friday and Saturday nights.
2620 Frederick Douglass Blvd. (bet. 139th and 140th Sts.), 234-6114, MC, V, AmEx, D, Entrées: $9-$16, ❶❷❸❹ *to 145th Street* &

Lucky Cheng's
The real reason Middle America never ventures below 14th Street. Imagine nibbling at Thai duck salad and then noticing that the innocuous

soft rock playing the background has become the anthem of a transvestite waiter dancing on your table. The subsequent spectacle of licking whipped cream off of her thighs to the shock (and secret personal relief) of the other patrons renders the experience so entertaining that no one will even notice the food. Free shows downstairs.
24 First Ave. (bet. 1st and 2nd Sts.), 473-0516, MC, V, AmEx, D, Diners, Entrées: $11-$18, ❻ *to Second Ave.*

Lucky Garden
Don't be intimidated by the Chinese families haggling over their lunch. Ask the waiter for an English menu and order a seafood dish. The small tank at the front proudly displays your meal.
34 Pell St., 233-8677, MC, AmEx, D, V, Entrées: $6-$11, ❻❻❻ *to Grand St.*

Luma
Though the decor may be minimalist, all-star chef Scott Bryan's cooking is anything but restrained. Leave your diet at the door and prepare for one of the wine-fueled, artery-clogging marathon meals that the French are famous for surviving.

200 Ninth Ave. (bet. 22nd and 23rd Sts.), 633-8033, MC, V, AmEx, D, Diners, Entrées: $18-$25, ❻❻ *to 23rd St.*

Luna's
Show up early or plan to spend time waiting in line for this favorite neighborhood haunt. The Plaza it's not, but expect hearty, down-home Italian cooking. The sagging floorboards might even remind you of grandmama's house.
112 Mulberry St. (near Canal St.) 226-8657, Cash Only, Entrées: $9-$17, ❻❻❻❻ *to Canal.St.*

M
M and R Bar
There is a peaceful, romantic garden in back, dining room is perfect for blustering parties of ten, and the bar in front is packed almost nightly: Best place for hard retro cocktails. The New American cuisine is low-cost, and the candle-lit atmosphere is dominated by garage-sale oil paintings of nudes adorning the walls.
264 Elizabeth St. (bet. Houston and Prince Sts.), 226-0559, MC, V, AmEx, D, Entrées: $7-$14, ❻❻❻ ❻❻ *to Prince St.*

Mabat
Like any ethnic neighborhood restaurant in the outer boroughs, this place may not be as fancy as its Manhattan counterparts, but makes up for it in terms of authenticity and price. Nearly everything here is very good.
1809 East 7th St. (bet. Clinton and King's Highway), (718) 339-3300, Cash Only, Entrées: $14-$16, ❻ *to King's Highway*

Madras Mahal
Vegetarian Kosher Indian food attracts an eclectic crowd, ranging from vegetarian Indians to Orthodox Jews. The atmosphere is friendly and service staff is dedicated.
104 Lexington Ave. (bet. 27th and 28th sts.), 684-4010, AmEx, D, MC, V, Entrées: $7-$12, ❻❻❻ *to 28th St.*

Mama's Food Shop
Mama's clients eat here many times a week. Mama is, in fact, a man who cooked so much food for his friends that his space evolved into a restaurant. All the food is excellent, and the portions are huge. Try the grilled salmon; don't miss the awesome mac-and-cheese.
200 East 3rd St. (bet. Aves. A and B), 777-4425, Cash Only, Entrées: $6-$8, ❻ *to Second Ave.*

Mama Joy's
In the front window a handwritten copy of a Zagats review sings the praises of this cramped deli's mind-boggling list of cheeses. Sandwiches here are great, but go elsewhere for standard grocery items. Columbia students come for the vast beer selection just before the 1am closing time.
2892 Broadway (at 113th St.), 662-0716, V, MC, ❻❻ *to 110th St.*

Mamá Mexico
Great margaritas, a friendly, festive atmosphere and traveling junior mariachis, make Mamá Mexico the spot to find South of the Border cuisine on the island of Manhattan. Both their traditional and inventive Mexican dishes are excellent and the guacamole is made fresh at the table! When they say, "comidas y bebidas con amor," they aren't kidding.
2671 Broadway 864-2323, V, MC, AmEx, Entrées: $9.95-$19.95, ❻❻ *to 103rd St.*

Man Ray
The sophisticated neighbor of the Joyce theater is perfect for preperformance martinis, which are encouraged by the overly spacious bar. While the decor may not do justice to its namesake, the avant-garde photographer who was instrumental in both American and European Dadaism and surrealism, it definitely incorporates upscale art and classy retro. The menu offers typical, slightly mediocre American cuisine and decent prix fixe.
69 Eighth Ave. (bet. 18th and 19th Sts.), 627-4220, Entrées: $9-$12, ❻❻ *to 23rd St.*

Mangia
Gourmet Mediterranean cuisine and friendly waitstaff at this lunch restaurant make it a culinary hot-spot for the surround-

---

mention this ad and receive 10% off

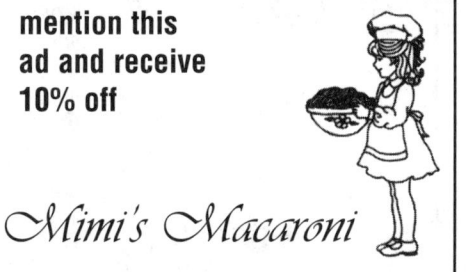

Mimi's Macaroni

718 Amsterdam Avenue
New York, NY 10025 • 212 866-6311

ing working worlds of businesses, galleries and museums. Mangia's diverse array of pastas, sandwiches, and entrées:, including an "antipasto table," with a wonderful selection of foods ranging from paella to rare tuna, is sure to quench anyone's desire for a gastronomic thrill. In a rush? Stop at the cafe downstairs for equally delicious take-out dining. *50 West 57th St. (bet. Fifth and Sixth Aves.), 582-5554/5882, MC, V, AmEx Entrées: $11-15,* **❶❸❺** *to Seventh Ave.,* **❻❼** *to 57th St.* & *(downstairs)* 🚲

Mappamondo; Mappamondo Due

This pair of small, inexpensive Italian eateries wink at each other across Abingdon Square. The menu consists of simple, serviceable pasta standards and reliable house wines; the ambiance is the attraction: the original is cramped and noisy, with distractingly loud music, while its younger sibling boasts a more low-key atmosphere. *581 Hudson St. (at Bank St.), 675-7474, 675-3100, Cash Only, Entrées: $6-$12,* **❶❸❹** *to 14th St.*

Mare Mare

Fresh seafood cooked to perfection is served in the soothing wood and wave interior of this West Side culinary treasure. Dishes are inventive and colorful. Outdoor seating is available on the terrace. Try the specials of the evening and leave room for coffee and dessert! *225 Columbus Ave. (at 70th St.), 579-3966, V, MC, AmEx, Entrées: $15-*

$21, **❶❷** *to 72nd St.* &

Margon

Only breakfast and lunch are served at this cheap find; it's a bit of a dive, but perfect for getting down and dirty with a couple of burritos along with the rat race crowd. *136 West 46th St. (bet. Sixth and Seventh Aves.), 354-5013, Cash Only, Entrées: $5-$7,* **❸❹❺❻** *to 42nd St.*

Mary Ann's

Between the spirited salsa piped through the dining room and the glowing jalapeño lights strung from the walls, every day feels like Cinco de Mayo at this wildly popular, calorie-conscious Latin kitchen. Homemade Mexican fare includes tofu jack cheese and nonfat sour cream; top it all off with a delicious chilled margarita composed of "special ingredients." *116 Eighth Ave. (at 16th St.), 633-0877, Entrées: $6-$11, Cash Only,* **❶❸❹** *to 14th St./Eighth Ave.* &

Match

Tireless style here has survived the neighborhood's oscillations with ease, due to an unwavering commitment to black. Join the thrifty crowd lunching on dim sum under twisted metal wall ornaments, all reflected by the mirrored back wall, or indulge in anything from steak to vegetarian concoctions. Dimly lit and intimate, the relative anonymity Match affords frequently draws celebrities. *160 Mercer St. (bet. Houston and Prince Sts.), 343-0020, MC, V, AmEx, Diners, Transmedia,*

Entrées: $15-$24, **❶❷** *to Prince St.*

Match Uptown

A dose of uptown swank and sophistication with a dash of pretension flavor this hip New American menu with its own in-house sushi bar, sit-in bar, and caviar service. Moody lighting, an older crowd, and comfortable seating make for a pleasant dining experience. Food is colorful, artfully prepared, and fabulous. Dessert is a must! *33 East 60th St. (bet. Madison and Park Aves.), 906-9177, V, MC, AmEx, Entrées: $25-30,* **❶❷** *to 59th St.* & ↵

Matthew's

Chef Matthew Kenney's light, airy upscale Mediterranean restaurant offers a wide variety of aromatic and flavorful fare. He is wonderfully inventive and equally proficient whether preparing toasted barley risotto, wild mushrooms roasted in hazelnut oil, or any one of the other dishes that have ensured his status as a world-class chef. *1030 Third Ave. (at 61st St.), 838-0020, V, MC, AmEx, D, Entrées: $20-$29,* **❶❷** *to Lexington Ave.,* **❹❺❻** *to 59th St.* &

Maya

Excellent cuisine, excellent service, and a comfortable atmosphere make dining at this "Gourmet Mexican" truly a euphoric experience. The food is that good. Colorful and flavorful, the dishes are inventive with surprising combinations. Try the mango margaritas and the guacamole with fresh chips. *1191 First Ave. (at 64th*

Métisse
French Bistro

"A taste of France in the Upper West Side"

239 West 105 Street
New York, NY 10025
(212) 666-8825

5:30 - 10:30pm Sunday through Thursday
5:30 - 11:00pm Friday and Saturday

250 restaurants

St.), 585-1818, V, MC, AmEx, Entrées: $17-$24, ❹❺❻ to 59th St.

McDonald's
If you want your Big Mac on a silver platter, sit among the orchids, listen to the pianist, and super-size your fries here. Complete with a doorman, table service, and a gourmet coffee bar, this is not your ordinary fast-food joint. But you can still "get fries with that." 160 Broadway (bet. Maiden and Liberty Sts.), 385-2063, MC, AmEx, V, Diners, Entrées: $2-$6, ❶Ⓜ︎Ⓩ❷❸❹❺ to Fulton St. ♿

Mekka
People of all types are drawn to the excellent Southern and Caribbean food at this urban, hip-hop restaurant. Difficult as it is to resist, don't devour too much of the complementary cornbread, or you may find yourself incapable of walking at the end of the night, or worse yet, you won't have room for the peach cobbler which is not to be missed. 14 Avenue A (bet. Houston and 2nd Sts.), 475-8500, MC, V, AmEx, MC, Diners, D, Entrées: $14, ❻ to Second Ave. ♿

Mekong
This laid-back Vietnamese outpost in Little Italy has varied, spicy fare like lightly fried bean curd with lemongrass, green peppers, and a crowning flourish of peanut crumbs. A wonderful introduction to the cuisine and a staple for those who are already fans. 44 Prince St. (at Mulberry St.), 343-8169, MC, V, AmEx, Entrées: $8-$12, ❻ to Spring St., ❺❻❼❽ to Broadway/Lafayette St.

Merchant's, NY
The downtown branch of a trio of sleek establishments of the same name, some actually order food here to go with their Martini or Cosmopolitan; check out the downstairs sofa scene for ultimate cushiness. The appetizer and dessert menus are truly excellent. 112 Seventh Ave. (bet. 16th and 17th Sts.), 832-1551, V, MC, AmEx, D, Entrées: $10-$14, ❶❾ to 18th St. ♿

Mesa Grill
Bobby Flay's limitless imagination has bestowed upon the city a masterful array of Southwestern flavors served in a light, airy space that pulses with festivity. A New Yorker favorite, this restaurant is an eye-opener for those yet un-acquainted with the exuberant classicality of Flay's cuisine. 102 Fifth Ave. (bet. 15th and 16th Sts.), 807-7400, V, MC, AmEx, D, Entrées: $18-$28, ❶ⓃⓇ❹❺❻ to 14th St./Union Sq. ♿

Mesopatamia
This East Village newcomer is a pleasant surprise. The mustard walls and plain wood tables create an unexciting atmosphere, but the hearty Belgian portions, specialty beers, and very friendly service make you forget the unassuming interior. Be sure to try the Belgian endives wrapped in jambon and the chocolate mousse for desert. 98 Avenue B (bet. 6th and 7th Sts.), 358-1166, MC, V, D, Transmedia, Entrées: $8.75-$12.95, ❻ to Second Ave. ↩

Metisse
Ooh la la! Morningside Heights has its own French bistro. With fresh flowers. blue tealights at each table, and rich, delicious, reasonably priced food, you might blink and think you've found Paris in New York City. 239 west 105th St. (at Broadway), 666-8825, V, MC, AmEx, Entrées: $10-$14, ❶❾ to 103rd St.

Metro Diner
Unique to the world of diners, this veggie-friendly establishment offers all the standard diner fare—only fresh!—with a splash of Mediterranean dishes including a variety of salads and vegetarian plates. Grab a booth and soak in its streamlined train car decor. A great postmovie hangout. 2641 Broadway (at 100th St.), 866-0800, V, MC, AmEx, Entrées: $5.00-25.95, ❶❾ to 96th St. ♿

Mi Cocina
Mexican cuisine, West Village-style: haute, pricey, and with a generous supply of liquor. The most savory south-of-the-border dishes here may not be authentic, but it sure is chic. 57 Jane St. (at Hudson St.), 627-8273, MC, V, AmEx, Diners, Entrées: $9-$20, ❶Ⓒ❺ to 14th St. ♿

Mike's Papaya
Cheap tasty and almost healthy if you get a fruit juice to go. Hot dogs are only 50 cents and their breakfast egg on a roll is the best bargain in Morningside Heights. Open 24 hours! 2832 Broadway (at 110th St.) Cash Only, ❶❾ to 110th St.

Milon Bangladesh
Blinking Christmas lights, metallic paper dolls, and flaming jalepeños beg the attention of the hungry pedestrian from the street. It may be a cheap ploy, but it works! The inexpensive menu resembles many in the city, but the kitschy and festive atmosphere of this little secret can be found no where else. 93 First Ave., 2nd Floor (bet. 5th and 6th Sts.), 228-4896, Cash Only, Entrées: $6-10, ❻ to Second Ave. ♿

Mimi's Macaroni
This quaint Italian newcomer to the Morningside Heights restaurant scene offers delicious pastas and

---

FRESH JUICE

Mike's Papaya

50¢ all beef hot dog

2832 BROADWAY AT 110TH STREET
(212) 663-5076
open 24 hours

restaurants 251

salads that are perfect for a light lunch. Heartier Italian delights are available for dinner and wine completes the Mimi's experience.
718 Amsterdam Ave. (at 95th St.), V, MC, Entrées: $8-$12, **1****9****2****3** *to 96th St.*

Mocca Hungarian
Throw your doctor's caveats regarding cholesterol to the wind and dig into peasant staples like ghoulash and stuffed cabbage. The decor takes its cues from communist functionalism.
1588 Second Ave. (bet. 82nd and 83rd Sts.), 734-6470, Cash Only, Lunch $7, Dinner $14, **4****5****6** *to 86th St.*

Mo's Caribbean
When city life has got you down and only live Reggae, Redstripe, and jerk chicken will cure you, Mo's is the closest you can get to island life without leaving Manhattan. Tuesdays feature $2.00 Carib bottles and all the good vibes you can handle so early in the week.
1454 Second Ave. (at 76th St.), 650-0561, MC, V, **6** *to 77th St.*

Monte's
Long after the taste has slipped away, the charm of this amicable basement trattoria will remain. Patrons bring visiting grandchildren for involved conversations with the loquacious waiter. The menu spares no calorie, so go all the way and try the zabaglione served cold with strawberries.
97 MacDougal St. (at West 3rd St.), 228-9194, MC, V, AmEx, D, Diners, Entrées: $7-$13, **A****B****C****D****E****F** *to West 4th Street*

Moomba
Make an effort to get past the velvet rope and superfluous doormen, because your dinning experience will be that enjoyable.
133 Seventh Ave. South (bet. 10th and Charles Sts.), 989-1414, MC V AmEx, Average main course: $23, **1****9** *to Christopher St.* ♿

Mott Su
Capitalizing on downtown's newfound sushi fetish, this newcomer's pair of Italian-American owners nevertheless deviate from the standards: sake is served chilled in bottles, rather than warm in ceramic flasks, and you'll be hard-pressed to find tempura, chicken teriyaki, and udon noodle soups on the menu. The sushi is unusually large and stylish enough to qualify as decor.
285 Mott St. (bet. Houston and Prince Sts.), 343-8017, MC, V, AmEx, D, Diners, $2.25-$2.50 per piece, **N****R** *to Prince St.* ♿

Moustache
Not pizza, but pitzas: yummy pita bread piled with toppings. These constitute the backbone of the menu, though the salads and falafel are worth sampling. It's possible to get in and out of here for less than $10. Located at one of the Village's most peaceful intersections.
90 Bedford St. (bet. Barrow and Grove Sts.), 229-2220, Cash Only, Entrées: $6-$12, **A****B****C****D****E****F** *to West 4th St.* ♿

Mr. Broadway
New York Deli waiters are not known for their friendliness, so the excellent service here is a unique plus as you hunker down with great overstuffed sandwich in a stylish room filled with Jewish momentos at this standard-bearer of authentic New York Deli.
1372 Broadway (near 38th St.), 921-2152, AmEx, MC, V, D, Entrées: $8-$15, **1****2****3****9** *to 34th St.*

My Cousin Vinny's
Lunch crowds giddily sample the range of hot and cold options that are all over the map, including Chinese, Italian, and good ol' American. Sicilian slices go for $1.65, and there's plenty of seating upstairs.
270 Park Ave. South (bet. 21st and 22nd Sts.), 982-8253, Cash Only, Entrées: $3-$6, **6** *to 23rd St* ♿

N

Nakisaki International Restaurant
This cozy haven of Chinese-Jamaican cooking takes the finest of each cuisine and creates some of the most flavorful dishes around, like pan-fried chicken and shrimp, scallops with garlic sauce, and brown-stewed jerk pork. Take-out available.
38-89 Francis Lewis Blvd., (718) 527-7355, MC, V, AmEx, D, Entrées: $8-$15, **E****J****Z** *to Parsons/Archer Street* ♿

Nam
Vietnamese cuisine, from the folks who brought you the Lemongrass Grill. The is prompt and reliable and the outdoor terrace is pleasant in good weather.
222 Seventh Ave. (at 3rd St.), (718) 788-5036, MC, V, AmEx, D, Diners, Entrées: $8-$14, **F** *to 9th St/Seventh Ave.*

Negril Caribbean Restaurant
Reggae bass sets the rhythm for the spirited crowd which flocks here to indulge in classics like jerk chicken and goat or to imbibe at the tropically-themed, brilliantly turquoise bar where an aquarium plays backdrop to the potables. Free coffee and muffins with weekend brunch.
362 West 23rd St. (bet. Eighth and Ninth Aves.), 807-6411, MC, V, AmEx, Entrées: $8-$15, **A****C** *to 23rd St.* ♿

New Pasteur
The thirty-four-year-old owner of this successful Vietnamese noodle shop left his country on a makeshift raft with nothing but a few changes of clothing and the recipes for flavorful rice, noodles, and beef dishes, which Wall Street suits, tourists, and locals have enjoyed for the past eight years
85 Baxter St. (bet. Canal and Bayard Sts.), 608-3656, Cash Only, Entrées: $3.50-7.50, **N****R** *to Canal Street* ♿

New York Noodletown
While its uniquely savory crab dishes best explain the mobs of people, any of the roasted meat entrées are a good bet for quick, cheap eats; this spot carries cachet with those who know the ins and outs of Chinatown eats.
28 Bowery (at Pell St.), 349-0923, Cash Only, Entrées: $4-$10, **B****D****Q** *to Grand St.*

252 restaurants

Nha Trang

You won't be bowled over by the decor—there really isn't any—but this place serves up some of the best Vietnamese food around and it's cheap. You'll most likely be sharing a table with the locals who frequent the place—including and not limited to, artists, musicians, and drag queens. The service is rapid and friendly.
87 Baxter St. (bet.Walker and Bayard Sts.) 233-5948, Cash Only, Entrées:$7.75
J M N R Z *to Canal St.*

Nice Restaurant

Boisterous parties, complete with karaoke, frequently flood the second-floor banquet hall of this friendly Cantonese restaurant deep in the heart of the 'hood. Such food may be more elaborately prepared elsewhere, but the unfailingly gracious service is enough to keep patrons loyal. Stop by for dim sum in the early afternoon.
35 East Broadway (bet. Market St. and Bowery), 406-9776, AmEx, Entrées: $7-$20, **B D Q** *to Grand Street*

Niko's

Nearly always crammed to capacity, this taverna offers a range of delicacies that take cues from all over the Mediterranean, particularly Greece and Lebanon. Noteworthy are the stuffed grape leaves and the rodos yuvetsi, a lamb stew. Afterwards, choose from among the cloying array of authentic honey-drenched Greek desserts.
2161 Broadway (at 76th St.), 873-7000, V, MC, D,
AmEx, Entrées: $10-$18, **1 2 3** *to 72nd St.*

Nino's

There must be a thousand different slice joints in this city, but this is without a doubt one of the very best. In addition to making great pizza, the place looks out on Thompkins Square Park and keeps hours as late as any bar. A plain slice is always a safe bet, but the more adventuresome shouldn't miss the white pizza with fresh tomatos.
131 St. Mark's Place (at Avenue A), 979-8688, Cash Only, $1.50 per slice, **6** *to Astor Pl.*

Nobu

One of the hottest and best restaurants in the city, offering exquisite L.A.-style Japanese cuisine served in a pristinely decorated, lofty, and uncluttered space for the rich, famous, and gourmands. Reservations must be made 30 days in advance, leaving you plenty of time to eagerly anticipate the meal.
105 Hudson St. (at Franklin St.), 219-8095, 219-0500 (reservations), MC, V, AmEx, Entrées: $12-$35, **1 9** *to Franklin Street*

Noodles on 28

Putting the kitchen on display has never been more fun: watching the chef from outside as he churns out dumplings at an awe-inspiring rate beats most live entertainment these days, and a sample of his work, or any of the other standard noodle dishes, won't disappoint. Indoors, the service runs around like so many speed freaks as well.
394 Third Ave. (at 28th St.), 679-2888, MC, V, AmEx, Entrées: $5-$10, **6** *to 28th St.*

O
Odeon

After many years, this place remains one of the most stylish eateries around. Their secret seems to be maintaining atmosphere and decor that are classically stylish rather than trendy and serving excellent brassiere food for the late-night dining crowd. More suitable for making the scene with a group than an intimate dinner for two.
145 West Broadway (bet Duane and Thomas Sts.), 233-0507, MC, V, AmEx, Diners, Entrées: $15, **1 2 3 9** *to Canal St.*

Odessa

The hippest of the East Village's Eastern European diners, open 24 hours. Everything from standard diner food to potato pancakes and other regional fare finds its way onto the menu. The location makes it perfect for a food break while cruising the Avenue A bar scene, and to continue drinking you need only walk next door to their lounge, recently opened in the restaurant's pre-expansion and remodeling digs.
119 Avenue A (bet. 7th and 8th Sts.), 253-1470, MC, V, AmEx, D, Entrées: $6-$12, **F** *to Second Ave.*

Ollie's Restaurant

If there is such a thing as Chinese and diner fusion, this is it. The unbeatable location, kitty corner from Columbia's main gates, and low prices keep it packed with students.
2957 Broadway (at 116th St.) 932-3300, V, MC, AmEx, Entrées $5-$12, **1 9** *to 116th St.*

147

Restaurant 147 is known as much for its fashionable clientele as its delicious menu. The decor is subtle yet elegant, the food simple yet scrumptious. You can't go wrong ordering, but we especially recommend the chilled vegetable rolls as an appetizer. After your meal, hang out until the wee hours at the stylish bar.
147 West 15th St. .(bet. Sixth and Seventh Aves.), 929-5000, Entrées: $15-$24, **1 2 3** *to 14th St.*

Oriental Garden

Cheap decor and rude waiters only add to the charm of this tiny eatery. The food is cheap and delicious, especially the seafood. Ask for everything to be made extra-spicy, and your tongue will never forgive you.
14 Elizabeth St. (bet. Canal and Bayard Sts.), 619-0085, AmEx, MC, V, Entrées: $6-$12, **J M Z** *to Canal St.,* **B D Q** *to Grand St.*

Oznot's Dish

The decor here is something akin to an LSD-induced Arabian Nights fantasy, with technicolor mosaics and art objects everywhere. The food is Mediterranean and middle eastern and unlike anything you've ever had. Brunch is the most popular meal here and the specials are always inspired. Dinner is equally good, and allows the opportunity to tap into their extensive beer and wine list.

restaurants 253

79 Berry St. (at North 9th St.), (718) 599-6596, Cash Only, Entrées: $6-$14, **L** to Bedford St. ♿

Ozu
Though prompt seating can be a problem, this small, Japanese macrobiotic, near-organic restaurant wins points for its creative tofu, grain, noodle, tempura, and vegetable dishes. The ambitious side orders will transport you to new levels of sensual awareness, especially the three-root sesame salad with carrot, burdock root, and daikon radish.
566 Amsterdam Ave. (at 87th St.), 787-8316, V, MC, Entrées: $7-$12, Delivery from 4-9pm, **1 9** *to 86th St.* ♿

P

Pamir
Savory pilaf complements the well-executed lamb and chicken dishes, from kebabs to quabilli palaw, at this cozy uptown enclave of Afghan cuisine adorned with hand-tooled metalwork and bright Afghan rugs. Denim-clad students will feel self-conscious in the upscale atmosphere..
1437 Second Ave. (bet. 74th and 75th Sts.), 734-3791, MC, V, Entrées: $11-$16, **6** *to 77th St.* ♿

Pao!
When dining at Pao! watch motorcycles zoom by and taxis clatter up the street. Huge framed menus feature delicious Portuguese seafood dishes, but the steak, topped with garlic and spicy cream sauce is their specialty. A small bar inside.
322 Spring St. (at

Greenwich St.) 334-5464, MC, V, AmEx, Entrées: $12.95-$15.95, **E C** to Spring St. 🚇 🚲

Paradise
Test the effectiveness of vodka at this Russian restaurant/nightclub, as knocking down a shot or two or three makes sense of the nouveau riche Mafiosi-slick-haired, wannabe-guidos sporting CK One-and subpar, heavily accented renditions of "Pink Cadillac" and "Lady in Red." Included is a night of raucous dancing, the unwelcome advances of middle-aged regulars with fuzzy mustaches (of both genders), and more mediocre smoked fish than you'd expect to consume in a lifetime. Whether kitsch or just plain inebriation is your cup of chai, you can't beat this mirror-and-velvet palace for ambiance.
2814 Emments Ave. (at 29th St.), (718) 934-2283, MC, V, Dinner and dancing $22 Friday, $42 Saturday, $30 Sunday, **D Q** *to Sheepshead Bay* ♿

Park Avalon
Elegant and stylish, sink back and soak up the self-esteem of this crowded, gothic hot spot, where the pleasures in the seeing as much as in the eating. In spite of its popularity, claustrophobia is avoidable due to the spaciousness of the interior. The staff, as beautiful as everyone else inside, doesn't let it go to its head. The New American food, by the way, isn't shabby either.
225 Park Ave. South (bet. Eighth and Ninth Aves.), 533-2500, V, MC, AmEx, Entrées: $14-$20,

4 5 6 N R to Union Sq.
Park Slope Brewing Company
Best-known for its award-winning micro-brews, such as the Belgian Amber, this brewpub doubles as a slightly polished burger joint, anomalous in the strictly residential Park Slope area. Generously portioned if limited menu offerings are designed to complement the beer, all brought by an efficient, amicable waitstaff.
356 Sixth Avenue (at 5th St.), (718) 788-1756, MC, V, Entrées: $7-$10, **F** *to Seventh Ave.*

Pasty Grimaldi's
Every New Yorker claims to know the best pizzeria in the city, but Grimaldi's is the real thing. Old Brooklyn ambiance is enhanced by Sinatra and Bennett crooning as you savor crisp, thin-crust pizza, topped with fresh mozzarella and organic tomato sauce, that will satisfy even the most discriminating pizza lovers.
19 Old Fulton St. (bet. Water and Front Sts.), (718) 858-4300, Cash Only, Entrées: $10-$20, **A** *to High St.* ♿

Patria
Professionals give way to cover girls as the sky darkens and the scene heats up in the multi-tiered dining area as lights stream through the huge windows. The menu includes Latin American cuisine from countries ranging from Brazil to Mexico and comes out meticulously styled, like tamales cradled in corn husks.
250 Park Avenue South (at 20th St.), 777-6211, MC, V, AmEx, Diners, $19-$29,

6 to 23rd St. ♿
Pearl Street Diner
For cheap eats amid all the Monday-thru-Friday suits, come here for all the diner essentials. Greasy fries and burgers will please your palate, and you'll still have enough change left over for a decent tip and a subway token.
212 Pearl St. (near Maiden Lane), 344-6620, AmEx, Entrées: $2.50-$10, **2 3** *to Wall St.*

Penang Malaysian Cuisine
This lively, decked out Malaysian/New American is usually packed on weekends and reasonably so; the food is innovative and tasty, the crowd generally young and hip, and there's live music and a lounge in the bar downstairs. Try eating down there to avoid the wait upstairs.
240 Columbus Ave. (at 71st St.), 769-3988, V, MC, AmEx, Entrées: $10-15, **1 9** *to 72nd St.* 🚇

Peter Luger Steak House
Simply the superlative steak house in New York City. Not for the faint of heart (and definitely not for vegetarians) the menu is limited to steak, salmon, and lamb chops, as well as an amazing array of à la carte side-dishes. Informal given the price of a meal, a reservation on a Friday or Saturday can be weeks in the waiting. Worth the wait, worth the cost, just plain worth it!
178 Broadway (at Driggs St.), (718) 387-7400, Cash Only, Entrées: $25-$35, **L** *to Bedford Ave.* 🚇

Pietrasanta
A Hell's Kitchen neighbor-

hood secret where the chef actually comes out of the kitchen to ask how customers are enjoying their meals. For an appetizer, try the succulent scallops in a rich pesto sauce, and order the pumpkin ravioli in sweet pepper sauce as an entrée. Delish!
683 Ninth Ave. (at 47th St.), 265-9471, MC, V, AmEx, Entrées: $7.95-15.95, ❶❸❸ to 50th St.

Pig Heaven
Chinese food with a difference: tasty, spicy dumplings, and one-of-a-kind scallion pancakes. Its Upper East Side locale means it's more upscale than most, with less turnover. Patrons are mostly locals, though people from outside the neighborhood will swing by based on its good reputation.
1540 Second Ave. (bet. 80th and 81st Sts.), 744-4333, MC, V, AmEx, D, Entrées: $11-$20, ❻ to 77th St.

Pintaile's Pizza
A meal of thin-crust, scrumptious brick-oven pizza at this counter-service shop is cheaper than eating at home.
26 East 91st St. (bet. Madison and Fifth Aves.), 722-1967, MC, V, AmEx, ❹❺❻ to 86th St. 1443 York Ave. (bet. 76th and 77th Sts.), 717-4990, MC, V, AmEx, ❻ to 77th St.

Pizza Fresca
The Italian waiters' detailed recitation of the daily specials is almost as enjoyable as the meal at this gourmet, brick-oven pizza joint; toppings range from four cheeses to salmon. Their specialty is pizza, Fresca, of course.
31 East 20th St. (bet. Broadway and Park Ave.), 598-0141, MC, V, AmEx, Entrées: $9-15, ❶❸❻ to 23rd St.

Plum Tree
Upper East Siders should be thankful for their proximity to Lin Tsend's delightful vegetarian, macrobiotic restaurant. All menu items are wholesome and flavorful, and Ms. Tsend prepares each dish from scratch using only organic fruits, vegetables, grains, and herbs when possible.
1501 First Ave. (bet. 78th and 79th Sts.), 734-1412, Cash Only, Entrées: $8-$11, Free Delivery, ❻ to 77th St.

Pó
With Food Network god Mario Batalli at the wheel, no detail is overlooked in preparing singularly divine pasta dishes. The chef's status may explain the droves of older, white-collar types that pack themselves into the narrow, low-lit interior, though moderate pricing coupled with local bonhomie makes it an ideal student splurge as well.
31 Cornelia St. (bet. Bleecker and West 3rd St.), 645-2189, MC, V, AmEx, ❶❾ to Christopher St.

Puccini
This small Italian cafe owned by Israelis serves huge portions of some of the best pasta in the area for unbelievably fair prices. It's great for a date or just to taste the authentic spaghetti carbonara.
475 Columbus Ave. (bet. 82nd and 83rd Sts.), 975-9533, MC, V, AmEx, Entrées: $8-$12, ❶❾ to 79th St., ❸❿ to 81st St.

Puglia
Like Pasta? Like Elvis? Then you're in luck—spend your time at large communal tables, chugging wine with your new friends as an Italian Elvis does his magic on a little Casio keyboard in the corner. By the time you leave, you'll be arm-in-arm with half the restaurant.
189 Hester St. (bet. Mott and Mulberry Sts.), 966-6066, Cash Only, Entrées: $5-10, ❶❻❹❷❻ to Canal St.

Q

Quantum Leap
Handpicking the best in natural dishes that Mexico, Japan, and the Middle East have to offer, this healthy kitchen excels at breakfasts which include wholegrain, buckwheat, or blue-corn waffles and/or pancakes smothered with organic maple syrup. Not exactly the ascetic way, but better than bacon.
188 West 3rd St. (bet. Thompson and Sullivan Sts.), 677-8050, Entrées: $5-$10, ❶❸❻❹❸ ❻❾ to West 4th St.

Queen's Restaurant
Downtown Brooklyn's pasta of choice for local suits and shoppers; try anything on the menu since it's difficult to go wrong. Spicy, crisp pizza is available to go or for delivery.
84 Court St. (bet. Livingston and Schermerhorn), (718) 596-5954, Cash Only, Entrées: $7- $25, ❹❻❸ to Hoyt/Schermerhorn Sts.

R

Radio Mexico
When the Wall Street suits want to loosen their ties, shoot some pool, and chug some Coronas, they come here. Complete with a juke box blasting all the country you could ever want, Tex-Mex food is served in abundant portions.
259 Front St. (at Dover s St.), 791-5416, AmEx, MC, V, Entrées: $4-$9, ❶❻❷❷❸❹ to Fulton St.

Redeye Grill
Vibrant Southern Californian fare is complemented by the warm mosaic tiled architecture of the main dining room, with its 28-foot-high floor-to-ceiling windows and columns wrapped in hand-painted canvas murals. From 11pm-3am, Tuesdays through Saturdays, "Jazz Into the Wee Hours of the Night" is no cover, no minimum. Pass over the restaurant's signature dish, dancing shrimp, in favor of the lobster maki with jalapeño-smoked salmon and sturgeon caviar.
888 Seventh Ave. (at 56th St.), 541-9000, MC, V, AmEx, D, Entrées: $11.50-$29, ❹❺❻ to 59th St.

Regal Restaurant
A bit too earnest to fall into the diner category, this low-key, family-run restaurant seems somewhat out of place in its urban environs, but what it lacks in atmosphere is offset by unbelievable prices for high-quality home-cooked food.
250 Eighth Ave., 243-0980, Cash Only, Entrées: $5-$14, ❹❸ to 23rd St.

restaurants 255

Restaurant Delphi
Large portions of Greek home cooking are served by the same people who opened the place twenty-five years ago. Locals flood the place, but the wait is worth it—especially for the calamari stew.
109 West Broadway (at Reade St.), 227-6322, AmEx, V, MC, Entrées: $5-$14, ❶❷❸❾ *to Chambers St.*

Rialto
First-time visitors are consistently wowed; the understated SoHo ambiance and first-rate American food entice stunning neighborhood folks time and again. A chatty bunch crowds around the bar, and an ambient glow settles on the curved red banquettes where others feast on the Chef's Tasting Menu (a 3-, 5-, or 8-course meal), which includes a potato leek soup infused with roasted garlic, served in a demitasse cup. The staff shuffles back and forth to the magnificent garden out back.
265 Elizabeth St. (bet. Houston and Prince Sts.), 334-7900, MC, V, AmEx, Transmedia, Entrées: $8-$18, ❻❶❹❺❻ *to Prince St.* ♿

Rib Shack
Owned by local businessman Po' Freddy, the venue's offerings of sweet potato pie, collard greens, and fried chicken will move the hearts of devoted soul food lovers. The employees are so friendly that they regularly garner tips, a wow considering that customers are only allowed to order take-out.
157-06 Linden Blvd (bet. Sutphin and Guy Brewer),

(718) 659-7000, Cash Only, Entrées: $6-$8, ❸ *to Sutphin/Archer Sts.* ♿

Rice
Take-out with a twist. The menu stakes everything on the grain which inspires the restaurant's name, offering six different varieties a number of South and Southeast Asian-inspired toppings. Minimalist bar stools and pulsing trance music transform the fast-food experience into a premillennium cultural interlude.
227 Mott St. (bet. Prince and Spring Sts.), 226-5775, Cash Only, Rice $4-$8, ❶❷ *to Prince St.* ♿

Richard's Place
Something about church just makes you hungry sometimes. Forget all you learned about gluttony and gorge yourself at Richard's scrumptious all-you-can-eat Sunday brunch. Prices leave enough for tithings.
200-05 Linden Blvd. (bet. Francis Lewis and Farmers Blvd.), St. Albans, (718) 723-0041 MC, V, Entrées: $8-$12, ❸ *to Parsons/Archer* ♿

Rikyu
The freedom to choose can be mind-boggling for early-bird diners taking advantage of the $9.95 prix fixe, with 17 dinner options. You can't go wrong with remarkably fresh sushi or any combination involving tempura, teriyaki, or cooked fish.
210 Columbus Ave. (bet. 69th and 70th Sts.), 799-7847, MC, V, AmEx, Entrées: $10-$17, ❶❷❸❾ *to 72nd St.*

Riss Diner
A gold-mine of grease with which to sate those after-hours munchies. Free delivery and 24-hour status earn it its diner stripes.
242 Eighth Ave. (bet. 22nd and 23rd Sts.), 627-2933, Entrées: $7-$14, Cash Only, ❶❸ *to 23rd St.*

Rock n' Roll Noodle House
Aside from it's name, this eatery has little to offer besides amusingly named dishes. Try anything sautéed in "Rock n' Roll wonderful taste hot spicy sauce." Basic appetizers are generally a safe bet, as are the noodle selections.
19 Murray St., 227-9794, AmEx, MC, V, Entrées: $4-$13, ❶❾ *to Chambers St.*

Rocky's Italian Restaurant
You'll feel like you're eating in Mama's kitchen when you step through the screen door of this tiny 20-seat room. There's only one guy back there cooking up pasta that might be even better than Mama's. If you're going for the true Little Italy experience, this is the place to have it.
45 Spring St. (at Mulberry St.) 274-0936, MC, V, AmEx, D, Discover, Entrées: $9.95-$14.95, ❻ *to Spring St.*

Rosa Mexicano
Well-heeled clientele sips pomegranate margaritas at the crowded bar while waiting for a taste of well ex-ecuted classics; guacamole is prepared tableside and desserts like the *tamal et cazuela dulce*, a sweetish, warm cornmeal swirled with a black sauce made from corn fungus is their specialty.
1063 First Ave. (bet. 57th and 58th Sts.), 753-7407, MC, V, AmEx, D, Diners, Entrées: $17-$26, ❻❹❺❻ *to 59th St/Lexington Ave.*

Royal Canadian Pancake House
Ever get a craving for a chocolate chip pancake, or one with lingonberries, boysenberries, or raspberries? How about going to any one of their three locations as fast as you can because the pancakes are out of this world! There's always a wait on the weekends and a single order is enough for two people, though it will cost you $5 extra to share.
2286 Broadway (near 83rd St.), 873-6052, V, MC, AmEx, Entrées: $8-$12, ❶❾ *to 86th St.* ♿

Royal Coach Diner
One of many well established around-the-way eateries. A weekend tradition for neighborhood residents; you can fill your stomach and spare your pockets, particularly with breakfast items. "Can't go wrong with the pancakes," according to one customer.
3260 Boston Road (at Gun Hill), (718) 653-1716, MC, AmEx, D, V, Entrées: $4-$15, ❺ *to Gun Hill Road.*

S

Saigon Grill
One of the best and best-priced Vietnamese restaurants in the city, and a favorite of Upper West Siders. Not much elbow room, go early to avoid the crowds, but you'll be craving the fresh summer rolls for days afterward.
2381 Broadway (at 87th St.), 875-9072, V, MC, AmEx, D, Entrées: $7-$13, ❶❾ *to 86th St.* ♿

256 restaurants

Sam Chinita's
The quintessential pit stop: chilled beer and hearty portions of Chinese-Cuban fusion fare served til late for prices that are hard to beat on the Eighth Avenue promenade.
176 Eighth Ave. (at 19th St.), 741-0240, Cash Only, Entrées: $5-$15, ❶❷ *to 23rd St.*

Samalita's Tortilla Factory
Bargain Tex-Mex basics here toe the "actually good for you" line. The mein is easy-going, but the Factory has difficulty accommodating its own popularity—both seating and your waiter's attention will be hard to come by.
1429 Third Ave. (bet 80th and 81st Sts.), 888-8100, MC, V, AmEx, ❹❺❻ *to 77th St.*

Sammy's Noodle Shop and Grill
Hurried urbanites took their time in warming up to this noodle shop's flavorful fare, though now it's an indispensable lunch fixture, with an annexed bakery serving fresh desserts. Try the roast meat soups and dumplings.
453 Avenue of the Americas, (bet. 10th and 11th Sts.), 925-6688, MC, V, AmEx, D, ❶❷❸ ❷❸❾ *to 14th St.*

Sammy's Roumanian
This bustling and lively restaurant hosts rich meals and a loud Yiddish band. Locals and other New Yorkers, none of whom are dieting, frequent the place. Red meat is a featured menu item. Chopped liver, and lots o' vodka are popular as well.
157 Chrystie St. (at Delancey St.), 673-0330, Average Entrée: $20, ❻❼❽ *to Grand St.,* ❻ *to Delancey St.*

Santa Fe Grill
The clientele at this Park Slope Mexican isn't the only thing that's upwardly mobile: the food here is excellent (especially the chimichangas) and the waitstaff is friendly, fun, and fast. Also stop by for multicolored nachos, above-average salsa, and drinks at the busy bar.
60 Seventh Ave., (718) 636-0279, V, MC, AmEx, D, Entrées: $10-16, ❷❸ *to 7th Ave.*

Screening Room Restaurant
Dinner and a movie is a classic date; find them both under one roof. Forgo popcorn for the house specialties like the pan-fried baby artichoke appetizer, cedar-planked salmon, and lemon icebox cake; the truly extravagant will splurge on one of the specialty cocktails. A less expensive lounge menu is available and the $30 prix fixe includes a three-course meal and movie admission.
54 Varick St. (at Canal St.), 334-2100, MC, V, AmEx, Diners, D, Entrées: $16-$23, ❶❾ *to Canal St.*

Second Avenue Deli
Hit this legendary deli for the matzoh balls, blintzes, and other traditional dishes that beat your Gramma's. Recent renovations have dispelled some of the old-country flair which made the Deli a kosher home away from home, but completely unmanageable sandwiches and the miniature museum honoring stars of the Yiddish theater with a "walk of fame" still remain.
156 Second Ave. (at 10th St.), 677-0606, AmEx, Entrées: $6-$16, ❻ *to First or Third Ave.*

Serendipity
If you ever wondered where all the sexual repression of Victorian England went, this restaurant sums it up in one word: decor. Frill upon frill of lace, cascading velvets, and intricate porcelain simulate the feeling of inhabiting a dollhouse. Luckily, the menu avoids the pitfalls of British cuisine, favoring countrified American fare like shepherd's pie and barbecue chicken casserole. Polish it all off with one of the decadently enormous desserts like frozen hot chocolate.
225 East 60th St. (bet. Second and Third Aves.), 838-3531, MC, V, AmEx, Diners, D, Transmedia, ❹❺❻ *to 59th St.*

Shun Lee Palace
Unlike its sister restaurants, Shun Lee and Shun Lee Cafe, on the West Side, this upscale version is rather low on the tofu quotient. Still, vegetarians have their choice of a few dishes, and the decor, with its painted wood walls and ceiling is quite nice.
155 East 55th St. (bet. Lexington and Third Aves.), 371-8844, V, MC, AmEx, D, Entrées: $13-$29, ❻❼❽ *to 51st St.*

Shun Lee
Quite possibly New York's finest upscale Chinese, spitting distance from Lincoln Center; its glamour is defined by old-school, bejeweled Upper West Side matrons and their wizened escorts, complemented by excessive mirrors and a tiered dining floor. Exquisite dishes are served family-style in silver bowls; the chicken is tender and savory. Complement that with a heated towelette proffered by the white-suited waitstaff.
43 West 65th St. (bet. Central Park West and Columbus Ave.), 595-8895, MC, V, AmEx, D, Diners, Entrées: $12-$20, ❶❾ *to 66th St./Lincoln Center*

Silver Spoon
Greasy spoon might be more like it, but everyone loves a diner, and the Spoon has the typically all-encompassing menu of that ilk of eatery. The place bustles for brunch on weekends and features outdoor seating in warm weather, if you don't mind the Flatbush Avenue fumes. Good for a quick, cheap bite.
218 Flatbush Ave. (bet. Bergen and Dean Sts.), (718) 622-1192, V, MC, AmEx, D, Entrées: $3-$10, ❷❸ *to Bergen St.*

Sister's Cuisine
Forget Sylvia's; you won't find tour buses here. Authentic eats draw a local crowd of those who know their stuff and where the deals are.
1931 Madison Ave. (at 124th St.), 410-3000, MC, V, Entrées: $6-$7, ❹❺❻ *to 125th St.*

Sloppy Louie's
Though the waterfront

restaurants 257

Sophia's BISTRO

Pasta • Panini • Salad • Desserts

998 Amsterdam Avenue (between 109th & 110th)

212.662.8822

HOURS:
Open 24 hours
Saturday & Sunday Brunch
10am – 3pm

Fast, Free, Delivery ($7.50 minimum)
Catering available Inquire about group rates

---

decor is reminiscent of a tiled bathroom, Wall Streeters hungry for king-sized portions of fresh fish don't seem to mind at this old-school favorite, family-run for sixty-five years. *92 South St. (bet. Fulton and John Sts.), 509-9694, MC, V, AmEx, Entrées: $13-$26, ❷❸❹❺ to Fulton St.* ♿

Smiler's Delicatessen Store

A colossal, cross-cultural salad bar awaits the hungry. Choose from roast beef, fried chicken, dim sum, fruits, and vegetables, all at $5 a pound. Not your style? Then try the pizzeria, deli, bakery, or juice bar. *49 Broadway (bet. Exchange and Morris Sts.), 425-5000, Cash Only, Entrées: $3-$6, ❹❺ to Bowling Green.*

Sophia's Bistro

Downtown style has been creeping into the local neighborhood during the last year. This little bistro leads the onslaught, offering the only hip, late-night dining in the area. Pale yellow and red brick, flickering candlelight, and wine-colored drapery create a laid-back, romantic atmosphere. *998 Amsterdam Ave. (bet. 109th and 110th Sts.), 662-8822, MC, V, AmEx, Entrées: $6-$10, ❶❾ to 110th St.* ♿

Sosa Borella

A favorite lunch stop for the crews and stars of the area's film shoots as well as neighborhood residents. Sandwiches, salads and soups that mix simple ingredients into exquisite combinations. An airy dining area provides the perfect respite from the bustle of more heavily traversed areas of TriBeCa. *460 Greenwhich St (3 blks south of Canal St.), 431-5093, MC, V, AmEx, Entrées: $8-$10, ❶❾ to Canal St.*

Souen

Downtown New Yorkers may delight in their manufactured indulgences, but this unassuming, primarily macrobiotic restaurant has been helping them get in touch with their earthier side for twenty years. The Japanese-influenced menu specializes in dishes featuring tempeh, seitan, and organic vegetables, and the sugar-free futomaki and tempeh croquettes are noteworthy. *28 East 13th St. (bet. University and Fifth Ave.), 627-7150, V, MC, D,* Entrées: $8-$15, ❶❷❹❺❻ to Union Sq.

Soup Kitchen

While Seinfeld fanatics are bemoaning the end of an era, one remnant lives on: the lines at this pop-culture landmark are unreal at lunch time, but have you noticed how smoothly it moves along? Patrons have made up their minds what to order by the time they reach the counter of this famous take-out. Otherwise it's "No soup for you!" *259-A West 55th St. (bet. Eighth Ave. and Broadway), 757-7730, Cash Only, Entrées: $6.50-$8, ❶❷ to 57th St. or ❶❷❸❹❾ to Columbus Circle*

Spring Street Natural

A twenty-five year veteran of the area' steady gentrification, this spacious, high-ceilinged restaurant was serving savory healthy dishes long before organic and unprocessed foods could command higher prices. Despite such foresight, it remains unpretentious, with some options for carnivores thrown in. The waitstaff is so nice you want to take them home. *62 Spring St. (at Lafayette St.), 966-0290, V, MC, ❶❷ to Prince St.*

Standard Notions

Bountiful cheap sides, like garlic mashed potatoes, save mediocre entrées: at this earnest Ludlow Street neophyte. Nightfall occasions the addition of votives to the back garden, and large picture windows flanking the front door lend the interi- or an airy, spacious feel. Service is charmingly eccentric, with none of the expected pretension, and everything comes at a price unusually low for such calculated ambiance. *161 Ludlow St. (at Stanton St.), 473-3535, MC, V, AmEx, Entrées: $6-$12.50, F to Second Ave.* ♿

Step Mama's

Located across the street from Mama's Food Shop, this delightful little take-out restaurant will prepare mouth-watering creations right before your very eyes. Check the specials board, but don't miss the veggie burgers with hand-cut fries or the homemade soups. Yum! *199 East 3rd St. (at Ave. B), 228-2663, Cash Only, ❻ to Second Ave.*

Strictly Roots

Words on a wall-hanging voice the establishment's proud motto: "We Serve Nothing That Crawls, Walks, Swims, or Flies." The nonexistent ambiance is irrelevant, customers devote themselves to indulging in veggie-plate permutations. For the best deal, order from the 4-12 dish combinations. *2058 A. C. Powell, Jr. Blvd. (at 124th St.), 866-1600, Cash only, Entrées: $5.45 - $10.30, ❶❷❸❹❷❸ to 125th St.,* 🚲

Sun Garden

This elegant yet casual lounge and restaurant overlooks the hustle and bustle of 42nd Street. Sip a coctail and have one of their perfect appetizers, lean back in your chair and remember why you love New York. *Grand Hyatt Hotel; Park Ave (at Grand Cental*

Station) 850-5997, V, MC, AmEx, D, Entrées: $13-$19, ④⑤⑥Ⓢ⑦ to Grand Cetnral Station.

Symposium
Hidden away in a side-Street basement, this Hellenic outpost way uptown serves reliable taverna fare like classic Greek salads drenched in olive oil and buttery spanikopita (spinach-filled pies), to patrons seated at long, wooden tables. Beware the curiosity of the resident cat, a quirk that's very Greek, though hardly in line with New York's health codes. 544 West 113th St. (bet. Broadway and Amsterdam Ave), 865-1011, MC, V, AmEx, Entrées: $7-$16, ①⑨ to 110th St.

Szechuan Empire
Free-flowing wine after 3pm is the selling point here. Local businessmen swing by for generously proportioned lunches; families and couples are the standard crowd at dinner. 117 Court St. (at State St.), (718) 858-8098, AmEx, Entrées: $4.50-$10, ②③④⑤ to Borough Hall

T

Tartine
Situated at one of the West Village's most bucolic intersections, there's nothing more pleasant on a Sunday morning than brunch with the sun shining through the floor to-ceiling windows and birds chirping. The menu is standard and portions are hardly generous, but the staff has orange juice on the table by the time patrons sit down. Alas, by noon the wait outside is 45 minutes, but here's a tip: they actually open at 10:00am, not the posted 10:30. 253 West 11th St. (at West 4th St.), 229-2611, Cash Only, Entrées: $8-$12, ⒶⒷⒸⒹⒺⒻⓆ to West 4th St.

Tavern on Jane
This tavern serves much more than pub food, but at pub food prices. While the fish and chips are a reliable delight, customers go crazy for the grilled leg-of-lamb with sour cherry sauce, potatoes o'gratin and garlic spinach, and the Moroccan tuna, served with saffron, lemon and garlic cous cous, and wilted watercress gets rave reviews. The atmosphere is cozy and inviting; regulars are bound to strike up a friendly conversation over a pint of beer. Simply put: you know a place is great when the staff hangs out there on their nights off. 31 Eighth Ave. (Corner of Jane St.), 675-2526, MC, V, AmEx, D, Entrées: $7-$13, ⒶⒸⒺ to 14th St. ♿

Tavern on the Green
Only the well-connected score the best seats, but the crystal chandeliers and tranquil setting are enjoyable from any area of this legendary Central Park outpost. The oysters and steak, along with a mind-boggling wine list, help to solidify the Tavern's reputation as one of New York's most prestigious restaurants; in winter, twinkling lights on the surrounding trees evoke the picturesque New York of Woody Allen's paeans. Central Park West (at 67th St.), 873-3200, MC, V, AmEx, Entrées: $13-$25, ⒷⒸ to 72nd St.

Terrace
The exquisite view of upper Manhattan from this upsale dining room may finally convince your parents that living next to Harlem isn't so bad, or it may impress your date by revealing your uncanny ability to find romance in the most unexpected places. After trying the house risotto or grilled salmon, visit the rooftop garden. The open air and a much-needed cocktail will help you recuperate from the bill. 400 West 119th St. (bet. Amsterdam Ave. and Morningside Dr.), 666-9490, MC, V, AmEx, Diners, D, Entrées: $25-$33, ①⑨ to 116th St.

Tevere '84
Elegantly presented upscale American cuisine will impress even the most hardened kvetch. Cozy dining and numerous waiters at your beck and call make this place a great date spot. 155 East 84th St. (bet. Third and Lexington Aves.), 744-0210, AmEx, Entrées: $15-$25, ④⑤⑥ to 86th St.

Tibet Shambala
An uptown outpost of authentic Tibetan cuisine. Sunshine-colored walls, the amiable and attentive waitstaff, and a hot cup of bocha—traditional monk's tea with salt, milk, and butter—transport you from the grit and grime of Amsterdam Avenue to the halcyon Himalayas for a breath of fresh air. The half-vegetarian menu relies primarily on dumplings and Indian-style starch medleys. 488 Amsterdam Ave. (bet. 83rd and 84th Sts.), 721-1270, MC, V, Entrées: $5.50-$9, ①⑨ to 86th St.

Tiengarden
Pause to calm your cholesterol levels at this vegan kitchen, located among the salami-oriented delis of Houston and Delancey. Flavorful Chinese concoctions like sweet and sour soy nuggets and sautéed bok choy, juro, and shiitake in ginger sauce ensure that any concessions to health won't compromise taste. 170 Allen St. (at East Houston St.), 388-1364, Cash Only, $4-$8, Ⓕ to Second Ave.

Time Out
Not your average pizzeria. The nearby Yeshiva community enjoys Israeli salads, falafel, knishes, and kosher slices with a superbly crisp crust. One-of-a-kind fare. 2549 Amsterdam Ave. (at 185th St.), 923-1180, Cash Only, Ⓐ to 181st St.

Tito Puente's
Forty-five years ago, a young jazz percussionist from Spanish Harlem rocked the Palladium nightly with his infectious mambo; on City Island, his spirit lives on. Live local talent pumps out Latin Jazz on Thursday and Friday nights, and Tito himself has been known to take the stage. Like at most theme restaurants, the decor impresses more than the actual food: check out the conga barstools, or see how many jazz greats you can name on the mural

restaurants 259

by Sergio.
64 City Island Ave. (bet. Horton and Buckley Sts.), (718) 885-3200, MC, V, AmEx, Diners, Entrées: $10-$40, ❻ *to Pelham Bay* ♿

Tom's Restaurant
"I came, I sat, I wrote" reads a note from Suzanne Vega on the wall of this venerable luncheonette, verifying that it is this Prospect Heights favorite, not Tom's on 112th Street in Manhattan, immortalized in Vega's "Tom's Diner." Worthy of immortality, Tom's is a charmer, founded in 1936 with prototypical Brooklyn fare, great egg creams, and terrific service. Closes at 4pm. *728 Washington Ave. (at Sterling Pl.), (718)636-9738, Cash Only, Entrées: $3-$12,* ❷❸ *to Eastern Parkway,* 🚲

Tom's
Once you push through the occasional crowd from a Kramer's Reality tour (the southern façade serves as a cutaway shot in Seinfeld), you'll be surprised to see what the fuss is all about. Low prices, huge platters, late hours, and thick "Broadway" shakes keep kids comin' back to this greasy spoon. *2880 Broadway (at 112th St), 864-6137, Cash Only, Entrées: $3-$10,* ❶❾ *to 110th St.*

Tomoe Sushi
Rare deviations from the standard sushi line-up such as cockle, abalone, and sweet shrimp are the superstars of a menu which boasts over 50 types of sushi; downtown trendsetters have latched on to the gourmet innovations, so expect a line out the door. *172 Thomspon St. (bet. Bleecker and Houston), 777-9346, AmEx, $1.75-$3.75 per piece,* ❹❺❻❼❽❾ *to West 4th St.* ♿

Tonic
Natural light pours in through the skylights of this cavernous space, as patrons feast on cheap, eclectic cafe fare. A former Lower East Side kosher winery, Tonic has a performance space in back, encircled in red velvet, featuring jazz and comedy acts; classic Hollywood films are played on Monday nights, and down stairs is a hair salon painted various shades of green. Most endearing feature is the downstairs cocktail lounge with circular booths built within 2,500-gallon hard-wood wine casks. *107 Norfolk St. (bet. Delancy and Rivington Sts.), 358-7503, Cash Only, Average Entrée: $5,* ❻ *to Delancy St.* ♿ 🍴 🚲

Torch
This supper club is the first elegant eatery to have touched down on bar-laden Ludlow Street. Delight in the French, southern infusion cuisine and nightly torch performances, or linger in the lounge area with a cocktail and smoke in hand. *137 Ludlow St. (bet. Rivington and Stanton Sts.), 228-5151, MC, V, AmEx, Entrées: $8-$19,* ❻ *to Delancy St.* ♿ 🍴

Torre Di Pisa
True to its namesake, everything's a little out of whack here. The dazzling decor makes one visit fun, but only the most tolerant become regulars. *19 West 44th St. (bet. Fifth and Sixth Aves.), 398-4400, MC, V, AmEx, Entrées: $15-$29,* ❽❹❻❼ *to 42nd St.*

Tout Va Bien
A tasty $20 prix-fixe dinner menu is one reason to choose this homey bistro from among the many theater-district establishments. Typically French; steak frites, coq au vin, crème brûlée. The proprietors are welcoming and attentive. You'll leave with both belly and wallet full. *311 West 51st St. (between Eighth and Ninth Aves.), 974-9051, V, MC, AmEx, D, Entrées: $10-$14,* ❻❺ *to 50th St.* 🍴

Trattoria dell'Arte
Tons of well-heeled Manhattanites dine here on their way to a show, but the decor is the biggest celebrity at his huge modern Italian restaurant opposite Carnegie Hall: busts of famous noses, enormous paintings of close-up body parts, and electric-colored walls make the space happening. This chic spot also boasts polished service, a well-heeled clientele, and the tastiest bread in New York City. *900 Seventh Ave. (bet. 56th and 57th Sts.), 245-9800, MC, V, AmEx, D, Entrées: $17-$25,* ❶❷❸❹❾ *to Columbus Circle* ♿

Tribeca Grill
This flagship of the DeNiro restaurant mini-empire is a haven for those who like to enjoy a little celebrity watching with their meal. Movie industry big shots from the nearby TriBeCa Film Center can be found sharing the spacious, dark wood and brick dining room with plenty of other notables and, of course, some commoners all there to enjoy New American cuisine delicious enough to distract you from your gape-eyed staring. *375 Greenwich St. (at Franklin St.), 941-3900, MC, V, AmEx, Entrées: $18-$28,* ❶❾ *to Franklin St.* ♿

Triple Eight Palace
After taking the escalator to the threshold of this Hong Kong extravaganza, you understand how they derived the "palace" part of the name. The multi-roomed restaurant assumes the air of a circus, what with the families chattering over fried and steamed noodles, shrieking toddlers playing chicken with rolling dim sum carts, and tables of heated woks threatening diners with third-degree burns. The dumplings, buns, and shellfish are excellent. *88 East Broadway (under the Manhattan Bridge), 941-8886, MC, V, AmEx, D, Diners, Entrées: $8,* ❽❷❻ *to Grand St.* ♿

Trois Jean
Decorative high-quality French cuisine, showcasing dishes like rabbit, duck, leeks, and tiny little salads on which the chef's lackey spent five minutes positioning the greens. Businessmen on expense accounts linger over aperitifs and appetizers and sweet talk clients for what seems like hours before their entrées: arrive. Students should dress up. *154 East 79th St. (bet.*

Lexington and Third Aves.), 988-4858, Cash Only, Entrées: $12-$24, ❻ to 77th St.

Trumpet's Cigar Room

The first cigar room in Manhattan, this restaurant/lounge will make you feel like one of Frank Sinatra's pals. With an excellent ventilation system and top shelf liquors, live music on the weekends and an attentive waitstaff, this is what New York in the 40's must have been like. A big steak, caviar, a fine cigar, Ahh! The good life!
The Grand Hyatt Hotel; Park Ave., (at Grand Central Station), 850-5999, MC, V, AmEx, D, Transmedia, Cigars:$12-$35, Entrées: $26-$34, ❹❺❻❼ to Grand Central Station

Tsampa

While it may not have the locomotive force of Beastie Boy Adam Yauch's Free Tibet concerts when it comes to raising mainstream awareness for the North Asian country's political plight, this hospitable newcomer is certainly doing is humble part. Four Tibetan sisters serve up flavorful Tibetan cooking to a loyal crowd of local converts.
9th St. (at Third Ave.), 614-3226, $9-$16, MC, V, AmEx, D, Diners, ❻❼ to 8th St.

Tsunami

Flotillas of rainbow-colored sushi drifting by patrons seated along the miniature canal built into the countertop. That's the only real novelty at this two-storied, neon-lit pit stop; stick with the cheap appetizers and forego the sushi.
70 West 3rd St. (bet. LaGuardia and Thompson Sts.), 475-7770, MC, V, AmEx, D, $1.50-$3.25 per piece, ❶❷❸❹❺❻❼ to West 4th St.

Turkish Kitchen

Turkish music brings to mind the minarets of Istanbul silhouetted across the Golden Horn, and shockingly red wallpaper coupled with a laundry list of kebabs strives to maintain exotic authenticity. Don't be afraid to experiment; just about anything with lamb is good.
386 Third Ave., 679-1810, MC, V, AmEx, Entrées: $10-$18, ❻ to Second Avenue

Tutta Pasta

The Brooklyn branch of the popular chain. Reserve in advance on weekend nights. Lots of business types show up after work, familes are drawn by Americanized Italian cuisine the kids will eat, and students gravitate toward the cheap house wines.
160 Seventh Ave. (bet. 1st and Garfield Sts.), (718) 788-9500, MC, V, Entrées: $7-$12, ❻❼ to Seventh Ave.

Twigs Bar and Restaurant

Straightforward Italian standards at reasonable prices attract a diverse neighborhood crowd of families and young couples, gay and straight. Steer clear on Mondays unless you feel comfortable next to the buff post-gym crowd flashing their gym membership cards for half-priced entrées.
196 Eighth Ave. (at 20th St.), 633-6735, MC, V, AmEx, Entrées: $9-$14, ❶❸❻❼ to 14th St.

Two Boots

Be sure to order a soda, since pies from this Cajun Pizzeria are made with a spicy sauce that will have you draining your water glass in record time. Topping choices include standards like pepperoni and mushrooms alongside unconventional options like artichokes, andouille sausage, and crayfish. places are colorful, noisy, and kid-friendly, so come ready for casual and festive dining fun.
37 Avenue A (bet. 2nd and 3rd Sts.), 505-2276, MC, V, AmEx, Entrees $8-$15, Slices around $2, ❻ to Second Ave.

Also at:

75 Greenwich St., 633-9096, MC, V, AmEx, ❶❾ to 14th St.

Two Steps Down

While the crew downstairs feasts on jerk chicken and shrimp stuffed with crabmeat, the livelier venture upstairs, where a full bar and occasional live entertainment create a social late-night setting. A basket of fried fish or cajun fries holds over the locals, who really just come to hang out.
240 DeKalb Avenue (bet. Vanderbilt and Cleremont Aves.), 718-399-2020, MC, V, AmEx, Entrées: $13-17, ❶ to Clinton/Washington Aves.

Two Two Two

Restaraunteur Frank Valenza is revolutionizing gourmet with renditions of New American cuisine

---

V&T

Pizzeria & Restaurant

Italian Food at Its Best

FULL MENU
PRIVATE PARTY ROOM

WE DELIVER

1024 Amsterdam

(between 110-111th Sts.)

OPEN 7 DAYS

663-1708
666-8051

restaurants 261

with European touches like Russian Beluga caviar, French duck and goose foie gras, char-grilled prime dry-aged rib steak drenched in red wine sauce and adorned with summer truffles. You may have to waddle back onto the sidewalk.
222 West 79th St. (bet. Broadway and Ambrosia), 799-0400, MC, V, AmEx, D, Diners, Entrées: $23-$49, ❶❾ *to 79th St.* ♿

U

U.S.A. Diner, Inc.
Everyone from local politicians to high school sweethearts finds a suitable dish here, since menu offerings range from chicken fingers to lobster. The linguini with chicken, shrimp, and scallops is especially tasty. Since the diner is open 24 hours, this place is a haven for club hoppers.
243-03 Merrick Blvd., (718) 949-7793, MC, V, AmEx, D, Diners, Entrées: $6-$25 ❺ *to Parson Cntr. then 5 Rosedale bus* ♿

Umberto's Clam House
Way back in 1973, mobster Joey "Crazy" Gallo had his last meal here before getting offed by his "pals." Since then, this place has become a relatively safe haven for hungry crowds in search of large plates of good pasta and seafood. Don't miss the fried calamari.
129 Mulberry St. (at Hester St.), 431-7545, AmEx Only, Entrées: $9-$15, ❶❶❶❶❶❶ *to Canal St.*

Uncle Nick's Greek Cuisine
Serving enormous kebobs, salads brimming with stuffed grape leaves and olives, and huge wedges of flaming saganaki cheese, Uncle Nick's Greek Cuisine won't leave you hungry. The bustling atmosphere, attentive waitstaff, and speedy service make this restaurant perfect for pre-theater dining.
747 Ninth Ave. (bet. 50th and 51st Sts.), 245-7992, MC, V, AmEx, D Entrées: $9-15 ❶❶❶ *to 50th St.* ♿

Uncle Vanya
Delicious, inexpensive, authentic—what more could you possibly want? To top it off, the vodka flows freely, the food is hardy (the Russian dumplings are out of this world!), and there's often live music, a pleasant folk singer, although incomprehensible to non-russo-phones. In regard to that last feature, this is a good place to practice your budding language skills: the staff and virtually the clientele are for real.
315 West 54th St. (bet. Eighth and Ninth Aves.), 262-0542, Cash Only, Entrées: $8-$12, ❶❶ *to 50th St.*

Under the Stairs
This bar/restaurant has been around for as long as anyone in the neighborhood can remember, and they still pack in for happy hour. Come for the lively crowd, the loud jazz, and Wednesday's bargain shrimp night.
688 Columbus Ave. (bet. 92nd and 93rd Sts.), 663-3103, MC, V, AmEx, Entrées: $10-$13, ❶❷ ❷❸ *to 96th St.* ♿

V

V and T Pizzeria and Restaurant
Pair a glass of cheap house red with one of the great, classic New York pies at a neighborhood mainstay that's hosted many a kiddie birthday party at its red and white checked tables. The only real sit-down pizza around; avoid the entrées. Sorry, no slices.
1024 Amsterdam Ave. (bet. 110th and 111th Sts.), 663-1708, MC, V, AmEx, Diners, Entrées: $3-$11, ❶❾ *to 110th St.* ♿

Vegetarian Dim Sum House
No need to suppress those 3am dim sum cravings with this primarily vegetarian outpost offering buns around the clock. Fried radish cakes and lotus-wrapped sticky rice stand on their own merits, even without the meat; no Hong Kong-style carts here-items are ordered individually from a menu and served steaming from the kitchen.
24 Pell St. (bet. Mott St. and Bowery), 577-7176, Cash Only, Dim Sum: $2-$3.75, ❶❶ *to Canal St.* ♿

Veniero's
Folks crowding into this ever-popular bakery, known for serving up Italian pastry par excellence, are far from the average East Village breed. The take-out line always requires a number, though seating in th area in back isn't too much of a hassle. Strawberry shortcake here is divine.
342 East 11th St. (at First Ave), 674-7264, MC, V, AmEx, D, ❶❶❶❶❶❶ *to Union Sq.* ♿

Veselka
Populated by a healthy mix of elderly immigrants, leisurely locals, and cogitating coffeehouse specimens, this is one of the last vestiges of Ukrainian culture in the 'hood; tasty kielbasa, pierogi, and kasha demonstrate its equally strong commitment to its roots. The sweet table bread is a meal in itself.
144 Second Ave. (at 9th St.), 228-9682, MC, V, AmEx, D, Diners, Entrées: $7-$9, ❻ *to Astor Pl.*

Viand
Greek banter from the cooks sounds out over the chatter of this hectic luncheonette on the border of Midtown. Breakfast comes for the price of the Sunday *Times*, though the turkey sandwiches and thick egg creams are what the suits who crowd the narrow take-out space would stake their portfolios on.
673 Madison Ave. (bet. 61st and 62nd Sts.), 751-6622, Cash Only, Entrées: $5-$10, ❶❻ *to Lexington Ave.,* ❹❺❻ *to 59th St.*

Viceroy
Come to this trendy spot for "see-food"—Chelsea's bold and beautiful are on display from the inside or out, with floor to ceiling windows providing a free peek. Viceroy features some great dishes (and the food's not half-bad either). Cool, comfortable, and art-deco make for a glam time. Plus, given who's biting, you never know what you'll catch...
160 Eighth Ave. (at 18th St.), 633-8484, V, MC, AmEx, D, Entrées: $12-$20, ❶❻❶ *to 14th St.,* ❶❾ *to 18th St.* ♿

262 restaurants

W

Wave
Enjoy this Japanese restaurant's outdoor terrace. The stunning views of New York Harbor and the Statue of Liberty are the perfect backdrop for some of the "finest sushi around." With the breeze off the water, and shade from the trees, there's no better place to chill on a hot summer day.
South End Avenue (West Thames), 240-9100, MC, V, AmEx, Entrées: $6.75-$18.00, ❶❾ *to Rector St.*

Well's
Since 1938, Harlemites have swooned over the homemade cornbread served with strawberry butter, as well as the waffles and fried chicken at this family-run legend.
2247 A.C. Powell, Jr. Blvd (at 132nd St.), 234-0700, MC, V, AmEx, Entrées: $11-$15, ❷❸ *to 135th Street,* ♿

Windows on India
It's difficult to decide when faced with the onslaught of restaurants on Sixth Street's "Little India," but loyal patrons swear that this corner favorite is a stand-out: unfailingly delicious food, authentically spiced, and with plenty of naan.
97 First Ave. (at 6th St.), 477-5956, MC, V, AmEx, Diners, Entrées: $5-$15, ❻ *to Second Ave.,* ♿

Wo Hop
This classic Chinatown haunt has been serving up Cantonese style dishes for 60 years. Open 24 hours this establishment has turned into a hot spot for the drunken late night munch. The food here will satisfy that Cantonese craving.
12 Mott St. (Chatham Sq.) 267-2536, Cash Only, Entrées: $5-$12.95 ❶❻❶❻❷ *to Canal St.*

Wok 'n Roll
They don't kick you out til 3am and you'll never significantly alter the level of your water glass at this airy new dumpling house, where the polished wood decor and predictable noodle and dumpling fare feels like a friend's mom's dinner you can always count on. Fair prices keep it packed with NYU kids.
169 Bleecker St. (at Sullivan St.), 260-6666, MC, V, AmEx, D, Entrées: $6.50-$13, ❶❻❶❻❶ *to West 4th St.*

Wrapp Factory
Burritos have been redefined into healthy low-fat rolls of delight. Try their famous thai chicken with peanut sauce and jasmine rice wrap or their comforting corn, mashed potatoes and fried chicken wrap. Vegetarian chili, fresh soups and refreshing smoothies make this a welcome, healthy stop for Columbia students.
2857 Broadway, 665-5870, Cash Only, ❶❾ *to 110th St.*

Y

Ye Waverly Inn
One of the vestiges of 19th-century Village life, this former carriage house exudes a quaint, Colonial feel with wooden ceiling beams and old-fashioned offerings from both north and south, like Yankee pot roast and southern fried chicken, with excellent

THE WRAPP FACTORY
HAND-WRAPPED SANDWICHES & SMOOTHIES

2857 BROADWAY
@ 111TH STREET
212.665.5870
WRAPPING BEGINS AT 11 AM
AND ENDS LATE
EAT IN / TAKE OUT / FREE DELIVERY
Catering is our Specialty

puddings and muffins. Occasionally, Village celebs drop by.
16 Bank St. (at Waverly Pl.), 929-4377, MC, V, AmEx, Entrées: $12-$17, ❶❾ to Christopher St.

Yum Thai Cuisine

The neighborhood dearth's of good cheap eats recommends this clean, congenial niche for fresh, tasty fast food in the heart of the theater district. Fill up on green curry and coconut rice before the show.
129 44th St. (bet. Sixth Ave. and Broadway), 819-0554, AmEx, Entrées: $6.50-$7.50, ❶❹❺❼ to 42nd St.

Z

Zen Palate

Mushrooms and nuts are featured prominently, spices are flavorful, and the decor is clean and slightly monkish at this Asian take on a vegetarian kitchen. Gramercy's branch is the most exciting and architecturally pleasing of the three in the chain.
34 Union Sq. East (at 16th St.), 614-9291, MC, V, AmEx, $7.50-$12, ❶❹❻❺❻ to 14th St./Union Sq.

Zöe

It is impossible to understate how wonderful the Zöe dining experience is. Attentive waitstaff, elegant decor, and intricate yet subtle food all await at this SoHo hot spot. The crowd is a pleasing mixture of downtown denizens and suited professionals on thieir way home from work. The crowd does get funkier as the evening wears on. Perfect for a romantic date.

90 Prince St. (bet. Broadway and Mercer St.) Entrées: $18-25, 966-6722, ❻ to Prince St. ♿

Zum Stantiszh

While German cuisine hardly qualifies as in vogue to chic Manhattan critics, its hearty, carnivorous slant goes over well with the locals in the quiet neighborhood of Glendale. Non-Queens residents drive in for a taste of the great sauerkraut and heavy meat-and-potato dishes. Stained glass windows and dim lights bring to mind stodgy 19th-century German intellectuals debating Hegel over steins.
69-46 Myrtle Ave., (718) 386-3014, MC, V, AmEx, Entrées: $7-$15.50, ❶ to Wycoff and Q55 to Myrtle on 69th Street

INDEX BY CUISINE

AFRICAN
Andalousia
Le Grenier
AMERICAN
Alley's End
Ambassador Grill
Amsterdam Cafe
AubudonBar & Grill
Bendix Diner
Bodega
Bouley Bakery
Bryant Park Grill
Cal's
Candy Bar and Grill
Clementine
Coogan's Restaurant
Corner Bistro
Donald Sacks
Duke's
Elaine's
El Fuerte
Empire Diner
Fanelli's
First
Friend of a Farmer
Fraunces Tavern
Gabriel's
Galaxy
The Garage
Ginger Ty
Gotham Bar and Grill
Gramercy Tavern
The Grange Hall

Granville Restaurant and Lounge
Harry's at Hanover Square
Home
Howard Johnson's Restaurant
Jake's Steakhouse
Jim McMullen
Joe Allen
Josephina
Keen's Chophouse
Kitchen Club
Lexington Candy Shoppe Luncheonette
Lincoln Tavern
M & R Bar
Man Ray
Mama's
Match
Merchant's N.Y.
Mike's Papaya
Moomba
Odeon
147
Park Avalon
Park Slope Brewing Company
Peter Luger Steakhouse
Pietrasanta
Regal Restaurant
Rialto
Richard's Place
Rock 'N' Roll Noodle House
Royal Canadian Pancake House
Screening Room Restaurant
Trumpet's Cigar Room
Serendipity
Sosa Borella
Standard Notions
Sun Garden
Step Mama's
Tavern on Jane
Tavern on the Green
Torre Di Pisa
Tonic
TriBeCa Grill
Two Two Two
Under the Stairs
The Viceroy
Wrapp Factory
Ye Waverly Inn
Zöe
ASIAN-EAST/SOUTHEAST
Atlantis Sushi
Bo Ky
Canton
Chi-Chi Steak
Columbia Cottage
Dish of Salt
Dok Suni's
Dynasty
East
Golden Unicorn
Hangawi
HSF
Joe's Shanghai

Kin Khao
Lemongrass Grill
Lucky Cheng's
Lucky Garden
Mekong
Mott Su
Nam
New Pasteur
New York Noodletown
Nha Trang
Nice Restauran
Nobu
Noodles on 28
Ollie's Restaurant
Oriental Garden
Penang Malayasian Cuisine
Pig Heaven
Rice
Rikyu
Saigon Grill
Sammy's Noodle Shop and Grill
Shun Lee Palace
Szechuan Empire
Tibet Shambala
Tiengarden
Tomoe Sushi
Triple Eight Palace
Tsampa
Tsunami
Wave
Wo Hop
Vegetarian Dim Sum House
Wok 'N' Roll
Yum Thai Cuisine
CARIBBEAN/LATIN
107 West
Boca Chica
Castillo de Jagua
Chi-Chi Steak
El Cid Tapas
El Nuevo Sambuca Restaurant
El Pollo
El Sitio II
Fiesta Mexicana
Jamaican Hot Pot
Jean's Restaurant
Mama Mexico
Maya
Mi Cocina
Mo's Caribbean
Nakisaki International Restaurant
Negril Carribean Restaurant
Patria
Sam Chinita's
DELIS
Deli Kasbah
Second Avenue Deli
Smiler's Delicatessen Store
34th Street Gourmet Market
DINERS
Around the Clock
The Flame
Golden Rule Diner

264 restaurants

Grand Lucheonette
Jimmy's Bronx Cafe
Junior's
Mama Joy's
Metro Diner
Pearl Street Diner
Riss Diner
Royal Coach Diner
Sliver Spoon
Tom's Restaurant
U.S.A. Diner, Inc.
EASTERN EUROPEAN
Mocca Hungarian
Odessa
Paradise
Sammy's Roumanian
Uncle Vanya
Velselka
FRENCH
Alison on Dominick
Alouette
Arcadia
Balthazar
Bistro Jules
Bistro Margot
Chanterelle
Dix et Sept
Florent
Gascogne
Indigo
L'Express
La Jumelle
Le Bilboquet
Les Halles
Luma
Metisse
Tartine
Terrace
Torch
Tout Va Bien
Trois Jean
GERMAN
Zum Stantiszh
INDIAN
A Taste of India II
Amin Indian Cuisine
Baluchi's
Madras Mahal
Milon Bangladesh
Windows on India
ITALIAN
Arqua
Aunt Suzie's
Basilio Inn
Camille's
Carmine's
Cucina
Cucina Della Nonna
Cucina Di Pesce
Da Nico
Dante Restaurant
Erinie's
Frutti De Mare
Grapino's
La Poeme
Lanza's
Lemon
Luna's
Mangia e Bevi

Mappamondo;
Mappamondo Due
Mimi's Macaroni
Monte's
Po
Puccina
Puglia
Queen's Restaurant
Rocky's Italian Restaurant
Sophia's Bistro
Torre di Pisa
Trattoria dell'Arte
Tutta Pasta
Twigs Bar and Restaurant
KOSHER
China Shalom II
Jerusalem II
Katz
Kosher Delight
Tevere '84'
MEDITERREAN
Babylon
Bolo
Mangia
Matthew's
Niko's
Pao!
Regal Restaurant
Restaurant Delphi
Symposium
Turkish Kitchen
Uncle Nick's Greek Cuisine
Viand
MIDDLE EASTERN
Amir's
Habib's Place
Layla
Mabat
Mesopotamia
Moustache
Oznot's Dish
Pamir's
PIZZA
Cafe Roma Pizzeria
Che Bella
Crocitto's II
Don Giovanni
Famiglia's
John's of Bleeker Street
Koronet's
My Cousin Vinny's
Nino's
Pasty Grimaldi's
Pintaile's Pizza
Pizza Fresca
Time Out
Two Boots
V & T Pizzeria and Restaurant
SEAFOOD
City Crab and Seafood Co.
Hudson River Club
Mare Mare
Redeye Grill
Sloppy Louie's
Umberto's Clam House
SOUTHERN
ACME
BBQs

Boulevard
Carmichael's
Chaz and Wilson
Copeland's
Cotton Club
Dallas BBQ
Dougie's BBQ and Grill
Londel's
Mama's
Mekka
The Rib Shack
Sister's Cuisine
Step Mama's
Two Steps Down
Virgil's BBQ
Well's
SOUTHWESTERN
Arizona 206
Bright Food Shop
Bubby's
Burritoville
Cowgirl Hall of Fame
El Teddy's
Hoppin Jalepenos
Margon
Mary Ann's
Mesa Grill
Redeye Grill
Rosa Mexicana
Samalita's Tortilla Factory
Sante Fe Grill
TAKE-OUT
Daily Soup
Desperados
McDonald's
Soup Kitchen
White Castle
VEGETARIAN
Angelica Kitchen
Annam Brahma Restaurant
Bachue
Dojo
Healthy Henrietta
Kate's Joint
KPNY
Le Roy's Restaurant and Coffee Shop
Lucky's Juice Joint
Ozu
Plum Tree
Quantum Leap
Souen
Spring Street Natural
Strictly Roots
Vegetarian Dim Sum House
Zen Palate

INDEX BY NEIGHBORHOOD

BROOKLYN
Aunt Suzie's
Cucina
Healthy Henrietta's
Junior's
Mabat
Nam
Oznot's Dish
Paradise
Park Slope Brewing

Company
Pasty Grimaldi's
Peter Luger Steakhouse
Queen's Restaurant
Richard's Place
Sante Fe Gril
Silver Spoon
Szechuan Empire
Tom's Restaurant
Tutta Pasta
Two Steps Down
BRONX
Jimmy's Bronx Cafe
Royal Coach Diner
CHELSEA
Alley's End
Amin Indian Cuisine
Bachue
Bendix Diner
Bolo
Bright Food Shop
Cal's
Candy Bar and Grill
Empire Diner
Gascogne
Luma
Man Ray
Mary Ann's
Merchant's N.Y
Negril Caribbean
147
Restaurant
Pietrasanta
Regal Restaurant
Riss Diner
Sam Chinita
Twigs Bar and Restaurant
Uncle Vanya
The Viceroy
CHINATOWN
Bo Ky
Canton
Golden Unicorn
The Grand Deli
HSF
Joe's Shanghai
New Pasteur
New York Noodletown
Nha Trang
Nice Restaurant
Oriental Garden
Rice
Triple Eight Palace
Vegetarian Dim Sum House
Wo Hop
EAST VILLAGE
Angelica Kitchen
Around the Clock
Bendix Diner
Cucina Di Pesce
Dok Suni
East Village
Eclectic
First
Frutti De Mare
Habib's Place
Kate's Joint

Lanza's
Lucky Cheng's
Lucky Garden
Mama's
Mekka
Mesopotamia
Milon Bangladesh
Nino's
Odessa
Second Avenue Deli
Step Mama's
Tsampa
Two Boots
Veniero's
Veselka
Windows on India

FINANCIAL DISTRICT
Donald Sacks
Fraunces Tavern
Harry's at Hanover Square
Hudson River Club
McDonald's
Pearl Street Diner
Rock 'N' Roll Noodle House
Sloppy Louie's
Wave

GRAMERCY
City Crab and Seafood Co.
Duke's
Friend of a Farmer
Galaxy
Gramercy Tavern
Granville Restaurant and Lounge
Grapino's
L'Express
Lemon
Les Halles
Mesa Grill
My Cousin Vinny's
Noodles on 28
Park Avalon
Patria
Pizza Fresca
Turkish Kitchen
Zen Palate

GREENWICH VILLAGE
Andalouisa
BBQs
Chi-Chi Steak
Corner Bistro
Dix et Sept
Dojo
East
El Cid Tapas
Florent
The Garage
Ginger Ty
Gotham Bar and Grill
The Grange Hall
Home
Indigo
John's of Bleeker Street
KPNY
Mappamondo;
Mappamondo Due

Mi Cocina
Monte's
Moomba
Moustache
Pó
Quantum Leap
Sammy's Noodle Shop and Grill
Souen
Tartine
Tavern on Jane
Tomoe Sushi
Tsampa
Tsunami
Wok 'N' Roll
Ye Waverly Inn

HARLEM
Copeland's
Cotton Club
House of Seafood
Jamaican Hot Pot
Le Grenier
Londel's
Sister's Cuisine
Strictly Roots
Well's

LITTLE ITALY
Bistro Margot
Da Nico
La Poeme
Luna's
Mekong
Mott Su
Puglia
Rice
Rocky's Italian Restaurant
Umberto's Clam House

LOWER EAST SIDE
Babylon
Boca Chica
Castillo de Jagua
Katz's Deli
Mama's
Sammy's Roumanian
Standard Notions
Step Mama's
Tiengarden
Tonic
Torch

MIDTOWN
Ambassador Grill
Bryant Park Grill
Daily Soup
Dish of Salt
Don Giovanni
Grand Luchenonette
Hangawi
Howard Johnson's Restaurant
Jerusalem II
Joe Allen
Keen's Chophouse
Kosher Delight
Madras Mahal
Mangia e Bevi
Margon
Redeye Grill
34th Street's Gourmet Market

Torre di Pisa
Trattoria dell' Arte
Yum Thai Cuisine

MORNINGSIDE HEIGHTS
107 West
Alouette
Amir's
Amsterdam Cafe
Cafe Roma Pizzeria
Camille's
Che Bella
Columbia Cottage
Desperados
Dynasty
Famiglia's
Fiesta Mexicana
Koronet's
Lemongrass Grill
Mama Mexico
Matthew's
Mimi's Macaroni
Ollie's Restaurant
Sophia's Bistro
Symposium
Terrace
Tom's Restaurant
V & T Pizzeria and Restaurant

QUEENS
Annam Brahma Restaurant
Carmichael's
Dante Restaurant
El Sitio II
Jean's Restaurant
Nakisaki International Restaurant
The Rib Shack
U.S.A. Diner Inc.
Zum Stantiszh

SOHO
ACME
Balthazar
Balucchi's
Clementine
Cucina Della Nonna
Fanelli's
Kin Khao
Kitchen Club
La Jumelle
M&R Bar
Match
Pao!
Rialto
Spring Street Natural
Zöe

STATEN ISLAND
A Taste of India II
Basilio Inn
Crocitto's II

TRIBECA
Allison on Dominick
Arqua
Bodega
Bouley Bakery
Chanterelle
El Teddy's
Layla
Le Roy's Restaurant and Coffee Shop

Nobu
Odeon
Restaurant Delphi
Screening Room
Sosa Borello
Tribeca Grill

UPPER EAST SIDE
Arcadia
Arizona 206
El Pollo
Elaine's
Jake's Steakhouse
Jim McMullen
Le Bilboquet
Lexington Candy and Shoppe Lucheonette
Matthew's
Maya
Mocca Hungarian
Pamir's
Pig Heaven
Pintaile's Pizza
Plum Tree
Restaurant Daniel
Rosa Mexicana
Samalita's Tortilla Factory
Serendipity
Shun Lee Palace
Teverne 84
Trois Jean
Viand

UPPER WEST SIDE
Boulevard
Carmine's
China Shalom II
Dallas BBQ
Deli Kasbah
Dougie's BBQ and Grill
Ernie's
Gabriel's
Josephina
Lincoln Tavern
Mare Mare
Mo's Caribbean
Ozu
Penang Malaysian Cuisine
Puccini
Rikyu
Royal Canadian Pancake House
Saigon Grill
Shun Lee
Soup Kitchen
Tavern on the Green
The Flame
Tibet Shambala
Tout Va Bien
Two Two Two
Uncle Nick's Greek Cuisine
Under the Stairs

WASHINGTON HEIGHTS
Coogan's Restaurant
El Nuevo Sambuca Restaurant
Golden Rule Diner
Hoppin' Jalapenos
Time Out

266 restaurants

cafes

In the early 1990s America gave birth to a coffee culture all its own. With Starbucks, New World and Timothy's on every corner, it's easy to see this culture has taken root in New York, a city whose citizens are always looking for something to keep the pace top speed. Is Manhattan buzzing with energy? Or is everyone just addicted to the java? Witness people scurrying about with big cups in their hands, and don't be afraid to call them on their professed one-cup-a-day limit; depending on the size of the cup, one might mean five.

While many New Yorkers could care less about hanging around in berets and rolling their own cigarettes, you will find a large quotient of European wannabes at Cafe Lalo, Veniero's, Le Gamin, Caffe Dante and The French Roast—to name a few. The nice thing about cafes like these is that it's just as acceptable to hang anonymously with your shades on, as it is to strike up conversations with total strangers. In fact, many a New Yorker has been known to come away with a good story after spending a morning in the cafe with their noses in the paper.

If you've got a secret you want to keep, don't go blabbing it in places like The Hungarian or The Cupcake Cafe. If there's one thing you'll learn while hanging out in New York City's cafes, it's that New Yorkers really do care.

A

alt.coffee
Everything from the comfy couches to the cereal by the bowl to the unintimidating $20 "Intro to the Internet" course strive to calm the cyberphobic. Eclectic nightly entertainment ranges from poetry readings to Monday night Klezmer jazz.
139 Avenue A (bet. St. Mark's Pl. and 9th St.), 529-2233, Cash Only, **L** *to First Ave.*

An Beal Bocht Café
The name means "the poor mouth" in Irish Gaelic, but this café will satisfy any appetite, cultural or gastronomical. The eats are traditional Irish favorites like Shepherd's Pie and fresh-baked scones. At night the place jumps with locals downing hearty pints of Guinness. Call ahead for a schedule of live performances of traditional Irish music and poetry readings.
445 West 238th St. (bet. Waldo and Greystone), (718) 549-5192, Cash Only, Entrées: $6, **1** *to 238th St.*

B

Bagel Bob's
The service couldn't be surlier, and don't be surprised if one of the Bagel Bob's boys gives girls a suspiciously friendly wink, but the carbo-packed rings are worth all the monkey business. Score fresh, warm bagels for only a quarter 4-7pm every weekday.
51 University Place (bet. 9th and 10th Sts.), 533-2627, **N R** *to 8th St.*

Bagel Cafe
Fluffy bagels (make sure you get 'em warm) are situated with assorted pastries, cakes, and pizza, a surprising and convenient culinary juxtaposition ideal for those on the go or who just pop in for a light snack.
657 West 181st St. (bet. Broadway and St. Nicholas Ave.), 781-1344, Cash Only, Entrees: $0.50-$4.50, **1 9 A** *to 181st Street*

Bagels & Cream Café
Tasty bagels and coffee, the friendly environment, all types of pastries, cappuccino, and espresso. The breakfast specials here are quite affordable.
80-02 Surrey Place (off of Union Turnpike), (718) 969-2640, Cash Only, Pastry $2.50-$5.75, **E F** *to Kew Gardens/Union Turnpike*

Bassett Coffee and Tea Co.
Coffee and tea are a foregone conclusion; the secret attraction here is the eats. What the locals call "that dog place" dishes out gourmet comfort food like garlic mashed potatoes and homemade mac-and-cheese Cafeteria-style, but without the hairnets.
123 West Broadway (at Duane), 349-1662, MC, V, AmEx ($15 minimum), Entrées: about $7, **1 9** *to Franklin St.*

Bell Cafe
It's rare that somewhere can be cool without lapsing into obnoxiousness; that's precisely what makes this place so special. The scene is definitely late-night, serving up huge portions of mostly vegetarian fare from around the globe until the wee hours of the morning, and it's equally accommodating for beverages and long conversation. There's really good free live music on Monday nights. A great alternative to the bar scene.
310 Spring St. (bet. Hudson and Greenwich Sts.), 334-BELL, MC, V, AmEx, D, Entrées under $10, **1 9** *to Houston St.,* **C E** *to Spring St.*

Bella's Coffee Shop and Luncheonette
Despite its name, this tiny joint serves up all the American favorites (such as grilled cheese), for less than $5. Snag an equally cheap—equally American—breakfast as well.
Elizabeth St. (at Prince St.), Cash Only, Entrées: $1.50-$5.50, **6** *to Spring Street*

Big Cup
Day-glo colors and paisley patterns might recall the '60s, but the very buff, short-coifed gay male clientele is pure '90s. Lounge all day in comfy chairs, sip a mocha, and watch the city tumble by.
228 Eighth Avenue (between 21st and 22nd Sts.), 206-0059, Cash Only, **C E** *to 23rd St.*

Bistro Jules
This cozy, authentic French cafe provides impoverished romantics with candles, trendy mood music, and wine affordable enough for cash-poor romantics to get sufficiently buzzed, leaving them enough change to pick up some roses on the way home. Spring through fall, the seating out front on the tiny sunken patio is ideal for leisurely afternoons of nursing lemonade and chain-smoking.
1 St. Mark's Pl. (bet. First and Second Aves.) 477-5560, **L** *to First Ave.*

Bread and Butter
This place has the best fries you'll ever taste. Bread and Butter serves soups, salads, pastries, and sandwiches. People either come in for take out or to sit on the benches lining the windows in this tiny yellow cafe leisurely sipping a cup of coffee. Owners, Sam and Sean, keep SoHoites eating morning 'til night, as they also own Rialto, another great dinner spot..
229 Elizabeth St. (bet. Prince and Houston Sts.), 925-7600, MC, V, AmEx, Sandwiches range from $3-$12.50, **N R** *to Prince St.* **B F** *to Broadway/Lafayette*

268 cafes

Bridge Cafe

Even if you're not a part of the city's political machine, the attentive staff will provide you with reliable standards at this adorable eatery just south of City Hall, one of former mayor Ed Koch's favorite haunts. Mostly a middle-aged crowd with spin doctors and other politicos.
279 Water St. (at Dover St.), 227-3344, MC, V, AmEx, Entrées: $10-$15, **N R** *to City Hall*

Bunnies' Feast

One of the neighborhood's newest and brightest lights when it comes to take out food, this bakery and pizza parlor has all the standard Italian selections, plus a whole caseful of wonderful desserts, including rum balls and brown sugar-glazed monkey bread.
3141 Broadway (at LaSalle St.), 666-4343, Cash Only, Pizza: $5-$15, Bakery: $1-$18, Free Delivery, **1 9** *to 125th St.* &

C

Cafe 18

This vegetarian kosher cafe uses meat substitutes to create classics like nonchicken chicken soup. The airy interior accommodates a bustling lunch crowd that comes from all over the city to sample the rare hybrids.
8 East 18th St., 640-4182, Entrées: $6-$8, **N R L 4 5 6** *to 14th St./Union Square*

Cafe Asean

While the candle-lit interior and backyard garden suggest rustic America, dishes here incorporate creative new Southeast Asian influences to perfection: mung bean-filled Vietnamese ravioli and Thai beef curry with pumpkin are consistently rewarding, and the service ever-helpful, just short of obsequious.
117 West 10th St., (bet. Sixth Ave. and Greenwich St.), 633-0348, Cash Only, Entrées: $7-$12 **A B C D E F** *to West 4th St.,* **1 9** *to Christopher St.* &

Cafe Con Leche

Cramped or cozy, depending on how tolerant you are of the neighboring conversation, this Cuban cafe pulses with upbeat salsa music and chatter that approaches a din during Monday night's sangria specials. Standard dishes are perfectly prepared, from empañadas to "filete de pollo al limon."
424 Amsterdam Ave. (at 90th St.), 595-7000, MC, V, AmEx, Entrées: $7-$14, **1 9** *to 79th St.*

Also at:

726 Amsterdam Ave. (bet. 95th and 96th Sts.), 678-7000 **1 9 2 3** *to 96th St.*

Cafe Della Artista

Wall art and paintings change monthly at this cozy West Village cafe where locals have flocked for over thirty years. Slip into the wooden and leather thrones and indulge a sweet tooth or craving for conversation.
46 Greenwich Ave. (bet. Charles and 7th Sts.), 645-4431, **A B C D E F** *to West 4th St.*

Cafe Europa

Übercoffees, replete with sprinkles and whipped cream, dominate the menu at this somewhat slick and meretricious coffeehouse located right at the hub of things. Veterans and neophytes alike can enjoy the ongoing spectacle of 57th Street through the oversized windows. The perky waitstaff also serves a limited menu of pizzas, crusty sandwiches, and elaborate desserts. Efficient, convenient, even pleasant-but hardly European.
205 West 57th St. (at Seventh Ave.), 977-4030, MC, V, AmEx, Diners, Entrées: $6-$8, **1 9** *to 59th St./Columbus Circle*

Also at:

1777 Sixth Ave. (at 46th St.), 575-7272, MC, V, AmEx, Diners, Entrées:: $6-$8, **B D F** *to Rockefeller Cntr.*

Cafe Gigi

Bring a good book and fine company to this underground haunt where locals lounge for hours, lost between the pages of Joyce while enjoying generously proportioned brunch dishes and the infamous pizzas in oh-so-comfy antique cushioned chairs. Perfect for an afternoon of lazy reflection and relaxation.
417 East 9th St. (bet. First Ave. and Avenue A), 505-3341, MC, V, AmEx, D, **L** *to First Ave.*

Cafe Gitane

A bastion of France on the edge of Little Italy, authentic from the menu offerings to the aloof waitstaff. Perfect ambiance for flipping through fashion rags, drinking coffee, and the standard downtown sports of posing and people-watching.
242 Mott St. (bet. Houston and Prince Sts.), 334-9552, Cash Only, Entrées: $7-$10, **N R** *to Prince St.* &

Cafe Kolonaki

The fun and cozy split-level coffeeshop is fairly new to the Steinway shopping area. The decor is contemporary, the staff, young and perky.
33-02 Broadway (at 33rd St.), (718) 932-8222, MC, V, AmEx, D, **N** *to Broadway* & ↩

Cafe Lalo

Perched in a brownstone, this bright and lively European Cafe serves night owls until 2am Sunday through Thursday, and until 4am on weekends. Come for the vast menu of decadent drinks and desserts; Sunday brunch available.
201 West 83rd St. (bet. Broadway and Amsterdam Ave.), 496-6031, Cash Only, Entrées: $5-$8, **1 9** *to 86th St.*

cafes 269

Cafe Love
Healthy vegan dining in low-key Brooklyn style. Choose from sit-down table service in the back or a quick bite from the juice and coffee bar in the front and enjoy anything from a sandwich to an entrée with ethnic inspiration in substantial portions that defy "rabbit food" stereotypes.
215 Court St. (at Warren St.), (718) 875-4568, MC, V, AmEx, Entrées: $5-$9, F to Bergen St.

Cafe Luna
It's not glamorous, but this neon-bedecked trattoria makes a mean pizza, and sauces and pastas are fresh and authentic enough to satisfy island natives. Extensive dessert offerings and the requisite demitasse cups of espresso attract crowds late into the evening.
1300 Hylan Blvd., (718) 351-3235, Entrées:$7-$22

Cafe Milou
Named after Tin Tin's dog, this new bistro opened in April, a breath of fresh air in the midst of trendy theme-oriented eateries on Seventh Avenue. Opened by the Abraham Merchant, of Merchant's, and with a menu created by a chef of Windows on the World fame, this place is a 24-hour surprise. Nowhere else is this kind of cuisine available at 4am.
92 Seventh Ave South, 414-9824, All Major Credit Cards, Average Entrée: $14, 1 9 to Christopher St.

Cafe Mona Lisa
Post-modern Art Nouveau meets Italian Renaissance: fragments of Lisa are spread across mint-green walls bathed in the soft glow of frosted bulbs in polished brass and wood fixtures. Graze on light lunch or decadent desserts.
282 Bleecker St. (bet. Jones St. and Seventh Avenue South), 929-1262, MC, V, AmEx ($15 minimum), Pastries around $3, 1 9 to Christopher St.

Cafe Mozart
Waitresses in starched aprons swivel around the baby grand with trays heaped with Austrian pastries and giant cups of cappuccino. A slice of Europe on the Upper West Side, perfect after the show or for late morning paper perusal.
154 West 70th St. (bet. Broadway and Columbus Ave.), 595-9797, MC, AmEx, V, 1 9 to 72nd St.

Cafe Noir
A trendy spot for late-night dining, the bar is generally inundated with well-dressed air-kissing types looking for fun. The atmosphere is French-Moroccan as is the food. Eschew the more expensive entrées in favor of lighter fare like sandwiches and tapas which combine simple ingredients to perfection and use the difference in price to splurge on a good bottle of wine from their extensive list of French vintages.
32 Grand St. (at Thompson St.), 431-7910, A C E to Canal St.

Cafe Orlin
Blend in by ordering an espresso and whipping out some sort of portfolio. Leave it open on the table and enjoy a smoky omelet or a slice of chocolate cake. Most regulars are artsy east-side chain smokers/aspiring directors. The low-angle view allows a glimpse of the shoes passing by on St. Mark's Place.
41 St. Mark's Pl. (bet. First and Second Aves.), 777-1447, Cash Only, Entrées: $7-$8, N R to 8th St., 6 to Astor Pl.

Cafe Palermo
"All it took was $50 and a load of dedication," manager and life-long Little Italy resident John De Lutro boasts, explaining the origins of the cafe he opened seventeen years ago. The family-run business still serves its familiar gelati and Italian pastries although these days, the clientele is mostly tourists.
148 Mulberry St. (bet. Grand and Hester Sts.) 431-4205, MC, V, AmEx, D, N R to Prince St.

Cafe Pick Me Up
Odd-shaped tables and mismatched lamps reveal this isn't Starbucks; someone must have raided their grandma's attic to decorate this charming cafe. Doors open up to Avenue A during warmer months, when many sip coffee and devour delectable deserts while looking out on the park.
145 Ave. A (at 9th St.), 673-7231, Cash Only, F to Second Ave.

Cafe Rafaella
Spacious and eclectic: table-lamps, high ceilings, stuffed armchairs, and a fashionable, slightly older crowd than the one found on the MacDougal-Bleecker axis. The charm can be mesmerizing, leaving the hours to slip by unnoticed.
134 Seventh Ave. (bet. 10th and Charles Sts.), 929-7247, Cash Only, Entrées: $5-$9, 1 9 to Christopher St.

Cafe Roma
Tiny marble-topped tables and an ancient, snorting espresso machine seem to whisk you into the back alleys of Rome while you enjoy old-world cannoli like mama used to make, in portions mama never would have imagined.
385 Broome St. (at Mulberry St.), 226-8413, Cash Only, Pastries $3-$7, 6 to Spring St.

Cafe Sha Sha
The summertime patio is a refuge amidst the midday mayhem. Relax with some java and read the entire Sunday Times.
510 Hudson St. (between Christopher and 10th Sts.), 242-3021, Cash Only, Entrees: $6-$10, 1 9 to Christopher St.

270 cafes

Cafe Un Deux Trois

Though a little strenuous on the wallet, this busy, touristy spot is perfect for a bowl of savory French onion soup or a delectable dish of creme brulee. Avoid the high prices by sitting at the bar. If you're up for a full meal, sit table side for a plate of steak and pomme frittes and let your imagination run wild as you design your own table cloth with a cup full of crayons.
123 W. 44th St. (bet. Sixth Ave. and Broadway), 354-4148/4397, MC, V, AmEx, Entrees: $15.75-23.95, **NRS1237** *to Times Sq.* ♿

Cafe Viva

Not every Italian restaurant has the kind of ambiance you'd expect when walking into a sidewalk cafe in Tuscany, and this one proves the point, but what an inspiration and breakthrough for eager vegetarians who crave pizza fully-loaded with gourmet veggie toppings, soy cheese, and marinated tofu. Other selections include a tasty faux sausage calzone and carob cake for dessert.
2578 Broadway (bet. 96th & 97th Sts.) 663-8482, Pizza: $4/slice, **19** *to 96th Street* ♿

Cafe Vivaldi

The espresso bar churns softly over classical music by everyone in the pantheon of Western music, including the place's namesake. The decor includes Xeroxed copies of composers' portraits, and does little to complement the music.
32 Jones St. (at Bleecker St.), 691-7538, Cash Only, Entrées: $7, **ABCDEF** *to West 4th St.,* **19** *to Christopher St.*

Cafe Yola

On a warm night, step through the cozy asymmetrical dining room into the back garden. Tucked in between apartment buildings, the outdoor space achieves a European atmosphere. Candlelight, ivy, and good wine make this the ideal place for a romantic dinner and quiet conversation.
337 East 10th St. (bet. Avenues A and B), 677-1913, Cash Only, Entrées: $8-17, **F** *to Second Ave.* ♿

Caffe Dante

Patience is a necessity at this classic Italian cafe, but the fresh mozzarella cold platters and the zuppa inglese are divine enough to justify anything, including Celine Dion playing in the background.
79 MacDougal St. (bet. Bleeker and Houston Sts.), 982-5275, MC, V, AmEx (Restaurant only), Entrées: $12-$16, **ABCDF** *to West 4th St.*

Caffe Pertutti

Bright and breezy, with a hard-tiled floor and marble-topped tables, this neighborhood cafe hosts intellectual tête-à-têtes while serving up Italian standards which hardly merit their above-average prices. The salads, however, are enormous and tasty, and the desserts usually taste as good as they look.
2888 Broadway (bet. 112th and 113th Sts.), 864-1143, Cash Only, Entrées: $7-$12, **19** *to 110th St.* ♿

Caffe Reggio

The standard by which Village cafes are measured, Caffe Reggio's charm makes it popular among students, hipsters, and aging bohemians. The dark interior is suitable for curling up and whiling away the hours with either a book or your significant other. Prices respect the starving artist's pocketbook.
119 MacDougal (bet. Bleecker and 3rd Sts.), 475-9557, Cash Only, Desserts around $4, **ABCDEF** *to West 4th St.*

Caffe Taci

Crowds of Columbia students eat adequately prepared Italian basics in the mock-ruin interior of this popular, dimly lit eatery. Manhattan School of Music students sing live opera on Friday and Saturday nights, and due to slow service, diners could theoretically hear one in its entirety.
2841 Broadway (at 110th St.), 678-5345, Cash Only, Entrées: $4.75-$12, **19** *to 110th St.*

Candle Cafe

"New York Naturally's" 1997 Restaurant of the Year, this environment-friendly lunch spot exhibits boundless creativity in options such as the "karmakazi," a wheat grass shot with ginger-veggie blend. Great lentil soup and delicious portobello mushroom sandwiches round out the more mainstream end of the menu, guaranteed to please the most finicky of carnivore converts.
1307 Third Avenue (at 75th St.), 472-0970, MC, V, D, Diners, **6** *to 77th St.*

Cargo Cafe

Just a stone's throw from the ferry terminal, this modern, trendy seafood house is hard to miss. A youngish local crowd congregates on the terrace in summer for delectable fresh fish specials like pan-seared tuna with cucumber-and-dill yogurt. Sandwiches, burgers, and salads make appearances as well. Local bands sometimes play, and local artists often showcase their work inside.
120 Bay St. (at Flosson Terrace), (718) 876-0539, MC, V, AmEx, D, Entrées: $10-$15, Walking distance from the ferry ♿

Ceci-Cela

Homemade sorbet and cafe au lait evoke La Cote d'Azur at this charming patisserie perched on the edge of Little Italy. The chat room in back is oh-so-perfect for nibbling on petit-fours and playing post-structuralist salon.
55 Spring St. (Mulberry

Coffeelounge
COFFEE · BAR · EATERY · GALLERY

Beer & Wine • Coffee and Espresso Drinks Deluxe & More
The Best Sandwiches • Healthy Wraps • Soups & Salads
Super Smoothies/Fresh Veggie Juices • Desserts & Ice Cream
Ongoing Events • Underground Environment

955 WestEnd Avenue at 107th St • 8am-late Everyday

and Lafayette Sts.), 274-9179, MC, V, Desserts: $1-$5, ⑥ to Spring St.

Cha Cha's in Bocca Al Lupo
Once a one hundred-and-ten-year-old Italian butcher shop, this eleven-year-old cafe moved in when the old locals' outward migration and the tourists' invasion was just beginning. The gelato may be half-melted and the desserts crumbling and meagerly proportioned, but who said that the Mulberry Street experience wouldn't come at a price? *113 Mulberry St. (bet. Canal and Hester Sts.), 431-9755, MC, V, AmEx, Entrées: $6-$9,* Ⓝ Ⓡ *to Canal St.*

The Chanting House Cafe
Inwood arty-types commiserate, quibble, and swap free verse at this tiny Irish coffeehouse. The food is nothing special, but this friendly little haunt attracts an esoteric crowd day and night.
634 West 207th St. (bet.

Broadway and Cooper St. 567-6716, Cash Only, Ⓐ *to 207th St.*

Chez Ma Tante Cafe
Dream of summering in Cannes while sipping Evian and nibbling bread fresh from the boulangerie at this intimate brassierie, where entrées: are prepared with a light and experienced hand and favor trendy ingredients like arugula and portabello mushrooms; the coq au vin and grilled dishes are also superb. Top it all off with one of the beautifully styled desserts—the fruit tarts are particularly sweet.
189 West 10th St. (bet. Bleecker and West 4th Sts.), 620-0223, MC, V, AmEx, D, Diners, Entrées: $11-$19, Ⓐ Ⓑ Ⓒ Ⓓ Ⓔ Ⓕ Ⓠ *to West 4th St.* ♿

Coffee Lounge
Practically hidden in its below street-level niche, this very mellow, laid-back hangout bedecked with books and artwork, offers comfy couches and mismatched furniture that give it a low-key, small-

city, loungey kind of vibe. Sample coffee drinks and other tasty morsels while reading or just lingering in the soothing ambiance. Live music on weekend evenings by announcement.
955 West End Ave. (at 107th St.), 531-4759, Cash Only, Prices: $1.50-$4.00,(evenings), ① ⑨ *to 110th St.* ↵

Columbia Bagels
The finest bagels in Manhattan, and just steps from Columbia's campus. Saturday morning finds bleary-eyed students lining up with cops, locals, and the occasional paramedic on break for one of the chewy, warm winners. Gourmet cream cheeses and toppings available.
2836 Broadway (at 110th St.), 222-3200, Cash Only, ① ⑨ *to 110th St.* ♿

Commodities
Exactly what you'd expect from the offspring of a gourmet health food supermarket: tasty organic lunch fare, a full juice bar, and the usual assortment of coffees. The front windows offer a great view of TriBeCans scurrying around the neighborhood.
117 Hudson St. (at North Moore St.), 334-8330, MC, V, AmEx, Salads about $6.50/lb, ① ⑨ *to Franklin Street*

Connecticut Muffin Co.
Marble tables and green lawn chairs bring a New England country flavor to Little Italy's cozy street.s.

The menu includes fresh sandwiches, soups, baked goods, and teas taken from a stock in tin jars on the back shelf.
10 Prince St. (at Elizabeth St.), 925-9773, Cash Only, Ⓝ Ⓡ *to Prince St.,* Ⓑ Ⓓ Ⓕ Ⓠ *to Broadway/Lafayette Sts.*

Cornelia Street Cafe
Neighboring restaurant Pó just lost one of their chefs to this refined cafe; the leisurely ambiance of soothing lights coupled with a background jazz and blues blend complements the similarly unforced take on simple New American cuisine. Venture downstairs after dinner to catch nightly theater, jazz, and poetry performances in the cabaret.
29 Cornelia St., 989-9318, MC, V, AmEx, Diners, Ⓐ Ⓑ Ⓒ Ⓓ Ⓔ Ⓕ Ⓠ *to West 4th St.*

Cupcake Cafe
A quaint little bakery with pink walls and tin ceilings on the raunchiest stretch in Hell's Kitchen. Great donuts, cakes, and waffles, with a few tables for immediate consumption. The location makes it an unfashionable destination for a food pilgrimage, but this is the place for old-fashioned sweets.
522 Ninth Ave. (at 39th St.), 465-1530, Cash Only, Ⓝ Ⓡ Ⓢ ① ② ③ ⑦ ⑨ *to Times Square*

272 cafes

The Cupping Room Cafe

A wonderful spot with an ambitious, if slightly pricey, brunch menu. Even at peak hours, there's plenty of space in the large, airy, main room, so the wait is never too long. Portions are generous; try the delicious eggs Florentine and the different types of pancakes. *359 West Broadway (at Broome St.), 925-2898, MC, V, AmEx, Brunch Entrées: $9-$15,* **C E** *to Canal St.*

Cybercafe

Spend serious quality time with computers; options extend beyond basic net access to the latest games and sophisticated design and desktop publishing programs. To top it all off, the cafe makes a mean mocha. *273 Lafayette St. (bet. Spring and Prince Sts.), 334-5140, MC, V, AmEx,* **N R** *to Prince St.*

D

Ditto Internet Cafe

One-stop shopping for those who want to surf the Net, design a webpage, and make color laser prints, all over a cup of mediocre coffee. A flat fee of $6 buys the first half hour of computer use, plus 20¢ each additional minute. *48 West 20th St. (bet. Fifth and Sixth Aves.), 242-0841, MC, V,* **N R** *to 23rd St.*

Drip

This coffee bar also has its liquor license so you can speed on caffeine, then come down with a microbrewed beer. Singles can leaf through binders chock full of bios while sipping lattes and nibbling on gargantuan rice-crispies treats. Atmosphere is casual, friendly, and relaxed unless, of course, you do find a match! *489 Amsterdam Ave. (bet. 83rd and 84th Sts.), 875-1032,* **1 9** *to 86th St.*

DTUT

A lazy cup of coffee is hard to come by in this part of town, making this couch-filled coffeeshop the perfect place to linger over the Sunday *Times* and an espresso concoction. Desserts are quite tasty. *1626 Second Ave. (bet. 84th and 85th Sts.), 327-1327, Cash Only,* **4 5 6** *to 86th St.*

Duane Park Patisserie

Get an entire cake, like those peddled by trendy TriBeCa restaurants for $7 per slice, for less than $20. Perfect for impressing dinner guests or treating yourself, if gluttony is a favorite deadly sin. *179 Duane St. (bet. Greenwich and Hudson Sts.), 274-8447, Cash Only,* **A C E 1 2 3** *to Chambers St.*

E

Ellen's Cafe and Bakery

Coffee ranks up there with air and water in the heart of the Financial District, and this busy cafe provides the best cup in town. Also a small selection of pastries and sandwiches. *270 Broadway (at Chambers St.), 962-1257, MC, V, AmEx, Entrées: $7-$8,* **1 9** *to Park Pl.*

F

Fa Cafe

East Village funkadelic cafe with reasonably priced selection of sandwiches, salads, pastas, omelets, and crepes as well as a handsome selection of vegetarian items and unbelievable desserts. Enjoy the kitschy decor and sit outdoors when the weather is fine and observe the goings-on on St. Mark's Pl. Open 24 hours. *97 St. Mark's Pl. (bet. 1st St. and Avenue A), 677-9001, Entrees: $6-10, V, MC, AmEx,* **6** *to Astor Pl.*

Fall Cafe

Cushy couches and chairs abound in this quiet cafe: settle into one and finish a physics problem set or dig into your first novel. Sustenance comes at starving student prices: $3 or less for soups and sandwiches, and a small coffee for less than $1. *307 Smith St. (bet. President and Union Sts.), (718) 403-0230, Cash Only, Sandwiches around $4,* **F G** *to Carroll St.*

The First Street Cafe

This one-man show is run with a certain admirable abandon, mirroring perfectly the quintessential style of this city. As you step through the cafe door, the man who runs the place is either foaming a latte behind the counter or doing a jig in the middle of the floor. His audience laughs merrily, welcoming the pleasant diversion. Then slowly, they bow their heads to their cups, magazines, or chess games. He's got a cropped goatee and a crush on every girl who enters the place. He'll chat with you or leave you alone for hours with your book; either way he always catches your vibe. *72 1st St. (bet First and Second Aves.), 358-7831, MC, V,* **L** *to First Ave.*

Fort Tryon Cafe

Housed in an old building with dark paneled wood walls and lead-framed windows, this airy cafe can't be beat for that rare, countrified ambiance so hard to come by in the city. Cakes are tasty, and sandwiches and frittata make for an excellent mid-afternoon interlude while visiting the Cloisters. *Fort Tryon Park, 923-2233, Cash Only, Entrées: $4-$9* **A** *to 190th St.*

cafes 273

Franklin Station Cafe

French and Malaysian bistro food is served up to the cellular phone toting set along TriBeCa's main drag. The French offerings are solidly good and the Malaysian fare is sublime and authentic, which is no wonder when you peer into the open kitchen and get a look at who's doing the cooking. Good for trying something new in a nonthreatening environment.
222 West Broadway (at Franklin St.), 274-8525, MC, V, AmEx, Diners, ❶❾ *to Franklin St.*

French Roast

Art Noveau dominates the decor at this airy, bustling cafe. Brunch and lunch available; try the consistently delicious soups.
458 Sixth Avenue (at 11th St.), 533-2233, MC, V, AmEx, Entrées: $6-$15,

❻❶❶❷❸❾ to 8th St.
Also at:
2340 Broadway (at 85th St.), 799-1533, ❶❾ *to 86th St.* ♿

G

Go Sushi

Pop culture's turning Japanese. This newcomer capitalizes on both the sushi trend and the still-burgeoning coffee-bar culture: sleek stools and a tattered copies of *Paper* meet sushi samples of fatty tuna and salmon prepared fresh around-the-clock by an in-house chef. Wash it all down with Go's own freshly brewed ginger ale.
3 Greenwich Ave.(bet. Sixth Ave. and 8th St.), 366-9272, Cash Only, $1.25 per piece,
❶❷❸❹❺❻❼ *to West 4th St.* ♿

Greenhouse Cafe

Nestle in among lovebirds basking in the glow of posies adorning the tables and light streaming through the glass ceiling.
New York Marriot World, 3 World Trade Cntr. (bet. Liberty and Vesey Sts.), 444-4010, MC, V, AmEx, D, $7-$12, ❶❾ *to Cortlandt St.,* ❸❹ *to World Trade Cntr.*

Greenwich Cafe

Skip the entrées: for the stylish array of appetizers at this spacious 24-hour cafe, staffed by waitpeople with the best cheekbones and chic-est wardrobe in the West Village. Weekend nighthawks might encounter a chic party for slinky models and their agents; brunch guests are serenaded with soothing jazz. Outdoor seating is available in the summer.
75 Greenwich Ave. (at Seventh Ave. South), 255-5450, MC, V, AmEx, D, Diners, ❶❾ *to Christopher St.*

The Grey Dog's Coffee

Bring a novel, your laptop, or your friends to this warm rustic cafe where sunlight pours in through the open French windows and casts shadows on the pressed tin ceilings above. Order a big chunk of fresh-baked bread, a terrific cup of coffee, and amble back to one of the artsy tables with apples, fish, or chili peppers painted on top. On the brick walls, resident artists display their art. A veritable community center, this cafe is where folks hang out all day doing their thing. At night the lights dim and the place transforms into a stylish yet equally casual wine bar.
33 Carmine St. (bet. Bleeker and Bedford Sts.), 462-0041, Cash Only, Average Entrée: $6,
❶❸❺ *to West 4th St.,* ❶❾ *to Houston St.* ↵

H

H & H Bagel

To certain New Yorkers, these bagels are good enough to qualify as a delicacy. The poppy and everything flavors go quickly, but the basic plain sourdough is something special, too. Call 1-800-NY-BAGEL to have mail orders delivered anywhere in the world. There's a "Seinfeld" episode lurking in that option.
2239 Broadway (at 80th St.), 595-8003, Cash Only, ❶❾ *to 79th St.*

274 cafes

Hard Rock Cafe

This chain's outposts are now a dime a dozen; overpriced but passable burgers and pseudo-healthy California fare like avocado-laden salads go down best with a Cherry Coke and a seat next to some Elvis relic at the New York Stateside mothership. Still, the place has seen better days: there are more Jersey teens here than at Garden State Plaza on a Saturday afternoon.
221 West 57th St. (at Broadway), 459-9320, MC, V, AmEx, D, Diners, Transmedia, Entrées: $8-$16, ❶❷❸❹❶❾ *to 59th St./ Columbus Circle* ♿

Hungarian Pastry Shop

The cafe's enduring reputation as Columbia University's intellectual hangout par excellence has suffered somewhat since the citywide smoking ban. Still the place of choice, however, to ostentatiously discuss Benjamin and Godard or write that dissertation on the hermeneutics of the Marquis de Sade while sipping chamomile tea and nibbling on a linzer torte
1030 Amsterdam Ave. (bet. 110th and 111th Sts.), 866-4230, Cash Only, ❶❾ *to 110th St.* ♿

I

Indian Cafe

Scrumptious curries, kebabs, and a mean chicken mahkni satisfy the Morningside crowd's cravings for spice. Watch locals making runs to the corner liquor store from floor-to-ceiling windows that jut out onto the sidewalk.
2791 Broadway (bet. 107th and 108th Sts.), 749-9200, MC, V, AmEx, Entrées: $6.50-$10, ❶❾ *to 110th St.*

Internet Cafe

New York's first cybercafe offers weekly classes for between $25 and $200. Alternately, pay the $5 cover to listen to striving artists unleash their souls in the cozy pub: bands play most nights; poetry readings are on Wednesdays. Gourmet beers, including a large Belgian selection, go well with the show.
82 East 3rd St. (bet. First and Second Aves.), 614-0747, MC, V, ❻ *to Second Ave.* ↩

J

Java Shop

Heroically proportioned brews could deliver enough caffeine to incite showtune-singing at this bar-like pit stop for pre- or post-theater coffee fixes. Tourists have heated discussions over which was better, Phantom or Cats.
1611 Broadway (bet. 48th and 49th Sts.), 246-1960, MC, V, AmEx, ❶❾ *to 50th Street* ♿

Jerry's

A longtime crowd pleaser, Jerry's still has a line out the door for weekend lunch and brunch. Try a plate of stellar tuna salad or citrus-marinated chicken: they're all the rage. This hot lunch spot draws a huge art crowd and plenty of celebrities, including Leonardo DiCaprio, who, on his last visit, attracted a horde of onlookers, which is unusual because hardly anyone looks up from the overflowing plates of French fries in this place. Jerry's has maintained a down-to-earth atmosphere, despite its popularity.
101 Prince St. (bet. Greene and Mercer Sts.), 966-9464, MC, V, AmEx, Entrees: $9-$13, ❼❽ *to Prince St.* ♿

K

Krispy Kreme

The very best around. Especially good are the dense, chewy blueberry and the classic glazed, still hot out of the ovens. Beware the frosted and sprinkled varieties; they melt in your mouth so fast and taste so good that it's impossible to eat fewer than three.
265 West 23rd St. (bet. Seventh and Eighth Aves.), 620-0111, Cash Only, One dozen around $5, ❻❼ *to 23rd St.*

Also At:

280 West 125th St. (at St. Nicholas Ave.), 531-0111, 60-65¢ apiece, $4.50-$4.99 a dozen, ❶❷❸❹ *to 125th St.*

L

L Cafe

This dark, smoky cafe functions as the center of Williamsburg social life before 2pm, serving up bagels with a wide range of toppings for under $2. Add a bottomless cup of admittedly mediocre coffee and cruise on the caffeine/carbo speedball for the rest of the day.
189 Bedford Avenue (bet. North 6th and North 7th Sts.), (718) 388-6792, Cash Only, Sandwiches around $4, ❶ *to Bedford Ave.* ↩

La Lantern

Across MacDougal from the NYU Law School, but surprisingly a lawyer-free zone. Two stories, but the downstairs is open only in the evenings. Order the chocolate mud pie.
129 MacDougal St. (bet. West 3rd and West 4th Sts.), 529-5945, Cash Only, ❶❷❸❹❺❻ *to West 4th St.* ↩

Le Figaro

A combination of cafe and diner, in the heart of the MacDougal-Bleecker coffee district. When the weather is nice, sit outside and soak up the Village as it meanders by.
184 Bleecker St. (bet. MacDougal St. and Sixth Ave.), 677-1100, Cash Only, Entrées: $7-$10, ❶❷❸❹❺❻ *to West 4th Street*

Le Gamin

A more successful stab than most at replicating a

cafes 275

Parisian cafe, this neighborhood joint serves crepes, croque monsieur, quiche, and salads to a laid-back, lingering crowd. Family types mix with the downtown chic; the lack of a liquor license encourages people to bring their own beer or wine. A great stopover for a cappuccino while club-hopping or a good setting for more lengthy leisure and a latte. The French menu has English subtitles.
183 Ninth Avenue (at 21st St.), 243-8864, Cash Only, Entrées $6.50-$10, **C E** *to 23rd St.*

Also at:
50 MacDougal St. (bet. Houston and Prince Sts.), 254-4678, Cash Only, Entrées: $7-$10, **A C E** *to Spring St.*

Les Deux Gamins
French-inspired omelets, salads, and rich entrées: consistently attract crowds at this endearing, perennially popular bistro; brunch goes down perfectly with cafe au lait or cocoa in warmed bowls on a lazy Sunday morning. Service can be harried, though the crowd of low-key locals in their late 20s is tolerant.
170 Waverly Pl. (at Grove St.), 807-7357, AmEx, Entrées: $14-$23, **1 9** *to Christopher St.*

Life Cafe
Two scenes from the Broadway play *Rent* take place at this eclectic source of healthful Cal-Mex, helping to solidify its reputation as an East Village landmark of laid-back creativity. Check out the rotating exhibits by local artists, preferably during the daily happy hour 5-7pm.
343 East 10th St. (at Avenue B), 477-8791, Entrées: $7-$9.50 (Sat/Sun Brunch Prix Fixe $7.95) **L** *to 14th St.*

Lucky's Juice Joint
This granola-y counterpart to the ubiquitous coffee bar is consistently packed with a trendy though democratic crowd eager to liquefy their diet in hopes of maxing out on vitamins and protein, as well as health-fad ingredients like ginseng and ginger. Try the delicious smoothies, made with soy milk and fresh fruit. Feels a like a little bit of Berkeley.
75 West Houston St. (off West Broadway), 388-0300, Drinks $2-$6 **1 9** *to Houston St.*

Luna Park
Primarily a haven of sugary decadence in the form of cakes, croissants, and gourmet ice cream, prix-fixe brunch brings the same level of indulgence to the mid-morning table, and the dinner buffet is a cheap alternative to home cooking. Kids overrun the premises in late afternoon; a more sedate, decaf-sipping crowd settles down in the evening.
249 Fifth Ave. (at Garfield St.), (718) 768-6868, Cash Only, Brunch $7.90, Dinner, $9.90

M
Masturbakers
This appropriately titled bakery is at the Old Devil Moon Restaurant. The most popular item here is the ass cake. Their breast cake bearing the words, "Breast Wishes" runs a close second. With moist devil's food cake, rich frosting and naughty details, their bakery lives up to their motto: 'tasty but tasteless.'
511 E 12th St. (bet. Avenues A and B), 475-4357, **6** *to Astor Pl.,* **L** *to First Ave.*

Mayflower Cafe & Bakery
Authentic foods and drinks of China, as well as conventional staples such as bagels and coffee. Local traffic purchases Chinese pastries and curry buns.
40-46 Main St., (718) 359-6655, Cash Only, Pastries approximately $4, **7** *to Main St.*

N
New Lung Fung Bakery
Chinese sweets and pastries, such as coconut rolls and the ever-present almond cookies, are just some of the delights offered here for your consumption. A highly affordable option for a snack or sugar binge.
41 Mott St. (bet. Pell and Bayard Sts.), 233-7447, Cash Only, Pastries: $.50-$3, **B D Q** *to Grand St.*

New Prospect Cafe
A diminutive cutie, the menu features wonderful seafood and vegetable dishes and nice, cheap wine. Not for New York's night owls, the kitchen closes by 10pm.; on the other hand, brunch is excellent and crowded.
393 Flatbush Ave. (bet.Plaza St. and Sterling Pl.), (718) 638-2148, V, MC, AmEx, Entrées $9-$14, **2 3** *to Grand Army Plaza,* **D Q** *to Seventh Ave.*

News Bar
Enjoy coffee, dessert, sandwiches, daily soup specials, and a new magazine to go with each course: racks inside offer a periodical to suit every fancy, fashion, or fetish. Seating is limited, so come during off-hours.
2 West 19th St. (at Fifth Ave.), 255-3996, MC, V ($10 minimum), Sandwiches around $5, **L N R 5 6** *to Union Square* ♿

Nussbaum & Wu
Not your ordinary coffee stop—the Chinese pastry shop and Kosher deli collided to form this one. Well-lit with a great wrap-around bar, you just may decide to stay a while. Fresh sandwiches and scrumptious pastries, both Asian and non, are available here, not to mention fresh bagels and, of course, coffee too.
2897 Broadway (at 113th St.), 280-5344, **1 9** *to 110th St.* ♿

O

Olive's
Even lunchtime takeout food is chic in SoHo. The selection of fresh, delicious sandwiches and salads changes daily, and offerings incorporate specialty ingredients like shitake mushrooms and prosciutto. Best of all, no matter how long the lines get inside it never takes more than 10 minutes to get lunch and be on your way.
120 Prince St. (bet. Greene and Wooster Sts.), 941-0111, MC, V, AmEx, Sandwiches $5-$7, ❶❷ to Prince St.

Omonia Cafe
Locals meet to hang out over espresso, baklava, and Italian pastries.
32-20 Broadway (at 33rd St.), (718) 274-6650, MC, V, AmEx, Diners, D, ❶ to Broadway

On the Park Cafe
Filling the vacuum left behind by the sorely missed Harlem Cafe next door, this stylish little coffeehouse promises to be Harlem's answer to the Jackson Hole chain further downtown. Smack dab in the middle of fashionable Striver's Row, Harlem's most up-and-coming neighborhood. The park in question is lovely and rustic. St. Nick's one block west.
301 West 135th St. (at Frederick Douglass Blvd.), 694-5469, Cash Only, ❷❸ to 135th St.

Once Upon A Tart
Delectable pastries, both savory and sweet, at lower prices than the standard coffeecakes served up by Manhattan's corporate chain espresso bars. Everything is made in their own bakery. Try one of the specials that include a tart and choice of salads.
135 Sullivan St. (bet. Houston and Prince Sts.), 387-8869, MC, V, AmEx, D, Tarts $4-$6.50, ❻ to Spring St. or ❶❷ to Prince St.

Ozzie's
Park Slope's aspiring writers and intellectuals come to this plain and pleasant space; no doubt the clientele provided inspiration for local author Paul Auster, who set scenes from *Smoke* in this coffee haven.
57 Seventh Ave. (bet. Lincoln and Berkeley), (718) 398-6695, Cash Only, ❶❷ to Seventh Ave.

P

Pasticceria Ferrara
At this self-proclaimed "America's first espresso bar since 1892," tourists have supplanted immigrants clamoring for a taste of home. While the mile-long glass case of whimsical puffs and cakes promises perfection, pastries don't always measure up; instead, take home biscotti by the pound.
195 Grand St. (bet. Mulberry and Mott Sts.), 256-6150, MC, V, AmEx, Diners, D, Pastry: $1.75-$3.75, ❻ to Spring St.,
Also in Greenwich Village and Midtown

Petite Abeille
Better be a big fan of Tintin if you plan on visiting one of these tiny spots—paraphernalia of the famous cartoon boy-reporter (et ses amis) plaster the walls, where limited indoor and outdoor seating is available to enjoy coffee, pastries, and an assortment of delicious soups and sandwiches. Fast, fun, and authentic, as much bakery as restaurant, you might try impersonating Captain Haddock, General Alcazar, or Snowy (Milou, en français) to score a free Tintin mug or watch.
107 West 18th St. (bet. Sixth and Seventh Aves.), 604-9350, V, MC, AmEx, D, Entrées: $5-$10, ❶❷ to 18th St.

Also at:
400 West 14th St. (at Ninth Ave.), 727-1505, V, MC, AmEx, D, Entrées: $5-$10, ❶❷❸ to 14th St.

Pink Pony
The "Ice Cream" sign outside is misleading, as the folks inside are all drinking coffee, though it is consistent with the kitsch theme. Neighbor to Max Fish, this '60s-style pit stop is perfect for lounging around and monopolizing the jukebox.
176 Ludlow St. (bet. Houston and Stanton Sts.), 529-3959, Cash Only, ❶ to Second Ave.

Popover Plum's
New England charm meets New York savvy at this convivial spot, one of the most popular brunch venues in the neighborhood. Feast upon gourmet omelets and excellent griddle specialties under cheery quilts and teddy bears—and don't forget the popovers.
551 Amsterdam Ave. (bet. 86th and 87th Sts.), 595-8555, MC, V, AmEx, Entrées: $8-$12, ❶❷ to 86th St.

R

The Rocking Horse Cafe Mexicano
One of a string of Mexican restaurants along Eighth Avenue, this is the most upscale, with fresh food, a perky waitstaff, and a popular brunch. Interesting twists on traditional fare include variations with crab and lobster, but the old standards are excellent as well—burritos, enchiladas, and margaritas.
182 Eighth Ave. (bet. 19th and 20th Sts.), 463-9511, V, MC, AmEx, Entrées: $9-$15, ❶❷❸ to 23rd St.

S

Salad Jazz Cafe
Paradise for those who want to be treated to a true variety of roughage at a reasonable rate. Don't expect to receive food for the ears; despite the title, the jazziness of the eatery's name has more to do with its modern-deco

cafes 277

aesthetics than its soundtrack.
162-03 Jamaica Ave. (bet. 162nd St. and Guy R. Brewer), (718) 526-5725, Cash Only, Entrees: $1.50-$4.50 (prices vary for salads depending on weight), ❶❷❸ to Jamaica/Sutphin Blvd.

Scharmann's
Paint-splattered walls and a vast wooden floor hold seating arrangements from a yellow velvet couch to a full-sized dining table. Nonstarving artists populate this somewhat intimidating coffee lounge. Best for refueling after a full day of gallery hopping.
380 West Broadway (bet. Spring and Broome Sts.) ❶❷❸❹ to Houston St.

Second Street Cafe
The bastion of Park Slope cafe culture serves up light meals and an appealing array of desserts, including chocolate cookies that would put mom's to shame. The cafe is packed during lunch hours, seven days per week; on weekend evenings, however, seats are plentiful.
189 Seventh Ave. (at Broadway), (718) 369-6928, Cash Only, Entrees: $5-$9, ❶ to Ninth Ave. &

Sette MoMA
Stark, sleek furniture, stunning artwork, and amazing views of the MoMA sculpture garden make the setting here the main attraction. This is no ordinary museum eatery, though; the food rivals, even surpasses, that of most upscale Italian cafes in Midtown. Consider the exceptionally slow service an opportunity to contemplate the world-class art.
11 West 53rd St. (bet. Fifth and Sixth Aves., at the MoMA), 708-9710, MC, V, AmEx, Entrees: $18-$28, ❶❷ to Fifth Ave. &

Space Untitled
No doubt the $7 sandwiches finance the rent payments on this capacious cafe/gallery, but those on meal plans can take advantage of the space for the price of a cup of coffee. The crowd ranges from networking financiers to the ragged artists who need their money; the wine bar perks up at sundown with a handful of votives and a decidedly classier crowd.
133 Greene St. (bet. Houston and Prince Sts.), 260-8962, Cash Only, Sandwiches around $6, ❶❷ to Prince St.

Sugar Shack Cafe
Amidst old brown-brick edifices lies this quaint and cozy haven. A relatively new addition to the Harlem restaurant canon, patrons can find relief in the sumptuous turkey burgers and the quirky mix of chicken fingers with waffles. Sometimes the chef comes out to see how everyone enjoyed the meal.
2611 Frederick Douglass Blvd.(at 139th St. and Eighth Ave.), 491-4422, MC, AmEx, D, V, Entrees: $8-$16, ❷❸ to 135th Street &

T

Time Cafe
Around mealtimes there are rarely many free tables in this vast, lofty space, and it's no wonder, since this is one of the few places filling the niche between greasy coffee shop and fancy restaurants. Health-conscious organic food and an extensive menu with selections like fancy tuna sandwiches and blue-corn ravioli guaranteed to satisfy nearly any craving.
380 Lafayette (bet. Great Jones and 4th Sts.), 533-7000, MC, V, AmEx, Entrees: $12-$18, ❻ to Bleecker St.

Tirami Su
Whimsically decorated with golden sun and moon masks dancing across the walls, this popular Italian café insists on offering its stylish patrons a good time. The menu boasts pizzas with both classic and daring toppings, homemade pastas with tangy, flavorful sauces, and a range of Italian desserts complemented by potent espresso.
1410 Third Ave. (at 80th St.), 988-9780, MC, V, ❻ to 77th St.

Tramps Cafe
Get your strength up before the show at this festive and boisterous, southern-themed cafe adjacent to the popular music. Live blues make digging into a plate of chili an even heartier experience on weekends, and portions cater to the long-haul trucker.
45 West 21st St. (bet. Fifth and Sixth Aves.), 633-9570, MC, V, AmEx, Diners, Entrees: $7-$22, ❶❷ to 23rd St., ❶ to 23rd St. &

Y

Yaffa Cafe
If you're craving healthy food at 4am, this is the place to go for an all night diner alternative. The fare is mainly Dojo-style veggie dishes along with a smattering of house specialties as eclectic as the kitschy junk shop decor. Suitable for bringing a larger group, especially when there's someone along for the ride who already ate, as no beatings are bestowed for beverage-only orders and the desserts are divine.
353 Greenwich St. (at Harrison St.), 966-0577, MC, V, AmEx, D, Diners, Entrees: $8-$18, ❶❷❸❹ to Chambers Street

Yaffa Tea Room
Alice in Wonderland collides with New York eclecticism at this delightful hamlet. Burgundy velvet and antique crystal chandeliers make you feel like bohemian royalty as you sip your tea. Reservations required for high tea, served Monday through Friday 2-5pm.
19 Harrison St.(at Greenwich Ave.), 966-

278 cafes

0577, MC, V, AmEx, Diners, D, High tea: $15, Entrées: $8-$18, ❶❷❸❾ to Chambers St.

Z
Zabar's Cafe
Stop in for a quick sandwich, especially after Zabar's gourmet grocery store next door puts an edge on the appetite. Check out the board on the back wall for cheap daily specials. Upper West Side intellectuals frequented this place in the '70s and '80s.
2245 Broadway (at 80th St.), 787-2000, MC, V, AmEx, Sandwiches around $5, ❶❾ *to 79th St.* &

BY NEIGHBORHOOD

BROOKLYN
Cafe Love
Cafe Luna
Fall Cafe
L Cafe
Luna Park
New Prospect Cafe
Ozzie's
Second Street Cafe
BRONX
An Beal Bocht Cafe
CHELSEA
Big Cup
Chelsea's Choice Expresso Bar
Krispy Kreme
Le Gamin
Petite Abeille
The Rocking Horse Cafe Mexicano
CHINATOWN
New Lung Fung Bakery

EAST VILLAGE
alt.coffee
Bistro Jules
Cafe Gigi
Cafe Orlin
Fa Cafe
Internet Cafe
Life Cafe
No Bar Cafe
Pink Pony
Time Cafe
Yaffa Cafe
FINANCIAL DISTRICT
Bridge Cafe
Ellen's Cafe and Bakery
Greenhouse Cafe
GRAMERCY
Cafe 18
Ditto Internet Cafe
News Bar
Petite Abeille
Tramps Cafe
GREENWICH
Bagel Bob's
Bread and Butter
Cafe Asean
Cafe Milou
Cafe Mona Lisa
Cafe Rafaella
Cafe Reggio
Cafe Sha Sha
Cafe Vivaldi
Caffe Dante
Chez Ma Tante Cafe
Cornelia Street Cafe
French Roast
Greenwich Cafe
The Grey Dog's Coffee
Go Sushi
Jerry's
La Lanterna
Le Figaro
Les Deux Gamins
Pasticceria Ferrara
HARLEM

Aubudon Bar and Grill
Bagel Cafe
Bunnies' Feast
Krispy Kreme
On the Park Cafe
Sugar Shack Cafe
LITTLE ITALY
Cafe Gitane
Cafe Palermo
Cafe Roma
Ceci-Cela
Cha-Cha's in Bocca Al Lupo
Pasticceria Ferrara
LOWER EAST SIDE
Cafe Pick Me Up
Cafe Yola
First Street Cafe
Masturbakers
MIDTOWN
Atlantis
Cafe Europa
Cupcake Cafe
Cafe Un Deux Trois
Hard Rock Cafe
Java Shop
Omonia Cafe
Pasticceria Ferrara
Sun Garden
Trumpet's Cigar Room
MORNINGSIDE HEIGHTS
Caffe Pertutti
Caffe Taci
Coffee Lounge
Columbia Bagels
Hungarian Pastry Shop
Indian Cafe
Metisse
Mike's Papaya
Nussbaum and Wu
QUEENS
Bagels and Cream Cafe
Cafe Kolonaki
Mayflower Cafe and Bakery

SOHO
Bella's Coffee Shop and Lucheonette
Bell Caffe
Cafe Noir
The Cupping Room Cafe
Cybercafe
Le Gamin
Lucky's Juice Joint
Olive's
Once Upon a Tart
Pasticceria Ferrara
Scharmann's
Space Untitled
STATEN ISLAND
Cafe Luna
Cargo Cafe
TRIBECA
Bassett Coffee and Tea Co.
Commodities
Connecticut Muffin Co.
Duane Park Patisserie
Franklin Station Cafe
Yaffa Tea Room
UPPER EAST SIDE
Candle Cafe
DTUT
Sette MoMA
Tirami Su
UPPER WEST SIDE
Cafe Con Leche
Cafe des Artistes
Cafe Lalo
Cafe Mozart
Cafe Viva
Drip
Empire Szechuan
French Roast
H & H Bagel
Popover Cafe
Zabar's Cafe
WASHINGTON HEIGHTS
Chanting House Cafe
Fort Tryon Cafe
Salad Jazz Cafe

soha

Uptown Lounge **SOUTH OF HARLEM**

988 Amsterdam Avenue (at 109th Street)

Jazz on Sundays

Live Music on Wednesdays

Available for Private Parties

212.678.0098

Open 4pm – 4am

Happy Hour 4pm – 7pm daily

nightlife

NYC nightlife — 282
*interview with writer/
tv personality michael musto* — 283
bars — 284
dance clubs — *313*
music venues — 321

nightlife

New York's diverse after-dark scene caters to the tastes of martini-sipping, cigar-toking lounge enthusiasts, the local chapter of beer-chugging tavern lovers, and the elite underground network of dance clubbers alike. This nightlife mecca offers something for everyone from country line-dancing at Denim and Diamonds to cabaret shows at famous gay establishments like The Duplex in Greenwich Village. Whether it's jazz in a basement dive, a crowded club throbbing with a trip-hop beat, or a spoken-word show in a smoky bar, New York is where it's at. Life for quite a few New Yorkers is nocturnal; many drunken revels demand a glimpse of sunrise before they end in exhausted sleep, and like no place else, this town accommodates.

As an amber hue settles on the skyscrapers of this city, and the workday recedes into distant memory, nightlife is launched in endless bars and clubs which offer happy-hour prices to giddy patrons. Note that while it's cost-effective to tank up on these cheap cocktails while you can, you might want to curb your appetite so that you avoid "bumbling-idiot" status before the wise ones even come out to play (around midnight), when the after-dark scene really gets going. Most New Yorkers not only consider 10pm an early start, they also have no concept of "the weeknight." On any given night of the week, after an extensive bar-hop, many a lively night-loving creature finds their way to live-music venues to catch a show of the latest local heroes, or they hurry to hit the hottest dance clubs before they lose their cache and fall into the category of "weak" as most upscale party joints do when they start admitting everyone under the sun (i.e., The "bridge and tunnel" set-see next paragraph). When bars and clubs wind down around dawn, after-hours joints open up to pick up the slack until long after the more health-conscious early-rising joggers have finished their runs.

The writhing masses who frequent the nightspots of this city are composed of two very distinct crowds: Manhattanites and bridge-and-tunnelers. The former consider themselves the true denizens of NYC's diverse nightlife universe, mostly because they can stick around the latest; there's no reason not to stay out until sunrise when home is, at worst, a ten-dollar cab ride away. Because distance is such a factor for bridge-and-tunnelers, they tend to inundate Manhattan's bars and clubs only on weekend nights. Many locals tend to steer clear of the massive weekend crowds, so they either take great pains in keeping their weekend favorites hush-hush for as long as they can, or they start their partying much earlier in the week.

Bar and club owners and party promoters pay very close attention to the social barometer of this city; they create a different theme party for every night of the week aimed at particular crowds, everything from ladies night to '80s night to gay night, and different styles of music from reggae to Latino to deep house or old-school groove, whether on the jukebox, on stage, or spun on a turntable courtesy of an in-house or a guest DJ. New York's hot nightspots supply the space and the tunes, but the mixed bag of people can go a long way toward characterizing the nightlife scene.

Nightlife is alive in the city that never sleeps

Michael Musto has written "La Dolce Musto," the weekly entertainment and gossip column in the Village Voice *since 1984. Known as the original diva of the after-dark party scene, Musto lives like a vampire, inhabiting the world behind the velvet rope, reporting all he sees for those who have day jobs.*

Q: How long have you lived in New York?
A: My entire life. I grew up in Brooklyn.

Q: When did you hit the party scene?
A: The second I graduated from college.

Q: How did you become "the original diva of the after-dark party scene"?
A: I started writing about nightlife, and when you're part of the press club owners want you there writing about their clubs. All that: free admission, free drinks, shmoozing, it's all intertwined with work.

Q: Any advice for diva wannabes?

A: Create an entire look so you stand out and get the attention of doormen. Be persistent. Hang out with somebodies. I'm not advocating using people, but it can't hurt.

Q: What do you love about New York?
A: People here are not characters from the *Truman Show*. New Yorkers tell you what they feel without being asked. And the culture, I mean I go to at least three somethings a night: play, party, club, whatever.

Q: What do you hate about New York?
A: How NY is becoming one big Disney Store. At first it was OK, because there was only, like, one store, but now it's too much. But New Yorkers are resilient, it's just challenging us to be even more resilient.

michael musto

"who me, gossip?"

Q: Why do doormen have so much power?
A: Everyone wants to get in. Some of these places have lines around the block. Attitude is the most famous thing that clubs deal in. Doormen get off on attitude. I've seen dinky little clubs with no one inside and they've got a velvet rope up and still won't let anyone in.

bars

NYC bar scene.285
bar listings.291
index by type.309
index by neighborhood.310

bars

"What is it about New York that makes sleep useless?" Simone de Beauvoir asked years ago, and the answer may well be the bars that are at the center of New York. Whether a place to unwind anonymously with a beer in a dark corner, a regular meeting spot for friends, a special night out, or just a pit stop on the way to somewhere else, these establishments are an integral part of the weekly routine of most city-dwellers.

College and sports bars tend to attract a predominantly male clientele who want to drink, watch the game, and absorb the sweaty masculinity that hovers around the pool table; these are (not surprisingly), located near colleges and frequently host fraternity events. Woman can take advantage of the ladies' nights which these bars throw in an attempt to even the gender ratio. Amsterdam Avenue in the high 70s to mid-80s boasts a string of very similar establishments which draw on the student populations of both Columbia University to the north and Fordham Law and Business Schools to the south; Hunter College and Manhattan Marymount students fill the bars on the Second Avenue strip from the 60s to the 80s. The scene around New York University is somewhat shaped by the hip cachet of going to school in Greenwich Village, but even the bastion of BoHo harbors some frat hang-outs. As a result, beer is the drink of choice (pitcher after pitcher of it)and none of the sissy microbrew crap; Bud and other American beers dominate.

Bleecker Street is a popular path for college students and out-of-towners clad in jeans and jerseys. Up and down the strip folkie-rock-n-roll bands play in places like the Bitter End and Cafe Wha? While much of the West Village is typically saturated with straight, horny, beer guzzling boys and girls, it is also highly concentrated with established gay and lesbian bars. Over the past ten years Chelsea has emerged as the most aggressive male-cruising scene in the city.

Twentysomethings who eschew the frat scene tend to congregate downtown at assorted holes-in-the-wall, usually in trendy neighborhoods like the Lower East Side and the East Village. The beautiful, well-groomed hipsters among the premarriage set may find themselves gravitating toward downtown's more upscale hideaways, where how your clothes hang starts to matter more as bouncers and their trusty velvet ropes begin to emerge like trolls beneath the bridge; if you have any aspirations of breaking into the elusive SoHo lounge scene, it's best to start by putting your self-image to the test in a friendlier environment.

Cabarets, piano bars, and hotel bars are part of a long tradition of metropolitan elegance where there are insiders and outsiders, and you know before entering into which category you fall. Such bars are often populated by the remaining New York blue bloods who gather uptown at Cafe Pierre and the Oak Room, where the drinks are so expensive you'll be nursing one all night, but the dress-up game is fun. Newer hotel bars like the SoHo Grand, invite a more modern bunch of fashionable artists into its classic SoHo-styled cast-iron building. Cabarets tend to attract a large gay male clientele. For a real treat, check out the nightlife renaissance in Harlem by traveling to the Seville, the Lenox Lounge, or Showman's.

ID

Underage would-be-drinkers, beware: despite rumors that you can get served anywhere in New York, in recent years the carte blanche with regard to serving the under-21 set that the NYPD used to bestow upon liquor-licensed establishments has been threatened by the quality-of-life crusader, Mayor Rudy Giuliani. The crackdown has resulted in much stricter ID policies at the doors of bars, clubs, and music venues, especially on the weekends. If someone asks you for ID and the best you can do is your library card, save the drama for your mama and leave quietly.

Neighborhood Haunts

The ultimate mixed bag descends upon neighborhood haunts and pubs, which are typically packed from Happy Hour (the time between 4 and 7pm being the longest and happiest hour of the day), until closing. All across the city, with the possible exceptions of the business strongholds of the Financial District and Midtown, students chat and jostle old men at the bar as they try to get the bartender's attention. Equal numbers of men and women flock to these low-key refugees but the pick up scene is nearly nil, since virtually no one is a stranger for long. These bars are easy to spot, since the people in them look genuinely happy to be there. Pubs are very similar in that they're friendly and populated mostly by regulars, and a fair share of them are Irish: Nevada Smiths, Paddy Reilly's, and Irish Times are just a few establishments where the bartender's brogue is no put-on; step in and enjoy a single-malt with an exiled IRA supporter, and watch as Guinness and McSorley's flow gracefully from the tap.

Lounges

Almost every year, there seems to be a new trend dominating the downtown bar scene that dictates the style of newcomers and causes old favorites to adopt new gimmicks in order to avoid losing business. Last year, martini madness was the thing; the rise or fall of a hip establishment rested on its ability to serve up an extensive list of innovative, candy-coated versions of the classic cocktails that never failed to include the omnipresent Cosmopolitan. But novelty drinks alone could not sustain bar culture for long; this year, the ever-present demand for something "new" coupled with a few dashes of inspiration from the SoHo-model bar scene has led to the explosion of the lounge scene. Now the East Village, West Village, and the Lower East Side are teeming with new or newly renovated bars, complete with all the requisite lounge trappings: DJs, mood lighting, cushy lounge furniture, and a different party theme for every night of the week. Variations on the theme cater to nearly every whim by offering different styles of music and party scenes ranging from youthful hip-hop to more subdued classic jazz. The crowds and levels of formality follow suit: the long-running Salon Wednesday party at Flamingo East, one of the original and best East Village lounges, attracts designer-clad, upscale industry types; while fourteen blocks down at SPOON, skaters (baggy jeans and all), are the mainstay of the scene. Finally, a trip west leads to the E&O, where Goth kids turn out for Vampiros Lesbos on Sundays. Go to the trouble of finding the right spot and you'll be rewarded: you'll have the perfect home away from home to drink, meet cool people and, well, lounge.

286 bars

A small bunch of bizarre theme bars can be found in the unlikely neighborhoods of the East Village and the Lower East Side, roughly 50 blocks away from mega-commercial theme spots like Planet Hollywood and the Hard Rock Cafe. These curious little joints are born when someone expresses his/her quirky vision, a couple of friends choreograph his/her design, the walls get dolled up, furniture gets collected, and the glamorous staff dresses accordingly. Viola! A wacky, and more often than not unique brainchild is born.

When Jerry Kuziw opened Burp Castle on East 7th Street six years ago, his vision was clear: Dress the staff in brown monks' robes, cover the walls with medieval murals, dim the lights, keep Gregorian chants and Classical music playing in the background, and serve world-class brews, like Chimay Grand Reserve ($12/25-oz bottle). Strangely enough, the most intoxicating relic at Burp Castle isn't the beer, it's Patrick Gorey, the 58-year-old bartender, who has stepped into dismal brown vestments and morphed into "Brother Patrick." People say Brother Patrick, "just looks the part... he brings out the atmosphere in a way that can't be described." Go to this East Village watering hole; soak up the drinks, the atmosphere, and the colorful stories that Patrick Gorey (supermonk) has gathered tending Manhattan bars for the past 35 years.

Another change from the standard stark-sofa-brick-wall-wood-floor places is down on East Houston at Idlewild, where the old Den of Thieves used to be. This place is the pioneering concept of Jim Chu, who also recently opened Torch in the Lower East Side. Jim and his partners, Eric and Rob, planned, researched, and with the help of friends, undertook all the labor to create its innovative design. Since "Idlewild" was once the name of JFK Airport, the design of the bar mimics the interior of a 1959 commercial plane. The replica's precision is remarkably accurate, from the shiny silver-paneled ceilings and leather-upholstered borders to the blue, beige, and white fabric wallpaper and brushed silver bathroom doors.

Seats line the "back" or the "front" of the imaginary plane where "passengers" sip Martinis, Metropolitans or Idlewilds (Cosmopolitans with a splash of Chambord). The gorgeous bartenders, dressed in white shirts and ties, act as pilots; the bar-back wears a bright orange baggage-handler jumpsuit, but instead of bags he's schlepping racks of clean glasses and cases of beer. The bar even has a ventilation system that filters out cigarette smoke and recirculates fresh air. The only thing that breaks the illusion is the lack of "vacant" and "occupied" switches on the bathroom doors. Idlewild, with its Lower East Side glam-makeover is worth jetting into, even if for only a cocktail and a little bag of airplane peanuts.

Two other funky theme bars worth mentioning are: Korova Milk Bar on Avenue A and Galaxy on Irving Place. Korova Milk Bar is a requisite stop for film buffs and lovers of eye candy; the bar glorifies and imitates the cult classic, *A Clockwork Orange*. Of course, there is always a showing of the strange and terrifying film noir on some eerie wall, as if the bar wasn't enough to remind patrons.

Galaxy is adorned in the sophisticated colors of the night sky. Fiber-optic stars splatter the ceiling, illuminating the room with a galactic glow, and huge windows let in the refreshing evening air. Some notable Galaxy drinks served are "Bloody Mars," and "Cosmic-politans," and maybe they are trying to keep you in space with their dizzying array of hemp-based menu items. Spend a whirlwind night hopping from one of these theme bars to the next, and you'll have traveled 500 years into the past and straight to the stars.

Burp Castle
(see Bars section)

Idlewild
(see Bars section)

Korova Milk Bar
(see Bars section)

Galaxy
(see Bars section)

The East Village: Is the Edge Really Gone?

Ah, Avenue A... a strip mall (of fun). As gentrification steadily invades the East Village, many still mourn the days gone by when finding a cabby to drop you off east of Avenue A on a Saturday night was a chancy endeavor. "Where have the real East Villagers gone?" people ask with bored disapproval, so characteristic of veteran New Yorkers. Where does anyone go when rising rents, increasing police presence and demolished city gardens make one feel less at home? Perhaps they've gone off to paint by the light of the moon in their Williamsburg, Brooklyn lofts or to tend bar on the booming Lower East Side. Lighten up! Change is good. And while it is true that the artists, punks, Puerto Rican immigrants, homeboys, and homeless have made room for a "cleaner," more homogenous (and more predictable) Bridge and Tunnel and uptown crowd (especially on the weekends), it is also true that the East Village bar scene has never been more diverse, with an unprecedented number of interesting new bars opening up. When the city stopped issuing liquor licenses on Avenue A (citing saturation), many called Avenue C the "new frontier" with recently opened Baraza and C Note blazing the way.

Yes it's true, you are less likely to step over heroin needles on Avenue C than you were two years ago and yes, that Wall Street guy on the next couch next to you is still wearing his shirt and tie, but don't stress; chances are there's an interesting new venue just down the block. Check out East Village newcomers Niagara at 7th Street and Avenue A, 9C (at 9th Street and Avenue C), and Barmacy on 14th Street, owned by Deb Parker of Beauty Bar fame.

Between 8th and 9th Streets on Avenue C is Baraza, possibly the best of a new crop of Avenue C bars. Before Baraza, the space was home to a bodega which fronted a notorious East Village cocaine operation. When the NYPD busted the operators and closed the

BOOMS
Bar Scene Booms on the Lower East Side

The red neon sign at Katz's kosher deli blazes like a beacon, a gateway to Barland on the Lower East Side. Not long ago, Lower East Side bar goers were limited to Max Fish, Ludlow Street Cafe, and The Orchard Bar, old neighborhood favorites. But a strong economy, relatively low rents, and saturation in the East Village have made opening a Lower East Side bar attractive to new owners; the densely populated dingy narrow streets of the Lower East Side, best known for their strong ethnic identities, are now peppered with eclectic bars. On any given evening, traveling packs of nightcrawlers from around the city and beyond can be seen milling through the streets south of Houston — loosely bound by the Bowery and Clinton Street to the west and east—in search of a good time. What they're finding is everything from burlesque and comedy, to belly dancing and jazz at new venues like Kush, Baby Jupiter, Dharma, Idlewild, Torch, and The Living Room. Check out these three "just opened" Orchard Street bars:

Dharma *(174 Orchard Street)* sits like a jewel, in stark contrast to the grungy fabric stores it's wedged between on Orchard Street. Like other newcomers to the neighborhood, Dharma's owner Josh Manson chose the location because he was attracted to the "up-and-coming, laid-back Lower East Side vibe. The name "Dharma," which symbolizes the religious laws and teachings of Buddha, was actually borrowed from Jack Kerouac's novel "Dharma Bums" to reflect the open and experimental musical scene at the club. Though many think of Dharma as a jazz club, the venue (which offers live music Monday through Saturday), also hosts top-notch Latin and world music performers. Performers such as the Brooklyn Funk Essentials and Groove Collective have made Dharma's groove/funk Tuesdays and Thursdays a big hit. The long narrow space, typical of the neighborhood, has two full-service bars and lounge seating in the front and back. Musicians play from an elevated performance space at the back of the bar. A cover is only charged for special performances.

The soft flickering candlelight and soothing music may tempt you to roll out your mat and bodega, Stephan Gerville-Reache and Dimitri Vlahakis decided to capitalize on the cleanup and realize their vision; Baraza was born. Four or five nights a week DJ's spin world music and some Mondays feature live music. Check out the funky fish tank in the back room, the penny-lined walls of the restroom, and $5 drink specials like Mojito Cubanos and Guava-Mango Margaritas.

Baraza
(see Bars section)

C Note
(see Bars section)

Niagara
(see Bars section)

Barmacy
(see Bars section)

Beauty Bar
(see Bars section)

begin your yoga practice at Kush, this new Lower East Side venue at 183 Orchard Street. Not possible, especially on the weekends when this Morrocan-themed Orchard Street bar packs a lively mixed crowd of uptown/downtown almost-30 types. Known for "achla" Tuesdays complete with belly dancers, middle eastern musicians, hookas, tarot readings and henna paintings, Kush also hosts Jazz Sundays with talent such as the Ben Alliston Trio. The decor at Kush, a "rustic North African interior," according to owner Mark Osborne, is reminiscent of North African "peasant" interiors, as opposed to a royal Moroccan aesthetic, which is "too busy" in his estimation. In the rear of the bar, an exterior stucco outcove (designed to resemble an outdoor veranda) houses a DJ seven nights per week, spinning "Global Music" beginning around 10pm. Osborne opened Kush because he was attracted to the "ethnic diversity and relatively low rent" of the Lower East Side. Relatively is the key word. Kush's rent nearly doubled in the first six months of operation, a testament to the Lower East Side real estate boom. Full-service bar, but nothing on tap. Light Mediterranean fare.

Another newcomer, Baby Jupiter *(at 170 Orchard Street)*, was first conceived of as a family-style establishment, according to proprietor Gary Auslander (also of Baby Jake's). Things seem to have taken on a life of their own, however, and seven nights per week beginning at 8pm, an eclectic array of entertainment can be found behind the maroon velvet curtain that separates the entertainment lounge from the restaurant and bar. Cabaret, vaudeville, "alternative" comedy, performance art, "pseudo film parties" and good ole' rock-n-roll attract a diverse crowd to Baby Jupiter, which is "pretty mellow until about 10" so as not to disturb the dinner crowd seated in diner-style booths, enjoying reasonably priced southern comfort food. Downtown music scene favorite Spook Engine performs regularly at Baby Jupiter, as does the highly controversial comedian Colt 45, a favorite of Howard Stern. Heavily promoted parties such as Electro Fetus (Wednesdays), Cool-Out Party (Fridays), and Sweet Cookie (Saturdays), bring in yuppie lounge lizards, bridge and tunnelers, wayward club kids, and "rockers" alike. Never a cover. Nothing on tap, but full bar.

Even in a city that's famous for its beautiful, aspiring model/actor/singer waitstaff and bartenders, Marvin is a standout. Check out this hunk of a bartender Tuesday and Saturday nights at Idlewild and Wednesday through Friday nights at Lava. Having worked in every capacity in the bar business for the past thirteen years, he is raising funds now to open his own place. More than his practical experience and education, Marvin, a self-proclaimed "child of the hospitality industry," says he has learned more about the business, watching other owners and managers screw up. He continues to bartend because, "the money's fantastic."

Certainly, some of his huge tips must stem from the bag of tricks he keeps behind the bar, complete with cigar-clipper, cigarette lighter, fifteen pens, loose cigarettes for those who are fiending, but can't get off their barstool. Rigged to his belt loop, he also has a key ring with an extending chain holding a bottle opener, so that in a flash the chain is yanked, it snaps back, and your beer is placed in front of you, label always facing out. As corny as it sounds, this guy loves what he does, he's good at it, and he makes people happy.

When asked if he felt like he was on stage behind the bar Marvin said, "yeah, that's why I like it." Because he's such a good-looking "ham," modeling (his side gig) comes naturally. One would think he'd have plenty of pretty young things at his beck and call, but Marvin prefers the nice type. "When the bar is three-deep, and I see a smiling face in the muck waiting patiently, I love that person," then he joked, "or if you throw me a C-note, you're golden!"

Lava
28 West 20th Street
bet. Fifth and Sixth Avenues
627-7867 *(see Bars section)*

Idlewild
145 East Houston Street
bet. First and Second Avenues
477-5005 *(see Bars section)*

{ m a r v i n }

Bull's Eye
Game Rooms Really Hit the Spot

Certain bars in New York add a competitive edge to the drinking scene. Most New Yorkers associate these game rooms with baseball-capped, plaid-shirted fraternity boys which may not be far from the truth in some cases. However, in some places the hipper-than-thou set has discovered the compounded joy of experiencing the glory of victory while simultaneously downing Cosmopolitans.

Regular gatherings about the pool table at the Stoned Crow in Greenwich Village foster conversation among friends and strangers alike. The Stoned Crow also features a jukebox, dart board, and a virtual reality race car video. Morningside Heights' 1020 bar also features a rather serious pool-playing crowd. In Gramercy, Revival, a low-key twentysome-things' bar, provides a much more laid-back approach to the game of pool. The Dive Bar, located on Amsterdam Avenue at 96th Street, is also a pretty tame spot. There is hardly ever a line for the free darts and even the resident pool sharks won't intimidate. The Tapas Lounge on First Avenue at 59th St. boasts that its customers can graze on tapas and sip sangria while playing backgammon. At Max Fish on Ludlow Street between Houston and Stanton Streets, a fishy decor provides the backdrop for numerous pool games involving fashionable regulars. Some bars are frequented solely for their pool tables. The ultimate game room--darts, pinball, etc.--can be found at the Ace Bar on East 5th Street between Avenues A and B. The SoHo Billiards on Mulberry Street at Houston is a smoky hangout which contains a ton of pool tables and blasts nostalgia-inducing '80s music for their chic patrons.

Though playing and drinking at the same time can be pricey, some spots offer discounts to help you out. Located on West 21st Street between Fifth and Sixth Avenues, the Chelsea Billiards offers pool tables at half-price on Thursday nights. Amsterdam Billiards, located on Amsterdam Avenue and 77th Street, allows up to four people to play from 11pm until 3am for a total of $19 on Sundays through Thursdays.

A

Abbey Pub
Both the food and the atmosphere are comforting at this ideal neighborhood bar where older locals mingle easily with the collegiate crowd; the perfect spot to meet for beers and share a basket of fish 'n chips.
237 West 105th St. (bet. Broadway and Amsterdam Aves.), 222-8713, MC, V, AmEx, Entrées: $6–$10, **1 9** *to 103rd St.*

Abbey Tavern
Gen-Xers love the warm atmosphere and dark wooden floors of this haunt where no one is trying too hard and the bartender has a brogue. An adjoining kitchen serves up standard pub fare.
354 Third Ave. (at 26th St.), 532-1978, MC, V, AmEx, Diners, **6** *to 28th St.*

Ace Bar
A Chuck E. Cheese for grown-ups: encounter counter culture scenesters of the '60s, but the allure of Tiffany lighting and monumental 19th-century bar remains.
82 University Pl. (bet. 11th and 12th Sts.), 929-9089, MC, V, AmEx, Diners, D **L N R 4 5 6** *to Union Sq.*

Alumni Hall
This Fordham-area bar boasts absolutely no "local flavor" as it's closed during the summer; that means it's strictly students on the dance floor. Here, the crowds flock to see, be seen, and check out the hook-up scene, which reportedly is the best in the neighborhood.
600 East Fordham Rd., (718) 933-1166, Cash Only, **C D** *to Fordham Rd.*

American Trash
Aaah, the great American melting pot. Bikers and bankers meet without colliding at this rare east side dive; its subtitle—"professional drinking establishment"—suggests democracy among lushes.
1471 First Ave. (bet. 76th and 77th Sts.), 988-9008, MC, V, AmEx, **6** *to 77th St.*

Amsterdam Billiards
This suburban-style pool hall is a good fallback when the tables at the area bars are booked till dawn. Alcoholic drinks are restricted to the cozy front room with its own working fireplace. Sunday through Thursday after 11pm, up to four people can play until 3am for a total of $19.
344 Amsterdam Ave. (at 77th St.), 496-8180, MC, V, AmEx, **1 9** *to 79th St.*

Amsterdam Cafe
Although it looks like a European hotel bar, this local favorite is a great place to visit either alone, at the padded bar, or in large thirsty groups. Columbia students and locals alike come for pitchers, pub grub and sports TV in a relaxed restaurant atmosphere.
1207 Amsterdam Ave. (bet. 119th and 120th Sts.), 662-6330, **1 9** *to 116th St.*

Anseo
Sometimes this no-attitude bar is kick-back, sometimes DJ Billy Shane spins, but this is a good stop on St. Mark's. The crowd is mostly youngish downtowners.
126 St. Mark's Pl. (between First Ave. and Ave. A), 475-4145, **L** *to First Ave.,* **4 5 6** *to Astor Pl.*

Arlene Grocery
This wood-paneled hangout's no-cover aspect makes it a decent pit stop to begin the night with ambitious bands which sound better from the back of the room; expect to stand. Only siblings and significant others of the band linger for more than an hour after the set.
95 Stanton St. (bet. Ludlow and Orchard Sts.), 358-1633, Cash Only, **F** *to Second Ave.*

Art Bar
Bring a chatty group of friends to the cozy, carpeted back room where velvet-draped divans, antique coffee tables, a score of paintings, and the consummate living room accessory, the crackling fire, set the stage for marathon conversation.
52 Eighth Ave. (at Horatio St.), 727-0244, MC, V, AmEx, D, Transmedia, **F L 1 2 3 9** *to 14th St.*

Au Bar
Eurotrashy area natives romp through this lavishly decorated retro bar. Among the pitfalls are $7 drinks, a large cover fee, and highly selective doormen, but as always, celebs and beautiful women are always welcome.
41 East 58th St. (bet. Park and Madison Aves.), 308-9455, Cover: $20–$25, **4 5 6** *to 59th St.*

Auction House
Mature customers populate this pricey, chic lounge which serves as a bastion of SoHo uptown, good-looking and fashionable women included.
300 East 89th St. (bet. First and Second Aves.), 427-4458, MC, V, AmEx, D, Diners, **4 5 6** *to 86th St.*

Audubon Bar and Grill
Midtown moves uptown at this swank, supper club located on the site of the Audubon Ballroom. Friday through Monday the place heats up when Latin and jazz music, complete with dancing, is featured in the spacious dining room. Pass on the overpriced menu. Local residents and exhausted medical students from nearby Columbia Presbyterian are doing their best to break in the sterile decor.
3956 Broadway (at 166th St.), 928-5200, MC, V, AmEx, Transmedia, Cover: $5 (Fridays and Saturdays only), **A B C 1 9** *to 168th St.*

Augie's
No refined elegance here, but a big-hearted audience crowds the tiny area where jazzmen ply their craft in hour-long sets and waitresses try their hardest to keep glasses full. The beer selection is limited and the mixed drinks are small, but there's no cover and the per-person table minimum is loosely enforced. Be kind when the trumpeter comes around with a hat for donations.
2751 Broadway (bet. 106th and 107th Sts.), 864-9834, Cash Only, **1 9** *to 103rd St.*

Australia
A friendly Aussie-inspired pub littered with boomerangs and an after-work crowd. Check out Ladies Nights on Wednesdays and Thursdays. No one will mind if you say "g'day".
1733 First Ave. (at 90th St.), 867-0203, **4 5 6** *to 86th St.*

bars 291

Automatic Slims
Go way west to find this happening hangout for locals. A friendly place, despite the deafening jukebox. Head downstairs if noise becomes a problem. When it gets late—very, very late—dancing on the bar is allowed; one might even say condoned. *733 Washington St. (at Bank St.), 645-8660, MC, V,* ❶❶❶❷❸❾ *to 14th St.*

B

The Bar
There's no mistaking the crowd here: all gay and all male, of all ages and styles, all drawn by those twin pleasures of cheap drinks and a lively crowd around the pool table. *68 Second Ave. (at 4th St.), 674-9714, Cash Only,* ❶ *to Second Ave.* ♿

Bar 89
A fancy, stylish crowd and pricey drinks are nothing unusual in this neck of the woods; the main attraction is the fabulous unisex bathroom, whose glass doors must be latched ever so precisely to prevent exposing everyone in the room to things better kept private. While someone's inside, the glass becomes opaque. *89 Mercer St. (bet. Spring and Broome Sts.), 274-0989, MC, V, AmEx,* ❶❾ *to Canal,* ❻❺ *to Spring St.*

Bar d'O
Arguably the place that initiated the lounge craze Tuesdays, Saturdays, and Sundays feature Joey Arias and Raven-O hosting teh festivities. $5 cover. *29 Bedford St. (bet. Sixth Ave. and Hudson St.), 627-1580, Cash Only, Cover: Free-$5,* ❶❾ *to Christopher St.*

Baraza
(see page 288)
133 Ave. C (between 8th and 9th Streets),539-0811, Cash Only, ❶ *to First Ave.*

Barmacy
Owner Deb Parker (also of the Beauty Bar) welcomes private functions, film shoots, photo shoots, and "anything else you'd like to shoot except drugs" at her new East Village establishment. It's not reserved most nights, however, and a downtown crowd gathers to mingle and mellow out with the in house DJ. Mon. through Fri. 5:30pm to 4am. *538 E. 14th St. (between Aves. A and B), 228-2240, MC, V,* ❶ *to First Ave.*

Bar None
A bit tacky, but the most consistently packed of the bars on Third Avenue's collegiate drinking strip. Enjoy the many diversions co-ed life has to offer: a frisky pick-up scene, dirt-cheap pitchers, cutthroat pool and "dancing" in the back room. *98 Third Ave. (bet. 12th and 13th Sts.), 777-6663, MC, V, AmEx,* ❶❶❶❹ ❺❻ *to Union Sq.*

Barracuda
This outing from the boys who brought Big Cup to Chelsea brings an East Village sense of ironic distance to the usually deadly serious Chelsea cruising game. Dark and cruisy in front, with a funky lounge complete with lava lamps, this recent offering attracts a young crowd of good-looking men and a smaller crowd of equally hip and attractive women more interested in chatting and having a good time than in proving how beautiful they all are. *275 West 22nd St. (bet. Seventh and Eighth Aves.), 645-8613, Cash Only,* ❻❸ *to 23rd St.* ♿

Barramundi
This stylish but unpretentious joint attracts a slightly older, more intellectual set than the grungy, giddy watering holes further up the block. Check out the funky club-room behind the bar, a taxidermist's dream, but come early to stake out territory on the weekend, when bartender Scott Cardwell mixes a mean margarita. *147 Ludlow St. (bet Stanton and Rivington Sts.), 529-6900, Cash Only,* ❶ *to Second Ave.* ♿

Beauty Bar
Glitter-sparkled walls shimmer, reflecting off vintage hair dryers that act as lounge chairs at this 50's beauty salon turned bar. Owner Deb Parker's own collection of '40's hairpins and pomade ads add the final touches. Wednesday afternoon manicure/drink specials are a must. *231 East 14th St. (bet. Second and Third Aves.), 539-1389, MC, V,* ❶❶❶❹❺❻ *to14th St.*

Belmont Lounge
The supercool Ave. A aesthetic migrates north and cleans itself up a bit at this dark and slightly sedate Union Square hotspot. *117 East 15th St. (bet. Park Ave. South and Irving Place), 533-0009, MC, V, AmEx, D, Diners,* ❶❶❶❹❻ *to Union Square* ♿

Bemelman's
Don't expect chips and Budweiser at this refined uptown bar, where Carlyle Hotel guests and those who wish they were congregate here for aperitifs. Named for illustrator Ludwig Bemelman who painted murals here, the bar's evening performances highlight jazz singers and pianists. *35 East 76th St. (at Madison Ave), 744-1600, MC, V, AmEx,* ❻ *to 77th St.* ♿

Big Sur
If the liveliness of the young working crowd enjoying rock music in comfortable seating doesn't please, attend the alternate social scene located by the unisex bathrooms. *1406 Third Ave. (at 80th St.), 472-5009, MC, V, AmEx, Diners,* ❻ *to 77th St.*

The Billiard Club
While the bar offers slim pickings for those who have a hankering for a brew while they shoot, the tables are flat, the juke box is loud, and there are other games like air hockey with which to while away the hours. *220 West 19th St. (bet. Seventh and Eighth Aves.), 206-7665, MC, V, AmEx, Diners,* ❶❾ *to 18th St.* ♿

Bleecker Street Bar
Coca-Cola paraphernalia and a fast-snax vending machine add a little kitsch to this smoky roadhouse wannabe. For the full consumer-culture experience, hop into the Polaroid photo booth in the pool room in the back. *56 Bleecker St. (bet. B'way & Lafayette), 334-0244, MC, V, AmEx,* ❶❶ *to 8th St.,* ❻ *to Astor Pl.*

Blind Tiger Ale House
With over 24 beers on tap and bottled beers from 12 countries, this haunt satisfies just about anyone's palate for brew. The crowd's strictly white-collar, after-work, and non-Budweiser drinking.
518 Hudson St. (at 10th St.), 675-3848, MC, V, AmEx, D, Diners, ❶❾ *to Christopher St.*

Blondie's
Don't be fooled, the windows looked soaped-over but they are open for business. Mounted televisions boasting an impressive range of sporting events play continuously above the blonde bartenders who helped, no doubt, to give this boisterous sports bar its name. Try the "world-famous atomic wings."
2180 Broadway (at 77th St.), 362-4360, MC, V, AmEx, Entrées: $5-$7, ❶❾ *to 79th St.*

Blue and Gold
A basement beer hall, great for drinking the night away without blowing your whole wad. Bring some bar snacks, commandeer a booth, and beware the regulars: answering obscure literary trivia questions can be a precondition for being allowed to exit.
79 East 7th Street (between First and Second Avenues), 473-8918, Cash Only, ❿ ® *to 8th St.*

The Boiler Room
More lounge than bar, the pool table is used only as seating, and classic disco mixed with current dance sets the stage for light cruising. Indulge after an expensive weekend with one-dollar beers and shots on Mondays. A mixed crowd in the early evening, but around nine, the boys take over.
86 East 4th St. (between First and Second Avenues), 254-7536, Cash Only, ❻ *to Second Avenue*

Boomer's
For the true sports fanatic: know your stats and be ready to talk some serious trivia. The crowd of cheering, jeering, thirtysomething men largely ignores the standby pool table in favor of the twenty-three televisions. New York home of the Celtic's soccer supporter club, so know what you mean when asking about the "football" game.
349 Amsterdam Ave. (bet. 76th & 77th Sts.), 362-5400, MC, V, AmEx, Entrées: $5-$7, ❶❾ *to 79th St.*

Boots and Saddle
Urban and rural cowboys flock to this Western veteran, proving denim the friendlier gay male counterpoint to leather. Features happy hour Monday to Friday, 3-9pm and Saturday and Sunday Beer Blasts that boast $1.50 cans and draft and $2.50 bottles.
76 Christopher Street (at Seventh Ave.) 929-9684, Cash Only, ❶❾ *to Christopher Street*

Botanica
The former site of the old Knitting Factory, recently converted into a paradise for twentysomething drinkers—one of the few chic spots where room to sit and converse can be found without resorting to someone's lap. Try to get a bar seat to be in the middle of all the action— if not hang out near the bathrooms where everyone ends up eventually.
47 Houston St. (between Mott and Mulberry Sts.), 343-7251, Cash Only, ❻❻❻❻ *to Broadway/Lafayette.*

Bourbon St.
A seamier joint than other Amsterdam watering holes, this down-home establishment welcomes those seeking a friendly bar to call their own, although seating is limited. Ladies nights Monday through Wednesday.
407 Amsterdam Ave. (bet. 79th and 80th Sts.), 721-1332, MC, V, AmEx, D, Diners, ❶❾ *to 79th Sts.*

Bowery Bar
Models pose beneath the chic, globular lights of this NoHo social scene staple, though it's not the shi-shi mecca it once was. The spacious, enclosed outdoor seating is popular.
40 East 4th Street (at Bowery), 475-2220, MC, V, AmEx, Diners, Entrées: $10-15, ❻ *to Bleecker or* ❻❻❻❻ *to Broadway/Lafayette*

Boxers
Yuppie paradise smack dab in the middle of the Village. Standard lunch and dinner fare, plus a bar with a television showing whatever game is on. In the summer, tables spill out onto the sidewalk, the better to see and be seen.
186 West 4th Street (at Barrow St.), 633-2275, Entrées: $8-12, MC, V, AmEx, D, Diners, Transmedia, ❶❻❻❻ ❻❻❻ *to West 4th St.*

The Break
Trendy club goers, gym boys, and Chelsea locals make this relatively low-key space the place to begin or end a night on the town. Recent renovations have made the small locale a little roomier, but be prepared to stand shoulder-to-shoulder with all sorts of attractive men. Weather permitting, enjoy the barbecued burgers available on Fridays and Saturdays for the happy hours, which begin at 6pm, in the small garden area in the back.
232 Eighth Avenue (between 21st and 22nd Streets), 627-0072, Cash Only, ❻❻ *to 23rd St.*

Brother Jimmy's
Anyone from south of the Mason-Dixon line will feel at home in this southern theme bar. Post collegiates and pre-professionals come for the generous bartenders and Sunday special of $18.95 for unlimited beer and all the ribs you can stomach.
1461 First Avenue at 76th Street), 288-0999, MC, V, AmEx, ❻ *to 77th Street*

Burp Castle
The great design and eccentric staff make this place a "must stop in."
41 East 7th St. (between Second and Third Avenues), 982-4576, ❻ *to Astor Place*

bars 293

C

C Note
Performers like working at C-Note, as its known for a superior sound system, designed by owner/sound engineer Jules Bailis. Seven nights a week a mixed-crowd comes to hear an eclectic mix of live jazz, Latin, Latin jazz, jazz singer showcases and more at this small club. One drink minimum. Music begins after 8pm.
57 Avenue C (at 10th St.), 677-8142, Cash Only, ⓛ *(to First Ave.)*

Cafe Pierre at the Pierre Hotel
Old money flocks to this posh, if somewhat stuffy, piano bar to sip V.S.O.P. and to enjoy staid renditions of Cole Porter tunes amidst the incongruous Louis Quartorze decor.
2 East 61st St. (at Fifth Ave.), 940-8195, MC, V, AmEx, $12 minimum, Monday-Saturday starting at 8pm, ❹❺❻ *to 59th St.* ♿

Cafe Un Deux Trois
The convivial crowd at the handsome bar of this tony French brasserie helps make it the ideal place to kick off a stylish evening in Midtown. Take in the classic Parisian ambiance, but forego the overprice and mediocre bistro food.
123 West 44th St. (at Sixth Ave. and Broadway), 354-4148/4397, MC, V, AmEx, ⓝⓡ❶❷❸❼❾ *to Times Square*

Caliente Cab
Try to taste each of the ten margarita flavors for which this Mexican style restaurant and bar is famous, but at $6 a glass don't expect to get too far. Still, the free nachos, mind-numbing rock music, and nine giant-screen TVs tuned to familiar sports teams sweating and grunting away are bound to entertain.
21 Waverly Place (at Greene), 529-1500, MC, V, ❻ *to Astor Place*

Candle Bar
Quite low-key, this bar is indeed lit largely by candles. The local clientele all seem to know each other, so the darkness isn't much of an impediment to anything. Tuesdays feature $1 off beers with presentation of a gym ID, and Wednesday is Latino Night, where Bacardi and Coke, known as Cuba Libre, is offered for a mere $2.50.
309 Amsterdam Ave. (bet. 74th and 75th St.), 874-9155, Cash Only, ❶❷❸❾ *to 72nd St.* ♿

Candy Bar & Grill
In synch with its name, this colorful bar mixes a Blakean world of "innocence" with "experience." While its theme and red-orange color scheme recall childhood memories of board games, the bar's extensive selection of martinis and other potables, including specialty summertime concoctions, sets the stage for more adult pleasures. The restaurant serves up global-fusion food blending flavors and dishes from around the world.
131 Eighth Ave. (bet. 16th and 17th Sts.), 229-9702, MC, V, D, Diners, Entrées: $6.95-$15.95, ❹ⓒ❹ⓛ *to 14th St./8th Ave.* ♿

Cannon's Pub
While an older crowd of regulars parks at the bar most hours, it's the baseball-capped herds from a certain university up the St. who determine whether it's empty or packed here. Equipped with a pool table and darts, this slightly seedy but arguably endearing haunt features low prices and McSorley's on tap.
1294 Broadway (at 108th St.), 678-9738, Cash Only, ❶❾ *to 110th St.*

Carnegie Bar and Books
This recently opened two-floor cigar kingdom attracts the same white-collar crowd as its city siblings. No smoking jackets but patrons do enjoy feeling literary among the bookshelves while nursing fabulous martinis. Live jazz rounds out the ambiance on weekends.
156 West 56th St. (at Seventh Ave.), 957-9676, MC, V, AmEx, Diners, ❻❼❼ *to Seventh Ave.* ♿

Carriage House
Home away from home for the cable-less of Park Slope who need their fix of the Knicks or the Rangers. If you're burnt on sports, amuse yourself at the pool table or with the occasional karoke night.
312 Seventh Ave. (bet. Seventh and Eighth Aves.), (718) 788-7747, MC, V, AmEx, D, Diners, ❼ *to Seventh Ave.* ♿

Cedar Tavern
Pay tribute to Willem de Kooning with a visit to this spacious tavern, which the famous abstract expressionist frequented. The patrons are no longer the counter-culture scenesters of the '60s, but the allure of the Tiffany lighting and the monumental 19th century bar remains.
82 University Place (bet. 11th and 12th Sts.), 929-9089, MC, V, AmEx, D, Diners, ⓝⓡ❹❺❻ *to Union Sq.* ♿

Champs
This king-sized bar gets rockin' just when most places are beginning to wilt. Buff beauties cruise a dance floor reminiscent of high school gym, complete with yellowish wood and brightly colored boundary lines. Work out with a crowd that's very fit, very young, very pretty, and very under-dressed.
17 West 19th St. (bet. Fifth and Sixth Aves.), 673-1717, Cash Only, ❶❾ *to 18th St.* ♿

Chelsea Billiard
Bring your own booze to this hall. Ladies, practice hustling Thursday nights when tables are half-price.
54 West 21st St. (bet. Fifth and Sixth Aves.), 989-0096, MC, V, AmEx, Diners, ❶❾ *to 23rd St.* ♿

The Chestnut Room
The perfect escape from the supercharged city, as well as one of its most affordable cabarets, despite being located in the ritzy Tavern on the Green. The soothing atmosphere and subdued crowd allow patrons to enjoy both the music and the dinner conversation.
Central Park West and 67th St., 873-3200, MC, V, AmEx, D, Diners, Entrées: $8-$34, ❶❾ *to 66th,* ⓐⓑⓒⓓ *to 72nd St.* ♿

294 bars

Chumley's

Professionals and other scene-making twenty-somethings inhabit this atmospheric basement bar; tucked away behind an unmarked entrance that recalls its days as a former bootlegger's paradise. The term "86ed" as in being thrown out, derives from the speakeasy's address. Breathing room is impossible to come by after nine on weekends.
86 Bedford St. (at Barrow St.), 675-4449, Cash Only, ❶❾ to Christopher St.

Ciel Rouge

Gaze into a date's eyes while reveling in the anonymity and intimacy of this hip hideaway. Sexy and swanky, with all the illicit glamour of a Prohibition-era speakeasy, this dark retreat offers drinks for a sophisticated palate in the scarlet lounge complete with comfy chairs and sporting the ultimate in retro chic, a baby grand
176 Seventh Ave. (bet. 20th and 21st Sts.), 929-5542, Cash Only, ❶❾ to 23rd St.

City Wine and Cigar Co.

Catering to celebrities, Wall Street suits and other who have "arrived," this Latin-style luxury lounge is firmly onboard the cigar bar bandwagon. Venture in only if you think you can pull it off.
62 Laight St. (at Greenwich), 334-2274, MC, V, AmEx, ❶❾ to Canal St.

Clarke's

"People don't drink like they used to anymore," laments owner Eugene.

"In the '80's on drink-up nights they used to bring guys out of here on stretchers." Be that as it may, the $5 all-you-can-drink-in-three-hours special on Thursday nights makes this the place for high-volume, '90's style, stress-antidote imbibing. The bar owes its spacious feel to extra-high ceilings, and a gallery of great athletes graces the walls. Free hot dogs and sauerkraut on Friday nights.
2541 Webster Ave. (near Fordham Rd.), (718) 364-9503, Cash Only, ❷❺ to Grand Concourse

Cody's

The crowd at Brooklyn's friendliest bar exudes a feel-good bonhomie. The kitchen stays open until 10pm, the bar until there are no more customers.
154 Court St. (bet. Amity and Pacific), (718) 852-6115, MC, V, AmEx, Entrées: $6-$15, ❻ to Bergen St.

Coffee Shop

Wide-slat blinds in the windows prevent pedestrians from gawking at the beautiful waitstaff serving mediocre Brazilian food to a post-collegiate crowd of painfully self-conscious hipsters in a '50's diner setting. The smart ones just come to drink
29 Union Square West (at 16th St.), 243-7969, MC, V, AmEx, Transmedia, ❶❽❾❹❺❻ to Union Square

The Cub Room

"I've sworn off martinis, except at this place," remarks a patron of this lovely bar. Business attire is the unwritten dress code for the young and affluent who enjoy expensive cocktails and the serious pick-up scene, while lounging on the comfy furniture.
131 Sullivan St. (second entrance at 183 Prince St.), 677-4100, AmEx, ❹❻❽ to Spring St.

Cubbyhole

Favored by friendly college aged women of various persuasions, this small, dark, dyke rendezvous spot lives up to the double or triple-entendre in its name. The bar is open with a $5 cover on Saturday nights from 8:30 to 10pm.
281 West 12th St. (at Fourth Ave.), 243-9041, Cash Only, ❶❽❾❹❺❻ to Union Square.

D

Danny's Skylight Room at the Grand Sea Palace

While it claims to have one of the best sound and lighting systems in the city, most people go to this reasonably priced singing bar for—surprise, surprise—the skylight.
346 West 46th St. (bet. Eighth and Ninth Aves.), 265-8130, Cover: $8-$15, $10 minimum, MC, V, AmEx, D, Diners, ❶❷❸❾❶❷❸ ❼❾ to 42nd St.

Dapper Dog

Undergrads unite at this typical dirty, sticky-floored college bar where baseball-capped, plaid-shirted fraternity boys abound. On Wednesdays, chug all you want (or can) till midnight for a measly $5.
1768 Second Ave. (at 92nd St.), 348-0879, Cash Only, ❻ to 96th St

DBA

Stands for "Doing Business As" but might as well stand for "Drink Best Ale," for the fine selection of both foreign and domestic beers and the best of nearly every type of liquor on the menu. The bartenders are knowledgeable and not condescending; watch the mostly male after-work crowd try to out-connoisseur one another. Special tasting events occur on Monday nights for a flat fee.
41 First Ave. (bet. Second and Third Aves.), 475-5097, MC, AmEx, D, ❻ to Second Ave.

Dharma

See bar scene sidebar
174 Orchard St., 780-0313, MC, V, ❻ (to Second Ave.).

Dive Bar

Sure, it's got dive written all over it, literally, but this clean haunt is pretty damn tame: there's hardly ever a line for the free darts, and even the resident pool sharks won't intimidate. Chug till 4am every day and don't overlook a menu strong enough to support a free delivery service.
732 Amsterdam Ave. (at 96th St.), 749-4358, MC, V, AmEx, Entrées: $5-$7, ❶❷❸❾ to 96th St.

Doc Holiday's

"I'm trapped in here with the convicts who love me," moans bartender Jessica—and she's just talking about the regulars. Weekends, this rollicking country-western joint in flooded with hell raisers who come from all over to admire the wild animal pelts on the walls and the

even wilder staff who can often be found dancing on the bar. Try the Vietnamese food.
141 Ave. A (bet. 9th and 10th Sts.), 979-0312, MC, V, AmEx, Diners, Entrées: $6-$12, ⓛ *to First Ave.*

Don Hill's

Don Hill's is consistently crowded with down town kids, especially on Wednesday nights for the Beauty party when kids come out to groove '70's and '80's style, and Hot Fudge Sundays, which features soul and hip hop music, and the Famous Squeeze Box on Friday nights: a gay rock drag queen party. Live bands and DJ's every night.
511 Greenwich St. (at Spring St.), 334-1390, MC V AmEx D, ⓒⓔ *to Spring St.;* ①⑨ *to Houston St.* ♿

Don't Tell Mama

Wrest control of the microphone away from fellow exhibitionists at this extrovert's paradise where patrons are invited to sing along with the waitstaff, the pianist, and the predominantly gay clientele. Ask about student discounts.
343 West 46th St. (bet. Eighth and Ninth Aves.), 757-0788, MC, V, AmEx, Cover: $10-$20 (two-drink minimum), ①⑨ *to 50th St.*

Down the Hatch

A good game of foosball might win you a free shot at this Upper West Side favorite. "Down the Hatch" means all the beer you can drink and all the wings you can eat on Saturday and Sundays. Find out how much you can take.
179 West 4th (bet. Sixth

and Seventh Aves.), 627-9747, MC, V, ⓐⓑⓒⓓ ⓔⓕⓠ *to West 4th St.*

The Duplex

This piano bar right off Sheridan Square has been providing live show tunes to the neighborhood for years. A mature contingent lingers here, so tweed is more prevalent than muscle-tees. Large and elegantly decorated, the legendary space offers cabaret upstairs; shows are varied and frequent, so make reservations. Younger men may find the paternalistic attitude grating.
61 Christopher St. (at Seventh Ave.), 255-5438, Cash Only, ①⑨ *to Christopher St.*

E

E & O

Sit back into one of the satin-covered couches in this basement rec room and watch the downtown trendies shuffle to tunes spun by a live DJ. Sundays command erotic lounge, Thursdays play trance-inducing house, while hip-hop Fridays are decidedly more active.
100 West Houston St. (bet. La Guardia and Thompson), 254-7000, MC, V, AmEx, D, Diners, ⓑⓓⓕⓠ *to Broadway/Lafayette,* ⓝⓡ *to Prince St.*

Ear Inn

A laid-back, homey atmosphere and reasonable prices on both food and liquor draws a crowd that's on the hip side of yuppie to this former brothel, located way west of the main drags. The sign once read BAR, but the burnt out 'B' gave way

to its present 'E'.
326 Spring St. (bet. Greenwich and Washington), 226-9060, MC, V, AmEx, Diners, Entrées: $5-$10, ⓒⓔ *to Spring St.*

Eighty-Eight's

The bar of course draws its name from the piano downstairs, where aspiring NYU talent is regularly showcased, while equally inspired cabaret is featured upstairs. Plenty of big names also. Call for reservations.
228 West 10th St. (bet. Bleecker and Hudson Sts.), 627-4351, MC, V, AmEx, Cover: $15-$20, ⓐⓑⓒ ⓓⓔⓕⓠ *to West 4th St.*

Element Zero

Submarines are the theme of this tiny one-room subterranean hotspot. DJs favor jungle and its many variations. Only the very tall can get any air, but survival pales in comparison to impressing even the trendiest of friends.
215 East 10th St. (bet. First and Second Aves.), 780-9855, Cash Only, ⓛ *to Third Ave.*

11th Street Bar

Locals hungry for bar action un-tainted by Ave. A herds are breaking in this addition to Alphabet City nightlife. Narrow in front at the crowded bar, it opens up in the back with a handful of tables large enough to fit all your roommates, or your new friends.
510 East 11th St. (bet. Aves. A and B), 982-3929, MC, V, AmEx, ⓛ *to First Ave.*

F

Fez

A chic, artsy clientele hides out at this Moroccan style bar whose decor is as lush as the menu offerings. Catch the legendary Mingus Big Band on Thursdays, arrive early to snag the comfiest seats.
380 Lafayette St. at Great Jones (Under Time Cafe, bet. Fourth Ave. and Great Jones), 533-2680, ⓝⓡ *to 8th St.,* ⑥ *to Astor Pl.,* ⓑⓓⓕⓠ *to Broadway/Lafayette.*

Flamingo East

Upstairs is chic and pretentious, full of film industry types, and usually reserved for private parties; the downstairs restaurant lounge is a bit more mellow. Wednesdays, observe them at their finest.
219 Second Ave. (bet. 13th and 14th Sts.), 533-2860, MC, V, AmEx, Diners, ⓛ *to First or Third Ave.*

Florio's Cigar Bar and Restaurant

Unwind, eat, and light up at this simple establishment located at the junction of Little Italy and Chinatown. Patrons range from upscale to postcollegiate, but it's thankfully not a pick-up scene; sometimes a cigar bar can just be a cigar bar.
192 Grand St. (bet. Mulberry and Mott Sts.), 226-7610, MC, V, AmEx, D, Diners, ⓑⓓⓠ *to Grand St.*

Four Seasons

Picasso and Miro grace the walls of this classic hotel bar. Break the piggybank and maybe you'll be able to afford a gimlet here.
99 East 52nd St. (bet. Lexington and Park Aves.), 754-9494, MC, V, AmEx, D,

Diners, Entrées: $37-$48, ❻ to 51st St. or ❺❻ to Lexington-Third. ♿

420 Bar and Lounge

This new, swank addition to the Amsterdam scene, populated with the requisite clothes hangers and the men who finance their drinking, could teach those SoHo types a thing or two. Local scenesters, spared the cab ride downtown, don't seem to mind the pricey cocktails, but if you've come for the strip's notorious drink specials, you may be better served up the St.
420 Amsterdam Ave. (at 80th St.), 579-8450, MC, V, AmEx, D, Diners, Transmedia, ❶❾ *to 79th St.* ♿

Fred's Beauty

This tribute to a popular 1940s cigar aims for universal appeal, incorporating classic cigar bar style and computer-age glassworks into the decor of a polished and spacious lounge. "What we wanted was a real hangout," explains the designers, Pattie and Kristin. The menu ranges from small sandwiches to caviar.
4 West 22nd St. (at Fifth Ave.), 463-0888, MC, V, AmEx, D, ❶❷ *to 23rd St.* ♿

G

"g"

An alternative to the gym-obsessed Chelsea scene, this hotspot has arrived with quite a bang. Casual elegance is the key here; expect to see Matsuda jackets rather than bare torsos. Subtly but well-lit, the bar is surrounded by lounges galore and, in an example of planning genius, a second bar in the back features coffee and gourmet juice drinks. This bar is so popular, the owners have recently ceased publishing their telephone number for fear of incurring the wrath of Giuliani's goons on account of noise and overcrowding.
223 West 19th St. (bet. Seventh and Eighth Aves.), Cash Only, ❶❾ *to 18th St.* ♿

Galaxy

Bedecked in colors of the night sky, this bar and restaurant serves up creative drinks and eclectic food to neighborhood folks and late-night carousers from nearby Irving Plaza. The chef specializes in food made from hemp extracts, claiming it lowers cholesterol.
15 Irving Pl. (at 15th), 777-3631, MC, V, Transmedia, Entrées: $6-$10, ❶❷❸❹❺❻ *to Union Sq.* ♿

Gantry's Pub

You'd never know it from the outside but this St. John's area pub is one of the most congenial around. Basic nightlife nourishment—beer, TV, jukebox and human contact—are provided.
177th St. and Union Turnpike, Fresh Meadows, (718) 969-1515, Cash Only, ❼ *to 179th St.*

Gin Mill

Multiple TVs, long picnic tables, and Atomic Cafe spicy wings keep the crowd busy upstairs; downstairs, exposed brick and a fireplace wrap weary souls in a more mellow mood.
442 Amsterdam Ave. (bet. 81st and 82nd Sts.), 580-9080, MC, V, AmEx, ❶❾ *to 79th St.*

Gingerman

The suits turn out in jaunty little three-piece numbers to mix networking with cruising over cigars and rather anonymous-looking drinks in oh-so-stylish cocktail glasses.
11 East 36th St. (at Fifth Ave.), 532-3740, MC, V, AmEx, D, Diners, ❻ *to 33rd St.* ♿

The Grange Hall

A combination bar/restaurant, frequented by an urbane crowd. Elegant, atmospheric, and delightfully hidden on one of the least-trafficked streets in the West Village. The bar jams up during dinner and on weekends, but after the rush subsides, spread out at a table and enjoy one of the finer things in Village life. Open until 3am, Thursday through Saturday, and until 2am all other nights.
50 Commerce St. (bet. Seventh Ave and Hudson St.), 924-5246, AmEx, ❶❾ *to Christopher St.* ♿

H

The Hangar Bar

Generally filled with young, T-shirt and jeans-clad men on the butch side and usually on their way to someplace else, this unassuming little bar on "the strip" has just enough of a sleaze factor to feel naughty. Highlights include a $100 pool tournament on Wednesdays, go-go men on Fridays, and various "Beer Blasts" on the weekends.
115 Christopher St. (bet. Hudson and Bleecker Sts.), 627-2044, Cash Only, ❶❾ *to Christopher St.* ♿

Heartland Brewery

Take the pulse of the after-work crowd at this hip Union Square bar; patrons move fast, talk fast, and drink fast, enjoying the award-winning house brews like Harvest Wheat while communing with cell phones, digital diaries, and sometimes even each other. For the more leisurely diner, plenty of seating is available, as well as a menu which ranges from your basic meatloaf falafel.
35 Union Sq. West (at 17th St.) 645-3400, MC, V, AmEx, Entrées $8-$12, ❶❷❸❹❺❻ *to Union Sq.*

The Heights

This slick restaurant bar now has a rooftop garden which is heated in the cooler months. Potent margaritas, fresh salsa with tri-colored chips, Boddington's on tap and an eager waitstaff make this a favorite among Columbia students. Start early by slurping $2.50 margaritas during happy hour between 5 and 7pm.
2867 Broadway (at 111th St.), 866-7055, MC, V, AmEx, Entrées: $8-$15, ❶❾ *to 110th St.*

Hell

Once again, the meatpacking district offers elegance amidst its oftentimes squalid warehouses.

bars 297

The boys who brought Big Cup to Chelsea now bring this cozy lounge that mirrors the festive and not the infernal aspect of the mythical hotspot from which it takes its name. The crowd is much like the Big Cup aficionados, with a Barracuda-like healthy mix of East Village.
59 Ganesvoort St. (bet. Washington and Greenwich), 727-1666, MC, V, AmEx, ACE to 14th St.

Henrietta Hudson
Both lipstick and flannel set the tone for this landmark room of her own. Minimal attitude make this mid-sized spot comfortable for cruising to the beat of a fierce jukebox, stand-up comedy on Tuesday nights starting at 10pm, and live music on Wedns. and Suns., with a $4 cover on both nights.
438 Hudson St. (bet. Morton and Barrow), 924-3347, MC, V, AmEx, 1 9 to Hudson St.

Her/She Bar
Popular Friday night party sponsored in part by the infamous and ubiquitous WOW promoters, where predominantly black and Latina women dance, cruise, and strut their stuff. Sports bras and bare midriffs abound below hot lesbian porn shown on the televisions above the bar.
366 Eighth Ave. (at 28th), 631-1093, Friday nights only, 10pm-4am, Cover: before 11pm, $8 thereafter, Cash Only, 1 to 28th St.

Hi-Life Bar and Grill
A friendly atmosphere and late-night menu draw crowds for sushi and live music in an atmosphe which time warps clientele back to the 1930s.
477 Amsterdam Ave. (at 83rd St.), 1 9 to 86th St.

Hogs 'n' Heifers
Appropriately named for the less-than-fragrant part of town in which it resides, this rowdy biker bar attracts the stars despite its meat-packing district address. Tim Roth was recently spotted exiting the dive, while Julia Roberts posed near the infamous bra-clad moose-head for *People*.
859 Washington, 929-0655, Cash Only, ACEL to 14th St.

Holiday Cocktail Lounge
No funky theme, DJs, or chic decor here; strong well drinks for $2.25 and lots of booth space lure a crowd of old barflies, cute young hipsters, and everything in between. Come early before the bartender gets too drunk to remember your order.
75 St. Mark's Pl. (bet. First and Second Aves.), 777-9637, Cash Only, NR to 8th St.

Hoops Bar
Great specials practically every day of the week: score chicken wings for a dime apiece on Mondays; Tuesdays, all aboard for one-dollar bottled beers. A live DJ spins tunes Tuesday through Saturday, seven TVs cater to the couch-bound athlete, and they'll even let you have your birthday party here!
179-11 Union Turnpike, (718) 969-5447, Cash Only, E F to Union Turnpike.

Hudson Bar & Books
Patches on the jacket are optional, but a smoke is de riguer at the finest cigar bar in the Village. The bookshelves sports volumes in several languages, but don't be intimidated: the upscale clientele is friendly and willing to converse—in English, happily enough.
636 Hudson (bet. Horatio and Jane Sts.), 229-2642, MC, V, AmEx, Diners, F L 1 2 3 9 to 14th St.

I

Idlewild
Its innovative design has people flocking from all over to check it out. The music is "consistently eclectic," the atmosphere is "loungy," and a DJ spins every night. The dress code is: clean and casual. (see Theme Bar sidebar)
145 East Houston St. (bet. First and Second Aves.), 477-5005, V MC, F to Second Ave. N R to Broadway/Lafayette.

Irish Brigade Pub
Feisty female bartender serves a much, much older crowd interested in letting loose. Beers start at $1.25, pitchers at $6. Sometimes as a special treat, there's a DJ for dancing. Thrill seeking seniors also flock to Irish Eyes up the Street. (5008 Broadway at 213th), where they have live Irish music Saturday nights.
4716 Broadway (at Arden St.), 567-8714, Cash Only, A to Dyckman St.

J

Jake's Dilemma
Stylish scene makers to low-key regulars inhabit this Amsterdam haunt. The half-price happy hour runs from 5-8pm each weekday. Free draft beer for ladies, on Monday nights.
430 Amsterdam Ave. (bet. 82nd and 83rd Sts.), 580-0556, MC, V, AmEx, 1 9 to 77th St.

Jekyll and Hyde
Busy local hangout advertising over 250 beers, populated by an eclectic crowd drawn to the bustle of Seventh Ave. Don't expect to get away from it all here. Waitstaff indulges in costume party outfits in keeping with the theme. Open late.
91 Seventh Ave. South (bet. Barrow and Grove Sts.), 989-7701, MC, V, AmEx, D, Diners, Entrées: $10-$17, 1 9 to Christopher St.

Jimmy Armstrong's Saloon
According to the menu, "tasty vittles, good grog, and sweet music" draw the uptown music set to this jovial neighborhood pub. which positively bursts with bonhomie. The top-rate jazz guitarists featured here four nights a week (Wednesday through Saturday) are good enough to please the picky crowd of professional musicians, composers, and Julliard students who frequent this friendly, lively place. Appease a hearty appetite with some of the scrumptious savories offered on the eclectic, moderately priced menu.
875 Tenth Ave. (at 57th

298 bars

St.), 581-0606, AmEx, Entrées: $7.50-$12, ❶❾ to 59th St.

Jimmy's Corner
Escape the giddiness and rapacity of the Theater District at this easy-going local dive, the site of some scenes in Raging Bull. Owner Jimmy Glen subsidizes his career as a boxing trainer and manager with the revenues from his hopping bar business. An eclectic crowd of boxing fanatics, literati, grad students, and the occasional movie star gathers here. *140 West 44th St. (bet. Sixth and Seventh Aves.), 221-9510, MC, V, AmEx,* ❿❺❶❷❸❼❾ to Times Sq.

Judy's Restaurant and Cabaret
Catering to high-strung middle-aged women in cocktail dresses and their gay male friends; guests are serenaded with renderings of favorite tunes by Porter, Rodgers and Hart, Mercer, and the like. *49 West 44th St. (bet. Fifth and Sixth Aves.), 764-8930, MC, V, AmEx, Cover: $10-$15, $10 minimum,* ❽ⒹⒻⓆ to 42nd St.

Julie's
This piano bar offers the mature elegance of the Townhouse Bar, but for women. The crowd is generally thirtysomething and professional, but don't mistake comfy couches and a sleek oak bar for boredom: Wednesday nights sizzle with salsa and Sundays prove that the women are not to be outdone by the men by featuring a sexy tea dance that begins at 6pm. Never a cover. *204 East 58th St. (bet.*

Second and Third Aves.), 688-1294, Cash Only, ❹❺❻ to 59th or ⓃⓇ to Lexington Ave.

Julius
Burgers on demand distinguish this long-time fixture. A neighborhood dive quite proud of its wood paneling, this defiant holdover from another era attracts a devoted following of mature men. The occasional smooching couple is at times the only reminder that this is a gay bar, as the ubiquitous graying beards, flannel shirts, and sports on the television set give no clue. *159 West 10th St. (off Seventh Ave.), 929-9672, Cash Only,* ❶❾ to Christopher St.

K

KGB
Old Soviet paraphernalia gives this small upstairs barroom an illicit feel, reinforced by the regular poetry readings and theater downstairs. Perfect for bringing out the inner subversive artist for a good stiff drink, preferably something with vodka. *85 East 4th St. (bet. First and Second Aves.), 505-3360, Cash Only,* Ⓕ to Second Ave.

King
Libido at its most forthright rules this three-tiered yet cramped dance bar. Monday nights promise boys $1 drinks if they take off their shirts, which should give a clue as to what the clientele doesn't wear. A perfect venue for gym boys to flaunt their hard work. Cover varies from $5 to $10. Wednesdays offer an Amateur Strip Contest worth $200, the tamest of

the many contests. *679 Sixth Ave. (bet. 16th and 17th Sts.), 366-5464, Cash Only,* ❶❾ to 18th St.

Knitting Factory
This multi-level venue hosts big names as well as local acts, from avant-garde to jazz to swing. Big couches make everyone feel at home; the multitude of performance spaces will satisfy even the most attention deficient. *74 Leonard St. (bet. West Broadway and Church St.), 219-3055, MC, V, AmEx,* ❶❾ to Franklin St.

Korova Milk Bar
Some wacky guys recreated the milk bar out of *A Clockwork Orange*, and the accuracy is amazing, from the naked mannequins to endless video screens all showing something appropriately strange and terrifying. A mandatory stop for film buffs and lovers of eye candy alike. Sadly, the drinks aren't cheap, except for specials like ladies' night on Wednesdays, when it's all you can drink for $5. *200 Ave. A (bet. 11th and 12th Sts.), 254-8838, Cash Only,* Ⓛ to First Ave.

Kush
(See Bar Scene sidebar) *183 Orchard St. (bet. Houston and Stanton), 677-7328, MC, V,* Ⓕ to Second Ave.

L

La Tour D'Or
Join stockbrokers and investment bankers in carrying on the legacy of J.P. Morgan by puffing cigars and sipping scotch on the rocks in his old library, the closest thing to a private

dining room in the city. The breakfast room overlooks the Harbor. *14 Wall St., 233-2780, MC, V, AmEx, Entrées: $15-$18,* ❷❸❹❺ to Wall St.

Lakeside Lounge
Come prepared to wait for your drinks since this hipster haunt deep in Alphabet City is packed even on nights the bartender calls "real slow." Live bands regularly. Open until 4am. *162 Ave. B (just off 10th St.), 529-8463, Cash Only,* Ⓛ to First Ave.

Landmark Tavern
The swanky, old-fashioned bar attracts yuppies, tourists, and the occasional free spirit. Come in the winter, when the fireplace is ablaze, or late on a summer afternoon, when warm western light streams through the large windows. Pub fare like fish and chips and steaks complement the $5 pints. *626 Eleventh Ave. (at 46th St.), 757-8595, MC, V, AmEx, Diner's, D, Entrées: around $15,* ⓃⓇ❺❶❷❸❼❾ to Times Sq.

Last Second Saloon
The dance floor near the bar overflows with Columbia students whose moves are probably not admired downtown. Thursdays all-you-can-drink from 10pm till 1am: $10 dollars for guys, free for girls; any ideas on what the goal is here? *1840 Second Ave. (at 95th St.), 860-4030, Cash Only,* ❻ to 96th St.

Lava
Lava is known for its sweet vodka drinks like, the Lava Flow, Blue Lagoon and Purple haze,

bars 299

all served in gigantic tiki bowls (good for six people), and if you'd like, the bartenders will set them on fire. Lava, of course, flows down the walls and trees litter the place. Live bands and DJ's play under enormously high ceilings. *28 West 20th St. (bet. Fifth and Sixth Aves.), 627-7867, MC V AmEx, NR19 to 23rd St.*

Lenox Lounge
Variety is key to this venerable "hideaway" established in 1939. Hosts jazz performances on some nights, while Tuesdays and Thursdays cater to a gay crowd. Don't allow the outdated facade to fool you; a good night on the town is timeless. *288 Lenox Ave., 427-0253, Cover varies depending on night, 23 to 125th St.*

Lexington Bar and Books
A pricey, high-class establishment with great ambiance and fantastic martinis make this cozy cigar bar a nice place to pretend you're all grown up along with the white-collar crowd. College students beware: "proper attire is required". Live jazz on Fridays and Saturdays. *1020 Lexington Ave. (at 73rd St.), 717-3902, MC, V, AmEx, Diners, 6 to 77th. St.*

Lickety Split
This small red room, catering to a middle-aged neighborhood group, swells nightly with the sounds of hearty jazz and blues; expect the best on Tuesdays, when marathon jam sessions usher in the morning light. *2361 Adam Clayton Powell Jr. Boulevard (at 138th St.), 283-9093, Cover: around $5, MC, V, AmEx, D, 23 to 135th St.*

Liquor Store Bar
Huge front windows, an oak bar, and sidewalk seating render this bar utterly irresistible. The charming, slightly motley group of neighborhood men welcome newcomers as a fresh audience for their stale jokes. Heaven for any true bar lover. *235 Broadway (at White), 226-7121, Cash Only, 19 to Franklin St.*

Live Bait
Located right on Madison Square Park, curious passers-by and neighborhood locals find it hard to resist this oxymoronic urban rendition of the Louisiana bayou. Force your way past the boisterous happy hour crowd at the bar to the tables in back in order to sample the Cajun shrimp or the mesquite BBQ. *14 East 23rd St. (bet. Broadway and Madison Ave.), 353-2400, MC, V, AmEx, Transmedia, Entrées: $7-$11, NR to 23rd St.*

Lucky Strike
Old-world refinement pervades this restaurant/bar with a pounded brass-topped wood bar, a menu written on huge mirrors and a small dining room in the back; downtown drinkers spice things up. *59 Grand St. (bet. Wooster St. and West Broadway), 941-0479, MC, V, AmEx, Diners, Entrées: $7-$14, ACE to Canal St.*

Ludlow Bar
Dependably cool, and-crowded on the weekends, this downstairs bar stakes all its seating on minimalist couches; the DJ changes night-to-night but the dancing never gets going until everyone's liquored up. Quite a pick-up scene, especially around the purple pool table. *165 Ludlow St. (bet. Houston and Stanton Sts.) 353-0536, MC, V, AmEx, F to Second Ave.*

Luna Lounge
No cover and no minimum draw a lively crowd of tattooed bohemians to this otherwise undistinguished bar. The dark, cavernous space hosts Alternative Comedy Nite on Mondays at 8pm. *171 Ludlow St. (bet. Houston and Stanton Sts.), 260-2323, Cash Only, F to Second Ave.*

M

Marechiaro Tavern
Oooh and Aaah at the huge photo of Frank Sinatra. Then go get yourself a drink at one of Little Italy's last genuine bars. Also known as "Tony's" in case you want to feel like a real local. *176 1/2 Mulberry St., 226-9345, Cash Only, NR to Prince St.*

Marion's
Drinking seems as natural as breathing at this 40s-style institution. Squeeze in at the bar or take a table for some fine continental dining: despite some modern touches like adding Thai elements to the menu, the overall retro style makes for guilt-free indulgence in red meat and other fatty but delicious fare. *354 Bowery St. (bet Great Jones and 4th Sts.), 475-7621, MC, V, AmEx, Entrées: $8-$13, 6 to Bleecker or BDFQ to Broadway/Lafayette*

Marriott Marquis Lounge
The eighth-floor revolving lounge, one of two in this hotel, is not for the faint of heart and affords a unique view of Times Square. Plush and amenable to expense accounts, but not pretentious. *1535 Broadway (at 45th St.), 398-1900, MC, V, AmEx, ACENRS1 279 to 42nd St.*

Mary Lou's
Elegant restaurant and bar sunken into the basement level of a fashionable townhouse. Entrées tend towards expensive seafood, but the bar is cozy and the crowd is made up of regulars. *21 West 9th St. (bet. Fifth and Sixth Aves.), 533-0012, 533-0013, MC, V, AmEx, D, Diners, Transmedia, Entrées: $8-$20, ABCDEFQ to West 4th St.*

Max Fish
Hipsters live it up at this comparatively bright and lively Ludlow fave, once a hotspot, now just comfortably cool. Play pool with the regulars or spend a week's wages on pinball while enjoying local artist's work which is proudly hung on the walls. *178 Ludlow St. (bet. Houston and Stanton Sts.), 529-3959, Cash Only, F to Second Ave.*

Meow Mix
Bohemians of all persuasions are welcome at this

campy but casual downtown dyke bar. The hub of the queer art scene, it hosts everything: comedy, poetry, performance art, theme parties, and both local and touring bands, usually of the post-punk girl variety. Pick up a calendar, and, if you're lucky, one of the cute, pierced, and tattooed chicks.
269 East Houston St. (at Suffolk St.), 254-1434, Cash Only, ❻ to Second Ave.

Merc Bar
Beyond the nondescript entrance lies a classic model bar, where even the servers are cover girls and half the clientele seems strung out. A soothing atmosphere means no one gets jolted unnecessarily out of their reverie (save that for the cab home).
151 Mercer St. (bet. Prince and Houston Sts.) 966-2727, MC, V, AmEx, Diners, ❻❻ to Prince St. &

Merchants
Yuppie nirvana. Drop twenties on exquisite food and patrician cocktails upstairs, then move downstairs for a stogie and some live jazz. Everyone comes decked out in their finest threads, including the occasional model.
1125 First Ave. (at 62nd St.), 832-1551, MC, V, AmEx, D, Diners, Transmedia, Entrées: $6.95-$13.95, ❹❺❻ to 59th St., ❻❻ to Lexington Ave./Third Ave.

Metronome
Slightly more polished and pricey than the other Gramercy bars, Metronome draws an older professional crowd. Call ahead; hours vary depending on the event, though live jazz is predominant.

915 Broadway (at 21st St.), 505-7400, MC, V, AmEx, Diners, ❻❻ to 23rd St. &

Milano's
Old men who look like they haven't left their barstools in a good twenty-years and the youngsters who love to drink with them fill this dark, narrow hallway. Come in for a beer and leave with the wisdom of the ages.
50 Houston St. (bet. Mott and Mulberry Sts.), 226-8632, Cash Only, ❻❻❻❻ to Broadway/Lafayette St.

Monkey Bar
"It's hip, it's hopping, and it's hot," said a fiftyish, dolled-up patron of this Art Deco masterpiece where a glamorous, older crowd sips cocktails and flaunts Chanel. The epitome of swank.
Hotel Elysée, 60 East 54th St. (bet. Madison and Park Aves.), 838-2600, MC, V, AmEx, Diners, ❻ to 53rd Street &

Motor City Bar
"Professional creative types" too old to be carded flock to this unlikely Detroit theme bar, a harbinger of gentrification this far south of Houston. Motown on weekdays, sliding into a rave scene Friday and Saturday, but the vehicular bric-a-brac adorning the walls may strike some as a little corny. Slicker and a little less funky than other joints in these parts, locals like it "cuz there's elbow room."
127 Ludlow Street (bet. Rivington and Delancey Sts.), 358-1595, Cash Only, ❻ to Second Avenue &

Mug's Ale House
So many good beers on tap, most people never investigate the vast selection in bottles. Add to this the local contingent and a decent juke-box for a good reason why people come from Manhattan to drink here. Join 'em and fill in the blanks.
125 Bedford Ave. (at North 10th St.), (718) 486-8232, Cash Only, ❻ to Bedford Ave. &

Mulligan's Pub
A friendly if somewhat macho Irish bar within spitting distance of New York Public Library and Grand Central Station: "Only real men here, no half-measures." Decent pub grub.
267 Madison Ave. (bet. 39th and 40th Sts.), 286-0207, MC, V, AmEx, ❻❻❻❻ to 42nd St. &

Mustang Harry's
Low lighting and wood paneling create a comfortable, elegant ambiance for yuppies in search of the perfect after-work cocktail. While the food plays second fiddle to the drinks, this watering hole boasts a good draught beer selection.
352 7th Ave. (bet. 29th and 30th Sts.), 268-8930, MC, V, AmEx, ❶❷❸❾ to 34th St. &

Mustang Sally's
Older sister to Mustang Harry's, this saloon caters to a mixed crowd of students, young professionals, and that rare bar species, the family. Above-average pub menu located under the televisions mounted on the walls.
324 7th Ave. (at 28th St.), 695-3806, MC, V, AmEx, Entrées: $7-$15, ❶❾ to 28th Street &

Myer Lansky Lounge at Ratner's
Named after Jewish Mafia kingpin Meyer Lansky, this sophisticated new nightspot channels the spirit of the celebrated speakeasy whose site the club now occupies. Beautiful people proffer fine cigars, spirits, and delectable kosher treats to the rhythms of classic jazz, lounge, and kontiki. Expect to run into Hasidim in the men's room, as the club shares its facilities with the deli out front. Humane door policy, but mixed groups of men and women have a better chance of making the cut. Closed on Shabbat; open 8pm -4am, six nights a week.
138 Delancey St. (entrance on Norfolk), 677-9489; around the corner; 102-106 Norfolk St.; follow the lights up the iron staircase to the unmarked door; MC, V, AmEx, Entrées: $6-$11, ❻ to Delancey St., ❻❻❻ to Essex Street

N

ñ
Savor pitchers of sangria while admiring the flamenco dancers who perform every Wednesday night. Don't even try to resist the tapas. It's tiny and little cramped, so stake out a space early and camp there all night.
33 Crosby St. (bet. Broome and Grand Sts.), 219-8856, Cash Only, ❻❻❻ to Canal St. &

Nancy Whiskey Pub
Lunch pub by day, taken over by a colorful cast of regulars by night. The

bars 301

jukebox is classic rock, the pastime is shuffleboard, and the drink of choice is Bud by the bottle. Order another by slamming the empty bottle on the counter; the timid take their pitchers and hide out upstairs.
One Lispenard St. (at West. Broadway), 226-9943, AmEx, ⒶⒸⒺ❶❾ *to Canal St.*

Niagara

Downstairs you'll find the only tiki bar in the East Village. DJs spin rockabilly and swing every night. Sundays Ivan reads Neruda and plays "wild B-Bop, R&B, and soul favorites" from his personal stock. Young crowd, but a breath of fresh air on Avenue A.
112 Avenue A (at 7th St.), 920-9517, MC, AmEx, D, V, Ⓛ *to First Ave.*

Night Cafe

No pitchers, but plenty of pool at one of the neighborhood's most popular watering holes, During the school year, Columbia's graduate writing students have a weekly open mike. Locals good-naturedly tolerate the Columbians and their metaphors, and by 3am the jolly bartender's trivia games and a jukebox packed with billboard hits have loosened everyone up.
938 Amsterdam Ave. (bet. 106th and 107th Sts.), 864-8889, Cash Only, ❶❾ *to 103rd St.* ♿

Nine C

Tiny space packs a down-to-earth crowd for the Sunday Blue Grass Jam and Alphabet City Oprey on Monday nights. Formerly the Red Bar.
700 East 9th St. (at Ave. C), 358-0048, Ⓛ *(to First Ave.), Cash Only*

North Star Pub

For the true pub grub fan: this is where limeys go to dine. Great ales, a quiet but cheerful ambiance, and the largest collection of single-malt scotch in New York make this place worth a visit. Be sure to take the tasting tour of Scotland.
93 South St. (at Fulton St.), 509-6757, MC, V, AmEx, Diners, Entrées: $9-$13, ❶Ⓜ︎Ⓩ❷❸❹❺ *to Fulton St.*

The Nowbar

Intimate without being cramped, the dance floor is complemented by an upstairs that generally serves as a lounge. Creative indirect lighting renders the crowd, gay and straight, hip and festive, surprisingly visible.
22 Seventh Ave. South (at Leroy St.), 293-0323, MC, V, AmEx (bills over $20), ❶❾ *to Houston St.*

O

Oak Bar at the Plaza Hotel

Mildly decadent amusements are encouraged per the motto at this dignified yet easy-going barroom: "We don't mind if you smoke. Living forever is vastly overrated." Posh without being stuffy, the Oak Bar is perfect for a tryst, comparing investment portfolios, or hosting family for special occasions. High drink prices are offset by the copious supply of free nuts. Light bar fare is available, and a humidor keeps stogies fresh.
Fifth Ave. (at Central Park South), 759-3000, MC, V, AmEx, ❶Ⓠ *to 57th St.,* ❺Ⓕ *to Fifth Ave.*

The Oak Room

One of two lounges at the Algonquin Hotel, where Dorothy Parker's mordant wit presided over a legendary circle of writers and critics in the 1920s. Dress up to fit in with the stylish crowd soaking up late-night cabaret performances in this stylized version of an English tea room.
768 Fifth Ave. (at 54th St.), 754-3000, MC, V, AmEx, ⒺⒻⓃⓇ *to Fifth Avenue* ♿

Oke Doke

Rumor has it that not even Jack Nicholson can always get past the octogenarian proprietor Elsie, the toughest doorwoman around, at this intimate, after-hours spot. Elsie's Austrian background explains the excellent selection of German beer and shots, as well as the lace curtains.
307 East 84th St. (bet. First and Second Aves.), 650-9424, Cash Only, ❹❺❻ *to 86th St.*

Old Town Bar

Over a century old, the mirror-backed bar, tiled floor, and brass cash register exude Edith Wharton-era charm, not poseur pretension. Do like the locals by burrowing into a dark booth for a burger.
45 East 18th St. (bet. Broadway and Park Ave. South), 529-6732, MC, V, AmEx, ⓁⓃⓇ❶❹❺❻ *to Union Square* ♿

147

An upscale bar, lounge and restaurant. The hustling staff and bustling patrons are equally beautiful and engaging.
147 West 15th St. (bet. Sixth and Seventh Aves.), 929-5000, MC V AmEx, *Average main course: $20,* ❶❷❸❾ *to 14th St.* ♿

The Opium Den

Find shockingly clean downtown kids at this gothic lock-in. Saints and candles plastered around the room bring on a creepiness that would prompt anyone to reach for another drink.
29 East 3rd St. (bet. Bowery St. and Second Ave.), 505-7344, Cash Only, Ⓕ *to Second Ave.* ♿

Orchard Bar

Enveloped in mellow music and dim blue lighting, low-key Ludlow types chat on the elongated sofas till dawn. Check it out to see what happens next.
200 Orchard St. (bet. Ludlow and Allen Sts.), 673-5350, MC, V, AmEx, D, Ⓕ *to Second Ave.*

Ozone

An up-scale crowd breathes rarefied air at this mood-lit, lush and elegant bar. The black-clad flock here to lounge on couches in the back room or to sample imported beers at the bar up front.
1720 Second Ave. (bet. 89th and 90th Sts.), 860-8950, ❹❺❻ *to 86th St.*

P

P & Gs

Go for the smoky atmosphere, a jukebox jam-packed with the Rolling Stones, and a shot at sighting a rock star unwinding after a couple sets at the nearby Beacon Theater.
279 Amsterdam Ave. (bet. 73rd and 74th Sts.), 874-8568, Cash Only, ❶❾ *to 79th St.*

302 bars

Paddy Reilly's

Live Irish tunes are an attraction for an all-ages crowd not afraid to flaunt the shamrock.
519 Second Ave. (at 29th St.), 686-1210, AmEx, ❻ to 28th St.

The Paramount

Ian Schrager's ritzy hotel offers a maze of mostly two person tables for those wishing to imbibe; there's a nice view of the lobby below with its checkered carpet and colorful chairs.
235 West 46th St. (bet. Broadway and 8th Ave.), 764-5500, MC, V, AmEx, D, ❶❷❸❹❼❾ to Times Square

Park Slope Brewing Company

Comfy and friendly, this bar is by far one of the city's best micro-breweries, boasting a number of tasty beers (try the Belgian Blonde), and killer burgers. Outdoor seating is available, weather permitting.
356 Sixth Ave. (at 5th St.), (718) 788-1756, MC, V, AmEx, Entrées: $7-$12, ❼ to Seventh Avenue

Parnell's Pub

"It'll kill ya' or cure ya'," explains the red-headed waitress in her lilting brogue to customers inquiring about Guinness. Outfitted with a dark wood bar and plenty of Irish pride this bar and restaurant serves traditional dishes along with the infamous, coffee-colored brew.
350 East 53rd St. (at First Ave.), 753-1761, MC, V, AmEx, ❶❷❸ to 51st Street/Lexington Ave.

Patrick's

A slightly seedy but extremely cheap bar: beers start at $1.25, mixed drinks at $2.50. The regulars look like they haven't moved from their barstools in recent memory, but the friendly atmosphere makes this a congenial spot for a quiet pint or two. Beware: the draught beers have a kick like a mule.
221 Dyckman St. (bet. Broadway and Seaman St.), 567-9229, Cash Only, Ⓐ to Dyckman St.

Peculiar Pub

Charming and dingy, this beer-lover's heaven boasts one of the largest selections of beers in the city.
145 Bleecker St. (between Thompson St. and La Guardia Pl.), 353-1327, Cash Only, ❻ to Bleecker Street

Perk's Fine Cuisine

"Every third person's a gangsta and the other two are Buppies," said one Harlemite about this Harlem hangout. Savor succulent baby back ribs while vocalist Robert Fox serenades the ladies with his super-slick renditions of "Me and Mrs. Jones" and other R&B standards. Terrific bar menu; gracious waitstaff in the plush, expensive dining room downstairs.
553 Manhattan Ave. (at 123rd St.), 666-8500, MC, V, AmEx, D, Entrées: $13-$22, ❶❷❸❹ to 125th Street

Pete's Tavern

An honest-to-God neighborhood establishment, Pete's has been a gathering place in Gramercy for ages. Although known mostly as a bar, its surprisingly Italian menu is certainly adequate. Still, more a slice of 19th century London than a piece of pizza from Pisa.
129 East 18th St. (at Irving Pl.), 858-3510, AmEx, V, DC, Entrées: $8-$12, ❹❺❻❼❽ to Union Square

Pete's Waterfront Ale House

Where everybody knows your name, sort of. A welcoming crowd, an impressive array of beers, and fair prices to boot.
155 Atlantic Ave. (bet. Clinton and Henry Sts.), (718) 522-3794, MC, V, AmEx, ❷❸❹❺ to Borough Hall.

The Piper's Kilt

The best neighborhood bar in Washington Heights serves Irish-American food, like "Nachos a la Piper's Kilt", in a plush setting. Specials include a $10 weekend brunch with lots of food and bottomless drinks between noon and 3pm, a weekday lunch special between noon and 3pm and dinner specials every night between 5 and 10pm. The wide selection of beer starts at $1.75, pitchers at $6.50.
4944 Broadway (at 207th St.), 569-7071, MC, V, AmEx, D, Diners, Ⓐ to 207th St.

Pollyesther's

Kitsch by the truckload here; psychedelia, beaded curtains and the requisite Brady Bunch and Sonny and Cher homages will satisfy every Gen-Xer's fantasy of Flower Power and free love. The prices aren't retro but at least they're reasonable.
186 West 4th St. (bet. Sixth and Seventh Aves.), 924-5707, MC, V, AmEx, D, Diners, Cover: $7, ❶❷❸❹❺❻❾ to West 4th St.

Also at

1487 First Ave. (bet. 77th and 78th Sts.), 628-4477, MC, V, AmEx, D, Diners, ❻ to 77th Street

Poppolini's

Come during the fall and witness the Greeks' initiation rites at this frat-boy haven over steaming pasta dishes and oodles of cheap beer.
16 Waverly Place (bet. Mercer and Greene Sts.), 475-1722, MC, V, AmEx, D, Entrées: $10, ❽❾ to 8th Street

Pravda

Go underground, literally. It's neither post-Soviet mayhem, nor is it a hardcore proletarian drinking establishment but the eighty flavors of vodka (including the decidedly bourgeois flavors mango and raspberry), caviar, and a rust-themed decor sort of justify the Russian name High-class SoHoites eschew communism for black market prices.
281 Lafayette (bet. Prince and Spring Sts.), 226-4696, MC, V, AmEx, Transmedia, ❷❹❺❻ to Broadway/Lafayette St., ❻ to Spring St.

Puffy's Tavern

Just a standard bar, which is why this place is so remarkably popular. The crowd is casual except for the obligatory after-work crowd who wish they were, and the atmosphere is quiet enough to sit down and have a conversation without yelling. Late-night patrons come

for the loud jukebox, frozen pizza, darts, and feisty bartender.
81 Hudson St. (bet. Harrison and Jay Sts.), 766-9159, MC, V, AmEx, Diners, 1 9 to Franklin St.

R

Rainbow Room
Pioneering the "windows on the world" concept, this very staid cocktail lounge and restaurant showcases staggering views from the 65th floor. Jacket and tie are essential for dinner and dancing; go next door to Rainbows and Stars for live cabaret. Closed Mondays and Sundays in the summer.
30 Rockefeller Plaza, 65th Floor, 632-5000, MC, V, AmEx, Cover: $20-$40 (jacket required), 6 to 68th St.

Rainbows and Stars
Floating sixty-five floors above St. level, this well-known 70s-style tourist attraction offers one of the finest views of the city in a romantic setting. Both the food and the crowd are bland, but the lively decor makes up for it. More intimate than its neighbor, The Rainbow Room, its the cabaret option of the two spaces.
30 Rockefeller Plaza, 65th Floor, 632-5000, MC, V, AmEx, Cover: $20-$40, 6 to 68th St.

Remedy
College kids congregate here to drink, drink, and maybe do a little drinking as well. While hardly distinctive, it's as good a place as any to kick off an evening of Amsterdam bar-hopping, as drinks here are always inexpensive and free for women on the frequent and well-attended ladies' nights.
462 Amsterdam Ave. (bet. 82nd and 83rd Sts.), 579-9625, MC, V, AmEx, 1 9 to 86th St.

Reminiscence
The name could very well refer to post-collegiate nostalgia for rec-room dance fests and makeout couches, judging by the antics of the clientele. A DJ spins most nights for a local crowd.
334 East 73rd St. (bet. First and Second Aves.), 988-6100, MC, V, AmEx, 6 to 77th St.

Revival
Perfect for a summer night out, this low-key, twentysomething bar offers an outdoor beer garden and pool table. The bar area is cramped, but it's worth waiting for the live DJ after 10pm
129 East 15th St. (bet. Third Ave. and Irving Pl.), 253-8061, Cash Only, L N R 4 5 6 to Union Sq.

Revolution
Larval yuppies gather 'round the fireplace, smoke long cigarettes, and toss their heads back in mock laughter at this unusually hip and upscale for Hell's Kitchen watering hole cum restaurant.
6 119th Ave. (bet. 43rd and 44th Sts.), 489-8451, MC, V, AmEx, D, Diners, A C E to 42nd St.

Reynolds' Cafe Bar
On the corner of a neighborhood known for its Latin flavor, this Irish-oriented pub always attracts Columbia students doing special "research." Shamrocks abound as the symbol of good times.
4241 Broadway (at 180th St.), 923-8927, Cash Only, A to 181st St., 1 9 to 181st St.

Rio Mar
The tapas stops being served in the early evening, but the Rio Mar stays open late, like any good bar in the meatpacking district. For sustenance, try their restaurant next door.
7 Ninth Ave. (at Little West 12th St.), 243-9015, AmEx, F L 1 2 9 to 14th St.

Rising Cafe
On any given night, this relaxed gathering place for Park Slope's sizable gay community hosts anything from readings to art openings. Equal parts coffeehouse and beer and wine bar, all are welcome here; kids can amuse themselves in a play space equipped with plenty of enticing toys.
186 Fifth Ave. (at Sackett), (718) 789-6340, Cash Only, N R to Union Sq.

Riverrun
Families coming in for an early dinner mingle with businessmen partaking of one of the twelve beers on tap. Entrées are outstanding, but no one goes hungry with the abundant bar snacks: complimentary chips, salsa, and hard-boiled eggs provide impoverished drinkers with a little nourishment. Upon leaving, consult TriBeCa's only neighborhood map, to the left of the door.
176 Franklin St. (bet. Hudson and Greenwich Sts.), 966-3894, MC, V, AmEx, D, Entrées: around $10, 1 9 to Franklin St.

The Riviera Cafe
A split-level tavern with two dozen televisions, a knowledgeable crowd, and friendly bartenders who will even change the channel upon request. Food is served and reservations are accepted, even during the NCAA championships.
225 West 7th St. (bet. West 4th and West 10th Sts.), 929-3250, MC, V, AmEx, Diners, Entrées: $7-$10, 1 9 to Christopher St.

Rodeo Bar & Grill
Don't expect cowboy hats and big belt buckles at this cozy wild west watering hole, but then again don't let the giant stuffed buffalo above the bar surprise you. The menu is limited, but live FREE rockabilly bands keep the place swingin' on weekends.
375 Third Ave. (at 27th St.), 683-6500, MC, V, AmEx, D, Diners, Transmedia, Entrées: $7-$12, 6 to 28th St.

Rome
An openly gay version of a fraternity party. War, conquest, sex, sports, chiseled bare chests, and other "male virtues" are celebrated without shame at this marble-walled, multi-leveled megabar with an Ancient Roman theme. Watch out for Ritual Mondays, celebrating even darker pleasures of testosterone than other nights.
290 Eighth Ave. (bet. 24th and 25th Sts.), 242-6969, Cash Only, A C E to 23rd St.

The Royalton
Grand, as is everything designed by Philip Stark,

304 bars

so be prepared to be overwhelmed. The clientele is a sampling of wealthy suits, both local and imported, and tourists who cough up ten bucks for a drink and nurse it till the waiter's sneer becomes too much.
44 West 44th St. (bet. Fifth and Sixth Aves.), 944-8844, MC, V, AmEx, ❸❹❼❾ *to 42nd St.* &

Rudy Bar and Grill

patrons of varying class and sexual orientations converge at this beer and hot dog joint, identifying with its large model pig outside. The $1.50 pint of Bud early bird special leaves plenty of spare change for the jukebox.
627 Ninth Ave. (bet. 44th and 45th Sts.), 974-9169, Cash Only, ❶❸❾ *to 42nd St.reet*

S

Saint's

The gay community meets the Columbia community at this recently opened Morningside Heights Bar. Saints has it all: savvy bartenders; a light tapas menu; and a crowd of mostly professionals and students, and a few sinners. Saint's is wonderful, not only because of the great atmosphere, but because it already has had a significant impact on a community that has very few gay and lesbian bars. Saint's is also available for private parties.
On the corner of 109th St. and Amsterdam Ave., 222-2431 V, MC, ❶❾ *to 110th St.*

Sardi's

Billing itself as "The Longest Running Show On Broadway," this celebrated theater hangout preserves its patina of class and sophistication despite its proximity to the bloated behemoths that now dominate mainstream theater in New York. Lots of red plush bestows an aura of celebration to an indifferent glass of house red. The countless celebrity caricatures adorning every nook and cranny of this cavernous affair provide a mild diversion for tourists while they fill up on bar mix before the show. There's live jazz in the upstairs lounge every Friday night.
234 West 44th St. (bet. Broadway and Eighth Ave.), 221-8440, MC, V, AmEx, Diners, Entrées: $14-$30, ❶❷❸❹❺ ❼❾ *to Times Square* &

Shades of Green

Weekend revelers at this Irish pub range from James Joyce look-alikes to college jocks who are more interested in the hockey game than the literary quotes lining the walls. Chat with Pat, the bartender/owner, and be sure to indulge in the homemade apple pie.
125 East 15th St. (at Third Ave. and Irving Pl.), 674-1394, MC, V, AmEx, Entrées: $6-$10, ❶❹❺❻ *to Union Sq.* &

Shark Bar

A well-known hangout for upscale African-Americans. Low lighting and polished wood accents make this hideaway a romantic alternative to the other, more raucous, Amsterdam bars. Bring a date to ward off the post-collegiate singles hovering around the bar.
307 Amsterdam Ave. (bet. 74th and 75th Sts.), 874-
8500, MC, V, AmEx, ❶❷❸❾ *to 72nd St.*

Ship of Fools

Locals come for the two pool tables and televised sporting events. Those in the neighborhood should stop to relax and have a few drinks. Pleasant but unexciting; not worth an extended commute.
1590 Second Ave. (bet. 82nd and 83rd Sts.), 570-2651, MC, V, AmEx, D, Diners, ❹❺❻ *to 86th St.*

Showman's Cafe

"Everything is copasetic" at this laid-back haunt, according to the Copasetics, Harlem's brotherhood of tap dancers, which makes this popular club its headquarters. Come for the world famous jazz acts Wednesday through Saturday.
2321 Frederick Douglass Blvd. (bet. 124th and 125th Sts.), 864-8941, AmEx, $10 minimum, ❶❾ *to 125th St.*

Sidewalk

A raucous crowd of locals congregates here to eat cheap, drink up, and occasionally take in some homegrown guitar riffs on the tiny stage in back. In the summer, the table area snaking around the corner is one of the Avenue's hottest sidewalk scenes.
94 Avenue A (at 6th St.), 473-7373, MC, V, AmEx, Diners, Transmedia, Entrées: $7-$12, one drink minimum in the back, ❻ *to Second Ave.,* ❻ *to Astor Pl.*

The Slaughtered Lamb

One of the Village's best-known pubs, tourists flock to this horror-film theme bar to watch the shocker
movies and consume slightly overpriced drinks.
182 West 4th St. (bet. Sixth and Seventh Aves.), 727-3350, MC, V, AmEx, D, Diners, Transmedia, ❶❸❹❺❻❾ *to West 4th St.*

Snug

Yuppies in denial pack this narrow Irish bar to exercise the jukebox's Dylan and play pool. The seven-foot screen ensures that a moment of the game will not be missed. Celebrate Monday nights with mixed drinks for $2.50 and draft beers for a mere two bucks.
450 Amsterdam Ave. (at 92nd St.), 595-5670, V, AmEx, ❶❾ *to 79th St.* &

SoHa

Stands for SOuth of HArlem and is a hip addition to Columbia's astonishingly limited bar scene. Vintage chandeliers, purple pool table and plenty of couches make patrons forget they're in the square heart of the ivy league. The smart crowd, excellent music, and extensive beer and liquor selection remind Morningside Heights dwellers that SoHo is So Far away.
1998 Amsterdam Ave. (at 105th St.), 678-0098, V, MC, AmEx, ❶❾ *to 110th St.* &

Soho Billiards

Rack 'em up in this smoky, multi-level hall outfitted with a healthy number of gleaming pool tables. The music calls to mind an As-Seen-On-TV 80s compilation but the patrons don't seem to mind. Bring a watch, as there are conveniently no clocks with which to time yourself.
256 East Houston (bet.

bars 305

Mulberry and Mott Sts.), 925-3753, Cash Only, ❶❷❸❹ to Broadway/Lafayette St.

The SoHo Grand Bar

This hotel bar is growing ever more popular. During the day guests and drop ins meet for business over lunch martini's, at night sophisticated SoHoites spiral up the cast-iron, bottle cap staircase for a pre-diner drink of night cap.
310 West Broadway (bet. Canal and Grand Sts.), 965-3000, MC, V, AmEx, D, ❶❷❸ *to Canal St.*

Splash

This cavernous gay bar is packed with Chelsea gym types and boyish guppies. The real draw is the center stage: a shower stall, with shows nightly. Straight women flock here to ogle the buff bartenders, who never, ever, wear shirts.
50 West 17th St. (off Sixth Ave.), 691-0073, Cash Only, ❶❷ *to 18th St.*

SPOON

Very chill: DJs churn out smooth, crowd-pleasing grooves, hardly anyone is spotted posing, and you don't have to pay through the nose for drinks to finance the ambiance.
12 Avenue A (bet. Houston St. and 2nd St.), 477-9050, MC, V, AmEx, D, ❶ *to Second Ave.*

The Sporting Club

You won't miss a minute of the game, thanks to huge television screens hanging from the ceiling; the ambiance is rounded out by a few football helmets and lots of greasy finger foods. For an exciting cultural lesson, come in while they're showing European matches
99 Hudson St. (between Franklin and Leonard Sts.), 219-0900, MC, V, AmEx, D, Diners, ❶❷ *to Franklin Street*

Sports Mania

Known for its daily specials, from Senior Citizen's Day to Sanitation Worker's day, this otherwise unexciting sports bar redefines "neighborhood haunt" with its summertime weekend barbecues and volleyball in the backyard, where all the food is free. Equipped with no fewer than twelve television screens, a kitchen, a jukebox, and video games.
1143-67 243rd St., (718) 525-9521, Cash Only, Entrées: around $5, ❶❷ *to Archer St., then Q5A to end of line.*

Spy

Wear the trendiest outfit you can find and approach the bouncers with all the arrogance you can muster. Just remember: money and beauty aren't everything.
101 Greene St. (bet Prince and Spring Sts.), 343-9000, MC, V, AmEx, Diners, ❶❷ *to Spring St.,* ❸❹ *to Prince St.*

Nick's Pub

Definitely a place with a loyal clientele: if a regular is a no-show, the manager calls to see what's wrong. Renowned jazz musicians play to this low-key crowd, and allow local musicians to join in (that doesn't mean you can bring your recorder). No cover and no minimum.
773 St. Nicholas Ave. (at 149th St.), 283-9728 or 234-3380, Cash Only, ❶❷❸❹ *to 145th St.*

Stan's Sports Bar

A lot of hi-fiving and boisterous talking goes on after games at this spot. The clientele consists mainly of college-age males.
836 River Ave. (across from Yankee Stadium), (718) 993-5548, Cash Only, ❶❷❸ *to Yankee Stadium*

The Stoned Crow

Thrills come cheap enough for cash-poor grad students at this local basement hangout: a jukebox, pool table, dart board, and to top it all off, a quarter-sucking virtual reality race car video game.
85 Washington Place (at MacDougal St.), 677-4022, Cash Only, ❶❷❸❹❺❻❼ *to West 4th St.*

Stonewall

Nothing but history really recommends this landmark. Garish red lighting dimly illuminates the space, itself a fraction of the establishment that housed the riot that launched the modern gay rights movement. Still, the bar is a good place to meet out-of-towners who flock here daily trying to connect with history. The most significant drink specials offered are Wednesday's all-night 2-for-1 event and a very long happy hour on weekdays, 3 to 9pm.
53 Christopher St. (off Seventh Ave., at Sheridan Sq.), 463-0950, Cash Only, ❶❷ *to Christopher St.*

Suzy Wong Room

The downstairs bar of the E & O Restaurant, this popular nightspot for trendy go-getters is bathed in a red glow and the decor is eastern and "oriental."
100 W Houston St. (bet Thompson St. and LaGuardia Pl.), 254-7000, ❶❷❸❹❺❻❼ *to West 4th St.-Washington Sq.*

T

Tap-a-Keg

Low key and a bit rough around the edges, this dive offers a respectable selection of draft beers but the real draw seems to be the colorful locals just sittin' around. No kitchen here, so feel free to pack your own junk food or even have something delivered.
Broadway (at 105th St.), 749-1734, Cash Only, ❶❷ *to 103rd St.*

The Tapas Lounge

An oasis of velvet couches and dripping candles. Graze on tapas and sip sangria while playing backgammon.
1078 First Ave. (at 59th St.), 421-8282, AmEx, Tapas: $3.95-$12.50, ❹❺❻ *to 59th St.*

Tatou

Rub shoulders with the young, chic and sartorially privileged at this swank little Murray Hill supper-club. The setting is dark and romantic, with a decidedly glitzy demeanor.
151 East 50th St. (bet. Lexington and Third Aves.),753-1144, MC, V, AmEx, Diners, Cover: $15 ($20 weekends), ❶❷❸ *to 53rd St*

Tavern on Jane

This tavern serves much more than pub food, but at pub food prices. While the fish and chips are a reliable delight, customers go crazy for the grilled leg-of-lamb with sour cherry sauce, potatoes gratin and savory garlic spinach, and the Moroccan tuna, served with saffron, lemon and garlic cous cous, and wilted water cress get rave reviews, not to mention the free-range duck is "phenomenal." The atmosphere is cozy and inviting; regulars are bound to strike up a friendly conversation over a pint of beer. Simply put: you know a place is great when the staff hangs out there on their nights off.
31 Eighth Ave. (Corner of Jane St.), 675-2526, MC V AmEx D, Entrées: $7-$13, ❶❸❹ *to 14th St.*

Teddy's

The best bar food in Brooklyn, with plenty of beverages to wash it down with. Try a burger or just go for dessert and sample the ice cream smothered in homemade hot fudge. One of the few places offering pitchers of really good beer like Bass and Sierra.
96 Berry St. (at North 8th St.), (718) 384-9787, Cash Only, Entrées: $6-$13, ❶ *to Bedford Ave.* ♿

Temple Bar

The epitome of understated elegance: the dark wood interior is quietly beautiful, rather than forcibly chic. The perfect place to impress a date if money is no object, since not much comes cheaply here.
332 Lafayette St. (bet. Bleecker and Houston Sts.), 925-4242, MC, V, AmEx, Diners, ❻ *to Bleecker St.,* ❷❸❹❺ *to Broadway/Lafayette St.*

1020

"Graduates" of the local college bars drink microbrews at this brick-and-wood home of Morningside's only ten-foot high television screen. Half-price Happy Hour features $2 pints.
1020 Amsterdam Ave. (at 110th St.), 961-9224, Cash Only, ❶❾ *to 110th St.*

Three of Cups

Come early to get first dibs on the make-out couch at this intimate dive aglow with candles and tucked underneath the restaurant of the same name. Hit the fairly cheap and typically strong well drinks for a quick buzz.
83 First Ave. (at 5th St.), 388-0059, Cash Only, ❻ *to Second Ave.*

Tommy Makem's Irish Pavillion

This oasis in a nearly barless desert serves to subdued nine-to-fivers during the week, but come weekend, spontaneous eruptions of Irish tunes are regular occurrences. The kitchen prepares food a cut above the usual pub fare.
130 East 57th St. (bet. Lexington and Park Aves.),759-9040, MC, V, AmEx, Diners, Entrées: around $11, ❹❺❻ *to 59th St.,* ❶❻ *to Lexington Ave.* ♿

The Townhouse Bar

An extremely professional gay bar catering to well-dressed men with big bank accounts and the boys who love 'em. A piano bar in back exploits the somewhat pretentious ambiance. Drinks are expensive (from $4 to $7) and the decor slightly over-ambitious.
236 East 58th St. (bet. Second and Third Aves.), 754-4649, Cash Only, ❹❺❻ *to 59th St.*

Triad

Both floors of this lounge and restaurant stage acts of surprisingly high quality seven nights a week. Check out the upstairs theater for Off-Broadway productions and jazz, blues, and comedy acts; head downstairs to the more relaxed Dark Star Lounge for open-mike on Mondays. Cover charge varies, but is usually doesn't stray far from $5 with a two-drink minimum at the tables.
58 West 72nd St. (bet. Broadway and Columbus Ave.), 799-4599, MC, V, AmEx, Entrées: $8-$34, ❶❷❸❾ *to 72nd St.* ♿

2A

Locals hunch over their drinks in the dark and dirty lower level before drifting upstairs and commandeering a couch or armchair as ska music drifts tinnily down from mounted speakers. Even Marisa Tomei has been spotted hustling a drink after last call.
25 Avenue A (at 2nd St.), Cash Only, ❻ *to Second Ave.*

200 5th

An upscale crowd goes for dinner as well as drinks, at one of Park Slope's most popular nightspots. Get there early on Friday nights for salsa dancing; other evenings are a bit more sedate. The cover varies and, more importantly, is negotiable.
200 Fifth Ave. (bet. Union Pl. and Second Ave.), (718) 638-2925, MC, V, AmEx, D, Diners, Entrées: $10-$16, ❶❷❸❹❺❻ *to West 4th St.*

Two Potato

Located at the end of "the strip," this cozy offering caters to an African-American and Latino clientele. Go-go boys provide distractions on Wed. and Sun. nights.
143 Christopher St. (at Greenwich St.), 255-0286, Cash Only, ❶❾ *to Christopher St.*

U

Uncle Charlie's

First among the super-sized bars, the meandering hallways of this legendary hub of the gay bar scene still constitute every city gay boy's first bar experience. Video monitors at every turn provide a prop to practice studied indifference. The crowd seems more earnest and less body-conscious than at Chelsea bars, though wood fixtures lit by garish post-modern lighting create a somewhat brooding atmosphere. Theme nights are the rule here, call for details.
56 Greenwich Ave. (off Seventh Ave.), 255-8787, Cash Only, ❶❷❸❹❺ ❻❾ *to West 4th St.*

V

Velvet Room

The name says it all: velvet-covered furniture helps set the mood at one of the east side's chillest spots. Never too crowded, the cool, artsy natives, starved for such unobtrusive ambiance, come to unwind.

bars 307

209 East 76th St. (bet. Second and Third Aves.), 628-6633, MC, V, AmEx, ➏ to 77th St. ♿

Velvet
No cover most nights, this is a laid-back but funky place. Sunday night features the drag king show 'Club Cassanova,' while most nights you can hear a mixture of lounge and techno-ish music. Other than Sunday night, the crowd is mostly hip, young East Village residents.
167 Avenue A (bet. 10th and 11th Sts.), 995-1963, ➊ to First Ave.

Viceroy
Experience the Chelsea phenomenon of celebrity look-alikes. Is that Larry Fishbourne drinking a Sam Adams at the glittering bar? Probably not, but people-watching is the preferred activity at this chic bar/diner.
160 8th Ave. (at 18th St.), 633-8484, MC, V, AmEx, Diners, Entrées: around $14, ➊➌➍➏ to 14th St./8th Ave. ♿

Void
Video and a great free film series are the heart of this nightspot. Find out what the event is ahead of time and be prepared to appreciate it; otherwise, there's no social scene, just people lining the walls, mesmerized by the big screen.
116 Mercer St. (at Howard St.), 941-6492, MC, V, AmEx, ➊➒ to Canal St.

W

Walker's
Scoring a seat is still tough as patrons flock here for a solid list of good beers and a menu

that ranges from standard pub fare to pastas and tasty portobello mushroom sandwiches.
16 No. Moore St. (at Varick St.), 941-0142, MC, V, AmEx, D, Diners, ➊➒ to Franklin St.

Wax
Spy rejects: try your luck here where both the models and the furniture are of the same species as those in every other pretentious lounge.
113 Mercer St. (bet. Prince and Spring Sts.), 226-6082, MC, V, AmEx, ➎➏ to Prince St. ♿

West End
This is Columbia students' favorite place to "Howl." All ages and majors dutifully carry on the legacy of beats Kerouac and Ginsberg at the writers' old hangout, though the ambiance is far from literary. Surprisingly good food, extensive beer selection, and stand-up comedy in the basement, draw a crowd that defies the frat boy stereotype.
2911 Broadway (bet. 113th and 114th Sts.), 662-8830, MC, V, AmEx, D, Diners, Entrées: $6-$10, ➊➒ to 116th St. ♿

The White Horse Tavern
A Village landmark, reputed to be the place where Dylan Thomas supposedly drank himself to death though the poets are long gone, supplanted by a decidedly pedestrian twentysomething crowd. Dinner essentials are served, including good burgers, and sidewalk dining is available, weather permitting. Half-price Happy Hour.
567 Hudson St. (at West 11th

St.), 243-9260, Cash Only, ➊➒ to Christopher St. ♿

Who's on First
The main bar is expansive, as is the dance floor, but be prepared to wait a few minutes for a drink on busy nights. Bartenders occasionally give out free shots to the Columbia-based crowd and are particularly friendly on slow nights when the crowd includes local private school rebels in search of booze. A DJ digs up your old jukebox faves.
1683 First Ave. (bet. 87th and 88th Sts.), 410-2780, MC, V, AmEx, ➍➎➏ to 86th St.

Wonder Bar
Unwind after work at this mellow dive whose decor is a bit of a circus what with the R&B and funk DJ peeking through a hole in the wall while a blue polka-dot strobe beats light against the zebra-striped walls.
505 East 6th St. (bet. Avenues A and B), 777-9105, Cash Only, ➏ to Second Ave. ♿

The Works
Generally packed, this cruisy but preppy hangout for gay yuppies, or guppies, and Columbia folk has recently been renovated and features new video screens, a fierce sound-

system, and a much nicer bathroom. Home of the original Beer Blast, The Works has raised over $150,000 dollars for various charities to date. Drink Specials are the rule, but check out their ten-ounce $4 martinis on Weds. Seemingly impossible considering the space, go-go boys grace the bar on weekends.
428 Columbus Ave. (bet. 80th and 81st Sts.), 799-7365, Cash Only, ➊➒ to 79th St. ♿

WXOU
It's surprisingly easy to find a table here, in the middle of the West Village, but not on the local tourist trail. The clientele ranges from long-time village residents to younger yuppies and the occasional famous musician. As its radio-inspired name predicts, the jukebox rocks.
558 Hudson St. (at Eleventh Ave.), 206-0381, Cash Only, ➊➌➋➊ to 14th St. ♿

X

XVI
A hip-hop vibe moves the crowd in the downstairs lounge while upstairs the mood mellows. Sophisticates gather in the front hallway and goths congregate in the back. A friskier-than-usual pick-up

---

The West End

Since 1918
A GREAT BAR & RESTAURANT
The Tradition, Music, and Atmosphere You Expect in New York.

BROADWAY (113TH & 114TH) @COLUMBIA UNIVERSITY. 662-8830

See us on our website
@ http//:www.Westend.Com

scene, guaranteed to be tourist-free.
16 First Ave. (bet. First and Second Aves.), Cash Only, **F** to Second Ave.

Z

Z Bar
The forest-meets-industrial decor exemplifies the incongruities of this alphabet city haunt. The specialty at the bar is beer, beer, and more beer, but there's also a DJ, a downstairs lounge open on weekends and special nights, and theme parties throughout the week. Accordingly, the crowd is an odd mix of neighborhood brew-swillers and the chic cocktail set.
206 Avenue A (bet. 12th and 13th Sts.), 982-9173, MC, V, AmEx, D, Diners, **L** to First Ave.

Zinc Bar
Don't be fooled by the compact quarters of this underground jazz bar: there's no dance floor, but an irrepressibly powerful rhythm keeps hips and shoulders smoothly swaying between the alley-like walls until 3am. Come for the pre-weekend line-up: Jazz Wednesdays, Latin Jazz on Thursdays, and Flamenco Fridays.
90 West Houston St. (at La Guardia Pl.), 477-8337, **BDFQ** to Broadway/Lafayette St. or **NR** to Prince St.

The Zone
After midnight a crowd, that's decidedly more down-to-earth than typical SoHo dwellers, warms the loud industrial interior of this laid-back haunt; an anomaly in this part of town.
357 West Broadway (bet. Broome and Grand Sts.), 431-9172, AmEx, **ACE** to Canal St. ♿

INDEX BY TYPE

CABARET
Audubon Bar and Grill
Cafe Pierre at the Pierre Hotel
Danny's Skylight Room at the Grand Sea Palace
Don't Tell Mama
Eighty-Eight's
Judy's Restaurant and Cabaret
Rainbow and Stars
The Chestnut Room
Triad
Cigar Bars
Carnegie Bar and Books
City Wine and Cigar Co.
Florio's Cigar Bar and Restaurant
Fred's Beauty
Hudson Bar and Books
Lexington Bar and Books
Oak Bar at the Plaza Hotel
The Bubble Lounge

COLLEGE
Alumni Hall
Amsterdam Cafe
Bar None
Bear Bar
Blondie's
Caliente Cab Co.
Cannon's
Clarke's
Dapper Dog
Down the Hatch
Jekyll and Hyde
Last Second Saloon
Petes' Tavern
Pollyesther's
Poppolini's
Remedy
Reminiscence
Revival
Reynold's Cafe Bar
Rio Mar
Shades of Green
Shark Bar
Ski Bar
Stoned Crow
The Slaughtered Lamb
West End
Who's on First

SAINTS
Gay and Lesbian Bar for the 90's and Beyond

212.222.2431

992 Amsterdam Avenue (Corner of 109th Street)

GAY AND LESBIAN
"g"
Barracuda
Boots and Saddle
Candle Bar
Champs
Crazy Nanny's
Cubbyhole
Hell
Henrietta Hudson
Her/She Bar
Julie's
Julius
King
Meow Mix
Nowbar
Rising Cafe
Rome
Saint's
Splash
Stonewall
The Boiler Room
The Break
The Duplex
The Hangar Bar
The Townhouse Bar
The Works
Two Potato
Wonder Bar
Hotel Bars
Four Seasons
Marriot Marquis Lounge
Monkey Bar
The Oak Room
The Paramount
The Royalton
The SoHo Grand Bar

JAZZ
Augie's
Jimmy Armstrong's Saloon
Lickety Split
Metronome
Showman's Cafe
St. Nick's Pub

LOUNGES
420 Bar and Lounge
Arlene Grocery
Art Bar
Au Bar
Auction House
Bar d'O
Belmont Lounge
Ciel Rouge
E&O
Element Zero
Flamingo East
Knitting Factory
Lenox Lounge
Luna Lounge
Merc Bar
Meyer Lansky Lounge at Ratner's
Niagara
Pravda
Rainbow Room
SPOON
Spy
The Opium Den
The Tapas Lounge
Velvet Room
Wax
XVI
Z Bar

MICROBREWERIES
Heartland Brewery
Park Slope Brewing Company

NEIGHBORHOOD HAUNTS
1020
11th Street Bar
200 Fifth
2A
Abbey Pub
Ace Bar
American Trash

bars 309

Automatic Slims
Blind Tiger Ale House
Blue and Gold
Bourbon Street
Cedar Tavern
Chumley's
Clarke's
Dive Bar
Doc Holiday's
Ear Inn
Hillside Inn
Hogs 'n' Heifers
Holiday Cocktail Lounge
Jake's Dilemma
Jimmy's Corner
Lenox Lounge
Liquor Store Bar
Mare Chiaro
Max Fish
McSorley's Old Ale House
Milano's
Night Cafe
Norh Star Pub
Old Town Bar
P&Gs
Puffy's Tavern
Revolution
Riverrun
Rodeo Bar and Grill
Rudy Bar and Grill
Ship of Fools
Showman's Cafe
Sidewalk
Soha
Tap-A-Keg
The Heights
The Subway Inn
Tommy Makem's Irish Pavilion
Walkers
WXOU

POOL HALLS
Abbey Tavern
Amsterdam Billiards
Chelsea Billiards
Gantry's Pub
Irish Brigade Pub
Mulligan's Pub
Nancy Whiskey Pub
North Star Pub
Paddy Reilly's
Parnell's Pub
Patrick's
Snug
Soho Billiards
Teddy's
The Billiard Club
The Piper's Kilt
The White Horse Tavern
Walker's

RESTAURANTS
Boxers
Cafe Un Deux Trois
Candy Bar and Grill
Hi-Life Bar and Grill
Landmark Tavern
Mary Lou's
Moomba
Sardi's
Tavern on Jane
Viceroy
Sports
Amsterdam Cafe
Boomer's
Carriage House
Cody's
Gin Mill
Hoops Bar
Sports Mania
Stan's Sports Bar
The Riviera Cafe
The Sporting Club
Wilson Bar

UPSCALE & TRENDY
147
Bar 89
Bowery Bar
Fez
Idlewild
Marion's
Motor City Bar
Ozone
Tatou
Temple Bar
The Grange Hall
Zinc Bar
ñ

YOUNG & TRENDY
Anseo
Barramundi
Big Sur
Bleeker Street Bar
Botanica
Brother Jimmy's
Burp Castle
Coffee Shop
Don Hill's
Galaxy
KGB
Korova Milk Bar
Lakeside Lounge
Lava
Live Bait
Lucky Strike
Ludlow Bar
Mug Ale House
Orchard Bar
Peculier Pub
Pollyesther's
Suzy Wong Room
Three of Cups
Velvet
Void

YOUNG PROFESSIONAL
Australia
Bemelman's
Doing Business As
Gingerman
La Tour D'Or
Merchants
Mustang Harry's
Mustang Sally's
Oke Doke
Perk's Fine Cuisine
Pete's Waterfront Ale House
The Cub Room

INDEX BY NEIGHBORHOOD

BROOKLYN
200 Fifth
Carriage House
Cody's
Mug's Ale House
Park Slop Brewing Company
Pete's Waterfront Ale House
Rising Cafe
Teddy's
Bronx
Alumni Hall
Clarke's
Stan's Sports Bar

CHELSEA
147
"g"
Barracuda
Candy Bar and Grill
Champs
Chelsea Billiards
Ciel Rouge
Hell
Her/She Bar
Hogs 'n' Heifers
King
Lava
Mustang Harry's
Mustang Sally's
Rome
Splash
Tavern on Jane
The Billiard Club
The Break
The NowBar
Viceroy
Wilson Bar

CHINATOWN
Florio's Cigar Bar and Restaurant

EAST VILLAGE
11th Street Bar
2A
Ace Bar
Anseo
Bar None
Blue and Gold
Bowery Bar
Burp Castle
Doc Holiday's
DBA
Element Zero
Fez
Flamingo East
Holiday Cocktail Lounge
Idlewild
KGB
Korova Milk Bar
Lakeside Lounge
Marion's
McSorley's Old Ale House
Niagara
Sidewalk
SPOON
Temple Bar
The Bar
The Boiler Room
The Opium Den
Three of Cups
Velvet
Wonder Bar
XVI
Z Bar

FINANCIAL DISTRICT
La Tour D'Or
MacMenamin's Irish Pub
North Star Pub
Gramercy
Belmont Lounge
Coffee Shop
Galaxy
Live Bait
Metronome
Old Town Bar
Pete's Tavern
Revival
Rodeo Bar and Grill

310 bars

Shades of Green

GREENWICH VILLAGE
Art Bar
Automatic Slims
Bar d'O
Bleeker St. Bar
Blind Tiger Ale
Boots and Saddle
Caliente Cab Co.
Cedar Tavern
Chumley's
Crazy Nanny's
Cubbyhole
E&O
Eighty-Eight's
Fred's Beauty
Henrietta Hudson
Hudson Bar and Books
Jekyll and Hyde
Julius
Moomba
Peculiar Pub
Pollyesthers
Poppolini's
Rio Mar
Riviera Cafe
Stoned Crow
Stonewall
Suzy Wong Room
The Duplex
The Grange Hall
The Hangar Bar
The Heartland Brewery
The Riviera Cafe
The Slaughtered Lamb
Two Potato
Uncle Charlie's
White House Tavern
WXOU
Zinc Bar

HARLEM
Lenox Lounge
Lickety Split
Perk's Fine Cuisine
Showman's Cafe
St. Nick's Pub

LITTLE ITALY
Marechiaro Tavern
Lower East Side
Arlene Grocery
Baby Jupiter
Barramundi
Ludlow Bar
Luna Lounge
Max Fish
Meow Mix

Meyer Lansky Lounge at Ratner's
Motor City Bar
Orchard Bar

MIDTOWN
Au Bar
Auction House
Cafe Pierre at the Pierre Hotel
Cafe Un Deux Trois
Carnegie Bar and Books
Danny's Skylight Room at The Grand Sea Palace
Don't Tell Mama
Four Seasons
Gingerman
Jimmy's Armstrong Saloon
Jimmy's Corner
Judy's Restaurant and Cabaret
Julie's
Landmark Tavern
Marriot Marquis Lounge
Merchants
Monkey Bar
Mulligan's Pub
Oak Bar at the Plaza
Parnell's Pub
Rainbow and Stars
Rainbow Room
Revolution
Rudy Bar and Grill
Sardi's
Tatou
The Oak Room
The Paramount
The Royalton
The Subway Inn
The Tapas Lounge
Tommy Makem's Irish Pavilion
Townhouse Bar

MORNINGSIDE HEIGHTS
1020
Abbey Pub
Amsterdam Cafe
Augie's
Dive Bar
Night Cafe
Saint's
SoHa
Tap-A-Keg
The Heights

QUEENS
Gantry's Pub
Hillside Inn

Hoops Bar
Sports Mania

SOHO
Bar 89
Botanica
Chelsea Billiards
Don Hill's
Ear Inn
Lucky Strike
Merc Bar
Milano's
n
Pravda
Soho Billiards
Spy
The Billiard Club
The Cub Room
The SoHo Grand Bar
Void
Wax

TRIBECA
City Wine and Cigar Co.
Knitting Factory
Liquor Store Bar
Nancy Whiskey Pub
Puffy's Tavern
Riverview
The Bubble Lounge
The Sporting Club
Walker's

UPPER EAST SIDE
American Trash
Australia
Bear Bar
Bemelman's
Big Sur
Brother Jimmy's
Dapper Dog
Last Second Saloon
Lexington Bar and Books

Oke Doke
Ozone
Pollyesthers
Reminiscence
Ship of Fools
Ski Bar
Velvet Room
Who's on First

UPPER WEST SIDE
420 Bar and Lounge
Amsterdam Billiards
Blondie's
Boomer's
Bourbon Street
Candle Bar
Cannon's
Down the Hatch
Gin Mill
Hi-Life Bar and Grill
Jake's Dilemma
P&Gs
Remedy
Shark Bar
Snug
The Chestnut Room
The Works
Triad
West End

WASHINGTON HEIGHTS
Audubon Bar and Grill
Irish Brigade Pub
Patrick's
Reynold's Cafe Bar
The Piper's Kit

MAMA JOY'S DELI
We Cater for all Occasions

COLD CUTS	2892 Broadway
CHEESE	(bet.112th & 113th Sts.)
FRUIT	212-662-0716
VEGETABLES	8 AM - 1 AM
	7 Days a Week

*With a personal touch:
A good variety of imported cheeses,
domestic & imported beers
along with a great selection of coffee.*

VISA / MC

JAKE'S DILEMMA

HAPPY HOUR
EVERY DAY 5-8PM
WHOLE BAR HALF PRICE

Melrose Monday 8-9pm
Ladies Drink Free Drafts

Monday Night Football
$1 Drafts & $6 Pitchers

Tuesday 8pm-Close
1/2 Price 1/2 Yards

WED. LADIES NIGHT
FREE DRAFT BEER

Thursday 8pm-Close
$10.00 Pitcher of Shots

POOL TABLE
FOOSBALL • DARTS

430 Amsterdam Avenue, bet. 80th & 81st Streets
PRIVATE PARTY ROOM AVAILABLE • Tel. 580-0556

MO'S CARIBBEAN BAR & GRILLE NEW YORK

LADIES NIGHT
Wed. 7-? Free Drafts and Frozen Drinks

LIVE REGGAE
every Tuesday 9-12
$2.00 Carib Bottles

$2 RED STRIPES
every Thursday

SATELLITE TV—LARGE SCREENS
INTERACTIVE TRIVIA GAMES · DJ BOOTH

LOBSTER MADNESS MONDAYS
$10.95 FOR 1ST LOBSTER (INCLUDES 2 SIDES)
$6 FOR EACH ADDITIONAL ONE

BRUNCH SATURDAY AND SUNDAY
11:30-4 $8.95 INCLUDES 2 DRINKS

1454 2nd Ave. Corner of 76th Street • Tel. 650-0561

It's all good at... THE GIN MILL

442 AMSTERDAM AVE
(bet. 81st & 82nd)
212-580-9080

FEATURING PLUCK-U WINGS

SAT & SUN 1-6pm All the beer you can drink, all the wings you can eat ONLY $12

Monday-Friday 4-7pm
HAPPY HOUR
HALF PRICE DRINKS

Monday 7pm-Close
$1 Drafts & $6 Pitcher

PABST CANS $1.75
4PM-10PM EVERY DAY

Tuesday 7pm-Close
LADIES NIGHT
FREE DRAFT BEER
$1 Frozen Margaritas

Wednesday 7pm-Close
1/2 Price Liters & Meters

Thursday 7pm-Close
Shot And Beer Specials

SATELLITE SPORTS
PRIVATE PARTY ROOM AVAILABLE

DOWN THE HATCH

SAT.-MON.
ALL PINTS $2

WED. 7-10
LADIES NIGHT
$1 MARGARITAS

TUES. $1 DRAFTS 7-10

SAT & SUN 1-6
ALL THE BEER YOU CAN DRINK,
ALL THE WINGS YOU CAN EAT
JUST $14

FOOSBALL
shot specials
SATELLITE TV
DJ BOOTH

179 West 4th Street (bet. 6th & 7th)
Tel. 627-9747

312 bars

clubs

WEBSTER HALL

PSYCHEDELIC THURSDAY
PRESENTS
GIRLS NITE OUT

NYC club scene.314
interviews:
club/owner jahan matin.316
DJ seth-K.316
club listings.317
index by neighborhood.320

dance clubs

While most of America heads to Disneyland to escape reality, New Yorkers look no further than the warehouses, caverns, and padded chambers of the city's nightclubs. Each of these spots provides a different array of diversions to help its cast of characters leave the world behind.

New York's myriad of dance clubs encompass every type of music, fashion, sexual preference, ego, and bank account. Mega-dance clubs like the Tunnel, Life, System, and Speed. pump almost as much money in to their fantasyland establishments as Disneyland does-- strobe lights and smoke abound. These large venues care what you wear, the cursed Velvet Rope standing between you and what you want (a night of crazy gyrating and drink slamming), cordoning off the rabble from the celebrities and hard-core club kids; towering bouncers will be eyeing the threads on the crowd, so if you want in, dress for the occasion.

Smaller clubs like bOb, Sapphire, Delia's, and E&O, are less trendy fashion conscious venues with a more intimate feel and local crowd. George Poneson at bOb describes small clubs as, "a living-room you don't have to clean up." But it's so much more. Small club venues, with their low lighting, cushy couches, and close-dancing-friendly clientele, are the wave of the '90s. Jahan Matin, owner of Sapphire, says, "you don't have to be "all that" to be at Sapphire, but if you are inside you probably are." Some of these smaller clubs haven't been granted cabaret licenses, which essentially means no dancing allowed, but a host of DJ's and live bands still play to the house, and dancing goes on.

New York's dance scene is notoriously fickle, and this week's hottest club may get boarded up the next. Also, a place can host completely different crowds depending on the night of the week--drag ball on Tuesdays, punk "battle of the bands" on Wednesdays--or even shut its doors temporarily to throw a private party, and many places are only open one or two (rotating) nights of the week. To avoid unwanted surprises, use resources like the *Voice*, *Time Out New York* and *Paper* magazine. Space and site don't usually concern the club kids who follow parties as they travel from club to club; for the rest of us, keeping abreast of the oscillations of cutting-edge club trends is nearly a full-time job. These resources are useful in following certain DJ's or parties. Pick up any of the eye-catching fliers circulating the downtown area; many offer half-price entrance fees or list promoters' beeper numbers for getting on the invite guest list. Be prepared, the light on your answering machine will be blinking like mad once your name is out here.

314 clubs

CLUBWORLD: Then and Now

The New York club scene is one of the largest industries in the city and tens of thousands of partygoers from around the world flood city clubs every week. Most people associate the dawn of club life with New York's Studio 54, though discotheques served Europe's hip and famous for twenty years before Studio 54 forefather Steve Rubell first opened the doors at 254 West 54th Street in 1976. There were early New York clubs like Cheetah, Le Club, and El Morocco, but the wild abandon that was to characterize New York's club life did not reach its pitch until Studio 54, when uptown, downtown, black, white, straight, gay and famous first came together to dance to the driving beats of Donna Summer, and to snort cocaine and swallow Quaaludes. Clubworld was born and a blurry mass swayed beneath giant glittering disco balls, illuminated by random strobes of light.

The magically seductive, otherworldly and sometimes dangerous night world of Studio 54 (whose heyday was brief and bright), soon gave birth to other clubs, like Xenon, The Mudd Club, Infinity, and later Palladium, The Tunnel, Mars, and Nell's (among many others) that enjoyed untethered success through the late '70s, early '80s and on into the '90s. The "Kill Disco" movement of the '80s, and the sharp rise of punk did not kill the club scene, but fueled it, both uptown and down. Music and style mutated and new wave and rap inspired dance music. Into the '80s, after-hours clubs enjoyed growing success and a new phenomenon known as the "party promoter" was born. The opening of Peter Gatien's Limelight in 1983 (recently reopened following controversy) marked a new era of club life, and club kids—young outcasts from around the country—became the heirs apparent of the old Studio 54 club scene.

During the 1990s, New York clubs have suffered under Mayor Guiliani's "quality-of-life campaign" and subsequent crackdown, but club life today offers abundant options, with new venues opening all the time. Though outrageous scandals involving club operators and staff have tarnished the scene's image, club goers are dancing and hanging out to hip hop, reggae and soul, house, disco, jungle and Latin music, in megadiscos, lounges, and illegal after-hours clubs all over the city. Door policies, which were very strict in the '70s, have been relaxed, and while there has been a trend toward homogenization, a great range of types (from homeboys to drag queens to yuppies) can still be found roaming the city night. A gay sensibility and presence are also common at many clubs. Beware though, club trends change here almost in the blink of an eye and heavily promoted parties and DJ's move from venue to venue and come and go with the sunrise.

Studio 54
(see Clubs section)
Palladium
(see Clubs section)
The Tunnel
(see Clubs section)
Nell's
(see Clubs section)

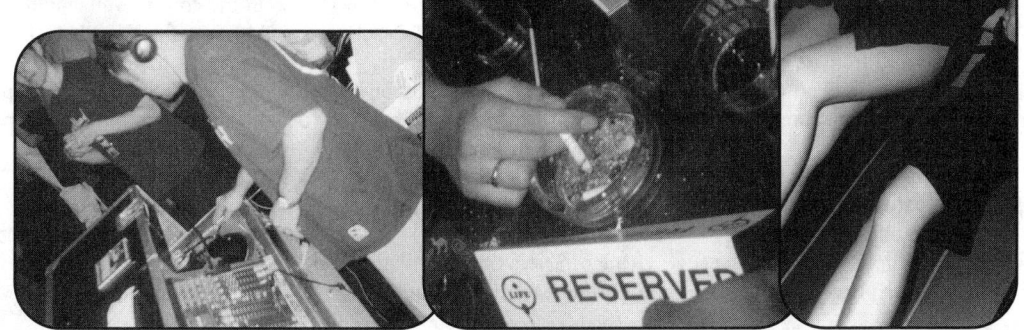

Name: Jahan Matin
Occupation: Owner of Sapphire since 1995.
Location: 249 Eldridge Street, south side of Houston Street near First Ave. ⓕ to Second Ave., 777-5153, open every day 7pm-4am

Q: Why did you decide to get involved in a small club rather than a larger venue?
A: I promoted a lot in the '70s and early '80s and was involved in a lot of big, big clubs, but I think the time of the big club is over. People are interested in lounges because they're smaller and more intimate. Unlike in big clubs, where everybody seems to be staying away from each other, you walk into this place and make friends in no time. In the '90s, small clubs are where it's at. The people going to big clubs right now are kids.
Q: Do you card heavily?
A: Yes, we ID everyone. Our crowd goes anywhere from 21 to 65 years old. People from all over come in and get into a groove and start dancing.

Q: What makes Sapphire distinctive?
A: Sapphire has a cabaret license, most small venues around here don't. Sapphire is the only place where the mixed crowd is attracted naturally.
Q: What factor, do you think is most responsible for the diversity?
A: Our DJ's are very accommodating. It's not a big crowd so we keep everybody satisfied. We don't play the same kind of music all night.
Q: Do you have different DJ's spinning every night?
A: Yes. DJ Seth-K spins a Groove School party on Tuesdays and house classics and old-school disco on Saturdays. On Thursday DJ Jazzy Nice, who used to play at Life, spins anything from acid jazz to funk and soul. On Fridays DJ Freddy Bastone spins a little bit of hip-hop and reggae dance music. The different themes and crowds and the cool atmosphere keep us hopping. If it keeps up we could last forever.

interview

DJ Seth-K plays to the house
interview

The behind-the-scenes work done by owners and promoters is often overshadowed by the role of the DJ. As the master or mistress of the mix, the DJ is responsible for guiding the writhing masses through the evening, sensing the mood of the crowd and spinning the appropriate jam to keep the dance floor packed.

No one works harder than DJ Seth-K. Sweat beads on his forehead and his above-the-shoulder locks bob rhythmically to the resonating throb of the record tracks which he's scratching, revolving, or flipping. He's lightning fast and always smiling as he whirls around, pulling another record from its jacket (with his fingers still on the system behind him), and gliding into the next beat.

DJ Seth-K is a man of the people. "I always zoom in on the crowd; I go out and talk to the people. I get a feel for what they want, and then I give it to them... that way you keep them in the palm of your hand."

Being raised in the Village, he comes from an artistic background; his parents are both bohemian-types who made clothing for the likes of Paul Simon, Art Garfunkel, and Bob Dylan, "We had lots of famous musicians coming in and out of our house," he says. "It was the biggest thrill. I've always loved music--from very young age."

Seth has been deejaying for eighteen years. "I kind of fell into it, I was a sound man for bands first, then one day they said they wanted me to spin and I said great. I liked doing it and realized I was good at it. Because I've collected records my whole life, I have this outrageous collection-- over 40,000. I have this 12' by 12' room in my house filled to the ceiling, and there's another ten thousand in my Dad's attic in Long Island."

One of Seth's first gigs was at Danceteria back in the '80s. Since then he has played long stretches at Nirvana, Limelight, Le BarBat, Sticky Mike's Frog Bar (which is now Time Cafe), and the China Club. He's done corporate and private parties at the Supper Club, private New York University parties, and parties for Annie Lenox and JFK Junior. Meanwhile, he looks 26 years-old, tops. "I'm 37, but this business really keeps me young, in spirit and in looks," he said, knocking on wood.

In his faded bell-bottom jeans, and his red mock-turtleneck, Seth looks like a regular guy, not like a DJ with a huge following. He made his mark by breaking the rules and not by playing one type of music all night. "I play it all, if I can toot my horn that's what I'd say. In the course of my night you'll hear every style of music and I weave it together in a coherent fashion and try to keep people dancing through it all. The people who come here know music and know me, they know I'm going to be a little predictable and a little bit crazy, and go a little bit off, but never too off that they can't dance to it."

316 clubs

B

The Bank
Black-caped and raven-garbed goth crowd into a dark, double-roomed realm where swaying and stomping approach a religious experience. Both Fridays and Saturdays boast the best selections of gothic, industrial, new wave, and alternative eighties music, with the occasional live band thrown in for variety.
225 East Houston St. (at Essex St.), 505-5033, Cash Only, Cover: $5-12, ⓕ to Second Ave. ♿

bOb
Like a rec-room on acid. The crowd starts out staid but succumbs to debauchery in the wee hours; between the funk music and the paucity of seats, there's no choice but to dance.
235 Eldridge Street (bet. Houston and Stanton Sts.), 777-0588, Cash Only, ⓕ to Second Ave.

Bowlmor Lanes
Mondays herald The Strike: How much do heavy house, drums-n-bass, and hip-hop improve your bowling technique? With glow-in-the-dark pins and shoes thrown in, a strike or two is bound to slip into the game.
110 University Place (bet. 12th and 13th), 255-8188, Cash Only, Cover: $10 for "Strike": ⓛⓝⓡ④⑤⑥ to Union Square ♿

C

Chaos
Rumor has it that this model-sporting, Armani-clad crowd will shell out $100 minimum for a seat on the sofa here. If the idea of three huge floors of this attitude seems appealing and your drinking budget exceeds your rent payments, join the largely heterosexual, late twenties and up crowd in savoring the extravagance of it all.
23 Watt Street (bet. Broadway and Broome), 925-8966, MC, V, AmEx, ⓐⓒⓔ to Canal St. ♿

Club Liguanea
Popular among the college crowd, this place plays an excellent blend of R&B, soul, reggae, and classic disco; Fridays attract hip-hop lovers. Catch the occasional performances by urban music faves.
220-30 Jamaica Avenue (bet. Springfield and 221st Sts.), Queens Village, (718) 776-0747, Cover: $10-20, LIRR to Queens Village

Club Vertigo
"Butter Sundays": A young, straight crowd dances to hip-hop and reggae downstairs while tribal house and classics play to the throng upstairs.
565 West 23rd Street (at Eleventh Ave.), 366-4181, Cash Only, ⓐⓒⓔ to 23rd St. ♿

Coney Island High
Variety keeps both floors of this joint jumping throughout the week. Parties cover themes across the spectrum, drawing crowds to match. Recently they've been exhuming some pretty interesting corpses of nightlife past, including Boy Bar and Max's Kansas City. What's next?
15 St. Marks Place (bet. Second and Third), 674-7959, AmEx, Cover: $5-$20, ⓝⓡ to 8th, ⑥ to Astor Pl.

Crazy Nanny's
Sundown finds working girls each other out at this comparatively conservative dyke bar. Pool tables and a fully-stocked bar help out a low-key atmosphere conducive to mingling.
21 Seventh Avenue South (at Leroy St.), 366-6312, MC, V, ①⑨ to Christopher St.

D

Decade
Sixties music, eighties crowd, and nineties decor are the parameters of this cheesy club and its patrons trying to relive their lost youth. More of a spectacle than anything. Closed Sundays and Mondays.
1117 First Avenue (bet. 61st and 62nd Sts.), 835-5979, MC, V, AmEx, Diners, D, Cover: $20 (Thurs., Fri., Sat.) ⓝⓡ to Lexington Ave., ④⑤⑥ to 59th St. ♿

Don Hill's
Wear pants or mama's best dress and you'll feel perfectly at home. This den of individuality attracts all sorts of people who want to get funky without getting judged. The mood intensifies for the long-running SqueezeBox, a queer party with punk attitude on Friday nights.
511 Greenwich Street (at Spring St.), 334-1390, MC, V, AmEx, ⓒⓔ to Spring St. ♿

Downtime
Part of the Recording and Rehearsal Arts building, this huge space, including a performance stage and a state-of-the-art sound system, is mostly populat-ed by a large contingent of after-work professionals
251 West 30th Street (bet. Seventh and Eighth Aves.), 695-2747, MC, V, AmEx, Cover: $10, 1239 or ⓐⓒⓔ to Penn Station

E

El Flamingo
An aura of noir-ish retro glamour attracts a cosmopolitan crowd-no crush of club kids here. The balcony lounge offers refuge from crowds and a view from which to scope out the dance floor.
547 West 21st St. (bet. Tenth and Eleventh Aves.), 243-2121, MC, V, AmEx, ⓒⓔ to 23rd St. ♿

Expo
Every Sunday from ten until dawn, Cafe con Leche draws lesbians, drag queens, and heteros with its seductive deep house, merengue, and salsa. A more mainstream crowd comes on Saturdays for Soul II Soul, a mix of hip-hop and pop. The cover varies with the party.
124 West 43rd St. (bet. Sixth Avenue and Broadway), 819-0377, Cash Only, ⓝⓡⓢ② ③⑦⑨ to Times Sq.

F

Fat Boy
Club kids gyrate to the pulse of a pop-oriented mix on the ample dance floor under a soaring ceiling. "It's the music that keeps me coming," quips one customer who's practicing to be a regular at this area neophyte.
409 W. 14th St. (bet. 9th and 10th Aves.), 367-9054, ⓐⓒⓛ to 14th St. ♿

clubs 317

H

Hell

Once again, the meat-packing district offers elegance amidst its oftentimes squalid warehouses. The boys who brought Big Cup to Chelsea now bring this cozy yet really quite spacious lounge that mirrors the festive and not the infernal aspect of the mythical hotspot from which it takes its name. Organizers continue proving their flair for the unique with Sunday tea in hell, a twist on the Sunday tea dance that features music 7PM to midnight. Monday nights feature Karma, with a DJ spinning all sorts of lounge sounds and fabulous martini specials are available from the bar. DJ Tina Alexander brings She Devils—a lounge for girls but where boys are quite welcome—on Tuesdays with specials on Stoli vodka drinks.
59 Gansevoort St. (bet. Greenwich and Washington Sts.), 727-1666, MC, V, AmEx, **A C E** *to 14th St.*

K

Krash

No doubt its namesake in San Juan would be proud of the Latin music this cavernous dance emporium serves up Mondays, Thursdays, Fridays, and Saturdays. Worth the tokens if you crave this beat.
34-48 Steinway St. (at Thirty-fifth Ave.), (718) 937-2400, MC, V, Cover: $1-$10, **G R** *to Steinway St.*

L

Las Vegas

With a predominantly Dominican population on hand, merengue rules at this well-known weekly fiesta. Salsa, bachata, hip-hop and house get spun as well. Admission can be costly for nights with live bands, with past prominent acts including La Banda Soberbia, Oro Solido, and Punto Fijo. 21 and over rule not always adhered to, as teens party alongside older clubbers.
179 Dyckman, (718) 942-1516, Cover $10-$30 (free for ladies on certain nights), **1** *to 207th St.*

Life

People throng in front of the massive doors as bouncers of the cooler-than-thou Spy variety let in a handful of poseur-types. Models and other self-involved people compose the clutter of heads found on the dance floor. Dancers in the know turn out for Sunday's gay party, without a doubt the home of the most grooveable music of the week.
158 Bleecker St. (bet. Thompson and Sts.), 420-1999, MC, V, AmEx, Cover: $5-$15, **A B C D F Q** *to West 4th St.*

The Lure

Leather-bound S&M boys manifest their darkest fantasies. Not exactly for the faint of heart
409 West 13th St. (bet. Ninth and Washington Aves.), 741-3919, Cash Only, Cover: free-$5, **F 2 3 9** *to 14th St.*

M

Mantra

Recent renovations have transformed this former neighborhood dive into a subterranean haven for house and techno lovers. All drinks are two dollars during the 5-7pm Happy Hour.
28 East 23rd St. (bet. Madison and Park Aves.), 254-6117, MC, V, AmEx, D, Cover: $7, **6** *to 23rd St.*

Metropolis

A predominantly Hispanic crowd jams to a unique mix of salsa, meringue, house and R&B at this out-of-the-way megaclub, which will require a cab ride after reaching the subway stop. Worth the trek if you're seeking an alternative to the Manhattan scene. Open Wednesday through Sunday.
31-99 123rd St. (718) 539-7172, Cash Only, Cover: $15-$20, **7** *to Main St.*

Mother

Catering to a largely gay crowd, this meat-packing district venue comes across as dicier than the others on the block but cut-rate drinks reward the courageous. Once inside, the lure of the three rooms obviates the unpleasant exterior: a front-room lounge, a dance floor, and a dark, cozy downstairs retreat. Classic club memorabilia like "Jackie 60" t-shirts are available at the "souvenir shop" *432 West 14th St. (at Washington), 366-5680, Cash Only,* **A C E L** *to 14th St./Eighth Ave.*

N

Nell's

Three rooms on two floors offer an eclectic mix of music ranging from reggae, hip-hop, and jazz to Latin, funk, and disco. The elegance of the capacious upstairs room calls for a sophisticated drink from the well-stocked bar. Downstairs, relax in a more intimate lounge or move to techno-groove aimed at a stylish crowd described by the bouncer as a mix of "tourists, regulars, and DJs."
246 West 14th St. (bet. Seventh and Eighth Aves.), 675-1567, MC, V, AmEx, **A C E L** *to 14th St./Eighth Ave.*

NV

Fashion types pout, air-kiss, and lounge as only they can inside this SoHo chicotorium. The DJs spin various genres, laced with Top Forty tunes. Leave the Airwalks at home: sneakers are strictly prohibited.
289 Spring St. (at Varick Ave., 929-NVNV, MC, V, AmEx, Cover: $10, **C E** *to Spring St.*

O

Opera

With great martinis to help the swing, the dance floors pack in late-night crowds. Considered small by club standards, it still lures many a club kid.
539 West 21st St. (bet. Tenth and Eleventh Aves.), 229-1618, MC, V, AmEx, Cover: $15-$20, **C E** *to 23rd St.*

P

Planet 28

Catered to a largely black and Latino crowd, the music blends R&B, hip-hop, and reggae. Check listings for gay/straight nights.
215 West 28th St. (bet. Seventh and Eighth Aves.), 643-1199, **C E 1 9** *to 23rd St.*

318 clubs

Plush

Two floors offer up deep techno, soul classics, and hip-hop. Downstairs the dimly lit dance floor pulsates to a driving beat while a relaxed lounge upstairs offers quiet refuge for chillin' hipsters. *31 West 14th St. (bet. Ninth and Tenth Ave.), 367-7035, Cash Only, Cover: $5-10,* ⒶⒸⒺⓁ *to 14th St./Eighth Ave.* ♿

Pyramid

Thursday's new wave and dark retro 80s tunes keep the goth crowd sweating, swaying, and stomping into the wee hours on the understated dance floor. Friday's 1984 and Saturday's Rapture promise more bob-inducing sets for the gay-boy and downtown hipster crowd, with 80s revival and pop exploding from the speakers. *101 Avenue A (bet. 6th and 7th Streets.), 604-4588, Cash Only,* Ⓕ *to Second Ave.*

Q

Q-Club International

Delight in hip-hop, R&B, and soul at this South Jamaica spot. Work up an appetite on the dance floor, then mosey downstairs for a bite to eat. Thursday through Saturday nights offer an upbeat blend of urban contemporary music; Sundays bring out the largest crowd of reggae listeners. *93-37 150th St. (718) 262-0733, Cash Only,* Ⓕ *to Parsons Blvd.* ♿

R

Rebar

Not the largest site in the area, but dubbed hip by the club kid crowd, which forms the lines snaking out onto Eighth Avenue. Parties vary. *127 Eighth Ave. (at 16th St.), 627-1680, MC, V, AmEx, Cover: $5/$10,* ⒶⒸⒺⓁ *to 14th St./Eighth Ave.*

Roxy

Almost always packed, the place plays host to track performers, AIDS benefits, and nonstop dancing. The crowd is different every night; Saturdays are gay. *515 West 18th St. (at Tenth Ave.), 645-5156, Cash Only,* ⒸⒺ *to 23rd St.*

S

Sapphire

Drink before coming to this claustrophobic den of hip-hop. Sweaty fun awaits the aggressor who makes it to the middle of the floor. Deserted on weeknights. Happy Hour from 7pm to 10pm. *249 Eldridge St. (bet. Houston and Stanton Sts.), 777-5153, Cash Only, Cover: $3-$5,* Ⓕ *to Second Ave.* ♿

The Shadow

Different theme nights, live performances, and dance offerings attract huge crowds of older men and mostly women. The main floor sports several dance floors, bars, and a small room for the immobile. Take a break in the upstairs lounge. Women must be twenty-three, men must be twenty-five; bring ID. A strict dress code is enforced. *229 West 28th St. (bet. Seventh and Eighth Aves.), 629-3331,* ①⑨ *to 28th Street*

Shane's Villa

Not-too-big and not-too-small reggae haunt that thrives on the middle road. With the decor geared towards the 25-35 year old set, expect to hear an accessible music-mix. Bar is just as accessible, as it's centered in the middle of the dance floor. *4012 Boston Rd. (at Bivona), Cover $10,* ⑤ *to Dyre Avenue*

Soca Paradise

Droves of Trinidadian and Guyanese natives come out every weekend as the sharp and calypso tunes blast until the wee hours, spun by various area DJs. Ladies get in free on Fridays and before 11pm on Saturdays. Delicious, traditional Caribbean cuisine is available. *25-20 Jamaica Ave. (at Frances Lewis Blvd.), (718) 464-3600, Cash Only, Cover: $10-$12,* ⒺⒿⓏ *to Jamaica Cntr.* ♿

Sound Factory

Riding on its reputation as a model hangout in the late 70s, these days this relocated club features edgeless music, and bridge and tunnel teens from Long Island and New Jersey and twentysomethings characterize the early scene. After hours, as the 'burbanites are paying their tolls to get home, expect deeper music and serious dancers. *618 West 46th St. (bet. Eleventh and Twelfth Aves.), 643-0728,* ⒶⒸⒺ *to 42nd St.*

System

Not as cool as it used to be, but still semi-respectable. In the sizable lounge area, middle-aged, sequin-sporting martini-sippers drink in the packs of guidos congregating at the couches. Ample space for dancing makes gyrating a necessity. Very Miami Beach. Call ahead to get on the guest list, as bouncers are choosy. *76 East 13th St. (bet. Broadway and Fourth Ave.), 388-1060, Cover: $20 (Wed.- Sat.), MC, V, AmEx,* ⓁⓃⓇ④⑤ ⑥ *to Union Sq.*

T

Thirteen

Preps and yups make up most of this late twenties/early thirties YMCA crowd; the cast of bouncers and bartenders are remarkably cool however, despite their slightly cheesy clientele. *35 East 13th St. (bet. Broadway and University Pl.), 979-6677, MC, V, AmEx, Cover: $10 and under,* ⓁⓃⓇ④⑤ ⑥ *to Union Sq.*

Tunnel

This monster club offers something for everyone: surf the web in the Cosmic Cavern to the tune of deep house and classics or join the bridge and tunnel types grinding to a hard house mix on the main dance floor. Occasional film screenings and fashion shows round out the offerings. Weekend "all-nighters" tempt those who must party beyond the break of dawn. Call (917) 244-8908 to get on the guest list for parties Friday and Saturday nights. *220 Twelfth Ave. (at 27th*

St.), 695-7292, Cash Only, Cover: $20 ($15 with invite), ❶❾ to 28th St.

Twilo

Party late in the old Sound Factory space, where funky decor brings new life to an old idea. No hard drinks are served after 4am, but a juice bar will keep the blood pumping. Maybe you can still make it to work...
530 West 27th St. (bet. Tenth and Eleventh Aves.), 268-1600, MC, V, AmEx, ⓒⓔ to 23rd St. ♿

205 Club

A dangling disco ball welcomes the predominantly hip-hop/R&B crowd into this spacious two-room social mecca. While it varies from party to party, the crowd is typically put-together and over twenty-five. Open Tuesday through Saturday till 4am. 205 Chrysty Street (at Stanton St.), 473-5816, Cover: never over $10, ⓕ to Second Avenue

U

Udder Club

A pint-sized dance club, complete with disco ball and 70s music. Food is available from the Holy Cow restaurant upstairs. Broadway and 86th St., 769-0000, MC, V, AmEx, ❶❾ to 86th St.

V

Velvet

Saturdays fill the room with Latin music and a wonderful mix of drag queens, heteros, and inconspicuous tourists; Sundays after midnight host a special drag show. Guest DJs perform every week, usually for no cover. 67 Avenue A (bet. 10th and 11th Sts.), 475-2172, Cash Only, ⓛ to First Ave.

Vinyl

Hordes of raver-kids palpitate to outer space-like tunes in a labyrinth of hazy rooms, converted from an old warehouse. Not for the timid. 157 Hudson St. (bet. Leight and Hubert Sts.), 343-1379, Cash Only, Cover: Usually $15, ❶❾ to Canal St.

W

The Warehouse

Venture to this two-level sweatfest near the outskirts of Manhattan. Catering to a mostly black and Latino gay male crowd, the club is a synthesis of New York's old Sound Factory Bar and Washington D.C.'s legendary Tracks. Walls are gray and sparsely decorated, hence the venue's title. Huge lounge area!
141 East 140th St., (718) 992-5974, Cover $10-$12, ❷❹❺ to 149th-Grand Concourse

Webster Hall

College boys seeking girls and college girls seeking no cover and free drinks flock here on Thursdays for ladies' night. Four separate dance floors, each with a different theme, allow you to find your niche or to floor-hop to ditch pesky wannabe pick-up artists. Especially good if you're a fan of alterna-pop or grunge.
125 East 11th St. (bet. Third and Fourth Ave.), 353-1600, MC, V, AmEx, ⓛⓝⓡ❹❺ ❻ to Union Sq.

CLUB INDEX BY NEIGHBORHOOD

BRONX
Shane's Villa
The Warehouse

CHELSEA
Club Vertigo
Downtime
El Flamingo
Fat Boy
Hell
Mother
Nell's
Rebar
Roxy
The Shadow
Tunnel
Twilo

EAST VILLAGE
Bowlmor Lanes
Coney Island High
Crazy Nanny's
Financial District
Gramercy
Greenwich Village
Life
Mantra
Opera
Planet 28
Plush
Pyramid
System
The Lure
Thirteen
Velvet
Webster Hall

LOWER EAST SIDE
205 Club
bOb
NV
Sapphire
The Bank

MIDTOWN
Expo
Sound Factory

QUEENS
Chaos
Club Liguanea
Don Hill's
Krash
Metropolis
Q-Club
International
Soca Paradise

TRIBECA
Vinyl

UPPER EAST SIDE
Decade

UPPER WEST SIDE
Udder Club

WASHINGTON HEIGHTS
Las Vegas

music

NYC music *scene*.322
music venue listings.326

music venues

Manhattan is the birthplace of such punk legends as the Velvet Underground, the Ramones, and poet-rocker Lou Reed. Brooklyn gave us the Beastie Boys; and Paul Simon came out of Queens. Strike up a conversation with most New Yorkers, and they'll tell you about the time when Eddie Vedder, Slash of Guns 'n Roses, or Joey Ramone cruised into their favorite bar and jammed for six hours straight, or how they'd catch every Blues Traveler show at Wetlands, years before the band became popular. These days, there are more opportunities than ever to check out a quality rock performance at local club. Ten years ago, Continental (nee Divide), Maxwell's (in Hoboken), and CBGB's were practically the only worthy scenes. But live-music venues have sprung up all over the city, especially in the East Village and Lower East Side, and a growing number of revolutionary local bands, such as Soul Coughing and Rasputina, have emerged on the New York music scene, many of whom deserve a hearty shove onto the national stage.

As much as musicians hate to be labeled and compartmentalized, it has to be said that music scenes exist. People with like tastes are drawn to one another and bands and cliques result. Your average blaring barroom hard-rock band still lives at Continental, '70s punk and glam bands still hold their heads high at esteemed outpost CBGB's, and Wetlands continues to specialize in cover bands, who pay earnest, hopelessly nostalgic homage to groups like the Grateful Dead, the Doors and Led Zeppelin. Chic crowds attracted to retro bands gather at Fez and Windows on the World. Hungry spoken-word artists arrange events at Nuyorican Poets Cafe and the Knitting Factory and appeal to a growing number of fans, and loyal Latin-music fans mob clubs like Copacabana, Bayamo, and Latin Quarter.

The New York jazz tradition has experienced a resurgence of popularity; in Greenwich Village, a thriving network of jazz clubs, some historic spots and some young upstarts, attests to this new trend, as tourists and residents alike clamor to hear old legends and young up and comers. While most of the big names tend to congregate at the more expensive clubs like The Blue Note, the Village Vanguard, and Lincoln Center, nights at Smalls and the no-cover brunch at Sweet Basil are good times to enjoy laid-back tunes without breaking the bank. A new craze in the city is the swing scene; at Club 46, the Supper Club, or Louisiana Grill you can immerse yourself in all that this scene has to offer from the sweaty energetic moves to the fashion which has made its mark coast to coast.

Musical movements-whether they be the newest trends or revivals of classic sounds-which register elsewhere as explosions can seem like the status quo in New York. This city's burgeoning contributions to the cutting edge are so manifold as to seem inconsequential, while the various subcultures which make up the city's music scene still pay tribute to the progenitors whose ground they now occupy. New York continues to foster young and old talent in its major venues like Madison Square Garden and Carnegie Hall and small venues like Coney Island High and the Mercury Lounge, like no other city in the world.

322 music

The Retro Swing Renaissance

The swing scene has exploded in New York City over the past year. People of all ages are flocking to clubs around town to celebrate the revival of a sound that sends your heart racing and your body rocketing through the legs and above the heads of ecstatically smiling partners. This new craze has got us all dancing together again, wildly reaching for each others hands and swinging each other about. The energetic Big Band sound of the '40s has evolved into a new form of swing called Jump Swing or Blues Jump and has sparked a special interest in the younger generation. Wild packs of kids rush the doors of Louisiana Bar and Grill on Monday nights; they pay no cover charge and their age is not an issue. The tables are stacked aside and a large dance floor awaits the loyal, enthusiastic hipster crowd. Louisiana gets its fair share of folks who "dress the part," in Zoot-suits, Spat-shoes, Fedoras and baggy slacks, but it also has a large contingent who make no attempt and have no airs, "they look like utter slobs, they show up with their trail-mix and spring water," says Louisiana owner, but he likes it that way. Louisiana Bar and Grill has been credited with kicking off the east coast swing scene; "we've been doing the swing thing for five years, and other venues have caught on slowly, which is nice." He goes on to say that the swing scene started out as an elitist fashion and than blew up into this big scene. Louisiana plans to inaugurate another swing night on Wednesdays to accommodate an older crowd. And every Saturday Louisiana features the Harlem Jazz Legends, "the guys who created this stuff."

The most obvious modern Swing push began with the 1996 release of the west-coast-based movie Swingers, and the Big Bad Voodoo Daddy band who rocks the house at the end of the flick; California has been swinging ever since, but most of New York lagged about a year behind. Some New York venues, which followed the movie trend are: Swing 46 which opened its doors a year ago, and the Supper Club. These places attract a more fashion-conscious, trendy crowd. Swing 46 features live swing bands Monday through Saturday nights, Thursday through Saturday they only let in 21-year-olds and over. Swing 46 holds Lindy and Jitterbug lessons at 9pm, for those who want a competitive edge, and than the bands play from 10pm until 1:30am. The Supper Club serves an à la carte dinner from 5:30 to 11:30pm, they offer a swing class to the dress-up kids from 11pm-12am, and a 17-piece Big Band plays from 8pm-12am. By midnight the club totally transforms to Swing. And let's not forget Big Daddy Swing featured every Thursday night at Lansky Lounge on the Lower East Side, which also offers dance lessons and live bands.

Like all trends, the swing craze is all encompassing. But even the new Gap commercial which features fantastic swingers boogying in basic baggies to a jump swing beat can't diminish the appeal of swing.

music 323

New York City --
The Jazz Capital of the World

New York has been the jazz capital of the world ever since Chicago ceded the title in the 1920s. Early 20th-century Harlem became a cradle for experimentation with ragtime and other precursors to jazz which spawned such diverse variations as James P. Johnson's and Fats Waller's stride, an intricate manipulation of ragtime syncopation and big-band jazz.

Populated by a remarkable pantheon of personalities, including big-band leaders like Cab Calloway and Duke Ellington and the great chanteuse Billie Holiday, New York became a jazz center. Soon, the heart of the city belonged to jazz, and by the '50s, 52nd Street was a solid wall of sound: legendary clubs like the Downbeat, the Hickory House, Jimmy Ryan's, Kelly's Stable, and Birdland converged on "Swing Street" to host the likes of Count Basie and Dizzy Gillespie. But as jazz powered the city's mainstream musical scene in the early 1950s, it also instigated a revolution that would take an entirely new direction. Jazz greats such as Ellington and Count Basie collaborated with Big Joe Turner to create a new style that was dubbed Rhythm and Blues, first broadcast in 1954 over the radio station WINS. DJ Alan Freed was the first to call this "rock 'n roll."

At the same time, John Coltrane was developing what would be known as modal jazz, frequently experimenting in front of audiences at the Village Vanguard. This new style opened up possibilities for the melodic improvisations which further dismantled the rules of traditional jazz and eventually led to free jazz in the late '60s and early '70s; Thelonious Monk and Ornette Coleman are products of this movement. Even as proponents of free jazz pushed forth, a young trumpeter named Miles Davis arrived on the scene to defend traditional tuneful jazz and was incredibly prolific until his death in the early '90s.

The R&B arm of jazz's development exploded into the pop music phenomenon of the '50s and '60s. The Brill Building, whose brass art deco façade still shines brightly next to Colony Records on Broadway at 50th Street, was the epicenter of the songwriting and recording world. The Alison Anders film, *Grace of My Heart* loosely chronicles a fictionalized account of the career of Carole King, who started as a songwriter for the girl-and-guy groups of this period before graduating to a solo career.

Though jazz went underground toward the end of the '70s and into the early '80s, it regained popularity with the revival of downtown clubs like the Blue Note and the Village Vanguard. Today, New York City is home to the most active jazz clubs in the world. The appropriately named club, Smalls, vaguely recalls the jazz clubs of the '50s. Located on W. 10th Street at Seventh Avenue, Smalls attracts a youthful crowd and features amateurs and headliners alike. Sweet Basil, located on Seventh Ave. South between Grove and Bleecker Sts., once labeled the Village Vanguard's chief Seventh Ave. South competitor, is now a prosperous West Village mainstay. Basil consistently draws its regular crowd by booking veterans and crowd-pleasing international jazz acts. The Blue Note, at 131 W. 3rd St. features open jam sessions on Fridays and Saturdays and highlights some of the hottest young talent in jazz.

Why linger on the fringes of New York's music scene when you could be one of the stars? Ponder these questions: Do you loiter at your favorite local pub for hours, feeding crisp dollar bills into the jukebox and belt out harmony to every song? Are you a shower singer? Do you sit around the living room all day in your underwear, with a guitar strapped around your shoulder, strumming away as your roommates pass back and forth, to and from the kitchen? Do you secretly wish they'd stop for a minute and clap along? Do you desire the opportunity to test out your skills in front of an audience that will listen? If you have answered "yes" to any of the above questions, you might want to take advantage of some of the weekly open mikes and jams hosted by local nightspots all over the city.

Every Sunday night, Chicago B.L.U.E.S, "New York's premiere Blues Club," welcomes "all musicians," to a no-cover, open-blues jam. Sign up is at 8:30pm, and these nights tend to be packed, so you may have to wait a while, but in time you'll have your long-awaited "15 minutes of fame." The Dark Star Lounge, on the upper west side, hosts an open mike for songwriters with "varying degrees of proficiency," on Mondays at 9pm. All songs must be original. Bring your guitar or other acoustic accompaniment, and there is a piano on stage. If jazz is your thing, Roy Campbell welcomes singers every Monday from 10pm to 1am, at the Lenox Lounge, where Billie Holiday was once a regular. Also on Monday nights, Spiral, in the East Village, hosts an open mike at 8pm, for acoustic, alternative pop, Southern rock, and swing lovers. Ask for a guy named George and take advantage of the $2 Buds to calm your nerves. At Sidewalk, it's open mike, anything goes--music, comedy, performance or spoken word (Mondays, 7:30pm sign-up). On Tuesday night, a live band accompanies each participant at Nell's, for a soul and R&B jam. Sign-up starts at 10pm, but you'll get up there after 11:30 pm. There is a strict "one song per participant policy." Bring sheet music if your selection is obscure, otherwise the band knows everything. The last Tuesday of every month is gospel. And finally, every night (except Sunday) Smalls on 10th Street has a jam session of the hardbop variety from 2-7am, for late-night music enthusiasts. You never know what might happen when you seize the limelight at any of these night-spots; maybe you'll get discovered, but most likely you'll make do with the rush of applause that will (temporarily) sate your performance lust. You need only a few things: a little talent, a lot of chutzpah, and a healthy tolerance for your fellow amateurs.

Open-Mike Nights and Jam Sessions

music 325

A

Acme Underground
All cleaned up and ready to rock and roll: this low-frills basement stage just got a makeover and a brand new sound system for its spruced-up lineups. Have legitimate ID ready; the doorman is not taking any more sorry excuses.
9 Great Jones St. (bet. Broadway and Lafayette), 420-1934, MC, V, ❶❷ to 8th St.

B

Beacon Theatre
Red velveteen and brass accents adorn the interior of this grand hall which now hosts rock concerts and gospel plays on its small stage. Best acoustics in New York City.
2124 Broadway (at 74th Street), 496-7070, MC, V, AmEx, ❶❷❸❹ to 72nd Street ♿

The Bitter End
Be prepared to keep collars well-buttoned and jeans tightly cuffed for maximum conformity, since it's strictly an older bridge-and-tunnel crowd crowding in these days at this garage-band stage that's been around since the sixties.
147 Bleecker St. (bet. Thompson and LaGuardia Pl.), 673-7030, MC, V, AmEx, D, Diners, ❶❷ to 8th St. ♿

The Blue Note
At the heart of New York's jazz scene in the heart of the Village, showcasing nationally-acclaimed acts with prices to match: cover and drinks will total at least thirty dollars. The real value is after 2am when the cover for the after-hours jam drops to five dollars. Often as hot as the main act, late-night entertainment generally consists of a free-form jam hosted by whichever top musicians decide to show up.
131 West 3rd St.(bet. MacDougal and Sixth Ave.), 475-8592, MC, V, AmEx, ❶❷❸❹❺❻ to West 4th St.

The Bottom Line
From Springsteen on, virtually everyone to emerge from the New York rock scene has played here. Nowadays, the acts range from emerging singer-songwriters to veteran performers.
5 West 4th St. (at Mercer), 228-6300, Cash Only, ❶❷❸❹❺❻ to West 4th Street

Brownie's
The club space remains physically unextraordinary despite some tinkering over the years, but no one seems to mind since they regularly book some of the best lineups in town, including the best bands in the city, regional outfits, and college radio faves. Every Sunday night is all ages.
169 Avenue A (bet. 10th and 11th Sts.), 420-8392, Cash Only, ❶ to First Ave.

C

CBGB's
Still punk after all these years. Loud, dirty and crowded-and those are the positive aspects of this EV landmark. But the raw energy of the music quickly overshadows all of that. Besides, where else will $5 buy thirteen different bands these days?
1315 Bowery (bet. First and Second Aves.), 982-4052, Cash Only, ❻ to Bleecker St.

CB's 313 Gallery
CBGB's with a day job. Similar to the original, but without the excessive racket and filth. Instead, the crowds behave themselves and seem to prefer acoustic music to simple destrucive behavior. A haven for folkies and anyone else with a hard time finding a niche. Stop by during the day to check out the art.
313 Bowery (bet. First and Second Aves.), 677-0455, Cash Only, ❻ to Bleecker St.

Chicago B.L.U.E.S.
The sophisticated crowd middle-aged crowd starts coming after five, and the good blues music usually starts around nine. Breathing room is hard to come by on weekends.
73 Eighth Ave. (bet. 13th and 14th Sts.), 924-9755, MC, V, Am Ex, ❶❷❸❹ to 14th/Eighth Ave.

Continental
A stereotypical rock joint, complete with garage bands and a floor like the bottom of a taxi cab. Most weekdays are no cover, and with a lot of effort, it's possible to find the occasional diamond in the rough.
23 Third Ave. (bet. St. Marks Pl. and 9th St.), 529-6924, Cash Only, ❻ to Astor Pl. ♿

The Cooler
A sky-blue door among drab neighbors leads the way into this slickly-renovated underground meat locker, now home to experimental jazz, reggae, and alternative rock shows. Cash only at the door; whip out the gold card to finance the overpriced drinks inside. Advance tickets are usually available at the Bleecker Street Kim's Underground.
416 West 14th St. (bet. Ninth and Washington Sts.), 229-0785, MC, V, AmEx, Cover: $5-$10, ❶❷❸❹❺ to 14th St.

326 music

Cotton Club

Once a speakeasy patronized by the likes of Bogie, this jazz venue is now a supper club serving up soul food to the middle-aged and tourists. While it lacks its former edge, everyone still has a good time. Call to make reservations for dinner seatings and for show times; gospel brunch every Saturday and Sunday is $25.
656 West 125th Street (bet. Broadway and Riverside Dr.), 663-7980, MC, V, Diners, D, ❶❾ to 125th St. ♿

I

Irving Plaza

A former dance club still retaining some of the charming architectural vestiges from days of yore, this mainstream spot's advance schedule can be found at www.irving-plaza.com or by checking the ads in the free weekly newspapers.
17 Irving Place (at 15th St.), 777-1224 (Box Office hours: 12-6pm, Mon.-Sat.), Cash Only (Credit cards call Ticketmaster), ❶❿❿❹❺❻ to Union Sq.

K

The Knitting Factory

One of the city's most intimate performance spaces for acts ranging from a jazz quartet to an indie rock group to an organist accompanying a silent film. A surefire interesting time.
74 Leonard St. (bet. West Broadway and Church St.), 219-3055, MC, V, Am Ex, ❶❾ to Franklin St.

L

Latin Quarter

Puerto Rican bands and Latino orchestras set the beat for salsa and merengue dancing on Thursday and Saturday nights. Tickets available in advance at a discount.
2551 Broadway (at 96th St.), 864-7600, Cash Only, Cover: $10-$15, ❶❷❸❾ to 96th St.

Les Poulets

Latin music and live bands on the weekends as well as savory Spanish cooking draws a crowd that is young, mixed and attractive. Free admission before 9pm.
16 West 22nd St. (at Fifth Ave.), 229-2000, MC, V, Am Ex, Cover: $5-$15, ❶❿ to 23rd St. ♿

The Lion's Den

An NYU-oriented crowd jams to a smorgasbord of acts, from alternative to punk to reggae. The stage is deep, but standing room is somewhat limited.
214 Sullivan Street (bet. Bleecker and 3rd), 477-2782, Cash Only, ❶❷❿❹ to West 4th St.

M

Manny's Car Wash and Blues

Renowned acts like Johnny (Clyde) Copland, Luther Allison, and Junior Wells play here. The Sunday night "World Famous Blues Jam" boasts no cover; expect to pay $3-$15 for other performances.
1558 Third Ave. (bet. 87th and 88th Sts.), 369-2583, MC, V, Am Ex, ❹❺❻ to 86th St. ♿

Mercury Lounge

Aspiring musicians consider this garage-smelling landmark a haven of inspiration. Expect established, non-mainstream bands and a quasi-hippie, musically-abreast crowd.
217 East Houston St. (at Essex), 260-4700, MC, V, AmEx, ❿ to Second Ave.

N

New Music Cafe

Cover is usually pretty cheap at this midsized club, since the bands are generally relative unknowns from the Northeast with small cult followings. The TriBeCa location draws the younger members of the lower Manhattan office set for music, drinks and pool at the table inconveniently located in the entryway. If this sounds like a recipe for fun, take advantage of yet another great deal on Canal.
380 Canal St. (at West Broadway), 941-1019, Cash Only, Cover under $10, ❶❾ to Canal St. ♿

O

Orange Bear

No pretension, just pool tables, a juke box, and some live rock, country, and jazz. The crowd is middle-aged and middle-income, but not mid-life crisis; they keep their cool and the atmosphere comfortable. According to the bartender, "they're usually just guys that work around here."
147 Murray St. (bet. Church and West Broadway), 566-3705, MC, V, Am Ex, ❶❷❿❾ to Chambers St. ♿

P

Postcrypt Coffee House

One of Columbia's best-kept secrets, this intimate basement space in St. Paul' Chapel hosts everyone from spoken-word artists to folk-singers; Suzanne Vega got her start here. Expect students and plenty of older folk in the know who love a plaintive acoustic guitar.
St Paul's Chapel Columbia University, 854-1953, Admission: Free, ❶❾ to 116th St.

music 327

R

Roseland

Interesting set-up in that it's not isolated from the passerbys like most teenage-oriented concert halls (even Susan Sarandon's been here). Dome-like, Victorian inside makes it a nice setting to hang around.
239 West 52nd Street (bet. Broadway and Eighth Ave.), 245-5761, Cash Only, NR to 49th St., 19 to 50th St.

Roulette

Experimental jazz and art music in an artist-style loft space. The shows always cost eight dollars for non-members and start at nine o'clock. Call for more information, since there's always something new going on.
223 West Broadway (at White), 219-3600, Cash Only, 19 to Franklin Street

S

Small's

Starting at 10pm, ten hours of jazz is for just ten dollars. A bring-your-own-booze policy, complimentary juice bar, and mellow setting make this cozy, living-room-like jazz haven a hit. All shows are open to all-ages.
183 West 10th St. (at Seventh Ave), 929-7565, 19 to Christopher St.

Sounds of Brazil (SOB's)

Latin and Caribbean musicians who can't be found anywhere else; stick around for the dance party afterwards. If dancing's more than an afterthought, turn out for Sunday's Tango event: free lessons and a handful of cocky pros.
204 Varick St. (at Houston St.), 243-4940, MC, V, Am Ex, 19 to Houston St.

Sweet Basil

Once a health food store, this homey jazz restaurant hasn't changed since it opened twenty-five years ago, demonstrated by the seventies-style lamp shades still dotting the room. Sunday brunch with no cover from 2pm to 6pm features legendary trumpeter Doc Cheatham; other days, Cho the Bartender is reason enough to stop by.
88 Seventh Avenue South (bet. Grove and Bleecker Sts.), 242-1785, Cover: $17.50, $10 minimum, MC, V, Am Ex, 19 to Christopher St.

T

Terra Blues

The local talent featured on weekends is among the best in the city; even with the weekend cover climbing as high as twenty bucks, it's worth it.
149 Bleecker St. (bet. Thompson St. and LaGuardia Pl.), 777-7776, MC, V, Am Ex, ABCDE FQ to West 4th St.

Tramps

An intimate stage in a large, dingy space with good acoustics hosts bands range from rising local talent like Skeleton Key and Yo La Tengo to nationally known bands with devoted followings that work best in smaller spaces.
51 West 21st St. (bet. Fifth and Sixth Aves.), 544-1666, MC, V, Am Ex (drinks only, cash at the door), NR to 23rd St.

V

Village Vanguard

Once the home of progressive jazz, New York's most fashionable and expensive jazz club offers a mix of young lions like Joshua Redman and Roy Hargrove and older boppers like Tommy Flanagan and Hank Jones. The basement location, candles, and wooden tables create an intimate setting.
178 Seventh Avenue South (at 11th St.), 255-4037, Cash Only, Cover: $25 including $10 minimum, FL123 9 to 14th St.

Visiones

Well-known locals and lesser-known national acts with a progressive slant play here.
125 MacDougal St. (at 3rd Ave.), 673-5576, Cover: $5-$15, $10/table or one drink minimum, MC, V, AmEx, ABCDEF to West 4th St.

W

Wetlands

The vibe at this hippie party palace makes it seem like a great time to dance around with ska-crazed high schoolers, and it isn't just the drinks. The club books with an emphasis on oodles of fun: ska, funk, and Dead cover bands; Thursday's no-cover Eco-Saloon is perfect for the cash-poor pothead.
161 Hudson St. (at Laight St.), 966-4225, MC, V, Am Ex (drinks only, cash at the door), 19 to Canal St.

328 music

Leisure

escaping from NYC ....▶ 330
relaxing in NYC ◀--------◀ *334*
sports + recreation ◀············▶ 338

leisure

Feel like there's no escape from the city? Hardly. There are plenty of places in and around New York to unwind, de-stress, calm down-or just get a tan. Central Park, for instance, is filled with verdant slopes, rustling tress, and tranquil, undisturbed pools. Bring a picnic basket and watch the city fauna at play. To keep the blood moving, take a hike across the Brooklyn Bridge. The views of Manhattan are unbelievable, especially at sunrise. For a break from the urban jungle, sample some of the natural beauty of Long Island. Head for the beaches; the beautiful white sand runs for miles. If wilderness sounds better, then venture upstate. Pitch a tent in one of the region's thick forests, or go skiing in the Catskills. For a real thrill ride, visit Six Flags in New Jersey. The roller coasters there are the quickest way to forget landlord problems.

If you want to devote your leisure time to the serious business of exercise, then visit one of the top-notch gyms in the city for an intense workout. Or stay outdoors and join the hundreds of other people who bike, blade, and jog in the various city parks. Manhattan offers several other exercise alternatives, like horseback riding, ice skating, and softball. Better yet, stay on the sidelines and take in a game at Yankee Stadium. Whatever you choose, New York City has an endless number of ways to keep the body busy and the mind clear.

great escapes

long island

Long Island has long served as a playground for New Yorkers. The Island, as it is lovingly known, is easily accessible by the Long Island Railroad and offers a variety of recreational possibilities. In the summer, celebrities, society notables, and others willing to rent a room in a house crowded with strangers and empty kegs, head out to the Hamptons, a conglomeration of small towns on the island's eastern end. They spend the warmer months in enormous private mansions on the shore, and their presence creates a flurry of business in the normally quiet towns. Tourists come as well, and not just for a glimpse of the rich and famous; the beaches in the Hamptons are beautiful, and some are relatively deserted. There are trendy shops and galleries to browse through in town, and for a real guilty pleasure, walk or drive through the residential blocks and stare at the mansions. Go to Southhampton to see the most legendary houses; Meadow and Gin Lanes, which run parallel to the ocean, are the best blocks to scope Hampton real estate. Long Island Railroad provides regular service to Hamptons. By car, take the Long Island Expressway to exit 70, then right for three miles to Route 27 (Sunrise Highway), which goes straight into South Hampton. When you're done checking out the lifestyles of the rich and famous, head farther out Route 27 toward Montauk and sample some of the tastiest lobster you've ever had from one of the many roadside seafood restaurants. For more mansions and spectacular views outside of the Hamptons, head to Old Westbury Gardens (71 Old Westbury Road, Old Westbury, 516-571-7900) and peruse the replica of an 18th-century English country estate. The grounds also offer excellent picnicking spots. The Sand's Point Park and Preserve (Middleneck Road, Port Washington, 516-571-7900) is another area filled with beautiful mansions and exquisite gardens.

For a trek off the beaten path, take a day trip to Shelter Island, a secluded and peaceful place nestled between the north and south forks of Long Island's east end. Shelter Island is about 12 square miles and can only be reached by ferry, so it's obviously not a huge hub for tourism. Rent a sailboat and go fishing, or hike over the varied terrain and enjoy the peace and quiet. Take the Sunrise Express Bus Service from Port Authority *(see Resources section)* to Shelter Island. Stony Brook, a little town on Long Island's North Shore, is an equally tranquil retreat. Stony Brook is one of the Island's most historic enclaves, and it is filled with white Colonial homes and other remnants of early America. A peaceful harbor and an 18th-century grist mill top it all off. Take the Long Island Expressway to exit 62, then proceed north on Nicolls Road and turn left on Route 25A, which runs straight into Stony Brook. Also on 25A is Oyster Bay, another charming and rustic town, which has two main attractions: Sagamore Hill (Cove Neck Road, Oyster Bay, 516-922-4447), the former home of Theodore Roosevelt, is found here, and the three-story, 22-room Victorian house is an impressive sight (the guided tours frequently sell out on weekends, so get there early); and the Planting Fields Arboretum (Planting Fields Road, 516-922-9200) which was recently named a State Historic Park. There is a 65-room Tudor mansion on the estate, as well as a rose garden and over 600 species of rhododendrons and azaleas. Visit during spring and enjoy the dazzling natural display.

Long Island has a number of beaches, but by far the most popular is Jones Beach (Ocean Drive, Wantagh, 516-785-1600), which is serviced by the Long Island Railroad. The beach is inundated with sunseekers on summer weekends, when people from all boroughs leave the city for some fresh air. Long Island's most famous boardwalk is found here, and it offers such amenities as 1920s bath houses, outdoor eateries, miniature golf, and swimming pools. The sand is white and usually devoid of litter, so it's worth the train trip. Get there early and save a spot. The island has lovely parks, as well, and Eisenhower Park (take the Hempstead Turnpike to East Meadow, 516-572-0348) is surely the prettiest. There are facilities for everything from golf to cross-country jogging to cricket, as well as a boating lake and an a lakeside theater.

leisure 331

upstate new york

When people think of New York they undoubtedly picture Manhattan. Truth is, there are many attractions north of the city that are worth visiting. Saratoga Springs, for instance, is a legendary resort town. Located just north of Albany, Saratoga Springs is famous for its healing mineral springs; it's also the site of America's oldest and most beautiful racetracks. The racing season attracts blue-bloods and tourists alike, as does the summer entertainment. From June until August, the Saratoga Performing Arts Center has something going on almost every night. Saratoga State Park has two beautiful golf courses, four swimming pools, a dozen picnic areas, and several tennis courts. Reserve a spot at the Roosevelt and Lincoln Bathhouses (518-584-2011) well in advance and enjoy the fizzy mineral baths and famous massages that made the town famous. Take Amtrak (from Penn Station; see Resources section) or Greyhound (from Port Authority) to Saratoga.

Some miles away from Saratoga Springs is Albany, the state capital. Visit in the fall and enjoy the spectacular foliage. Albany is the home of the New York State Museum, which chronicles the development of New York State and its cities. There are, among other things, full-size replicas of Manhattan stores, buses, and government offices. The Museum is housed in a 98-acre complex in the heart of downtown Albany known as Empire State Plaza, which was a gift from the late Governor Nelson Rockefeller. There is an art collection and a 42nd-floor observation deck, along with an enormous assortment of stores. Visit the Albany Urban Cultural Park Visitor's Center to learn more about the city and its unique history. Take Amtrak to Albany; the tracks run along the Hudson River, so it's bound to be a scenic trip.

For a more spectacular view of the Hudson River, travel along its east bank. Enormous mansions line the shore, and the Catskill and Shawangunk mountains provide an incredible backdrop. Most of the historical estates are open to the public now, so spend a weekend hopping from mansion to mansion. The town of Rhinebeck is a good starting point; it's home to the oldest hotel in America (see Bed and Breakfasts, this section). Tour the old homes of FDR and painter Frederic Edwin Church, among others. Contact Hudson River Heritage (P.O. Box 287, Rhinebeck, NY 12572) for more information on the estates. Take Amtrak to Rhinecliff, which is three miles from Rhinebeck.

The Catskill Mountains are filled with ski resorts; however, their popularity can lead to over-crowding. To experience the scenery of the mountains in peace and quiet, try a less frequented town like Woodstock. Set against a mountain, the town affords spectacular views. Take a scenic drive up Mead's Mountain to enjoy the vantage point from Overlook Trail. Travel to the town of Phonecia nearby for more dramatic view of the wilderness. Esopus Creek, which follows the road (Route 28), for many miles, and is a favorite for fly fishing and tubing. Ride the Catskill Mountain Railroad for unobstructed views of the waterway. If skiing is on the agenda, try Hunter Mountain; it's just a short drive from Phonecia. From the ski-lift, there is a 360-degree view of the surrounding mountains. Belleayre Mountain also has excellent skiing. For more information, contact the Woodstock Chamber of Commerce (P.O. Box 36, Woodstock, NY 12498). Take the Adirondack Trailways Bus (967-2900, or 800-858-8555) to Woodstock and Phonecia.

On the other side of the city lies New Jersey, accessible by the PATH (234-7284) for only a dollar. Make a beeline for Hoboken, Frank Sinatra's birthplace. Maxwell's on Washington Street books acts rivaling those of New York's best rock clubs. Exploring the rest of the city can be a hit-or-miss affair, but some worthwhile shops, thrift stores, bars and restaurants can be found along and just off of Washington Street. Venture across the state to the Jersey border on the Delaware River, where a small group of towns offer some excellent shopping. Lambertville in particular is a choice place for antiques, and the town has some lovely restaurants and inns as well. Enjoy the nearby shopping in Princeton and cruise the magnificent university campus. There is a major outlet center in Flemington, which includes big names like Calvin Klein and Adidas. Reach these areas via the New Jersey Turnpike (the Flemington/Princeton exit), or take the Trans-Bridge Lines bus to Lambertville.

Atlantic City is a hotbed of glitz and conspicuous consumption. All the major hotels, casinos, and shops line the famous boardwalk; straying from it might be dangerous at night. "Vegas on the Atlantic it is not," said a native New Yorker and long-time Atlantic City visitor, "but it's fun for a weekend." Call the Atlantic City Convention Center and Visitor's Bureau for travel information. Get there by bus from the Port Authority in Manhattan (see the Resources section). Spend all the winnings at the Paramus Park Mall (in Paramus) or the Roosevelt Field Shopping Mall (in Garden City, 516-742-8000); both are spectacular examples of the suburban ideal. Clothes are tax-free in New Jersey, so hop a bus at the Port Authority and stock up.

For outdoor fun, take a New Jersey Transit shuttle bus to the beautiful New Jersey shoreline. Ocean Grove's wide, clean beach is complemented by the surrounding Victorian architecture, while Bayhead is reminiscent of New England, with fine sand, rough seas, and Cape Cod-style houses. Spring Lake boasts fine sandy beaches, tree-lined streets, mansions, cottages, and shops. Point Pleasant Beach is home to a boardwalk filled with cruising teens, while Belmar supports the majority of the shore's nightlife. For the ultimate in outdoor thrills, visit New Jersey's best amusement park, Six Flags Great Adventure. Don't pay the full cost of admission; look for special offers on Coke bottles and Burger King placemats.

For a special retreat, visit Cape May, the nation's oldest seaside resort. The whole town was declared a historic landmark; there are over 600 gingerbread Victorian houses within the city limits. It's most appealing at the tail end of summer, just after Labor Day. Have tea at the Mainstay Inn (see Bed and Breakfasts, this section) and stroll down the beach promenade. Cape May Point State Park boasts one of the country's oldest lighthouses. Contact the Greater Cape May Chamber of Commerce (P.O. Box 109, Cape May, NJ 0824) for more information.

Getting There

Long Island Railroad
(516) 766-6722
Long Island Bus
(516) 766-6722
New Jersey Transit
(800) 582-5946
Port Authority Bus Terminal
564-8484
Amtrak
(800) USA-RAIL

leisure 333

best places to swim + picnic

Despite its seductive magnetism, New York City can be overwhelming at times. Escape the hellish heat and humidity of Gotham's concrete jungle and head to the beaches for some urban purification. The kaleidoscopic rush of bright bikinis, sun and skin offers welcome relief for most city dwellers. Jocks can show off their muscle at the numerous basketball and tennis courts and the social set can try their hand at miniature golf or shuffleboard. Lounge lizards can relax and dream away the sounds of honking horns on the sand and picnic areas. For music lovers there are the diverse sounds of outdoor concerts set against the backdrop of crashing surf. Nature trails keep the environmentalist inspired. So, no more excuses-be a water baby and go sun-worshipping at these paradises. NYC-surf city? Of course!

Jones Beach State Park

With 6.5 miles of sand and surf, beach diehards will find a slice of heaven in this granddaddy of beaches. West Bathhouse, Central Mall, and East Bathhouse comprise the three most famous of the eight sections that make up this Long Island haven for hedonists. People mostly flock to the Central Mall section because of its many landmarks, like the famous 200-foot water tower and the Boardwalk Restaurant, where everything from a down-to-earth hamburger deluxe to a sophisticated grilled North Atlantic salmon with lime and tequila sauce are served. Because of its popularity, Central Mall does get crowded with the scantily clad, so for tranquil moments head for the other sections. East Bathhouse could be the best sanctuary for mediators and peace seekers with its picturesque Zach's Bay. With its sacred expanse of green, Parking Field 10 is also a good bet for a quiet picnic. Further east along the beach, things get a little less mainstream with nudists, bongo bangers, and gay sunbathers. Make sure to check out the many top-name concerts at the 11,200-seat outdoor theater near the *park entrance. Wantagh, L.I. (516) 679-7222 $9.50 round-trip weekends, $14.50 round-trip weekdays. Long Island Railroad to Freeport, Long Island*

Sandy Hook

Since the ten beach sections of Sandy Hook stretch over several miles of widely spaced roadways, navigating can be limited without wheels. As a barrier peninsula, this New Jersey beach is visually stunning. At the northern tip, bring the sunblock and check out the panoramic views of the Twin Towers and the Verrazano Narrows Bridge. For the active, daring bunch, whip out the wind-surfing gear and head for the cove area. After a refreshing wipeout, sample refreshing drinks and relish the ambiance at the full-service concession stand and bar within a mile and a half of the beach's entrance. Not only do surf and sand dominate the landscape, but also 250 historic sites keep visitors coming, including the nation's oldest operating lighthouse. Also legendary is the clothing-optional stretch of beach located in area G. *Highlands, NJ. (908) 872-5900. $12.75 round-trip. Academy Bus Line from Port Authority to Highlands Bridge.*

Coney Island Beach

Even more famous than the Coney Island hotdog is the beach. Come revel in the amusement park, which features the quintessential rollercoaster, the Cyclone. Despite the 2.9 mile shoreline, the rides are what keep this beach the most popular of any of the city's sun havens, alluring up to 30,000 beach bums to its shores, especially on a bright Fourth of July. By late evening, the thrill seekers leave-and leave behind their refuse. With the help of heavy machinery, crews tidy up the sand for another day of fun. To avoid the herds, head toward the boardwalk by the New York Aquarium, between West 8th

334 leisure

Street and West 5th Street. For the height of body traffic, head toward the area between Steeplechase Pier at West 17th Street and West 8th Street. On the Atlantic Ocean, between West 37th Street and Ocean Parkway (718) 946-1350. *Subway: B D F N to Stillwell Avenue/Coney Island; D F to West 8th Street/NY Aquarium.*

When trying to capture a definitive picture of New York City, nature doesn't usually come to mind. Nevertheless, the symbiosis between nature and man remains a dazzling feature of the city. Take advantage of the grassy refuges that pepper Manhattan and for a few hours, pretend the city has disappeared. No concrete or pavement can beat the resilience of the tree-lined parks. There are plenty of perfect places to spread a blanket and dig into a well-stocked picnic basket. No matter what you've heard, even alligators cannot live in the city's sewers, but many varieties of benign wildlife scamper over New York's grassy hills. Stick to these places for a communal visit with nature.

Central Park

For a peaceful respite from the stress of urban living, picnic at Strawberry Fields at the 72nd Street entrance on the west side. Here, nature is coiffed to perfection with plenty of grass for lounging and hanging out with friends. Contemplate John Lennon while supporting world peace in the garden which features 161 varieties of flora and fauna, one for each nation in the world. At the center of this garden of Eden lies a circular Italian mosaic with the word "Imagine" set in the middle. Another great picnic spot is Sheep's Meadow at the southwestern part of the park by the 65th Street transverse. A little more effervescent than most areas, watch out for UFOs--kites, Frisbees, and sticks thrown by dog owners. "How can I compare thee to a summer's day?" Be wooed by the eloquence of Shakespeare by starlight at the Delacorte Theater where the Bard's plays are performed outdoors.

Battery Park

Located from State Street to the New York harbor, this park provides picnic-perfect promenades. Misty breezes from the Atlantic Ocean, the East River, and the Hudson River combine to add the final refreshing touch to an amazing view of the lower Manhattan skyline. New York offers itself to you with panoramic visions of Governors Island, Staten Island, the Statue of Liberty, Ellis Island, and the intricate span of the Verrazano Narrows Bridge. Soak it all in while munching, lounging, and chatting on the green.

Washington Square Park

Known more for voyeuristic spectacle than quiet seclusion, this park showcases Greenwich Village's activity. Street musicians, acrobats, NYU students, flame swallowers and players of Go, an ancient Chinese board game, animate this park. The visual centerpiece is the Arch, designed by Stanford White, marking the 100-year anniversary of George Washington coming to New York. Many New Yorkers don't know that the park was formerly used as a cemetery and people enjoying the park are really dancing on the graves of over 10,000 bodies. In the northwest corner, the notorious Hanging Elm stands as a reminder of the public executions that happened in the early 1800s. Still, the eerie history does not deter picnickers. Pack some popcorn too and watch the show.

The Cloisters

Fort Tyron boasts lush, grassy lawns, landscaped terraces, footpaths, and flower gardens for the emotionally spent city dweller. Come here after an educational tour of the medieval museum exhibits known for their collections of tapestries, illuminated manuscripts, stained glass, and precious metal work. Bask in the self-satisfaction of getting a dose of culture as you relax on a sun-drenched hill south of the museum, perfect for relaxing. At the end of the day, watch a romantic sunset and check out the superb views of the towering Palisades across the Hudson River
Fort Tyron Park, 923-3700. Tuesday through Sunday 9:30am-5:15 pm. Subway: A to 190th St.

leisure 335

{bed+breakfast getaways}

Bed and Breakfasts usually conjure up images of sleeping in canopied four posters and waking up to the gentle ringing of Vermont cow bells and the scent of freshly brewed coffee. This gentrified picture is not as out of place as you would imagine in the tristate area. Accommodations can range from tiny pieds-à-terre to huge SoHo lofts to Cape Cod houses on the Jersey shore. For good deals, prices at B&B's can't be beat. So go indulge and take a mini-vacation. Shh! The boss will never know.

Abingdon Guest House

Find no perky, air-kissing inn owners or gratuitous socialization over fruit salad in this quaintly furnished nine-room house. Seclusion and independence are usually the norm. In the mornings, wake up to a complimentary continental breakfast provided by Brew Bar.
13 Eighth Ave. bet. 12th and Jane Sts. 243-5384. $80-$145.

Akwaaba Mansion

"Enchanting" and a "return to bygone elegance" is what visitors call a stay in this Stuyvesant Heights bed and breakfast. As a restored 1860s Italianate villa with an Afrocentric soul, this antique-furnished home has eighteen suites featuring different themes. Choose from the Ashante Suite, which contains African artifacts and textiles; the Regal Suite, a room with deep burgundy colors and rich textiles surrounding a Victorian style bed; the Black Memorabilia Suite, a retreat that combines the ambiance of a noble ancestral past with the liberating free-spirit of youth; and finally the Jumping the Broom Suite, a retreat into romance complete with a canopy bed draped in gauzy tulle and a complementary gift of champagne, strawberries, and fresh whipped cream. After spending a night or two in these luxurious rooms, enjoying a drink on the wraparound porch, getting cozy by the fireplace, receiving a personal massage, day-dreaming in the fairytale gardens, "Akwaaba," which means "welcome" in Akan, the language of Ghana, will become the password to a tranquil and serene affair.
347 MacDonough Street, Brooklyn, NY 11233. (718) 455-5958. $100-$125

Baisley House

Velvet drapes heavy with fringe, elegant silk-moiré wallpaper, and a delicately hand-painted ceiling of clouds give this cozy Carroll Garden row house a divine, ethereal atmosphere lifted from a page of an Edith Wharton novel. The feel of genteel New York pervades this bed and breakfast. During warm weather, guests are invited outside by Henry Paul, the interior decorator and landscape designer, for dessert and coffee at Victorian tables and chairs amidst a vivid rose garden.
294 Hoyt Street between Union and Sackett Streets, Carroll Gardens, Brooklyn. (718) 935-1959 $80-$170.

Bed and Breakfast on the Park

By Prospect Park, a bigger version of the Baisley House, this B&B offers seven bedrooms and garden-level suites. Inside, the patrons get spoiled with elaborately carved moldings, lush, ankle-skimming oriental carpets, and beds fit for kings and queens. The guilt-free decadence extends to the dining hall where guests eat sumptuously while brilliant light filters through stained-glass windows.
113 Prospect Park West bet. 6th and 7th Sts, Park Slope, Brooklyn (718) 449-6115. $110-$250.

Foy House

Originally built in 1894, this bed and breakfast brownstone still holds most of its late 19th-century furnishings in pristine condition. An aura of authenticity and classicism permeate the three rooms and garden apartment. The large wood silver holders in the dining hall and the love seat in the lower level are original pieces. For the real, homey bed and breakfast experience, come here.
819 Carroll Street bet. Eighth Avenue and Prospect Park West, Park Slope, Brooklyn. (718) 636-1492. $79-$150.

Hotel Alternatives

Visitors to Manhattan will thank you for directing them to these accommodation services that offer lodging more charming and less expensive than their chain-hotel counterparts. Whether you're searching for a cozy bed and breakfast for a weekend visit or an entire furnished apartment for an extended stay, these agencies can book you into fabulous apartments during your time in New York. Breakfast is usually provided, but check with the agency for details.

Hospitality Inc.
965-1102, fax: 965-1149,
www.acompanies.com

Bed, Breakfast and Books:
865-8740

Assured Accommodations:
431-0569, fax: 431-7088,
www.assurednyc.com

336 leisure

Outward Bound...

Three Village Inn

Picture old, white Colonial homes, a Melville-esque harbor packed with fishermen, kids chasing a trail of ducks to ponds, 18th-century grist mills and suddenly this Early American style of bed and breakfast comes to mind. Once the home of Captain Jonas Smith, a New York Ship builder who became Long Island's first millionaire, it evolved from being a tea service to being one of the most charming, personalized inns in the area. Relax in one of the seven rooms upstairs in the main house or one of the peripheral cottages tucked into pretty landscaping out back. For traditional, early-American food try the chicken pot pie and Yankee pot roast served as Continental fare in the flowery dining hall and at the almost 300-year-old Country House located in the village. Then take a walk down the Colonial-influenced Main Street for a real time-warp experience into the past, a truly atypical historic enclave of Long Island.
150 Main Street, Stony Brook, New York 11790.
(516) 751-0555. $100-$135.

Mainstay Inn

Go to Cape May, a historic seaside retreat town, especially around late summer, for the most authentic sampling of Victorian living. Otherwise known as the "Victorian Mansion," this bed and breakfast is the centerpiece of the 600 prize Victorian homes within the 2.2 square miles of heaven. Graceful 14-foot ceilings, tall mirrors, ornate plaster moldings, bejeweled chandeliers, and cupola with ocean views treat guests to more than just an innocuous getaway. Come in October and bring the cameras, corsets, and Victorian morals for the Victorian Week extravaganza complete with house tours, period fashions shows, and lectures on period art. Attracting luminaries and celebrities has been Cape May's historic legacy. Over the years local guests have included presidents, actors, media mavens, and other stars.
635 Columbia Avenue, Cape May, New Jersey 08204.
(201) 884-8690. $70-$150.

Centennial House

Hollywood potentates and posh New York society converge in the lush precincts of the Hamptons. For a captivating, high-styled getaway come here. Socialites flock to Southampton, while writers and artists look for inspiration in the monastic seclusion of the East Hamptons. None of these things? Go anyway, because the beaches here are the some of the most gorgeous stretches of sand and the numerous historical sites, mostly Colonial-style homes, are a summer's stroll away from this three-bedroom bed and breakfast. Built in 1876, this charmer offers an intimate flavor with its exquisitely decorated rooms with fabrics and prints adorning the walls. The excellent house breakfast includes buttermilk pancakes. For more pampering, head to the back of the inn for a dip in the swimming pool.
13 Woods Lane (Route 27), East Hampton, NY, 11937.
(516) 324-9414. $135-$250.

leisure 337

SPORTS AND RECREATION

Perhaps in response to the daunting challenge of maintaining a human form while working a desk job, New Yorkers pursue physical activity with an almost pathological fervor; the gym social set and company softball teams trying to salvage their blood pressure are just the most obvious examples of a serious subculture of exercise. The cult of the body, coupled with an almost burdensome desire to have fun may drive yuppies to the racquetball court and models to the Stairmaster, but it is possible to utilize the city's manifold resources as opportunities of true, uncomplicated relaxation time without letting the muscled and Spandex-ed masses kill your runner's high. Hit off-peak hours at the gym: a mid-afternoon workout is a luxury afforded by the college student's uneven scheduling, as is late-night exercise. Venture into the outer boroughs for expansive, serene parks, and take advantage of any private spaces to which you may have access through affiliation with a university.

PARKS

Manhattan is speckled with pockets of green that accommodate Frisbee, volleyball, sunbathing, and the like, though for large-scale undertakings-a long run, a game of softball—the more defined parks are usually in order. Each borough of the city maintains at least one major park: Manhattan's Central Park, immortalized in paeans and crime stories alike; Brooklyn's Prospect Park, designed by the man who planned Central Park; sprawling Van Cortlandt Park in the Bronx; and Corona Park in Queens, offering respite from urban anxiety.

Central Park, designed by Frederick Law Olmstead and opened in 1859, runs from 59th Street to 110th Street and is bordered by Central Park West and Fifth Avenue; it is accessible from virtually every subway line imaginable. Another major Manhattan Park for recreation is the three-tiered Riverside Park on the Upper West Side also designed by Olmstead, a slim strip of green following the Hudson River down the upper half of the island and accessible by all the red subway lines.

Prospect Park, designed by Olmstead as well, is bordered by Park Slope to the West, Prospect Heights to the North, and Flatbush to the east. Olmstead's hand is evident in both spaces, though in keeping with the Brooklyn mien, Prospect Park is mellower and isn't as claustrophobic on weekends, with family barbecues and pick-up soccer games lending a more residential feel. Also of note are the Prospect Park Zoo and the Carousel just to the south.

Van Cortlandt Park, bordered by Riverdale to the west and Kingsbridge to the south, is accessible by the 1, 9, A, C trains. Though a bit more dilapidated then Central and Prospect Parks, with a design that lacks such cleanly defined scenic accents and elegant mapping, "Vannie" succeeds by being more modern and utilitarian. The city's third largest park further redeems itself with a couple of authentic golf greens, recently renovated tennis courts, several reasonably well-kept softball diamonds, and a six mile trail for joggers and bikers.

Corona Park, New York City's largest, and the site of the 1939 and 1964 World's Fairs, is bordered by both its namesake, Jackson Heights to the east, and Flushing to the west. The 7, E, F subway lines all stop nearby. By virtue of its sheer size, one would be hard-pressed to find fault with the park's resources. Sites of special note include the enormous World's Fair Ice Skating Rink, the nearby United States Tennis Center, and the Shea Stadium. When the weather turns warm, head over to Meadow Lake for sailing lessons or be a kid at the carousel located on 111th Street and 54th Avenue.

Finally, Floyd Bennett Field in Brooklyn is the ideal spot for model airplane builders to test-fly their toys.

RUNNING

The opportunities afforded by the city are accompanied by precautions unique to the area that even the most seasoned athlete should note. Some of the most scenic jogging paths, like those in Riverside Park on the Upper West Side, provide very poor support for knees and ankles, so if you plan on running regularly, invest in high-quality shoes which will absorb the impact of concrete. Always be aware of your surroundings, including other runners, bikers, rollerbladers, cars, kids, strollers, or pedestrians.

The reservoir at Central Park, located roughly in the middle of the park from about 86th to 96th Streets, is circumscribed by a scenic, if somewhat narrow 1.57 soft-surface path ideal for jogging. Beware the onslaught of shuffling and huffing "runners" on weekends, and women should be forewarned that in the late evening hours, the path is notoriously dangerous. More ambitious types should try the Outer Loop (7.02 miles) along the circular drive, or the Middle Loop (4.04 miles), which begins at 72nd Street and follows the drive around the southern periphery. Runners seeking camaraderie should contact the New York Road Runner's Club (860-4455), headquartered near the newly-christened Jackie O. Reservoir at the eastern entrance to the park on 90th Street. The club's activities include twice-nightly runs in Central Park at 6:30pm and 7:15pm, a weekend jog at 10am, a marathon prep, a New Year's Eve run, and a Central Park Safety Patrol. During summer evenings, the traffic is closed off in the Park.

Riverside Park is a beautiful place to run for those who don't mind the pavement, since the infrequent strips of dirt are ill-maintained and subject to ruts and mud. Avoid the relatively steep hill at the junction of the Upper West Side and Morning-side by staying on the lower level at 96th Street. The best place to veer down towards the riverside path, where a small houseboat community docks and optimistic fishermen occasionally cast their lines, is at around 86th Street since the West Side Highway is too close for comfort further north. A quarter of a mile track is maintained at 72nd Street. Further north, on top of the 145th Street incinerator, there's a quality track, though on hot, windless days, a nose plug for heavy breathing may be in order.

Also in Manhattan, a jogging path follows the East River from Sutton Place all the way down to Gracie Mansion, though don't expect to catch Rudy, flanked by bodyguards à la Bill, running alongside you. Down in the Village, the Westside Highway Path is a newly refurbished strip for downtown joggers, bladers, and bikers that can seem as circus-like as the boardwalk on Coney Island on busy days.

When traffic is cut off on Saturdays and Sundays in Prospect Park, the roughly two-and-a-half-mile route looping around the park makes a good jog. For post-jog relaxation, the interior path offers shady groves and gaggles of swans.

RUNNING CLUBS

New York Road Runners Club
860-4455

Achilles Track Club
A nation-wide club for athletes with disabilities ranging from blindness to epilepsy to heart disease.
354-0300

Atalanta
Women only. *737-7480*

Central Park Track Club
838-1120

Front Runners
A gay and lesbian running group.
724-9700

Milrose Team
Ideal for the amatuer looking to get serious. $15 membership fee.
663-5641

Moving Comfort
Ladies only, but you've got to be able to do 10K in forty minutes.
222-7216

Warren Street Social and Athletic Club
Training and competition.
807-7422

World Runners
595-9310

CYCLING

Riding a bike in Manhattan is an excellent and inexpensive means of transportation and exercise, but it can get a bit wild so observing the following precautions can help you to avoid falling prey to cabs and MTA bus drivers:

Claim space in a lane so as to avoid pedestrians and opening car doors; many major avenues have bike paths as well.

Always ride on the right with traffic; drivers don't always watch out for obstacles to their left side, which is where you'll be when riding against traffic.

Wear a helmet without fail.

When in Central Park path or on other bike paths, don't hang a U-turn.

leisure 339

For clearly defined bike paths, all the running paths mentioned above suffice as well as specific bike trails like the one-mile Brooklyn Bridge bike lane across the East River; if you have a couple hours to kill, try the Ocean Parkway bike path which begins in Prospect Park Church Avenue and ends up at Coney Island. It's perfectly permissible to take your bike on the subway (you'll get buzzed through the door after depositing a token), though the commuter trains require a pass for bikes.

CYCLING CLUBS
Century Club
222-8062
Five Boroughs Club
www.bikenewyork.org
New York Cycle Club
242-3900
Sundance Outdoor Adventure Society
For gays and lesbians
598-4726

SOFTBALL
The Sheep Meadow in Central Park, closed in the winter, overflows in summer with loads of scantily-clad sunbathers, Frisbee players, and picnickers. Regulation-sized softball and baseball diamonds are located around 100th Street on the eastern side of the park; the Heckscher fields around 64th Street are well-maintained but often claimed by amateur, fiercely territorial leagues known more for mild spectator value than for open field policies, since most harken from the high-strung cubicles of nearby Midtown. There are huge, underutilized Astroturf fields atop the 145th Street incinerator in Riverside that are a good alternative to the Central Park melee.

Five softball diamonds and two baseball diamonds, accessible from the 9th Street and Park West entrance, are well-maintained at Prospect Park and a bit friendlier than their Manhattan counterparts.

MANHATTAN
Batting Cages at Chelsea Piers
23rd Street at the Hudson, 336-6500
Hackers, Hitters and Hoops
123 West 18th Street, 929-7482
To reserve a field in a city park of any borough:
Manhattan: 408-0309
Bronx: (718) 822-4282
Queens: (718) 520-5933
Brooklyn: (718) 965-8919
Staten Island: (718) 816-6172

ROLLERBLADING & ICE-SKATING
Some words of wisdom: Central Park, in particular on weekends and in the spring and summer, is packed with people who have not yet perfected maneuvering on blades, so don't assume they'll honor the right-of-way or even be able to brake. Other parks, where it's not such a social scene, are a little less like a circus.

In-line skaters can attempt the advanced slalom courses in Central Park by the Bandstand and west of the Great Lawn by the restaurant Tavern on the Green, where on weekends experienced skaters do informal exhibitions for a large crowds of spectators. Watch and learn, but if you've just fitted your knee-pads for the first time, you may be better accommodated on The Dead Road, from about 66th to 69th Streets in the middle of the park.

CENTRAL PARK SKATING
Wollman Rink
Mid-park at 63rd St., 517-4800
Lasker Rink
Near 110th St. and Lenox Ave. 396-0388, Winter Ice Skating: Adults $4, Skate Rental: $6.50, In-Line Skating: Adults: $4 in the rink, $15 for two hours in the park, $25 for all day

World's Fair Rink in Flushing Meadows-Corona Park
(718) 271-1996
Abe Stark Rink at Coney Island
On Boardwalk (at West 19th St.), (718) 946-3135, Admission: $6 (adults); Skate Rental: $4 (wknds only)
Kate Wollman Rink in Central Park
East Drive (bet. Lincoln and Parkside Aves.), (718) 282-7789, Adults: $2.50, Skate Rental: $3.50

SWIMMING
Two city pools are particularly clean and accessible although invariably crowded on weekends and especially during the sweltering summer months: Carmine Street Pool (Seventh Ave. South at Clarke St.), 242-5228, and John Jay Park (East 77th St. and Cherokee Pl.), 794-6566.

New York City beaches are open from Memorial Day through Labor Day weekends from 10am to 6pm. The main ones are all found in the outer boroughs.

BEACHES
Orchard Beach
(718) 885-3273, ⑥ *to Pelham Bay Pk.*
Manhattan Beach
(718) 941-1373
Coney Island and Brighton Beach
(718) 946-1350, ⒹⓆ *to Brighton*

Beach, **B****D****F** to Stillwell Ave./Coney Island
Rockaway Beach
(718) 318-4010, **A****S** to Rockaway Park Beach/116th St.
South and Midland Beaches (Staten Island)
(718) 987-0709

INDOOR POOLS
MANHATTAN
Luye Aquafit
310 East 23rd St. 505-2400
McBurney YMCA
215 West 23rd St. 787-3356
Aerobics West Fitness
131 West 86th St. 787-3356
Asphalt Green
555 East 90th St., 369-8890
Doug Stern's
700 Columbus Ave. (at 95th St.), 222-0720
Hansborough
134th St. (bet. Fifth and Lenox Aves.), 234-9603
Harlem YMCA
180 West 135th St. 281-4100
92nd Street YMCA
1395 Lexington Ave.(at 92nd St.), 415-5729

OUTDOOR POOLS
Hamilton Fish
Pitt and Houston Sts., 387-7687
Dry Dock
East 10th St. (bet. Aves. C and D)
John Jay Park Pool
East 77th Street and Cherokee Place, 794-6566
Lasker Pool
West 110th St. (at Lenox Ave.), 534-7639
Thomas Jefferson
East 112th St. and First Ave., 860-1372
Wagner
East 112th St.(bet. First and Second Aves.), 543-4238
Jackie Robinson
Bradhurst Ave. and West 146th St., 234-9606
Highbridge
Amsterdam Ave. and West 173rd St., 927-2400

INDOOR/OUTDOOR POOLS
MANHATTAN
Asser Levy
Asser Levy Pl. (at East 23rd St.), 447-2020
Carmine Street Pool
Clarkson St. (at 7th Ave. South), 242-5228

BRONX
Claremont
170th St. and Clay Ave., (718) 901-4792
Crotona
173rd St. and Fulton Ave., (718) 822-4440
Mapes
East 180th St.(bet. Mapes and Prospect), 364-8876
St. Mary's
St.Anne's Ave. and East 145th St., (718) 548-2415
Van Cortlandt
West 242nd St. and Broadway, (718) 548-241

QUEENS
Astoria
19th St. and 23rd Dr. (718) 626-9620
Fisher
99th St. and Thirty-Second Ave., (718) 779-8356
Liberty
173rd St. and 106th Ave. (718) 657-4995
Roy Wilkins
119th St. and Merrick Blvd., (718) 276-4630

BROOKLYN
Betsy Head
Boyland, Livonia, and Dumont Aves., (718) 965-6581
Brownsville
Linden Blvd. and Christopher Ave., (718) 485-4633
Bushwick Houses
Flushing Ave. and Humbolt St., (718) 452-2116
Commodore Barry
Flushing and Park Aves., Navy and North Elliot Sts., (718) 243-3593
Douglas and DeGraw
3rd Avenue and Nevins Street, (718) 625-3268
Howard Houses
Glenmore and Mother Gatson Blvd.,, East New York Avenue, (718) 385-1023
Kosciusko
Kosciusko (bet Marcy and Dekalb Sts.), (718) 622-5271

Metropolitan
Bedford and Metropolitan Aves., (718) 965-6576
Red Hook
Bay and Henry Sts., (718) 771-3213
St. Johns
Prospect Pl. (bet 10th and 11th Sts.), (718) 771-2787
Sunset
7th Avenue (bet. 41st and 44th Sts.), (718) 965-6578

STATEN ISLAND
Faber Street and Richmond Terrace
(718) 816-5259
Lyons
Pier 16 and Victory Blvd., (718) 816-9571
Tottenville
Hylan Blvd. and Joline Ave., (718) 356-8242
West Brighton
Henderson Ave.(near Chappet St.), (718) 816-5019

TENNIS

If you have an affiliation with a university you will most likely have access to courts, though the issue of maintenance is a bit dicier. If you prefer to search out city courts, Central Park's mid-area around 93rd (280-0205) are among the most happening, though only those with season permits can reserve a court in advance. However if you don't mind the wait, join the others waiting to plunk down five bucks to play on an unreserved court for an hour; bring a deck of cards and join the others in line in a game of bridge or poker. Riverside Park's clay courts near 96th are well-maintained by neighborhood volunteers. If you don't mind the trek to Queens, tennis courts abound at the prestigious USTA National Center (718) 592-8000), the site of the US Open.

ALL BOROUGHS
Parks and Recreation General Information

leisure 341

(800) 201-PARK

MANHATTAN

New York Health and Racket Club
Piers 13 and 14 (at Wall St.), 422-9300

NYHRC Tennis Courts
110 University Place (bet 12th and 13th Sts.), 989-2300

Central Park Tennis Center
West 93rd St. and Central Park West, 280-0201/0205

Tower Tennis
1725 York Ave. (at 89th St.), 860-2464

Columbus Tennis Club
795 Columbus Ave. (bet. 97th and 100th Sts.), 622-8367

Riverside Park
96th St. and Riverside Dr. 496-2006, 119th St. and Riverside Dr., 486-2103

Harlem Tennis Center
143rd St. (bet Lenox and 7th Aves.), 283-4028

Riverbank State Park
145th St. and Riverside Dr., 694-3600

Fred Johnson Playground
151st St. and Seventh Ave., 234-9609

Columbia Tennis Center
575 West 218th Str. at Seaman Ave. (behind Baker's Field), 842-7100

BRONX

Stadium Tennis Center in Mullaly Park
11 East 162nd St. (718) 322-4191, (718) 293-2386

QUEENS

Alley Pond Tennis Club
79-20 Winchester Blvd., Queens Village. (718) 468-1239

Long Island City Indoor Tennis
50-01 Second St., (718) 784-9677

The U.S.T.A. National Center
Flushing Meadows Corona Park, (718) 583-8000

BROOKLYN

Breakpoint Tennis Club in Bensonhurst
9000 Bay Parkway, (718) 372-6878

Prospect Park Tennis Center
305 Coney Island Ave. (at Parkside), (718) 438-1200

Expert Rider Elizabeth Barnett

HORSEBACK RIDING

While the only horses you may ever see are pulling mon-eyed tourists through Central Park, the serious equestrian can seek out several options for horseback-riding within the city limits, though costs are often high. Central Park has a bridle path for experienced riders, and Van Cortlandt Park has a fairly extensive riding center.

By far the best option for horseback-riding is the newest addition to the sleek recreation supercenter Chelsea Piers. The members-only full riding facility is geared toward the serious urban rider who before now didn't have the option of staying in the city to pursue such passions as jumping, dressage, and polo. Offering classes to the novice as well as to the seasoned equestrian, the center is a private club where the distinguished, long-established world of horseback-riding teams up with the new world of educational and entertaining multimedia equipment to further the sport that doubles as a recreational pastime for the wealthy. Thanks to huge glass doors along the east and west of the building, both indoor and outdoor arenas sport exquisite views of the Hudson River in a 30,000-square-foot space. Definitely a stylish addition to a burgeoning waterfront, though avid riding enthusiasts will have to plunk down $2500 as an initial membership fee, and $250 a month thereafter.

Chelsea Piers
63 North River, Pier 63 (at 23rd St. and the West Side Highway), 367-9090

Claremont Riding Academy
175 West 89th St., 724-5100

BRONX

Pelham Bit Stable
9 Shore Road, (718) 885-0551

The Riverdale Equestrian Center
West 254th Street and Broadway, (718) 548-4848

QUEENS

Lynne's Riding School
88-03 70th Rd., (718) 261-7679

Dixie Dew Stables
88-11 70th Rd., (718) 263-3500

GYMS

The fitness craze culminated in the '90s with a saturation of sleek, comfortable weightlifting and fitness facilities all over the city. They attract all walks of life: dancers tone up on dance machines; grade-school teachers work on their deltoids; and stockbrokers take on the Stairmasters. The social underpinnings of the city gym experience might merit a separate write-up in this book's nightlife section, but suffice it to say that the following conversation was overheard on Broadway near Reebok Sports Club: "Haven't I seen you at the gym? My name's Rick." "Oh yeah, you're the ab guy, right?"

Location is the biggest determinant of atmosphere: Midtown clubs attract a more corporate mix, while gyms in the Village cater to a younger crowd. All the spandex and muscle at these places can be intimidating but don't give up. Many gyms, including the ubiquitous Crunch, pride themselves on a "non-judgmental," laid-back policy. Shop around since most facilities cheerfully allow trial-periods on a no-strings-attached basis. The prices can be prohibitive but look for special seasonal deals.

Bally Total Fitness
144 East 86th St., and 8 other NYC Branches, (800) 230-0606, 3-year memberships around $2,000.

Bally Vertical Clubs
More costly but more features such as towel service + personal training
350 West 50th St,, 265-9400

Chelsea Gym
267 West 17th St., 255-1150, $425 per year, $80 per month

Crunch
Flagship location features a climbing wall.
1109 Second Ave. (bet. 58th and 59th Sts.), 4 other Manhattan locations, 758-3434, $949 per year, $20 per day for non-members

Lucille Roberts
Body-shaping for women
103rd St. and B'way, yearly/monthly memberships available, 961-0500

New York Health and Racquetball Club
39 Whitehall St., 269-9800

New York Sports Club
50 West 34th St., other Manhattan locations, 868-0820

Reebok Sports Club
150 Columbus Ave. (at 67th St.), 362-6800, $1,100 to join, $157 fee per month

World Gym
232 Mercer St. (at West 3rd St.) and 1926 B'way (at 64th St.), 780-7407, $799 per year, $325 for 3 months

RECREATION CENTERS

Membership in this city-run Manhattan Recreation Centers costs $25 a year for adults from 18 to 50 years, $10 for youths 13-17, and is free for those 12 years and under. Most have locker rooms and showers, but patrons must bring their own locks, towels, and toiletries. The centers have gyms, weightrooms, aerobics classes, and pools. Call for particular programs.

In Midtown, the Manhattan recreation centers located on 54th Street between First and Second Avenues and on West 59th Street between Tenth and Eleventh Avenues offer indoor swimming running, aerobics, weightrooms, and all the basics, and the member ship fee will only set you back $25! The 168th Street Armory (281-9376) offers one of the finest track and field facilities in the city.

In the outer boroughs, world-class gyms, weightrooms, basketball courts, and pools are available for a fee that's often cheaper than in Manhattan.

MANHATTAN

Alfred E. Smith
Catherine St. (bet. Cherry and Monroe Sts.), 285-0300

Asser Levy
Asser Levy Place (Ave. A and East 23rd Street) 447-2020

Carmine Street
Clarkson St. and Seventh Ave. South, 242-5228

East 54th
East 54th St. and First Ave., 397-3154

West 59th
West 59th St. and Tenth Ave., 397-3166

Hamilton Fish
Houston and Pitt Sts., 767-7688

Hansborough
West 134th St. (bet. Fifth and Lenox Aves.), 234-9603

Highbridge
Amsterdam Ave. (at West 173rd St.) 927-2400

Jackie Robinson
Bradhurst Ave. (at West 146th St.) 234-9606

North Meadow
Central Park (at 97th St.), 348-4867

Pelham Fritz
Mount Morris Park West, (at West 122nd St.), 860-1380

Thomas Jefferson
East 112th St. and First Ave., 860-1372

BRONX

Crotona
East 173rd and Fulton Sts., (718) 822-4272

Mullaly
East 164th St. and Jerome Ave., (718) 822-4191

Saint Mary's
East 145th St. and St. Anne's Ave., (718) 402-5155

Williams Bridge Oval
East 208th St. and Bainbridge Ave. (718) 543-8672

QUEENS

The Lost Batallion Hall
93-29 Queens Blvd., (718) 520-5366

Roy Wilkins
177th St. and Baisley Blvd., (718) 276-4630

Sorrentino
Beach 19th St. and Cornaga Ave., (718) 471-4818

BROOKLYN

Betsy Head
Hopkinson and Livonia Aves., (718) 965-6581

Brownsville
Linden and Mother Gaston Blvds. (at Christopher St.), (718) 485-4633

Herbert Von King
Lafayette Ave. (bet. Marcy and Tompkins Sts.), (718) 965-6567

Red Hook
Bay and Henry St, (718) 722-3213

St. John's
Troy and Schenectady Aves, (718) 771-2787

Sunset Park
44th St. and Seventh Ave., (718) 965-6578

leisure 343

STATEN ISLAND
Cromwell
Pier 6 and Murray Hulbert Ave., (718) 816-6172

BOATING

Genteel dreams of whiling away the afternoon in a trim rowboat can be realized in the Loeb Boathouse that also rents canoes for those inclined to the wilderness aesthetic.

MANHATTAN
Loeb Boathouse in Central Park
East Drive (at 74th St.), $10 for the first hour, $2.50 for each additional hour, and a $30 refundable deposit, 517-2233.

BRONX
Crotona Lake
East 173rd St. and Crotona Park, (718) 587-0096

BROOKLYN
Kate Wollman Rink in Prospect Park
Between Lincoln and Parkside, pedalboats for 4 people at $12/hr, $10 refundable deposit required

PROFESSIONAL SPORTS

Watching others expend their energies in athletic pursuits can be just as satisfying; New York boasts several notable arenas hosting our beloved home teams.

Although the house that Ruth built has a tentative date with a wrecking ball scheduled for sometime in the early 21st century, Yankee Stadium (See the Bronx) remains, after nearly seventy-five years of witnessing baseball history, the most scenic and historic venue the city offers for viewing professional sports.

Shea Stadium, home of the Mets, has served as baseball's other home in the city since its 1964 opening brought National League baseball back after the Dodgers ignominious departure in 1957. While Shea and the Mets lack the tradition and lore of the Yankees, its more accessible location and the revitalization of the team in the '97 season help keep Shea packed with higher attendance.

Madison Square Garden, New York City's primary indoor arena, located above Penn Station, has been an exciting place to go lately with both the Knicks and the Rangers enjoying strong teams and exciting playoff runs through the nineties. Although the '96-'97 seasons failed to produce a championship for Ewing's Knicks or Messier's Rangers, optimism remains high this fall. At the spacious Garden, fans can see the floor even from the worst seats, and the crowd is often raucous enough to qualify as a secondary attraction. Other events at the Garden include Rangers games, college basketball, ice shows, dog shows, tennis tournaments, and big-name concerts.

Yankee Stadium
(718) 293-6000, Tickets: $6- $21, ❹❻❼ to 161st St./ Yankee Std.

Shea Stadium
126th St. and Roosevelt Ave. (718) 507-8499, Tickets: $7-$19, ❼ to Willis Point/Shea Stadium

Madison Square Garden
Knicks, 465-5867, Tickets: $25-$425
Rangers, 465-6741, Tickets: $22-$125, ❶❷❸❹❺❻❼ to Penn Sta.

HIKING AND CAMPING

Sometimes one must embrace the raging animal within and get off this face-paced, soul-sucking island. These clubs can help you resurrect the serenity you lost during your last subway ride

Appalachian Mountain Club
679-3111

Hudson River Waterway Association
724-5069

New York/New Jersey Trail Conference
685-9699

Campers' Group
(718)897-1448, www.panix.com/~levner/camping/

SOCCER CLUBS

During the 1998 World Cup, the UN lobby was crowded with diplomats cheering on their favorite teams; The Cosmopolitan League can help you find places to play "the beautiful game"

The Cosmopolitan Soccer League: 355-6700

WALKING CLUBS

Pedestrians unite! Racewalkers can find kindred spirits by calling the following:

East Side Racewalk Team
737-9255

Park Racewalkers
628-1317

344 leisure

Resources

moving + storage ············→ 346
getting to and from NYC ←----→ 348
budget travel ·················→ 349
hotel listings ———————— 351
resources ←————— 353
services ——————————→ 358

moving + storage

Nearly all recent transplants to the city move frequently during the first few years they are here, so a number of industries thrive on the desperation that accompanies the undertaking of such a feat in the midst of the urban melee. The luxury of a private car is accessible only to those with dutiful friends or relatives in the vicinity, leaving most prospective movers with that omnipresent resource, the U-Haul (562 West 23rd, at Eleventh, 620-4177.) Note the emphasis on "U": if you are carting heavy boxes and/or furniture, movers are an additional investment, easy to come by and worth the expense provided you're not transporting Czech crystal. Do not hire other people to pack for you. Most universities have connections with moving and storage companies, as well as shipping companies, that allow you to leave your boxes at some check-off point near campus, saving you the trouble of trekking across town with a thousand pounds of books in tow. While you pay dearly for such convenience, it definitely beats moving boxes yourself.

Planning Ahead

While some of the following tips may seem self-evident, most people who move frequently will admit to overlooking or undervaluing these precautions once or twice; the resulting mishaps make for excellent, self-mocking cocktail party conversation. First, if you are a college student, do not invest in furniture or other unwieldy items of decor unless you plan on disposing of them upon departure. Also keep in mind that college storage facilities are not conducive to objects which do not fit into boxes.

Begin looking for boxes early on, especially if you are moving out at the end of the school year when cardboard becomes a valuable commodity. Liquor stores and bookstores are best, since their boxes are very sturdy; Starbucks is particularly useful if you tell them ahead of time to save the boxes from their shipment, and their boxes are in good condition and clean, not to mention the burgeoning chain is just about on every corner these days. Go at night when it's less busy to ask when you can pick them up. Always get twice as many boxes as you think you'll need; most people grossly underestimate their material possessions, and any spares will be appreciated by friends who were not as forward-thinking.

If you are leaving for the summer, have a plan for where to store valuables. Ask around and see if any of your friends and acquaintances will have summer housing with a little extra space for a refrigerator or a stereo. Allow lots of time for packing, since inevitably you will have a minor emergency, i.e. having a box break, running out of room, etc.

Packing

When packing, distribute the weight of items, and use lots of smaller boxes as opposed to several large ones. Only use large boxes for clothing, blankets, and other light items. Try to pack a few books in each of the boxes. If you are shipping anything, don't wrap breakables in clothing; pack each thing in its own box with appropriate padding, and if necessary, place all those boxes in a larger box. If you must ship books, place them in their own box so that they can be sent at the book rate, but again, don't pack too many books into one box. You should always save the manufacturer's boxes for computers, stereos, and other electronic equipment, since the fitted Styrofoam will cushion the product. Make sure when packing mixed boxes that heavier items are on the bottom, and constantly check the weight of the box while packing to ensure that it will not be too heavy for the cardboard.

Boxes and tubs for packing are quite easy to come by. If your attempts to get free boxes fail, the post office, FedEx, and UPS all sell boxes at exorbitant prices ($3-$5 per box), and private companies take advantage of mass moving days at universities by setting up shop on the street or in dorm lobbies. Again, the boxes they sell are vastly overpriced.

There are several places throughout the city where you can stock up on boxes and other moving supplies if you plan in advance: boxes are relatively cheap at Moving Supplies & More (772-2555, phone orders only), where advice about how to pack, how much you should pay for movers, and more, comes along free with your purchase; free delivery with a $25 purchase. Another option is Robert Karp Container Corp. (618 West 52nd Street, bet. Eleventh and Twelfth Avenues, 586-4474) which stocks picture and mirror boxes along with the standards, and offers free delivery for orders over $100.

Storing

If you plan on using college storage, you should forego boxes for Rubbermaid tubs, since storage rooms are usually in basements which flood frequently. Avoid storing valuables since security is more lax than at professional storage companies, and don't pack items in computer or stereo boxes, since potential thieves may mistake them for the real thing. Tubs are also useful because there's a chance that overweight boxes might be placed on top of your own, causing them to cave under the pressure.

Many apartment buildings in Manhattan make storage facilities available to their residents. These facilities involves some of the same risks as dorm storage, often consisting of little more than a large basement room with a single lock on the door.

Commercial storage is a great choice for those who don't have the option or desire to use apartment storage. Storage companies such as Whitehall Mini-Storage and Tuck-It-Away offer storage space on a monthly basis, with customers providing locks for their own spaces. Most contracted storage companies claim to offer some form of free moving to the storage facility for their customers. However, it's best to inquire regarding the specifics because some storage companies, such as Tuck It-Away on Broadway and 131st Street, only provide free moving for a few hours and require that you call well in advance to schedule a pickup. Others, such as Hudson Moving & Storage on Broadway and 130th Street, limit free moving to those items below a certain total volume.

When to Move

Take advantage of street-cleaning days to get closest to your building. Moving in the early morning or late at night is clearly a better choice, since traffic isn't as bad and, if you're moving out of a dorm, you may just get a shot at the elevator. Summer weekends are the best times to move into the city. In many sections of Manhattan, residents flee New York's steamy weather and traffic within the city is relatively light during these time periods. Weekends can be a problem, however, if you are using a U-Haul, since vans are only rented out for six hours then. Those moving into or out of apartment buildings should call supers in case there are times when you aren't allowed to move, especially if you will involve doormen or elevators.

If you plan on utilizing a cab, definitely move late at night or in mid-morning, since drivers get surly and unhelpful it they feel they're wasting time with you instead of picking up more fares at a peak time. Even better than a cab is a car service, since drivers have huge cars with body-bag sized trunks, and are a bit more helpful with loading and unloading. Be sure to agree on a price before getting into the car, since Gypsy Cabs have no meters and the driver may get greedy; when calling a car service, don't let them know you'll be requiring help with boxes; they may send an even larger boat of a Cadillac and charge an exorbitant amount. If a driver helps unload and load boxes, make sure to tip well, since they are going above and beyond the call of duty. Moving in a taxi or Gypsy Cab is okay with a few boxes; with large boxes and breakables, invest in a van, especially since within the city, a U-Haul cargo van only costs $19.95 a per day.

resources 347

Commuter Trains

Several commuter trains provide transportation to Westchester county, Long Island, New Jersey, Connecticut, or Pennsylvania. They are remarkably efficient and quite cheap.

Metro-North services Westchester County, directly north of the city. It departs from Grand Central station, located at 42nd Street and Lexington Avenue and accessible by the S, 4, 5, 6, 7 lines. The trains are relatively slow, don't run after 1:30am, and have varying fares. The New Haven line services Connecticut, and the Hudson and Harlem lines go to upstate New York.

The Long Island Railroad, or LIRR, originates at the Penn Station/34th Street station on the 1, 2, 3, 9, A, C, E lines and services both Nassau and Suffolk counties. Be sure to buy tickets either at the ticket window or from the automated machines, as a surcharge is added onboard. For especially distant or out-of-the-way destinations, passengers may need to transfer to another train en route.

Also departing from Penn Station is New Jersey Transit, whose several lines service New Jersey. Getting to Pennsylvania is as easy as riding New Jersey Transit to a connection with SEPTA, another commuter rail.

The Port Authority Trans-Hudson (PATH), which departs from the Manhattan Mall/34th Street and Sixth Avenue subway stop, a block east of Penn Station, is the best buy for transportation out of the city. For a paltry dollar, travelers can ride and transfer among this subway's four lines: 33rd Street - Journal Square, 33rd Street-Hoboken, World Trade Center Newark, or World Trade Center-Hoboken. This routing only applies Monday through Friday, days and evenings. Overnight, weekends, and major holidays, there are only two lines: Newark-World Trade Center and 33rd Street-Journal Square via Hoboken. The lines originating from 33rd also stop at 23rd, 14th, 9th, and Christopher Streets, making transportation cheaper than the MTA subway. In Newark, PATH also arrives at Penn Station. Hoboken supposedly has more bars per square mile than anywhere in the country, so many New Yorkers find themselves passing out there from time to time.

Long Island Railroad
(718) 217-LIRR or (516) 822-LIRR; Lost Articles (212) 643-5228

Metro North
532-4900, 1-800-638-7646 (outside of NYC), Lost Articles 340-2555, Commuter Relations 340-2144

New Jersey Transit
(973) 762-5100, Lost Articles 630-7389 (New York)

PATH
1-800-234-PATH, Lost Articles 435-2611

SEPTA
(215) 580-7800

Long-Distance Buses

Out-of-state buses leave from Port Authority at 42nd Street and Eighth Avenue; the station also houses the A, C, E lines and is connected to the 42nd Street/Times Square stop on the N, R, 1, 2, 3, 7, 9 lines by an underground tunnel. Heavily-traveled routes, such as those to Boston and Washington, D.C., have regularly-scheduled departures; round-trip tickets go for roughly $50 to either city. Be sure to either buy tickets in advance or show up at least an hour before scheduled departure, as ticket lines are generally very long, especially on weekends. Even with a previously purchased ticket, plan to arrive at the station a good half-hour in advance of scheduled departure, or find out the hard way that a ticket in hand does not necessarily guarantee a seat. Most companies do not sell tickets for a specific departure time, just for a particular route, although for Greyhound treks to other cities, you are restricted to a specific destination and time of departure after purchasing the ticket.

Greyhound Bus Information
1-800-231-2222 (Fares and Schedules)

Peter Pan Bus Lines
1-800-343-9999

New Jersey Transit
(973) 762-5100

Port Authority
For information on bus transportation to all three airports, the Meadowlands, and Six Flags Great Adventure Park
564-8484

Long-Distance Trains

Train travel along the eastern seaboard is cleaner and more pleasurable than the bus, but not necessarily faster: bus travel from New York to Boston clocks in at four and a half hours; the train takes more than five, due to the number of stops in between. Amtrak runs regularly-scheduled trains out of Penn Station at 34th Street and Broadway on the 1, 2, 3, 9 and A, C, E lines to locations all over the country. Reservations are available, but these seats tend to be more expensive, especially on holidays, and prices also depend on whether the route is local, making many stops, or express, making one or no stops. Amtrak also operates an express, the Metroliner, to Washington D.C. running throughout the week; reservations are required.

Amtrak, including Metroliner
1-800-USA-RAIL

Airports

There are three main airports accessible from Manhattan: La Guardia in Queens, JFK International in Queens, and Newark International in New Jersey. Although accessible by cab, the cheapest ways to reach the airports are by shuttles (if you have a lot of luggage) and buses.

LaGuardia in Flushing, Queens, only services domestic flights. A cab ride from the Upper West Side to LaGuardia averages only twenty-five minutes for $19 plus a $3.50 toll. More time-consuming but cheaper is the M60 bus, which departs from 116th Street and Broadway on the 1·9 line and arrives at the airport in about forty-five minutes, stopping at all major terminals. The fare is the same as all other buses: $1.50. From the East Side, take the privately-operated Carey Express from 42nd and Park Avenue for $13.

JFK International Airport in eastern Queens is quite a hike. If time is not a concern, take the A from 59th Street/Columbus Circle to Howard Beach, Queens, where a shuttle runs back and forth to JFK; the cost is a mere $1.50, but not ideal with more than two pieces of luggage. Another option is the $13 Carey Bus.

Newark International Airport can also be reached by a shuttle, run by the always dependable New Jersey Transit, which departs from Port Authority: seven dollars one-way, $12 round-trip.

JFK International Airport
(718) 244-4444, 24 hours
LaGuardia Airport
(718) 533-3400

Newark Airport
(973) 961-6000, (973) 961-6154

(Hearing Impaired)
New Jersey Transit Express
(973) 762-5100
Carey Express
(718) 632-0500

AIRLINES
American
1-800-433-7300
British Airways
1-800-247-9297
Continental
1-800-525-0280
Delta
1-800-221-1212
Northwest
1-800-225-2525
TWA
1-800-221-2000
United
1-800-241-6522
USAir
1-800-428-4322
Virgin Atlantic Airways
1-800-862-8621

BUDGET TRAVELING

Many airlines offer significant student discounts; USAir, Delta, and Continental run shuttles between New York and Boston and New York and Washington D.C. The student rate is $75 for a single ticket and increasingly less when tickets are bought in four- or eight-packs. Booking a flight for the cheapest fare possible can be incredibly complex since fare structures change all the time, and factors like two-to-three-week advance sales can raise ticket costs considerably. Use all the travel resources available, including student travel agencies, newspaper listings, and the advice of friends and acquaintances, to get the best deal.

The easiest method is to book directly through the airline of your choice. The fare will not be a bargain, but if the flight is overbooked, they are accountable and will put you on the next available flight. Join as many Frequent Flier clubs as possible; in the long run, the benefits of free flights or upgrades will appear. Frequent flyers also often get hotel and car rental discounts.

Agencies of different stripes provide bargains of varying value. The less aggressive traveler only needs a couple of numbers, which will yield good, if not great, deals. These agencies also provide other services like Eurail passes, International Student IDs, and hostel information.

A favorite method of travel is signing up for an American Express card. American Express sends its members travel coupons for Continental domestic flights: $159 for anywhere east of the Mississippi, $229 anywhere in the continental United States, if you book twenty-one or fewer days in advance. The Optima Card charges no annual fee, so there is little reason not to enroll (800-678-4629). A special note on the Optima Card and travel: if you are abroad, having a student American Express card means that you are not entitled to the typical member benefits, such as being able to draw cash from your home account without an ATM card. If you expect to travel, and would like to receive these benefits, sign up for a regular American Express card.

Also read the page in the *New York Times* or *Village Voice* travel sections with tiny ads from dozens of travel agencies. Although all advertise incredible prices, chances are the seats won't be available. They still might offer better fares than otherwise available. Most are consolidators: they buy large chunks of tickets and sell them without hangups about advance fares. Also, they sometimes get nervous when they occasionally find themselves with extras. Call all of them, and reserve a lot of tickets at will, as long as they're not binding. Go to the office in person and make sure a real ticket is there when a credit card number is handed over. This entire process takes plenty of time and energy, but the savings can be impressive.

One last option for those seeking cheap air tickets comes in the form of free e-mail service. A number of airlines have developed FlightSaver accounts which send out weekly lists of cheap flights from the airport closest to you. The savings vary greatly and there are usually a number of limitations. Contact the airlines through their web pages or toll-free numbers:

American
http://www2.amrcorp.com/cgi-bin/intaans or 1-800-344-6702

Council Travel
205 East 42nd Street (bet Second and Third Aves), 822-2700, ❹❺❻ to Grand Central

Liberty Travel
This agency can provide assistance in arranging vacations, or any type of trip. Convenient locations throughout Queens.
Locations in Manhattan, Bayside, Flushing, Forest Hills, Fresh Meadows, Middle Village, Kew Gardens and Jamaica, Main Office: 201-934-3500

STA Travel
These guys can turn up student discounts on just about any fare. Pay cash to avoid waiting two weeks for tickets.
10 Downing Street, 627-3111 and 627-3387, MC, V, ❶❾ to Houston Street

Also at
2871 Broadway (bet. 111th and 112th Sts.), 865-2700, MC, V, AmEx, ❶❾ to 110th Street

COURIER FLIGHTS
Leave the country on a moment's notice: courier companies offer last-minute week or two-week long trips. As a rule, the sooner the departure, the cheaper the ticket. Unfortunately, only carry-on luggage is allowed, since the company is basically buying your cargo space. Leave tomorrow for Paris? Why not? It's only $259!

Now Voyager
74 Varick Street, 431-1616, MC, V, *Discount for paying with cash*, ❶❾ to Houston Street

---

STUDENT TRAVEL

Journey. Voyage. Expedition. Quest. Pilgrimage.

Call it what you want. JUST GO.

STA TRAVEL...
THE WORLD'S LARGEST
STUDENT TRAVEL ORGANIZATION.

627-3111
10 Downing Street
(6TH AVE. & BLEECKER)

865-2700
COLUMBIA UNIVERSITY
2871 Broadway

STA TRAVEL
We've been there.

BOOK YOUR TICKET ONLINE
WWW.STA-TRAVEL.COM

HOTELS

New York City boasts more hotel rooms than any other city in the world, barring Las Vegas. That doesn't, however, make finding an affordable hotel in New York an easy process. While in Midtown and the Financial District, hotels seem a dime a dozen, outside these districts lodgings are significantly harder to come by, and no matter where you are, hotels will milk you for all you're worth. Space is often at a premium, and the city also gets in on the action by levying a hefty "hotel occupancy tax" of 13.25% making an under-$200-a-night deal a bargain. If you foresee a trip in high season, for example during December, book well in advance since rooms go quickly.

Upper End ($200+)

Four Seasons Hotel

Don't let the grand walk up from the lobby to the reception desk intimidate you, and forget all those models and celebrities milling around the lobby bar, too; if you've got the funds to sign on as a guest, the service is warm and welcoming without being obsequious. You could fit several average New Yorkers' apartments into the coolly elegant rooms with impressive cityscape views to boot. A list of premium amenities could fill pages. Everything here is state-of-the-art and sophisticated, down to the Magrittes and Kandinskys distributed liberally throughout. Drawbacks? This luxurious experience comes at a very hefty price.
57 East 57th St. (bet. Madison and Park Aves.), 758-5700, Rooms start at $500, MC, V, Am Ex, D, **N R** *to 69th St.* &

Grand Hyatt New York

This fabulous hotel in the heart of the city is located just steps away from what makes New York, New York: Broadway theatres; museums; Fifth Avenue shopping; the United Nations Building; the Empire State Building, etc. Staying at the Grand Hyatt will afford you a premier location while enjoying the comforts of a first-class and newly renovated hotel.
Park Avenue (at Grand Central Station), 850-5900, MC, V, AmEx, D, Diners, Rooms range from $189 to $365, **4 5 6 S 7** *to Grand Central Sta.*

Loews

With jacuzzis, personal trainers at your request, and a concierge on two levels to direct you to all the sights and stores the hotel rests in the center of, Loews has big city accommodations with a friendly staff ready to make you feel right at home.
569 Lexington Ave. (at 51st St.), 752-7000, MC,V,AmEx, Weekend Rates: around $240, **6** *to 51st St.*

Peninsula

A neophyte in the parade of luxury properties along the spine of upper Fifth Avenue, the Peninsula was born with a silver spoon in its mouth, namely a million-dollar location. Fantastic views abound from the renowned rooftop bar, the Pen-Top, and the outlook from the opulent day spa on the 21st floor is far from shabby. Though small and a bit minimalist, rooms are nice, and for the money, views should be better than an air shaft. Still, the Peninsula is a classy place, and the well-heeled visitors who stay here can attest to that.
700 Fifth Ave. (at 55th St.), 247-2200, Rooms start at $390, MC, V, AmEx, D, **E F** *to Fifth Ave.*

Plaza

The stuff of legends, the epitome of old New York, where every middle-American dreams of staying. Tons of movies, from *Home Alone II* to *Plaza Suite*, pay homage to the Edwardian romance of this classic. The parkside hotel seems dedicated to preserving this mystique, from its opulent lobby to the delicate splendor of the Palm Court restaurant. This vision of elegance is marred somewhat by the scores of gawking halter-topped tourists from Iowa, though if you escape to your room, old-style sinks and marble fireplaces will re-orient you in the hotel's tradition.
Central Park South (at Fifth Ave.), 759-3000, Rooms start at $290, MC, V, AmEx, D, Diners, **E F** *to Fifth Ave.* &

SoHo Grand

Currently the hottest hotel in New York, this newcomer made headlines and angered neighborhood residents as the first hotel in SoHo. Everything is in sync with the neighborhood: artsy, avant-garde types walk through the cutting-edge industrial lobby to their custom-designed digs. You can request a black goldfish to accompany you during your stay. In keeping with the cyber-sexy image, you can even make reservations on their website: http://www.SoHoGrand.com
310 West Broadway (at Grand St.), 965-3000, Rooms start at $250, MC, V, AmEx, D, Diners, **A C E 1 9** *to Canal St.*

UN Plaza-Park Hyatt New York

Often overlooked by tourists, this pleasant Hyatt outpost is a good bet in Midtown East. Directly across from the United Nations and the East River, all of the rooms have incredible views. The mood, evoked by an abundance of mirrors, brass, marquee lights, and dark walls, is subdued, even stodgy, but who wants to complain when the rooms are this comfortable?
One UN Plaza 44th St. (bet. First and Second Aves.), 758-1234, Rooms start at $225, MC, V, AmEx, D, **S 4 5 6 7** *to 42nd St./Grand Central Station* &

OLYMPIA TOURS & TRAVEL INC.

- for last minute bookings -

1270 BROADWAY SUITE #302 (bet. 32nd + 33rd)
NEW YORK, N.Y. 10001
TEL: (212) 695-6699 FAX: (212) 695-0918
TOLL FREE (888) 665-9674(6-OLYMPIA)
www.enjoyasia.com - www.enjoychina.com

resources 351

The Bell Atlantic Yellow Pages cover Manhattan...and Bell Atlantic Community Directories cover many New York City neighborhoods, offering money-saving coupons, up-to-date listings and more.

Manhattan Community directories:
- Harlem, Morningside Heights
- Washington Heights, Inwood
- Upper West Side
- Chelsea, Greenwich Village
- Beekman Place, Sutton Place, Turtle Bay
- Upper East Side, Yorkville
- Lower Manhattan
- Gramercy Park, Murray Hill

Call us for your FREE book!
1-800-346-9639
Bell Atlantic Yellow Pages

Mid-Range ($100-$200)

Gramercy Park Hotel
With lovely pre-war architecture, this established outpost onGramercy Park attracts a genteel clientele. Charm abounds here, and the neighborhood is an interesting one to explore, but more importantly, visitors here will be the secret envy of every New Yorker: the hotel holds a coveted key to the beautiful, private Gramercy Park. *2 Lexington Ave. (at Gramercy Park, 21st St.), 475-4320, MC, V, Am Ex, D, Diners, Rooms start at $145, 6 to 23rd St.*

Marriott Marquis
Look for the garish yellow Hertz billboard and you won't miss this Times Square staple for theater-bound tourists and other visitors who equate flashiness with luxury. With two thousand rooms, a revolving rooftop restaurant, an ultra-glitzy lobby, and its own Broadway theater, the Marquis dispenses with the need to even leave the premises for a taste of overwrought glamour. *1535 Broadway (at 45th St.), 398-1900, Rooms start at $200, MC, V, Am Ex, NR1379 to Times Square*

Millenium Hilton
A sleek and modern monolith, this hotel of choice for out-of-town suits is smack dab in the middle of the hectic world of stocks and trading and just steps away from the World Trade Center. Rooms here put your average Hiltons to shame, and with everyone taking their blood pressure pills, the atmosphere is surprisingly calm like the eye of the storm. *55 Church St. (bet. Fulton and Dey Sts.), 693-2001, Rooms start at $139 (but prices change frequently), MC, V, AmEx, D, Diners, NR19 to Cortlandt St.*

Paramount
Cheap by New York standards, this snazzy hotel offers reasonable prices for well-appointed rooms, trendy clientele, and smart chic. Designed by master hotelier Phillipe Starck, everything here is too cool: the lobby decor looks like Dr. Seuss himself moonlit as the interior decorator, while bathrooms have funky, pyramid-shaped aluminum sinks. Expect showbiz types (guests of "Saturday Night Live" stay here) who don't mind being shoehorned into microscopic rooms. *235 West 46th St. (bet. Broadway and Eighth Ave.), 764-5500, Rooms start at $145, MC, V, Am Ex, D, Diners, ACE to Port Authority*

Radisson Empire
Near Lincoln Center, this budget-conscious hotel is a real find for visitors who want to explore the Upper West Side or catch an opera at the Met. The attractive rooms have a surprising number of amenities for the price, including CD players and VCRs. Columbia University relatives get a discount. *44 West 63rd St. (opposite Lincoln Sq.), 265-7400, Rooms start at $165, MC, V, Am Ex, D, Diners, 19 to 66th St.*

Wales Hotel
An anomaly among the luxury properties of the Upper East Side, this homey, attractive hotel in venerable Carnegie Hill provides very nice rooms in an unexpectedly charming atmosphere. Its proximity to Museum Mile and Madison Avenue shopping is an added bonus. *1295 Madison Avenue (bet. 92nd and 93rd Sts.), 876-6000, Rooms start at $199, MC, V, Am Ex, 456 to 86th St.*

Budget (under $100)

The De Hirsh Residence (at the 92nd St. YMCA)
Dormitory style residence hall where one can stay by the day (minimum 3-day stay), or apply to stay by the month for up to a year. The activities available at the Y are open to De Hirsh residents. *1395 Lexington Ave. (at 92nd St.), 415-5650, Rooms are $35/doubles (apiece), $49/singles, 456 to 86th St.*

East Campus Hotel
Columbia University guest accommodations offers rooms for visitors. *Columbia University, 854-2946, MC, V, Rooms are $75/single, $90/double*

352 resources

1 9 to 116th St.

Herald Square Hotel
One can get a "very small single" with a shared bathroom for just $50 a day; add $25 for a private shower.
19 West 31st St. (bet. Thea and Broadway), 279-4017, MC, V, Am Ex, D, Rooms start at $55, **1 9 2 3** *to 34th St.*

New York International House AYH-Hostel
Vistors can stay in large ten-to-twelve-person bedrooms. Members get a better deal. Maximum stay is one week.
891 Amsterdam Ave. (at 103rd St.), 932-2300, MC, V, Rooms are $27/$24 (members), **1 9** *to 103rd St.*

NYU Guest Accommodations
One bedroom accommodations are available for guests; prices are twenty bucks cheaper on weekends.
52 William Street, 229-3802, MC, V, Am Ex, Rooms start at $99 (weekends), **1 9** *to Christopher St.*

Park West Studio Hotel
Extended stay prices are the best deal at $165/wk.
465 Central Park West (at 107th St.), 866-1880, Cash Only, Rooms start at $50, **B C** *to Cathedral Pkwy.*

Pickwick Arms
No frills, but it's often the best bet for savvy budget travelers who appreciate the warm lobby and the safe neighborhood and don't mind the forgettable rooms. The rooftop garden overlooking the skyscrapers makes this place an even bigger bargain.
230 East 51st Street (bet. Second and Third Aves.), 355-0300, Rooms start at $60, MC, V, Am Ex, **E F** *to Lexington,* **6** *to 51st St.*

Washington Square
Experience the quintessential trade-off of a resident New Yorker: location vs. space. Shoebox rooms at the only hotel in the Village, but in return, you're within walking distance of Washington Square Park, which beats the sleaze of Times Square any day.
103 Waverly Pl.(off Washington Sq. Park), 777-9515, Rooms start at $110, MC, V, AmEx, **A B C D E F Q** *W. 4th St.*

The Outer Boroughs
There aren't very many choices for lodging in Brooklyn, Bronx, Queens, and Staten Island. There are a few motels and inns sprinkled throughout, although they usually tend to be located along the major expressways out of town. Luxury options are pretty much confined to bed and breakfasts. Here is a partial listing.

Holiday Motel
2291 New England Thruway, (718) 324-4200

Le Refuge Bed and Breakfast
620 City Island Ave., City Island, (718) 885-2478

Best Western City View Motor Inn
33-17 Greenpoint Ave., (718) 392-8400

Marriott LaGuardia Airport
102-05 Ditmars Blvd., (718) 565-8900

Comfort Inn Brooklyn
8315 Fourth Ave., Bay Ridge, (718) 238-3737

Staten Island Hotel
1415 Richmond Ave., (718) 698-5000

RESOURCES

ANIMALS

ASPCA Humane Organization
876-7700

Emergency Animal Care
838-7053, Open 24 hours daily.

Bureau of Animal Complaints
442-1999

CONSUMER RESOURCES

Better Business Bureau
533-6200, Monday-Friday, 9am-5pm

New York City Department of Consumer Affairs, Complaints Department
487-4444

New York State Consumer Frauds Helpline and Protection Bureau
Office of the Attorney General, 120 Broadway, 416-8345, Monday-Friday, 9:30am-4:30pm

Small Claims Court/ Civil Court
You don't need a lawyer to file a suit to claim under $3000; over 60,000 New Yorkers go to Small Claims Court every year, though winning in court doesn't mean you will necessarily get the money due to poor enforcement mechanisms.
791-6000

CHILDCARE

Babysitter's Guild
It's best to call a day ahead.
60 East 42nd St., 682-0227, 9am-9pm daily

Barnard College Babysitting Service
You must call to pre-register with your name, address, phone, and name of your pediatrician. Call two days in advance, and a student sitter will call back to confirm.
Barnard College, 11 Milbank, 606 West 120th St., 854-2035, **1 9** *to 116th St.*

Columbia University Career Services
Call in with a semipermanent position, and they will post it on the part-time employment board. Students call for more information and to negotiate a baysitting rate.
116th St. and Amsterdam Ave., 854-5497, Fax: 663-9398

Hand-In-Hand Agency
This agency provides temporary and permanent sitters; it's about $7 and hour for one or two children, and $1 more for each extra child. Live-in-sitters are also available.
116-55 Queens Blvd., Forest Hills, Queens, (718) 268-6666, Monday-Friday, 9pm-5pm

Town & Country's Gilbert Child Care
For children over nine months, the hourly rate is $7.25 with a four hour minimum; it's about a $1-$2 more for children under nine months. Same-day service is possible, but definitely call ahead for weekends.
157 West 57th St., 245-8400 (reservation office), Monday-Friday, 9pm-5pm

Parents League
Join for $35 a year and gain access to the League's baby-sitting service, which includes sitters age thirteen to eighteen who attend one of the member schools. Check out the sitters' files, arranged by neighborhood, on the premises.
115 East 82nd St., 737-7385, Mon., Wed., Thurs., 9am-4pm, Tuesday, 9am-6pm,

resources 353

Friday, 9am-12pm,
❹❺❻ *to 86th St.*

DAYCARE AND OTHER RESOURCES

Agency for Child Development
Pre-school and referral information, as well as a free directory of daycare services.
(718) 523-6826

Child Care Inc./ The Pre-School Association
This nonprofit group offers parents telephone counseling, information of day care and early childhood programs, and names of day care providers in your neighborhood.
275 Seventh Ave., 929-4999, ❶❾ *to 27th street*

The New York Public Library's Early Childhood Resource Center
There is an entire floor devoted to resource materials for parents, and appropriately enough, a playroom for kids.
66 Leroy St. (at Seventh Ave.), 929-0815, ❶❾ *to Houston St.*

CRISIS LINES, HOTLINES AND MEDICAL NUMBERS

Bellevue Hospital Rape Crisis Service
Free medical treatment for rape victims, as well as counseling referral.
562-3755, Monday-Friday, 9am-5pm

Crime Victims Hotline
Victims of any personal crime, including domestic violence, rape, and theft, as well as legal advice.
577-7777, Open 24 hours daily

St. Luke's/ Roosevelt Hospital Rape Crisis Center
Trained volunteers talk victims through dealing with rape, both legally and emotionally.
523-4728, Monday-Friday, 9am-5pm

Sex Crimes Report Line
A female detective from the NYPD handles reports of all sex crimes, child victimization, hate crimes against gays, send an ambulance, provide counseling referrals, and set up an interview with a Sex Crimes Squad detective; you may request to be interviewed in your home.
267-7273, Open 24 hours daily

DOMESTIC VIOLENCE AND CHILD ABUSE

Domestic Violence Helpline
Trained social workers offer advice and use of shelter space, though working women pay a fee.
(800) 621-4673, Open 24 hours daily

New York State Child Abuse and Maltreatment Register
Call to report suspected child abuse.
(800) 342-3720, Open 24 hours daily

New York State Domestic Violence Helpline
Information on legal options and referrals to local programs and shelters.
(800) 942-6906, Open 24 hours daily, (800) 621-4673 (Spanish), Monday-Friday, 9am-5pm

ENTERTAINMENT

Broadway Show Line
573-BWAY

Cultural Affairs Department Line
765-2787

NYC/ OnStage
768-1808

Parks and Recreation Department
Special events: 360-8146; Summer Stage: 360-2777

GAMBLING

Gamblers Anonymous
903-4400, Open 24 hours daily

GAY AND LESBIAN

Gay and Lesbian Switchboard
A good resource for visitors to get advice about the city.
777-1800, 10am-12am daily

Gay Men's Health Crisis Hotline
Advice for people concerned about HIV/AIDS.
807-6655, Monday-Friday, 10am-9pm, Saturday, 12:00pm-3pm

Lesbian and Gay Community Services Center
(See sidebar in the Gay Feature for more information.)
208 West 13th St. (at Eighth Ave.), 620-7310, 9am-11pm daily, ❺❻ ❶❷❸❾ *to 14th St.*

New York City Gay and Lesbian Anti-Violence Project
647 Hudson St. (at Gansevoort St.), 807-0197, Monday-Thursday, 10am-8pm, Friday, 10am-6pm, Hotline open 24 hours daily, ❺❻❶❷❸❾ *to 14th St.*

HEALTH

Bailey House
Deals with emergency situations for people with AIDS/HIV.
275 Seventh Ave. (at 25th St.), 633-2500, Monday-Friday, 9:30am-5:30pm, ❶❷ *to 28th St.*

Emergency Dental Associates
(800) 439-9299, 9am-7pm daily

Fire Department and Emergency Medical Service
Report problems, including delayed service, poor treatment, or no-shows.
(718) 416-7000

Herpes Hotline and Advice Center
Advice and treatment run by a private medical practice.
213-6150, Monday-Thursday, 9am-6:45pm, Friday, 9am-3pm, 684-7455

Mental Health Counseling Hotline
Therapists will talk you through any emotional problems and issue referrals.
734-5876, Open 24 hours daily

New York City AIDS Information Hotline
447-8200, 9am-9pm daily

New York City Department of Health STD Information Hotline
158 East 115th St. (at Lexington Ave.), 427-5120, Monday-Friday, 9am-4pm, ❹❺❻ *to 116th St.*

New York University Student Dental Plan
Affordable, one-fee yearly dental care for college or university students
David B. Kriser Dental Center, 345 East 24th St. (at First Ave.), 998-9870

Poison Control Center
Call with questions.
764-7667

HOUSING

Housing Complaints (general)
960-4800

Rent Stabilization Association. (owners)
214-9200

Rent Stabilization Association. (tenants)
961-8930

Division of Housing and Community Renewal
240-6010

MOTOR VEHICLES

Alternate Side of the St. Parking Regulations
442-7080

Highway Emergencies
442-7094

Parking Violations Help Hotline (NYC Dept. of Transportation)
477-4430

Towed-Away Cars (NYC Bureau of Traffic Operations)
971-0070

RUNAWAYS

National Runaway Switchboard
Help for runaways, parents and friends of runaways, and homeless children. The switchboard gives advice on places to stay, and the hotline will send messages to parents, if asked.
(800) 621-4000, Open 24 hours daily

SANITATION

New York City Department of Sanitation
219-8090

Environmental Action Coalition (recycling)
677-1601

New York City Bureau of Highways (potholes)
768-4653

New York City Bureau of Electrical Control (street lights)
669-8353

New York City Department of Environmental Protection (water mains and sewers)
(718) 699-9811

SUBSTANCE ABUSE

Alateen Information Center
260-0407, Open 24 hours daily

Alcoholics Anonymous
647-1680, 9am-10:30pm

Pills Anonymous
874-0700, Open 24 hours daily

SUICIDE PREVENTION

The Samaritans
Volunteers help those suffering from depression, thoughts of suicide, and alcoholism.
673-3000, Open 24 hours daily

Suicide Prevention
Trained volunteers help talk people through thoughts of suicide.
532-2400 (interpretation service), 9am-10pm daily

DISABILITY INFORMATION

Although New York City may appear daunting at first, armed with information and determination, any disabled individual can take advantage of most of what the City has to offer. The best resources on accessibility can be found at:

Hospital Audiences, Inc. (HAI)
575-7676

Mayor's Office for People with Disabilities
788-2830

New York City Transit Authority Travel Information Center
(718) 330-1234

Lighthouse Incorporated
Information on resources for the blind
111 East 59th St. (bet. Park and Lexington Aves.), 821-9200/(800)829-0500, Mon.-Fri., 9am-5pm,
N R to Lexington Ave.

New York Society for the Deaf
Information on resources for the deaf.
817 Broadway (at 12th St.), 777-3900, Monday-Friday, 9am-5pm, **N R**
4 5 6 to Union Sq.

Andrew Heiskell Library for the Blind and Physically Handicapped
206-5400

WIRE SERVICES

MoneyGram
Fifty offices throughout the city.
(800) 926-9400

Credit Union National Association
(800) 358-5710

Western Union
(800) 325-6000 for nearest location.

GOVERNMENT OFFICES

Birth Records
788-4520

Department of Motor Vehicles
516 and 914 area codes: (800) DIAL-DMV,
Manhattan: 645-5550,
Outer Boroughs: 966-6155

Directory Assistance
Outer Boroughs: (718) 555-1212, Manhattan: 411

Immigration And Naturalization Service
206-6500

Passport Agency
630 Fifth Ave., Room 230, 206-3500, Monday-Friday, 7:30am-4pm.

United States Postal Service Zip Code Information
967-8585

LEGAL SERVICES

Community Action For Legal Services
Government-funded referral service.
431-7200

Legal Aid Society
Free advice on legal matters and referrals, but you must live below 34th Street in order to qualify.
577-3300, Monday-Friday, 9am-5pm

LIBRARIES

Queens Central Library
(718) 990-0778 (also extensions, 0779, 0781, 0700)

New York Public Library
340-0849

The New York Public Library For The Performing Arts
870-1630

Science, Industry and Business Library (NYPL)
592-7000

Brooklyn Central Library
(718) 230-2100

Bronx Central Library
(718) 579-4200

Telephone Reference Service
Librarians are extremely helpful about answering reference questions; they will refer you to the department with the most data.
Manhattan: 340-0849
Bronx: (718) 220-6576
Brooklyn: (718) 780-7700
Queens: (718) 990-0714

INSTITUTIONAL LIBRARIES

Andrew Heiskell Library for the Blind and Physically Handicapped
206-5400

Archive of Contemporary Music
54 White St., (bet. Broadway and Church Sts.), 226-6967

Baha'i Center and Library
53 East 11th St. (bet. University Pl. and Broadway), 674-8998

Donnell Library Center
621-0618

Frick Art Reference Library
10 East 71st St., 288-8700

resources 355

Gilder-Lehrman Library
481-6299
Hampdenbooth Theatre Library
228-7610
Independent Schools Multi-Media Center, Inc.
16 Gramercy Park South (bet. Park Ave. and Irving Pl.), 873-0844
Jewish Theological Seminary of America
678-8000
Morgan Library
29 East 36th St. (bet. Madison and Park Aves.), 685-0008
New York Law Institute
120 Broadway (bet. Cedar and Pine Sts.), 732-8720

THE CITY ON THE NET

Guides to New York:
www.insideny.com
www.columbia.edu/~hauben/nyc.guides.html
www.citysearch.com
www.ny.yahoo.com
www.sidewalk.com

Museums/Libraries:
Metropolitan Museum of Art: www.metmuseum.org
American Museum of Natural History: www.amnh.org
New York Public Library: www.nypl.org

Nightlife:
Playbill Online: www.playbill.com
New York City Ballet: www.nycballet.com
New York City Opera: www.interport.net/nyc-opera
New York Philharmonic: www.nyphilharmon.org
MovieLink: www.777film.com
Village Voice Essentials Guide to New York at Night: www.villagevoice.com/e/nighttit.html

ClubNYC: www.clubnyc.com
Metrobeat: www.metro.com

Food:
Zagat's Dining: pathfinder.com/Travel/Zagat/Dine
New York Food: www.nyfood.com
Kosher Restaurant database: www.shamash.org/kosher/\krestqquery.html
New York City Beer Guide: www.nycbeer.com

Transportation:
Subway Navigator Site: metro.gaius.fr:1001/bin/select/english/usa/new-york
Metropolitan Transit Authority: www.mta.nyc.ny.us

Sports:
Knicks: www.nba.com/knicks
Yankees: www.yankees.com
Giants: www.nfl.com/giants
Jets: www.nfl.com/jets

Government
New York City government: www.ci.nyc.by.us
Public Advocate's Office: www.pubadvocate.nyc.gov/~advocate
New York City Council Homepage: www.council.ny.us
United Nations: www.un.org

Parks and Recreation:
Central Park: www.centralpark.org
Parks and Recreations Special events: www.user.interport.net/~jerdugal/nycpark.specialevents.html

POST OFFICES

US General Post Office
Twenty-four hour postal service, except for money orders and registered mail, in the famous McKim, Mead, White masterpiece of design. Call to find the branch is closest to you.
380 West 33rd St. (at Eighth Ave.), (800) 725-2161 (Info Line), **A C E** to Penn Sta.

RELIGION

Baptist:
Calvery Baptist
123 West 57th St. (bet. Sixth and Seventh Aves.), 975-0170, **N R** to Fifth Ave.
Judson Memorial Baptist
55 Washington Sq. South, 477-0351, **A B C D F Q** to West 4th St.

Buddhist:
New York Buddhist Temple
331 Riverside Dr. (bet. 105th and 106th Sts.), 678-0305, **1 9** to 103rd St.

Episcopal:
Cathedral Church of St. John the Divine
Amsterdam Ave. (at 112th St.), 316-7400, **1 9** to 110th St.
Church of the Ascension
Fifth Ave. (at 10th St.), 254-8620, **N R** to 8th St.
Church of the Transfiguration
1 East 29th St. (bet. Fifth and Madison Aves.), 684-6770, **4 5** to Lexington Ave.
Grace Episcopal
802 Broadway (at 10th St.), 254-2000, **N R** to 8th St.
Holy Trinity
316 East 88th St. (bet 1st and 2nd Sts.), 289-4100, **4 5 6** to 86th St.
St. Bartholomew's
Park Ave. (at 51st St.), 751-1616, **6** to 51st St.
St. George's
209 East 16th St. (bet. Second and Third Aves.), 475-0830, **4 5 6 L N R** to Union Sq.
St. James
865 Madison Ave. (at East 71st St.), 288-4100, **6** to 68th St.
St. Luke's Chapel
487 Hudson St. (bet Christopher and Grove Sts.), 924-0562, **1 9** to Christopher St.
St. Mark's-in-the-Bowery
Second Ave. and East 10th St., 674-6377, **6** to Astor Pl.
St. Martin's Episcopal
230 Lenox Ave. (at 122nd St.), 534-4531, **2 3** to 125th St.
St. Thomas
Fifth Ave. and 53rd St., 757-7013, **6** to 51st St., **E F** to Lexington Ave.
Trinity Church
74 Broadway and Wall St., 602-0800, **1 2 3 9 A C** to Chambers St.

Greek Orthodox:
Holy Trinity Cathedral
319 East 74th St. (bet. First and Second Aves.), 288-3215, **6** to 77th St.

Jewish:
Central Synagogue
123 East 55th St. (bet. Park and Lexington Aves.), 838-5122, **6** to 51st St., **E F** to Lexington Ave.
Congregation Rodeph Shalom
7 West 83rd St. (at Central Park West), 362-8800, **B C** to 81st St.
Fifth Ave. Synagogue
5 East 62nd St. (at Fifth Ave.), 838-2122, **4 5 6** to 59th St., **N R** to Lexington Ave.
Park Avenue Synagogue
50 East 87th St. (bet. Madison and Fifth Aves.), 369-2600, **4 5 6** to 86th St.
Shearith Israel Spanish and Portuguese Synagogue
2 West 70th St. (at Central Park West), 873-0300, **B C** to 72nd St.

356 resources

Stephen Wise Free Synagogue
30 West 68th St. (at Central Park West), 877-4050, ❶❾ to Lincoln Cntr.**Lutheran:**
Holy Trinity
Central Park West (at 65th St.), 877-6815, ❶❾ to Lincoln Cntr.

St. John's Lutheran
81 Christopher St. (at Seventh Ave.), 242-5737, ❶❾ to Christopher St.
Methodist:
Christ Church
520 Park Ave. (at 60th St.), 838-3036, ❹❺❻ to 59th St., ❿❼ to Lexington Ave.
John Street United Methodist
44 John St. (at Nassau St.), 269-0014, ❹❺ to Wall St.
Mormon:
Church of Jesus Christ of Latter-Day Saints
Columbus Ave. (at West 65th St.), 875-8197, Family History Center 873-1690, ❶❾ to Lincoln Cntr.
Muslim:
Mosque of Islamic Brotherhood
130 West 113th St. (at St. Nicholas St.), 662-4100, ❷❸ to 116th St.
Non-Denominational:
Church of the UN
777 UN Plaza (bet. East 44th St. and First Ave.), 661-1762, ❹❺❻❼ to Grand Central Sta.
Riverside Church
Riverside Drive (at 122nd St.), 870-6700, ❶❾ to 125th St.
Presbyterian:
Church of the Covenant
310 East 42nd St. (at Second Ave.), 697-3185, 4567 to Grand Central Sta.
Fifth Avenue Presbyterian
Fifth Ave. (at 55th St.), 247-0490, ❹❺❻ to 59th St., ❿❼ to Lexington Ave.
Roman Catholic:
Church of Our Saviour
59 Park Ave. (at 38th St.), 679-8166, ❹❺❻❼ to Grand Central Sta.
Holy Apostles
296 Ninth Ave. (at 28th St.), 807-6799, ❻❼ to 23rd St.
Holy Trinity Chapel
58 Washington Square South, 674-7236, ❶❷❸❹❺❻❼ to West. 4th St.
Immaculate Conception
414 East 14th St. (at First Ave.), 254-0200, ❶ to First Ave.
St. Ignatius Loyola
980 Park Ave. (at East 84th St.), ❹❺❻ to 86th St.
St. Jean Baptiste
184 East 76th St. (at Lexington Ave.), 288-5082, ❻ to 77th St.
St. Patrick's Cathedral
Fifth Ave. (at 50th St.), 753-2261, ❻❼❻❿ to Rockefeller Cntr.
St. Paul the Apostle
415 West 59th St. (bet. Ninth and Tenth Aves.), 265-3209, ❶❾❼❼❿ to Columbus Circle
St. Vincent Ferrer
Lexington Ave. (at 66th St.), 744-2080, ❻ to 68th St.
Unitarian:
All Souls Unitarian
1157 Lexington Ave. (at East 80th St.), 535-5530
Community Church of New York
40 East 35th St. (bet. Park and Madison Aves.), 683-4988, ❻ to 33rd St.
Other:
Metropolitan Community Church of New York
446 West 36th St. (bet. 9th and 10th Aves.), 629-7440,
❶❼❼ to Penn Station

RENTALS
Furniture:
AFR The Furniture Rental People
711 Third Ave. (at 44th St.), 867-2800, Monday-Saturday, First month's rental plus a two-month security fee is required.
I.S. Furniture Rentals
49 West 23rd St., 924-4800, Monday-Friday, First month's rent and two months security.
International Furniture Rentals
345 Lexington Ave. (bet. 51st and 52nd Sts.), 421-0340, Monday-Saturday, One-and-a-half month's rent required as deposit.
Air Conditioners:
AABCO Amber Corp.
1594 York Ave., 535-9578, MC, V, AmEx, Average cost during the hot season (May through October) is $200.
Ace Air Conditioning Service Corp.
24-81 47th St., Astoria, Queens, (718) 406-2256, MC, V, Room size determines price.
Columbus Air Conditioning Center
529 Columbus Ave., 496-2626, MC, V, AmEx, Service and Delivery included.
Bicycles:
Bicycles Plus
400 Third Ave., 794-2929; 301 East 87th St., 722-2201.
Fourteenth St. Bicycle Discount House
332 East 14th St. (at First Ave.), 228-4344
Metro Bicycles
1311 Lexington Ave. (at 88th St.), 427-4450; 360 West 47th St., 581-4500; 231 West 96th St., 663-7531; 417 Canal St., 334-8000; 546 Avenue of the Americas (at 15th St.)

Pedal Pusher Bike Shop
1306 Second Ave. (at 69th St.), 288-5592.
Stuveysant Bicycle
349 West 14th St., 254-5200
Roller Blades:
Blades East and West Skate and Sport
160 East 86th St., 996-1644; 105 West 72nd St., 787-3911, Open 7 days a week.
Manhattan Sports
2188 Broadway (at 78th St.), 580-4753; 2901 Broadway (at 113th St.), 749-1454, Rents and Repairs.
Village Wheels
63-73 East 8th St., 505-6753.

TOURS
Adventures on a Shoestring
Walking tours through Greenwich Village, SoHo, Chinatown, the Lower East Side, and other neighborhoods according to demand. Guides are committed to helping the low-budget explorer and refuse to raise their rates, which have remained at five bucks a tour for the thirty-five years of the organization's existence. 265-2663, $5 per tour

Architectural Tours through the 92nd St. Y
Tours of Manhattan's historic cast-iron districts in Gramercy and SoHo, and other architecturally interesting spots in the city, are led by experts Joyce Mendelsohn, Barry Lewis, and Andrew Dolkart. c/o 92nd St. Y, 1395 Lexington Ave. (at 92nd St.), 415-5628, ❹❺❻ to 86th St.

Backstage on Broadway
Get a group of twenty-

resources 357

five together to tour behind the scenes of a Broadway theater; tours led by actors, directors, and stage managers. Call for reservations.
228 West 47th St. (bet. Broadway and Eighth Ave.), 575-8065, $8 (students), Cash Only, **A C E** *to 42nd St.*

Big Onion Walking Tours
A group of Columbia University graduate students in American History gives tours of New York's ethnic neighborhoods. Find out why New York City used to be called the big onion.
439-1090, Tour: $7

CityQuest Audio Tours
The best way to see New York! Enjoy an hour long trip through Greenwich Village, Wall Street, Fifth Avenue or Central Park with James Earl Jones and other special surprise guests. Sound effects, music and excellent commentary bring the history, culture and myths of each neighborhood to life. CDs and players can be rented from kiosks located throughout the city.
For more information, call: 1-888-HEAR NYC

Harlem Your Way Tours
Tours of Harlem tailored to your particular interest—historical or current.
690-1687, Tour: $25

Israel Israelowitz Tours
Guided tours of the Lower East Side, as well as boat tours of Jewish New York. Lecture programs as well.
(718) 951-7072

Urban Park Rangers
Rangers take you around the city's parks; where you go and what you see all depends on what you're interested in, whether it be bird-watching, fishing, or Native American history.
1234 Fifth Ave. (at 104th St.), 360-2774, 9am-5pm Daily, **6** *to 103rd St.*

UTILITIES

Con Ed Emergency Line
Call to report problems. Only gas leaks are treated as true emergencies.
Gas Emergency: 683-8830, Open 24 hours daily
Electrical or Steam Emergency: 683-0862, Open 24 hours daily

Public Service Commission Emergency Hotline
If your gas or electricity is cut off because you haven't paid the bills, they will give advice.
(800) 342-3355, Monday-Friday, 7:30am-7:30pm

YMCA's
Harlem
281-4100
McBurney
741-9210
Prospect Park
(718) 768-7100
Vanderbilt
756-9600
West Side
787-4400
Beacon Center
(718) 961-6014
Bronx
(718) 792-9736

SERVICES

COPY SERVICES

Chelsea Copy and Printing
255 West 23rd Street (bet. Seventh and Eighth Aves.), 924-4953

Kinko's
Notorious among college students for catering to those last-minute needs, Kinko's is open 24 hours. Some services include: copying, faxing, computer use and enlargements.
118-10 Queens Boulevard (at 70th Ave.), (718) 286-7700, MC, V, AmEx, D, Diners, **E F** *to Union Tpke* &

Village Copier
Reasonable rates; conveniently located to Columbia.
601 West 115th Street (bet. Broadway and Riverside Drive), 666-0600, MC, V, AmEx, **1 9** *to 116th St.* &

DRY CLEANERS

Joe Far Laundry
Fast and efficient, this inconspicuous laundry is the cheapest in Morningside.
B'way and 113th St., cash only, **1 9** *to 116th St.*

M+N Cleaners
Speedy and organized and they offer delivery.
292 Eighth Avenue (bet. 25th and 26th Sts.), **1 9** *to 23rd St.*

Piermont Cleaners
Pick up that suit en route to the show.
845 Seventh Avenue (at 54th Street), 242-2865, MC, V, **B D E** *to 117 Orchard Street at Delancey*

HAIRCARE

Aveda
Haircuts that would normally set you back $65 are free in the training class. Expect to wait a month. No coloring.
233 Spring Street (bet. Varick and Prince Sts.), 807-1492, Call for specific times, by appointment, **C E** *to Spring St.*

Bumble and Bumble
Leave a message explaining what you want done, and they'll get back to you if they think they can use you for the training class. Just remember: no one said this was democratic, and lying to the assistant's voicemail isn't gonna pay off in the long run.
146 East 56th Street (bet. Third and Lexington), Call for specific times and appointment, 521-6500, Cut: $10, Color: $20, 456 to 59th St. or **N R** *to Lexington Ave.*

Columbia Barber
These barbers cut hair two ways: short and shorter. Perfect for cash-strapped Columbia guys, but those who require a more creative clip should look elsewhere. Try to get David Azimov, the owner; his cuts are the best.
Broadway and 114th Street, 678-9259, Cash Only, **1 9** *to 116th Broadway* &

Crisca Hair Salon
Stop in for a moderately priced haircut with no appointment necessary.
21 East 51st Street (bet. Fifth and Madison Aves.), 759-4743, MC, V, **E F** *to Fifth Avenue*

Headlines
This busy salon that does the basics from hair to manicures. First-time walk-in clients can take advantage of a $15 cut if someone's free. Otherwise, cuts start at $26.
220 Eighth Ave. (bet. 20th and 21 Sts.), 243-0533, MC, V, **1 9** *to 23rd St.*

Jacques Dessange
By appointment only.
505 Park Avenue (bet. 59th and 60th), 308-1400, Cut: $10, Color: $20, 456 to 59th St. or **N R** *to Lexington Ave.*

Jean Louis David
Moderately priced, but cuts are hit or miss unless you latch onto a regular stylist. Check out their training center for great deals on Mondays, Tuesdays, and Wednesdays.
Broadway (bet. 73rd and

358 resources

74th Sts.), 873-1850, cash only, ❶❾ to 79th St.

Jeffrey's Manhattan Eyeland
Small selection of unique frames. Check out the window displays.
Broadway (bet. 87th and 88th Sts.), 787-3232, MC, V, AmEx, ❶❾ to 86th St.

Louis Licari
A great colorist. Call between 2 and 2:30pm on the first Tuesday of the month to qualify for a reduced price with the trainees.
797 Madison (bet. 67th and 68th Sts.), 517-8084, Single process color: $30, Highlights: $45, ❻ to 68th St.

Peter Coppola Salon
If you wade through the waiting list, you still have to pass a consultation before they turn you over to the trainees.
746 Madison Avenue (at 65th St.), Call for specific times and appointment, 988-9404, MC, V, AmEx, Cut: $20 (Color: $30 (Wed., 6pm), ❻ to 68th St.

Pierre Michel Salon
Call to sign up.
The Plaza Hotel, 768 Fifth Avenue (bet. 58th and 59th Sts.), 759-3000, Cash Only, Cut: $25, ❿❻ to Fifth Avenue

Saks Fifth Avenue Beauty Salon
Same procedure, but if you have patience you'll end up with a free cut.
611 Fifth Avenue, ninth floor, (bet. 49th and 50th Sts.), Call for specific times, 753-4000, ❺❻ to Lexington/Third Aves.

Salon Dada
By appointment only.
4 West 16th Street (at Fifth), 741-3232, Cut: $10, Color: $15, Call for specific times, ❶❿❷❹❺❻ to Union Square

Scott J.
Columbia students pamper themselves with professional cuts, colors, and massages.
2929 Broadway (bet. 114th and 115th Sts.), 666-6429, MC, V, ❶❾ to 116th St.

Sister African Hair Braiding Center
Let these experts do box braids, corn rows, Senegalese twists, and other styles at affordable prices.
307 West 125th Street (bet. Frederick Douglass and St. Nicholas Boulevards), 749-9300, Cash only, ❶❷❸❹❺ to 125th St.

The Service Station
Bodies in need of a tune-up, look toward the twelve-foot Gulf sign. Cuts start at $40. The shop offers an array of body tweakings, including manicures, tanning, and electrolysis.
137 Eighth Avenue (bet. 17th and 18th Sts.), 243-7770, ❶❾ to 18th St.

Vartoli
Model nights offer discount rates. Call for details.
48 East 57th Street (bet. Madison and Park), 935-4640, MC, V, Cut: $20, ❻❿ to 57th St.

Vidal Sassoon
You can't get scheduled till they take a look at your hair. Twenty percent off the already cut-rate prices for students.
90 Fifth Avenue (bet. 14th and 15th Sts.), 229-2000, Model Call by appointment, ❶❿❷❹❺❻ to Union Square (Also in Midtown)

SHOE REPAIR

Ambassador Luggage and Leather Goods
Repair of all types of leather goods.
371 Madison Avenue (bet 45th and 46th Sts.), 972-0965, MC, V, AmEx; ❹❺❻❼❽ to 42nd St./Grand Central Station

Drago
Shoe shine, repairs, shoe polish, and other shoe needs.
2455 Broadway (bet. 110th and 111th), 663-7060, MC, V, ❶❾ to 110th St.

Ham Shoe Repair
Conviniently located in the downtown Jamaica area, this place is excellent for all footwear repairs. Very reasonable prices as well.
160-09 Jamaica Avenue, (718) 526-5191

OPTICIANS

Charles Alexander Opticians
Find a large selection of stylish frames, at Madison Avenue.
400 Madison Avenue (at 47th Street), 753-8883, MC, V, AmEx, ❺❻ to Rockefeller Center

Columbia Opticians
Fittings and frames.
1244 Amsterdam Avenue (at 119th Street), 316-2020, MC, V, ❶❾ to 116th St.

Confucius Plaza Optical
One of the least expensive vision alternatives in this area.
17 Bowery, 431-4910, MC, V, AmEx, ❻ to Second Ave.

Jeffrey's Manhattan Eyeland
Small selection of unique frames.
Broadway (bet. 87th and 88th Sts.), 787-3232, MC, V, AmEx, ❶❾ to 86th St.

Ocean-View Optical
Stylish specs, but be prepared to pay the high-end prices.
Union Square East bet. 16th and 17th Street, 477-9515, MC, V, AmEx, ❹❺❻❻❿ to Union Square

PHOTO SERVICES

Fotorush
One-hour processing, also passport photos, video transfer, and slide transfers.
2889 Broadway (at 113th Street), 749-0065, MC, V, ❶❾ to 110th St.

STORAGE

Access Self Storage
Open 7 days a week, Access has 24-hour security, ample free parking, insurance and exceptional clean service for their customers.
29-00 Review Avenue (at 29th St.), (718)729-0442, MC, V, AmEx, D, ❼ to Hunter's Point

Chelsea Moving & Storage Inc.
601 West 26th Street (bet. Eleventh and Twelfth Aves.) and 300 West 23rd Street (bet. Seventh and Eighth Aves.), 243-8000, ❶❾ to 28th St.

Chelsea Mini Storage
224 Twelfth Avenue, 564-7735, ❶❾ to 28th St.

Guarantee Storage Centers Inc.
531 West 21st Street, 620-7387, ❶❾ to 23rd St.

TAILORS

Czarina
Besides baggy linens for sale, tailoring is also available.
2876 Broadway (bet. 112th and 113th Sts.), 222-4285, MC, V, AmEx, ❶❾ to 110th Street

WHY FOTORUSH IS BETTER IN FILM PROCESSING

1. **QUALITY CONTROL**
   We process C-41 film, RA4 paper control strips every day to (read by densitometer) monitor processing chemicals and processor for best quality.

2. **DEDICATED FILM CHANNEL**
   Our Printer has dedicated channels for different types of film: 100, 200, 400, 1600, etc. We run Bull's Eye to balance these channels for Normal Under and Over exposures to ensure constant high quality printing. We use Aperion True Color Balance Bull's Eye.

3. **TEST PRINT: WE INSPECT OUR PRINTS TWICE**
   Even if we do our part right, there still exist variations of color such as heat effected film, foreign-made Kodak film (which has different emulsion), artificial lights, etc. As a result, when we see something wrong with the negatives we test the prints, printing only 3 or 4 frames at first. After we examine the outcome of the tests we make the necessary color corrections.

4. **19 YEARS EXPERIENCE IN PHOTOFINISHING**

FOTORUSH
ONE HOUR PROCESSING

2878 Broadway at 113th Street • 749-0065

230 Park Avenue (West Arcade) • 687-3479

2585 Broadway at 97th Street • 662-8542

INDEX

A

A Different Light 208, 213
A Taste of India II 235
A.L. Bazzini 156
Abbey Pub 291
Abbey Tavern 291
ABC Carpet and Home 159
Abyssinian Baptist Church 114
Academy Bookstore 213
Ace Bar 290-291
ACME 235
Acme Underground 326
Actor's Playhouse 198
Actors 225
African American Wax Museum 178
African Poetry Theater, Inc. 198
Aggie's 234
AIRLINES 349
Airports 349
Albany 332
Algonquin Hotel 190, 234
Alice Underground 152
Alley's End 85, 235
Alliance Française 186
Allison on Dominick 235
Alouette 235
Alphabet City 69
Alternative Museum 178
Alumni Hall 291
Alvin Ailey American Dance Theater 198
Amato Opera House 198
Ambassador Grill 235
American Ballet Theater 186, 198
American Craft Museum 178
American Folk Art Institute 186
American Jewish Theater 198
American Movie Theater 125
American Museum of Moving Image 178
American Museum of Natural History 103, 106, 178
American Museum of the Moving Image 227
American Numismatic Society 117, 186
American Trash 291
Americas Society 187
Amin Indian Cuisine 235
Amir's 235
Amsterdam Billiards, 290
Amsterdam Cafe 235, 291
Amtrak 348
An Beal Bocht Café 268
Anbar Shoe Steal 162
Andalousia 235
Andrew J. Tobin Plaza 44
Andy's Chee-Pees 143, 152
Angelica Kitchen 235
Angelika Film Center 227
Anglers and Writers 235
Anglican Church 109
ANIMALS 354
Anime Crash 163
Anna Sui 148
Annam Brahma Restaurant 235
Annex Antique Fair & Flea Market 152
Anseo 291
Ansonia 104
Anthology Film Archives 227
Anthropologie 150
Antique Boutique 142, 150
APARTMENTS 21-22
APC 150
Apex 183
Aphrodisia 163
Apollo Theater 198
Applause Theatre and Cinema Books 213
Apthorp 104
Arcadia 236
Argosy Bookstore 213
Arizona 206 236
Arlene Grocery 291
Around the Clock 236
Art Bar 291
Art Expo New York 36
Art Greenwich Village Twin 227
ART SUPPLY 147
Artist's Space 183
ARTS 169, 171-182, 184-187, 189-199, 201, 203, 205-217, 220-224, 226-229
Asia Society 178, 187
Asian American Arts Center 178
Astroland Park 134
AT&T Long Lines Building 49
Atlantic City 333
Atlantis 236
Atomic Passion 159
Atrium 150
Au Bar 291
Aubudon Bar and Grill 236
Auction House 291
Audubon Bar and Grill 291
Augie's 291
Aunt Suzie's 236
Automatic Slims 292
Avery Fisher Hall 105-106

B

Baby Jupiter 63, 288-289
Babylon 62, 236
Bagel Bob's 268
Bagels & Cream Café 130, 268
Bags O' Bags 71
Baisley House 336
Baker Field 119
Balaman Gallery 155
Balducci's 72, 156
Bally 148
Balthazar 236
Baluchi's 237
The Bank 317
Bank St. College Bookstore 213
Bank Street College 108
Banks 13-14
Bar 89 66, 292
Bar None 292
Baraza 289, 292
Barbara Gladstone 183
Barmacy 289, 292
Barnard 108,109, 111
Barnes & Noble 80, 38, 208, 210, 225
Barney's 143, 154
Barramundi 292
Bars 28, 282, 284-290, 292-303, 305-309, 318
BARS INDEX BY TYPE 309
BARS INDEX BY NEIGHBORHOOD 310
Basilio Inn 140, 237
Bassett Coffee and Tea Co. 268
Battery Park City 43-44
Bay Plaza Shopping Mall 126
BBQs 237
Beaches 331, 334, 341
Beacon Theatre 107, 326
Beauty Bar 289, 292
Bed and Breakfasts 336
Bell Cafe 268
Bella's Coffee Shop 268
Belmont Lounge 292
Belmont Stakes 37
Belvedere Castle 98, 100
Bemelman's 292
Bendix Diner 237
Bergdorf Goodman 154
Bessie Schomberg Theater 198
Betsey Johnson 150
Beyond Words 213
Biblio's 48, 50
Bicycle Habitat 163
Big Cigar Co. 163
Big Cup 84, 268
Biography Bookshop 213
Bistro Jules 268
Bitter End 285, 326
Black Book 16
Black Books Plus 214
Black Fashion Museum 178
Black Spectrum Theater 198
Blackout Books 214
Blades Boards & Skates 163
Bleecker Bob's 160
Bleecker Street Bar 292
Bleecker Street Records 160
Blind Tiger Ale House 293
Blondie's 293
Bloomingdale's 154
Blue and Gold 293
Blue Note 322, 324, 326
Bo Ky 55, 237
Board Games 100
Boathouse Cafe 35
BOATING 100, 344
BOb 317
Boca Chica 237
Bodega 237
Boiler Room 293
Bolo 85, 237
Book Ark 214
Bookberries 214
Booklink/Booklink Too 214
BOOKSTORE INDEX BY NEIGHBORHOOD 218
BOOKSTORE INDEX BY TYPE 219
Bookstore Listings 213
Boomer's 293
Boots and Saddle 293
Borders Bookstore 208
Boroughs 24
Botanic Gardens 135
Botanica 293
Bottom Line 326
Boulevard 237
Bourbon St. 293
Bouwerie Lane Theater 198
Bowery Bar 293
Bowling Green 44
BowlMor Lanes 34, 317
Bowne House 129
Boxers 293
Boy's Choir of Harlem 198
Break 293
Bridge Cafe 47, 268
Bright Food Shop 237
Brighton Beach 132
Broadway 190, 192, 195
Bronfman Jewish Center 187
Bronx 11, 24-25, 56, 122-123, 126-127, 166, 188, 218, 265, 277, 320, 343, 344
Bronx Museum of the Arts 124-125, 178
Bronx Zoo/Wildlife Conservation Park 123, 124, 126
BROOKLYN 11, 24-25, 32, 35, 56, 132-137, 139, 143, 166, 171, 188, 204, 218, 265, 277, 283, 310, 336, 338, 341-342, 344
Brooklyn Academy of Music 132, 198
Brooklyn Botanical Gardens 132
Brooklyn Brewery 157
Brooklyn Bridge 29, 34, 134, 171, 175, 330, 339
Brooklyn galleries 175
Brooklyn Heights 29, 132
Brooklyn Heights Press 21
Brooklyn Heights Promenade 134
Brooklyn Historical Society 75
Brooklyn Mod 137
Brooklyn Moon Cafe 135
Brooklyn Museum of Art 136, 175, 178
Brooklyn Promenade Show 37
Bryant Park 89, 93, 37, 225
Bryant Park Grill 238
BUDGET TRAVEL 349
Burlington Antique Toys 155
Burlington Coat Factory 147
Burp Castle 287, 293
Buses 9, 11, 348

C

C Note 289, 294
Cabs 9-10, 12
CAFES 18, 267-272, 274-277
Cafe Asean 269
Cafe Con Leche 269
Cafe Della Artista 269
Café Des Artistes 107
Cafe Europa 92

Cafe Gigi 269
Cafe Gitane 59, 269
Cafe Kolonaki 269
Cafe Lalo 267, 269
Cafe Love 269
Cafe Luna 269
Café Milou 76, 269
Cafe Mona Lisa 270
Cafe Mozart 270
Cafe Noir 270
Cafe Orlin 270
Cafe Palermo 270
Cafe Pick Me Up 270
Cafe Pierre at the Pierre Hotel 285, 294
Cafe Rafaella 270
Cafe Roma 270
Cafe Roma Pizzeria 238
Cafe Sha Sha 270
Cafe Un Deux Trois 270, 294
Cafe Viva 270
Cafe Vivaldi 270
Cafe Wha? 285
Cafe Yola 270
CAFE INDEX BY NEIGHBORHOOD 277
Caffe Dante 267, 271
Caffe Pertutti 271
Caffe Reggio 271
Caffé Taci 111, 271
Cal's 238
Caliente Cab 294
Calvin Klein 148, 150, 333
Calypso 150
Camille's 238
Canal Jean Co. Inc. 153
Candle Bar 294
Candle Cafe 271
Candy Bar and Grill 238, 294
Cannon's Pub 294
Canton 238
Car services 12
Card-o-Mat 155
Cargo Cafe 271
Carl Schurz Park 95-96
Carmine's 239
Carnegie Bar and Books 294
Carnegie Hall 199, 322
Carriage House 294
Carrot Top Cafe 120
Casa Italiana 179
Castillo de Jagua 239
Castillo Theater 199
Catch a Rising Star 199
Cathedral of St. John the Divine 109-110
Catskills 330, 332
CB's 313 Gallery 326
CBGB's 322, 326
Ceci-Cela 271
Cedar Tavern 294
Celeste Bartos Forum 93
Centennial House 337
Center for the Arts 199
Centerfold Coffeehouse at Church of St. Paul and St. Andrew 199
Central Park 29, 34-35, 95, 98-104, 107 335, 338-340, 344
Century 21, 47, 143, 147

Champs 294
Chanel 149
Chanterelle 239
Chaos 317
Chatham Square Library 53
Che Bella 239
Cheap Jack's 143, 153
CHELSEA 78, 82-85, 166, 171, 188, 204, 218, 229, 265, 277, 310, 320
Chelsea Flower District 83
Chelsea Gym 85
Chelsea Hotel 82-83, 85
Chelsea Piers 34, 83, 342
Cherry 153
Cherry Lane Theater 199
Chestnut Room 294
Chez Ma Tante Cafe 271
Chi-Chi Steak 239
Chicago B.L.U.E.S. 326
Chicago City Limits 199
CHILDCARE 353
Children's Museum of Manhattan 179
China Institute 187
China Shalom II 239
Chinatown 52-55, 166, 188, 218, 229, 232, 265, 277, 310
Chinatown Fair 54-55
Chinatown Ice Cream Factory 55, 157, 239
Chinatown Manpower Project 53
Chinese New Year 36
Christie's 183
Chrysler Building 90
Chumley's 295
Church Street Surplus 153
Ciel Rouge 295
CINEMA LISTING 227
CINEMA INDEX BY NEIGHBORHOOD 229
Cinema Village 227
CINEMA INDEX BY TYPE 229
Cinematographe 227
Cineplex Odeon Chelsea West 227
Cineplex Odeon Worldwide Cinema 105
Cineplex Waverly 227
Circle Repertory Theater 199
Citarella 106, 157
City Cinemas Village East 227
City College of the City University of New York 115
City Hall 44
City Island 122, 124
City Wine and Cigar Co. 295
CityKids Foundation 48, 196-197
CITY ON THE NET 356
Civil and Criminal Court Division of Jurors 26
Clarke's 125, 295
Clementine 239
Clinton Hill 132
Clocktower Gallery 45
Cloisters 118, 120, 179, 335
Clothes-Out Connection 147

CLOTHING 147
CLUB INDEX BY NEIGHBORHOOD 320
Club Las Vegas 120
Club Liguanea 317
Club Listings 317
Club Vertigo 317
CLUBS 28, 282-283, 286, 313-317, 319-320
Cody's 295
Coffee Lounge 271
Coffee Shop 295
Colden Center For the Performing Arts at Queens College 199
Cole Haan 162
Coliseum 163
Collective Unconscious 199
Colony 160
Columbia Bagels 108, 271
Columbia Cottage 239
Columbia University 16, 108-111, 115, 210, 285
Columbia University Bookstore 214
Columbia-Presbyterian Medical Center 118
Columbus Circle 88
Columbus Day Parade 38
Columbus Park 53
COMEDY CLUBS 203
Comic Strip 199
Comme de Garçons 149
Commodities 272
Community Book Store and Cafe 214
Community Bookstore 208
Community Gardens 69-70
Commuter Trains 348
Complete Traveller 214
COMPUTING 153
Condomania 164
Coney Island 9, 132, 134, 136-137, 334, 317
Connecticut Muffin Co. 272
Conservatory Garden 98, 100
CONSUMER RESOURCES 354
Context Studios 199
Continental 322, 326
Conway Stores 147
Coogan's Restaurant 239
Cooler 84, 326
Cooper Union 69
Cooper-Hewitt Museum 179
Copeland's 239
COPY SERVICES 358
Cornelia Street Cafe 272
Corner Bistro 234, 239
COSMETICS 154
Costume Jewelry 146
Cotton Club 234, 240, 326
courier flights 350
Cowgirl Hall of Fame 240
Craft Museum 144
Crawford Doyle Booksellers 214
Crazy Nanny's 32, 317
CRISIS LINES 354
Crocitto's II 240

Cub Room 295
Cubbyhole 295
Cucina 240
Cucina Della Nonna 240
Cucina Di Pesce 240
CULTURAL INSTITUTIONS AND SOCIETIES 186
Cunningham Park 129
Cupcake Cafe 267
Cupping Room Cafe 272
Cut & Dried 164
Cybercafe 272
CYCLINGCLUBS 340
Cynthia Rowley 150
Czarina 150
Czech Center 179

D

D&G Bakery 157
Da Nico 240
Daffy's 147
Daily News 16
Daily Soup 240
Dakota Apartments 104
Dallas BBQ 241
Damrosch Park 105-106
Dana Discovery Center 101
DANCE CLUBS 282, 314
Dance Theater of Harlem 199
DANCE THEATERS 204
Dance Theatre of Harlem 115
Dance Tracks 160
Danese 183
Danny's Skylight Room 295
Dapper Dog 295
Datavision 153
Dating 28-29
DAY CARE AND OTHER RESOURCES 353
DBA 295
De Hirsh Residence 352
Dean & Deluca 157
Decade 317
Dee & Dee 147
Delacorte Theater 101
Deli Kasbah 241
Delia's 314
Depression Modern 159
Desperados 241
Deutsches Haus 179
Dharma 63, 288, 295
Dia Center for the Arts 183
Diamond District 146
Dick Clark's Rockin' New Year's Eve 36
Diesel 147
Dim sum 54
Dina Magazines 214
Dining and entertainment 234
DISABILITY INFORMATION 355
Disc-o-Rama 160
Dish of Salt 241
Ditto Internet Cafe 272
Dive Bar 290, 295
Dix et Sept 241
Dixon Place 194
DJ Reynold's 92
Doc Holiday's 295
Dog Walking 100

Dojo 241
Dok Suni's 241
Dolce & Gabanna 149
Dom 159
Domsey's 143, 153
Don Giovanni 241
Don Hill's 67, 296, 317
Don't Tell Mama 32, 296
Donald Sacks 241
Donna Karan 150
Double Day Book Shop 214
Down the Hatch 296
Downtime 317
Dö Kham 155
Dr. Jay's 150
Drama Bookshop 214, 225
Drawing Center 179, 210
Drip 32, 272
DTUT 272
Duane Park Patisserie 272
Duke's 241
Duplex 296
Dyckman Farmhouse Museum 179
Dyckman Street Marina 119
Dynasty 241
Dynasty Supermarket 157

E
E & R Video 227
E&O 286, 296, 314
E. Rossi & Co. 155
Ear Inn 234, 296
Earl River Mart 155
Earwax 160
East Campus Hotel 352
East River 42, 112
East River Park 61, 63
EAST VILLAGE 30, 68-71, 145, 151, 166, 192, 204, 208, 218, 229, 232, 277, 286, 288, 310, 322, 325
East-West Books 214
Easter Parade 36
Eastern States Buddhist Temple 53, 54
EAST VILLAGE 265, 320
Economy Candy 157
Ed's Book Exchange, Inc. 214
Edgar Allan PoeCottage 124
Edigio's 127
Eighty-Eight's 32, 296
El Cid Tapas 241
El Diario 16
El Flamingo 317
El Museo del Barrio 95, 179
El Nuevo Sambuca Restaurant 242
El Pollo 242
El Sitio II 242
El Teddy's 242
11th Street Bar 296
Elaine'S 242
Eldridge Street Synagogue 61
Electronics 146
Element Zero 296
Elephant + Castle 234
Elizabeth Street Company Garden Sculpture 57
Elk Candy 96, 157

Ellen's Cafe and Bakery 272
Ellis Island 12, 44, 46
Empire Diner 34, 242
Empire State building 31, 35, 91, 93
Empire State Plaza 332
Empire Szechuan 242
Emporio Armani 149
Enchanted Forest 144
ENTERTAINMENT RESOURCES 354
Erminia 35
Ernie's 242
Esso 184
Exit 9 155
Exit Art 184
Expo 317

F
Fa Cafe 272
Fab 208 150
Fabbricatore Jewelry Design 164
Face Stockholm Ltd. 154
Fairway 157
Fall Cafe 273
Famiglia's 242
Fanelli's 66, 243
FAO Schwartz 92
FASHION 142
Fashion Design Books 214
Fashion Institute of Technology 179
Fat Beats 160
Fat Boy 317
Federal Reserve Bank of New York 45
Ferrara 59
Festival of San Gennaro, 56
Fez 296, 322
555 Soul 149
Fiesta Mexicana 243
Fifth Avenue 31, 35, 86, 90, 93-95, 97
Filene's Basement 147
FILM AND TELEVISION 221-224, 226-229
Film festivals 225
Film Forum 227
FINANCIAL DISTRICT 42-44, 46, 166, 188, 204, 218, 265, 277, 286, 310
Financial services 13-15
Finding a job 18-20
Finding an apartment 21-22
FIRE Museum 179
First 243
First Street Cafe 70, 273
Fish's Eddy 159
Fishing 100
Flame 243
Flamingo East 286, 296
Flatiron Building 79, 81
Flatiron District 21, 78
Flea Markets 142
Fleet Week 36
Floral Park 180
Florent 243
Florio's Cigar Bar and Restaurant 296
Flower District 85

Flowers and Plants 146
Floyd Bennett Airfield 135
Flushing Meadow Park 128-129
420 Bar 297
42nd Street 194
Folk Art Museum 144
Forbidden Planet 215
Fordham Law School 102
Fordham University 16, 124
Forest Hills 128
Fort Greene 132, 135, 137
Fort Tryon Cafe 120, 273
Fort Tryon Park 119
Fountain Pen Hospital 164
Four Seasons Hotel 296, 351
Foy House 336
Franklin Furnace 48
Franklin Station Cafe 273
Fraunces Tavern 46, 180, 243
Free Time 16
French Connection 151
French Roast 273
Frick Collection 180
Friend of a Farmer 80, 243
Fulton Fish Market 45, 47

G
Gabriel's 243
Gagosian 184
Galaxy 243, 287, 297
GALLERIES 171, 174-176, 183
Gantry's Pub 297
Garage 243
Garden of Eden Farmers Market 157
Garment District 146
Gates of Marrakesh 156
Gay and lesbian 30-31,33, 355
General Post Office 83
General Theological Seminary 83, 84
George Washington Bridge 119, 121
GIFTS 155
Gin Mill 297
Ginger Ty 244
Gingerman 297
Giuliani 25, 286, 315
Givenchy 149
Go Sushi 273
Golden Rule Diner 244
Golden Unicorn 244
Golf 331
Goodwill Superstore 159
Gotham Bar and Grill 244
Gotham Bikes 163
GOVERNMENT OFFICES 356
Grace Church 74
Gracie Mansion 95-96
GRAMERCY 34-35, 78-79, 143, 166, 188, 218, 265, 277
Gramercy Park 21, 78-80, 352
Gramercy Park Hotel 352
Gramercy Tavern 244
Grand Army Plaza 135
Grand Central Terminal 10, 38 90, 93
Grand Deli 244
Grand Luncheonette 244
Grandma Sylvia's Funeral at

The SoHo Playhouse 200
Grange Hall 244, 297
Grant's Tomb 109-110
Grapino's 297
Great American Backrub 164
Great Lawn 100
Greene Naftali Gallery 184
GREENWICH VILLAGE 30, 35, 65, 72-75, 82, 102, 166, 188, 190, 192, 218, 229, 266, 282, 285, 310, 277, 310, 335
Grey Art Gallery 184
Grey Dog's Coffee 76, 273
Greyhound Bus 348
GROCERY STORES 156
Gryphon 215
Guggenheim Museum 177
Guggenheim SoHo 180
GYMS 343

H
H&H Bagel 273
H.T. Dance Company 53
Habib's Place 244
Hacker Art Books 215
HAIRCARE 358
Halloween Parade 38
Hamilton Fish Pool and Recreation Center 61
Hamilton Grange 114
Hamilton Heights 112
Hamptons 331
Hanae Mori 149
Hangar Bar 297
Hangawi 244
Hard Rock Cafe 274, 287
Harkness Dance Center 200
HARLEM 112-117, 143, 166, 188, 204, 218, 266, 277, 311, 323
Harlem Meer 100
Harlem Mine Records 161
Harlem River 118
Harrison Street Row 49
Harry's at Hanover Square 245
Hayden Planetarium 180
HEALTH 355
Healthy Henrietta's 245
Heartland Brewery 297
Heights 246
Hell 298, 318
Hell's Kitchen 21, 86
Henderson Place 95
Henrietta Hudson 298
Her/She Bar 298
Herald Square Hotel 352
HERE 200
Hester Street Shoe Outlet 162
Hi-Life Bar and Grill 298
HIKING AND CAMPING 344
Hilton Rockefeller Center 351
HMV 161
Hogs and Heifers 77, 298
Holiday Cocktail Lounge 298
Holiday Motel 353
Home 234, 245
Hong Kong Supermarket 157
Hoppin' Jalapeños 121, 245
HORSEBACK RIDING 101, 330,

Hotalings 215
Hotel Carlyle 35
HOTELS 351
HOTLINES 354
House of Seafood 245
House of Vegetarian 245
HOUSEWARES 159
Housing market 26
HOUSING resources 355
Housing Works Used Bookstore Cafe 215
Howard Johnson's Restaurant 245
Hudson River 42, 83-84, 332
Humanities Library 35, 93
Hungarian 267
Hungarian Pastry Shop 274
Hunter Mountain 332

I

ICE-SKATING 101, 330, 340
Idlewild 287-288, 290, 298
Il Buco 76
INA 151
Indian Cafe 274
Indigo 245
INDOOR POOLS 341
INSTITUTIONAL LIBRARIES 356
International Center for Photography 180
Internet Cafe 274
Internships 19
Intrepid Sea-Air-Space Museum 88
Inwood Hill Park 118-119
Irish Brigade Pub 298
Irish Repertory Theatre 200
Irving Plaza 326
Isamu Noguchi Garden Museum 180
Islamic Cultural Center and Mosque 180
Italian Belmont 127
Italian Food Center 59, 158

J

J&R Music World 161
J. Crew 142, 147
Jackie Robinson Park 114
Jackson Diner 131
Jackson Heights 32
Jacques Marchais Center of Tibetan Art 139-140
Jake's Dilemma 298
Jake's Steakhouse 245
Jamaica Arts Center 200
Jamaica Market 158
Jamaican Hot Pot 246
Japan Society 187
Java Shop 274
jazz 324
Jean Claude 35
Jean's Restaurant 246
Jefferson Market Library 74
Jekyll and Hyde 77, 298
Jerry Ohlinger's Movie Mania 164
Jerry's 66, 274
Jerusalem II 246

Jessica Fredericks Gallery 184
Jewelry 144
Jewish Museum 180
Jewish Theological Seminary 108
JFK International Airport 9, 349
Jim Deitsch Projects 184
Jim McMullen 246
Jimmy Armstrong's Saloon 298
Jimmy's Bronx Café 246
Jimmy's Corner 299
JOBS 18-20
Joe Allen 246
Joe's Shanghai 246
John Fluevog 162
John's of Bleecker Street 246
Jones Beach State Park 331,334
José Tailor 67
Joseph Papp Public Theater 200
Josephina 246
Joyce SoHo 200
Joyce Theater 200
Judson Memorial Church 74
Judy's Restaurant and Cabaret 299
Juilliard School 105
Julie's 32, 299
Junior's 246
jury duty 26
Just Bulbs 159
Just Jake 164

K

K & W Books & Stationary 215
K.C.C. International Trading 164
Kam Kuo Food Corp. 158
Kam Wo Trading Co. 164
Kate Wollman Rink 344
Kate's Joint 246
Kate's Paperie 164
Katz's Delicatessen 60, 62, 246
Keen's Chophouse 247
Kew Gardens 128
KGB 299
Kiehl's 154
Kim's Video 227
Kin Khao 247
King 299
King Manor 129
Kinokuniya Bookstore 215
Kitchen 200
Kitchen Arts and Letters 215
Kitchen Club 247
Kitchenette 51
Knickerbocker Club 96
Knicks 86, 88, 344
Knitting Factory 51, 299, 326
Knoedler Gallery 184
Koronet 110, 247
Korova Milk Bar 70, 299
Kosher Delight 247
Kossars Bakery 60
KPNY 247
Krash 318
Krispy Kreme 116, 274

Kush 288, 299

L

L Cafe 274
L'Express 247
La Jumelle Inc. 247
La Lantern 274
La Maison du Chocolat 158
La Maison Française 187
La MaMa etc. 200
La Mela 59
La Piccola Cucina 158
La Poeme 247
La Tour D'Or 299
Labyrinth Books 215
Lady Mendl's Tea Salon 81
LaGuardia Airport 349
Lakeside Lounge 71, 299
Landmark Tavern 299
Langston Hughes House 114, 116
Lansky Lounge 62
Lanza's 247
Las Vegas 318
Last Word 215
Latin Quarter 327
Lava 290, 300
Layla 247
Le Bilboque 247
Le Figaro 274
Le Gamin 267, 274
Le Grenier 248
Lectorum Book Store 215
Lee's Art Shop 147
LEGAL SERVICES 356
LEISURE 330, 332-344
Lemongrass Grill 248
Lenox Lounge 115, 117, 300
Leo Castelli 184
Les Deux Gamins 274
Les Halles 248
Les Poulets 327
Lesbian + Gay Community Services Center 31
Lexington Bar and Books 300
Liberation Book Store 215
LIBRARIES 356
Lickety Split 300
Life 314, 318
Limbo 70
Lincoln Center 37, 102-103, 105-106, 322
Lincoln Plaza Cinemas 228
Lincoln Tavern 248
Linda Kirkland Gallery 184
Lion's Den 327
Liquid Sky 151
Liquor Store Bar 300
Literary walking tours 212
LITERATURE 34, 205-218, 220
LITTLE ITALY 34, 56, 58-59, 122, 127, 167, 188, 266, 277, 311
Little Ricky's 156
Little Spain 83
Live Bait 300
Living Room 288
Liz Christy Garden 63
Loeb Boathouse 34, 344
Loehmann's 143, 148
Loews Hotel 351

Londel's 248
Long Island 122, 331
Long Island City 131
Long Island City Art Loop 130
Long Island Railroad 331, 348
Lord of the Fleas 151
Louisiana Bar and Grill 322, 323
LOUNGES 286
Love NYC 151
Low Memorial Library 108, 110
LOWER EAST SIDE 21, 53, 60-62, 69, 167, 171, 188, 204, 218, 266, 285-286, 288, 320,322
Lower East Side Tenement Museum 61-62, 181
Lucille Lortel Theater 200
Lucky Cheng's 234, 248
Lucky's Juice Joint 275
Ludlow Bar 300
Ludlow Street Cafe 288
Luna Lounge 63, 300
Luna Park 275

M

M + G Diner 116
M+R Bar 67,249
M. Rohrs Fine Teas & Coffee 158
Mabat 249
MAC Cosmetics 154
Macondo 215
Macy's 20, 38, 154
Madison Square Garden 86, 88, 322,344
Madison Square Park 79
Mainstay Inn 333, 337
Malcolm Shabazz Masjid (Mosque of Islam) 114
Malik Yoba 196-197
Mama Joy's 249
Mamá Mexico 249
Mama's 70
Mama's Food Shop 249
Man Ray 249
Mangia 249
MANHATTAN 11-12, 21, 23-25, 35, 93, 95, 112, 128, 133, 138, 142, 322, 338, 341
Manhattan Books 216
Manhattan Bridge 52
Manhattan College 122
Manhattan Comics and Cards 216
Manhattan Futon 159
Manhattan Mall 155
Manhattan School of Music 201
Manhattan Spirit 16
Manhattan's Democratic County Committee 25
Manic Panic 154
Manny's Car Wash and Blues 97, 327
Manny's Closet 153
Mantra 318
Marc Jacobs 142
Marcus Garvey Park 114
Mare Mare 249

Marechiaro Tavern 300
Margon 249
Marine Park 134
Marion's 300
Mariposa 46, 164
Marriot Marquis Hotel 89, 352
Marriott Marquis Lounge 300
Mart 125 116, 155
Mary Ann's 250
Mary Boone Gallery 184
Masturbakers 275
Match 250
Match Uptown 97, 250
Matt Umanov Guitars
Matthew's 250
Max + Roebling 151
Max Fish 288, 290, 301
Maxilla and Mandible 164
Maxwell's 322
Maya 250
Mayflower Cafe & Bakery 275
Mayor Fiorello La Guardia 25
McDonald's 250
McNulty's Tea and Coffee 158
McRae Furniture 160
Mead's Mountain 332
Meat-Packing District 85
Media 16
MEDICAL NUMBERS 354
Meghan Kinney 151
Mekka 250
Mekong 250
Meow Mix 32, 301
Merc Bar 301
Merchants 250, 301
Mercury Lounge 327
Mermaid Parade 37
Mesa Grill 251
Mesopotamia 71, 251
Met in the Parks 37
Metisse 251
Metro Diner 110, 251
Metro Pictures 184
Metro-North 348
MetroCard 11, 26
Metroliner 348
Metronome 301
Metropolis 153, 318
Metropolitan Museum of Art 35, 95, 176, 181
Metropolitan Opera 101, 105, 106, 201
MetroSource 31
Mets 344
Mi Cocina 251
Michael Musto 283
Midnight Records 161
Midsummer Night's Swing 37
MIDTOWN 35, 86-87, 89-93, 167, 188, 204, 218, 229, 266, 278, 286, 311, 320
Mike's Papaya 251
Milano's 301
Milk Bar 287
Millenium Hilton 352
Miller Theater 201, 210
Milon Bangladesh 251
Mimi's Macaroni 251

Minetta Lane Theater 201
Minor Latham Playhouse 201
Miriam and Ira D. Wallach Art Gallery 184
MISCELLANEOUS stores 164
Mister Roger 151
Miu Miu 149
Mo's Caribbean 251
Mocca Hungarian 251
Moe Ginsburg 148
MoMA 38, 176-177
Momenta Art 185
Mondel Chocolates 158
Mondo Kim's 161
Monkey Bar 301
Monkey Wrench Theater 201
Montauk 331
Monte's 251
MONY 151
Mood Indigo 160
Moomba 251
Moon Bike Ride 38
MORNINGSIDE HEIGHTS 21, 108-109, 111, 167, 188, 204, 218, 229, 266, 278, 311
Morningside Park 112, 115, 119
Morris-Jumel Mansion 181
Mother 318
Motor City Bar 301
MOTOR VEHICLES 27, 355
Mott Su 252
Mount St. Vincent 122
Moustache 252
Movie Place 228
Moving and storage 346-347
Mulligan's Pub 301
Municipal Art Society Urban Center Books 216
Murder Ink 216
Murray Hill 86
Museo del Barrio 115-116
Museum and Gallery Index by Neighborhood 188
Museum culture 176
Museum for African Art 181
MUSEUM LISTINGS 178
Museum Mile 95, 97
Museum of African American History and Arts 181
Museum of American Folk Art 181
Museum of American Illustrators 181
Museum of Modern Art 177, 181
Museum of Modern Art Design Store 156
Museum of Television and Radio 181
Museum of the Chinese in the Americas 53, 55
Museum of the City of New York 95, 181
MUSEUMS 175-176
MUSIC 160, 321
MUSIC VENUES 204, 286, 322-327
Mustang Harry's 301
Mustang Sally's 301

My Cousin Vinny's 252
Myer Lansky Lounge at Ratner's 301
Mysterious Bookshop 216
N
Ñ 66, 302
Nada 201
Nakisaki International Restaurant 252
Nathan's 35
National Arts Club 78, 80
National Black Theatre 201
National Museum of the American Indian 44
Negril Caribbean Restaurant 252
Nell's 315, 318
New Jersey 330, 333
New Jersey Transit 333, 348
New Lung Fung Bakery 275
New Music Cafe 327
New Prospect Cafe 136, 275
New York Aquarium 134
New York Botanical Garden 123, 124, 126
New York Buddhist Temple 109
NEW YORK BY SEASON 36-37
New York City Opera 202
New York City Transit Museum 182
New York Hall of Science 182
New York Historical Society 101, 105, 187
New York AYH-Hostel 353
New York Noodletown 252
New York Open Center 65
New York Philharmonic 36, 105, 202
New York Post 16
New York Press 16
New York Public Library 89-90, 164
New York State Museum 332
New York Stock Exchange 45
New York Transit Authority 10
New York University 16, 73, 72, 74, 174, 210, 216
Newark Airport 349
News Bar 275
Nha Trang 252
Niagara 302
Nice Restaurant 252
Nicholas Roerich Museum 182
Nick's Pub 306
NIGHTCLUB LISTINGS 326
NIGHTCLUBS 314
NIGHTLIFE 282-290, 292-308, 313, 315-327
Niko's 252
Nino's 253
Nobu 253
Noodles on 28 253
Norman's Sound and Vision Too 161
North Park 44
North Star Pub 302
Nowbar 302

Nutcracker Suite 38
Nuyorican Poet's Cafe 202
NYC Marathon 38
O
Oak Bar at the Plaza Hotel 302
Oak Room 285, 302
Odeon 253
Odessa 253
Off-Broadway 190-192
Oke Doke 302
St. Patrick's Cathedral 57
Old Town Bar 302
Ollie's Restaurant 253
Once Upon A Tart 275
Opaline 71
OPERA HOUSES 204
Opium Den 302
OPTICIANS 360
Orange Bear 327
Orchard Bar 288, 302
Oriental Dress Company 151
Oriental Garden 253
Original Levi's Store 147
Oscar Wilde Memorial Bookstore 216
Our Name's Mud 76, 156
OUTDOOR POOLS 341
Oznot's Dish 253
Ozone 303
Ozu 253
Ozzie's 276
P
P&Gs 303
P.S.1 131
Pace Wildenstein Gallery, SoHo 185
Paddy Reilly's 303
Palladium 315
Pão! 77, 253
Paper 16, 314
Papyrus 216
Paragon 163
Paramount 303
Paramount Hotel 352
Park Avalon 254
Park Avenue 92, 94-95
Park Slope Brewing Company 254, 303
Park West Studio Hotel 353
Parnell's Pub 303
Parsons School of Design 75
Partners & Crime 217
Pasticceria Ferrara 276
Pasty Grimaldi's 254
PATH 348
Patria 254
Patricia Field 142, 152
Paula Cooper Gallery 185
Pearl Paint 147
Pearl Theater 202
Peculiar Pub 303
Pelham Park 123
Penang 254
Peninsula Hotel 351
Pennsylvania Station 10, 83, 88, 348
PERFORMANCE ART 175, 189-200, 203

PERFORMANCE SPACES 202, 204
PERFORMING ARTS LISTINGS 198
PERFORMING ARTS INDEX BY TYPE 203
Perk's Fine Cuisine 303
Pete's Tavern 80, 303
Peter Luger Steak House 254
Petite Abeille 276
Phoenix Import 165
Phone company 27
Phyllis Kind 185
Pickwick Arms 353
Picnics 334
Pier 17 165
Pierogi 2000 175, 185
Pierpont Morgan Library 182
Pietrasanta 254
Pig Heaven 254
Pink Pony 276
Pink Pussycat 165
Pink Tea Cup 35
Pintaile's Pizza 254
Piper's Kilt 303
Pizza Fresca 254
Planet 28 318
Plaza Hotel 351
Plum Tree 255
Plush 319
Pó 255
Poet's House 65
Police Academy Museum 182
Politics 21, 24-26
Pommes Frites 70
Poor Richard's Flip A Disc 161
Poppolini's 303
Port Authority Bus Terminal 86, 331, 348
Porto Rico Importing Co. 158
Posman's 217
Postcrypt Coffee House 327
Postermat 165
POST OFFICES 356
Pottery Barn 160
PPOW 185
Pravda 303
Price Mart 148
PROFESSIONAL SPORTS 344
Prospect Park 132, 135, 137, 338, 339, 344
Public sculpture 174
Public Theaters 195
Puccini 255
Puck Building 65
Puffy's Tavern 304
Puglia 255
Pyramid 319

Q
Q-Club International 319
Quad Cinema 228

R
RESOURCES 353
Roosevelt Island Aerial Tramway 34, 89
Ropa 203 121,143, 148
Rosa Mexicano 256
Rose Is Vintage 153
Roseland 327

Rosemarie's 51
Roulette 327
Roundabout Theater 202
Route 66 Records 161
Roxy 319
Royal Coach Diner 126, 256
Royalton 305
Rudy Bar and Grill 305
Rumsey Playfield 101
RUNNING 338
Russian Bathhouse 71, 165

S
S.O.B's 234
Sacco 162
Saigon Grill 256
Saint's 305
Saks Fifth Avenue 155
Sakura Park 109
Salad Jazz Cafe 276
Salander-O'Reilly Galleries 185
Salon 75 175
Salvation Army 143, 153
Sam Flax 147
Samalita's Tortilla Factory 256
Sammy's Noodle Shop and Grill 256
Sammy's Roumanian 256
San Gennaro Feast 38, 58
Santa Fe Grill 257
Sapphire 314, 316, 319
Sara Delano Roosevelt Park 54
Sarabeth's 35
Sardi's 305
Saturday Night Live 226
Scharmann's 35, 276
Schomburg Center for Research in Black Culture 115, 188
School of Visual Arts 171
Science Fiction, Mysteries and More! 217
Screaming Mimi 153
Screening Room 51, 228, 257
Sea Grape Wines 158
Second Avenue Deli 257
Second Coming Records 161
Second Street Cafe 276
Serendipity 257
SERVICES 358
Sette MoMA 276
Shades of Green 305
Shadow 319
Shakespeare & Co. 217
Shakespeare Garden 100
Shakespeare in the Park 98, 101, 191, 195
Shane's Villa 319
Shark Bar 107, 305
Shea Stadium 128, 156, 338, 344
Shelter Island 331
Sheridan Square 30, 73, 75
Shine 152
Ship of Fools 305
Shoes 146, 162
SHOPPING 142-147, 149-154, 156, 158, 162-164
SHOPPING INDEX BY NEIGH-

BORHOOD 166
Showman's Cafe 305
Shun Lee Palace 257
Sidewalk 305
Sigerson Morrison 163
Sightseeing tours 358
Silver Spoon 257
Singles scene 28
Sister's Cuisine 257
Six Flags 330
Slaughtered Lamb 305
Smalls 322, 327, 324
Smiler's Delicatessen Store 257
Smylonylon 152
Snug Harbor Cultural Center 139
Soca Paradise 319
SOCCER CLUBS 344
Socrates Sculpture Park 130
SoHa 306
SOHO 48, 53, 64-67, 83, 142, 145, 150, 167, 171, 175, 188, 194, 204, 218, 229, 266, 278, 311
SoHo Billiards 290, 306
SoHo Books 217
SoHo galleries 173
SoHo Grand Bar 67, 285, 306
SoHo Grand Hotel 351
SoHo Photo Gallery 186
SoHo Rep 202
Solomon R. Guggenheim Museum 95, 182
Sony IMAX at Lincoln Center 228
Sony Theaters Lincoln Square 228
Sophia's Bistro 257
Sosa Borella 257
Sotheby's 182
Sound Factory 319
Sounds of Brazil (SOB's) 327
Soup Kitchen 258
South Beach 139-140
South Bronx 122-123
South St. Seaport Museum Shop 217
South Street Seaport 45-46
Space Untitled 276
Spanish Harlem 112
Spanish Institute 188
SPECIALTY stores 163
Speed 314
Spiral 325
Splash 306
SPOON 306
SPORTS AND RECREATION 163, 338-344
Sports Mania 306
Sporty Weekend Itinerary 34
Spring St. Books 217
Spring Street 258
Spy 66, 306
St. Charles Borromeo Roman Catholic Church 115
St. Clement's Church 202
St. John the Divine 111
St. John the Divine Gift Shop 156

St. Luke's in the Fields 75
St. Mark's Books 217
St. Mark's Comics 217
St. Marks Church in the Bowery 202
St. Michael's Russian Catholic Church 57
St. Nicholas Park 115
St. Patrick's Cathedral 91
St. Patrick's Church 57
St. Patrick's Day Parade 36
St. Paul's Chapel 44, 202
Staley-Wise 186
Stand-Up NY 202
Standard Notions 258
Starlight Fashion 148
STATEN ISLAND 25, 138-140, 167, 204, 266, 278
Staten Island Ferry 12, 42, 47, 140, 341, 344
Statue of Liberty 12, 44, 46
Stella Dallas 153
Step Mama's 258
Steve Madden 163
Steven Alan Outlet 148
Steven Madden Shoes 163
Stoned Crow 290, 306
Stonewall 30, 32, 75, 306
Stony Brook 331
STORAGE 360
STORE LISTINGS 147
Stowell and Sons Bookstore 217
Strand Bookstore 206, 218
Strawberry Fields 98, 100
Street Fairs 142
Striver's Row 112
Studio 54 315
Studio Museum in Harlem 183
subway 9-10
Sufi Books 218
Sugar Hill 114, 117
Sugar Hill Thrift Shop 148
Sugar Shack Cafe 277
Sullivan St. Theater 203
SummerStage 101
Supper Club 234, 322-323
Supreme Court of New York 125
Surf Reality 203
Swedish Cottage Marionette Theater 101
Sweet Basil 322, 324, 327
SWIMMING 331, 341
Sylvia's 116-117
Symphony Space 203, 206
Symposium 258
Syms 148
System 314, 319
Szechuan Empire 258

T
Tamarind Seed Health Food 108, 158
Tap-a-Keg 306
Tapas Lounge 290, 307
Tartine 258
Tavern on Jane 258, 307
Tavern on the Green 35, 99, 259

Taxis 12
Taylor's 158
1020 Bar 290
Tea and Sympathy 32
Teddy's 307
Temple Bar 307
Ten Ren Tea and Ginseng Co., Inc. 158
Ten's the Limit 148
TENNIS 341-342
Tents & Trails 165
Terra Blues 328
Terrace 259
Tevere '84 259
TG-170 152
Thalia Spanish Theater 203
The Billiard Club 292
The Chanting House Cafe 271
The Chorus Tree 38
The Fun Factory 131
The Ramble 100
The Reservoir 100
The Screening Room 34
The Strand 34
Theater Development Fund 195
Theater District 88, 233
THEATERS 190, 192, 204
Three of Cups 307
Three Village Inn 337
Tiengarden 259
Time Cafe 277
TimeOut New York 16, 31, 143, 259, 314
Times Square 348
Times Square 87, 89, 192, 194
Times Square New Year's Eve Countdown 38
Tipping 233
Tisch School of the Arts 36
Tito Puente's 259
TKTS 195
TMC Asian Music 162
Tom's 137, 259
Tom's Restaurant 110, 259
Tommy Makem's Irish Pavillion 307
Tomoe Sushi 259
Tompkins Square Park 68-69
Tonic 62, 259
Torch 63, 260, 287-288
Torre di Pisa 92, 260
Tout Va Bien 260
Tower Records 162
Tower Video and Books 218
Townhouse Bar 307
Trains 348
Tramps 328
Tramps Cafe 277
Transportation 348-349
Trash and Vaudeville 163
Trendy clothing 149
Triad 307
TriBeCa 42, 48-51, 167, 188, 204, 218, 229, 266, 278, 311, 320
TriBeCa Film Center 49
TriBeCa Grill 49, 260
TriBeCa Performing Arts Center 203

TriBeCa Potters 50
TriBeCa Trib 50
Trinity Cemetery and Church of the Intercession 114
Trinity Church 45, 203
Triple Eight Palace 260
Trois Jean 260
Trumpet's Cigar Room 260
Tsampa 260
Tsunami 260
Tunnel 315, 319
Turkish Kitchen 260
Tutta Pasta 260
200 5th 307
2A 307
Twigs Bar and Restaurant 261
Twilo 320
Twin Towers 334
Two Boots 261
Two Potato 307
Two Steps Down 261
Two Two Two 261
U
U.S.A. Diner, Inc. 261
UDO 77
Ugly Luggage 153
Ukrainian Museum 69
Umberto's Clam House 56, 261
Uncle Nick's Greek 261
Uncle Vanya 261
Under the Stairs 262
Union Square 34, 79, 80
Union Square Cafe 81
Union Square Greenmarket 108
Union Theological Seminary 108
Unisphere 129-130
United Nations 86, 90
United States Tennis Center 338
Unterberg Poetry Center 210
UPPER EAST SIDE 21, 31, 34-35, 95, 167, 188, 204, 218, 266,278, 311 320
UPPER WEST SIDE 21, 102-104, 106-107, 114, 188, 204, 219, 229, 266, 278, 320
Urban Bird 165
Urban Outfitters 152
UTILITIES 358
V
V and T Pizzeria and Restaurant 262
Van Cortlandt Park 124
Variety Arts Theater 203
Vegetarian Dim Sum House 262
Velvet 308, 320
Velvet Room 308
Venus Records 162
Verrazano Narrows Bridge 132, 140, 334
Veselka 262
Viand 262
Victory Outreach Church 114
Village Vanguard 322, 324, 328
Village Voice 16, 19, 21, 29, 283

Vinegar Factory 159
VINTAGE CLOTHING 62, 143, 152
Vinyl 320
Vinylmania 162
Virgin Megastore 162
Visiones 328
VISUAL ARTS 170-182, 184-188
Vivian Beaumont Theater 106
Void 308
W
Wa Fun Company 165
Wales Hotel 352
Walker's 308
WALKING CLUBS 344
Walter Reade Theater/Film Society of Lincoln Center 228
Warehouse 320
WASHINGTON HEIGHTS 118-119, 121, 143, 188, 266, 278, 320
Washington Market Park 159
Washington Square Outdoor Art Exhibit 37
Washington Square Park 35, 72, 74-76, 335
Wave Hill 125
Wax 308
Weather 11
Webster Hall 320
Weeping Beech Tree 129
Well's 262
West 4th Street Flea Market 166
West End 111, 308
West Side Community Garden 105
West Side Judaica 218
WEST VILLAGE 30-31, 34, 75, 286, 324
Wetlands 322, 328
White Horse Tavern 308
White Street 49
White Trash 160

Whitney Museum 144
Whitney Museum of American Art 95, 156, 171, 176, 183
Who's on First 308
WIGSTOCK 38
William Greenberg Jr. 159
William Secord Gallery 186
Williams-Sonoma Outlet Center 160
Williamsbridge 122
Williamsburg 132, 135
Williamsburg Bridge 60
Wind Water 156
Windmill Shoppe 156
Windows on India 262
Windows on the World 322
WIRE SERVICES 356
Wo Hop 262
Wok 'n Roll 262
Wollman Rink 101
Wonder Bar 308
Woodstock 332
Wooster Gardens 186
Works 308
World Financial Center 45, 148
World Trade Center 45, 208
World's Fair Ice Skating Rink 129, 338
Worldwide Cinemas 229
Worth St. Theater 203
Wow Comics 166, 218
Wrapp Factory 262
Wu Wear 152
X
X-Large 152
XVI 309
Y
Yaffa Cafe 277
Yaffa Tea Room 277
Yankee Stadium 9, 36, 123, 125, 330, 344
Ye Waverly Inn 263
Yeshiva University 118, 183
YMCA 23

PHOTO CREDITS

Courtesy of Helen Schulman 221
Courtesy of the New York City Mayor's Office 96
Courtesy of the New York Historical Society 14, 25,43, 44, 45, 56, 57, 61, 69, 73, 99, 103, 105, 133, 176
Courtesy of the New York Philharmonic 107
Courtesy of Roshumba Williams 144
Courtesy of the Solomon J. Guggenheim Museum 94, 176
Courtesy of Stewart Wilson 145
Courtesy of the Village Voice 283
Courtesy of the Whitney Museum of American Art 176
Tali Gai 30, 33, 42, 51, 60, 71, 77, 83, 92, 93, 107 119,121,125, 137, 170, 174, 281, 282, 286, 289, 314, 315
Connie Hwong 82, 130
Laura Kearney 28, 41, 50, 86, 93, 107, 119, 121,125, 137, 169, 189, 209, 226, 333, 337
Stephen McBride 196
Remainder of photographs property of Inside New York